PRAISE FOR *LINUX QUICK FIX NOTE*

"Where has this book been all my professio book. The author covers many basic, practic that makes for a great troubleshooting refere of books available that give a broad overvie there are a lot of detailed books on each spe know of any other place where I can get so wide range of topics in such a concise and readable found. I will easily recommend it to my friends and colleagues who are trying to man show it to our instructors who teach data communications and networks as a possible text or lab manual."
—Ron McCarty, instructor and program chair, Computer Science, Penn State Erie

"This book takes a very unique approach and is very flexible. It offers a great deal to the home user, students, small businesses—all the way to any Linux sys admin that needs a handy reference. I found it very refreshing in terms of style, stated goals, presentation, ease of use, direction, and the "present and future" value of the content. In other words the author is very current and knowledgeable. I would recommend this book to every level from programmer to manager."
—Joe Brazeal, Information Technician III, Southwest Power Pool

"This book is an excellent resource for new Linux administrators. I was impressed with the comprehensive set of 35 topic chapters, making this book a very useful reference. I know of no other work like this."
—George Vish II, Linux curriculum program manager and senior education consultant, Hewlett-Packard Education

"I would recommend this book to novice Linux users and administrators. It covers a lot of topics, and makes it easy for readers to follow along."
—Bret Strong, education consultant, Hewlett-Packard Company

"*Linux Quick Fix Notebook* is a well-written guide to designing, installing, and maintaining Linux servers. Many Linux reference texts are just simple rewrites of Linux "man" and "info" pages, but this book addresses the real issues that systems administrators encounter when working with Linux. The author provides a pedagogical guide to learning Linux server administration. In addition, the book includes step-by-step information so that users can quickly take advantage of the best that open source software has to offer today. I would recommend this book to both beginning and intermediate users of Linux."
—Joseph Naberhaus, Professor of Networking, Universidad Del Mar

Linux® Quick Fix Notebook

Bruce Perens' Open Source Series

http://www.phptr.com/perens

Linux® Quick Fix Notebook

Peter Harrison

Upper Saddle River, NJ • Boston • Indianapolis • San Francisco
New York • Toronto • Montreal • London • Munich • Paris
Madrid • Capetown • Sydney • Tokyo • Singapore • Mexico City

PRENTICE
HALL
PTR

Many of the designations used by manufacturers and sellers to distinguish their products are claimed as trademarks. Where those designations appear in this book, and the publisher was aware of a trademark claim, the designations have been printed with initial capital letters or in all capitals.

The author and publisher have taken care in the preparation of this book, but make no expressed or implied warranty of any kind and assume no responsibility for errors or omissions. No liability is assumed for incidental or consequential damages in connection with or arising out of the use of the information or programs contained herein.

The publisher offers excellent discounts on this book when ordered in quantity for bulk purchases or special sales, which may include electronic versions and/or custom covers and content particular to your business, training goals, marketing focus, and branding interests. For more information, please contact:

U. S. Corporate and Government Sales
(800) 382-3419
corpsales@pearsontechgroup.com

For sales outside the U. S., please contact:

International Sales
international@pearsoned.com

Visit us on the Web: www.phptr.com

Library of Congress Number: 2004117224

Copyright © 2005 Pearson Education, Inc.

Printed in the United States of America.

This material may be distributed only subject to the terms and conditions set forth in the Open Publication License, v1.0 or later (the latest version is presently available at http://www.opencontent.org/openpub/).

ISBN 0-13-186150-6
Text printed in the United States on recycled paper at R.R. Donnelley and Sons Company in Crawfordsville, Indiana.
First printing, March 2005

Dedicated to

Diana
"Turn off the light and come to bed."

Blaze and Jade
"Daddy, can we stop being quiet now?"

Jack and Barbara
By my side every day.

About Prentice Hall Professional Technical Reference

With origins reaching back to the industry's first computer science publishing program in the 1960s, and formally launched as its own imprint in 1986, Prentice Hall Professional Technical Reference (PH PTR) has developed into the leading provider of technical books in the world today. Our editors now publish over 200 books annually, authored by leaders in the fields of computing, engineering, and business.

Our roots are firmly planted in the soil that gave rise to the technical revolution. Our bookshelf contains many of the industry's computing and engineering classics: Kernighan and Ritchie's *C Programming Language*, Nemeth's *UNIX System Administration Handbook*, Horstmann's *Core Java*, and Johnson's *High-Speed Digital Design*.

PH PTR acknowledges its auspicious beginnings while it looks to the future for inspiration. We continue to evolve and break new ground in publishing by providing today's professionals with tomorrow's solutions.

Contents

Part 1   The Linux File Server Project

Part 2   The Linux Web Site Project

Part 3   Advanced Topics

Preface

Without question, Linux is rapidly becoming the operating system of choice in many core areas of business. It is transforming information technology in many exciting ways, from being used in products ranging from cell phones and PDAs to cars and mainframe computers.

Like its many uses, Linux has a variety of printed and electronic guides to show you what to do. The specialist guides are highly detailed, focusing on narrow areas of excellence. The encyclopedic guides for beginners focus on Linux fundamentals and only then introduce you to more specialized topics. Unfortunately, there are few practical texts in between that help you to make the transition from being a beginner to having the confidence of an expert.

WHY IS THIS BOOK NECESSARY?

Most Linux "encyclopedias" are split in three sections: an introductory section covering topics such as CD-based Linux installation, GUI interfaces, and text editors; an intermediate section covering Microsoft Office clone productivity suites; and an advanced section covering the topics most nondesktop-support IT professionals use on a day-to-day basis. Unfortunately the "advanced sections" in these guides cover the underlying theory reasonably well, but often are short on space to adequately cover detailed configuration instructions. IT professionals frequently have to purchase additional specialist books on each topic.

Linux® Quick Fix Notebook takes these "advanced sections" and expands them sufficiently to provide a practical tutorial guide on how to do basic configuration of many popular Linux back-office applications with command-by-command instructions.

To avoid confusion between the many flavors of Linux, each with its own GUI interface, this guide exclusively uses the command line to illustrate the tasks needed to be done. It provides all the expected screen output when configuring the most commonly used Linux applications to help assure readers that they are doing the right thing. The notebook also includes many of the most commonly encountered errors with explanations of their causes and how to fix them.

PREREQUISITES

The book's format is aimed at proficient beginners, students, and IT professionals who often have to do advanced tasks in which the underlying theory is understood, but the commands to do it are forgotten or at the tips of their tongues. To maintain its appeal as a compact guide, only the essential supporting theory is provided to help end users implement their projects under budget and ahead of schedule.

A great deal of attention has been paid to troubleshooting techniques that are often needed to remedy unexpected behavior, and every chapter has real-world practical examples in the form of tutorials.

Because the readers are assumed to be exposed to the theory of Linux, many of the introductory topics are not covered, which provides room for much more coverage of the steps needed to get the more difficult jobs done. Two to three months of hands-on Linux experience is an ideal prerequisite. Additionally, basic Windows exposure to the concept of sharing directories between servers is needed.

APPROACH

With this in mind, the persons most likely to be interested in this book would be IT professionals and consultants, power users, computer literate business owners, community college and trade school professors and students, and SOHO workers.

The book creates a typical departmental, small-office, or home network and shows you how to set up the Linux servers most businesses need. Three sections have been created to make this process easier. The first starts as an introduction to networking and extends into using Linux as a main departmental server. The next section expands on this knowledge to show you how to create, manage, and monitor your own Linux-based Web site running on a simple DSL or cable modem line. Finally, the third section covers more advanced topics that will become invaluable as your Linux administration role expands

Explanations are given not as a lecturer, but as a trusted and experienced coworker. The chapters have a logical flow of information starting with concise backgrounders and ending with a troubleshooting section. They cover these essential topics:

Software installation	MRTG server performance monitoring
Networking setup and troubleshooting	Linux firewalls and VPNs
Samba for Windows files on Linux servers	Squid for Web access control
Linux-to-Linux file sharing with NFS	Mail, Web, and DNS server setup
Simple MySQL database administration	Web sites on DHCP Internet links
LDAP and NIS for centralized logins	Time synchronization with NTP
FTP and SCP file transfers	Error reporting with syslog
Disk drive redundancy with software RAID	Restricting users' disk space usage
Wireless Linux networks	with quotas

Many of the topics are covered in Linux certification exams making the book a valuable study guide for those seeking new areas of professional development.
In summary, this book

☞ Shows how to expand inexpensively an existing IT investment in Windows using Linux as the anchor of a network and Web site

☞ Shows how to do this command by command

☞ Is highly focused on being task-oriented

☞ Illustrates how to create a simple network for small business, corporate departments, and homes

☞ Provides an excellent networking familiarization and troubleshooting guide

As the line between power users and administrators continues to blur, as computers move from the data center to the desktop, and as Linux and Windows gain equal footing in business, it becomes harder to remember and do it all. This is the guide that will give you enough time to eat lunch.

BREAKDOWN OF BOOK

PART 1   The Linux File Server Project

Chapter 1   Why Host Your Own Site?
A discussion on the pros and cons of hosting your own Web site. Also includes a discussion on how to simply migrate a Web site from a third-party provider to your office or home.

Chapter 2   Introduction to Networking
Covers the basic concepts needed to make the advanced user comfortable with many frequently encountered networking scenarios. Describes 30 of the most commonly used terms with simple one-paragraph discussions.

Chapter 3   Linux Networking
A practical guide to configuring a network interface and simple Internet routing using Linux.

Chapter 4   Simple Network Troubleshooting
Very detailed yet simply explained coverage of the various methods you can use to identify network trouble spots.

Chapter 5   Troubleshooting Linux with *syslog*
Explanations on how to view and use Linux system error messages as part of the troubleshooting process.

Chapter 6   Installing RPM Software
All you need to know on installing Linux software using popularly available RPM installation files.

Chapter 7   The Linux Boot Process
Explanations of how Linux starts up after turning on the power switch. Coverage of how to activate/deactivate the startup of various important system programs when the system boots up.
     Details on how to choose between using the graphical and regular text interfaces on the Linux VGA console.

Chapter 8   Configuring the DHCP Server
Essential topics on how to configure a DHCP server so that PCs are automatically assigned their Internet addresses when they boot up. Targets usage in the simple networks found in small offices and schools.

Chapter 9 Linux Users and *sudo*

The basics on how to create Linux user accounts. Not all the features—just enough so that a user will be comfortable in creating one if software installation requires it.

Also provides explanations, with examples, of how to grant regular trusted users with temporary system administrator privileges and track what they do. This makes it easier to determine precisely who did what on a system, which can be virtually impossible to determine if everyone shares the administrator password.

Chapter 10 Windows, Linux, and Samba

How to make your Linux server act transparently as a Windows file server using the Samba package. Uses a sample network of a few PCs, which is the typical scenario in schools, corporate departments, and homes.

Chapter 11 Sharing Resources with Samba

Explains how to share a Linux attached printer or CD-ROM drive with other Windows users.

Chapter 12 Samba Security and Troubleshooting

Simple Samba problem resolution outlined in a logical step-by-step fashion.

Chapter 13 Linux Wireless Networking

Coverage of how to install, configure, and test a wireless network that includes Linux servers.

PART 2 The Linux Web Site Project

Chapter 14 Linux Firewalls Using *iptables*

Security is an essential part of Web life. This chapter gives an explanation of the most popular Linux-based firewall software with step-by-step examples of a script/program you can write to protect your network.

Chapter 15 Linux FTP Server Setup

Shows how to set up a Linux server to allow uploading and downloading of files from the Internet using the File Transfer Protocol (FTP) package. FTP can be tricky to configure with firewalls, and a sample iptables script is provided. There is also a tutorial on how to set up an FTP server to allow people to download only, not upload, files for the sake of security.

Chapter 16   Telnet, TFTP, and *xinetd*

Coverage of how to log into a Linux server from a remote PC using the commonly available Telnet program. Also offers an example of how to save the configuration files of various Cisco networking devices to a Linux server using TFTP. Both the Telnet and TFTP packages are governed by the xinetd program, which is also explained.

Chapter 17   Secure Remote Logins and File Copying

Telnet is very insecure as the data passing between the client and server is unencrypted. This chapter covers how to set up a secure shell (SSH) server for encrypted communications as an alternative to Telnet.

Also covers how to configure SSH to allow you to log in to a remote Linux server without a password and to execute commands on a remote Linux server on demand.

Chapter 18   Configuring DNS

How to configure the Domain Name Services (DNS) on a Linux server that will enable you to map an Internet address to a Web site name. Explains the different types of DNS servers and discusses simple methods of how to make them serve your departmental network.

Chapter 19   Dynamic DNS

In many cases you might want to host a Web site on a DSL line. Regular DNS relies on an Internet network whose Internet address doesn't change. Many home and office networks get their Internet addresses dynamically assigned. This chapter covers how to track this constant change so that your Web site's name (URL) always points to your new Internet address.

Chapter 20   The Apache Web Server

After DNS is configured you need to set up a server to handle your Web site's pages. The Apache Web server package is the most commonly used Linux software for this task, but the configuration file can be difficult to understand. This chapter explains how to create a Web site simply by tacking on easy-to-understand customizations to the end of the configuration file. Full examples provided.

Chapter 21   Configuring Linux Mail Servers

Covers how to configure the sendmail mail server to manage mail for your Web site. `sendmail` can be difficult to configure, but it can be easily simplified using macros that are provided with it, which is all explained in this chapter. Methods on how to combat SPAM, one of the Internet's greatest nuisances, are also explained, as are the steps needed to retrieve your mail from your sendmail server.

Chapter 22   Monitoring Server Performance

Very detailed coverage on how to monitor your server's performance, and even get Web-based Internet traffic graphs, using the SNMP, MRTG, Webalizer, TOP, VMSTAT, and FREE utilities.

Chapter 23   Advanced MRTG for Linux

Expanded coverage of MRTG, which explains how to get graphs of CPU, memory, and disk usage statistics with examples.

Chapter 24   The NTP Server

Explanations on how to synchronize the time on your Linux server with well-known time servers on the Internet, as well as how to make your Linux server the primary time source for your network.

PART 3   Advanced Topics

Chapter 25   Network-Based Linux Installation

How to install Linux quickly over a network without the need for CDs. Also covers how to automate installation for large-scale deployments, with examples.

Chapter 26   Linux Software RAID

Coverage of how to configure Linux software to create redundant arrays of identical disk drives (RAID) to provide fail-safe data storage.

Chapter 27   Expanding Disk Capacity

Sometimes you run out of space on a Linux partition and need to expand it onto another hard disk. This chapter explains how to do it.

Chapter 28   Managing Disk Usage with Quotas

Examples of how to limit the amount of disk space individual Linux users can use on a filesystem.

Chapter 29   Remote Disk Access with NFS

A practical guide on how to use the network file system (NFS) to share files between Linux systems.

Chapter 30   Configuring NIS

A description of how to use name information services (NIS) to create a centralized username/password database for all your Linux servers.

Chapter 31 Centralized Logins Using LDAP and RADIUS

NIS has its limitations because it is geared toward Linux logins and does unencrypted authentication. The lightweight directory access protocol (LDAP) can also be used to store username/password data in a rapid access database format over an encrypted network connection. When used in conjunction with RADIUS, it can be used to authenticate users logging into a variety of devices, such as networking equipment, that don't run Linux. This chapter explains how.

Chapter 32 Controlling Web Access with Squid

This chapter focuses on how to use Squid to limit the amount of time users can spend browsing the Internet using the Squid Linux package. Also covers how to provide password-only access to the Internet.

Chapter 33 Modifying the Kernel to Improve Performance

A brief explanation with examples on how to configure the Linux kernel to improve system performance.

Chapter 34 Basic MySQL Configuration

Many add-on Linux applications require interaction with a database of some sort; one of the most popular is MySQL. This chapter discusses basic MySQL configuration for the purposes of supporting the installation of third-party Linux applications, such as accounting packages and message boards.

Chapter 35 Configuring Linux VPNs

Details of how to create a permanent site-to-site VPN between two offices.

Appendix I Miscellaneous Linux Topics

Covers a variety of useful, yet often overlooked, topics for Linux servers, including additional security using TCP wrappers, a description of Security Enhanced Linux, adjusting dynamic kernel parameters, and how to manage your Linux server via a connection to the COM port.

Appendix II Codes, Scripts, and Configurations

Provides the library of useful sample configuration files and productivity enhancing scripts that are used as references in the main text.

Appendix III Differences Between The Fedora Versions

Describes many of the subtle differences in the functioning and configuration of the various versions of Fedora and Red Hat Linux. This is a handy brief reference when you are considering an upgrade of your operating system.

Appendix IV *syslog* Configuration and Cisco Devices

Shows how to configure many popular Cisco network devices to send their status and error messages to a Linux server. This was included because many Linux administrators also have a networking and security management role as well.

Acknowledgments

There have been numerous people who have provided me with the inspiration to write, too many to completely acknowledge on a single page.

I must first thank my family—Diana, Blaze, Jade, Jack, Barbara, Pauline, and Helene—who provided encouragement since the book was a single Web page on wireless Linux.

Ever since that simple start, visitors to the site have sent numerous e-mails of encouragement, suggesting new directions, correcting errors, and finding omissions. One of them, Keith Lofstrom, provided me with the extra push to seek publication. Without them all the cake would have no icing.

But the real dessert was reading the reviews of (alphabetically listed) Joseph Brazeal, Robert Husted, Ron McCarty, Joseph Naberhaus, Bret Strong, and George Vish, who challenged me to improve the technical content and readability of the book.

It would also be unthinkable not to mention Jill Harry of Prentice Hall, who had the vision to take a chance, with Brenda Mulligan, Nancy Albright, Christy Hackerd, and Linda Laflamme who always directed me along the right path. Also, without the combined knowledge of my coworkers the task would have been nearly impossible.

Thank you all.

About the Author

Peter Harrison has been fascinated by computers since the early 1980s. He was the founding president of PCJAM, Jamaica's first computer user group, and was the principal systems engineer responsible for the computerization of the island's tax collection and social security systems.

He then sought new opportunities as the western Caribbean representative for a Fortune 500 pharmaceuticals firm and later became the international sales manager for a West Indian rum company. Before moving to Silicon Valley he ran Trinidad and Tobago's first industrial trade office to Latin America.

Peter has since worked extensively in the Internet sector deploying large-scale data centers and Web sites. Extensive use of Linux in this environment combined with his varied business background has helped him create this highly readable book for the newbie, the techie, and their bosses.

In his quieter moments, Peter enjoys the art and literature of the Caribbean and Latin America. Long rides on his bicycle provide another guilty pleasure. Peter likes to relax with his family on short weekend trips to the many attractions of the San Francisco Bay Area.

The Linux File Server Project

Why Host Your Own Site?

In This Chapter

- ☞ Our Network
- ☞ Alternatives to In-House Web Hosting
- ☞ Factors to Consider Before Hosting Yourself
- ☞ How to Migrate From an External Provider
- ☞ In-House Server Considerations
- ☞ Conclusion

Web sites have proliferated greatly over the years to become a part of everyday life for many people. People use them to create Web logs of their daily lives, provide family members with a place to store their memories, or tell people of their experiences in getting things to work. The following is a typical Web site address: www.linuxhomenetworking.com.

Businesses originally used Web sites primarily as a marketing tool, but later expanded them to become an important part of their operations. Many companies rely almost exclusively on their Web sites to sell their products and provide both customer and supplier support services.

The decision as to whether to host your own Web site can be difficult. You have to consider factors of cost and convenience as well as service and support. This chapter briefly addresses the most common issues and outlines the simple network architecture for use in a small office or home on which the focus of the rest of the book will be based.

Not all businesses departments and homes require a Web site, but the process of establishing one touches many aspects of not only Linux, but information technology as well. This book is about setting up Linux servers to do the things that most businesses and homes need. It's about getting the job done.

With this in mind, the book is divided into three sections of gradually increasing complexity to make this process easier. After this chapter, the first section introduces you to networking, software installation, and troubleshooting before the first major project of using Linux as a main departmental file server for Windows PCs. The next section expands upon this knowledge to show you how to create, manage, and monitor your own Linux-based Web site on this network using a simple DSL or cable modem Internet connection. Finally, the third section covers more advanced topics that will become invaluable as your Linux administration role expands.

OUR NETWORK

The typical small office or home network is usually quite simple, with a router/firewall connected to a broadband Internet connection protecting a single network on which all servers and PCs are connected, as seen in Figure 1.1.

As stated before, the rest of the book shows how you can make a simple layout such as this become a functional low-volume Web site, but before you do it would be best to weigh the pros and cons of doing this.

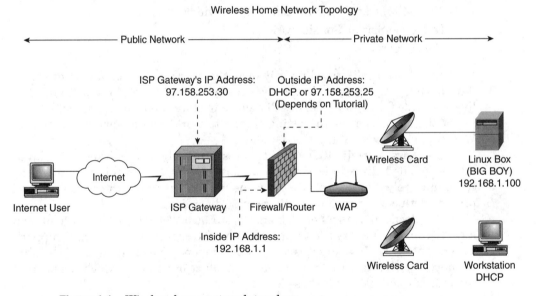

Figure 1.1   Wireless home network topology.

ALTERNATIVES TO IN-HOUSE WEB HOSTING

There are two broad categories of hosting options for small Web sites. There are companies that host multiple Web sites on the same server and are called **virtual hosting providers**. There are also those that allow you to use servers completely dedicated to your site, these are called **dedicated hosting**

providers. Dedicated providers might provide you with only a network connection for a server you purchase and install in their data center, or they might offer a menu of services, from monitoring to backups, from which to choose.

Virtual Hosting

It is easy to find virtual hosting companies on the Web that offer to host a simple Web site for about $10 per month.

The steps are fairly straightforward:

1. Sign up for the virtual hosting service. They will provide you with a user account, the IP address of your site, and the name of a private directory on a shared Web server in which you'll place your Web pages.
2. Register your domain name, such as `my-web-site.org`, with companies like Register.com, Verisign, or RegisterFree.com. You must make sure your new domain name's DNS records point to the DNS server of the virtual hosting company.
3. Upload your Web pages to your private virtual hosting directory.
4. Start testing your site using your IP address in your Web browser. It takes about 3-4 days for DNS to propagate across the Web, so you'll probably have to wait at least that long before you'll be able to view your site using your sub-domain, `www.my-web-site.org`.

The virtual hosting provider will also offer free backups of your site, technical support, a number of e-mail addresses and an easy-to-use Web-based GUI to manage your settings. For an additional charge, many will also provide an e-commerce feature, which allows you to have a shopping cart and customer loyalty programs.

The disadvantage of virtual hosting is that, though it is cheap, you often have no control over the operation of the server and have to rely on the staff and operational procedures of the hosting company to get your changes implemented. These may not necessarily be to your liking.

Dedicated Hosting

In this scenario, you typically have to make contact with a live sales representative who represents an Internet data center. At a minimum, you have to pay for the amount of space your server occupies in the data center, the amount of power it consumes, and the amount of Internet bandwidth you expect to use. Additional services such as backups, monitoring, on-call engineering time, firewall management, and bandwidth graphing information often can be purchased as extra line items on your bill.

As you can imagine, these services can be fairly expensive. A 1 ½-inch slot in a computer cabinet for a Web server can easily cost $200 per month for

1Mbps of bandwidth. The advantage over virtual hosting is that you can customize the server to your needs.

Despite the relative merits of external hosting, you may also want to consider doing it yourself.

FACTORS TO CONSIDER BEFORE HOSTING YOURSELF

Hosting your Web site externally, especially virtual hosting, is the ideal solution for many small Web sites but there are a number of reasons why you may want to move your Web site to your home or small office. The pros and cons of doing this are listed in Table 1.1.

Table 1.1   Factors to Consider When Hosting In-House

Savings	Costs	Risks
Monthly outsourced Web hosting fee	New hardware and software	Likelihood of a failure and its expected duration
Elimination of the cost of delays to implement desired services	Possible new application development	The cost of both the failure and post-failure recovery (hardware, software, data restoration, time)
	Training	
	The percentage of IT staff's time installing and maintaining the site	Irregular procedures that could increase the vulnerability of your site to failure
	Potential cost of the risks (% likelihood of failure per month × cost of failure)	

Is In-House Hosting Preferred?

There are a number of advantages and disadvantages to hosting Web sites that are physically under your own control.

Pros

☞ **Increased Control and Flexibility:** You will be able to manage all aspects of your Web site if it is hosted on a server based either in-house or within your control at a remote data center. You won't have to wait before changes are made and you can select the IT solution that best meets your needs, not those of the hosting provider. You can install the software you need, not what the ISP dictates.

There is also the possibility of offsetting the cost of your server by subleasing space on it to other companies in your community, so that you can become a small virtual hosting service yourself.

☞ **Cost:** It is possible to host a Web site on most DSL connections. A Web site can be hosted on this data circuit for only the additional hardware cost of a network switch and a Web server. You should be able to buy this equipment secondhand for about $100. If your home already has DSL there would be no additional network connectivity costs. So for a savings of $10 per month the project should pay for itself in less than a year.

The cost of using an external Web hosting provider will increase as you purchase more systems administration services. You will eventually be able to justify hosting your Web site in-house based on this financial fact.

☞ **New Skills:** An additional benefit is learning the new skills required to set up the site. Changes can be made with little delay.

☞ **Availability:** Reliable virtual hosting facilities may not be available in your country, and/or you may not have access to the foreign currency to host your site abroad.

☞ **Language:** ISPs often provide technical support in only a few languages. If you can't get adequate support for billing, engineering, and customer care services, an in-house solution may be better.

Cons

☞ **Lost Services:** You lose the convenience of many of the services—such as backups, security audits, load balancing, DNS, redundant hardware, database services, and technical support—offered by the virtual hosting company.

☞ **Security:** One important factor to consider is the security of your new server. Hosting providers may provide software patches to fix security vulnerabilities on your Web servers and may even provide a firewall to protect it. These services may be more difficult to implement in-house. Always weigh the degree of security maintained by your hosting provider against the security you expect to provide in-house. Proceed with the server migration only if you feel your staff can handle the job.

☞ **Technical Ability:** Your service provider may have more expertise in setting up your site than you do. You may also have to incur additional training costs to ensure that your IT staff has the necessary knowledge to do the job internally.

☞ **Availability:** In many cases the reliability of a data center's Internet connectivity is usually higher than that of your broadband connection.

☞ **Cost:** Though you may be able to save money on a data circuit, there are other costs to consider. You may not have access to cheap real estate in which to host your servers. Commercial office space is often more expensive than basic data center space. You may have to purchase additional equipment and services to support your servers, such as UPSs, backup systems, software patch management, maintenance contracts, monitoring systems, and additional power feeds, all of which may be already bundled in with the services of an external data center.

How to Migrate From an External Provider

Chapter 18, "Configuring DNS," which covers DNS, has a detailed explanation of the steps involved in migrating your Web site from an external hosting provider to your home or small office. You should also read Chapters 20, "The Apache Web Server," and 21 "Configuring Linux Mail Servers," on Web and mail server configuration to help provide a more rounded understanding of the steps involved.

In-House Server Considerations

For small Web sites without a great deal of database activity and where "hot standby" hardware isn't a great need, a basic desktop system will work fine. www.linuxhomenetworking.com, which was the inspiration for this book, receives more than half a million page views per month and runs on a 1GHz Intel Celeron with 1GB of RAM. A secondhand PC is adequate in this case.

Purpose-built Web servers tend to use multiple CPUs, dual redundant power supplies, high-speed redundant SCSI disks that can be replaced while the system is running without affecting performance, special error-correcting ECC RAM, multiple PCI buses, special built-in diagnostic tools, and slim-line cases only a few inches high. They cost significantly more, but you pay for the peace of mind when your only source of income is your Web site.

Try to have a dedicated area for your server that's clean, cool, and dry, and that uses UPS-protected power. Label all your cables at both ends and try to create an updated network diagram that you can show anyone who will provide you assistance.

Another good idea is to color-code your cables. Some companies use one color for networks using private IP addresses and another for Internet-facing networks; others use one color for straight-through and another for crossover cables.

Wireless technology for a home-based Web site can be extremely convenient. You can place your small wireless router near your DSL/cable modem and the server anywhere in the house. In my little lab, I have one server behind a bookcase, another behind the TV, one under a bed, and a couple around my desk. When you live in an apartment, there may be no other choice, but the risk is that a book falling behind a bookcase or a bounce from a vacuum cleaner could take your site off the air.

Selecting an Internet connection for your Web site is not as easy as it seems. There are many data circuit technologies such as cable modem, DSL, and wireless links, but they may not be available in your area or the installation times may not be acceptable. High-speed links are usually marketed to businesses and their cost per megabyte of data transfer is usually higher because the service may be combined with data center space, be more reliable, offer more bandwidth, and provide better customer support. Some technologies, such as T1 links, can optionally provide a dedicated circuit between two locations external to the Internet, but the service also has a per kilometer monthly distance charge.

DSL and wireless services are sometimes asymetrical, in that the incoming downstream data rate from the Internet is different than the reverse outgoing upstream speed. You should be most concerned about upstream speed for your Web site to the Internet. Inbound Web browser queries don't use a lot of data bandwidth, but the Web pages that contain the outbound replies do. Internet service providers (ISPs) provide asymmetric services for residential users and the downstream rate is almost always higher than the upstream. They reserve symmetrical data circuits for businesses that usually need high bandwidth to both surf the Web and serve Web pages. The ISP will usually provide the business with a fixed range of Internet addresses as part of the service; residential customers usually get a dynamic address allocation. This can have an impact on your Web site preparation and will be discussed in more detail in later chapters.

Another source of concern would be deciding on the operating system to use. A popular one is Windows, which may be the only product your Web or business application will work with and with which your staff is most familiar. These issues are becoming less important as software vendors are increasingly porting their applications to Linux, an increasingly strong rival to Windows, which also has a lower overall total cost of ownership, especially for smaller companies.

This book focuses on Fedora Linux with some references to Red Hat Linux, its popular corporate cousin. What's the difference? Until Version 9, Red Hat Linux was a free product. The company then decided to create enterprise and desktop versions that had paid service contracts bundled with them, and these maintained the Red Hat brand. At the same time Red Hat decided to create Fedora Linux as a support-free product with an aggressive development cycle, which is generally unsuitable for businesses that often require more stability and support. New versions of Fedora are released every six months. Though the original applications may be developed by volunteers, the Fedora versions are maintained by Red Hat. Once Fedora updates are proven stable, they are incorporated into the Red Hat Linux releases, which are updated every 12–18 months. Constant communication between Red Hat and the developers help to keep the updates synchronized.

I chose Fedora because it's free. You don't have to get a purchase order to play with Fedora. When you become comfortable with it and have proven the concept to yourself, your peers, and management, you can then consider the more stable Red Hat equivalent.

I also chose Fedora Linux because it's popular and it's the Linux flavor I've worked with most frequently at home and at work. This may not be the one suitable for you, and other Linux distributions should also be considered.

CONCLUSION

The decision to manage your Web site in-house can be difficult. Whatever you choose to do, plan carefully. Always get a professional opinion, even if it's informal, and always be aware of the potential risks of the decision you make.

If you decide to do it, this book will provide a lot of guidance in completing a successful project.

## CHAPTER 2

Introduction to Networking

IN THIS CHAPTER

☞ The OSI Networking Model
☞ An Introduction to TCP/IP
☞ How IP Addresses Are Used to Access Network Devices
☞ How Subnet Masks Group IP Addresses Into Networks
☞ The Physical and Link Layers
☞ Networking Equipment Terminology
☞ Additional Introductory Topics
☞ Conclusion

Installing the Linux operating system is only the first step toward creating a fully functional departmental server or Web site. Almost all computers are now networked in some way to other devices; therefore, a basic understanding of networking and issues related to the topic will be essential to feeling comfortable with Linux servers.

This introductory chapter forms the foundation on which the following network configuration and troubleshooting chapters will be built. These chapters will then introduce the remaining chapters that cover Linux troubleshooting, general software installation, and the configuration of many of the most popular Linux applications used in corporate departments and Small Office/Home Office (SOHO) environments.

Familiarity with the concepts explained in the following sections will help answer many of the daily questions often posed by coworkers, friends, and even you. It will help make the road to Linux mastery less perilous, a road that begins with an understanding of the OSI networking model and TCP/IP.

THE OSI NETWORKING MODEL

The Open System Interconnection (OSI) model, developed by the International Organization for Standardization, defines how the various hardware and software components involved in data communication should interact with each other.

A good analogy would be a traveler who prepares herself to return home through many dangerous kingdoms by obtaining permits to enter each country at the very beginning of the trip. At each frontier, our friend has to hand over a permit to enter the country. Once inside, she asks the border guards for directions to reach the next frontier and displays the permit for that new kingdom as proof that she has a legitimate reason for wanting to go there.

In the OSI model each component along the data communications path is assigned a layer of responsibility—in other words, a kingdom over which it rules. Each layer extracts the permit, or header information, it needs from the data and uses this information to correctly forward what's left to the next layer. This layer also strips away its permit and forwards the data to the next layer, and so the cycle continues for seven layers.

The very first layer of the OSI model describes the transmission attributes of the cabling or wireless frequencies used at each link or step along the way. Layer 2 describes the error correction methodologies to be used on the link; layer 3 ensures that the data can hop from link to link on the way to the final destination described in its header. When the data finally arrives, the layer 4 header is used to determine which locally installed software application should receive it. The application uses the guidelines of layer 5 to keep track of the various communications sessions it has with remote computers and uses layer 6 to verify that the communication or file format is correct. Finally, layer 7 defines what the end user will see in the form of an interface, graphical on a screen or otherwise. A description of the functions of each layer in the model can be seen in Table 2.1.

Table 2.1 The Seven OSI Layers

Layer	Name	Description	Application
7	Application	The user interface to the application.	telnet FTP
6	Presentation	Converts data from one presentation format to another—for example, e-mail text entered into Outlook Express being converted into SMTP mail formatted data.	sendmail
5	Session	Manages continuing requests and responses between the applications at both ends over the various established connections.	

Layer	Name	Description	Application
4	Transport	Manages the establishment and tearing down of a connection. Ensures that unacknowledged data is retransmitted. Correctly resequences data packets that arrive in the wrong order. After the packet's overhead bytes have been stripped away, the resulting data is said to be a **segment**.	TCP UDP
3	Network	Handles the routing of data between links that are not physically connected. After the link's overhead bytes have been stripped away, the resulting data is said to be a **packet**.	IP ARP
2	Link	Error control and timing of bits speeding down the wire between two directly connected devices. Data sent on a link is said to be structured in **frames**.	Ethernet ARP
1	Physical	Defines the electrical and physical characteristics of the network cabling and interfacing hardware.	Ethernet

AN INTRODUCTION TO **TCP/IP**

TCP/IP is a universal standard suite of protocols used to provide connectivity between networked devices. It is part of the larger OSI model upon which most data communications is based.

One component of TCP/IP is the Internet Protocol (IP), which is responsible for ensuring that data is transferred between two addresses without being corrupted.

For manageability, the data is usually split into multiple pieces or packets, each with its own error detection bytes in the control section or **header** of the packet. The remote computer then receives the packets and reassembles the data and checks for errors. It then passes the data to the program that expects to receive it.

How does the computer know what program needs the data? Each IP packet also contains a piece of information in its header called the **type** field. This informs the computer receiving the data about the type of layer 4 transportation mechanism being used.

The two most popular transportation mechanisms used on the Internet are Transmission Control Protocol (TCP) and User Datagram Protocol (UDP).

When the type of transport protocol has been determined, the TCP/UDP header is then inspected for the **port** value, which is used to determine which network application on the computer should process the data. This is explained in more detail later.

TCP Is a Connection-Oriented Protocol

TCP opens up a virtual connection between the client and server programs running on separate computers so that multiple and/or sporadic streams of data can be sent over an indefinite period of time between them. TCP keeps track of the packets sent by giving each one a sequence number with the remote server sending back acknowledgment packets confirming correct delivery. Programs that use TCP therefore have a means of detecting connection failures and requesting the retransmission of missing packets. TCP is a good example of a **connection-oriented protocol**.

How TCP Establishes a Connection

Any form of communication requires some form of acknowledgment for it to become meaningful. Someone knocks on the door to a house, the person inside asks, "Who is it?", to which the visitor replies, "It's me!" Then the door opens. Both persons knew who was on the other side of the door before it opened and a conversation can now begin.

TCP acts in a similar way. The server initiating the connection sends a segment with the SYN bit set in TCP header. The target replies with a segment with the SYN and ACK bits set, to which the originating server replies with a segment with only the ACK bit set. This SYN, SYN-ACK, ACK mechanism is often called the "three-way handshake."

The communication then continues with a series of segment exchanges, each with only the ACK bit set. When one of the servers needs to end the communication, it sends a segment to the other with the FIN and ACK bits set, to which the other server also replies with a FIN-ACK segment. The communication terminates with a final ACK from the server that wanted to end the session.

This is the equivalent of ending a conversation by saying "I really have to go now, I have to go for lunch," to which the reply is, "I think I'm finished here too, see you tomorrow." The conversation ends with a final "bye" from the hungry person.

Here is a modified packet trace obtained from the `tethereal` program discussed in Chapter 4, "Simple Network Troubleshooting." You can clearly see the three-way handshake to connect and disconnect the session:

```
hostA -> hostB TCP 1443 > http [SYN] Seq=9766 Ack=0 Win=5840 Len=0
hostB -> hostA TCP http > 1443 [SYN, ACK] Seq=8404 Ack=9767 Win=5792
Len=0
hostA -> hostB TCP 1443 > http [ACK] Seq=9767 Ack=8405 Win=5840 Len=0
hostA -> hostB HTTP HEAD / HTTP/1.1
hostB -> hostA TCP http > 1443 [ACK] Seq=8405 Ack=9985 Win=54 Len=0
hostB -> hostA HTTP HTTP/1.1 200 OK
hostA -> hostB TCP 1443 > http [ACK] Seq=9985 Ack=8672 Win=6432 Len=0
hostB -> hostA TCP http > 1443 [FIN, ACK] Seq=8672 Ack=9985 Win=54
Len=0
hostA -> hostB TCP 1443 > http [FIN, ACK] Seq=9985 Ack=8673 Win=6432
Len=0
hostB -> hostA TCP http > 1443 [ACK] Seq=8673 Ack=9986 Win=54
```

In this trace, the sequence number represents the serial number of the first byte of data in the segment. So in the first line, a random value of 9766 was assigned to the first byte, and all subsequent bytes for the connection from this host will be sequentially tracked. This makes the second byte in the segment number 9767, the third number 9768, etc. The acknowledgment number, or Ack, not to be confused with the ACK bit, is the sequential serial number of the first byte of the next segment it expects to receive from the other end, and the total number of bytes cannot exceed the Win or window value that follows it. If data isn't received correctly, the receiver will re-send the requesting segment asking for the information to be sent again. The TCP code keeps track of all this along with the source and destination ports and IP addresses to ensure that each unique connection is serviced correctly.

UDP, TCP's "Connectionless" Cousin

UDP is a connectionless protocol. Data is sent on a "best effort" basis with the machine that sends the data having no means of verifying whether the data was correctly received by the remote machine. UDP is usually used for applications in which the data sent is not mission-critical. It is also used when data needs to be broadcast to all available servers on a locally attached network where the creation of dozens of TCP connections for a short burst of data is considered resource-hungry.

TCP and UDP Ports

The data portion of the IP packet contains a TCP or UDP segment sandwiched inside. Only the TCP segment header contains sequence information, but both the UDP and the TCP segment headers track the port being used. The source/destination port and the source/destination IP addresses of the client and server computers are then combined to uniquely identify each data flow.

Certain programs are assigned specific ports that are internationally recognized. For example, port 80 is reserved for HTTP Web traffic, and port 25 is reserved for SMTP e-mail. Ports less than or equal to 1024 are reserved for privileged system functions, and those above 1024 are generally reserved for non-system third-party applications.

Usually when a connection is made from a client computer requesting data to the server that contains the data:

☞ The client selects a random previously unused source port greater than 1024 and queries the server on the destination port specific to the application. If it is an HTTP request, the client will use a source port of, say, 2049 and query the server on port 80 (HTTP).

☞ The server recognizes the port 80 request as an HTTP request and passes on the data to be handled by the Web server software. When the Web server software replies to the client, it tells the TCP application to respond back to port 2049 of the client using a source port of port 80.

☞ The client keeps track of all its requests to the server's IP address and will recognize that the reply on port 2049 isn't a request initiation for "NFS," but a response to the initial port 80 HTTP query.

The TCP/IP Time to Live Feature

Each IP packet has a **Time to Live (TTL)** section that keeps track of the number of network devices the packet has passed through to reach its destination. The server sending the packet sets the initial TTL value, and each network device that the packet passes through then reduces this value by 1. If the TTL value reaches 0, the network device will discard the packet.

This mechanism helps to ensure that bad routing on the Internet won't cause packets to aimlessly loop around the network without being removed. TTLs therefore help reduce the clogging of data circuits with unnecessary traffic.

Remember this concept because it will be helpful in understanding the traceroute troubleshooting technique outlined in Chapter 4 that covers network troubleshooting.

The ICMP Protocol and Its Relationship to TCP/IP

There is another commonly used protocol called the Internet Control Message Protocol (ICMP). It is not strictly a TCP/IP protocol, but TCP/IP-based applications use it frequently.

ICMP provides a suite of error, control, and informational messages for use by the operating system. For example, IP packets will occasionally arrive at a server with corrupted data due to any number of reasons including a bad connection, electrical interference, or even misconfiguration. The server will usually detect this by examining the packet and correlating the contents to what it finds in the IP header's error-control section. It will then issue an ICMP reject message to the original sending machine saying that the data should be re-sent because the original transmission was corrupted.

ICMP also includes echo and echo reply messages used by the Linux `ping` command to confirm network connectivity. ICMP `TTL expired` messages are also sent by network devices back to the originating server whenever the TTL in a packet is decremented to 0. More information on ICMP messages can be found in both Appendix II, "Codes, Scripts, and Configurations," and Chapter 4.

How IP Addresses Are Used to Access Network Devices

All TCP/IP-enabled devices connected to the Internet have an Internet Protocol (IP) address. Just like a telephone number, it helps uniquely identify a user of the system. The Internet Assigned Numbers Authority (IANA) is the organization responsible for assigning IP addresses to Internet Service Providers (ISPs) and deciding which ones should be used for the public Internet and which ones should be used on private networks.

IP addresses are in reality a string of 32 binary digits or **bits**. For ease of use, network engineers often divide these 32 bits into four sets of 8 bits (or octets), each representing a number from 0 to 255. Each number is then separated by a period (.) to create the familiar **dotted decimal notation**. An example of an IP address that follows these rules is 97.65.25.12.

Note

Chapter 3, "Linux Networking," which covers Linux specific networking topics, explains how to configure the IP address of your Linux box.

Private IP Addresses

Some groups of IP addresses are reserved for use only in private networks and are not routed over the Internet. These are called **private IP addresses** and have the following ranges:

```
     10.0.0.0 - 10.255.255.255
   172.16.0.0 - 172.31.255.255
  192.168.0.0 - 192.168.255.255
```

Home networking equipment/devices usually are configured in the factory with an IP address in the range 192.168.1.1 to 192.168.1.255.

You may be wondering how devices using private addresses could ever access the Internet if the use of private addresses on the Internet is illegal.

The situation gets even more confusing if you consider the fact that hundreds of thousands of office and home networks use these same addresses. This must cause networking confusion. Don't worry; this problem is overcome by NAT.

The *localhost* IP Address

Whether or not your computer has a network interface card it will have a built-in IP address with which network-aware applications can communicate with one another. This IP address is defined as 127.0.0.1 and is frequently referred to as `localhost`. This concept is important to understand, and will be revisited in many later chapters.

Network Address Translation (NAT) Makes Private IPs Public

Your router/firewall will frequently be configured to give the impression to other devices on the Internet that all the servers on your home/office network have a valid **public IP address** and not a private IP address. This is called **network address translation (NAT)** and is often also called **IP masquerading** in the Linux world. There are many good reasons for this; the two most commonly stated are:

☞ No one on the Internet knows your true IP address. NAT protects your home PCs by assigning them IP addresses from private IP address space that cannot be routed over the Internet. This prevents hackers from directly attacking your home systems because packets sent to the private IP will never pass over the Internet.

☞ Hundreds of PCs and servers behind a NAT device can masquerade as a single public IP address. This greatly increases the number of devices that can access the Internet without running out of public IP addresses.

You can configure NAT to be **one to one**, in which you request your ISP to assign you a number of public IP addresses to be used by the Internet-facing interface of your firewall, and then you pair each of these addresses to a corresponding server on your protected private IP network. You can also use **many to one** NAT, in which the firewall maps a single IP address to multiple servers on the network.

As a general rule, you won't be able to access the public NAT IP addresses from servers on your home network. Basic NAT testing requires you to ask a friend to try to connect to your home network from the Internet.

Examples of NAT may be found in the IP masquerade section of Chapter 14, "Linux Firewalls Using `iptables`," that covers the Linux `iptables` firewall. Some of the terms mentioned here might be unfamiliar to you, but they will be explained in later sections of this chapter.

Port Forwarding with NAT Facilitates Home-Based Web Sites

In a simple home network, all servers accessing the Internet will appear to have the single public IP address of the router/firewall because of many to one NAT. Because the router/firewall is located at the border crossing to the Internet, it can easily keep track of all the various outbound connections to the Internet by:

☞ Monitoring the IP addresses and TCP ports used by each home-based server

☞ Mapping it to the TCP ports and IP addresses of the Internet servers with which they want to communicate

This arrangement works well with a single NAT IP trying to initiate connections to many Internet addresses. The reverse isn't true.

New connections initiated from the Internet to the public IP address of the router/firewall face a problem. The router/firewall has no way of telling which of the many home PCs behind it should receive the relayed data because the mapping mentioned earlier doesn't exist beforehand. In this case the data is usually discarded.

Port forwarding is a method of counteracting this. For example, you can configure your router/firewall to forward TCP port 80 (Web/HTTP) traffic destined to the outside NAT IP to be automatically relayed to a specific server on the inside home network

As you may have guessed, port forwarding is one of the most common methods used to host Web sites at home with DHCP DSL.

DHCP

The Dynamic Host Configuration Protocol (DHCP) is a protocol that automates the assignment of IP addresses, subnet mask default routers, and other IP parameters.

The assignment usually occurs when the DHCP-configured machine boots up or regains connectivity to the network. The DHCP client sends out a query requesting a response from a DHCP server on the locally attached network. The DHCP server then replies to the client PC with its assigned IP address, subnet mask, DNS server, and default gateway information.

The assignment of the IP address usually expires after a predetermined period of time, at which point the DHCP client and server renegotiate a new IP address from the server's predefined pool of addresses. Configuring firewall rules to accommodate access from machines that receive their IP addresses via DHCP is therefore more difficult because the remote IP address will vary from time to time. You'll probably have to allow access for the entire remote DHCP subnet for a particular TCP/UDP port.

Most home router/firewalls are configured in the factory to be DHCP servers for your home network. You can also make your Linux box into a DHCP server, once it has a fixed IP address.

The most commonly used form of DSL will also assign the outside interface of your router/firewall with a single DHCP-provided public IP address.

You can check Chapter 3 for how to configure your Linux box to get its IP address via DHCP. You can also look at Chapter 8, "Configuring the DHCP Server," to find out how to make your Linux box provide the DHCP addresses for the other machines on your network.

How DNS Links Your IP Address to Your Web Domain

The domain name system (DNS) is a worldwide server network used to help translate easy-to-remember domain names like www.linuxhomenetworking.com into an IP address that can be used behind the scenes by your computer. Here is a step-by-step description of what happens with a DNS lookup.

1. Most home computers get the IP address of their DNS server via DHCP from their router/firewall.

2. Home router/firewall providing DHCP services often provides its own IP address as the DNS name server address for home computers.

3. The router/firewall then redirects the DNS queries from your computer to the DNS name server of your ISP.

4. Your ISP's DNS server then probably redirects your query to one of the 13 root name servers.

5. The root server then redirects your query to one of the Internet's .com DNS name servers, which then redirects the query to the linuxhomenetworking.com domain's name server.

6. The linuxhomenetworking.com domain name server then responds with the IP address for www.linuxhomenetworking.com.

As you can imagine, this process can cause a noticeable delay when you are browsing the Web. Each server in the chain will store the most frequent DNS name to IP address lookups in a memory cache that helps speed up the response. Chapter 18, "Configuring DNS," explains how you can make your Linux box into a caching or regular DNS server for your network or Web site if your ISP provides you with fixed IP addresses. Chapter 19, "Dynamic DNS," explains how to configure DNS for a Web site housed on a DHCP DSL circuit where the IP address constantly changes. It explains the auxiliary DNS standard called **dynamic DNS (DDNS)**, which was created for this type of scenario.

IP Version 6 (IPv6)

Most Internet-capable networking devices use version 4 of the Internet Protocol (IPv4), which I have described here. You should also be aware that there is now a version 6 (IPv6) that has recently been developed as a replacement.

With only 32 bits, the allocation of version 4 addresses will soon be exhausted between all the world's ISPs. Version 6, which uses a much larger 128-bit address, offers 80 billion, billion, billion times more IP addresses, which it is hoped should last for most of the 21st century.

IPv6 packets are also labeled to provide quality-of-service information that can be used in prioritizing real-time applications, such as video and voice, over less time-sensitive ones, such as regular Web surfing and chat. IPv6 also inherently supports the IPSec protocol suite used in many forms of secured networks, such as virtual private networks (VPNs).

Most current operating systems support IPv6 even though it isn't currently being used extensively within corporate or home environments. Expect it to become an increasingly bigger part of your network planning in years to come.

HOW SUBNET MASKS GROUP IP ADDRESSES INTO NETWORKS

Subnet masks are used to tell which part of the IP address represents the network on which the computer is connected (network portion) and the computer's unique identifier on that network (host portion). The term **netmasks** is often used interchangeably with the term **subnet masks**; this book uses the latter term for the sake of consistency.

A simple analogy would be a phone number, such as (808) 225-2468. The (808) represents the area code, and the 225-2468 represents the telephone within that area code. Subnet masks enable you to specify how long you want the area code to be (network portion) at the expense of the number of telephones that are in the area code (host portion).

Most home networks use a subnet mask of 255.255.255.0. Each 255 means this octet is for the area code (network portion). So if your server has an IP address of 192.168.1.25 and a subnet mask of 255.255.255.0, the network portion would be 192.168.1 and the server or host would be device #25 on that network.

In all cases, the first IP address in a network is reserved as the network's base address and the last one is reserved for broadcast traffic that is intended to be received by all devices on the network. In our example, 192.168.1.0 would be the network address and 192.168.1.255 would be used for broadcasts. This means you can then use IP addresses from #1 to #254 on your private network.

Calculating the Number of Addresses Assigned to a Subnet

Most office and home networks use networks with 255 IP addresses or less in which the subnet mask starts with the numbers 255.255.255. This is not a pure networking text, so I'll not discuss larger networks because that can become complicated; but in cases where less than 255 IP addresses are required a few rules apply. There are only seven possible values for the last octet of a subnet mask. These are 0, 192, 128, 224, 240, 248 and 252. You can calculate the number of IP addresses for each of these by subtracting the value from 256.

In many cases the subnet mask isn't referred to by the dotted decimal notation, but rather by the actual number of bits in the mask. So for example a mask of 255.255.255.0 may be called a **/24** mask instead. A list of the most commonly used masks in the office or home environment is presented in Table 2.2.

Table 2.2   The Dotted Decimal and Slash Subnet Mask Notations

Dotted Decimal Format	Slash Format	Available Addresses
255.255.255.0	/24	256
255.255.255.128	/25	128
255.255.255.192	/26	64
255.255.255.224	/27	32
255.255.255.240	/28	16
255.255.255.248	/29	8
255.255.255.252	/30	4

So for example, if you have a subnet mask of 255.255.255.192, you have 64 IP addresses in your subnet (256 − 192).

Calculating the Range of Addresses on Your Network

If someone gives you an IP address of 97.158.253.28 and a subnet mask of 255.255.255.248, how do you determine the network address and the broadcast address—in other words, the boundaries of your network? The following section outlines the steps to do this using both a manual and programmed methodology.

Manual Calculation

Take out your pencil and paper—manual calculation can be tricky. Here we go!

1. Subtract the last octet of the subnet mask from 256 to give the number of IP addresses in the subnet (256 − 248 = 8).
2. Divide the last octet of the IP address by the result of step 1; don't bother with the remainder (for example, 28 / 8 = 3). This gives you the theoretical number of subnets of the same size that are below this IP address.

3. Multiply this result by the result of step 1 to get the network address (8 × 3 = 24). Think of it as the third subnet with 8 addresses in it. The network address is therefore 97.158.253.24.

4. The broadcast address is the result of step 3 plus the result of step 1 minus 1. (24 + 8 −1 = 31). Think of it as the broadcast address being the network address plus the number of IP addresses in the subnet minus 1. The broadcast address is 97.158.253.31.

Let's do this for 192.168.3.56 with a mask of 255.255.255.224:

1. 256 − 224 = 32
2. 56 / 32 = 1
3. 32 × 1 = 32. Therefore the network base address is 192.168.3.32.
4. 32 + 32 − 1 = 63. Therefore the broadcast address is 192.168.3.63.

Let's do this for 10.0.0.75 with a mask of 255.255.255.240:

1. 256 − 240 = 16
2. 75 / 16 = 4
3. 16 × 4 = 64. Therefore the network base address is 10.0.0.64.
4. 64 + 16 −1 = 79. Therefore the broadcast address is 10.0.0.79.

Note

As a rule of thumb, the last octet of your network base address must be divisible by the "256 minus the last octet of your subnet mask" and leave no remainder. If you are sub-netting a large chunk of IP addresses it's always a good idea to lay it out on a spreadsheet to make sure there are no overlapping subnets. Once again, this calculation exercise only works with subnet masks that start with "255.255.255".

Calculation Using a Script

There is a BASH script in Appendix II that will do this for you. Here is an example of how to use it; just provide the IP address followed by the subnet mask as arguments. It will accept subnet masks in dotted decimal format or **/value** format:

```
[root@bigboy tmp]# ./subnet-calc.sh 216.151.193.92 /28

IP Address             : 216.151.193.92
Network Base Address   : 216.151.193.80
Broadcast Address      : 216.151.193.95

Subnet Mask            : 255.255.255.240
Subnet Size            : 16 IP Addresses

[root@bigboy tmp]#
```

Subnet Masks for the Typical Business DSL Line

If you purchased a DSL service from your ISP that gives you fixed IP addresses, they will most likely provide you with a subnet mask of 255.255.255.248 that defines 8 IP addresses. For example, if the ISP provides you with a public network address of 97.158.253.24, a subnet mask of 255.255.255.248, and a gateway of 97.158.253.25, your IP addresses will be

```
97.158.253.24 - Network base address
97.158.253.25 - Gateway
97.158.253.26 - Available
97.158.253.27 - Available
97.158.253.28 - Available
97.158.253.29 - Available
97.158.253.30 - Available
97.158.253.31 - Broadcast
```

THE PHYSICAL AND LINK LAYERS

TCP/IP can be quite interesting, but knowledge of the first two layers of the OSI model is important, too, because without them, even the most basic communication would be impossible.

There are very many standards that define the physical, electrical, and error-control methodologies of data communication. One of the most popular ones in departmental networks is Ethernet, which is available in a variety of cable types and speed capabilities, but the data transmission and error correction strategy is the same in all.

Ethernet used to operate primarily in a mode where every computer on a network section shared the same Ethernet cable. Computers would wait until the line was clear before transmitting. They would then send their data while comparing what they wanted to send with what they actually sent on the cable as a means of error detection. If a mathematical comparison, or cyclic redundancy check (CRC), detected any differences between the two, the server would assume that it transmitted data simultaneously with another server on the cable. It would then wait some random time and retransmit at some later stage when the line was clear again.

Transmitting data only after first sensing whether the cable, which was strung between multiple devices, had the correct signaling levels is a methodology called **carrier sense, multiple access** or CSMA. The ability to detect garbling due to simultaneous data transmissions, also known as **collisions**, is called **collision detect** or CD. You will frequently see references to Ethernet being a CSMA/CD technology for this reason, and similar schemes are now being used in wireless networks.

Ethernet devices are now usually connected via a dedicated cable, using more powerful hardware capable of simultaneously transmitting and receiving without interference, thereby making it more reliable and inherently faster than its predecessor versions. The original Ethernet standard has a speed of 10Mbps; the most recent versions can handle up to 40Gbps!

The 802.11 specifications that define many wireless networking technologies are another example of commonly used layer 1 and 2 components of the OSI model. DSL, cable modem standards, and T1 circuits are all parts of these layers.

The next few sections describe many physical and link layer concepts and the operation of the devices that use them to connect the computers in our offices and homes.

NETWORKING EQUIPMENT TERMINOLOGY

Up to this point you have had only an introduction to the theory of the first two OSI layers. Now we'll cover the hardware used to implement them.

Network Interface Cards

Your network interface card is also frequently called a NIC. Currently, the most common types of NIC used in the home and office are Ethernet and wireless Ethernet cards.

The Meaning of the NIC Link Light

The link light signifies that the NIC card has successfully detected a device on the other end of the cable. This indicates that you are using the correct type of cable and that the duplex has been negotiated correctly between the devices at both ends.

Duplex Explained

Full duplex data paths have the capability of allowing the simultaneous sending and receiving of data. Half duplex data paths can transmit in both directions too, but in only one direction at a time.

Full duplex uses separate pairs of wires for transmitting and receiving data so that incoming data flows don't interfere with outgoing data flows.

Half duplex uses the same pairs of wires for transmitting and receiving data. Devices that want to transmit information have to wait their turn until the coast is clear, at which point they send the data. Error-detection and data-retransmission mechanisms ensure that the data reaches the destination correctly and are specifically designed to remedy data corruption caused when multiple devices start transmitting at the same time.

A good analogy for full duplex communications is the telephone, in which both parties can speak at the same time. Half duplex, on the other hand, is more like a walkie-talkie in which both parties have to wait until the other is finished before they can speak.

Data transfer speeds will be low and error levels will be high if you have a device at one end of a cable set to full duplex and a device at the other end of the cable set to half duplex.

Most modern network cards can autonegotiate duplex with the device on the other end of the wire. It is for this reason that duplex settings aren't usually a problem for Linux servers.

The MAC Address

The media access control (MAC) address can be equated to the serial number of the NIC. Every IP packet is sent out of your NIC wrapped inside an Ethernet frame that uses MAC addresses to direct traffic on your locally attached network.

MAC addresses therefore have significance only on the locally attached network. As the packet hops across the Internet, its source/destination IP address stays the same, but the MAC addresses are reassigned by each router on the way using a process called ARP.

How ARP Maps the MAC Address to Your IP Address

The Address Resolution Protocol (ARP) is used to map MAC addresses to network IP addresses. When a server needs to communicate with another server it takes the following steps:

1. The server first checks its routing table to see which router provides the next hop to the destination network.
2. If there is a valid router, let's say with an IP address of 192.168.1.1, the server checks its ARP table to see whether it has the MAC address of the router's NIC. You could very loosely view this as the server trying to find the Ethernet serial number of the next hop router on the local network, thereby ensuring that the packet is sent to the correct device.
3. If there is an ARP entry, the server sends the IP packet to its NIC and tells the NIC to encapsulate the packet in a frame destined for the MAC address of the router.
4. If there is no ARP entry, the server issues an ARP request asking that router 192.168.1.1 respond with its MAC address so that the delivery can be made. When a reply is received, the packet is sent and the ARP table is subsequently updated with the new MAC address.
5. As each router in the path receives the packet, it plucks the IP packet out of the Ethernet frame, leaving the MAC information behind. It then inspects the destination IP address in the packet and uses its routing

table to determine the IP address of the next router on the path to this destination.

6. The router then uses the "ARP-ing" process to get the MAC address of this next hop router. It then reencapsulates the packet in an Ethernet frame with the new MAC address and sends the frame to the next hop router. This relaying process continues until the packet reaches the target computer.

7. If the target server is on the same network as the source server, a similar process occurs. The ARP table is queried. If no entry is available, an ARP request is made asking the target server for its MAC address. When a reply is received, the packet is sent and the ARP table is subsequently updated with the new MAC address.

8. The server will not send the data to its intended destination unless it has an entry in its ARP table for the next hop. If it doesn't, the application needing to communicate will issue a timeout or time exceeded error.

9. As can be expected, the ARP table contains only the MAC addresses of devices on the locally connected network. ARP entries are not permanent and are erased after a fixed period of time depending on the operating system used.

Chapter 3, which covers Linux network topics, shows how to see your ARP table and the MAC addresses of your server's NICs.

The Two Broad Types of Networking Equipment

There are two main types of networking equipment: Data Communications Equipment (DCE), which is intended to act as the primary communications path, and Data Terminal Equipment (DTE), which acts as the source or destination of the transmitted data.

Data Terminal Equipment

DTE devices were originally computer terminals located at remote offices or departments that were directly connected modems. The terminals would have no computing power and only functioned as a screen/keyboard combination for data processing.

Nowadays most PCs have their COM and Ethernet ports configured as if they were going to be connected to a modem or other type of purely networking-oriented equipment.

Data Communications Equipment

DCE is also known as Data Circuit-Terminating Equipment and refers to such equipment as modems and other devices designed primarily to provide network access.

Using Straight-Through/Crossover Cables to Connect DTEs and DCEs

When a DCE is connected to a DTE, you need a **straight-through cable**. DCEs connected to DCEs or DTEs connected to DTEs require **crossover cables**. This terminology is generally used with Ethernet cables.

The terminology can be different for cables used to connect serial ports together. When connecting a PC's COM port (DTE) to a modem (DCE) the straight-through cable is frequently called a **modem cable**. When connecting two PCs (DTE) together via their COM ports, the crossover cable is often referred to as a **null modem cable**.

Some manufacturers configure the Ethernet ports of their networking equipment to be either of the DTE or the DCE type, and other manufacturers have designed their equipment to flip automatically between the two types until it gets a good link. As you can see, confusion can arise when selecting a cable. If you fail to get a link light when connecting your Ethernet devices together, try using the other type of cable.

A straight-through Ethernet cable is easy to identify. Hold the connectors side by side, pointing in the same direction with the clips facing away from you. The color of the wire in position #1 on connector #1 should be the same as that of position #1 on connector #2. The same would go for positions #2 through #8— that is, the same color for corresponding wires on each end. A crossover cable has them mixed up. Table 2.3 provides some good rules of thumb.

Table 2.3   Cabling Rules of Thumb

Scenario	Likely Cable Type
PC to PC	Crossover
Hub to hub	Crossover
Switch to switch	Crossover
PC to modem	Straight through
PC to switch	Straight through
PC to hub	Straight through

Connectivity Using Hubs

A **hub** is a device into which you can connect all devices on a network so that they can talk together. Hubs physically cross-connect all their ports with one another, which causes all traffic sent from a server to the hub to be blurted out to all other servers connected to that hub whether they are the intended recipient or not.

Hubs have no, or very little, electronics inside and therefore do not regulate traffic. It is possible for multiple servers to speak at once, with all of them receiving garbled messages. When this happens the servers try again, after a random time interval, until the message gets through correctly.

It is for these reasons that Ethernet devices that plug into hubs should be set to half duplex.

Note

Hubs can add a lot of delays to your network because of the message garbling collisions and retransmissions. A switch is a much more reliable and predictable alternative, and ones made for the home often cost only a few dollars more.

Using Switches as a Faster Alternative to Hubs

A **switch** is also a device into which you can connect all devices on a home network so that they can talk together. Unlike a hub, traffic sent from Server A to Server B will be received only by Server B. The only exception is broadcast traffic, which is blurted out to all the servers simultaneously.

Switches regulate traffic, thereby eliminating the possibility of message garbling and providing a more efficient traffic flow.

Devices that plug into switches should be set to full duplex to take full advantage of the dedicated bandwidth coming from each switch port.

Local Area Networks

A local area network (LAN) is a grouping of ports on a hub, switch, or tied to a wireless access point (WAP) that can communicate only with each other.

It is possible to connect multiple switches and/or hubs in a chain formation to create a LAN with more ports. This is often called **daisy chaining**.

Switches and hubs provide no access control between servers connected to the same LAN. This is why network administrators group trusted servers having similar roles on the same LAN.

Servers use their IP address and subnet mask and the IP address of the remote server to determine whether they are both on the same network. If not, they attempt to communicate with each other via routers that interconnect their LANs. Routers are also capable of filtering traffic passing between the two LANs, therefore providing additional security.

Larger, more expensive switches can be configured to assign only certain ports to prespecified virtual LANs (VLANs) chosen by the network administrator. In this case, the switch houses ports on multiple LANs. A router still needs to be connected to each VLAN for internetwork communication.

How Routers Interconnect LANs

As stated before, switches and hubs usually have only servers connected to them that have been configured as being part of the same network. By connecting its NIC cards to multiple LANs, a correctly configured router is capable of relaying traffic between networks.

Routers can also be configured to deny communication between specific servers on different networks. They can also filter traffic based on the TCP port section of each packet. For example, it is possible to deny communication between two servers on different networks that intend to communicate on TCP port 80 and allow all other traffic between them. Routers therefore direct and regulate traffic between separate networks, much like a traffic policeman.

If you intend to route between networks, you must reserve an IP address for a router for each network and make sure that the router is directly connected to the LAN associated with that network.

In home networks, routers most frequently provide connectivity to the Internet using network address translation or NAT. In other words, routers act as gateways to the wider world and it won't be surprising to learn that routers are frequently referred to as "gateways."

Note

The term **gateway** specifically refers to a device that routes traffic between dissimilar network protocols (IP to Appletalk) or access methods (Ethernet to DSL). Routers transfer traffic where both the protocols and communications medium are the same. The terms are frequently used interchangeably, especially if only one network protocol is being used. Therefore a home DSL router that provides IP Internet access to an Ethernet network is technically a gateway. The distinction can be important in complicated networking environments where newer technologies need to talk with older ones using incompatible communications protocols.

How Simple Routing Works

In the broader networking sense, a "route" refers to the path data takes to traverse from its source to its destination. Each router along the way may also be referred to as a **hop**.

Usually when we speak about a route on a Linux box, we are referring to the IP address of the first hop needed to reach the desired destination network. It is assumed that this first hop will know how to automatically relay the packet.

Routers are designed to exchange routing information dynamically and can therefore intelligently redirect traffic to bypass failed network links. Home Linux boxes frequently don't run a dynamic routing protocol and therefore rely on **static** routes issued by the system administrator at the command line or in configuration files to determine the next hop to all desired networks.

Chapter 3, which covers Linux network topics, shows how to add static routes to your Linux box and also how you can convert it into a simple router.

Default Gateways, the Routers of Last Resort

A default gateway is the router that is used when no alternative devices can be found to relay the traffic. They are often called **routers of last resort**.

Say for example you have two routers, R1 and R2. R1 is connected to both your SOHO home network and the Internet. R2 is connected to SOHO home network and is capable of relaying data to other corporate networks with addresses starting with 10.X.X.X via another NIC card.

You could put a route on your SOHO servers that states:

☞ Go to network 10.0.0.0 255.0.0.0 via router R2.

☞ Go to everything else via router R1. R1 therefore would be considered your default gateway.

For most home networks, your default gateway would be the router/ firewall connected to the Internet.

Chapter 3, which covers Linux network topics, shows how to configure the default gateway on your Linux box.

Firewalls Help Provide a Secure Routing Environment

Firewalls can be viewed as routers with more enhanced abilities to restrict traffic, not just by port and IP address as routers do. Specifically, firewalls can detect malicious attempts to subvert the TCP/IP protocol. A short list of capabilities includes the following:

☞ Throttling traffic to a server when too many unfulfilled connections are made to it

☞ Restricting traffic being sent to obviously bogus IP addresses

☞ Providing network address translation or NAT

Routers are designed to make packets flow as quickly as possible with the minimum amount of inspection. Firewalls are used as close to the source or target of data communication as possible to try to ensure that the data hasn't been subverted.

Firewalls can often create an encrypted data path between two private networks across the Internet providing secure communication with a greatly reduced chance of eavesdropping. These VPNs are frequently used to connect branch offices to the corporate headquarters and also to allow sales representatives to get access to sensitive pricing information when traveling from town to town.

ADDITIONAL INTRODUCTORY TOPICS

The last few topics of this chapter may not appear to be directly related to networking, but they cover Linux help methods that you'll use extensively and the File Transfer Protocol (FTP) package, which enables you to download all the software you need to get your Linux server operational as quickly as possible.

The File Transfer Protocol

FTP is one of the most popular applications used to copy files between computers via a network connection. Knowledge of FTP is especially important and is a primary method of downloading software for Linux systems.

There are a number of commercially available GUI-based clients you can load on your PC to do this, such as WSFTP and CuteFTP. You can also use FTP from the command line, as shown in Chapter 5, "Troubleshooting Linux with Syslog," on RPM software installation.

From the remote user's perspective, there are two types of FTP. The first is **regular FTP**, which is used primarily to allow specific users to download files to their systems. The remote FTP server prompts you for a specific username and password to gain access to the data.

The second method, **anonymous FTP**, is used primarily to allow any remote user to download files to their systems. The remote FTP server prompts you for a username, at which point the user types `anonymous` or `ftp` with the password being any valid e-mail address.

From the systems administrator's perspective, there are two more categories. These are **active** and **passive** FTP, which are covered in more detail in Chapter 15, "Linux FTP Server Setup."

Remember that FTP isn't very secure because usernames, passwords, and data are sent across the network unencrypted. More secure forms—such as SFTP (Secure FTP) and SCP (Secure Copy)—are available as a part of the Secure Shell package (covered in Chapter 17, "Secure Remote Logins and File Copying") that is normally installed by default with Fedora.

Linux Help

Linux help files are accessed using the `man` or manual pages. From the command line you issue the `man` command followed by the Linux command or file about which you want information. If you want to get information on the `ssh` command, you use the command `man ssh`:

```
[root@bigboy tmp]# man ssh
```

If you want to search all the `man` pages for a keyword, use the `man` command with the `-k` switch—for example, `man -k ssh`, which gives a list of all the `man` pages that contain the word `ssh`:

```
[root@bigboy tmp]# man -k ssh
...
...
ssh                    (1)  - OpenSSH SSH client (remote login program)
ssh [slogin]           (1)  - OpenSSH SSH client (remote login program)
ssh-agent              (1)  - authentication agent
ssh-keyscan            (1)  - gather ssh public keys
ssh_config             (5)  - OpenSSH SSH client configuration files
sshd                   (8)  - OpenSSH SSH daemon
sshd_config            (5)  - OpenSSH SSH daemon configuration file
...
...
[root@bigboy tmp]#
```

This book is targeted at proficient Linux beginners and above, so I'll be using a wide variety of commands in this book without detailed explanations to help keep the flow brisk. If you need more help on a command, use its man page to get more details on what it does and the syntax it needs. Linux help can sometimes be cryptic, but with a little practice the man pages can become your friend.

CONCLUSION

Congratulations! Now that you have an understanding of basic networking, it's time to read Chapter 3 to learn how to configure Linux networking.

Feel free to return to this chapter whenever you need to refresh your memory on these foundation concepts.

Linux Networking

IN THIS CHAPTER

Now that you have a firm grasp of many of the most commonly used networking concepts, it is time to apply them to the configuration of your server. Some of these activities are automatically covered during a Linux installation, but you will often find yourself having to know how to modify these initial settings whenever you need to move your server to another network, add a new network interface card, or use an alternative means of connecting to the Internet.

In Chapter 2, "Introduction to Networking," we started with an explanation of TCP/IP, so we'll start this Linux networking chapter with a discussion on how to configure the IP address of your server.

HOW TO CONFIGURE YOUR NIC'S IP ADDRESS

You need to know all the steps to configure IP addresses on a NIC card. Web site shopping cart applications frequently need an additional IP address dedicated to them. You also might need to add a secondary NIC interface to your server to handle data backups. Last but not least, you might just want to play around with the server to test your skills.

This section shows you how to do the most common server IP activities with the least amount of headaches.

Determining Your IP Address

Most modern PCs come with an Ethernet port. When Linux is installed, this device is called `eth0`. You can determine the IP address of this device with the `ifconfig` command:

```
[root@bigboy tmp]# ifconfig -a

eth0 Link encap:Ethernet HWaddr 00:08:C7:10:74:A8
BROADCAST MULTICAST MTU:1500 Metric:1
RX packets:0 errors:0 dropped:0 overruns:0 frame:0
TX packets:0 errors:0 dropped:0 overruns:0 carrier:0
collisions:0 txqueuelen:100
RX bytes:0 (0.0 b) TX bytes:0 (0.0 b)
Interrupt:11 Base address:0x1820

lo Link encap:Local Loopback
inet addr:127.0.0.1 Mask:255.0.0.0
UP LOOPBACK RUNNING MTU:16436 Metric:1
RX packets:787 errors:0 dropped:0 overruns:0 frame:0
TX packets:787 errors:0 dropped:0 overruns:0 carrier:0
collisions:0 txqueuelen:0
RX bytes:82644 (80.7 Kb) TX bytes:82644 (80.7 Kb)

wlan0 Link encap:Ethernet HWaddr 00:06:25:09:6A:B5
inet addr:192.168.1.100 Bcast:192.168.1.255 Mask:255.255.255.0
UP BROADCAST RUNNING MULTICAST MTU:1500 Metric:1
RX packets:47379 errors:0 dropped:0 overruns:0 frame:0
TX packets:107900 errors:0 dropped:0 overruns:0 carrier:0
collisions:0 txqueuelen:100
RX bytes:4676853 (4.4 Mb) TX bytes:43209032 (41.2 Mb)
Interrupt:11 Memory:c887a000-c887b000

wlan0:0 Link encap:Ethernet HWaddr 00:06:25:09:6A:B5
inet addr:192.168.1.99 Bcast:192.168.1.255 Mask:255.255.255.0
UP BROADCAST RUNNING MULTICAST MTU:1500 Metric:1
Interrupt:11 Memory:c887a000-c887b000


[root@bigboy tmp]#
```

In this example, eth0 has no IP address because this box is using wireless interface wlan0 as its main NIC Interface. wlan0 has an IP address of 192.168.1.100 and a subnet mask of 255.255.255.0

You can see that this command gives good information on the interrupts, or PCI bus ID, used by each card. On very rare occasions you may find that your NIC card doesn't work because it shares both an interrupt and memory access address with some other device. You can look at the contents of the /proc/interrupts file to get a listing of all the interrupt IRQs used by your system. In the example below we can see that there are no conflicts with each IRQ from 0 to 15 having only a single entry. Devices eth0 and eth1 use interrupts 10 and 5, respectively:

```
[root@bigboy tmp]# cat /proc/interrupts
             CPU0
  0:  2707402473       XT-PIC   timer
  1:          67       XT-PIC   i8042
  2:           0       XT-PIC   cascade
  5:      411342       XT-PIC   eth1
  8:           1       XT-PIC   rtc
 10:     1898752       XT-PIC   eth0
 11:           0       XT-PIC   uhci_hcd
 12:          58       XT-PIC   i8042
 14:     5075806       XT-PIC   ide0
 15:         506       XT-PIC   ide1
NMI:           0
ERR:          43
[root@bigboy tmp]#
```

If there are conflicts, you might need to refer to the manual for the offending device to try to determine ways to either use another interrupt or memory I/O location.

Changing Your IP Address

If you wanted, you could give this eth0 interface an IP address using the ifconfig command:

```
[root@bigboy tmp]# ifconfig eth0 10.0.0.1 netmask 255.255.255.0 up
```

The up at the end of the command activates the interface. To make this permanent each time you boot up you have to add this command in your /etc/rc.local file, which is run at the end of every reboot.

Fedora Linux also makes life a little easier with interface configuration files located in the /etc/sysconfig/network-scripts directory. Interface eth0 has a file called ifcfg-eth0, eth1 uses ifcfg-eth1, and so on. You can place your IP address information in these files, which are then used to autoconfigure your NICs when Linux boots. See Figure 3.1 for two samples of interface eth0. One assumes the interface has a fixed IP address, and the other assumes it requires an IP address assignment using DHCP.

Fixed IP Address

```
[root@bigboy tmp]# cd /etc/sysconfig/network-scripts
[root@bigboy network-scripts]# less ifcfg-eth0
DEVICE=eth0
IPADDR=192.168.1.100
NETMASK=255.255.255.0
BOOTPROTO=static
ONBOOT=yes
#
# The following settings are optional
#
BROADCAST=192.168.1.255
NETWORK=192.168.1.0
[root@bigboy network-scripts]#
```

Getting the IP Address Using DHCP

```
[root@bigboy tmp]# cd /etc/sysconfig/network-scripts
[root@bigboy network-scripts]# less ifcfg-eth0
DEVICE=eth0
BOOTPROTO=dhcp
ONBOOT=yes
[root@bigboy network-scripts]#
```

Figure 3.1   File formats for network-scripts.

As you can see, eth0 will be activated on booting, because the parameter ONBOOT has the value yes and not no. You can read more about netmasks and DHCP in Chapter 2, which acts as an introduction to networking.

The default Red Hat/Fedora installation will include the broadcast and network options in the network-scripts file. These are optional.

After you change the values in the configuration files for the NIC you have to deactivate and activate it for the modifications to take effect. The ifdown and ifup commands can be used to do this:

```
[root@bigboy network-scripts]# ifdown eth0
[root@bigboy network-scripts]# ifup eth0
```

Your server will have to have a default gateway for it to be able to communicate with the Internet. This will be covered later in the chapter.

How DHCP Affects the DNS Server You Use

Your DHCP server not only supplies the IP address your Linux box should use, but also the desired DNS servers. Make sure your `/etc/resolv.conf` file has the `servers` configuration lines commented out to prevent any conflicts.

Multiple IP Addresses on a Single NIC

In the previous section, "Determining Your IP Address," you may have noticed that there were two wireless interfaces: wlan0 and wlan0:0. Interface wlan0:0 is actually a child of interface wlan0, a virtual subinterface also known as an IP alias. IP aliasing is one of the most common ways of creating multiple IP addresses associated with a single NIC. Aliases have the name format *parent-interface-name:X*, where *X* is the subinterface number of your choice.

The process for creating an IP alias is very similar to the steps outlined for the real interface in the previous section, "Changing Your IP Address:"

1. First ensure the parent real interface exists.

2. Verify that no other IP aliases with the same name exist with the name you plan to use. In this we want to create interface `wlan0:0`.

3. Create the virtual interface with the `ifconfig` command:

```
[root@bigboy tmp]# ifconfig wlan0:0 192.168.1.99 \
    netmask 255.255.255.0 up
```

4. You should also create a `/etc/sysconfig/network-scripts/ifcfg-wlan0:0` file so that the aliases will all be managed automatically with the `ifup` and `ifdown` commands. Here is a sample configuration:

```
DEVICE=wlan0:0
ONBOOT=yes
BOOTPROTO=static
IPADDR=192.168.1.99
NETMASK=255.255.255.0
```

The commands to activate and deactivate the alias interface would therefore be:

```
[root@bigboy tmp]# ifup wlan0:0
[root@bigboy tmp]# ifdown wlan0:0
```

Note

Shutting down the main interface also shuts down all its aliases. Aliases can be shut down independently of other interfaces.

After completing these four simple steps you should be able to ping the new IP alias from other servers on your network.

IP Address Assignment for a Direct DSL Connection

If you are using a DSL connection with fixed or static IP addresses, the configuration steps are the same as those outlined earlier. You plug your Ethernet interface into the DSL modem, configure it with the IP address, subnet mask, broadcast address, and gateway information provided by your ISP and you should have connectivity when you restart your interface. Remember that you may also need to configure your DNS server correctly.

If you are using a DSL connection with a DHCP or dynamic IP address assignment, the process is different. Your ISP will provide you with a PPP authentication over Ethernet (PPPoE) `username` and `password` that will allow your computer to log in transparently to the Internet each time it boots up. Fedora Linux installs the `rp-pppoe` RPM software package required to support this.

Note

Unless you specifically request static IP addresses, your ISP will provide you with a DHCP-based connection. The DHCP IP address assigned to your computer and/or Internet router will often not change for many days and you may be fooled into thinking it is static.

Downloading and installing RPMs isn't hard. If you need a refresher, Chapter 6, "Installing RPM Software," covers how to do this in detail. When searching for the file, remember that the PPPoE RPM's filename usually starts with the word `rp-pppoe` followed by a version number like this: `rp-pppoe-3.5-8.i386.rpm`.

After installing the RPM, you need to go through a number of steps to complete the connection. The PPPOE configuration will create a software-based virtual interface named `ppp0` that will use the physical Internet interface `eth0` for connectivity. Here's what you need to do:

1. Make a backup copy of your `ifcfg-eth0` file:

```
[root@bigboy tmp]#
[root@bigboy tmp]# cd /etc/sysconfig/network-scripts/
[root@bigboy network-scripts]# ls ifcfg-eth0
ifcfg-eth0
[root@bigboy network-scripts]# cp ifcfg-eth0
DISABLED.ifcfg-eth0
```

2. Edit your `ifcfg-eth0` file to have no IP information and also to be deactivated on boot time.

```
DEVICE=eth0
ONBOOT=no
```

3. Shut down your `eth0` interface:

```
[root@bigboy network-scripts]# ifdown eth0
[root@bigboy network-scripts]#
```

4. Run the `adsl-setup` configuration script:

```
[root@bigboy network-scripts]# adsl-setup
```

It will prompt you for your ISP username, the interface to be used (`eth0`), and whether you want the connection to stay up indefinitely. We'll use defaults wherever possible:

```
Welcome to the ADSL client setup.  First, I will run some checks on
your system to make sure the PPPoE client is installed properly...

LOGIN NAME

Enter your Login Name (default root): bigboy-login@isp

INTERFACE

Enter the Ethernet interface connected to the ADSL modem
For Solaris, this is likely to be something like /dev/hme0.
For Linux, it will be ethX, where 'X' is a number.
(default eth0):

Do you want the link to come up on demand, or stay up continuously?
If you want it to come up on demand, enter the idle time in seconds
after which the link should be dropped.  If you want the link to
stay up permanently, enter 'no' (two letters, lower-case.)
NOTE: Demand-activated links do not interact well with dynamic IP
addresses.  You may have some problems with demand-activated links.
Enter the demand value (default no):
```

It will then prompt you for your DNS server information. This step edits your `/etc/resolv.conf` file. If you're running BIND on your server in a caching DNS mode then you may want to leave this option blank. If you want your ISP to provide the IP address of its DNS server automatically, enter the word `server`.

Please refer to Chapter 18, "Configuring DNS," for more information on BIND and DNS.

```
DNS

Please enter the IP address of your ISP's primary DNS server.
If your ISP claims that 'the server will provide dynamic DNS
addresses', enter 'server' (all lower-case) here.
If you just press enter, I will assume you know what you are
doing and not modify your DNS setup.
Enter the DNS information here:
```

The script will then prompt you for your ISP password:

```
PASSWORD

Please enter your Password:
Please re-enter your Password:
```

Then it will ask whether you want regular users (not superuser `root`) to be able to activate/deactivate the new `ppp0` interface. This may be required if non-root members of your family or home office need to get access to the Internet:

```
USERCTRL

Please enter 'yes' (three letters, lower-case.) if you want to allow
normal user to start or stop DSL connection (default yes):
```

The `rp-pppoe` package has two sample iptables firewall scripts located in the `/etc/ppp` directory named `firewall-standalone` and `firewall-masq`. They are very basic and don't cover rules to make your Linux box a Web server, DNS server, or mail server. I'd recommend selecting `none` and using a variant of the basic script samples in Chapter 14, "Linux Firewalls Using iptables," or the more comprehensive one found in the Appendix.

```
FIREWALLING

Please choose the firewall rules to use.  Note that these rules are
very basic.  You are strongly encouraged to use a more sophisticated
firewall setup; however, these will provide basic security.  If you
are running any servers on your machine, you must choose 'NONE' and
set up firewalling yourself. Otherwise, the firewall rules will deny
access to all standard servers like Web, e-mail, ftp, etc.  If you
are using SSH, the rules will block outgoing SSH connections which
allocate a privileged source port.

The firewall choices are:
0 - NONE: This script will not set any firewall rules.  You are
          responsible for ensuring the security of your machine.  You
          are STRONGLY recommended to use some kind of firewall rules.
1 - STANDALONE: Appropriate for a basic stand-alone web-surfing
          workstation
2 - MASQUERADE: Appropriate for a machine acting as an Internet
          gateway for a LAN
Choose a type of firewall (0-2): 0
```

You'll then be asked whether you want the connection to be activated upon booting. Most people would say `yes`:

```
Start this connection at boot time

Do you want to start this connection at boot time?
Please enter no or yes (default no):yes
```

Just before exiting, you'll get a summary of the parameters you entered and the relevant configuration files will be updated to reflect your choices when you accept them:

```
** Summary of what you entered **

Ethernet Interface: eth0
User name:          bigboy-login@isp
Activate-on-demand: No
DNS:                Do not adjust
Firewalling:        NONE
User Control:       yes
Accept these settings and adjust configuration files (y/n)? y

Adjusting /etc/sysconfig/network-scripts/ifcfg-ppp0
Adjusting /etc/ppp/chap-secrets and /etc/ppp/pap-secrets
  (But first backing it up to /etc/ppp/chap-secrets.bak)
  (But first backing it up to /etc/ppp/pap-secrets.bak)
```

At the very end it will tell you the commands to use to activate/deactivate your new ppp0 interface and to get a status of the interface's condition:

```
Congratulations, it should be all set up!

Type '/sbin/ifup ppp0' to bring up your xDSL link and '/sbin/ifdown
ppp0'to bring it down.
Type '/sbin/adsl-status /etc/sysconfig/network-scripts/ifcfg-ppp0'
to see the link status.
```

Note

This example recommends using the adsl-status command with the name of the PPPoE interface configuration file. This command defaults to show information for interface ppp0, and therefore listing the ifcfg-ppp0 filename won't be necessary in most home environments.

After you have completed installing rp-pppoe you should be able to access the Internet over your DHCP DSL connection as expected.

Some Important Files Created by adsl-setup

The adsl-setup script creates three files that will be of interest to you. The first is the ifcfg-ppp0 file with interface's link layer connection parameters:

```
[root@bigboy network-scripts]# more ifcfg-ppp0
USERCTL=yes
BOOTPROTO=dialup
NAME=DSLppp0
DEVICE=ppp0
TYPE=xDSL
ONBOOT=yes
PIDFILE=/var/run/pppoe-adsl.pid
FIREWALL=NONE
PING=.
PPPOE_TIMEOUT=20
LCP_FAILURE=3
LCP_INTERVAL=80
```

```
CLAMPMSS=1412
CONNECT_POLL=6
CONNECT_TIMEOUT=60
DEFROUTE=yes
SYNCHRONOUS=no
ETH=eth0
PROVIDER=DSLppp0
USER= bigboy-login@isp
PEERDNS=no
[root@bigboy network-scripts]#
```

The others are the duplicate /etc/ppp/pap-secrets and /etc/ppp/chap-secrets files with the username and password needed to login to your ISP:

```
[root@bigboy network-scripts]# more /etc/ppp/pap-secrets
# Secrets for authentication using PAP
# client          server  secret              IP addresses
"bigboy-login@isp" *       "password"
[root@bigboy network-scripts]#
```

Simple Troubleshooting

You can run the adsl-status command to determine the condition of your connection. In this case the package has been installed but the interface hasn't been activated:

```
[root@bigboy tmp]# adsl-status
Note: You have enabled demand-connection; adsl-status may be
inaccurate.
adsl-status: Link is attached to ppp0, but ppp0 is down
[root@bigboy tmp]#
```

After activation, the interface appears to work correctly:

```
[root@bigboy tmp]# ifup ppp0

[root@bigboy tmp]# adsl-status
adsl-status: Link is up and running on interface ppp0
ppp0: flags=8051<UP,POINTOPOINT,RUNNING,MULTICAST> mtu 1462 inet
...
...
...
[root@bigboy tmp]#
```

For further troubleshooting information you can visit the Web site of rp-ppoe at Roaring Penguin (www.roaringpenguin.com). There are some good tips there on how to avoid problems with VPN clients.

IP Address Assignment for a Cable Modem Connection

Cable modems use DHCP to get their IP addresses, so you can configure your server's Ethernet interface accordingly.

HOW TO ACTIVATE/SHUT DOWN YOUR NIC

The `ifup` and `ifdown` commands can be used respectively to activate and deactivate a NIC interface. You must have an `ifcfg` file in the `/etc/sysconfig/network-scripts` directory for these commands to work. Here is an example for interface `eth0`:

```
[root@bigboy tmp]# ifdown eth0
[root@bigboy tmp]# ifup eth0
```

HOW TO VIEW YOUR CURRENT ROUTING TABLE

The `netstat -nr` command will provide the contents of the routing table. Networks with a gateway of 0.0.0.0 are usually directly connected to the interface. No gateway is needed to reach your own directly connected interface, so a gateway address of 0.0.0.0 seems appropriate. Your default gateway is the route with a destination address of 0.0.0.0.

☞ In this example there are two gateways, the default and one to 255.255.255.255 which is usually added on DHCP servers. Server bigboy is a DHCP server in this case:

```
[root@bigboy tmp]# netstat -nr
Kernel IP routing table

Destination      Gateway      Genmask          Flags MSS Window irtt Iface
255.255.255.255  0.0.0.0      255.255.255.255  UH    40  0      0    wlan0

192.168.1.0      0.0.0.0      255.255.255.0    U     40  0      0    wlan0

127.0.0.0        0.0.0.0      255.0.0.0        U     40  0      0    lo

0.0.0.0          192.168.1.1  0.0.0.0          UG    40  0      0    wlan0

[root@bigboy tmp]#
```

☞ In this example, there are multiple gateways handling traffic destined
for different networks on different interfaces:

```
[root@bigboy tmp]# netstat -nr
Kernel IP routing table

Destination    Gateway        Genmask         Flags MSS Window irtt
Iface

172.16.68.64   172.16.69.193  255.255.255.224 UG    40  0      0    eth1

172.16.11.96   172.16.69.193  255.255.255.224 UG    40  0      0    eth1

172.16.68.32   172.16.69.193  255.255.255.224 UG    40  0      0    eth1

172.16.67.0    172.16.67.135  255.255.255.224 UG    40  0      0    eth0

172.16.69.192  0.0.0.0        255.255.255.192 U     40  0      0    eth1

172.16.67.128  0.0.0.0        255.255.255.128 U     40  0      0    eth0

172.160.0      172.16.67.135  255.255.0.0     UG    40  0      0    eth0

172.16.0.0     172.16.67.131  255.240.0.0     UG    40  0      0    eth0

127.0.0.0      0.0.0.0        255.0.0.0       U     40  0      0    lo

0.0.0.0        172.16.69.193  0.0.0.0         UG    40  0      0    eth1

[root@bigboy tmp]#
```

HOW TO CHANGE YOUR DEFAULT GATEWAY

Your server needs to have a single default gateway. DHCP servers automatically assign a default gateway to DHCP-configured NICs, but NICs with configured, static IP addresses will need to have a manually configured default gateway. This can be done with a simple command. This example uses a newly installed wireless interface called wlan0; most PCs would be using the standard Ethernet interface eth0:

```
[root@bigboy tmp]# route add default gw 192.168.1.1 wlan0
```

In this case, make sure that the router/firewall with IP address 192.168.1.1 is connected to the same network as interface wlan0!

When this is done, you need to update your /etc/sysconfig/network file to reflect the change. This file is used to configure your default gateway each time Linux boots:

```
NETWORKING=yes
HOSTNAME=bigboy
GATEWAY=192.168.1.1
```

Some people don't bother with this step and just place the `route add` command in the script file `/etc/rc.d/rc.local` which is run at the end of every reboot.

It is possible to define default gateways in the NIC configuration file in the `/etc/sysconfig/network-scripts` directory, but you run the risk of inadvertently assigning more than one default gateway when you have more than one NIC. This will cause packets to be sent to alternating gateways and could cause connectivity problems. If one of the default gateways has no route to the intended destination, every other packet will become lost. Firewalls that are designed to block packets with irregular sequence numbers and unexpected origins could also obstruct your data flow.

HOW TO CONFIGURE TWO GATEWAYS

Some networks may have multiple router/firewalls providing connectivity. Here's a typical scenario:

☞ You have one router providing access to the Internet that you'd like to have as your default gateway (see the default gateway example earlier).

☞ You also have another router providing access to your corporate network using addresses in the range 10.0.0.0 to 10.255.255.255. Let's assume that this router has an IP address of 192.168.1.254

The Linux box used in this example uses interface `wlan0` for its Internet connectivity. You may be most likely using interface `eth0`, please adjust your steps accordingly.

There are a number of ways to add this new route.

Adding Routes from the Command Line

The `route add` command can be used to add new routes to your server. It has the advantage of being universal to all versions of Linux and is well documented in the `man` pages. In our example the reference to the 10.0.0.0 network has to be preceded with a `-net` switch, and the subnet mask and gateway values also have to be preceded by the `netmask` and `gw` switches, respectively:

```
[root@bigboy tmp]# route add -net 10.0.0.0 netmask 255.0.0.0 \
   gw 192.168.1.254 wlan0
```

If you wanted to add a route to an individual server, the `-host` switch would be used with no netmask value. (The route command automatically knows the mask should be 255.255.255.255.) Here is an example for a route to host 10.0.0.1:

```
[root@bigboy tmp]# route add -host 10.0.0.1 gw 192.168.1.254 wlan0
```

A universal way of making this change persistent after a reboot would be to place this `route` `add` command in the file `/etc/rc.d/rc.local`, which is always run at the end of the booting process.

Adding Routes with */etc/sysconfig/network-scripts/* Files

In Fedora Linux, permanent static routes are added on a per interface basis in files located in the `/etc/sysconfig/network-scripts` directory. The filename format is `route-interface-name`, so the filename for interface `wlan0` would be `route-wlan0`.

The format of the file is quite intuitive with the target network coming in the first column followed by the word `via` and then the gateway's IP address. In our routing example, to set up a route to network 10.0.0.0 with a subnet mask of 255.0.0.0 (a mask with the first 8 bits set to 1) via the 192.168.1.254 gateway, we would have to configure file `/etc/sysconfig/network-scripts/route-wlan0` to look like this:

```
#
# File /etc/sysconfig/network-scripts/route-wlan0
#
10.0.0.0/8 via 192.168.1.254
```

Note

The `/etc/sysconfig/network-scripts/route-*` filename is very important. Adding the wrong interface extension at the end will result in the routes not being added after the next reboot. There will also be no reported errors on the screen or any of the log files in the `/var/log/` directory.

You can test the new file by running the `/etc/sysconfig/network-scripts/ifup-routes` command with the interface name as the sole argument. In the next example we check the routing table to see no routes to the 10.0.0.0 network and execute the `ifup-routes` command, which then adds the route:

```
[root@bigboy tmp]# netstat -nr
Kernel IP routing table
Destination  Gateway       Genmask        Flags MSS Window irtt Iface
192.168.1.0  0.0.0.0       255.255.255.0  U     0   0      0    wlan0
169.254.0.0  0.0.0.0       255.255.0.0    U     0   0      0    wlan0
0.0.0.0      192.168.1.1   0.0.0.0        UG    0   0      0    wlan0
[root@bigboy tmp]#

[root@bigboy tmp]# ./ifup-routes wlan0

[root@bigboy tmp]# netstat -nr
Kernel IP routing table
Destination  Gateway       Genmask        Flags MSS Window irtt Iface
192.168.1.0  0.0.0.0       255.255.255.0  U     0   0      0    wlan0
169.254.0.0  0.0.0.0       255.255.0.0    U     0   0      0    wlan0
10.0.0.0     192.168.1.254 255.0.0.0      UG    0   0      0    wlan0
0.0.0.0      192.168.1.1   0.0.0.0        UG    0   0      0    wlan0
[root@bigboy tmp]#
```

How to Delete a Route

Here's how to delete the routes added in the previous section:

```
[root@bigboy tmp]# route del -net 10.0.0.0 netmask 255.0.0.0 \
   gw 192.168.1.254 wlan0
```

The file `/etc/sysconfig/network-scripts/route-wlan0` will also have to be updated so that when you reboot, the server will not reinsert the route. Delete the line that reads

```
10.0.0.0/8 via 192.168.1.254
```

Changing NIC Speed and Duplex

There is no better Linux investment than the purchase of a fully Linux-compatible NIC card. Most Linux vendors have a list of compatible hardware on their Web sites; read this carefully before you start hooking up your machine to the network. If you can't find any of the desired models in your local computer store, a model in the same family or series should be sufficient. Most cards will work, but only the fully compatible ones will provide you with error-free, consistent throughput.

Linux defaults to negotiating the speed and duplex of its NIC automatically with that of the switch to which it is attached. Configuring a switch port to autonegotiate the speed and duplex often isn't sufficient because there are frequently differences in the implementation of the protocol standard.

Typically, NICs with failed negotiation will work, but this is usually accompanied by many collision-type errors being seen on the NIC, when using the `ifconfig -a` command, and only marginal performance. Don't limit your troubleshooting of these types of errors to just failed negotiation; the problem could also be due to a bad NIC card, switch port, or cabling.

Using *mii-tool*

One of the original Linux tools for setting the speed and duplex of your NIC card was the `mii-tool` command. It is destined to be deprecated and replaced by the newer `ethtool` command, but many older NICs support only `mii-tool`, so you need to be aware of it.

Issuing the command without any arguments gives a brief status report, as seen in the next example, with unsupported NICs providing an `Operation not supported` message. NICs that are not compatible with `mii-tool` often will still work, but you have to refer to the manufacturer's guides to set the speed and duplex to anything but `auto-negotiate`.

```
[root@bigboy tmp]# mii-tool
SIOCGMIIPHY on 'eth0' failed: Operation not supported
eth1: 100 Mbit, half duplex, link ok
[root@bigboy tmp]#
```

By using the verbose mode -v switch you can get much more information. In this case, negotiation was OK, with the NIC selecting 100Mbps, full duplex mode (FD):

```
[root@bigboy tmp]# mii-tool -v
eth1: negotiated 100baseTx-FD, link ok
   product info: vendor 00:10:18, model 33 rev 2
   basic mode:    autonegotiation enabled
   basic status: autonegotiation complete, link ok
   capabilities: 100baseTx-FD 100baseTx-HD 10baseT-FD 10baseT-HD
   advertising:   100baseTx-FD 100baseTx-HD 10baseT-FD 10baseT-HD
   link partner: 100baseTx-FD 100baseTx-HD 10baseT-FD 10baseT-HD flow-
control
[root@bigboy tmp]#
```

Setting Your NIC's Speed Parameters with mii-tool

You can set your NIC to force itself to a particular speed and duplex by using the -F switch with any of the following options: 100baseTx-FD, 100baseTx-HD, 10baseT-FD, or 10baseT-HD. Remember that you could lose all network connectivity to your server if you force your NIC to a particular speed/duplex that doesn't match that of your switch:

```
[root@bigboy tmp]# mii-tool -F 100baseTx-FD eth0
```

Unfortunately there is no way to set this on reboot permanently except by placing the command in the /etc/rc.local file to let it be run at the very end of the booting process or by creating your own startup script if you need it set earlier. Creating your own startup scripts is covered in Chapter 7, "The Linux Boot Process."

Using ethtool

The ethtool command is slated to be the replacement for mii-tool in the near future and tends to be supported by newer NIC cards.

The command provides the status of the interface you provide as its argument. Here we see interface eth0 not doing autonegotiation and set to a speed of 100Mbps, full duplex. A list of supported modes is also provided at the top of the output:

```
[root@bigboy tmp]# ethtool eth0
Settings for eth0:
```

```
            Supported ports: [ TP MII ]
            Supported link modes:   10baseT/Half 10baseT/Full
                                    100baseT/Half 100baseT/Full
            Supports auto-negotiation: Yes
            Advertised link modes:  10baseT/Half 10baseT/Full
                                    100baseT/Half 100baseT/Full
            Advertised auto-negotiation: No
            Speed: 100Mb/s
            Duplex: Full
            Port: MII
            PHYAD: 1
            Transceiver: internal
            Auto-negotiation: off
            Supports Wake-on: g
            Wake-on: g
            Current message level: 0x00000007 (7)
            Link detected: yes
[root@bigboy tmp]#
```

Setting Your NIC's Speed Parameters with ethtool

Unlike `mii-tool`, `ethtool` settings can be permanently set as part of the interface's configuration script with the `ETHTOOL_OPTS` variable. In our next example, the settings will be set to 100Mbps, full duplex with no chance for autonegotiation on the next reboot:

```
#
# File: /etc/sysconfig/network-script/ifcfg-eth0
#
DEVICE=eth0
IPADDR=192.168.1.100
NETMASK=255.255.255.0
BOOTPROTO=static
ONBOOT=yes
ETHTOOL_OPTS = "speed 100 duplex full autoneg off"
```

You can test the application of these parameters by shutting down the interface and activating it again with the `ifup` and `ifdown` commands.

These settings can also be changed from the command line using the `-s` switch followed by the interface name and its desired configuration parameters.

```
[root@bigboy tmp]# ethtool -s eth1 speed 100 duplex full autoneg off
[root@bigboy tmp]#
```

The Linux `man` pages give more details on other `ethtool` options, but you can get a quick guide by just entering the `ethtool` command alone, which provides a quicker summary:

```
[root@bigboy tmp]# ethtool
...
...
```

```
ethtool -s DEVNAME \
        [ speed 10|100|1000 ] \
        [ duplex half|full ]      \
        [ port tp|aui|bnc|mii|fibre ] \
...
...
[root@bigboy tmp]#
```

HOW TO CONVERT YOUR LINUX SERVER INTO A ROUTER

Router/firewall appliances that provide basic Internet connectivity for a small office or home network are becoming more affordable every day, but when budgets are tight you might seriously want to consider modifying an existing Linux server to do the job.

Details on how to configure Linux firewall security are covered in Chapter 14, but you need to understand how to activate routing through the firewall before it can become a functioning networking device.

Configuring IP Forwarding

For your Linux server to become a router, you have to enable packet forwarding. In simple terms packet forwarding enables packets to flow through the Linux box from one network to another.

The Linux kernel configuration parameter to activate this is named net.ipv4.ip_forward and can be found in the file /etc/sysctl.conf. Remove the # from the line related to packet forwarding.

Before:

```
# Disables packet forwarding
net.ipv4.ip_forward=0
```

After:

```
# Enables packet forwarding
net.ipv4.ip_forward=1
```

This enables packet forwarding only when you reboot, at which time Linux will create a file in one of the subdirectories of the special RAM memory-based /proc filesystem. To activate the feature immediately you have to force Linux to read the /etc/sysctl.conf file with the sysctl command using the -p switch. Here is how it's done:

```
[root@bigboy tmp] sysctl -p
sysctl -p
net.ipv4.ip_forward = 1
net.ipv4.conf.default.rp_filter = 1
```

```
kernel.sysrq = 0
kernel.core_uses_pid = 1
[root@bigboy tmp]#
```

Please refer to Appendix I, "Miscellaneous Linux Topics," for more information on adjusting kernel parameters.

Configuring Proxy ARP

If a server needs to send a packet to another device on the same network, it sends out an `ARP request` to the network asking for the MAC address of the other device.

If the same server needs to send a packet to another device on a remote network the process is different. The server first takes a look at its routing table to find out the IP address of the best router on its network that will be able to relay the packet to the destination. The server then sends an ARP request for the MAC address that matches the router's IP address. It then sends the packet to the router using the router's MAC address and a destination IP address of the remote server.

If there is no suitable router on its network, the server then sends out an ARP request for the MAC address of the remote server. Some routers can be configured to answer these types of ARP requests for remote networks. This feature is called proxy ARP. There are some disadvantages with this. One of the most common problems occurs if two routers are on the network configured for proxy ARP. In this scenario there is the possibility that either one will answer the local server's ARP request for the MAC address of the remote server. If one of the routers has an incorrect routing table entry for the remote network, there is the risk that traffic to the remote server will occasionally get lost. In other words you can lose routing control.

Note

It is for this and other reasons that it is generally not a good idea to configure proxy ARP on a router. It is also good to always configure a default gateway on your server and use separate routing entries via other routers for all networks your default gateway may not know about.

Some types of bridging mode firewalls need to have proxy ARP enabled to operate properly. These devices are typically inserted as part of a daisy chain connecting multiple network switches on the same LAN while protecting one section of a LAN from traffic originating on another section. The firewall typically isn't configured with an IP address on the LAN and appears to be an intelligent cable capable of selectively blocking packets.

If you need to enable proxy ARP on a Linux server the `/proc` filesystem comes into play again. Proxy ARP is handled by files in the `/proc/sys/net/ipv4/conf/` directory. This directory then has subdirectories corresponding to each functioning NIC card on your server. Each subdirectory then has a file called `proxy_arp`. If the value within this file is 0, proxy ARP on the interface is disabled; if the value is 1, it is enabled.

You can use the `/etc/sysctl.conf` file mentioned in Appendix II to activate or disable proxy ARP. The next example activates proxy ARP, first for all interfaces and then for interfaces `eth0` and `wlan0`:

```
#
# File: /etc/sysctl.conf
#

# Enables Proxy ARP on all interfaces
net/ipv4/conf/all/proxy_arp    = 1

# Enables Proxy ARP on interfaces eth1 and wlan0
net/ipv4/conf/eth1/proxy_arp   = 1
net/ipv4/conf/wlan0/proxy_arp = 1
```

You can then activate these settings with the `sysctl` command:

```
[root@bigboy tmp] sysctl -p
```

Configuring Your */ETC/HOSTS* File

The `/etc/hosts` file is just a list of IP addresses and their corresponding server names. Your server will typically check this file before referencing DNS. If the name is found with a corresponding IP address, DNS won't be queried at all. Unfortunately, if the IP address for that host changes, you also have to update the file. This may not be much of a concern for a single server, but can become laborious if it has to be done companywide. For ease of management, it is often easiest to limit entries in this file to just the `loopback` interface and also the server's own hostname, and use a centralized DNS server to handle most of the rest. Sometimes you may not be the one managing the DNS server, and in such cases it may be easier to add a quick /etc/hosts file entry until the centralized change can be made:

```
192.168.1.101     smallfry
```

In this example, server `smallfry` has an IP address of 192.168.1.101. You can access 192.168.1.101 using `ping`, `telnet`, or any other network-aware program by referring to it as `smallfry`. Here is an example using the `ping` command to see whether `smallfry` is alive and well on the network:

```
[root@bigboy tmp]# ping smallfry
PING zero (192.168.1.101) 56(84) bytes of data.
```

```
64 bytes from smallfry (192.168.1.101): icmp_seq=0 ttl=64 time=0.197
ms
64 bytes from smallfry (192.168.1.101): icmp_seq=1 ttl=64 time=0.047
ms

--- smallfry ping statistics ---
2 packets transmitted, 2 received, 0% packet loss, time 2017ms
rtt min/avg/max/mdev = 0.034/0.092/0.197/0.074 ms, pipe 2
[root@bigboy tmp]#
```

You can also add aliases to the end of the line, which enable you to refer to the server using other names. Here we have set it up so that `smallfry` can also be accessed using the names `tiny` and `littleguy`:

```
192.168.1.101    smallfry  tiny  littleguy
```

You should never have an IP address more than once in this file because Linux will use only the values in the first entry it finds:

```
192.168.1.101    smallfry     # (Wrong)
192.168.1.101    tiny         # (Wrong)
192.168.1.101    littleguy    # (Wrong)
```

The *loopback* Interface's *localhost* Entry

Usually the first entry in `/etc/hosts` defines the IP address of the server's virtual `loopback` interface. This is usually mapped to the name `localhost.localdomain` (the universal name used when a server refers to itself) and `localhost` (the shortened alias name). By default, Fedora inserts the hostname of the server between the 127.0.0.1 and the `localhost` entries like this:

```
127.0.0.1    bigboy    localhost.localdomain    localhost
```

When the server is connected to the Internet, this first entry after the 127.0.0.1 needs to be the fully qualified domain name (FQDN) of the server—for example, `bigboy.mysite.com`:

```
127.0.0.1    bigboy.my-web-site.org    localhost.localdomain    localhost
```

Some programs such as Sendmail are very sensitive to this and if they detect what they feel is an incorrect FQDN they will default to using the name `localhost.localdomain` when communicating with another server on the network. This can cause confusion, because the other server also feels it is `localhost.localdomain`.

> **Note**
> You *must* always have a `localhost` and `localhost.localdomain` entry mapping to
> 127.0.0.1 for Linux to work properly and securely.

CONCLUSION

As you can imagine, configuring Linux networking is just a first step in providing Internet access to your server. There always things that can go wrong
that may be totally out of your control. Good systems administrators know the
tools needed to be able to identify the probable causes of these types of problem, which enables them to know the type of help they need to fix it.

The next two chapters show you how to test your network and Linux
server applications confidently when things appear to go wrong. The skills you
develop to identify and rectify these issues could prove to be invaluable to your
company and career.

## CHAPTER 4

Simple Network Troubleshooting

IN THIS CHAPTER

- ☞ Doing Basic Cable and Link Tests
- ☞ Testing Your NIC
- ☞ How to See MAC Addresses
- ☞ Using `ping` to Test Network Connectivity
- ☞ Using `telnet` to Test Network Connectivity
- ☞ Testing Web Sites with the `curl` and `wget` Utilities
- ☞ The `netstat` Command
- ☞ The Linux `iptables` Firewall
- ☞ Using `traceroute` to Test Connectivity
- ☞ Using MTR to Detect Network Congestion
- ☞ Viewing Packet Flows with `tcpdump`
- ☞ Viewing Packet Flows with `tethereal`
- ☞ Basic DNS Troubleshooting
- ☞ Using `nmap`
- ☞ Determining the Source of an Attack
- ☞ Who Has Used My System?
- ☞ Conclusion

You will eventually find yourself trying to fix a network related problem, which usually appears in one of two forms. The first is slow response times from the remote server, and the second is a complete lack of connectivity. These symptoms can be caused by:

Sources of Network Slowness

☞ NIC duplex and speed incompatibilities

☞ Network congestion

☞ Poor routing

☞ Bad cabling

☞ Electrical interference

☞ An overloaded server at the remote end of the connection

☞ Misconfigured DNS (Covered in Chapter 18, "Configuring DNS," and Chapter 19, "Dynamic DNS")

Sources of a Lack of Connectivity

All sources of slowness can become so severe that connectivity is lost. Additional sources of disconnections are:

☞ Power failures

☞ The remote server or an application on the remote server being shut down.

We discuss how to isolate these problems and more in the following sections.

DOING BASIC CABLE AND LINK TESTS

Your server won't be able to communicate with any other device on your network unless the NIC's link light is on. This indicates that the connection between your server and the switch/router is functioning correctly.

In most cases a lack of link is due to the wrong cable type being used. As described in Chapter 2, "Introduction to Networking," there are two types of Ethernet cables: crossover and straight-through. Always make sure you are using the correct type.

Other sources of link failure include:

☞ The cables are bad.

☞ The switch or router to which the server is connected is powered down.

☞ The cables aren't plugged in properly.

If you have an extensive network, investment in a battery-operated cable tester for basic connectivity testing is invaluable. More sophisticated models on the market will be able to tell you the approximate location of a cable break and whether an Ethernet cable is too long to be used.

TESTING YOUR NIC

It is always a good practice in troubleshooting to be versed in monitoring the status of your NIC from the command line. The following sections introduce a few commands that will be useful.

Viewing Your Activated Interfaces

The `ifconfig` command without any arguments gives you all the active interfaces on your system. Interfaces will not appear if they are shut down:

```
[root@bigboy tmp]# ifconfig
```

Note

Interfaces will appear if they are activated but have no link. We'll soon discuss how to determine the link status using commands.

Viewing All Interfaces

The `ifconfig -a` command provides all the network interfaces, whether they are functional or not. Interfaces that are shut down by the systems administrator or are nonfunctional will not show an IP address line and the word UP will not show in the second line of the output. This can be seen in the next examples.

Shut Down Interface

```
wlan0     Link encap:Ethernet  HWaddr 00:06:25:09:6A:D7
          BROADCAST MULTICAST  MTU:1500  Metric:1
          RX packets:2924 errors:0 dropped:0 overruns:0 frame:0
          TX packets:2287 errors:0 dropped:0 overruns:0 carrier:0
          collisions:0 txqueuelen:100
          RX bytes:180948 (176.7 Kb)  TX bytes:166377 (162.4 Kb)
          Interrupt:10 Memory:c88b5000-c88b6000
```

Active Interface

```
wlan0     Link encap:Ethernet  HWaddr 00:06:25:09:6A:D7
          inet addr:216.10.119.243  Bcast:216.10.119.255
          UP BROADCAST RUNNING MULTICAST  MTU:1500  Metric:1
          RX packets:2924 errors:0 dropped:0 overruns:0 frame:0
          TX packets:2295 errors:0 dropped:0 overruns:0 carrier:0
          collisions:0 txqueuelen:100
          RX bytes:180948 (176.7 Kb)  TX bytes:166521 (162.6 Kb)
          Interrupt:10 Memory:c88b5000-c88b6000
```

Testing Link Status from the Command Line

Both the mii-tool and ethtool commands provide reports on the link status and duplex settings for supported NICs.

When used without any switches, mii-tool gives a very brief report. Use it with the -v switch because it provides more information on the supported autonegotiation speeds of the NIC, and this can be useful in troubleshooting speed and duplex issues.

The ethtool command provides much more information than mii-tool and should be your command of choice, especially because mii-tool will be soon deprecated in Linux. In both of the following examples, the NICs are operating at 100Mbps, full duplex, and the link is ok.

Link Status Output from mii-tool

```
[root@bigboy tmp]# mii-tool -v
eth0: 100 Mbit, full duplex, link ok
  product info: Intel 82555 rev 4
  basic mode:   100 Mbit, full duplex
  basic status: link ok
  capabilities: 100baseTx-FD 100baseTx-HD 10baseT-FD 10baseT-HD
  advertising:  100baseTx-FD 100baseTx-HD 10baseT-FD 10baseT-HD
flow-control
  link partner: 100baseTx-HD
[root@bigboy tmp]#
```

Link Status Output from ethtool

```
[root@bigboy tmp]# ethtool eth0
Settings for eth0:
        Supported ports: [ TP MII ]
        Supported link modes:   10baseT/Half 10baseT/Full
                                100baseT/Half 100baseT/Full
        Supports auto-negotiation: Yes
        Advertised link modes:  10baseT/Half 10baseT/Full
                                100baseT/Half 100baseT/Full
        Advertised auto-negotiation: No
        Speed: 100Mb/s
        Duplex: Full
        Port: MII
        PHYAD: 1
        Transceiver: internal
        Auto-negotiation: off
        Supports Wake-on: g
        Wake-on: g
        Current message level: 0x00000007 (7)
        Link detected: yes
[root@bigboy tmp]#
```

Viewing NIC Errors

Errors are a common symptom of slow connectivity due to poor configuration or excessive bandwidth utilization. They should always be corrected whenever possible. Error rates in excess of 0.5% can result in noticeable sluggishness.

Ifconfig *Error Output*

The `ifconfig` command also shows the number of overrun, carrier, dropped packet, and frame errors.

```
wlan0     Link encap:Ethernet  HWaddr 00:06:25:09:6A:D7
          BROADCAST MULTICAST  MTU:1500  Metric:1
          RX packets:2924 errors:0 dropped:0 overruns:0 frame:0
          TX packets:2287 errors:0 dropped:0 overruns:0 carrier:0
          collisions:0 txqueuelen:100
          RX bytes:180948 (176.7 Kb)  TX bytes:166377 (162.4 Kb)
          Interrupt:10 Memory:c88b5000-c88b6000
```

ethtool *Error Output*

The `ethtool` command can provide a much more detailed report when used with the `-s` switch:

```
[root@probe-001 root]# ethtool -S eth0
NIC statistics:
     rx_packets: 1669993
     tx_packets: 627631
     rx_bytes: 361714034
     tx_bytes: 88228145
     rx_errors: 0
     tx_errors: 0
     rx_dropped: 0
     tx_dropped: 0
     multicast: 0
     collisions: 0
     rx_length_errors: 0
     rx_over_errors: 0
     rx_crc_errors: 0
     rx_frame_errors: 0
     rx_fifo_errors: 0
     rx_missed_errors: 0
     tx_aborted_errors: 0
     tx_carrier_errors: 0
     tx_fifo_errors: 0
     tx_heartbeat_errors: 0
     tx_window_errors: 0
     tx_deferred: 0
     tx_single_collisions: 0
     tx_multi_collisions: 0
     tx_flow_control_pause: 0
     rx_flow_control_pause: 0
     rx_flow_control_unsupported: 0
     tx_tco_packets: 0
     rx_tco_packets: 0
[root@probe-001 root]#
```

Possible Causes of Ethernet Errors

The following are possible causes of Ethernet errors:

☞ **Collisions:** The NIC card detects itself and another server on the LAN attempting data transmissions at the same time. Collisions can be expected as a normal part of Ethernet operation and are typically below 0.1% of all frames sent. Higher error rates are likely to be caused by faulty NIC cards or poorly terminated cables.

☞ **Single Collisions:** The Ethernet frame went through after only one collision.

☞ **Multiple Collisions:** The NIC had to attempt multiple times before successfully sending the frame due to collisions.

☞ **CRC Errors:** Frames were sent but were corrupted in transit. The presence of CRC errors, but not many collisions, usually is an indication of electrical noise. Make sure that you are using the correct type of cable, that the cabling is undamaged, and that the connectors are securely fastened.

☞ **Frame Errors:** An incorrect CRC and a noninteger number of bytes are received. This is usually the result of collisions or a bad Ethernet device.

☞ **FIFO and Overrun Errors:** The number of times that the NIC was blocked from transferring data from the network to its memory buffers because of the speed limitations of the hardware. This is usually a sign of excessive traffic.

☞ **Length Errors:** The received frame length was less than or exceeded the Ethernet standard. This is most frequently due to incompatible duplex settings.

☞ **Carrier Errors:** Errors are caused by the NIC losing its link connection to the hub or switch. Check for faulty cabling or faulty interfaces on the NIC and networking equipment.

HOW TO SEE MAC ADDRESSES

There are times when you lose connectivity with another server that is *directly* connected to your local network. Taking a look at the ARP table of the server from which you are troubleshooting will help determine whether the remote server's NIC is responding to any type of traffic from your Linux box. Lack of communication at this level may mean:

☞ Either server might be disconnected from the network.

☞ There might be bad network cabling.

☞ A NIC might be disabled or the remote server might be shut down.

☞ The remote server might be running firewall software such as iptables or the Windows XP built-in firewall. Typically in this case, you can see the MAC address, the server is running the correct software, but the desired communication doesn't appear to be occurring to the client on the same network.

Here is a description of the commands you may use to determine ARP values:

☞ The `ifconfig -a` command shows you both the NIC's MAC address and the associated IP addresses of the server that you are currently logged in to:

```
[root@bigboy tmp]# ifconfig -a

wlan0 Link encap:Ethernet HWaddr 00:06:25:09:6A:B5
inet addr:192.168.1.100 Bcast:192.168.1.255 Mask:255.255.255.0
UP BROADCAST RUNNING MULTICAST MTU:1500 Metric:1
RX packets:47379 errors:0 dropped:0 overruns:0 frame:0
TX packets:107900 errors:0 dropped:0 overruns:0 carrier:0
collisions:0 txqueuelen:100
RX bytes:4676853 (4.4 Mb) TX bytes:43209032 (41.2 Mb)
Interrupt:11 Memory:c887a000-c887b000

wlan0:0 Link encap:Ethernet HWaddr 00:06:25:09:6A:B5
inet addr:192.168.1.99 Bcast:192.168.1.255 Mask:255.255.255.0
UP BROADCAST RUNNING MULTICAST MTU:1500 Metric:1
Interrupt:11 Memory:c887a000-c887b000
[root@bigboy tmp]#
```

Here you can see the `wlan0` interface has two IP addresses 192.168.1.100 and 192.168.1.99 tied to the NIC hardware MAC address of 00:06:25:09:6A:B5:

☞ The `arp -a` command will show you the MAC addresses in your server's ARP table and all the other servers on the directly connected network. Here we see we have some form of connectivity with the router at address 192.168.1.1:

```
[root@bigboy tmp]# arp -a
bigboypix (192.168.1.1) at 00:09:E8:9C:FD:AB [ether] on wlan0
? (192.168.1.101) at 00:06:25:09:6A:D7 [ether] on wlan0
[root@bigboy tmp]#
```

☞ Make sure the IP addresses listed in the ARP table match those of servers expected to be on your network. If they don't, your server may be plugged into the wrong switch or router port.

☞ You should also check the ARP table of the remote server to see whether it is populated with acceptable values.

USING *PING* TO TEST NETWORK CONNECTIVITY

Whether or not your troublesome server is connected to your local network, it is always a good practice to force a response from it.

One of the most common methods used to test connectivity across multiple networks is the `ping` command. `ping` sends ICMP echo packets that request a corresponding ICMP echo-reply response from the device at the target address. Because most servers will respond to a `ping` query, it becomes a very handy tool. A lack of response could be due to:

☞ A server with that IP address doesn't exist.

☞ The server has been configured not to respond to pings.

☞ A firewall or router along the network path is blocking ICMP traffic.

☞ You have incorrect routing. Check the routes and subnet masks on both the local and remote servers and all routers in between. A classic symptom of bad routes on a server is the ability to ping servers only on your local network and nowhere else. Use `traceroute` to ensure you're taking the correct path.

☞ Either the source or destination device has an incorrect IP address or subnet mask.

☞ You may have lost connectivity to the gateway router on the network. If you can't get to the first network hop, your traffic won't be able to leave the LAN. Try pinging the gateways to make sure they are responsive.

There are a variety of ICMP response codes that can help in further troubleshooting. See the appendix for a full listing of them.

The Linux `ping` command sends continuous pings, once a second, until stopped with a Ctrl-C. Here is an example of a successful ping to the server `bigboy` at 192.168.1.100:

```
[root@smallfry tmp]# ping 192.168.1.101
PING 192.168.1.101 (192.168.1.101) from 192.168.1.100 : 56(84) bytes
of data.
64 bytes from 192.168.1.101: icmp_seq=1 ttl=128 time=3.95 ms
64 bytes from 192.168.1.101: icmp_seq=2 ttl=128 time=7.07 ms
64 bytes from 192.168.1.101: icmp_seq=3 ttl=128 time=4.46 ms
64 bytes from 192.168.1.101: icmp_seq=4 ttl=128 time=4.31 ms

--- 192.168.1.101 ping statistics ---
4 packets transmitted, 4 received, 0% loss, time 3026ms
rtt min/avg/max/mdev = 3.950/4.948/7.072/1.242 ms
[root@smallfry tmp]#
```

You may get a `Destination Host Unreachable` message. This message is caused by your router or server knowing that the target IP address is part of a valid network, but is getting no response from the target server. There are a number of reasons for this.

If you are trying to ping a host on a directly connected network:

☞ The server might be down or disconnected for the network.

☞ Your NIC might not have the correct duplex settings; you may verify this with the `mii-tool` command.

☞ You might have the incorrect type of cable connecting your Linux box to the network. There are two basic types: straight through and crossover.

☞ In the case of a wireless network, your SSID or encryption keys might be incorrect

If you are trying to ping a host on a remote network:

☞ The network device doesn't have a route in its routing table to the destination network and sends an ICMP reply type 3, which triggers the message. The resulting message may be `Destination Host Unreachable` or `Destination Network Unreachable`:

```
[root@smallfry tmp]# ping 192.168.1.105
PING 192.168.1.105 (192.168.1.105) from 192.168.1.100 : 56(84) bytes
of data.
From 192.168.1.100 icmp_seq=1 Destination Host Unreachable
From 192.168.1.100 icmp_seq=2 Destination Host Unreachable
From 192.168.1.100 icmp_seq=3 Destination Host Unreachable
From 192.168.1.100 icmp_seq=4 Destination Host Unreachable
From 192.168.1.100 icmp_seq=5 Destination Host Unreachable
From 192.168.1.100 icmp_seq=6 Destination Host Unreachable
--- 192.168.1.105 ping statistics ---
8 packets transmitted, 0 received, +6 errors, 100% loss, time 7021ms,
pipe 3
[root@smallfry tmp]#
```

USING *TELNET* TO TEST NETWORK CONNECTIVITY

An easy way to tell if a remote server is listening on a specific TCP port is to use the `telnet` command. By default, `telnet` will try to connect on TCP port 23, but you can specify other TCP ports by typing them in after the target IP address. HTTP uses TCP port 80, HTTPS uses port 443.

Here is an example of testing server 192.168.1.102 on the TCP port 22 reserved for SSH:

```
[root@bigboy tmp]# telnet 192.168.1.102 22
```

When using `telnet` troubleshooting, here are some useful guidelines to follow that will help isolate the source of the problem:

☞ Test connectivity from the remote PC or server.

☞ Test connectivity on the server itself. Try making the connection to the loopback address as well as the NIC IP address. If the server is running a firewall package, such as the Linux iptables software, all loopback connectivity could be allowed, but connectivity to desired TCP ports on the NIC interface may be blocked. Further discussion of the Linux iptables package is covered in a later section.

☞ Test connectivity from another server on the same network as the target server. This helps eliminate the influence of any firewalls protecting the entire network from outside.

LINUX *TELNET* TROUBLESHOOTING

The following sections illustrate the use of `telnet` troubleshooting from a Linux box.

Note

Always remember that many Linux servers have the iptables firewall package installed by default. This is often the cause of many connectivity problems and the firewall rules should be correctly updated. In some cases where the network is already protected by a firewall, iptables may be safely turned off. You can use the `/etc/init.d/iptables status` command on the target server to determine whether iptables is running.

Successful Connection

With Linux, a successful `telnet` connection is always greeted by a `Connected to` message like this one when trying to test connectivity to server 192.168.1.102 on the SSH port (TCP 22):

```
[root@bigboy tmp]# telnet 192.168.1.102 22
Trying 192.168.1.102...
Connected to 192.168.1.102.
Escape character is '^]'.
SSH-1.99-OpenSSH_3.4p1
^]
telnet> quit
Connection closed.
[root@ bigboy tmp]#
```

To break out of the connection you have to press the Ctrl and] keys simultaneously, not the usual Ctrl-C.

> **Note**
> In many cases you can successfully connect on the remote server on the desired TCP port, yet the application doesn't appear to work. This is usually caused by there being correct network connectivity but a poorly configured application.

Connection Refused Messages

You will get a `Connection refused` message for one of the following reasons:

☞ The application you are trying to test hasn't been started on the remote server.

☞ There is a firewall blocking and rejecting the connection attempt.

Here is some sample output:

```
[root@bigboy tmp]# telnet 192.168.1.100 22
Trying 192.168.1.100...
telnet: connect to address 192.168.1.100: Connection refused
[root@bigboy tmp]#
```

telnet Timeout or Hanging

The `telnet` command will abort the attempted connection after waiting a predetermined time for a response. This is called a **timeout**. In some cases, `telnet` won't abort, but will just wait indefinitely. This is also known as **hanging**. These symptoms can be caused by one of the following reasons:

☞ The remote server doesn't exist on the destination network. It could be turned off.

☞ A firewall could be blocking and *not* rejecting the connection attempt, causing it to time out instead of being quickly refused.

```
[root@bigboy tmp]# telnet 216.10.100.12 22
Trying 216.10.100.12...
telnet: connect to address 216.10.100.12: Connection timed out
[root@bigboy tmp]#
```

TELNET TROUBLESHOOTING USING WINDOWS

Sometimes you have to troubleshoot Linux servers from a Windows PC. The `telnet` commands are the same, but the results are different. Go to the command line and type the same `telnet` command as you would in Linux.

Screen Goes Blank—Successful Connection

If there is connectivity, your command prompt screen will go blank. Using the `Ctrl-C` key sequence enables you to exit the `telnet` attempt.

Connect Failed Messages

The `Connect  failed` messages are the equivalent of the Linux `Connection refused` messages explained earlier and are caused by the same reasons:

```
C:\>telnet 172.16.1.102 256
Connecting To 172.16.1.102...Could not open connection to the host, on
port 256:

Connect failed
C:\>
```

telnet Timeout or Hanging

As explained previously, if there is no connectivity, the session will appear to hang or time out. This is usually caused by the target server being turned off or by a firewall blocking the connection.

```
C:\>telnet 216.10.100.12 22
Connecting To 216.10.100.12...
```

TESTING WEB SITES WITH THE *CURL* AND *WGET* UTILITIES

Testing a Web site's performance using a Web browser alone is sometimes insufficient to get a good idea of the source of slow Web server performance. Many useful HTTP error codes are often not displayed by browsers, making troubleshooting difficult. A much better combination of tools is to use `telnet` to test your site's TCP port 80 response time in conjunction with data from the Linux `curl` and `wget` HTTP utilities.

Rapid TCP response times, but slow `curl` and `wget` response times, usually point not to a network issue, but to slowness in the configuration of the Web server or any supporting application or database servers it may use to generate the Web page.

Using *curl*

The `curl` utility acts like a text-based Web browser in which you can select to see either the header or complete body of a Web page's HTML code displayed on your screen.

A good start is to use the `curl` command with the `-I` flag to view just the Web page's header and HTTP status code. By not using the `-I` flag you will see all the Web page's HTML code displayed on the screen. Either method can provide a good idea of your server's performance:

```
[root@ bigboy tmp]# curl -I www.linuxhomenetworking.com
HTTP/1.1 200 OK
Date: Tue, 19 Oct 2004 05:11:22 GMT
Server: Apache/2.0.51 (Fedora)
Accept-Ranges: bytes
Vary: Accept-Encoding,User-Agent
Connection: close
Content-Type: text/html; charset=UTF-8

[root@bigboy tmp]#
```

In this case the Web server appears to be working correctly because it returns a `200 OK` code. Please refer to Chapter 20, "The Apache Web Server," for a more complete listing of possibilities.

Using *wget*

You can use `wget` to recursively download a Web site's pages, including the entire directory structure of the Web site, to a local directory.

By not using recursion and activating the time stamping feature (the `-N` switch), you view not only the HTML content of the Web site's index page in your local directory, but also the download speed, file size, and precise start and stop times for the download. This can be very helpful in providing a simple way to obtain snapshots of your server's performance:

```
[root@zippy tmp]# wget -N www.linuxhomenetworking.com
--23:07:22--  http://www.linuxhomenetworking.com/
           => `index.html'
Resolving www.linuxhomenetworking.com... done.
Connecting to www.linuxhomenetworking.com[65.115.71.34]:80...
connected.
HTTP request sent, awaiting response... 200 OK
Length: unspecified [text/html]
Last-modified header missing -- time-stamps turned off.
--23:07:22--  http://www.linuxhomenetworking.com/
           => `index.html'
Connecting to www.linuxhomenetworking.com[65.115.71.34]:80...
connected.
HTTP request sent, awaiting response... 200 OK
Length: unspecified [text/html]

    [ <=>                                          ] 122,150
279.36K/s

23:07:22 (279.36 KB/s) - `index.html' saved [122150]

[root@zippy tmp]#
```

THE *NETSTAT* COMMAND

Like curl and wget, netstat can be very useful in helping determine the source of problems. Using netstat with the -an option lists all the TCP ports on which your Linux server is listening, including all the active network connections to and from your server. This can be very helpful in determining whether slowness is due to high traffic volumes:

```
[root@bigboy tmp]# netstat -an
Active Internet connections (servers and established)
Proto Recv-Q Send-Q Local Address      Foreign Address       State
tcp        0      0 127.0.0.1:25       0.0.0.0:*             LISTEN
tcp        0      0 :::80              :::*                  LISTEN
...
...
...
[root@bigboy tmp]#
```

Most TCP connections create permanent connections. HTTP is different because the connections are shut down on their own after a predefined inactive timeout or time_wait period on the Web server. It is therefore a good idea to focus on these types of short-lived connections. You can determine the number of established and time_wait TCP connections on your server by using the netstat command filtered by the grep and egrep commands, with the number of matches being counted by the wc command, which in this case shows 14 connections:

```
[root@bigboy tmp]# netstat -an | grep tcp | egrep -i \
'established|time_wait' | wc -l
14
[root@bigboy tmp]#
```

The netstat -nr command can also be used to view your routing table. It is always good to ensure that your routes are correct and that you can ping all the gateways in your routing table. The traceroute command, which I'll discuss later, can then be used to verify that your routing table is correct by displaying the path a packet takes to get to a remote destination. If the first hop is incorrect, then your routing table needs to be examined more carefully.

```
[root@bigboy tmp]# netstat -nr
Kernel IP routing table
Destination     Gateway         Genmask         Flags MSS Window irtt
Iface
172.16.68.64    172.16.69.193   255.255.255.224 UG    40  0      0    eth1
172.16.11.96    172.16.69.193   255.255.255.224 UG    40  0      0    eth1
172.16.68.32    172.16.69.193   255.255.255.224 UG    40  0      0    eth1
172.16.67.0     172.16.67.135   255.255.255.224 UG    40  0      0    eth0
172.16.69.192   0.0.0.0         255.255.255.192 U     40  0      0    eth1
172.16.67.128   0.0.0.0         255.255.255.128 U     40  0      0    eth0
172.160.0       172.16.67.135   255.255.0.0     UG    40  0      0    eth0
172.16.0.0      172.16.67.131   255.240.0.0     UG    40  0      0    eth0
127.0.0.0       0.0.0.0         255.0.0.0       U     40  0      0    lo
0.0.0.0         172.16.69.193   0.0.0.0         UG    40  0      0    eth1
[root@bigboy tmp]#
```

THE LINUX *IPTABLES* FIREWALL

An unexpected source of server connectivity issues for brand new servers is frequently the `iptables` firewall. This is installed by default under Fedora and Red Hat and usually allows only a limited range of traffic.

Determining Whether *iptables* Is Running

You can easily test whether iptables is running by using the `/etc/init.d/iptables` script with the `status` qualifier. If it isn't running you'll get a very short listing of the firewall rules. Here is some sample output:

```
[root@zero root]# service iptables status
Firewall is stopped.
[root@zero root]#
```

How to Stop *iptables*

If your Linux box is already protected by a firewall, you may want to temporarily disable iptables using the same `/etc/init.d/iptables` script with the `stop` qualifier:

```
[root@bigboy tmp]# service iptables stop
Flushing firewall rules: [  OK  ]
Setting chains to policy ACCEPT: filter [  OK  ]
Unloading iptables modules: [  OK  ]
[root@bigboy tmp]#
```

How to Configure *iptables* Rules

Stopping iptables may not be a good permanent solution, especially if your network isn't protected by a firewall. You can read more about configuring iptables in Chapter 14, "Linux Firewalls Using iptables."

USING *TRACEROUTE* TO TEST CONNECTIVITY

Another tool for network troubleshooting is the `traceroute` command. It gives a listing of all the router hops between your server and the target server. This helps you verify that routing over the networks in between is correct.

The `traceroute` command works by sending a UDP packet destined to the target with a TTL of 0. The first router on the route recognizes that the TTL has already been exceeded and discards or drops the packet, but also sends an ICMP time exceeded message back to the source. The `traceroute` program records the IP address of the router that sent the message and knows that

that is the first hop on the path to the final destination. The `traceroute` program tries again, with a TTL of 1. The first hop sees nothing wrong with the packet, decrements the TTL to 0 as expected, and forwards the packet to the second hop on the path. Router 2 sees the TTL of 0, drops the packet and replies with an ICMP time exceeded message. `traceroute` now knows the IP address of the second router. This continues around and around until the final destination is reached.

Note

In Linux the `traceroute` command is `traceroute`. In Windows it is `tracert`.

Note

You receive `traceroute` responses only from functioning devices. If a device responds, it is less likely to be the source of your problems.

Sample *traceroute* Output

Here is a sample output for a query to 144.232.20.158. Notice that all the hop times are under 50 milliseconds (ms) which is acceptable:

```
[root@bigboy tmp]# traceroute -I 144.232.20.158
traceroute to 144.232.20.158 (144.232.20.158), 30 hops max, 38 byte
packets
1 adsl-67-120-221-110.dsl.sntc01.my-isp-provider.net (67.120.221.110)
14.408 ms 14.064 ms 13.111 ms
2 dist3-vlan50.sntc01.my-isp-provider.net (63.203.35.67) 13.018 ms
12.887 ms 13.146 ms
3 bb1-g1-0.sntc01.my-isp-provider.net (63.203.35.17) 12.854 ms 13.035
ms 13.745 ms
4 bb2-p11-0.snfc21.my-isp-provider.net (64.161.124.246) 16.260 ms
15.618 ms 15.663 ms
5 bb1-p14-0.snfc21.my-isp-provider.net (64.161.124.53) 15.897 ms
15.785 ms 17.164 ms
6 sl-gw11-sj-3-0.another-isp-provider.net (144.228.44.49) 14.443 ms
16.279 ms 15.189 ms
7 sl-bb25-sj-6-1.another-isp-provider.net (144.232.3.133) 16.185 ms
15.857 ms 15.423 ms
8 sl-bb23-ana-6-0.another-isp-provider.net (144.232.20.158) 27.482 ms
26.306 ms 26.487 ms
[root@bigboy tmp]#
```

Possible *traceroute* Messages

There are a number of possible message codes `traceroute` can give; these are listed in Table 4.1.

Table 4.1   `traceroute` Return Code Symbols

Traceroute Symbol	Description
* * *	Expected 5-second response time exceeded. Could be caused by the following: ☞ A router on the path not sending back the ICMP time exceeded messages ☞ A router or firewall in the path blocking the ICMP time exceeded messages ☞ The target IP address not responding
!H, !N, or !P	Host, network, or protocol unreachable.
!X or !A	Communication administratively prohibited. A router Access Control List (ACL) or firewall is in the way.
!S	Source route failed. Source routing attempts to force `traceroute` to use a certain path. Failure may be due to a router security setting.

traceroute Time Exceeded False Alarms

If there is no response within a 5-second timeout interval, an asterisk (*) is printed for that probe, as seen in the following example:

```
[root@bigboy tmp]# traceroute 144.232.20.158
traceroute to 144.232.20.158 (144.232.20.158), 30 hops max, 38 byte
packets
1 adsl-67-120-221-110.dsl.sntc01.my-isp-provider.net (67.120.221.110)
14.304 ms 14.019 ms 16.120 ms
2 dist3-vlan50.sntc01.my-isp-provider.net (63.203.35.67) 12.971 ms
14.000 ms 14.627 ms
3 bb1-g1-0.sntc01.my-isp-provider.net (63.203.35.17) 15.521 ms 12.860
ms 13.179 ms
4 bb2-p11-0.snfc21.my-isp-provider.net (64.161.124.246) 13.991 ms
15.842 ms 15.728 ms
5 bb1-p14-0.snfc21.my-isp-provider.net (64.161.124.53) 16.133 ms
15.510 ms 15.909 ms
6 sl-gw11-sj-3-0.another-isp-provider.net (144.228.44.49) 16.510 ms
17.469 ms 18.116 ms
7 sl-bb25-sj-6-1.another-isp-provider.net (144.232.3.133) 16.212 ms
14.274 ms 15.926 ms
8 * * *
9 * * *
[root@bigboy tmp]#
```

Some devices will prevent `traceroute` packets directed at their interfaces, but will allow ICMP packets. Using `traceroute` with an `-I` flag forces `traceroute` to use ICMP packets that may go through. In this case the * * * status messages disappear:

```
[root@bigboy tmp]# traceroute -I 144.232.20.158
traceroute to 144.232.20.158 (144.232.20.158), 30 hops max, 38 byte
packets
1 adsl-67-120-221-110.dsl.sntc01.my-isp-provider.net (67.120.221.110)
14.408 ms 14.064 ms 13.111 ms
2 dist3-vlan50.sntc01.my-isp-provider.net (63.203.35.67) 13.018 ms
12.887 ms 13.146 ms
3 bb1-g1-0.sntc01.my-isp-provider.net (63.203.35.17) 12.854 ms 13.035
ms 13.745 ms
4 bb2-p11-0.snfc21.my-isp-provider.net (64.161.124.246) 16.260 ms
15.618 ms 15.663 ms
5 bb1-p14-0.snfc21.my-isp-provider.net (64.161.124.53) 15.897 ms
15.785 ms 17.164 ms
6 sl-gw11-sj-3-0.another-isp-provider.net (144.228.44.49) 14.443 ms
16.279 ms 15.189 ms
7 sl-bb25-sj-6-1.another-isp-provider.net (144.232.3.133) 16.185 ms
15.857 ms 15.423 ms
8 sl-bb23-ana-6-0.another-isp-provider.net (144.232.20.158) 27.482 ms
26.306 ms 26.487 ms
[root@bigboy tmp]#
```

traceroute Internet Slowness False Alarm

The following `traceroute` gives the impression that a Web site at 80.40.118.227 might be slow because there is congestion along the way at hops 6 and 7 where the response time is over 200ms:

```
C:\>tracert 80.40.118.227

    1      1 ms      2 ms      1 ms   66.134.200.97
    2     43 ms     15 ms     44 ms   172.31.255.253
    3     15 ms     16 ms      8 ms   192.168.21.65
    4     26 ms     13 ms     16 ms   64.200.150.193
    5     38 ms     12 ms     14 ms   64.200.151.229
    6    239 ms    255 ms    253 ms   64.200.149.14
    7    254 ms    252 ms    252 ms   64.200.150.110
    8     24 ms     20 ms     20 ms   192.174.250.34
    9     91 ms     89 ms     60 ms   192.174.47.6
   10     17 ms     20 ms     20 ms   80.40.96.12
   11     30 ms     16 ms     23 ms   80.40.118.227

Trace complete.

C:\>
```

This indicates only that the devices on hops 6 and 7 were slow to respond with ICMP TTL exceeded messages, but not an indication of congestion, latency, or packet loss. If any of those conditions existed, all points past the problematic link would show high latency.

Many Internet routing devices give very low priority to traffic related to `traceroute` in favor of revenue-generating traffic.

traceroute Dies at the Router Just Before the Server

In this case the last device to respond to the `traceroute` just happens to be the router that acts as the default gateway of the server. The problem is not with the router, but with the server. Remember, you will only receive `traceroute` responses from functioning devices.

Possible causes of this problem include the following:

☞ The server has a bad default gateway.

☞ The server is running some type of firewall software that blocks `traceroute`.

☞ The server is shut down or disconnected from the network, or it has an incorrectly configured NIC.

```
C:\>tracert 80.40.100.18

Tracing route to 80.40.100.18 over a maximum of 30 hops

  1    33 ms    49 ms    28 ms   192.168.1.1
  2    33 ms    49 ms    28 ms   65.14.65.19
  3    33 ms    32 ms    32 ms   81.25.68.252
  4    47 ms    32 ms    31 ms   80.40.97.1
  5    29 ms    28 ms    32 ms   80.40.96.114
  6     *        *        *      Request timed out.
  7    ^C
C:\>
```

Always Get a Bidirectional *traceroute*

It is always best to get a `traceroute` from the source IP to the target IP and also from the target IP to the source IP. This is because the packet's return path from the target is sometimes not the same as the path taken to get there. A high `traceroute` time equates to the round-trip time for both the initial `traceroute` query to each hop and the response of each hop.

Here is an example of one such case, using disguised IP addresses and provider names. There was once a routing issue between telecommunications carriers FastNet and SlowNet. When a user at IP address 40.16.106.32 did a `traceroute` to 64.25.175.200, a problem seemed to appear at the 10th hop with OtherNet. However, when a user at 64.25.175.200 did a `traceroute` to 40.16.106.32, latency showed up at hop 7 with the return path being very different.

In this case, the real traffic congestion was occurring where FastNet handed off traffic to SlowNet in the second trace. The latency appeared to be caused at hop 10 on the first trace not because that hop was slow, but because that was the first hop at which the return packet traveled back to the source via the congested route. Remember, `traceroute` gives the packet round-trip time:

```
Trace route to 40.16.106.32 from 64.25.175.200

1   0    ms 0     ms 0     [64.25.175.200]
2   0    ms 0     ms 0     [64.25.175.253]
3   0    ms 0     ms 0     border-from-40-tesser.my-isp-provider.net
[207.174.144.169]
4   0    ms 0     ms 0     [64.25.128.126]
5   0    ms 0     ms 0     p3-0.dnvtco1-cr3.another-isp-provider.net
[4.25.26.53]
6   0    ms 0     ms 0     p2-1.dnvtco1-br1.another-isp-provider.net
[4.24.11.25]
7   0    ms 0     ms 0     p15-0.dnvtco1-br2.another-isp-provider.net
[4.24.11.38]
8  30    ms 30    ms 30    p15-0.snjpca1-br2.another-isp-provider.net
[4.0.6.225]
9  30    ms 30    ms 30    p1-0.snjpca1-cr4.another-isp-provider.net
[4.24.9.150]
10 1252 ms 1212 ms 1202 h0.webhostinc2.another-isp-provider.net
[4.24.236.38]
11 1252 ms 1212 ms 1192 [40.16.96.11]
12 1262 ms 1212 ms 1192 [40.16.96.162]
13 1102 ms 1091 ms 1092 [40.16.106.32]
Trace route to 64.25.175.200 from 40.16.106.32

1   1    ms 1     ms 1     ms [40.16.106.3]
2   1    ms 1     ms 1     ms [40.16.96.161]
3   2    ms 1     ms 1     ms [40.16.96.2]
4   1    ms 1     ms 1     ms [40.16.96.65]
5   2    ms 2     ms 1     ms border8.p4-2.webh02-1.sfj.fastnet.net
[216.52.19.77]
6   2    ms 1     ms 1     ms core1.ge0-1-net2.sfj.fastnet.net
[216.52.0.65]
7  993   ms 961   ms 999   ms sjo-edge-03.inet.slownet.net
8  [208.46.223.33]
1009 ms 1008 ms 971   ms sjo-core-01.inet.slownet.net [205.171.22.29]
9  985   ms 947   ms 983   ms svl-core-03.inet.slownet.net [205.171.5.97]
10 1028 ms 1010 ms 953   ms [205.171.205.30]
11 989   ms 988   ms 985   ms p4-3.paix-bi1.another-isp-provider.net
[4.2.49.13]
12 1002 ms 1001 ms 973   ms p6-0.snjpca1-br1.another-isp-provider.net
[4.24.7.61]
13 1031 ms 989   ms 978   ms p9-0.snjpca1-br2.another-isp-provider.net
[4.24.9.130]
14 1031 ms 1017 ms 1017 ms p3-0.dnvtco1-br2.another-isp-provider.net
[4.0.6.226]
15 1027 ms 1025 ms 1023 ms p15-0.dnvtco1-br1.another-isp-provider.net
[4.24.11.37]
16 1045 ms 1037 ms 1050 ms p1-0.dnvtco1-cr3.another-isp-provider.net
[4.24.11.26]
17 1030 ms 1020 ms 1045 ms p0-0.cointcorp.another-isp-provider.net
[4.25.26.54]
18 1038 ms 1031 ms 1045 ms gw234.my-isp-provider.net [64.25.128.99]
19 1050 ms 1094 ms 1034 ms [64.25.175.253]
20 1050 ms 1094 ms 1034 ms [64.25.175.200]
```

ping and *traceroute* Troubleshooting Example

In this example, a `ping` to 186.9.17.153 gave a TTL timeout message. Ping TTLs will usually timeout only if there is a routing loop in which the packet bounces between two routers on the way to the target. Each bounce causes the TTL to decrease by a count of 1 until the TTL reaches 0, at which point you get the timeout.

The routing loop was confirmed by the `traceroute`, in which the packet was proven to be bouncing between routers at 186.40.64.94 and 186.40.64.93:

```
G:\>ping 186.9.17.153

Pinging 186.9.17.153 with 32 bytes of data:

Reply from 186.40.64.94: TTL expired in transit.
Reply from 186.40.64.94: TTL expired in transit.
Reply from 186.40.64.94: TTL expired in transit.
Reply from 186.40.64.94: TTL expired in transit.

Ping statistics for 186.9.17.153:
    Packets: Sent = 4, Received = 4, Lost = 0 (0% loss),
Approximate round trip times in milli-seconds:
    Minimum = 0ms, Maximum =  0ms, Average =  0ms


G:\>tracert 186.9.17.153

Tracing route to lostserver.my-isp-provider.net [186.9.17.153]
over a maximum of 30 hops:

  1    <10 ms    <10 ms    <10 ms   186.217.33.1
  2     60 ms     70 ms     60 ms   rtr-2.my-isp-provider.net [186.40.64.94]
  3     70 ms     71 ms     70 ms   rtr-1.my-isp-provider.net [186.40.64.93]
  4     60 ms     70 ms     60 ms   rtr-2.my-isp-provider.net [186.40.64.94]
  5     70 ms     70 ms     70 ms   rtr-1.my-isp-provider.net [186.40.64.93]
  6     60 ms     70 ms     61 ms   rtr-2.my-isp-provider.net [186.40.64.94]
  7     70 ms     70 ms     70 ms   rtr-1.my-isp-provider.net [186.40.64.93]
  8     60 ms     70 ms     60 ms   rtr-2.my-isp-provider.net [186.40.64.94]
  9     70 ms     70 ms     70 ms   rtr-1.my-isp-provider.net [186.40.64.93]
...
...
...
Trace complete.
```

This problem was solved by resetting the routing process on both routers. The problem was initially triggered by an unstable network link that caused frequent routing recalculations. The constant activity eventually corrupted the routing tables of one of the routers.

traceroute Web Sites

Many ISPs will provide their subscribers with the facility to do a `traceroute` from purpose-built servers called **looking glasses**. A simple Web search for the phrase `Internet looking glass` will provide a long list of alternatives. Doing a `traceroute` from a variety of locations can help identify whether the problem is with the ISP of your Web server or the ISP used at home/work to provide you with Internet access. A more convenient way of doing this is to use a site like `traceroute.org`, which provides a list of looking glasses sorted by country.

Possible Reasons for a Failed *traceroute*

A `traceroute` can fail to reach its intended destination for a number of reasons including the following:

☞ `traceroute` packets are being blocked or rejected by a router in the path. The router immediately after the last visible one is usually the culprit. It's usually good to check the routing table and/or other status of this next hop device.

☞ The target server doesn't exist on the network. It could be disconnected or turned off. (!H or !N messages may be produced.)

☞ The network on which you expect the target host to reside doesn't exist in the routing table of one of the routers in the path. (!H or !N messages may be produced.)

☞ You may have a typographical error in the IP address of the target server.

☞ You may have a routing loop in which packets bounce between two routers and never get to the intended destination.

☞ The packets don't have a proper return path to your server. The last visible hop is the last hop in which the packets return correctly. The router immediately after the last visible one is the one at which the routing changes. It's usually good to do the following

   ☞ Log on to the last visible router.

   ☞ Look at the routing table to determine what the next hop is to your intended `traceroute` target.

   ☞ Log on to this next hop router.

   ☞ Do a `traceroute` from this router to your intended target server.

   ☞ **If this works**: Routing to the target server is OK. Do a `traceroute` back to your source server. The `traceroute` will probably fail at the bad router on the return path.

   ☞ **If it doesn't work**: Test the routing table and/or other status of all the hops between it and your intended target.

Note

If there is nothing blocking your `traceroute` traffic, the last visible router of an incomplete trace is either the last good router on the path or the last router that has a valid return path to the server issuing the `traceroute`.

USING MTR TO DETECT NETWORK CONGESTION

Matt's Traceroute is an application you can use to do a repeated `traceroute` in real time; it dynamically shows the round-trip time to reach each hop along the `traceroute` path. The constant updates enable you not only to visually determine which hops are slow, but also to determine when they appear to be slow. It is a good tool to use whenever you suspect there is some intermittent network congestion.

You type `mtr` followed by the target IP address to get output similar to the following:

```
[root@bigboy tmp]# mtr 192.168.25.26

                        Matt's traceroute  [v0.52]
Bigboy                                        Fri Feb 20 17:19:17 2004
Keys:  D - Display mode    R - Restart statistics    Q - Quit
                            Packets                Pings
Hostname                    %Loss Rcv  Snt  Last Best  Avg  Worst
   1. 192.168.1.1             0%   17   17    32   10   15    32
   2. 192.168.2.254           0%   17   17    12   11   18    41
   3. 192.168.3.15            0%   17   17    23   14   18    25
   4. 192.168.18.35           0%   16   16    24   23   29    42
   5. 192.168.25.26           0%   16   16    23   21   26    37
^C
[root@bigboy tmp]#
```

One of the nice features of MTR is that it gives you the best, worst, and average round-trip times in milliseconds for the probe packets between each hop along the way to the final destination. The advantage of this is that you can let MTR run for an extended period of time, acting as a constant monitor of communication path quality. The constant refreshing of the screen also enables you to instantaneously spot transient changes in quality fairly easily, making it much more convenient than a regular `traceroute`.

MTR is automatically installed as part of Fedora Linux. If MTR isn't installed on your system, you can download the RPM software installation package from many of the Fedora download sites. The installation of RPMs is covered in Chapter 6, "Installing RPM Software." There is even a free Windows version called WinMTR.

VIEWING PACKET FLOWS WITH *TCPDUMP*

The `tcpdump` command is one of the most popular packages for viewing the flow of packets through your Linux box's NIC card. It is installed by default on Red Hat/Fedora Linux and has very simple syntax, especially if you are doing simpler types of troubleshooting.

One of the most common uses of `tcpdump` is to determine whether you are getting basic two-way communication. Lack of communication could be due to the following:

☞ Bad routing

☞ Faulty cables, interfaces of devices in the packet flow

☞ The server not listening on the port because the software isn't installed or started

☞ A network device in the packet path blocking traffic; common culprits are firewalls, routers with access control lists and even your Linux box running iptables

Analyzing `tcpdump` in much greater detail is beyond the scope of this section.

Like most Linux commands, `tcpdump` uses command-line switches to modify the output. Some of the more useful command-line switches are listed in Table 4.2.

Table 4.2   Possible `tcpdump` Switches

Tcpdump Command	Switch Description
-c	Stop after viewing *count* packets.
-t	Don't print a timestamp at the beginning of each line.
-i	Listen on *interface*. If this is not specified, `tcpdump` uses the lowest numbered interface that is UP.
-w	Dump the output to a specially formatted `tcpdump` dump file.
-C	Specify the size the dump file must reach before a new one with a numeric extension is created.

You can also add expressions after all the command-line switches. These act as filters to limit the volume of data presented on the screen. You can also use keywords such as `and` or `or` between expressions to further fine-tune your selection criteria. Some useful expressions are listed in Table 4.3.

Table 4.3   Useful `tcpdump` Expressions

Tcpdump Command Expression	Description
host host-address	View packets from the IP address *host-address*.
icmp	View icmp packets.
tcp port port-number	View TCP packets with either a source or destination TCP port of *port-number*.
udp port port-number	View UDP packets with either a source or destination UDP port of port-number.

The following is an example of `tcpdump` being used to view ICMP `ping` packets going through interface `wlan0`:

```
[root@bigboy tmp]# tcpdump -i wlan0 icmp

tcpdump: listening on wlan0
21:48:58.927091 smallfry > bigboy: icmp: echo request (DF)
21:48:58.927510 bigboy > smallfry: icmp: echo reply
21:48:58.928257 smallfry > bigboy.my-web-site.org: icmp: echo request (DF)
21:48:58.928365 bigboy. > smallfry: icmp: echo reply
21:48:58.943926 smallfry > bigboy.my-web-site.org: icmp: echo request (DF)
21:48:58.944034 bigboy > smallfry: icmp: echo reply
21:48:58.962244 bigboy > smallfry: icmp: echo reply
21:48:58.963966 bigboy > smallfry: icmp: echo reply
21:48:58.968556 bigboy > smallfry: icmp: echo reply

9 packets received by filter
0 packets dropped by kernel
[root@bigboy tmp]#
```

In this example:

☞ The first column of data is a packet timestamp.

☞ The second column of data shows the packet source and then the destination IP address or server name of the packet.

☞ The third column shows the packet type.

☞ Two-way communication is occurring as each echo gets an echo reply.

The following example shows `tcpdump` being used to view packets on interface `wlan0` to/from host 192.168.1.102 on TCP port 22 with no timestamps in the output (`-t` switch):

```
[root@bigboy tmp]# tcpdump -i wlan0 -t host 192.168.1.102 and tcp port
22

tcpdump: listening on wlan0
smallfry.32938 > bigboy.ssh: S 2013297020:2013297020(0) win 5840 <mss
1460,sackOK,timestamp 75227931 0,nop,wscale 0> (DF) [tos 0x10]
bigboy.ssh > smallfry.32938: R 0:0(0) ack 2013297021 win 0 (DF) [tos
0x10]
smallfry.32938 > bigboy.ssh: S 2013297020:2013297020(0) win 5840 <mss
1460,sackOK,timestamp 75227931 0,nop,wscale 0> (DF) [tos 0x10]
bigboy.ssh > smallfry.32938: R 0:0(0) ack 1 win 0 (DF) [tos 0x10]
smallfry.32938 > bigboy.ssh: S 2013297020:2013297020(0) win 5840 <mss
1460,sackOK,timestamp 75227931 0,nop,wscale 0> (DF) [tos 0x10]
 7 packets received by filter
0 packets dropped by kernel
[root@bigboy tmp]#
```

In this example:

☞ The first column of data shows the packet source and then the destination IP address or server name of the packet.

☞ The second column shows the TCP flags within the packet.

☞ The client named `bigboy` is using port 32938 to communicate with the server named `smallfry` on the TCP SSH port 22.

☞ Two-way communication is occurring.

Analyzing *tcpdump* files

By using the `-w filename` option you can send the entire Ethernet frame, not just brief IP information that normally goes to the screen, to a file. This can then be analyzed by graphical analysis tools such as Ethereal, which is available in both Windows and Linux, with customized filters, colorization of packet records based on criteria deemed interesting, and the capability of automatically highlighting certain error conditions such as data retransmissions:

```
tcpdump -i eth1 -w /tmp/packets.dump tcp port 22
```

Covering Ethereal is beyond the scope of this book, but that shouldn't discourage you from using it. The application is part of the Fedora RPM suite, and a Windows version is also available.

Common Problems with *tcpdump*

By default `tcpdump` will attempt to determine the DNS names of all the IP addresses it sees while logging data. This can slow down `tcpdump` so much that it appears not to be working at all. The `-n` switch stops DNS name lookups and makes `tcpdump` work more reliably.

The following are examples of how the `-n` switch affects the output.

Without the `-n` switch:

```
[root@bigboy tmp]# tcpdump -i eth1 tcp port 22
tcpdump: verbose output suppressed, use -v or -vv for full protocol
decode
listening on eth1, link-type EN10MB (Ethernet), capture size 96 bytes
02:24:34.818398 IP 192-168-1-242.my-web-site.org.1753 > bigboy-100.my-
web-site.org.ssh: . ack 318574223 win 65471
02:24:34.818478 IP bigboy-100.my-web-site.org.ssh > 192-168-1-242.my-
web-site.org.1753: P 1:165(164) ack 0 win 6432
02:24:35.019042 IP 192-168-1-242.my-web-site.org.1753 > bigboy-100.my-
web-site.org.ssh: . ack 165 win 65307
02:24:35.019118 IP bigboy-100.my-web-site.org.ssh > 192-168-1-242.my-
web-site.org.1753: P 165:401(236) ack 0 win 6432
```

```
02:24:35.176299 IP 192-168-1-242.my-web-site.org.1753 > bigboy-100.my-
web-site.org.ssh: P 0:20(20) ack 401 win 65071
02:24:35.176337 IP bigboy-100.my-web-site.org.ssh > 192-168-1-242.my-
web-site.org.1753: P 401:629(228) ack 20 win 6432

6 packets captured
7 packets received by filter
0 packets dropped by kernel
[root@bigboy tmp]#
```

With the -n switch:

```
[root@bigboy tmp]# tcpdump -i eth1 -n tcp port 22
tcpdump: verbose output suppressed, use -v or -vv for full protocol
decode
listening on eth1, link-type EN10MB (Ethernet), capture size 96 bytes
02:25:53.068511 IP 192.168.1.242.1753 > 192.168.1.100.ssh: . ack
318576011 win 65163
02:25:53.068606 IP 192.168.1.100.ssh > 192.168.1.242.1753: P
1:165(164) ack 0 win 6432
02:25:53.269152 IP 192.168.1.242.1753 > 192.168.1.100.ssh: . ack 165
win 64999
02:25:53.269205 IP 192.168.1.100.ssh > 192.168.1.242.1753: P
165:353(188) ack 0 win 6432
02:25:53.408556 IP 192.168.1.242.1753 > 192.168.1.100.ssh: P 0:20(20)
ack 353 win 64811
02:25:53.408589 IP 192.168.1.100.ssh > 192.168.1.242.1753: P
353:541(188) ack 20 win 6432

6 packets captured
7 packets received by filter
0 packets dropped by kernel
[root@bigboy tmp]#
```

VIEWING PACKET FLOWS WITH *TETHEREAL*

The tethereal program is a text version of the graphical Ethereal product that is part of the Fedora Linux RPM suite. The command-line options and screen output mimic that of tcpdump in many ways, but tethereal has a number of advantages.

The tethereal command has the capability of dumping data to a file like tcpdump and creating new files with new filename extensions when a size limit has been reached. It can additionally limit the total number of files created before overwriting the first one in the queue, which is also known as a **ring buffer**.

The tethereal screen output is also more intuitive to read, though the dump file format is identical to tcpdump. Tables 4.4 and 4.5 show some popular command switches and expressions that can be used with tethereal.

Table 4.4 Possible `tethereal` Switches

`tethereal` Command Switch	Description
`-c`	Stop after viewing *count* packets.
`-i`	Listen on *interface*. If this is not specified, `tethereal` will use the lowest numbered interface that is UP.
`-w`	Dump the output to a specially formatted `tethereal` dump file.
`-C`	Specify the size the dump file must reach before a new one with a numeric extension is created.
`-b`	Determine the size of the ring buffer when the `-C` switch is selected.

Table 4.5 Useful `tethereal` Expressions

`tethereal` Command Expression	Description
`host host-address`	View packets from the IP address *host-address*.
`Icmp`	View icmp packets.
`tcp port port-number`	View TCP packets with packets either a source or destination TCP port of port-number.
`udp port port-number`	View UDP packets with either a source or destination UDP port of port-number.

In the next example we're trying to observe an HTTP (TCP port 80) packet flow between server `smallfry` at address 192.168.1.102 and `bigboy` at IP address 192.168.1.100. The `tethereal` output groups the IP addresses and TCP ports together and then provides the TCP flags, followed by the sequence numbering. It may not be apparent on this page, but the formatting lines up in neat columns on your screen, making analysis much easier. Also notice how the command line mimics that of `tcpdump`:

```
[root@smallfry tmp]# tethereal -i eth0 tcp port 80 and host
192.168.1.100
Capturing on eth0
  0.000000 192.168.1.102 -> 192.168.1.100 TCP 1442 > http [SYN]
Seq=3325831828 Ack=0 Win=5840 Len=0
  0.000157 192.168.1.100 -> 192.168.1.102 TCP http > 1442 [SYN, ACK]
Seq=3291904936 Ack=3325831829 Win=5792 Len=0
  0.000223 192.168.1.102 -> 192.168.1.100 TCP 1442 > http [ACK]
Seq=3325831829 Ack=3291904937 Win=5840 Len=0
  2.602804 192.168.1.102 -> 192.168.1.100 TCP 1442 > http [FIN, ACK]
Seq=3325831829 Ack=3291904937 Win=5840 Len=0
  2.603211 192.168.1.100 -> 192.168.1.102 TCP http > 1442 [ACK]
Seq=3291904937 Ack=3325831830 Win=46 Len=0
  2.603356 192.168.1.100 -> 192.168.1.102 TCP http > 1442 [FIN, ACK]
Seq=3291904937 Ack=3325831830 Win=46 Len=0
  2.603398 192.168.1.102 -> 192.168.1.100 TCP 1442 > http [ACK]
Seq=3325831830 Ack=3291904938 Win=5840 Len=0
[root@smallfry tmp]#
```

Using graphical Ethereal to analyze `tethereal` dump files is beyond the scope of this book, but that shouldn't discourage you from using it. The application is part of the Fedora RPM suite and a Windows version is also available.

BASIC DNS TROUBLESHOOTING

Sometimes the source of problems can be due to misconfigured DNS rather than poor network connectivity. As mentioned before, DNS is the system that helps map an IP address to your Web site's domain name and your site may suddenly become unavailable if the mapping is incorrect.

Using *nslookup* to Test DNS

The `nslookup` command can be used to get the associated IP address for your domain and vice versa. The `nslookup` command is very easy to use; you just need to type the command, followed by the IP address or Web site name you want to query.

The command actually queries your DNS server for a response, which is then displayed on the screen. Failures can be caused by your server not having the correct value set in the `/etc/resolv.conf` file, as explained in Chapter 18, poor connectivity to your DNS server, or an incorrect configuration on the DNS server.

Using nslookup *to Check Your Web Site Name*

Here we see `nslookup` returning the IP address 216.151.193.92 for the site `www.linuxhomenetworking.com`:

```
[root@bigboy tmp]# nslookup www.linuxhomenetworking.com
...
...
Name:    www.linuxhomenetworking.com
Address: 216.151.193.92

[root@bigboy tmp]#
```

Using nslookup *to Check Your IP Address*

The `nslookup` command can operate in the opposite way in which a query against the address 216.151.193.92 returns the Web site named `www.linux-homenetworking.com`:

```
[root@bigboy tmp]# nslookup 216.151.193.92
...
...
Non-authoritative answer:
92.193.151.216.in-addr.arpa     name = extra193-92.my-isp-provider.net.
```

```
Authoritative answers can be found from:
193.151.216.in-addr.arpa       nameserver = dns1.my-isp-provider.net.
193.151.216.in-addr.arpa       nameserver = dns2.my-isp-provider.net.
dns1.my-isp-provider.net    internet address = 216.151.192.1

[root@bigboy tmp]#
```

Using nslookup *to Query a Specific DNS Server*

Sometimes you might want to test the DNS mapping against a specific DNS server; this can be achieved by adding the DNS server's IP address immediately after the IP address of the Web site name you intend to query:

```
[root@bigboy tmp]# nslookup www.linuxhomenetworking.com 68.87.96.3
...
...
Server:        68.87.96.3
Address:       68.87.96.3#53

Name:    www.linuxhomenetworking.com
Address: 216.151.193.92

[root@bigboy tmp]#
```

Note

The nslookup command will probably be removed from future releases of Linux, but can still be used with Windows. The Linux host command can be used as a good replacement.

Using the *host* Command to Test DNS

More recent versions of Linux have started to use the host command for basic DNS testing. Fortunately, syntax is identical to that of nslookup and the resulting output is very similar:

```
[root@bigboy tmp]# host 216.151.193.92
92.193.151.216.in-addr.arpa domain name pointer extra193-92.my-isp-
provider.net.
[root@bigboy tmp]#

[root@bigboy tmp]# host www.linuxhomenetworking.com
www.linuxhomenetworking.com has address 216.151.193.92
[root@bigboy tmp]#

[root@zippy root]# host www.linuxhomenetworking.com 68.87.96.3
Using domain server:
Name: 68.87.96.3
Address: 68.87.96.3#53
Aliases:

www.linuxhomenetworking.com has address 65.115.71.34
[root@zippy root]#
```

USING *NMAP*

You can use nmap to determine all the TCP/IP ports on which a remote server is listening. It isn't usually an important tool in the home environment, but it can be used in a corporate environment to detect vulnerabilities in your network, such as servers running unauthorized network applications. It is a favorite tool of malicious surfers and therefore should be used to test external as well as internal servers under your control.

Whenever you are in doubt, you can get a list of available nmap options by just entering the command without arguments at the command prompt:

```
[root@bigboy tmp]# nmap
Nmap V. 3.00 Usage: nmap [Scan Type(s)] [Options] <host or net list>
Some Common Scan Types ('*' options require root privileges)
* -sS TCP SYN stealth port scan (default if privileged (root))
  -sT TCP connect() port scan (default for unprivileged users)
* -sU UDP port scan
  -sP ping scan (Find any reachable machines)
...
...
[root@bigboy tmp]#
```

Some of the more common nmap options are listed in Table 4.6, but you should also refer to the nmap man pages for full descriptions of them all.

Table 4.6   Commonly Used nmap Options

Argument	Description
-P0	Attempts to ping a host before scanning it. If the server is being protected from ping queries, you can use this option to force it to scan anyway.
-T	Defines the timing between the packets set during a port scan. Some firewalls can detect the arrival of too many nonstandard packets within a predetermined time frame. This option can be used to send them from 60 seconds apart with a value of 5, "insane mode," to 0.3 seconds with a value of 0 in "paranoid mode."
-O	Tries to detect the operating system of the remote server based on known responses to various types of packets.
-p	Lists the TCP/IP port range to scan.
-s	Defines a variety of scan methods that use either packets that comply with the TCP/IP standard or are in violation of it.

Here is an example of trying to do a scan using valid TCP connections (-sT) in the extremely slow insane mode (-T 5) from ports 1 to 5000:

```
[root@bigboy tmp]# nmap -sT -T 5 -p 1-5000 192.168.1.153

Starting nmap V. 3.00 ( www.insecure.org/nmap/ )
Interesting ports on whoknows.my-site-int.com (192.168.1.153):
(The 4981 ports scanned but not shown below are in state: closed)
Port       State        Service
```

```
21/tcp        open         ftp
25/tcp        open         smtp
139/tcp       open         netbios-ssn
199/tcp       open         smux
2105/tcp      open         eklogin
2301/tcp      open         compaqdiag
3300/tcp      open         unknown

Nmap run completed -- 1 IP address (1 host up) scanned in 8 seconds
[root@bigboy tmp]#
```

Full coverage of the possibilities on nmap as a security scanning tool are beyond the scope of this book, but you should go the extra mile and purchase a text specifically on Linux security to help protect you against attempts at malicious security breaches.

DETERMINING THE SOURCE OF AN ATTACK

Sometimes you realize that your system is under a denial-of-service attack. This could be either malicious or simply someone rapidly downloading all the pages of your Web site with the Linux wget command. Symptoms include a large number of established connections when viewed with the netstat command or an excessive number of entries in your firewall or Web server logs.

Sometimes the attack isn't in the form of a constant bombardment that your server can't handle, but of the type that *you* can't handle, such as e-mail SPAM. ISPs are usually very sensitive to complaints about SPAM, but though you may have the IP address, a traceroute won't provide any contact information for the ISP.

Sometimes DNS lookups aren't enough to determine who owns an offending IP address. You need another tool.

One of the better ones to use is the whois command. Use it with an IP address or DNS domain as its sole argument and it will provide you with all the administrative information you need to start your hunt. Here is an example for the yahoo.com domain:

```
[root@bigboy tmp]# whois yahoo.com
...
...
    Administrative Contact:
        Domain Administrator
        (NIC-1382062)
        Yahoo! Inc.
        701 First Avenue
        Sunnyvale
        CA
        94089
        US
        domainadmin@yahoo-inc.com
        +1.4083493300
```

```
        Fax- +1.4083493301
...
...
[root@bigboy tmp]#
```

WHO HAS USED MY SYSTEM?

It is always important to know who has logged into your Linux box. This isn't just to help track the activities of malicious users, but mostly to figure out who made the mistake that crashed the system or blew up Apache with a typographical error in the httpd.conf file.

The *last* Command

The most common command to determine who has logged into your system is last, which lists the last users who logged into the system. Here are some examples:

```
[root@bigboy tmp]# last -100
root      pts/0          reggae.my-web-site.org Thu Jun 19 09:26    still
logged in
root      pts/0          reggae.my-web-site.org Wed Jun 18 01:07 - 09:26
(1+08:18)
reboot    system boot  2.4.18-14          Wed Jun 18 01:07
(1+08:21)
root      pts/0          reggae.my-web-site.org Tue Jun 17 21:57 - down
(03:07)
root      pts/0          reggae.my-web-site.org Mon Jun 16 07:24 - 00:35
(17:10)
wtmp begins Sun Jun 15 16:29:18 2003
[root@bigboy tmp]#
```

In this example someone from reggae.my-web-site.org logged into bigboy as user root. I generally prefer not to give out the root password and let all the systems administrators log in with their own individual logins. They can then get root privileges by using sudo. This makes it easier to track down individuals rather than groups of users.

The *who* Command

The who command is used to see who is currently logged in to your computer. Here we see a user logged as root from server reggae.my-web-site.org:

```
[root@bigboy tmp]# who
root      pts/0        Jun 19 09:26 (reggae.my-web-site.org)
[root@bigboy tmp]#
```

CONCLUSION

One of the greatest sources of frustration for any systems administrator is to try to isolate whether poor server performance is due to a network issue or problems with an application or database. The worry can be amplified, especially as network instability is often under the control of network engineers who need evidence pointing to problems in their domain of expertise before they will be convinced to act.

These tips should help provide you with a definitive answer by enabling you to isolate the source of most network problems and helping you make their resolution much faster.

The next chapter builds on this new knowledge and expands your troubleshooting skills to include the reading of Linux error log files to assist in the diagnosis of unexpected Linux application behavior.

## CHAPTER 5

Troubleshooting Linux with *syslog*

IN THIS CHAPTER

☞ `syslog`

☞ `logrotate`

☞ Conclusion

There are hundreds of Linux applications on the market, each with their own configuration files and help pages. This variety makes Linux vibrant, but it also makes Linux system administration daunting. Fortunately, in most cases, Linux applications use the `syslog` utility to export all their errors and status messages to files located in the `/var/log` directory.

This can be invaluable in correlating the timing and causes of related events on your system. It is also important to know that applications frequently don't display errors on the screen, but will usually log them somewhere. Knowing the precise message that accompanies an error can be vital in researching malfunctions in product manuals, online documentation, and Web searches.

`syslog` and the `logrotate` utility that cleans up log files are both relatively easy to configure but they frequently don't get their fair share of coverage in most texts. I've included `syslog` here as a dedicated chapter to both emphasize its importance to your Linux knowledge and prepare you with a valuable skill that will help you troubleshoot all the Linux various applications that will be presented throughout the book.

SYSLOG

syslog is a utility for tracking and logging all manner of system messages from the merely informational to the extremely critical. Each system message sent to the syslog server has two descriptive labels associated with it that makes the message easier to handle:

☞ The first describes the function (facility) of the application that generated it. For example, applications such as mail and cron generate messages with easily identifiable facilities named mail and cron.

☞ The second describes the degree of severity of the message. There are eight in all and they are listed in Table 5.1.

You can configure syslog's /etc/syslog.conf configuration file to place messages of differing severity and facilities in different files. This procedure will be covered next.

Table 5.1   syslog Facilities

Severity Level	Keyword	Description
0	emergencies	System unusable
1	alerts	Immediate action required
2	critical	Critical condition
3	errors	Error conditions
4	warnings	Warning conditions
5	notifications	Normal but significant conditions
6	informational	Informational messages
7	debugging	Debugging messages

The /etc/syslog.conf File

The files to which syslog writes each type of message received is set in the /etc/syslog.conf configuration file. This file consists of two columns: The first lists the facilities and severity of messages to expect, and the second lists the files to which they should be logged. By default, Red Hat/Fedora's /etc/syslog.conf file is configured to put most of the messages in the file /var/log/messages. Here is a sample:

```
.info;mail.none;authpriv.none;cron.none          /var/log/messages
```

In this case, all messages of severity "info" and above are logged, but none from the mail, cron, or authentication facilities/subsystems. You can make this logging even more sensitive by replacing the line above with one that captures all messages from debug severity and above in the /var/log/ messages file. This may be more suitable for troubleshooting:

```
*.debug                                    /var/log/messages
```

Certain applications will additionally log to their own application specific log files and directories independent of the syslog.conf file. Here are some common examples:

Files

```
/var/log/maillog           : Mail
/var/log/httpd/access_log  : Apache web server page access logs
```

Directories

```
/var/log
/var/log/samba             : Samba messages
/var/log/mrtg              : MRTG messages
/var/log/httpd             : Apache webserver messages
```

Note

In some older versions of Linux the /etc/syslog.conf file was very sensitive to spaces and would recognize only tabs. The use of spaces in the file would cause unpredictable results. Check the formatting of your /etc/syslog.conf file to be safe.

Activating Changes to the *syslog* Configuration File

Changes to /etc/syslog.conf will not take effect until you restart syslog. Issue this command to do so:

```
[root@bigboy tmp]# service syslog restart
```

How to View New Log Entries as They Happen

If you want to get new log entries to scroll on the screen as they occur, you can use this command:

```
[root@bigboy tmp]# tail -f /var/log/messages
```

Similar commands can be applied to all log files. This is probably one of the best troubleshooting tools available in Linux. Another good command to use apart from `tail` is `grep`. `grep` will help you search for all occurrences of a string in a log file; you can pipe it through the `more` command so that you only get one screen at a time. Here is an example:

```
[root@bigboy tmp]# grep string /var/log/messages | more
```

You can also just use the plain old `more` command to see one screen at a time of the entire log file without filtering with `grep`. Here is an example:

```
[root@bigboy tmp]# more /var/log/messages
```

Logging *syslog* Messages to a Remote Linux Server

Logging your system messages to a remote server is a good security practice. With all servers logging to a central `syslog` server, it becomes easier to correlate events across your company. It also makes covering up mistakes or malicious activities harder because the purposeful deletion of log files on a server cannot simultaneously occur on your logging server, especially if you restrict the user access to the logging server.

Configuring the Linux syslog *Server*
By default, `syslog` doesn't expect to receive messages from remote clients. Here's how to configure your Linux server to start listening for these messages.

As we saw previously, `syslog` checks its `/etc/syslog.conf` file to determine the expected names and locations of the log files it should create. It also checks the file `/etc/sysconfig/syslog` to determine the various modes in which it should operate. `syslog` will not listen for remote messages unless the SYSLOGD_OPTIONS variable in this file has an `-r` included in it:

```
# Options to syslogd
# -m 0 disables 'MARK' messages.
# -r enables logging from remote machines
# -x disables DNS lookups on messages received with -r
# See syslogd(8) for more details
SYSLOGD_OPTIONS="-m 0 -r"
# Options to klogd
# -2 prints all kernel oops messages twice; once for klogd to decode,
and
#    once for processing with 'ksymoops'
# -x disables all klogd processing of oops messages entirely
# See klogd(8) for more details
KLOGD_OPTIONS="-2"
```

You have to restart `syslog` on the server for the changes to take effect. The server will now start to listen on UDP port 514, which you can verify using either one of the following `netstat` command variations:

```
[root@bigboy tmp]# netstat -a | grep syslog
udp        0         0 *:syslog                 *:*
[root@bigboy tmp]# netstat -an | grep 514
udp        0         0 0.0.0.0:514              0.0.0.0:*
[root@bigboy tmp]#
```

Configuring the Linux Client

The `syslog` server is now expecting to receive `syslog` messages. You have to configure your remote Linux client to send messages to it. This is done by editing the `/etc/hosts` file on the Linux client named `smallfry`. Here are the steps:

1. Determine the IP address and fully qualified hostname of your remote logging host.
2. Add an entry in the `/etc/hosts` file in the format:

   ```
   IP-address    fully-qualified-domain-name    hostname    "loghost"
   ```

   Example:

   ```
   192.168.1.100    bigboy.my-web-site.org    bigboy    loghost
   ```

   Now your `/etc/hosts` file has a nickname of "loghost" for server `bigboy`.
3. The next thing you need to do is edit your `/etc/syslog.conf` file to make the `syslog` messages get sent to your new loghost nickname:

   ```
   *.debug                          @loghost
   *.debug                          /var/log/messages
   ```

You have now configured all debug messages and higher to be logged to both server `bigboy` ("loghost") and the local file `/var/log/messages`. Remember to restart `syslog` to get the remote logging started.

You can now test to make sure that the `syslog` server is receiving the messages with a simple test, such as restarting the `lpd` printer daemon and making sure the remote server sees the messages.

Linux Client

```
[root@smallfry tmp]# service lpd restart
Stopping lpd: [  OK  ]
Starting lpd: [  OK  ]
[root@smallfry tmp]#
```

Linux Server

```
[root@bigboy tmp]# tail /var/log/messages
...
...
Apr 11 22:09:35 smallfry lpd: lpd shutdown succeeded
Apr 11 22:09:39 smallfry lpd: lpd startup succeeded
...
...
[root@bigboy tmp]#
```

syslog Configuration and Cisco Network Devices

syslog reserves facilities local0 through local7 for log messages received from remote servers and network devices. Routers, switches, firewalls, and load balancers—each logging with a different facility—can each have their own log files for easy troubleshooting. Appendix IV has examples of how to configure syslog to do this with Cisco devices using separate log files for the routers, switches, PIX firewalls, CSS load balancers, and LocalDirectors.

syslog and Firewalls

syslog listens by default on UDP port 514. If you are logging to a remote syslog server via a firewall, you have to allow traffic on this port to pass through the security device. syslog messages usually have UDP port 514 for both their source and destination UDP ports.

LOGROTATE

The Linux utility logrotate renames and reuses system error log files on a periodic basis so that they don't occupy excessive disk space.

The */etc/logrotate.conf* File

The /etc/logrotate.conf file is logrotate's general configuration file in which you can specify the frequency with which the files are reused:

☞ You can specify either a weekly or daily rotation parameter. In the case below, the weekly option is commented out with a #, allowing daily updates.

☞ The rotate parameter specifies the number of copies of log files logrotate will maintain. In the case below, the 4 copy option is commented out with a #, while allowing 7 copies.

☞ The create parameter creates a new log file after each rotation.

Therefore, our sample configuration file will create daily archives of *all* the logfiles and store them for seven days. The files will have the following names, with `logfile` the current active version:

```
logfile
logfile.0
logfile.1
logfile.2
logfile.3
logfile.4
logfile.5
logfile.6
```

Sample Contents of */etc/logrotate.conf*

```
# rotate log files weekly
#weekly

# rotate log files daily
daily

# keep 4 weeks worth of backlogs
#rotate 4

# keep 7 days worth of backlogs
rotate 7

# create new (empty) log files after rotating old ones
create
```

The */etc/logrotate.d* Directory

Most Linux applications that use `syslog` put an additional configuration file in this directory to specify the names of the log files to be rotated. It is a good practice to verify that all new applications that you want to use the `syslog` log have configuration files in this directory. Here are some sample files that define the specific files to be rotated for each application.

The /etc/logrotate.d/syslog *File (for General System Logging)*

```
/var/log/messages /var/log/secure /var/log/maillog /var/log/spooler
/var/log/boot.log /var/log/cron {
    sharedscripts
    postrotate
    /bin/kill -HUP `cat /var/run/syslogd.pid 2> /dev/null` 2>
/dev/null || true
    endscript
}
```

The /etc/logrotate.d/apache *File (for Apache)*

```
/var/log/httpd/access_log /var/log/httpd/agent_log
/var/log/httpd/error_log /var/log/httpd/referer_log {
    missingok
    sharedscripts
    postrotate
    /bin/kill -HUP `cat /var/run/httpd.pid 2>/dev/null` 2> /dev/null
|| true
    endscript
}
```

The /etc/logrotate.d/samba *File (for Samba)*

```
/var/log/samba/*.log {
    notifempty
    missingok
    sharedscripts
    copytruncate
    postrotate
    /bin/kill -HUP `cat /var/lock/samba/*.pid 2> /dev/null` 2>
/dev/null || true
    endscript
}
```

Activating *logrotate*

The `logrotate` settings in the last section will not take effect until you issue
the following command:

```
[root@bigboy tmp]# logrotate -f
```

If you want `logrotate` to reload only a specific configuration file, and not
all of them, issue the `logrotate` command with just that filename as the
argument:

```
[root@bigboy tmp]# logrotate -f /etc/logrotate.d/syslog
```

Compressing Your Log Files

On busy Web sites the size of your log files can become quite large.
Compression can be activated by editing the `logrotate.conf` file and adding
the `compress` option.

```
#
# File: /etc/logrotate.conf
#

# Activate log compression
compress
```

The log files will then start to become archived with the `gzip` utility, each file having a `.gz` extension.

```
[root@bigboy tmp]# ls /var/log/messages*
/var/log/messages        /var/log/messages.1.gz /var/log/messages.2.gz
/var/log/messages.3.gz /var/log/messages.4.gz /var/log/messages.5.gz
/var/log/messages.6.gz /var/log/messages.7.gz
[root@bigboy tmp]#
```

Viewing the contents of the files still remains easy because the `zcat` command can quickly output the contents to the screen. Use the command with the compressed file's name as the argument:

```
[root@bigboy tmp]# zcat /var/log/messages.1.gz
...
...
Nov 15 04:08:02 bigboy httpd: httpd shutdown succeeded
Nov 15 04:08:04 bigboy httpd: httpd startup succeeded
Nov 15 04:08:05 bigboy sendmail[6003]: iACFMLHZ023165:
to=<tvaughan@clematis4spiders.info>, delay=2+20:45:44,
xdelay=00:00:02, mailer=esmtp, pri=6388168,
relay=www.clematis4spiders.info. [222.134.66.34], dsn=4.0.0,
stat=Deferred: Connection refused by www.clematis4spiders.info.
[root@bigboy tmp]#
```

CONCLUSION

In the next chapter we cover the installation of Linux applications, and the use of `syslog` will become increasingly important especially in the troubleshooting of Linux-based firewalls, which can be configured to ignore and then log all undesirable packets; the Apache Web server, which logs all application programming errors generated by some of the popular scripting languages such as PERL and PHP; and finally, Linux mail, whose configuration files are probably the most frequently edited system documents of all and which correspondingly suffer from the most mistakes.

This `syslog` chapter should make you more confident to learn more about these applications via experimentation because you'll at least know where to look at the first sign of trouble.

Installing RPM Software

You'll frequently need to install additional software on your Linux server that you didn't think you'd need when you first installed the operating system. This could be because of new business requirements for additional packages or the need to install new administrative tools to make your job easier.

Fedora Linux software is primarily available in Red Hat Package Manager (RPM) files. Regular RPM package files are used for installations in which the kernel, or master program, hasn't been customized in any way. This is the usual scenario for most departmental servers. Source RPMs are used when the kernel has been customized to add or drop support selectively for various devices or features for the sake of performance or functionality. The procedure for installing source RPMs involves recompiling source code to fit the needs of these kernel customizations. This makes life easier for the software developer who wrote the package as he or she now has only to create a single package to support all types of customizations. Both package types use standardized commands for installing the software contained inside, making RPMs relatively easy to use.

Software developers who want to use a universally recognizable file format across all flavors of Linux also will make their products available as TAR packages. TAR packages are generally more difficult to work with than RPM packages because the archived files within them may or may not need to be compiled and the commands to install the software may vary from package to package. Instructions are usually contained within a file inside the TAR package to help guide the installation.

This chapter focuses on the RPM format, which is the format of choice for Fedora Linux software, but also devotes a small section on TAR packages near the end because they are still very important.

WHERE TO GET COMMONLY USED RPMS

There are three commonly used sources for RPMs: Fedora distribution CDs; RPMs manually downloaded via a browser, File Transfer Protocol (FTP) client, or the wget utility; and automated downloads using yum. Each of these methods is introduced here, but is covered in greater detail in sections to follow.

RPMs on Your Installation CDs

Installing from your distribution CDs is usually easier than having to download files from a remote Web site, but they are never up to date for very long. We discuss using this method in more detail later.

RPMs Downloaded from Fedora

The two most common ways of getting RPMs from Fedora are by manually using FTP or a Web browser, or by using the automatic yum utility.

Using FTP or Your Web Browser

```
You can download RPMs from Fedora using the following link:
http://download.fedora.redhat.com/pub/fedora/linux/core/
```

You also can use FTP to download Fedora from the download.fedora.red hat.com site. Start your search in the /pub/fedora/linux/core/ directory and move down the directory tree. If you're new to FTP, don't worry, it's explained later.

Remember that Fedora RPMs may not work on Red Hat operating systems.

Using yum

The yum program is installed on Fedora systems by default. It enables you to keep the versions of your software up to date by downloading the required packages with the option of installing them afterward. This is discussed in more detail in a later section.

RPMs Downloaded from *rpmfind.net*

Red Hat and Fedora have only their approved software on their sites. A good general purpose source for additional software is www.rpmfind.net.

This site offers packages for a wide variety of software in various formats for many of the popular versions of Linux. It has an easy-to-use search function that enables you to locate the software you need quickly. Most downloads can be done using HTTP by either clicking on the link or using the wget command, which is explained later.

Note

Always remember to select the RPM that matches your version of Linux. Installing an incorrect version could adversely affect your system.

GETTING RPMs USING WEB-BASED FTP

There are numerous Web sites from which you can download Fedora RPM software; two of the most popular are the Fedora Web site and rpmfind.net. The methods used to get the software from either site are simple, but different enough to be treated separately.

Let's say you are running Fedora Core 2 and need to download an RPM for the DHCP server application; you can select either of these methods in the following sections to get the software.

Using the Fedora Web site

To use the Fedora Web site:

1. Use your Web browser to go to the Fedora link given earlier.
2. Go to the pub/fedora/linux/core/2/i386/os/Fedora/RPMS directory.
3. Click on the dhcp-3.0pl2-6.16.i386.rpm link.
4. Save the file to your hard drive.

Using the *rpmfind* Web site

To use the rpmfind Web site:

1. Go to the rpmfind link.

2. Type dhcp in the Search box.

3. Click the Search button.

4. Scroll down for the RPM that matches your version of Fedora. The right column has links with the actual names of the rpm files.

5. Click the link.

6. Save the file to the Linux box's hard drive.

It is best to download RPMs to a directory named RPM, or something similar, so you can find them later.

GETTING RPMs USING COMMAND-LINE ANONYMOUS FTP

The Web-based method in the last section transparently uses anonymous FTP. Anonymous FTP enables you to log in and download files from a FTP server using the username anonymous or the shorter username ftp and a password that matches your e-mail address. This way anyone can access the data. Let's illustrate this with an example of using anonymous FTP to download the SSH package from download.fedora.redhat.com.

1. First, we issue the FTP command targeting download.fedora.redhat.com at the command line:

```
[root@bigboy tmp]# ftp download.fedora.redhat.com
Trying 66.187.232.35...
Connected to download.fedora.redhat.com (66.187.232.35).
220 Fedora FTP server ready. All transfers are logged.
Name (download.fedora.redhat.com:root): anonymous
331 Please specify the password.
Password:
230 Login successful. Have fun.
Using binary mode to transfer files.
ftp> pwd
257 "/"
ftp> ls
227 Entering Passive Mode (66,187,232,35,57,155)
150 Here comes the directory listing.
drwxr-xr-x    3 ftp         ftp          4096 Oct 29 15:59 pub
226 Directory send OK.
ftp>
```

2. After we've logged in, we can use the help command to see what options we have at our disposal:

```
ftp> help
Commands may be abbreviated. Commands are:
```

!	Debug	mdir	sendport	Site
$	dir	mget	put	size
account	disconnect	mkdir	pwd	status
append	exit	mls	quit	struct
ascii	form	mode	quote	system
bell	get	modtime	recv	sunique
binary	glob	mput	reget	tenex
bye	hash	newer	rstatus	tick
case	help	nmap	rhelp	trace
cd	idle	nlist	rename	type
cdup	image	ntrans	reset	user
chmod	lcd	open	restart	umask
close	ls	prompt	rmdir	verbose
cr	macdef	passive	runique	?
Delete	Mdelete	proxy	Send	

```
ftp>
```

The commands you'll most likely use are listed in Table 6.1.

Table 6.1   FTP Commands

Command	Description
binary	Copy files in binary mode.
cd	Change directory on the FTP server.
dir	List the names of the files in the current remote directory.
exit	Bye bye.
get	Get a file from the FTP server.
lcd	Change the directory on the local machine.
ls	Same as dir.
mget	Same as get, but you can use wildcards like *.
mput	Same as put, but you can use wildcards like *.
passive	Make the file transfer passive mode.
put	Put a file from the local machine onto the FTP server.
pwd	Give the directory name on the local machine.

3. By using the Web browsing feature on the Web site ahead of time, I know that the Fedora Core 2 RPMs are located in the pub/fedora/linux/core/2/i386/os/Fedora/RPMS/ directory and will use the cd command to change my directory to there. We can use the ls command to get a listing of files in this directory:

```
ftp> cd pub/fedora/linux/core/2/i386/os/Fedora/RPMS/
250 Directory successfully changed.
ftp> ls open*
227 Entering Passive Mode (66,187,232,35,58,3)
150 Here comes the directory listing.
...
...
-rw-r--r--   ... ... 184281 Oct 28 23:29 openssh-3.6.1p2-
34.i386.rpm
...
...
226 Directory send OK.
ftp>
```

4. Next we get the file we need and place it in the local directory /usr/rpm.
The hash command prints # hash signs on the screen during the
download:

```
ftp> hash
Hash mark printing on (1024 bytes/hash mark).
ftp> lcd /usr/rpm
Local directory now /usr/rpm
ftp> get openssh-3.6.1p2-34.i386.rpm
local: openssh-3.6.1p2-34.i386.rpm remote: openssh-3.6.1p2-
34.i386.rpm
227 Entering Passive Mode (66,187,232,35,58,25)
150 Opening BINARY mode data connection for openssh-3.6.1p2-
34.i386.rpm (184281 bytes).
###############################################################
###############################################################
#########################################################
226 File send OK.
184281 bytes received in 3.41 secs (53 Kbytes/sec)
ftp>
```

Note
You can also use wildcards to download the RPMs you need using the mget command. You'll be prompted for each of the matching RPM files. In the next example,
we just aborted this download by typing n.

```
ftp> mget openssh-3.6*
mget openssh-3.6.1p2-34.i386.rpm? n
ftp>
```

5. Finally we use the exit command to leave FTP:

```
ftp> exit
221 Goodbye.
root@bigboy tmp]#
```

GETTING RPMS USING *WGET*

The `wget` command can be used to download files quickly when you already know the URL at which the RPM is located. This is especially convenient if you are logged into your Linux box from another machine running a Web browser. You can browse the download site for the RPM you need, right-click on the desired link, and select `copy shortcut` (**Windows**) or `Copy Link Location` (**Linux**). After you have done this, you can then select your SSH/telnet/Linux Terminal login window and type the command `wget URL`. Here is an example downloading a DHCP update from Fedora:

```
[root@bigboy tmp]# wget
http://linux.stanford.edu/pub/mirrors/fedora/linux/core/2/i386/os/
Fedora/RPMS/dhcp-3.0pl2-6.16.i386.rpm
--17:38:36--
ftp://linux.stanford.edu/pub/mirrors/fedora/linux/core/2/i386/os/
Fedora/RPMS/dhcp-3.0pl2-6.16.i386.rpm
           => `dhcp-3.0pl2-6.16.i386.rpm.5'
Resolving linux.stanford.edu... done.
Connecting to linux.stanford.edu[171.66.2.18]:21... connected.
Logging in as anonymous ... Logged in!
==> SYST ... done.    ==> PWD ... done.
==> TYPE I ... done.  ==> CWD
/pub/mirrors/fedora/linux/core/2/i386/os/Fedora/RPMS ... done.
==> PASV ... done.    ==> RETR dhcp-3.0pl2-6.16.i386.rpm ... done.
Length: 529,890 (unauthoritative)

100%[================================>] 529,890      889.12K/s    ETA
00:00

17:38:36 (889.12 KB/s) - `dhcp-3.0pl2-6.16.i386.rpm.5' saved [529890]

[root@bigboy tmp]#
```

AUTOMATIC UPDATES WITH *YUM*

The `yum` automatic RPM update program comes as a standard feature of Fedora Core. It has a number of valuable features:

☞ You can configure the URLs of download sites you want to use. This provides the added advantage of choosing the most reliable sites in your part of the globe.

☞ `yum` makes multiple attempts to download RPMs before failing.

☞ `yum` automatically figures out not only the RPM packages that need updating, but also all the supporting RPMs. It then installs them all.

Note

Updating packages could cause programs written by you to stop functioning, especially if they rely on the older version's features or syntax.

Configuring *yum*

All the configuration parameters for yum are stored in the /etc/yum.conf file. The three basic sections are listed in Table 6.2:

Table 6.2   File Format—yum.conf

Section	Description
[main]	Contains logging and fault-tolerance parameters, which can usually be left alone
[base]	Contains the URL (ftp:// or http://) of a mirror site that contains the Fedora base configuration RPMs
[updates-released]	Contains the URL (ftp:// or http://) of a mirror site that contains updated Fedora RPMs

The easiest way to determine the exact URLs to use in the baseurl parameters of the [base] and [updates-released] sections of the file is to go to the http://fedora.redhat.com/download/mirrors.html Web site to get a listing of alternative download sites. Browse the sites to find the correct locations of the files:

☞ The baseurl URL for [base] would be that of the fedora-version/ architecture-type/os subdirectory of your version of Fedora. Make sure there is a headers subdirectory here, or it won't work. There *will not* be RPMs in this subdirectory.

☞ The baseurl URL for [updates-released] would be that of the updates/fedora-version/architecture-type subdirectory of your version of Fedora. Make sure there is a headers subdirectory here, or it won't work. There *will* be RPMs in this subdirectory.

Here is a sample yum.conf file to update Fedora from one of the mirror sites:

```
[main]
cachedir=/var/cache/yum
debuglevel=2
logfile=/var/log/yum.log
pkgpolicy=newest
distroverpkg=fedora-release
tolerant=1
exactarch=1
```

```
[base]
name=Fedora Core $releasever - $basearch - Base
baseurl=http://mirrors.xmission.com/fedora/core/$releasever/$basearch/
os/

[updates-released]
name=Fedora Core $releasever - $basearch - Released Updates
baseurl=http://mirrors.xmission.com/fedora/core/updates/$releasever/
$basearch/
```

Note

yum accepts the use of variables in the configuration file. The `$releasever` variable refers to the current version of Fedora Core running on your server, and the `$basearch` variable maps to the base architecture of your server, which is determined automatically.

Note

It is probably best to select yum update sites that use HTTP instead of FTP. There are a number of reasons for this. FTP firewall rules are more difficult to implement than HTTP, outbound HTTP access to the Internet is often already allowed in offices, and Web servers are less likely to have connection limits imposed on them, unlike FTP servers, which often have limits on the number of user logins.

Note

You can list multiple URLs in a `baseurl` statement like this and `yum` will try them all. If you use multiple `baseurl` statements in each section, `yum` may act strangely, frequently only selecting the last one in the list:

```
baseurl=url://server1/path/to/files/
        url://server2/path/to/files/
        url://server3/path/to/files/
```

Creating Your Own *yum* Server

An obvious advantage of using yum is that you can use it to update a yum server at your office with the same directory structure of the mirror download sites on the Fedora Web site.

A small desktop PC with about five to six gigabytes of free disk space per distribution should be sufficient to start with for a dedicated small business yum server. Large RPMs are about twenty-five megabytes in size, and they are updated infrequently, so your network load should be minimal on average with an update once or twice a week per server. The problem is timing. There is a yum script file in the /etc/cron.daily directory that runs as a cron job every day at 4:00 a.m. Your `yum` server could get overwhelmed with simultaneous update requests from all your `yum` clients. If the load gets too high, you could move this script to another location and schedule it as a `cron` job for different times for each server. You can also consider throttling the NIC card of the `yum` server to 10Mbps as another interim means of reducing the problem. Finally, if these measures don't work, you can upgrade the server. For most small businesses/departments this should not be a major concern, and you can use MRTG on the server to get trend data for its network load. MRTG monitoring is covered in Chapter 22, "Monitoring Server Performance."

When established, you can then configure all your Fedora servers to use this local `yum` server for all updates, which will significantly reduce your Internet congestion and the associated bandwidth costs.

`yum` clients can access the `yum` server using either FTP or HTTP requests. If you need help in setting these up, Chapter 15, "Linux FTP Server Setup," discusses Linux FTP servers and Chapter 20, "The Apache Web Server," covers the Apache Web server for HTTP requests.

Note

When setting up an HTTP-based `yum` server, you need to enable the viewing of directory structures so that it will be easy for someone to use his or her Web browser to navigate down the directories and double-check the location of the `yum` files.

Before You Start

As of Fedora Core version 3, the `yum` utility checks the downloaded RPMs against checksum files to help protect against file corruption and malicious forgeries. This is set using the `gpgcheck` variable in the `/etc/yum.conf` file. When the value is set to 1, then checks are done, when set to 0, they are disabled:

```
#
# File: /etc/yum.conf
#
gpgcheck=1
```

This is a valuable feature to have but you need to load the checksum files in order for `yum` to work properly. Please refer to the section titled "Signature Keys" later in the chapter before proceeding.

Keeping Your System Current with *yum*

You can make the installed RPM packages on your system up to date with the latest patches using the `yum update` command. When used without listing any packages afterward, `yum` will attempt to update them all. The `yum update package-name` command updates only a particular RPM package.

It is always advisable to use `yum` after installing Linux to make sure the latest versions of software are installed for the sake of improved security and functionality. Here is an example of output with `yum` updating your system:

```
[root@bigboy tmp]# yum update
Gathering header information file(s) from server(s)
Server: Fedora Core 2 - i386 - Base
Server: Fedora Core 2 - i386 - Released Updates
Finding updated packages
Downloading needed headers
Resolving dependencies
Dependencies resolved
I will do the following:
[install: kernel 2.4.22-1.2166.nptl.i686]
[update: samba-client 3.0.2-7.FC1.i386]
[update: binutils 2.14.90.0.6-4.i386]
...
...
...
Is this ok [y/N]: y
Getting samba-client-3.0.2-7.FC1.i386.rpm
samba-client-3.0.2-7.FC1. 100% |=========================| 128 kB
05:01
...
...
...
Running test transaction:
Test transaction complete, Success!
glibc-common 100 % done 1/127
glibc 100 % done 2/127
Stopping sshd:[  OK  ]
Starting sshd:[  OK  ]
bash 100 % done 3/127
mozilla-nspr 100 % done 4/127
sed 100 % done 5/127
...
...
...
Completing update for pango  - 65/127
Completing update for samba-client  - 66/127
Completing update for binutils  - 67/127
...
...
...
Completing update for XFree86-font-utils  - 127/127
Kernel Updated/Installed, checking for bootloader
Grub found - making this kernel the default
Installed:  kernel 2.4.22-1.2166.nptl.i686
Updated:  pango 1.2.5-4.i386 samba-client 3.0.2-7.FC1.i386 binutils
2.14.90.0.6-4.i386 XFree86-Mesa-libGLU 4.3.0-55.i386 initscripts
[root@bigboy tmp]#
```

Note

If you don't want to be prompted to install the files, use the yum with the -y switch.

Example of a *yum* Package Installation

Here is a sample installation of an individual package using yum. In this case the RPM installed is the net-snmp-utils package:

```
[root@bigboy tmp]# yum -y install  net-snmp-utils
Repository updates-released already added, not adding again
Repository base already added, not adding again
Setting up Install Process
Setting up Repo:  base
repomd.xml           100% |=========================| 1.1 kB    00:00
Setting up Repo:  updates-released
repomd.xml           100% |=========================|  951 B    00:00
Reading repository metadata in from local files
base       : #########################################  2622/2622
primary.xml.gz       100% |=========================|  88 kB    00:00
MD Read    : ############################################## 229/229
updates-re: ############################################## 229/229
Resolving Dependencies
--> Populating transaction set with selected packages. Please wait.
---> Package net-snmp-utils.i386 0:5.1.2-11 set to be installed
--> Running transaction check

Dependencies Resolved
Transaction Listing:
   Install: net-snmp-utils.i386 0:5.1.2-11
Downloading Packages:
net-snmp-utils-5.1.2-11.i 100% |===================| 6.2 MB    00:48
Running Transaction Test
Finished Transaction Test
Transaction Test Succeeded
Running Transaction
Installing: net-snmp-utils 100 % done 1/1

Installed: net-snmp-utils.i386 0:5.1.2-11
Complete!
[root@bigboy tmp]#
```

Remember the following facts about yum:

☞ You can place a list of packages you never want automatically updated in the [main] section. The list must be separated by spaces. Kernel RPMs may be one of the first sets to go on this list, as in this example:

```
[main]
exclude=kernel
```

☞ yum does its updates using TCP port 80 for http:// update URLs and uses passive FTP for ftp:// update URLs in /etc/yum.conf. This will have importance for your firewall rules.

☞ More details on configuring yum can be obtained by running the man yum.conf command.

☞ yum runs automatically each day. The cron file is located in /etc/cron.daily/.

☞ Don't limit yourself to the default yum.conf URLs because they can become overloaded with requests and make yum perform poorly.

HOW TO INSTALL RPMS MANUALLY

There are generally two ways to install RPM files manually. The first method is by using a file previously downloaded to your hard drive, and the other is to install the RPM from some sort of removable media, such as a CD-ROM drive.

Using Downloaded Files

Download the RPMs (which usually have a file extension ending with .rpm) into a temporary directory, such as /tmp. The next step is to issue the rpm -Uvh command to install the package.

The -U qualifier is used for updating an RPM to the latest version, the -h qualifier gives a list of hash # characters during the installation, and the -v qualifier prints verbose status messages while the command is run. Here is an example of a typical RPM installation command to install the MySQL server package:

```
[root@bigboy tmp]# rpm -Uvh mysql-server-3.23.58-9.i386.rpm
Preparing...          ##################### [100%]
   1:mysql-server     ##################### [100%]
[root@bigboy tmp]#
```

Using CD-ROMs

The underlying steps to install RPMs from CDs are similar to those used when installing from your hard disk. The main difference is that you have to access your CD-ROM drive by mounting it first to the mnt/cdrom directory. Your RPMs will then be located in the CD-ROM's Fedora/RPMs subdirectory. The procedure is as follows:

1. Insert the CD-ROM, check the files in the /mnt/cdrom/Fedora/RPMS directory, and then install the RPM:

```
[root@bigboy tmp]# mount /mnt/cdrom
[root@bigboy tmp]# cd /mnt/cdrom/Fedora/RPMS
[root@bigboy RPMS]# ls filename*
filename.rpm
[root@bigboy RPMS]# rpm -Uvh filename.rpm
Preparing...            ####################### [100%]
   1: filename          ####################### [100%]
[root@bigboy RPMS]#
```

2. When finished, eject the CD-ROM:

```
[root@bigboy RPMS]# cd /tmp
[root@bigboy tmp]# eject cdrom
[root@bigboy tmp]#
```

Note

You can use the `rpm` command's `--aid` switch to make it search the CD-ROM for any other RPM dependencies and install them automatically.

How to Install Source RPMs

Sometimes the packages you want to install need to be compiled in order to match your kernel version. This requires you to use source RPM files:

☞ Download the source RPMs or locate them on your CD collection. They usually have a file extension ending with (`.src.rpm`).

☞ Run the following commands as root.

☞ Compiling and installing source RPMs with Fedora can be done simply with the `rpmbuild` command:

```
[root@bigboy tmp]# rpmbuild --rebuild filename.src.rpm
```

☞ Here is an example in which we install the TACACS plus package:

```
[root@bigboy rpm]# rpmbuild --rebuild tac_plus-4.0.3-2.src.rpm
Installing tac_plus-4.0.3-2.src.rpm
Executing(%prep): /bin/sh -e /var/tmp/rpm-tmp.61594
+ umask 022
+ cd /usr/src/redhat/BUILD
+ cd /usr/src/redhat/BUILD
+ rm -rf tac_plus-4.0.3
+ /usr/bin/gzip -dc /usr/src/redhat/SOURCES/tac_plus-4.0.3.tgz
+ tar -xvvf -
...
...
...
+ umask 022
+ cd /usr/src/redhat/BUILD
+ rm -rf tac_plus-4.0.3
+ exit 0
[root@bigboy rpm]#
```

The compiled RPM file can now be found in one of the architecture subdirectories under /usr/src/redhat/RPMS directory. For example, if you compiled an i386 architecture version of the RPM it will be placed in the i386 subdirectory.

You will then have to install the compiled RPMs found in their respective subdirectories as you normally would.

RPM INSTALLATION ERRORS

Sometimes the installation of RPM software doesn't go according to plan and you need to take corrective actions. This section shows you how to recover from some of the most common errors you'll encounter.

Failed Dependencies

Sometimes RPM installations will fail, giving Failed dependencies errors, which really means that a prerequisite RPM needs to be installed. In the next example we're attempting to install the MySQL database server application, which fails because the mysql MySQL client RPM, on which it depends, needs to be installed beforehand:

```
[root@bigboy tmp]# rpm -Uvh mysql-server-3.23.58-9.i386.rpm
error: Failed dependencies:
        libmysqlclient.so.10 is needed by mysql-server-3.23.58-9
        mysql = 3.23.58 is needed by mysql-server-3.23.58-9
[root@bigboy tmp]#
```

Installing the MySQL client also fails because it requires the perl-DBD-MySQL package:

```
[root@bigboy tmp]# rpm -Uvh mysql-3.23.58-9.i386.rpm
error: Failed dependencies:
        perl-DBD-MySQL is needed by mysql-3.23.58-9
[root@bigboy tmp]# rpm -Uvh perl-DBD-MySQL-2.9003-4.i386.rpm
error: Failed dependencies:
        libmysqlclient.so.10 is needed by perl-DBD-MySQL-2.9003-4
[root@bigboy tmp]#
```

Strangely enough, the installation of the perl-DBD-MySQL package fails because it needs the mysql client package. To get around this problem you can run the rpm command with the --nodeps option to disable dependency checks. In the next example we install the MySQL client ignoring dependencies, followed by successful installation of perl-DBD-MySQL and mysql-server:

```
[root@bigboy tmp]# rpm -Uvh --nodeps mysql-3.23.58-9.i386.rpm
Preparing...               ###################### [100%]
   1:mysql                 ###################### [100%]
```

```
[root@bigboy tmp]# rpm -Uvh perl-DBD-MySQL-2.9003-4.i386.rpm
Preparing...          ####################### [100%]
   1:perl-DBD-MySQL ####################### [100%]
[root@bigboy tmp]# rpm -Uvh mysql-server-3.23.58-9.i386.rpm
Preparing...          ####################### [100%]
   1:mysql-server   ####################### [100%]
[root@bigboy tmp]#
```

Note

If all the installation RPMs are located in the same directory, the rpm command can automatically install all the prerequisite RPMs using the --aid option. One of the advantages of using the yum facility is that you don't have to worry about this dependency process as much because the dependency RPMs are always downloaded and installed automatically also.

Signature Keys

Fedora digitally signs all its RPM files, so it's best to import their public encryption key beforehand so that the RPM installation program will be able to verify the validity of the RPM file. This can be done using the rpm command as seen in the next example. It is a good idea to import both the Red Hat and Fedora keys:

```
[root@bigboy tmp]# rpm --import /usr/share/rhn/RPM-GPG-KEY
[root@bigboy tmp]# rpm --import /usr/share/rhn/RPM-GPG-KEY-fedora
[root@bigboy tmp]#
```

If you don't install the keys you get a DSA signature warning that alerts you to the fact that the RPM file might be bogus:

```
[root@bigboy tmp]# rpm -Uvh dhcp-3.0pl2-6.16.i386.rpm
warning: dhcp-3.0pl2-6.16.i386.rpm: V3 DSA signature: NOKEY, key ID
4f2a6fd2
Preparing...          ################################### [100%]
   1:dhcp             ################################### [100%]
[root@bigboy tmp]#
```

It is always good to install the key files. If they are not there, the RPMs will install with only a warning message. If the RPM's digital signature doesn't match that in the key file, the rpm installation program also alerts you and fails to install the RPM package at all:

```
[root@bigboy tmp]# rpm -Uvh dhcp-3.0pl2-6.16.i386.rpm
error: dhcp-3.0pl2-6.16.i386.rpm: V3 DSA signature: BAD, key ID
4f2a6fd2
error: dhcp-3.0pl2-6.16.i386.rpm cannot be installed
[root@bigboy tmp]#
```

Signatures are therefore useful because they help protect you against tampered and otherwise corrupted RPMs being installed.

HOW TO LIST INSTALLED RPMs

The rpm -qa command lists all the packages installed on your system:

```
[root@bigboy tmp]# rpm -qa
perl-Storable-1.0.14-15
smpeg-gtv-0.4.4-9
e2fsprogs-1.27-9
libstdc++-3.2-7
audiofile-0.2.3-3
...
...
...
[root@bigboy tmp]#
```

You can also pipe the output of this command through the grep command if you are interested in only a specific package. In this example we are looking for all packages containing the string ssh in the name, regardless of case (-i means ignore case).

```
[root@bigboy tmp]# rpm -qa | grep -i ssh
openssh-server-3.4p1-2
openssh-clients-3.4p1-2
openssh-askpass-gnome-3.4p1-2
openssh-3.4p1-2
openssh-askpass-3.4p1-2
[root@bigboy tmp]#
```

Note

You could use the rpm -q package-name command to find an installed package because it is much faster than using grep and the -qa switch, but you have to have an exact package match. If you are not sure of the package name and its capitalization, the latter method is probably more suitable.

LISTING FILES ASSOCIATED WITH RPMs

Sometimes you'll find yourself installing software that terminates with an error requesting the presence of a particular file. In many cases the installation program doesn't state the RPM package in which the file can be found. It is therefore important to be able to determine the origin of certain files by listing the contents for RPMs in which you suspect the files might reside.

Listing Files for Already Installed RPMs

This can be useful if you have to duplicate a working server that is already in a production environment. Sometimes the installation of an application fails on the new server due to the lack of a file that resides on the old one. In this case you need to know which RPM on the old server contains the file.

You can use the -ql qualifier to list all the files associated with an installed RPM. In this example we test to make sure that the NTP package is installed using the -q qualifier, and then we use the -ql qualifier to get the file listing:

```
[root@bigboy tmp]# rpm -q ntp
ntp-4.1.2-0.rc1.2
[root@bigboy tmp]# rpm -ql ntp
/etc/ntp
/etc/ntp.conf
/etc/ntp/drift
/etc/ntp/keys
...
...
...
/usr/share/doc/ntp-4.1.2/rdebug.htm
/usr/share/doc/ntp-4.1.2/refclock.htm
/usr/share/doc/ntp-4.1.2/release.htm
/usr/share/doc/ntp-4.1.2/tickadj.htm
[root@bigboy tmp]#
```

Listing Files in RPM Files

Sometimes you make a guess and download what you think is the RPM with the missing file. You can use the -qpl qualifier to list all the files in an RPM archive to make sure before installing it:

```
[root@bigboy updates]# rpm -qpl dhcp-3.0pl1-23.i386.rpm
/etc/rc.d/init.d/dhcpd
/etc/rc.d/init.d/dhcrelay
/etc/sysconfig/dhcpd
/etc/sysconfig/dhcrelay
...
...
...
/usr/share/man/man8/dhcrelay.8.gz
/var/lib/dhcp
/var/lib/dhcp/dhcpd.leases
[root@bigboy updates]#
```

Listing the RPM to Which a File Belongs

You might need to know the RPM that was used to install a particular file. This is useful when you have a suspicion about the function of a file but are not entirely sure. For example, the MySQL RPM uses the `/etc/my.cnf` file as its configuration file, not a file named `/etc/mysql.conf` as you'd normally expect. The following example confirms the origin of the `/etc/my.cnf` file:

```
[root@zippy tmp]# rpm -qf /etc/my.cnf
mysql-3.23.58-9
[root@zippy tmp]#
```

UNINSTALLING RPMs

The `rpm -e` command erases an installed package. The package name given must match that listed in the `rpm -qa` command because the version of the package is important:

```
[root@bigboy tmp]# rpm -e package-name
```

WHICH RPMs START AT BOOT TIME?

The best way to view and configure which RPMs will start at boot time is by using the `chkconfig` command with the `--list` switch. A more detailed explanation will be provided in Chapter 7, "The Linux Boot Process," which covers the Linux boot process.

INSTALLING SOFTWARE USING *TAR* FILES

Another popular software installation file format is the `tar` file, which can frequently be obtained from the Web sites of software developers, and online software libraries such as www.sourceforge.net.

The Linux `tar` command is used to archive files, which typically have a `.tar` file extension in the filename. These files are also frequently compressed in the `gzip` format, and when they are, their file extensions end with `.tar.gz` or `.tgz`. The commands to extract the data from either type are similar. When a `tar` file is uncompressed, the command to extract the data is `tar -xvf filename.tar`. When the archive is compressed, the command to use is `tar -xzvf filename.tar.gz`.

The `tar` file installation process usually requires you first to uncompress and extract the contents of the archive in a local subdirectory, which frequently has the same name as the `tar` file. The subdirectory usually contains a file called README or INSTALL, which outlines all the customized steps to install the software.

Here are the initial steps to install `tar`-based software:

1. Issue the `tar` command to extract the files:

```
[root@bigboy tmp]# tar -xvzf linux-software-1.3.1.tar.gz
linux-software-1.3.1/
linux-software-1.3.1/plugins-scripts/
...
...
...
linux-software-1.3.1/linux-software-plugins.spec
[root@bigboy tmp]#
```

This creates a subdirectory with the installation files inside:

```
[root@bigboy tmp]# ls
linux-software-1.3.1   linux-software-1.3.1.tar.gz
[root@bigboy tmp]#
```

2. Use the `cd` command to enter the subdirectory and follow the directions listed in the INSTALL and README files:

```
[root@bigboy tmp]# cd linux-software-1.3.1
[root@bigboy linux-software-1.3.1]# ls
COPYING     install-sh   missing                    plugins
depcomp     LEGAL        mkinstalldirs              plugins-
scripts
FAQ         lib          linux-software.spec        README
Helper.pm   Makefile.am  linux-software.spec.in     REQUIREMENTS
INSTALL     Makefile.in  NEWS                       subst.in
[root@bigboy linux-software-1.3.1]#
```

Software installation with `tar` files can be frustrating, frequently requiring the installation of other supporting `tar` files, each with its own customized installation commands. RPMs, with the single standardized command format, are usually easier to use and may be the better method to use for newer Linux users.

CONCLUSION

This is just the beginning. If the software you install is intended to make your Linux machine permanently run an application—such as a Web server, mail server, or any other type of server—you have to know how to get the software activated when the system reboots. This is covered in Chapter 7. Subsequent chapters cover the use, configuration, testing, and troubleshooting of many of the most popular Linux server applications used today.

The Linux Boot Process

IN THIS CHAPTER

☞ The Fedora Boot Sequence
☞ Determining the Default Boot `runlevel`
☞ Getting a GUI Console
☞ Get a Basic Text Terminal Without Exiting the GUI
☞ System Shutdown and Rebooting
☞ How to Set Programs to Run at Each `runlevel`
☞ Conclusion

Learning how Linux boots up is critical. When you have this information you can use it to alter the type of login screen you get as well as which programs start up. Read on for the details.

THE FEDORA BOOT SEQUENCE

You might remember when you installed Linux that the installation process prompted you for a list of partitions and the sizes of each in which your filesystems would be placed.

When allocating disk space for the partitions, the first sector, or data unit, for each partition is always reserved for programmable code used in booting. The very first sector of the hard disk is reserved for the same purpose and is called the **master boot record (MBR)**.

When booting from a hard disk, the PC system BIOS loads and executes the **boot loader code** in the MBR. The MBR then needs to know which partitions on the disk have boot loader code specific to their operating systems in their boot sectors and then attempts to boot one of them.

Fedora Linux is supplied with the GRUB boot loader, which is fairly sophisticated and therefore cannot entirely fit in the 512 bytes of the MBR.

The GRUB MBR boot loader merely searches for a special **boot partition** and loads a **second stage boot loader**. This then reads the data in the `/boot/grub/grub.conf` configuration file, which lists all the available operating systems and their booting parameters. When this is complete, the second stage boot loader then displays the familiar Fedora branded splash screen that lists all the configured operating system kernels for your choice.

Figure 7.1 shows a typical `grub.conf` file for a system that can boot both Fedora Linux and Windows 2000. The structure of this file is discussed further in Chapter 33, "Modifying the Kernel to Improve Performance."

```
default=0
timeout=10
splashimage=(hd0,0)/grub/splash.xpm.gz
title Fedora Core (2.6.8-1.521)
        root (hd0,0)
        kernel /vmlinuz-2.6.8-1.521 ro root=LABEL=/
        initrd /initrd-2.6.8-1.521.img
title Windows 2000
        rootnoverify (hd0,1)
        chainloader +1
```

Figure 7.1   Example of a `grub.conf` file.

When Linux begins to boot with its kernel, it first runs the `/sbin/init` program, which does some system checks such as verifying the integrity of the file systems, and starts vital programs needed for the operating system to function properly. It then inspects the `/etc/inittab` file to determine Linux's overall mode of operation or runlevel. A listing of valid runlevels can be seen in Table 7.1.

Table 7.1   Linux Runlevels

Mode/Runlevel	Directory	Runlevel Description
0	/etc/rc.d/rc0.d	Halt
1	/etc/rc.d/rc1.d	Single-user mode
2	/etc/rc.d/rc2.d	Not used (user-definable)
3	/etc/rc.d/rc3.d	Full multiuser mode (no GUI interface)
4	/etc/rc.d/rc4.d	Not used (user-definable)
5	/etc/rc.d/rc5.d	Full multiuser mode (with GUI interface)
6	/etc/rc.d/rc6.d	Reboot

Based on the selected runlevel, the `init` process then executes startup scripts located in subdirectories of the `/etc/rc.d` directory. Scripts used for runlevels 0 to 6 are located in subdirectories `/etc/rc.d/rc0.d` through `/etc/rc.d/rc6.d`, respectively.

Here is a directory listing of the scripts in the `/etc/rc.d/rc3.d` directory:

```
[root@bigboy tmp]# ls /etc/rc.d/rc3.d
...      ...    K75netfs      K96pcmcia     ...    ...
...      ...    K86nfslock    S05kudzu      ...    ...
...      ...    K87portmap    S09wlan       ...    ...
...      ...    K91isdn       S10network    ...    ...
...      ...    K92iptables   S12syslog     ...    ...
...      ...    K95firstboot  S17keytable   ...    ...
[root@bigboy tmp]#
```

As you can see, each filename in these directories either starts with an s, which signifies the script should be run at startup, or a κ, which means the script should be run when the system is shutting down. If a script isn't there, it won't be run.

Most Red Hat/Fedora packages place their startup script in the `/etc/init.d` directory and place symbolic links (pointers) to this script in the appropriate subdirectory of `/etc/rc.d`. This makes file management a lot easier. The deletion of a link doesn't delete the file, which can then be used for another day.

The number that follows the κ or s specifies the position in which the scripts should be run, in ascending order. In our example, kudzu with a value of 05 will run before wlan with a value of 09.

Fortunately you don't have to be a scripting/symbolic linking guru to make sure everything works right because Fedora comes with a nifty utility called chkconfig to do it for you. This is explained later.

DETERMINING THE DEFAULT BOOT *RUNLEVEL*

The default boot runlevel is set in the file `/etc/inittab` with the initdefault variable. When set to 3, the system boots up with the text interface on the VGA console; when set to 5, you get the GUI. Here is a snippet of the file (delete the initdefault line you don't need):

```
# Default runlevel. The runlevels used by RHS are:
# 0 - halt (Do NOT set initdefault to this)
# 1 - Single user mode
# 2 - Multiuser, without NFS (The same as 3, if you do not have
networking)
# 3 - Full multiuser mode
# 4 - unused
# 5 - X11
# 6 - reboot (Do NOT set initdefault to this)
```

```
#
id:3:initdefault:                           # Console Text Mode
id:5:initdefault:                           # Console GUI Mode
```

Note the following:

☞ Most home users boot up with a Windows like GUI (runlevel 5).

☞ Most techies tend to boot up with a plain text-based command-line-type interface (runlevel 3).

☞ Changing `initdefault` from 3 to 5, or vice versa, has an effect on your next reboot. See the following section on how to get a GUI login all the time until the next reboot.

☞ Of course, don't set the `initdefault` value to 6 or your system will constantly reboot. Setting it to 0 will never allow it to start!

GETTING A GUI CONSOLE

You have two main options if your system comes up in a text terminal mode on the VGA console and you want to get the GUI:

☞ **Manual Method:** You can start the X terminal GUI application each time you need it by running the `startx` command at the VGA console. Remember that when you log out you will get the regular text-based console again:

```
[root@bigboy tmp]# startx
```

☞ **Automatic Method:** You can have Linux automatically start the X terminal GUI console for every login attempt until your next reboot by using the `init` command. You will need to edit your `initdefault` variable in your `/etc/inittab` file, as mentioned in the preceding section, to keep this functionality even after you reboot.

```
[root@bigboy tmp]# init 5
```

When the CPU capacity or available memory on your server is low or you want to maximize all system resources, you might want to operate in text mode runlevel 3 most of the time, using the GUI only as necessary with the `startx` command.

Servers that double as personal workstations, or servers that might have to be operated for an extended period of time by relatively nontechnical staff, may need to be run at runlevel 5 all the time through the `init 5` command. Remember you can make runlevel 5 permanent even after a reboot by editing the `/etc/inittab` file.

GET A BASIC TEXT TERMINAL WITHOUT EXITING THE GUI

There are a number of ways for you to get a command prompt when running a Linux GUI. This can be important if you need quick access to commands or you are not familiar with the GUI menu option layout.

Using a GUI Terminal Window

You can open a GUI-based window with a command prompt inside by doing the following:

☞ Click on the Fedora logo button in the lower-left corner of the screen.
☞ Click on Systems Tools and then Terminal.

Using Virtual Consoles

By default, Linux runs six virtual console or TTY sessions running on the VGA console. These are defined by the `mingetty` statements in the `/etc/inittab` file. The X terminal GUI console creates its own virtual console using the first available TTY that is not controlled by `mingetty`. This makes the GUI run as number 7:

☞ You can step through each virtual console session by using the Ctrl-Alt-F1 through F6 key sequence. You'll get a new login prompt for each attempt.
☞ You can get the GUI login with the sequence Ctl-Alt-F7, only in runlevel 5, or if the GUI is running after launching `startx`.

SYSTEM SHUTDOWN AND REBOOTING

It is usually not a good idea to immediately power off your system when you are finished using it. This can cause files that are being updated to become corrupted, or worse, you could corrupt the filesystem directory structure. Linux has a number of ways to gracefully shut down and reboot your system, which will be outlined in this section.

Halt/Shut Down the System

The `init` command enables you to change the current runlevel, and for a shut-down, that value is 0. Here is an example:

```
[root@bigboy tmp]# init 0
```

Fedora also has a `shutdown` command, which can be used to the same effect. It often prompts you as to whether you are sure you want to execute the command, which can be avoided with the `-y` switch. The `-h` switch forces the system to halt, and the first argument tells it how long to wait before starting the procedure, in this case 0 minutes. You can also specify shutting down at a specific time of the day; please refer to the `man` pages for details. Another advantage of the `shutdown` command is that it warns people that the shutdown is going to occur:

```
[root@bigboy tmp]# shutdown -hy 0

Broadcast message from root (pts/0) (Sat Nov  6 13:15:27 2004):

The system is going down for system halt NOW!
[root@bigboy tmp]#
```

Reboot the System

You can also use the `init` command to reboot the system immediately by entering runlevel 6:

```
[root@bigboy tmp]# init 6
```

The `reboot` command has the same effect, but it also sends a warning message to all users:

```
[root@bigboy tmp]# reboot

Broadcast message from root (pts/0) (Sat Nov  6 12:39:31 2004):

The system is going down for reboot NOW!
[root@bigboy tmp]#
```

More graceful reboots can be done with the `shutdown` command using the `-r` switch and specifying a delay, which in this case is 10 minutes:

```
[root@bigboy root]# shutdown -ry 10

Broadcast message from root (pts/0) (Sat Nov  6 13:26:39 2004):

The system is going DOWN for reboot in 10 minutes!

Broadcast message from root (pts/0) (Sat Nov  6 13:27:39 2004):

The system is going DOWN for reboot in 9 minutes!
```

```
...
...
...

Broadcast message from root (pts/0) (Sat Nov  6 13:36:39 2004):

The system is going down for reboot NOW!
```

Entering Single-user Mode

Some activities require you to force the system to log off all users, third-party applications, and networking so that only the systems administrator has access to the system from the VGA console. A typical scenario is the addition of a new hard disk, as mentioned in Chapter 27, "Expanding Disk Capacity," or the troubleshooting of a failed boot process.

Another reason is the recovery of your root password.

Switching to Single-user Mode

When the system is running normally, this can be done by using the init command to enter runlevel 1. It is best to do this from the console, because if you do it from a remote terminal session you'll be logged out:

```
[root@bigboy root]# init 1
...
...
bash-2.05b#
```

Unfortunately, this gives no prior warning to users, and the shutdown command doesn't have a single-user mode option. This can be overcome by running the shutdown command with a delay in minutes as the only argument:

```
[root@bigboy tmp]# shutdown 1

Broadcast message from root (pts/0) (Sat Nov  6 13:44:59 2004):

The system is going DOWN to maintenance mode in 1 minute!

Broadcast message from root (pts/0) (Sat Nov  6 13:45:59 2004):

The system is going down to maintenance mode NOW!

...
...
bash-2.05b#
```

Entering Single-user Mode at the Grub Splash Screen

You can enter single-user mode directly after turning on the power to your system:

1. Power on your system.
2. When the Linux logo screen appears, the one which allows you to select the various installed kernels on the system, type the letter a for "append." You will get a prompt like this to add boot options to the boot string found in your grub.conf file:

   ```
   grub append> ro root=LABEL=/
   ```

3. Add a 1 to the end of the string:

   ```
   grub append> ro root=LABEL=/ 1
   ```

4. Press enter. The system will continue to boot, but will go straight to the root # prompt without first asking for a username and password.

Reverting to Your Default runlevel *from Single-user Mode*

The exit command forces the system to exit runlevel 1 and revert to the default runlevel for the system. You can also use the init command (for example, init 3 and init 5) to alter this default behavior:

```
bash-2.05b# exit
INIT: Entering runlevel: 3
...
...
...
Fedora Core release 2 (Tettnang)
Kernel 2.6.8-1.521 on an i686

bigboy login:
```

Root *Password Recovery*

Sometimes you might forget the root password, or the previous systems administrator might move on to a new job without giving it to you. To recover the root password, follow these steps:

1. Go to the VGA console and press Ctrl-Alt-Del. The system will then shut down in an orderly fashion.
2. Reboot the system and enter single-user mode.
3. When at the command prompt, change your password. Single-user mode assumes the person at the console is the systems administrator root, so you don't have to specify a root username.
4. Return to your default runlevel by using the exit command.

HOW TO SET PROGRAMS TO RUN AT EACH *RUNLEVEL*

As stated earlier, the chkconfig command can be used to adjust which applications start at each runlevel. You can use this command with the --list switch to get a full listing of packages listed in /etc/init.d and the runlevels at which they will be on or off:

```
[root@bigboy tmp]# chkconfig --list
keytable 0:off 1:on  2:on  3:on 4:on  5:on 6:off
atd      0:off 1:off 2:off 3:on 4:on  5:on 6:off
syslog   0:off 1:off 2:on  3:on 4:on  5:on 6:off
gpm      0:off 1:off 2:on  3:on 4:on  5:on 6:off
kudzu    0:off 1:off 2:off 3:on 4:on  5:on 6:off
wlan     0:off 1:off 2:on  3:on 4:on  5:on 6:off
sendmail 0:off 1:off 2:off 3:on 4:off 5:on 6:off
netfs    0:off 1:off 2:off 3:on 4:on  5:on 6:off
network  0:off 1:off 2:on  3:on 4:on  5:on 6:off
random   0:off 1:off 2:on  3:on 4:on  5:on 6:off
...
...
```

chkconfig Examples

You can use chkconfig to change runlevels for particular packages. Here we see that sendmail starts with a regular startup at runlevel 3 or 5. Let's change it so that sendmail doesn't start up at boot.

Use chkconfig to Get a Listing of sendmail's Current Startup Options

The chkconfig command can be used with grep to determine the runlevels in which sendmail will run. Here we see it will run at levels 3 and 5:

```
[root@bigboy tmp]# chkconfig --list | grep mail
sendmail 0:off 1:off 2:off 3:on 4:off 5:on 6:off
[root@bigboy tmp]#
```

Switch Off sendmail Starting Up in Levels 3 and 5

The chkconfig command with the --level switch indicates that some action needs to be done at the runlevels entered as its values. The first argument in the command is the package you want to affect, and the second defines whether you want it on or off. In this case we want sendmail not to be started when entering runlevels 3 and 5:

```
[root@bigboy tmp]# chkconfig --level 35 sendmail off
[root@bigboy tmp]#
```

By not specifying the runlevels with the `--level` switch, chckconfig
makes the changes for runlevels 3 and 5 automatically:

```
[root@bigboy tmp]# chkconfig sendmail off
```

Because the intention is to shut down sendmail permanently, we might
also have to stop it from running now:

```
[root@bigboy tmp]# service sendmail stop
Shutting down sendmail: [  OK  ]
Shutting down sm-client: [  OK  ]
[root@bigboy tmp]#
```

Double-check that sendmail Will Not Start Up

We can then use chkconfig to double-check our work:

```
[root@bigboy tmp]# chkconfig --list | grep mail
sendmail 0:off 1:off 2:off 3:off 4:off 5:off 6:off
[root@bigboy tmp]#
```

Turn On sendmail Again

To reactivate sendmail, we can use chkconfig once more, but with the on argument. Start sendmail again to get it running immediately, not just after the
next reboot.

```
[root@bigboy tmp]# chkconfig sendmail on
[root@bigboy tmp]# chkconfig --list | grep mail
sendmail 0:off 1:off 2:off 3:on 4:off 5:on 6:off
[root@bigboy tmp]# service sendmail start
Starting sendmail: [  OK  ]
Starting sm-client: [  OK  ]
[root@bigboy tmp]#
```

Using chkconfig to Improve Security

A default Fedora installation automatically starts a number of daemons that
you may not necessarily need for a Web server. This usually results in your
system listening on a variety of unexpected TCP/IP ports that could be used as
doors into your system by hackers.

The screen output of the netstat -an command shows a typical case.
Some ports are relatively easy to recognize. TCP ports 25 and 22 are for mail
and SSH, respectively, but some others are less obvious. Should you use the
chkconfig command and the scripts in the /etc/init.d directory to shut these
down permanently?

```
[root@bigboy tmp]# netstat -an
Active Internet connections (servers and established)
Proto Recv-Q Send-Q Local Address          Foreign Address
State
tcp    0      0 0.0.0.0:32768      0.0.0.0:*      LISTEN
tcp    0      0 127.0.0.1:32769    0.0.0.0:*      LISTEN
tcp    0      0 0.0.0.0:111        0.0.0.0:*      LISTEN
tcp    0      0 127.0.0.1:631      0.0.0.0:*      LISTEN
tcp    0      0 127.0.0.1:25       0.0.0.0:*      LISTEN
tcp    0      0 :::22              :::*           LISTEN
udp    0      0 0.0.0.0:32768      0.0.0.0:*
udp    0      0 0.0.0.0:930        0.0.0.0:*
udp    0      0 0.0.0.0:68         0.0.0.0:*
udp    0      0 0.0.0.0:111        0.0.0.0:*
udp    0      0 0.0.0.0:631        0.0.0.0:*
...
...
[root@bigboy tmp]#
```

For example, how do you know which startup script is responsible for TCP port 111? The answer is to use the `lsof` command, which lists all open or actively used files and can be given additional options to extend its scope to include the TCP/IP protocol stack.

In the next examples, we see that TCP ports 111 and 32769, and UDP port 123 are being used by the `portmap`, `xinetd`, and `ntp` daemons, respectively. The `portmap` daemon is required for the operation of NFS and NIS, topics that are covered in Chapters 29, "Remote Disk Access with NFS," and 30, "Configuring NIS." `portmap` also has many known security flaws that makes it advisable to be run on a secured network. If you don't need any of these three applications, it's best to shut down `portmap` permanently. `ntp`, which is covered in Chapter 24, "The NTP Server," is required for synchronizing your time with a reliable time source and may be necessary. A number of network applications are reliant on `xinetd`, as explained in Chapter 16, "Telnet, TFTP, and XINETD," and it might be required for their operation:

```
[root@ bigboy tmp]# lsof -i tcp:111
COMMAND  PID USER   FD   TYPE DEVICE SIZE NODE NAME
portmap 1165 rpc    4u   IPv4   2979      TCP *:sunrpc (LISTEN)
[root@ bigboy tmp #

[root@bigboy tmp]# lsof -i tcp:32769
COMMAND  PID USER   FD   TYPE DEVICE SIZE NODE NAME
xinetd  1522 root   5u   IPv4   2764      TCP probe-001:32769
(LISTEN)
[root@bigboy tmp]#

[root@bigboy root]# lsof -i udp:123
COMMAND  PID USER   FD   TYPE DEVICE SIZE NODE NAME
ntpd    1321 ntp    4u   IPv4   3390      UDP *:ntp
...
...
[root@bigboy root]#
```

In some cases it's tricky to determine the application based on the results of the lsof command. In the example below, we've discovered that TCP port 32768 is being used by rpc.statd, but there is no rpc.statd file in the /etc/init.d directory. The simple solution is to use the grep command to search all the files for the string rpc.statd to determine which one is responsible for its operation. We soon discover that the nfslock daemon uses it. If you don't need nfslock, then shut it down permanently:

```
[root@bigboy tmp]# lsof -i tcp:32768
COMMAND     PID    USER   FD   TYPE DEVICE SIZE NODE NAME
rpc.statd 1178 rpcuser    6u   IPv4   2400          TCP *:32768 (LISTEN)
[root@bigboy tmp]# ls /etc/init.d/rpc.statd
ls: /etc/init.d/rpc.statd: No such file or directory
[root@bigboy tmp]# grep -i statd /etc/init.d/*
/etc/init.d/nfslock:[ -x /sbin/rpc.statd ] || exit 0
...
...
[root@bigboy tmp]#
```

As a rule of thumb, applications listening only on the loopback interface (IP address 127.0.0.1) are usually the least susceptible to network attack and probably don't need to be stopped for network security reasons. Those listening on all interfaces, depicted as IP address 0.0.0.0, are naturally more vulnerable and their continued operation should be dependent on your server's needs. I usually shut down nfs, nfslock, netfs, portmap, and cups printing as standard practice on Internet servers. I keep sendmail running as it is always needed to send and receive mail (see Chapter 21, "Configuring Linux Mail Servers," for details). Your needs may be different.

Remember to research your options thoroughly before choosing to shut down an application. Use the Linux man pages, reference books, and the Internet for information. Unpredictable results are always undesirable.

Shutting down applications is only a part of server security. Firewalls, physical access restrictions, password policies, and patch updates need to be considered. Full coverage of server and network security is beyond the scope of this book, but you should always have a security reference guide on hand to guide your final decisions.

Final Tips on *chkconfig*

Remember the following:

☞ In most cases, you want to modify runlevels 3 and 5 simultaneously *and* with the same values.

☞ Don't add/remove anything to other runlevels unless you absolutely know what you are doing. Don't experiment, unless in a test environment.

☞ `chkconfig` doesn't start the programs in the `/etc/init.d` directory, it just configures them to be started or ignored when the system boots up. The commands for starting and stopping the programs covered in this book are covered in each respective chapter.

CONCLUSION

The topics discussed in this chapter might seem simple, but like `syslog`, which was covered in Chapter 5, "Troubleshooting Linux with syslog," they are an essential part of Linux administration that gets frequently overlooked—especially when new software is installed.

Whenever possible, always try to reboot your system to make sure all the newly installed applications start up correctly. Sometimes they start but give errors listed only in the `/var/log` directory. Taking the time to configure and test your startup scripts could prevent you from being awakened in the middle of the night while you are on vacation! It is really important.

## CHAPTER 8

Configuring the DHCP Server

IN THIS CHAPTER

- ☞ Download and Install the DHCP Pacakge
- ☞ The `/etc/dhcpd.conf` File
- ☞ How to Get DHCP Started
- ☞ DHCP Servers with Multiple NICs
- ☞ Configuring Linux Clients to Use DHCP
- ☞ Configuring Windows Clients to Use DHCP
- ☞ Simple DHCP Troubleshooting
- ☞ Conclusion

Normally if you have a cable modem or DSL, you get your home PC's IP address dynamically assigned from your service provider. If you install a home cable/DSL router between your modem and home network, your PC will most likely get its IP address at boot time from the home router instead. You can choose to disable the DHCP server feature on your home router and set up a Linux box as the DHCP server.

This chapter covers only the configuration of a DHCP server that provides IP addresses. The configuration of a Linux DHCP client that gets its IP address from a DHCP server is covered in Chapter 3, "Linux Networking."

DOWNLOAD AND INSTALL THE DHCP PACKAGE

Most Red Hat and Fedora Linux software products are available in the RPM format. Downloading and installing RPMs isn't hard. If you need a refresher, Chapter 6, "Installing RPM Software," covers how to do this in detail.

When searching for the file, remember that the DHCP server RPM's file-name usually starts with the word dhcp followed by a version number like this: dhcp-3.0.1rc14-1.i386.rpm.

THE /ETC/DHCPD.CONF FILE

When DHCP starts, it reads the file /etc/dhcpd.conf. It uses the commands here to configure your network. The standard DHCP RPM package doesn't automatically install a /etc/dhcpd.conf file, but you can find a sample copy of dhcpd.conf in the following directory, which you can always use as a guide:

```
/usr/share/doc/dhcp-<version-number>/dhcpd.conf.sample
```

You have to copy the sample dhcpd.conf file to the /etc directory and then you have to edit it. Here is the command to do the copying for the version 3.0p11 RPM file:

```
[root@bigboy tmp]# cp /usr/share/doc/dhcp-3.0p11/dhcpd.conf.sample \
    /etc/dhcpd.conf
```

Here is a quick explanation of the dhcpd.conf file: Most importantly, there *must* be a subnet section for each interface on your Linux box:

```
ddns-update-style interim
ignore client-updates

subnet 192.168.1.0 netmask 255.255.255.0 {
    # The range of IP addresses the server
    # will issue to DHCP enabled PC clients
    # booting up on the network

    range 192.168.1.201 192.168.1.220;

    # Set the amount of time in seconds that
    # a client may keep the IP address

    default-lease-time 86400;
    max-lease-time 86400;

    # Set the default gateway to be used by
    # the PC clients

    option routers 192.168.1.1;

    # Don't forward DHCP requests from this
    # NIC interface to any other NIC
    # interfaces

    option ip-forwarding off;
```

```
            # Set the broadcast address and subnet mask
            # to be used by the DHCP clients

            option broadcast-address 192.168.1.255;
            option subnet-mask 255.255.255.0;

            # Set the DNS server to be used by the
            # DHCP clients

            option domain-name-servers 192.168.1.100;

            # Set the NTP server to be used by the
            # DHCP clients

            option nntp-server 192.168.1.100;

            # If you specify a WINS server for your Windows clients,
            # you need to include the following option in the dhcpd.conf file:

            option netbios-name-servers 192.168.1.100;

            # You can also assign specific IP addresses based on the clients'
            # ethernet MAC address as follows (Host's name is "laser-printer":

            host laser-printer {
                hardware ethernet 08:00:2b:4c:59:23;
                fixed-address 192.168.1.222;
            }
        }
        #
        # List an unused interface here
        #
        subnet 192.168.2.0 netmask 255.255.255.0 {
        }
```

There are many more options statements you can use to configure DHCP. These include telling the DHCP clients where to go for services such as finger and IRC. Check the dhcp-options man page after you do your install:

```
[root@bigboy tmp]# man dhcp-options
```

Note

The host statement seen in the sample dhcpd.conf file can be very useful. Some devices such as network printers default to getting their IP addresses using DHCP, but users need to access them by a fixed IP address to print their documents. This statement can be used to always provide specific IP address to DHCP queries from a predefined NIC MAC address. This can help to reduce systems administration overhead.

How to Get DHCP Started

To start DHCP:

1. Some older Fedora/Red Hat versions of the DHCP server will fail unless there is an existing `dhcpd.leases` file. Use the command `touch` `/var/lib/dhcp/dhcpd.leases` to create the file if it does not exist:

```
[root@bigboy tmp]# touch /var/lib/dhcp/dhcpd.leases
```

2. Use the `chkconfig` command to get DHCP configured to start at boot:

```
[root@bigboy tmp]# chkconfig dhcpd on
```

3. Use the `service` command to instruct the `/etc/init.d/dhcpd` script to start/stop/restart DHCP after booting:

```
[root@bigboy tmp]# service dhcpd start
[root@bigboy tmp]# service dhcpd stop
[root@bigboy tmp]# service dhcpd restart
```

4. Remember to restart the DHCP process every time you make a change to the `conf` file for the changes to take effect on the running process. You also can test whether the DHCP process is running with the following command; you should get a response of plain old process ID numbers:

```
[root@bigboy tmp]# pgrep dhcpd
```

5. Finally, always remember to set your PC to get its IP address via DHCP.

DHCP Servers with Multiple NICs

When a DHCP configured PC boots, it requests its IP address from the DHCP server. It does this by sending a standardized DHCP broadcast request packet to the DHCP server with a source IP address of 255.255.255.255.

If your DHCP server has more than one interface, you have to add a route for this 255.255.255.255 address so that it knows the interface on which to send the reply; if not, it sends it to the default gateway. (In both of the next two examples, we assume that DHCP requests will be coming in on interface `eth0`.)

Note

More information on adding Linux routes and routing may be found in Chapter 3.

Note

You can't run your DHCP sever on multiple interfaces because you can have only one route to network 255.255.255.255. If you try to do it, you'll discover that DHCP server working on only one interface.

Temporary Solution

You can temporarily add a route to 255.255.255.255 using the `route` `add` command:

```
[root@bigboy tmp]# route add -host 255.255.255.255 dev eth0
```

If you want this routing state to be maintained after a reboot, use the permanent solution that's discussed next.

Permanent Solution

The new Fedora Linux method of adding static routes doesn't seem to support sending traffic out an interface that's not destined for a specific gateway IP address. The DHCP packet destined for address 255.255.255.255 isn't intended to be relayed to a gateway, but it should be sent using the MAC address of the DHCP client in the Ethernet frame. To avoid this problem add the `route add` command to your `/etc/rc.local` script.

CONFIGURING LINUX CLIENTS TO USE DHCP

A Linux NIC interface can be configured to obtain its IP address using DHCP with the examples outlined in Chapter 3. Please refer to this chapter if you need a quick refresher on how to configure a Linux DHCP client.

CONFIGURING WINDOWS CLIENTS TO USE DHCP

Fortunately, Windows defaults to using DHCP for all its NIC cards so you don't have to worry about doing any reconfiguration.

SIMPLE DHCP TROUBLESHOOTING

The most common problems with DHCP usually aren't related to the server; after the server is configured correctly there is no need to change any settings and it therefore runs reliably. The problems usually occur at the DHCP client's end for a variety of reasons. The following sections present simple troubleshooting steps that you can go through to ensure that DHCP is working correctly on your network.

DHCP Clients Obtaining 169.254.0.0 Addresses

Whenever Microsoft DHCP clients are unable to contact their DHCP server they default to selecting their own IP address from the 169.254.0.0 network until the DHCP server becomes available again. This is frequently referred to as Automatic Private IP Addressing (APIPA). Here are some steps you can go through to resolve the problem:

1. Ensure that your DHCP server is configured correctly and use the `pgrep` command discussed earlier to make sure the DHCP process is running. Pay special attention to your 255.255.255.255 route, especially if your DHCP server has multiple interfaces.

2. Give your DHCP client a static IP address from the same range that the DHCP server is supposed to provide. See whether you can ping the DHCP server. If you cannot, double-check your cabling and your NICs.

CONCLUSION

In most home-based networks, a DHCP server isn't necessary because the DSL router/firewall usually has DHCP capabilities, but it is an interesting project to try. Just remember to make sure that the range of IP addresses issued by all DHCP servers on a network doesn't overlap because it could possibly cause unexpected errors. You might want to disable the router/firewall's DHCP server capabilities to experiment with your new Linux server.

A DHCP server may be invaluable in an office environment where the time and cost of getting a network engineer to get the work done may make it simpler for Linux systems administrators to do it by themselves.

Creating a Linux DHCP server is straightforward and touches all the major themes in the previous chapters. Now it's time to try something harder, but before we do, we'll do a quick refresher on how to create the Linux users who'll be using many of the applications outlined in the rest of the book.

## CHAPTER 9

Linux Users and *sudo*

In This Chapter

☞ Adding Users
☞ Using sudo
☞ Conclusion

Before we proceed, it would be best to cover some basic user administration topics that will be very useful in later chapters.

Adding Users

One of the most important activities in administering a Linux box is the addition of users. Here you'll find some simple examples to provide a foundation for future chapters. It is not intended to be comprehensive, but is a good memory refresher. You can use the command man useradd to get the help pages on adding users with the useradd command or the man usermod to become more familiar with modifying users with the usermod command.

Who Is the Super User?

The super user with unrestricted access to all system resources and files in Linux is the user named root. This user has a user ID of 0, which is universally identified by Linux applications as belonging to a user with supreme privileges. You need to log in as user root to add new users to your Linux server.

How to Add Users

Adding users takes some planning; read through these steps before starting:

1. Arrange your list of users into groups by function. In this example there are three groups: parents, children, and soho:

   ```
   Parents    Children    Soho
   Paul       Alice       Accounts
   Jane       Derek       Sales
   ```

2. Add the Linux groups to your server:

   ```
   [root@bigboy tmp]# groupadd parents
   [root@bigboy tmp]# groupadd children
   [root@bigboy tmp]# groupadd soho
   ```

3. Add the Linux users and assign them to their respective groups:

   ```
   [root@bigboy tmp]# useradd -g parents paul
   [root@bigboy tmp]# useradd -g parents jane
   [root@bigboy tmp]# useradd -g children derek
   [root@bigboy tmp]# useradd -g children alice
   [root@bigboy tmp]# useradd -g soho accounts
   [root@bigboy tmp]# useradd -g soho sales
   ```

   If you don't specify the group with the -g, Red Hat/Fedora Linux creates a group with the same name as the user you just created; this is also known as the User Private Group Scheme. When each new user first logs in, they are prompted for their new permanent password.

4. Each user's personal directory is placed in the /home directory. The directory name will be the same as the user's username:

   ```
   [root@bigboy tmp]# ll /home
   drwxr-xr-x    2 root        root         12288 Jul 24 20:04
   lost+found
   drwx------    2 accounts soho            1024 Jul 24 20:33 accounts
   drwx------    2 alice       children      1024 Jul 24 20:33 alice
   drwx------    2 derek       children      1024 Jul 24 20:33 derek
   drwx------    2 jane        parents       1024 Jul 24 20:33 jane
   drwx------    2 paul        parents       1024 Jul 24 20:33 paul
   drwx------    2 sales       soho          1024 Jul 24 20:33
   sales [root@bigboy tmp]#
   ```

How to Change Passwords

You need to create passwords for each account. This is done with the passwd command. You are prompted once for your old password and twice for the new one:

☞ User root changing the password for user paul:

```
[root@bigboy root]# passwd paul
Changing password for user paul.
New password: your new password
Retype new password: your new password
passwd: all authentication tokens updated successfully.
[root@bigboy root]#
```

☞ Users might want to change their passwords at a future date. Here is how unprivileged user paul would change his own password:

```
[paul@bigboy paul]$ passwd
Changing password for paul
Old password: your current password
Enter the new password (minimum of 5, maximum of 8 charac-
ters)
Please use a combination of upper and lower case letters and
numbers.
New password: your new password
Re-enter new password: your new password
Password changed.
[paul@bigboy paul]$
```

How to Delete Users

The userdel command is used to remove the user's record from the /etc/passwd and /etc/shadow used in the login process. The command has a single argument, the username:

```
[root@bigboy tmp]# userdel paul
```

There is also an optional -r switch that additionally removes all the contents of the user's home directory. Use this option with care. The data in a user's directory can often be important even after the person has left your company:

```
[root@bigboy tmp]# userdel -r paul
```

How to Tell the Groups to Which a User Belongs

Use the groups command with the username as the argument:

```
[root@bigboy root]# groups paul
paul : parents
[root@bigboy root]#
```

How to Change the Ownership of a File

You can change the ownership of a file with the chown command. The first argument is the desired username and group ownership for the file separated by a colon (:) followed by the filename. In the next example we change the ownership of the file named text.txt from being owned by user root and group root to being owned by user testuser in the group users:

```
[root@bigboy tmp]# ll test.txt
-rw-r--r--  1 root root 0 Nov 17 22:14 test.txt
[root@bigboy tmp]# chown testuser:users test.txt
[root@bigboy tmp]# ll test.txt
-rw-r--r--  1 testuser users 0 Nov 17 22:14 test.txt
[root@bigboy tmp]#
```

You can also use the chown command with the -r switch for it to do recursive searches down into directories to change permissions.

USING *SUDO*

If a server needs to be administered by a number of people, it is normally not a good idea for them all to use the root account. This is because it becomes difficult to determine exactly who did what, when, and where if everyone logs in with the same credentials. The sudo utility was designed to overcome this difficulty.

The sudo utility allows users defined in the /etc/sudoers configuration file to have temporary access to run commands they would not normally be able to due to file permission restrictions. The commands can be run as user root or as any other user defined in the /etc/sudoers configuration file.

The privileged command you want to run must first begin with the word sudo followed by the command's regular syntax. When running the command with the sudo prefix, you will be prompted for your regular password before it is executed. You may run other privileged commands using sudo within a five-minute period without being re-prompted for a password. All commands run as sudo are logged in the log file /var/log/messages.

Example of a User Using *sudo*

In this example, user bob attempts to view the contents of the /etc/sudoers file, which is an action that normally requires privileged access. Without sudo, the command fails:

```
[bob@bigboy bob]$ more /etc/sudoers
/etc/sudoers: Permission denied
[bob@bigboy bob]$
```

Bob tries again using `sudo` and his regular user password and is successful:

```
[bob@bigboy bob]$ sudo more /etc/sudoers
Password:
...
...
[bob@bigboy bob]$
```

The details of configuring and installing `sudo` are covered in later sections.

Downloading and Installing the *sudo* Package

Fortunately the package is installed by default by Red Hat/Fedora, which eliminates the need to anything more in this regard.

The visudo *Command*

The `visudo` command is a text editor that mimics the `vi` editor that is used to edit the `/etc/sudoers` configuration file. It is not recommended that you use any other editor to modify your `sudo` parameters because the `sudoers` file isn't located in the same directory on all versions of Linux. `visudo` uses the same commands as the `vi` text editor. The `visudo` command must run as user `root` and should have no arguments:

```
[root@bigboy tmp]# visudo
```

The /etc/sudoers *File*

The `/etc/sudoers` file contains all the configuration and permission parameters needed for `sudo` to work. There are a number of guidelines that need to be followed when editing it with `visudo`.

General /etc/sudoers *Guidelines*

The `/etc/sudoers` file has the general format shown in Table 9.1.

Table 9.1   Format of the `/etc/sudoers` File

General sudoers **File Record Format**
`usernames/group servername = (usernames command can be run as) command`

There are some general guidelines when editing this file:

☞ Groups are the same as user groups and are differentiated from regular users by a `%` at the beginning. The Linux user group `users` would be represented by `%users`.

☞ You can have multiple usernames per line, separated by commas.

☞ Multiple commands also can be separated by commas. Spaces are considered part of the command.

☞ The keyword ALL can mean all usernames, groups, commands, and servers.

☞ If you run out of space on a line, you can end it with a back slash (\) and continue on the next line.

☞ sudo assumes that the sudoers file will be used networkwide, and therefore offers the option to specify the names of servers, which will be using it in the servername position in Table 9.1. In most cases, the file is used by only one server and the keyword ALL suffices for the servername.

☞ The NOPASSWD keyword provides access without prompting you for your password.

Simple */etc/sudoers* Examples

This section presents simple examples of how to do many commonly required tasks using the sudo utility.

Granting All Access to Specific Users

You can grant users bob and bunny full access to all privileged commands with this sudoers entry:

```
bob, bunny  ALL=(ALL) ALL
```

This is generally not a good idea because this allows bob and bunny to use the su command to grant themselves permanent root privileges, thereby bypassing the command logging features of sudo. The example on using aliases in the sudoers file shows how to eliminate this problem.

Granting Access to Specific Users to Specific Files

This entry allows user peter and all the members of the group operator to gain access to all the program files in the /sbin and /usr/sbin directories, plus the privilege of running the command /usr/local/apps/check.pl. Notice how the trailing slash (/) is required to specify a directory location:

```
peter, %operator ALL= /sbin/, /usr/sbin, /usr/local/apps/check.pl
```

Notice also that the lack of any username entries within parentheses () after the = sign prevents the users from running the commands automatically masquerading as another user. This is explained further in the next example.

Granting Access to Specific Files as Another User

The `sudo -u` entry enables you to execute a command as if you were another user, but first you have to be granted this privilege in the `sudoers` file.

This feature can be convenient for programmers who sometimes need to kill processes related to projects they are working on. For example, programmer `peter` is on the team developing a financial package that runs a program called `monthend` as user `accounts`. From time to time the application fails, requiring `peter` to stop it with the `/bin/kill`, `/usr/bin/kill`, or `/usr/bin/pkill` commands but only as user `accounts`. The `sudoers` entry would look like this:

```
peter ALL=(accounts) /bin/kill, /usr/bin/kill /usr/bin/pkill
```

User `peter` is allowed to stop the `monthend` process with this command:

```
[peter@bigboy peter]# sudo -u accounts pkill monthend
```

Granting Access Without Needing Passwords

This example allows all users in the group `operator` to execute all the commands in the `/sbin` directory without the need for entering a password. This has the added advantage of being more convenient to the user:

```
%operator ALL= NOPASSWD: /sbin/
```

Using Aliases in the sudoers File

Sometimes you need to assign random groupings of users from various departments very similar sets of privileges. The `sudoers` file allows users to be grouped according to function with the group and then be assigned a nickname or `alias`, which is used throughout the rest of the file. Groupings of commands can also be assigned aliases.

In the next example, users `peter`, `bob`, and `bunny` and all the users in the `operator` group are made part of the user alias ADMINS. All the command shell programs are then assigned to the command alias SHELLS. Users ADMINS are then denied the option of running any SHELLS commands and `su`:

```
Cmnd_Alias    SHELLS = /usr/bin/sh,  /usr/bin/csh, \
                       /usr/bin/ksh, /usr/local/bin/tcsh, \
                       /usr/bin/rsh, /usr/local/bin/zsh


User_Alias    ADMINS = peter, bob, bunny, %operator
ADMINS        ALL    = !/usr/bin/su, !SHELLS
```

This attempts to ensure that users don't permanently su to become root, or enter command shells that bypass sudo's command logging. It doesn't prevent them from copying the files to other locations to be run. The advantage of this is that it helps to create an audit trail, but the restrictions can be enforced only as part of the company's overall security policy.

Other Examples

You can view a comprehensive list of /etc/sudoers file options by issuing the command man sudoers.

Using syslog to Track All sudo Commands

All sudo commands are logged in the log file /var/log/messages, which can be very helpful in determining how user error might have contributed to a problem. All the sudo log entries have the word sudo in them, so you can easily get a thread of commands used by using the grep command to filter the output accordingly.

Here is sample output from a user bob failing to enter his correct sudo password when issuing a command, immediately followed by the successful execution of the command /bin/more sudoers.

```
[root@bigboy tmp]# grep sudo /var/log/messages
Nov 18 22:50:30 bigboy sudo(pam_unix)[26812]: authentication failure;
logname=bob uid=0 euid=0 tty=pts/0 ruser= rhost= user=bob
Nov 18 22:51:25 bigboy sudo: bob : TTY=pts/0 ; PWD=/etc ; USER=root ;
COMMAND=/bin/more sudoers
[root@bigboy tmp]#
```

CONCLUSION

It is important to know how to add users, not just so they can log in to our system. Most server-based applications usually run via a dedicated unprivileged user account—for example, the MySQL database application runs as user mysql and the Apache Web server application runs as user apache. These accounts aren't always created automatically, especially if the software is installed using TAR files.

Finally, the sudo utility provides a means of dispersing the responsibility of systems management to multiple users. You can even give some groups of users only partial access to privileged commands depending on their roles in the organization. This makes sudo a valuable part of any company's server administration and security policy.

## CHAPTER 10

Windows, Linux, and Samba

IN THIS CHAPTER

☞ Download and Install Packages
☞ How to Get Samba Started
☞ The Samba Configuration File
☞ How SWAT Makes Samba Simpler
☞ Creating a Starter Configuration
☞ Samba Passwords
☞ How to Create a Samba PDC Administrator User
☞ How to Add Workstations to Your Samba Domain
☞ How to Add Users to Your Samba Domain
☞ Domain Groups and Samba
☞ How to Delete Users from Your Samba Domain
☞ How to Modify Samba Passwords
☞ Conclusion

Samba is a suite of utilities that allows your Linux box to share files and other resources, such as printers, with Windows boxes. This chapter describes how you can make your Linux box into a Windows **Primary Domain Controller** (**PDC**) or a server for a Windows Workgroup. Either configuration will allow everyone at home to have:

☞ Their own logins on all the home Windows boxes while having their files on the Linux box appear to be located on a new Windows drive
☞ Shared access to printers on the Linux box
☞ Shared files accessible only to members of their Linux user group.

What's the difference between a PDC and Windows Workgroup member? A detailed description is beyond the scope of this chapter, but this simple explanation should be enough:

149

☞ A PDC stores the login information in a central database on its hard drive. This allows each user to have a universal username and password when logging in from all PCs on the network.

☞ In a Windows Workgroup, each PC stores the usernames and passwords locally so that they are unique for each PC.

This chapter will cover only the much more popular PDC methodology used at home. By default, Samba mimics a Windows PDC in almost every way needed for simple file sharing. Linux functionality doesn't disappear when you do this. Samba domains and Linux share the same usernames so you can log into the Samba-based Windows domain using your Linux password and immediately gain access to files in your Linux user's home directory. For added security, you can make your Samba and Linux passwords different.

When it starts up, and with every client request, the Samba daemon reads the configuration file `/etc/samba/smb.conf` to determine its various modes of operation. You can create your own `smb.conf` using a text editor or the Web-based SWAT utility, which is easier. Keep in mind, however, that if you create `/etc/samba/smb.conf` with a text editor then subsequently use SWAT to edit the file, you will lose all the comments you inserted with the text editor. I'll explain how to use both SWAT and a text editor to configure Samba later in this chapter.

Tip

As your `smb.conf` is constantly being accessed, you're better off editing a copy of it if you decide not to use SWAT. After completing your modifications, test the validity of the changes using the `testparm` utility outlined in Chapter 12, "Samba Security and Troubleshooting," and when you are satisfied with your changes, copy the file back to its original location.

DOWNLOAD AND INSTALL PACKAGES

Most Red Hat and Fedora Linux software products are available in the **RPM** format. Downloading and installing RPMs isn't hard. If you need a refresher, Chapter 6, "Installing RPM Software," covers how to do this in detail.

Samba is comprised of a suite of RPMs that come on the Fedora CDs. The files are named

☞ samba

☞ samba-common

☞ samba-client

☞ samba-swat

When searching for the file, remember that the RPM's filename usually starts with the RPM name followed by a version number, as in `samba-client-3.0.0-15.i386`.

How to Get Samba Started

You can configure Samba to start at boot time using the chkconfig command:

```
[root@bigboy tmp]# chkconfig smb on
```

You can start, stop, and restart Samba after boot time using the smb initialization script as in the examples below:

```
[root@bigboy tmp]# service smb start
[root@bigboy tmp]# service smb stop
[root@bigboy tmp]# service smb restart
```

Note

Unlike many Linux packages, Samba does not need to be restarted after changes have been made to its configuration file, as it is read after the receipt of every client request.

You can test whether the smb process is running with the pgrep command; you should get a response of plain old process ID numbers:

```
[root@bigboy tmp]# pgrep smb
```

The Samba Configuration File

The /etc/samba/smb.conf file is the main configuration file you'll need to edit. It is split into five major sections, which Table 10.1 outlines.

Table 10.1   File Format of smb.conf

Section	Description
[global]	General Samba configuration parameters.
[printers]	Used for configuring printers.
[homes]	Defines treatment of user logins.
[netlogon]	A share for storing logon scripts. (Not created by default.)
[profile]	A share for storing domain logon information such as favorites and desktop icons. (Not created by default.)

You can edit this file by hand or more simply through Samba's SWAT Web interface.

How SWAT Makes Samba Simpler

SWAT, Samba's Web-based configuration tool, enables you to configure your smb.conf file without needing to remember all the formatting. Each SWAT screen is actually a form that covers a separate section of the smb.conf file into which you fill in the desired parameters. For ease of use, each parameter box has its own online help. Figure 10.1 shows the main SWAT login screen.

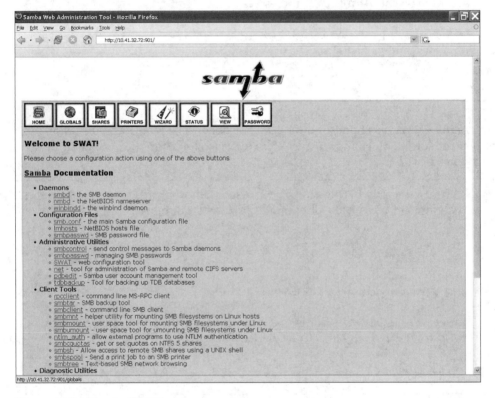

Figure 10.1   Samba SWAT main menu.

Basic SWAT Setup

You must always remember that SWAT edits the smb.conf file but also strips out any comments you may have manually entered into it beforehand. The original Samba smb.conf file has many worthwhile comments in it, you should save a copy as a reference before proceeding with SWAT. For example, you could save the original file with the name /etc/samba/smb.conf.original, as in

```
[root@bigboy tmp]# cp /etc/samba/smb.conf /etc/samba/smb.conf.original
```

As you can see, using SWAT requires some understanding of the smb.conf file parameters, because it eliminates these comments. Become familiar with the most important options in this file before proceeding with SWAT.

SWAT doesn't encrypt your login password. Because this could be a security concern in a corporate environment, you might want to create a Samba administrator user that has no root privileges or only enable SWAT access from the GUI console or localhost.

The enabling and disabling, starting and stopping of SWAT is controlled by **xinetd**, which is covered in Chapter 16, "Telnet, TFTP, and xinetd," via a configuration file named /etc/xinetd.d/swat. Here is a sample:

```
service swat
{
     port            = 901
     socket_type     = stream
     protocol        = tcp
     wait            = no
     user            = root
     server          = /usr/sbin/swat
     log_on_failure  += USERID
     disable         = no
     only_from       = localhost
}
```

The file's formatting is fairly easy to understand, especially as there are only two entries of interest.

☞ The disable parameter must be set to no to accept connections. This can automatically be switched between yes and no, as you will see later.

☞ The default configuration allows SWAT Web access from the VGA console only as user root on port 901 with the Linux root password. This means you'll have to enter http://127.0.0.0:901 in your browser to get the login screen.

You can make SWAT accessible from other servers by adding IP address entries to the only_from parameter of the SWAT configuration file. Here's an example of an entry to allow connections only from 192.168.1.3 and localhost. Notice that there are no commas between the entries.

```
only_from = localhost 192.168.1.3
```

Therefore in this case you can also configure Samba on your Linux server bigboy IP with address 192.168.1.100 from PC 192.168.1.3 using the URL http://192.168.1.100:901.

Remember that most firewalls don't allow TCP port 901 through their filters. You may have to adjust your rules for this traffic to pass.

Controlling SWAT

As with all `xinetd`-controlled applications, the `chkconfig` command automatically modifies the `disable` field accordingly in the configuration file and activates the change.

To activate SWAT use

```
[root@bigboy tmp] chkconfig swat on
```

To deactivate SWAT use

```
[root@bigboy tmp] chkconfig swat off
```

Encrypting SWAT

By default SWAT is configured via an unencrypted Web link using the Linux `root` account. When running SWAT in the unsecured mode above you should take the added precaution of using it from the Linux console whenever possible.

You can configure SWAT to work only with securely encrypted HTTP (HTTPS) versus the regular HTTP method shown above. Here is how it's done. (Please refer to the VPN section of Appendix I, "Miscellaneous Linux Topics," for more details on encryption methods.)

Create an stunnel *User*
You can create a `stunnel` user via the `useradd` command:

```
[root@smallfry tmp]# useradd stunnel
```

Create the Certificates
From the `/usr/share/ssl/certs` directory, you can create the encryption key certificate using the `make` command. Use all the defaults when prompted, but make sure you use the server's IP address when prompted for your server's Common Name or `hostname`.

```
[root@bigboy tmp]# cd /usr/share/ssl/certs
[root@bigboy certs]# make stunnel.pem
...
Common Name (eg, your name or your server's hostname) []: 172.16.1.200
...
[root@bigboy certs]#
```

The resulting certificate has only a 365 day lifetime. Remember to repeat this process next year.

Modify Certificate File Permissions

The certificate needs to only be read by `root` and the `stunnel` user. Use the `chmod` and `chgrp` commands to do this.

```
[root@bigboy certs]# chmod 640 stunnel.pem
[root@bigboy certs]# chgrp stunnel stunnel.pem

[root@bigboy certs]# ll /usr/share/ssl/certs
-rw-r----- 1 root stunnel    1991 Jul 31 21:50 stunnel.pem
[root@bigboy certs]#
```

Create an /etc/stunnel/stunnel.conf Configuration File

You can configure the `stunnel` application to:

☞ Intercept encrypted SSL traffic received on any TCP port
☞ Decrypt this traffic
☞ Funnel the unencrypted data to any application listening on another port.

For example, you can configure the `/etc/stunnel/stunnel.conf` file to intercept SSL traffic on the SWAT port 901 and funnel it decrypted to a SWAT daemon running on port 902. Here's how:

```
# Configure stunnel to run as user "stunnel" placing temporary
# files in the /home/stunnel/ directory
chroot  = /home/stunnel/
pid     = /stunnel.pid
setuid  = stunnel
setgid  = stunnel

# Log all stunnel messages to /var/log/messages
debug   = 7
output  = /var/log/messages

# Define where the SSL certificates can be found.
Client  = no
cert    = /usr/share/ssl/certs/stunnel.pem
key     = /usr/share/ssl/certs/stunnel.pem

# Accept SSL connections on port 901 and funnel it to
# port 902 for swat.
[swat]
accept  = 901
connect = 902
```

Create a New /etc/xinetd.d *File for Secure SWAT*

To start, copy the swat file and name it swat-stunnel. Configure the new file to be enabled, listening on port 902 and accepting connections only from local-host. Also make sure that the service is set to swat-stunnel.

```
[root@bigboy certs]# cd /etc/xinetd.d
[root@bigboy xinetd.d]# cp swat swat-stunnel
```

Your new swat-tunnel file should look like this:

```
service swat-stunnel
{
        port            = 902
        socket_type     = stream
        wait            = no
        only_from       = 127.0.0.1
        user            = root
        server          = /usr/sbin/swat
        log_on_failure  += USERID
        disable         = no
        bind            = 127.0.0.1
}
```

Edit the /etc/services *File to Create a Secure SWAT Entry*

The xinetd daemon searches the /etc/services file for ports and services that match those listed in each configuration file in the /etc/xinetd.d directory. If the daemon doesn't find a match, it ignores the configuration file.

You now have to edit /etc/services to include your new swat-stunnel file:

```
swat-stunnel    902/tcp     # Samba Web Administration Tool (Stunnel)
```

Activate swat-stunnel

You can then start the new swat-stunnel application with the chkconfig command. You'll also need to shutdown regular SWAT beforehand.

```
[root@bigboy xinetd.d]# chkconfig swat off
[root@bigboy xinetd.d]# chkconfig swat-stunnel on
Start stunnel
```

Now start stunnel for the encryption to take place:

```
[root@bigboy xinetd.d]# stunnel
```

In Fedora Core 2, you may get a **cryptonet error** when starting stunnel, as in:

```
Unable to open "/dev/cryptonet"
```

This is caused by an incompatibility with the hwcrypto RPM used for hardware- not software-based encryption. You need to uninstall hwcrypto to get stunnel to work correctly:

```
[root@bigboy xinetd.d]# rpm -e hwcrypto
```

You then have to stop stunnel, restart xinetd, and start stunnel again. After this, stunnel should begin to function correctly. Unfortunately stunnel doesn't have a startup script in the /etc/init.d directory and needs to be terminated manually using the pkill command.

```
[root@bigboy xinetd.d]# pkill stunnel
[root@bigboy xinetd.d]# stunnel
```

Test Secure SWAT

Your Samba server should now be listening on both port 901 and 902 as shown in the netstat -an command that follows. The server will accept remote connections on port 901 only.

```
[root@bigboy xinetd.d]# netstat -an
...
...
tcp        0      0 0.0.0.0:901       0.0.0.0:*        LISTEN
tcp        0      0 127.0.0.:902      0.0.0.0:*        LISTEN
...
...
[root@bigboy xinetd.d]#
```

Test the Secure SWAT Login

Point your browser to the Samba server to make an HTTPS connection on port 901:

```
https://server-ip-address:901/
```

You will be prompted for the Linux root user username and password. Expect a delay of about 60 to 75 seconds with each login.

Troubleshooting Secure SWAT

Sometimes you'll make mistakes in the `stunnel.conf` file, but changes to this file take effect only after `stunnel` has been restarted. Unfortunately, there is no `stunnel` script in the `/etc/init.d` directory to easily stop and restart it. You have to use the `pkill` command to stop it and the `stunnel` command to start it again:

```
[root@bigboy tmp]# pkill stunnel ; stunnel
```

Make sure the file permissions and ownership on the `stunnel.pem` file are correct and that SWAT is always permanently off but `swat-stunnel` is permanently on.

You can also refer to Chapter 4, "Simple Network Troubleshooting," to isolate connectivity issues between the SWAT client and Samba server on TCP port 901 amongst other things.

As mentioned previously, `stunnel` doesn't start automatically when the system reboots because it doesn't have its own startup script. You will have to add the command `stunnel` in the `/etc/rc.local` file for this to occur.

How to Make SWAT Changes Immediate

SWAT immediately changes the functioning of Samba whenever you commit your changes through the Web GUI.

CREATING A STARTER CONFIGURATION

The easiest way to configure a Samba server to be the PDC for a small network is by using SWAT. You'll need to edit the various sections of the `smb.conf` file, so I'll walk you through what you'll find in each.

The [global] Section

The [global] section governs the general Samba settings. Table 10.2 explains the parameters you need to set to create a PDC.

Table 10.2   Minimum Settings for the [global] Section of `smb.conf`

Parameter	Value	Description
domain logons	Yes	Tells Samba to become the PDC.
preferred master	Yes	Makes the PDC act as the central store for the names of all Windows clients, servers, and printers on the network. Very helpful when you need to browse your local network for resources. Also known as a **local master browser**.
domain master	Yes	Tells Samba to become the **master browser** across multiple networks all over the domain. The local master browsers register themselves with the domain master to learn about resources on other networks.

Parameter	Value	Description
Os level	65	Sets the priority the Samba server should use when negotiating to become the PDC with other Windows servers. A value of 65 usually makes the Samba server win.
wins support	Yes	Allows the Samba server to provide name services for the network. In other words, it keeps track of the IP addresses of all the domain's servers and clients.
time server	Yes	Lets the Samba server provide time updates for the domain's clients.
domain	"homenet"	The name of the Windows domain you'll create. The name you select is your choice. I've decided to use homenet.
security	User	Makes domain logins query the Samba password database located on the Samba server itself.

Here's how to set the values using SWAT:

1. Log into SWAT, and click on the [global] section.
2. Click the Advanced button to see all the options.
3. Make your changes, and click on the Commit Changes button when finished.
4. Your smb.conf file should resemble the example below when you're finished. You can view the contents of the configuration file by logging into the Samba server via a command prompt and using cat /etc/samba/smb.conf to verify your changes as you do them.

```
[global]
        workgroup = HOMENET
        time server = Yes
        domain logons = Yes
        os level = 65
        preferred master = Yes
        domain masterc = Yes
```

Be aware: security [eq] user and WINS support [eq] yes are default settings for Samba, and they may not show up in your smb.conf file, even though you may see them in SWAT.

Using the SWAT Wizard

The SWAT utility has a Wizard button that can be used to configure your server as a PDC quickly. However the defaults may not be to your liking. For example, the default domain is MYGROUP, and some of the [global] parameters mentioned previously will be set to Auto.

The [homes] Section

Part of the process of adding a user to a Samba domain requires you to create a Linux user on the Samba PDC itself. When you log into the Samba PDC, you'll see a new drive, usually named z:, added to your PC. This is actually a virtual drive that maps to the corresponding Linux users' login directories on the Linux PDC.

Samba considers all directories to be **shares** that can be configured with varying degrees of security. The [homes] section governs how Samba handles default login directories.

Table 10.3 explains the minimum settings you need to create a functional [homes] section.

Table 10.3   Minimum Settings for [home] Section of `smb.conf`

Parameter	Value	Description
browseable	No	Doesn't allow others to browse the contents of the directory.
read only	No	Allows Samba users to also write to their Samba Linux directories.
create mask	0664	Makes new files created by the user to have 644 permissions. You want to change this to 0600 so that only the login user has access to files.
directory mask	0775	Makes new subdirectories created by the user to have 775 permissions. You want to change this to 0700 so that only the login user has access to directories.

Here's how to set the values using SWAT:

1. Click on the SWAT shares button to proceed to where shared directories are configured.
2. Click the Advanced button to see all the options.
3. Choose the [homes] share section.
4. Make your changes, and click on the Commit Changes button when finished.

Your `smb.conf` file should resemble this when finished. You can view the contents of the configuration file by logging into the Samba server via a command prompt and using `cat /etc/samba/smb.conf` to verify your changes as you do them.

```
[homes]

    read only = No
    browseable = No
    create mask = 0644
    directory mask = 0755
```

The [netlogon] and [profiles] Share Sections

The [netlogon] share section contains scripts that the Windows clients may use when they log into the domain. The [profiles] share section stores settings related to the look and feel of Windows so that the user has the same settings no matter which Windows PC is logged into. The [profiles] share section stores such things as favorites and desktop icons.

Your smb.conf file should look like this when you're finished:

```
[netlogon]
        path = /home/samba/netlogon
        guest ok = Yes

[profiles]
        path = /home/samba/profiles
        read only = No
        create mask = 0600
        directory mask = 0700
```

Here's how to do it:

1. Click the Shares button.
2. Create a [netlogon] share section.
3. Modify the path and guest ok settings.
4. Click on the Commit Changes button.
5. Create a [profiles] share section.
6. Modify the path, mask, and read only settings. The mask settings allow only the owner of the netlogon subdirectory to be able to modify its contents.
7. Click on the Commit Changes button.

Remember to create these share directories from the command line afterwards:

```
[root@bigboy tmp]# mkdir -p /home/samba/netlogon
[root@bigboy tmp]# mkdir -p /home/samba/profile
[root@bigboy tmp]# chmod -R 0755 /home/samba
```

The [printers] Share Section

Samba has special shares just for printers, and these are configured in the [printers] section of SWAT. There is also a share under [printers] called printers that governs common printer settings. Print shares always have the printable parameter set to yes. The default smb.conf [printers] share section looks like this:

```
[printers]
    comment = All Printers
    path = /var/spool/samba
    printable = Yes
    browseable = No
```

Shares for Specific Groups of Users

The default Samba Version 3 `smb.conf` file you saved at the beginning of this exercise has many varied examples that you may use and apply to your particular environment. You can find the steps for creating a simple shared directory for home users in Chapter 11, "Sharing Resources Using Samba."

SAMBA PASSWORDS

You should be aware that your Linux password and Samba passwords are stored in two different locations. This provides the Samba administer the flexibility of allowing only some of the Linux users to have Samba accounts.

Use the `passwd` command to change Linux passwords, which are stored in the `/etc/shadow` file. Samba passwords are stored in the `/etc/samba/smbpasswd` file, and you can change them with the `smbpasswd` command.

This difference is important, as you will see throughout the chapter.

HOW TO CREATE A SAMBA PDC ADMINISTRATOR USER

To do both SWAT and user administration with Samba, you'll need to create administrator accounts on the Samba PDC Linux server.

Home Environment

By default, the root user is the Samba administrator, and SWAT requires you to use the Linux `root` password. Fortunately, you can add workstations to the Windows domain by creating a Samba-specific `root` password using the `smbpasswd` command.

```
[root@bigboy tmp]# /usr/bin/smbpasswd -a root password
```

Note

Remember that regular Linux logins via the console, TELNET, or SSH require the Linux `passwd` command. Samba domain logins use the `smbpasswd` password. Samba passwords are stored in the `/etc/samba/smbpasswd` file.

Corporate Environment

In a corporate environment, you might want more than one person to administer Samba, giving each an individual username. Here are the steps to follow:

1. Create a Linux user group, such as `sysadmin`, with the `groupadd` command.
2. Use SWAT to update your `smb.conf` file so that the `sysadmin` group is listed in the [global] parameter settings:

```
domain admin group = @sysadmin
admin users = @sysadmin
printer admin = @sysadmin
```

3. Create individual Linux users that are part of this group.
4. Use the `smbpasswd` command to create Samba passwords for domain logins for this group. For security reasons this password may be different from the Linux password used to log into the Linux system from the console, via `telnet` or `ssh`. (Remember that Linux passwords are changed with the `passwd` command.)

HOW TO ADD WORKSTATIONS TO YOUR SAMBA DOMAIN

Adding workstations to a Samba domain is a two-step process involving the creation of workstation **trust accounts** on the Samba server and then logging into each workstation to add them to the domain.

Create Samba Trust Accounts for Each Workstation

PDCs accept user logins only from trusted PCs that have been placed in its PC client database. Samba can create these **Machine Trusts** either manually or automatically.

Manual Creation of Machine Trust Accounts (NT Only)

The commands in the example create a special Linux group for Samba clients and then add a special machine user that's a member of the group. Next, the commands disable the password for this user and add the machine added to the `smbpasswd` file to help keep track of which devices are members of the domain. In summary, a machine trust account needs to have corresponding entries in the `/etc/passwd` and `/etc/smbpasswd` files. Pay careful attention to the $ at the end, and replace `machine_name` with the name of the Windows client machine.

```
[root@bigboy tmp]# groupadd samba-clients
[root@bigboy tmp]# /usr/sbin/useradd -g samba-clients \
```

```
-d /dev/null -s /bin/false machine_name$
[root@bigboy tmp]# passwd -l machine_name$
[root@bigboy tmp]# smbpasswd -a -m machine_name
```

This is the only way to configure machine trusts using Windows NT.

Dynamic Creation of Machine Trust Accounts

Although you can use the manual method, the recommended way of creating machine trust accounts is simply to allow the Samba server to create them as needed when the Windows clients join the domain, which is known as making a machine account on the fly. You can set this up by editing /etc/samba/smb.conf to automatically add the required users.

The easiest way is to use SWAT in the Global menu to modify the add machine script parameter.

```
[global]
# <...remainder of parameters...>
add machine script = /usr/sbin/useradd -d /dev/null -g samba-clients -
s /bin/false -M %u
```

When you've completed the modifications, you'll need to create the samba-clients Linux group that will help identify all the domain's Windows clients listed in the /etc/passwd file.

```
[root@bigboy tmp]# groupadd samba-clients
```

In Samba version 2, you need to add the client to the smbpasswd file also.

```
[root@bigboy tmp]# smbpasswd -a -m machine_name
```

Samba version 3 adds it automatically.

Make Your PC Clients Aware of Your Samba PDC

There are many types of Windows installed on PCs, and each version has its own procedure for joining a domain. The next sections show you how to add the most popular versions of Windows clients to your domain.

Windows 95/98/ME and Windows XP Home

Windows 9x machines do not implement full domain membership and, therefore, don't require machine trust accounts. Here's what you need to do:

1. Navigate to the Network section of the Control Panel (Start>Settings>Control Panel>Network).
2. Select the Configuration tab.

3. Highlight Client for Microsoft Networks.

4. Click the Properties button.

5. Check Log onto Windows NT Domain, and enter the domain name.

6. Click all the OK buttons.

Now, simply reboot and you're done!

Windows NT

For Windows NT, you must first create a manual Samba machine trust account as explained earlier, then follow these steps:

1. Navigate to the Network section of the Control Panel (Start>Settings>Control Panel>Network).

2. Select the Identification tab.

3. Click the Change button.

4. Enter the domain name and computer name, do *not* check the box Create a Computer Account in the Domain. In this case, the existing machine trust account joins the machine to the domain.

5. Click OK. You should get a "Welcome to <DOMAIN>" message as confirmation that you've been added.

6. Reboot.

You can now log in using any account in the `/etc/smbpasswd` file with your domain as the domain name.

Windows 200x and Windows XP Professional

For the 200x and XP Professional varieties of Windows, create a dynamic Samba machine trust account, then go through these steps:

1. Press the Windows and Break keys simultaneously to access the System Properties dialog.

2. Click on the Network Identification or Computer Name tab on the top.

3. Click the Properties button.

4. Click on the Member of Domain button.

5. Enter your domain name and computer name, and then click OK.

6. You will be prompted for a user account and password with rights to join a machine to the domain. Enter the information for your Samba administrator. In this home environment scenario, the user would be root with the corresponding `smbpasswd` password. Now, you should get a "Welcome to <DOMAIN>" message confirming that you've been added.

7. Reboot.

You can now log in using any account in the `/etc/smbpasswd` file with your domain as the domain name.

With Samba version 2, however, you may also have to make a few changes to your system's registry using the regedit command:

```
[HKEY_LOCAL_MACHINE\SYSTEM\CurrentControlSet\Services\Netlogon\
Parameters]
"requiresignorseal"=dword:00000000
"signsecurechannel"=dword:00000000
```

After making these changes, reboot before continuing.

HOW TO ADD USERS TO YOUR SAMBA DOMAIN

Adding users to a domain has three broad phases. The first is adding a Linux user on the Samba server, the second is creating a Samba smbpasswd that maps to the new Linux user, and the third is to map a Windows drive letter to the user's Linux home directory. Take a closer look.

Adding the Users in Linux

First, go through the process of adding users in Linux just as you would normally. Passwords won't be necessary unless you want the users to log into the Samba server via TELNET or SSH.

To create the user, use the command

```
[root@bigboy tmp]# useradd -g 100 peter
```

Giving them a Linux password is necessary only if the user needs to log into the Samba server directly. If the user does, use this method:

```
[root@bigboy tmp]# passwd peter
Changing password for user peter.
New password:
Retype new password:
passwd: all authentication tokens updated successfully.
[root@bigboy tmp]#
```

Mapping the Linux Users to an *smbpassword*

Next, you need to create Samba domain login passwords for the user:

```
[root@bigboy tmp]# /usr/bin/smbpasswd -a username password
```

The `-a` switch adds the user to the `/etc/smbpasswd` file. Use a generic password then have users change it immediately from their workstations in the usual way.

Remember the `smbpasswd` sets the Windows domain login password for a user, which is different from the Linux login password to log into the Samba box.

Mapping a Private Windows Drive Share

By default, Samba automatically gives each user logged into the domain an H: drive that maps to the `/home/username` directory on the Linux box.

Mapping Using My Computer
If the auto-mapping doesn't work, then try:
1. Let the user log into the domain.
2. Right-click on the My Computer icon on the desktop.
3. Click on Map Network Drive.
4. Select a drive letter.
5. Browse to the HOMENET domain, then the Samba server, then the user's home directory.
6. Click on the check box Reconnect at Logon, to make the change permanent.

If you're more a typist than a clicker, try the next method.

Mapping from the Command Line
If you find the My Computer method too time consuming for dozens of users or if the PC doesn't have the feature available, then you can use the command-line method and possibly make it into a script:

1. Create a master logon batch file for all users.
   ```
   [root@bigboy tmp]# vi /home/samba/netlogon/login.bat
   ```

2. Add the following lines to mount the user's share as drive P: (for private):
   ```
   REM Drive Mapping Script
   net use P: \\bigboy\
   ```

3. Make the file world readable using:
   ```
   [root@bigboy tmp]# chmod 644 /home/samba/netlogon/login.bat
   ```

4. Linux and Windows format text files differ slightly. As the file resides on a Linux box, but will be interpreted by a Windows machine, you'll have to convert the file to the Windows format. Use the `unix2dos` command:
   ```
   [root@bigboy tmp]# unix2dos /home/samba/netlogon/login.bat
   unix2dos: converting file /home/samba/netlogon/login.bat
    to DOS format ...
   [root@bigboy tmp]#
   ```

5. The final step is to edit your `smb.conf` file's [global] section to have a valid entry for the logon script parameter. This can be done using SWAT via the Globals menu.

```
[global]
logon script = login.bat
```

Now your users will have additional disk space available on a Windows P: drive whenever they login.

Domain Groups and Samba

Samba supports domain groups that allow users who are members of the group to have administrator rights on each PC in the domain. This enables them to add software and configure network settings, among other tasks. In Windows, domain groups also have the ability to join machines to the domain; however, Samba does not support this currently.

The `domain admin group` parameter specifies users who will have domain administrator rights. The argument is a space-separated list of user names or group names (group names must have an @ sign prefixed). For example:

```
domain admin group = USER1 USER2 @GROUP
```


How to Delete Users from Your Samba Domain

Deleting users from your Samba domain is a two-stage process in which you have to remove the user from the Linux server and also remove the user's corresponding `smbpasswd` entry:

1. Delete the users using the `smbpasswd` with the `-x` switch:

```
[root@bigboy tmp]# smbpasswd -x john
Deleted user john.
[root@bigboy root]#
```

2. Delete the Linux user by following the normal deletion process. For example, to delete the user `john` and all `john`'s files from the Linux server, use:

```
[root@bigboy tmp]# userdel -r john
```

Sometimes you may not want to delete the user's files so that they can be accessed by other users at some other time. In this case, you can just deactivate the user's account using the passwd -l username command.

How to Modify Samba Passwords

You can set your Samba server to allow users to make changes in their domain passwords and have these changes mirrored automatically in their Linux login passwords. Table 10.4 explains the `[global]` `smb.conf` parameters that you need to change.

Table 10.4   The `smb.conf` Settings for Enabling Online Password Changes

Parameter	Value	Description
`unix passwd sync`	Yes	Enables Samba/Linux password synchronization.
`passwd program`	Use the SWAT defaults	Lists the location of the Linux password file, which is usually `/bin/passwd`.
`passwd chat`	Use the SWAT defaults	A short script to change the Linux password using the Samba password.

Conclusion

By now you should have a fairly good understanding of adding users and PCs to a Samba domain. The next step is to take better advantage of Samba's file sharing features, which is Chapter 11's task.

Sharing Resources Using Samba

IN THIS CHAPTER

- ☞ Adding a Printer to a Samba PDC
- ☞ Creating Group Shares in Samba
- ☞ Sharing Windows Drives Using a Linux Samba Client
- ☞ Automating Mounting with Linux Samba Clients
- ☞ Conclusion

Now that you have Samba up and running, you may want to allow users to share such resources as floppy drives, directories, and printers via the Samba server. This chapter tells you how to do it all.

ADDING A PRINTER TO A SAMBA PDC

Sharing printers amongst all your PCs is one of the advantages of creating a home network. Here's how to connect your printer directly to your PDC. Not only does this method make your printer available to all your Windows workstations, it also makes your Samba PDC a print server! The only potential snag is that you need the Windows printer driver loaded on every client machine. This may be okay for a small home network but impractical for a huge corporate network.

Adding the Printer to Linux

By far, the easiest way to add a printer in Linux is to use one of the many menu-based printer utilities available. For the example, I'll use `system-config-printer` (Figure 11.1), which is easy to find and can be accessed from the command line:

```
[root@bigboy tmp]# system-config-printer
```

171

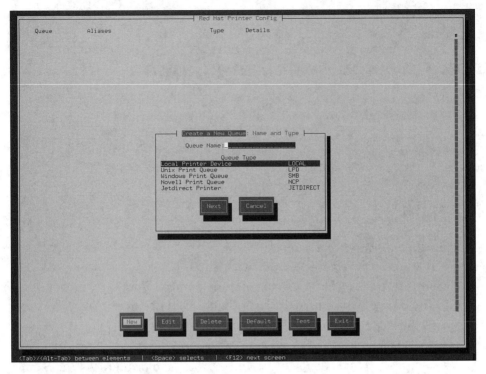

Figure 11.1   Printer configuration screen.

Note

Sometimes the graphics in `system-config-printer` don't work as expected due to your environment variables. You can temporarily set the required variable to the correct output with the command

```
[root@bigboy tmp]# env LANG=C system-config-printer
```

Assuming your printer is locally attached to the parallel port, here are the steps to use:

1. Using the Tab key, move to the New button and press the Enter key.
2. When the Create a New Queue menu appears, give the printer a name that's easy to remember, select Local Printer Device, and move to the "next" button before pressing Enter.
3. From the resulting Setting Up Local Printer Device menu, select `/dev/lp0`, assuming the printer is on the parallel port as opposed to the USB port. Click the Next button to go to the Queue Driver menu.
4. Scroll to your manufacturer's entry, press Enter. Scroll further to your model, and press Enter again. You'll now get a choice of drivers, select the

default device, which is marked with an asterisk. Click Next to go to the Create a New Queue confirmation menu.

5. Move to the Finish button, and press Enter. There will be a slight delay.

At this stage, it's wise to do a test print to make sure all is okay.

Make Samba Aware of the Printer

The easiest way to let Samba know the printer is available is via the Samba SWAT Web interface. Once you are in SWAT:

1. Click the Printers button.
2. Find your printer in the pull-down menu. If the printer name has an asterisk beside it, it has been auto-configured by Samba. It might not be visible on your network, however, if Samba hasn't been restarted since creating the printer. If this is the case, restart Samba. You can now skip ahead to the "Configure the Printer Driver on the Workstations" section.
3. If Samba did not auto-configure your printer, you need to edit or create it yourself. Click on the Commit Changes button to create an updated `/etc/samba/smb.conf` file.
4. Click on the Status tab at the top of the screen, and restart smbd and nmbd to restart Samba.

Your printer will now be available for use by all Windows workstations.

Configure the Printer Driver on the Workstations

With the printer ready to go on the Linux side, you now need to prepare things in Windows.

1. Download the appropriate Windows printer driver from the manufacturer and install it.
2. Go to the Add Printer menu. Click the Next button.
3. Select the Network Printer button to access the Local or Network Printer menu. Click the Next button, again.
4. You now should be on the Locate Your Printer menu. Don't enter a name, instead click Next so you can browse for your printer.
5. From the Browse for Printer menu, double-click on the name of your Linux Samba server. You should see the new printer. Click on the printer name, then click Next.
6. You may get the message "The server on which the printer resides does not have the correct printer driver installed. If you want to install the

driver on your local computer, click OK." Fortunately, you pre-installed the driver. Click the OK button.

7. When the Add Printer Wizard appears, select the manufacturer of your printer, select the printer model, and then click OK.

8. The Add Printer Wizard will ask you whether you want to use this new printer as the default printer. Select Yes or No depending on your preference. Click the Next button

9. From the resulting Completing the Add Printer Wizard menu, click the Finish button.

The new printer should now show up on the Windows Printers menu in the Control Panel. Send a test print, to be sure all is well.

CREATING GROUP SHARES IN SAMBA

On occasion, subgroups of a family need a share that is fully accessible by all members of the group. For example, parents working in a home office environment may need a place where they can share, distribute, or collaboratively work on documents. Here's how it's done.

Create the Directory and User Group

As with any group activity, the first step is to get organized.

1. Create a new Linux group named parents:

```
[root@bigboy tmp]# /usr/sbin/groupadd parents
```

2. Create a new directory for the group's files. If one user is designated as the leader, you might want to change the chown statement to make that person owner:

```
[root@bigboy tmp]# mkdir /home/parent-files
[root@bigboy tmp]# chgrp parents /home/parent-files
[root@bigboy tmp]# chmod 0770 /home/parent-files
```

3. Add the group members to the new group. For instance, the command to add a user named father to the group is

```
[root@bigboy tmp]# /usr/sbin/usermod -G parents father
```

All your members are in the group; now they need to share.

Configure the Share in SWAT

Next, you need to create the share in Samba using SWAT.

1. Click on the Shares button, then enter the name of the share you want to create, such as only-parents.

2. Click on the Create Share button. Make sure the path maps to `/home/parent-files,` and make the valid users be `@parents,` where parents is the name of the Linux user group.

3. Click on the Commit Changes button to create a new `/etc/samba/smb.conf` file.

4. Click on the Status tab at the top of the screen and restart `smbd` and `nmbd` to restart Samba.

Your `/etc/samba/smb.conf` file should have an entry like this at the end

```
# Parents Shared Area
[only-parents]
        path = /home/parent-files
        valid users = @parents
```

If it does, all is well and you can move on. If not, double check your work in the last steps.

Map the Directory Using My Computer

Finally, let the user log into the domain from a remote PC:

1. Right click on the My Computer icon on the desktop.

2. Click on Map Network Drive.

3. Select a drive letter.

4. Browse to the HOMENET domain, then the Samba server, then the share named only-parents.

5. Click on the check box Reconnect at Logon, to make the change permanent.

Now the files located in the Linux /home/parent-files directory will be accessible to the parents only and your job is complete!

SHARING WINDOWS DRIVES USING A LINUX SAMBA CLIENT

Up to this point I have focused on your Linux server being a Samba server, but it can also mimic a Windows client using Samba's client software.

For example, you can also access a CD-ROM, DVD, Zip, floppy, or hard drive installed on a Windows machine from your Linux box. In this section I'll show you how to share a CD-ROM drive.

Windows Setup

The Windows client box should be set up first as a member of a Samba domain or workgroup. The next step is to make the CD-ROM drive shared. The steps you use depend on which version of Windows you have.

For Windows 98/ME:

1. Double-click My Computer.
2. Right-click on the CD-ROM drive, and choose Sharing.
3. Set the Share Name as cdrom with the appropriate access control.
4. Restart Windows.

For Windows 2000:

1. Double-click My Computer.
2. Right-click on the CD-ROM drive, and choose Sharing.
3. Set the Share Name as cdrom with the appropriate access control.
4. Log out, and log in again as normal using your current login.

Finally, for Windows XP:

1. Double-click My Computer.
2. Right-click on the CD-ROM drive, and choose Sharing and Properties.
3. Set the Share Name as cdrom, and set the appropriate access control.
4. Log out and log in again as normal using your current login.

After you have completed this task, you'll have to go to the next step of testing your configuration.

Test Your Windows Client Configuration

Use the smbclient command to test your share. You should substitute the name of your Windows client PC for "WinClient," and in place of "username" provide a valid workgroup/domain username that normally has access to the Windows client. You should get output like this when using the username's corresponding password:

```
[root@bigboy tmp]# smbclient -L WinClient -U username
added interface ip=192.168.1.100 bcast=192.168.1.255
nmask=255.255.255.0
added interface ip=127.0.0.1 bcast=127.255.255.255 nmask=255.0.0.0
Got a positive name query response from 192.168.1.253 ( 192.168.1.253
)
Password:
Domain=[HOMENET] OS=[Windows 5.1] Server=[Windows 2000 LAN Manager]

Sharename Type Comment
--------- ---- -------
IPC$ IPC Remote IPC
D$ Disk Default share
print$ Disk Printer Drivers
SharedDocs Disk
cdrom Disk
Printer2 Printer Acrobat PDFWriter
```

```
ADMIN$ Disk Remote Admin
C$ Disk Default share

Server Comment
--------- -------

Workgroup Master
--------- -------
```

You can get the same result with

```
[root@bigboy tmp]# smbclient -L WinClient -U username%password
```

but this method is less secure as your password is echoed on the screen.

Create a CD-ROM Drive Mount Point on Your Samba Server

You'll now need to create the mount point on the Linux server to mount and access the CD-ROM drive. In this case, I've named it /mnt/winclient-cdrom, and you'll use the mount command to get access to this device from the Linux server.

Password Prompt Method

The Linux mount command will try to access the CD-ROM device as user username by using the username [eq] option. You will be prompted for a password:

```
[root@bigboy tmp]# mkdir /mnt/winclient-cdrom
[root@bigboy tmp]# mount -t smbfs -o username=username \
 //winclient/cdrom /mnt/winclient-cdrom
```

No Prompt Method

Linux won't prompt you for a password if you embed the access password into the mount command string along with username:

```
[root@bigboy tmp]# mkdir /mnt/winclient-cdrom
[root@bigboy tmp]# mount -t smbfs -o \
 username=username,password=password \
 //winclient/cdrom /mnt/cdrom
```

The smbmount Command Method

Some versions of Linux support the smbmount command to mount the remote drive. Incompatible versions will give errors like this:

```
[root@bigboy tmp]# smbmount //winclient/cdrom \
 /mnt/winclient-cdrom -o username=username
```

```
Password:
27875: session setup failed: ERRDOS - ERRnoaccess (Access denied.)
SMB connection failed
```

To be safe, stick with using the Linux mount command.

AUTOMATING MOUNTING WITH LINUX SAMBA CLIENTS

You can also automate the mounting of shares by placing entries in your /etc/fstab file. In the example below the home directory of user peter on server 192.168.1.100 will be mounted on the /mnt/smb mount point as a Samba filesystem (smbfs) using the login information in the file named /etc/cred.

```
#
# File: /etc/fstab
#
//192.168.1.100/peter    /mnt/smb     smbfs    credentials=/etc/cred 0 0
```

The contents of the /etc/cred file needs to have the username and password for the account in this format

```
#
# File: /etc/cred
#
username = peter
password = peterspassword
```

Once finished, you can use mount -a to mount the new /etc/fstab entry, and the /mnt/smb directory will contain the contents of the share.

```
[root@smallfry tmp]# mount -a
[root@smallfry tmp]# ls /mnt/smb
backups  profile  docs  data  music
[root@smallfry tmp]#
```

CONCLUSION

Both this chapter and the last have detailed the steps needed to configure a Samba network that is adequate for a small office or home. There are many steps to take, none are particularly complex, but you run the risk of not getting Samba to work if you omit any of them. For this reason, the next chapter is a dedicated troubleshooting guide to help you diagnose and recover from the most common Samba mistakes that we all tend to make.

## CHAPTER 12

Samba Security and Troubleshooting

In This Chapter

- ☞ Testing the `smb.conf` File
- ☞ Samba and Firewall Software
- ☞ Testing Basic Client/Server Network Connectivity
- ☞ Testing Samba Client/Server Network Connectivity
- ☞ Checking the Samba Logs
- ☞ Samba Network Troubleshooting
- ☞ Basic Samba Security
- ☞ Conclusion

Configuring Samba for your office or home can provide many advantages. By encouraging users to store files on a central file server you can simplify data backup and, in some cases, software installation and maintenance.

Unfortunately, the initial configuration of Samba can be tricky. Many simple steps need to be executed in the correct order, and one small slip up can have big repercussions. This chapter explores the ways in which you can recover from those mistakes that you couldn't avoid.

Testing the SMB.CONF File

Samba has a test utility called `testparm` that alerts you to errors in the `smb.conf` file. If you used SWAT to edit the file, you will usually pass the test successfully, as shown:

```
[root@bigboy tmp]# testparm -s
Load smb config files from /etc/samba/smb.conf
Processing section "[homes]"
Processing section "[printers]"
```

```
Loaded services file OK.
...
...
[root@bigboy tmp]#
```

A successful test only means that Samba will load the configuration file. There are other causes for Samba problems.

Tip

You can use `testparm` to test a file that's different from the default `/etc/samba/smb.conf` configuration file. Simply provide the filename as the first argument:

```
[root@bigboy tmp]# testparm -s filename
```

SAMBA AND FIREWALL SOFTWARE

Firewall software installed both on your Windows PCs and on the Samba server may prevent Samba from functioning. Two popular packages—`iptables` and Zone Alarm—offer solutions.

Linux *iptables*

The Fedora installation process configures the `iptables` firewall package by default. You have two options for working with it. You can ensure that this is deactivated, which may be desirable on a secured network. Or, you can configure it to allow through such Microsoft protocols as NetBIOS (UDP ports 137 and 138, TCP ports 139) and TCP port 445 for SMB file sharing without NetBIOS. Here is sample script snippet:

```
#!/bin/bash

SAMBA_SERVER="192.168.1.100 "
NETWORK="192.168.1.0/24"      # Local area network
BROADCAST="192.168.255.255"   # Local area network Broadcast Address

iptables -A INPUT -i lo -j ACCEPT
iptables -A OUTPUT -o lo -j ACCEPT
iptables -A INPUT -p udp -s $NETWORK -d $SAMBA_SERVER \
-m multiport --dports 137,138 -j ACCEPT
iptables -A INPUT -p tcp -s $NETWORK -d $SAMBA_SERVER -m multiport \
--dports 139,445 -j ACCEPT
iptables -A INPUT -p udp -s $NETWORK -d $BROADCAST --dport 137 \
-j ACCEPT
iptables -A INPUT -p udp -d $SAMBA_SERVER -m multiport \
--dports 137,138 -j DROP
iptables -A INPUT -p tcp -d $SAMBA_SERVER -m multiport \
--dports 139,445 -j DROP
iptables -A OUTPUT -s $SAMBA_SERVER -d $NETWORK -m state --state \
ESTABLISHED,RELATED -j ACCEPT
```

For more information, please refer to Chapter 14, "Linux Firewalls Using `iptables`."

Windows-based Zone Alarm

The default installation of Zone Alarm assumes that your PC is directly connected to the Internet. This means that the software will deny all inbound connections that attempt to connect with your PC. The NetBIOS traffic that Samba uses to communicate with the PCs on the network, therefore, is considered as hostile traffic.

The easiest way around this is to configure Zone Alarm to consider your home network as a trusted network too. To do so, click on the Firewall tab and edit the settings for your home network; it will most likely have a 192.168.x.x/255.255.255.0 type entry. Make this network a trusted network, instead of an Internet network, and Zone Alarm should cease to interfere with Samba.

The Windows XP Built-In Firewall

You may also need to disable the firewall feature of Windows XP. Follow these steps:

1. Bring up the Control Panel.
2. Double-click on the Network Connections icon.
3. Right-click on your LAN connection icon, and select Properties.
4. Click on the Advanced tab and then on the Windows Firewall Settings button.
5. Turn off the Internet Connection Firewall by clearing its check box. You may also leave the firewall on, but allow Windows file sharing traffic through this connection. This can be done by clicking on the Exceptions tab of the Windows Firewall dialog box and clicking on the File and Printer Sharing check box.

After you get SAMBA to work, you may want to experiment with the firewall software settings to optimize your security, keeping in mind the need to maintain a valid relationship with the Samba server.

TESTING BASIC CLIENT/SERVER NETWORK CONNECTIVITY

You can perform several tests to ensure that the Samba server and all its workstations can do basic communication with each other.

From the Samba server:

1. Ping the server's IP address and loopback address (127.0.0.1).
2. Ping the client's IP address.
3. Ping the client using its DNS name.

Next, from the Samba client:

1. Ping the client's IP address and loopback address (127.0.0.1).
2. Ping the server's IP address.
3. Ping the server using its DNS name.

If any of these fail, check your cabling, your routing, or the presence of a firewall running on either the server or client.

TESTING SAMBA CLIENT/SERVER NETWORK CONNECTIVITY

After configuring basic network connectivity, you need to go through a variety of tests to determine whether Samba has been configured correctly both on the server and client. As part of a thorough troubleshooting procedure:

1. Make sure your Samba server can see all the shares available on the network with the `smbclient -l samba_server` command. Press the Enter key when prompted for a password. Check your SWAT configuration for invalid `hosts allow`, `hosts deny`, and invalid `users` entries. Failure of this test may mean that Samba isn't running on the server at all and may need to be started.

```
[root@bigboy tmp]# smbclient -L bigboy
Password:
Anonymous login successful
Domain=[HOMENET]  OS=[Unix]  Server=[Samba 3.0.2-7.FC1]

        Sharename        Type        Comment
        ---------        ----        -------
        IPC$             IPC          IPC Service (Samba Server)
        ADMIN$           IPC          IPC Service (Samba Server)
Anonymous login successful
Domain=[HOMENET]  OS=[Unix]  Server=[Samba 3.0.2-7.FC1]

        Server                   Comment
        ---------                -------
        SILENT                   Samba Server

        Workgroup                Master
        ---------                -------
        HOMENET                  BIGBOY
        OTHERNET                 SILENT
[root@bigboy tmp]#
```

2. Use the `nmblookup -B samba-server-IP-address _SAMBA_` command on the server to determine whether the Samba software is running correctly. This should return the server's IP address if the software is running correctly.

```
[root@bigboy tmp]# nmblookup -B 192.168.1.100 __SAMBA__
querying __SAMBA__ on 192.168.1.100
192.168.1.100 __SAMBA__<00>
[root@bigboy tmp]#
```

3. Use the `nmblookup -B client-IP-address "*"` command on the server to determine whether the client is accepting Samba queries. This should return the client's IP address if it is running correctly. If the test fails, check to see whether the client is running firewall software that could prevent communication. Another source of the problem could be that the Client for Microsoft Windows or File and Printer Sharing for Microsoft Networks settings on the client's NIC haven't been selected. You also could have entered an incorrect IP address.

```
[root@bigboy tmp]# nmblookup -B 192.168.1.103 "*"
querying * on 192.168.1.103
192.168.1.103 *<00>
[root@bigboy tmp]#
```

4. Use the `nmblookup -d 2 "*"` command on the server to tell it to broadcast a query message to the network. This should return answers from all locally connected clients and servers. This test actually sends out a broadcasted request for information; it usually fails if either your client or server has an incorrect subnet mask configured on their NIC cards.

```
[root@bigboy tmp]# nmblookup -d 2 '*'
added interface ip=192.168.1.100 bcast=192.168.1.255
nmask=255.255.255.0
added interface ip=192.168.1.100 bcast=192.168.1.255
nmask=255.255.255.0
querying * on 192.168.1.255
Got a positive name query response from 192.168.1.100 (
192.168.1.100 )
Got a positive name query response from 192.168.1.103 (
192.168.1.103 )
Got a positive name query response from 192.168.1.100 (
192.168.1.100 )
192.168.1.100 *<00>
192.168.1.103 *<00>
192.168.1.100 *<00>
[root@bigboy tmp]#
```

5. Use the `smbclient //samba-server/tmp` command to attempt a command-line login to the Samba server. When prompted for a password, use the Linux password of the account with which you logged in. You can test other accounts by adding the `-U accountname` option at the end of the command line. This should return a message that the login was successful. If you are doing this as user root, press the Enter key when prompted for a password.

```
[root@bigboy tmp]# smbclient //bigboy/TMP
Password:
Anonymous login successful
Domain=[HOMENET] OS=[Unix] Server=[Samba 3.0.2-7.FC1]
tree connect failed: NT_STATUS_BAD_NETWORK_NAME
[root@bigboy tmp]#
```

A message that warns of an invalid or bad network name could mean that the tmp service on the Samba server isn't correctly configured.

Messages related to bad passwords could mean that the user's account doesn't exist, that their smbpasswd wasn't created, or that the password entered is incorrect.

6. Log into the Windows workstation as a Samba user. (In the example below, the username is peter.) Use the net view \\samba-server command to log into the Samba server from the command line and get a listing of your shares.

If it fails, then make sure your hosts allow, hosts deny, and invalid users parameters are set correctly in your smb.conf file.

This test attempts to log in using the username and password with which you logged into the PC. Make sure the corresponding Samba user has been created.

A "Network name not found" message usually points to an incorrect NetBIOS configuration on the client. Add the IP address of the Samba server to the WINS server settings, and enable Windows name resolution via DNS using the advanced TCP/IP settings menu on the PC. You can get to this menu using the following method:

1. Click on the Network Connections icon in the Windows Control Panel.

2. Right-click on the network connection and select Properties.

3. Click on the Internet Properties (TCP/IP) menu option and then click on the Properties button.

4. Click on the Advanced button and then on the WINS tab.

You may also need to add the name of the Samba server to the PC's C:\WINDOWS\system32\drivers\etc\lmhosts file.

If you're successful you should see:

```
C:\>net view \\bigboy
Shared resources at \\bigboy
Samba Server
Share name   Type   Used as   Comment

---------------------------------------------------
peter            Disk              Home Directories
The command completed successfully.
C:\>
```

If there is no user account, the test will fail and you will see:

```
C:\> net view \\bigboy
System error 5 has occurred.

Access is denied.
C:\>
```

7. Log into the Windows workstation as a Samba user. Try to map a drive letter to the user's default login directory on the Samba server. This is done with the `net use x: \\samba-server\share` command. Here we want user **"peter"** to have a DOS drive X: map to Peter's Linux home directory on the Samba server.

```
C:\>net use x: \\bigboy\peter
The command completed successfully.
C:\>
```

Make sure your password encryption is set correctly in the `smb.conf` file. As stated in Chapter 10, "Windows, Linux, and Samba," newer versions of Windows send encrypted passwords only. Make sure you have correctly configured the `encrypt passwords` option in the `[global]` section of `smb.conf`.

Failure could also mean that the server's `smb.conf` file hasn't been configured to automatically use the PC user's username as the Samba login name. You can do this by setting the `user=username` option in the `[tmp]` section of the `smb.conf` file.

8. From the Samba server, issue the `nmblookup -M domain` command to ensure that there is a master browser for the domain. Successful attempts should list the IP address of the master browser server. If not, you'll need to make sure that the `preferred master` parameter is set to yes in the [global] section of `smb.conf`.

```
[root@bigboy home]# nmblookup -M homenet
querying fedora on 192.168.1.255
192.168.1.100 homenet<1d>
[root@bigboy home]#
```

This may fail with some Windows NT clients if the Samba server has been configured not to use encrypted passwords. You will need to set the `encrypt passwords` option in the [global] section of the `smb.conf` file to yes. Remember that doing so may make logins from Windows 95/98/ME clients fail. As you can see, it is sometimes best to make all your clients run similar versions of the Windows operating system.

Once all this has tested positively, you should be able to see your domain under Windows' My Network Places located in file manager or in the Start Menu. You should also be able to browse through the shares as well.

CHECKING THE SAMBA LOGS

Samba stores all its log files in the /var/log/samba directory. If you find your-self having difficulties, try searching the nmbd.log and smbd.log files for clues.

SAMBA NETWORK TROUBLESHOOTING

It is always a good idea to use such network troubleshooting tools as tcpdump to do detailed troubleshooting, especially if you're not sure whether there is any bidirectional connectivity between the Samba server and the workstation.

BASIC SAMBA SECURITY

You can restrict connections to your server on both a per-interface and a per-network basis in the [global] section of the smb.conf file. Always remember to include your loopback interface lo and the loopback interface's network 127.0.0.0/8 in your configuration.

This type of security is activated by:

☞ Setting the bind interfaces only parameter to yes.

☞ Configuring Samba to deny all connections by default and then allowing specified hosts through with the hosts allow and hosts deny settings. In this case, the 192.168.1.0/24 has been included as a valid network. You also can include the IP addresses of individual hosts in this list.

☞ Specifying the interfaces on which Samba will be active. Interface eth0 is on the 192.168.1.0/24 network, so I have included it here.

```
[global]
...
bind interfaces only = Yes
hosts deny = ALL
hosts allow = 192.168.1.0/24 127.
interfaces = eth0 lo
```

CONCLUSION

By now you should have a fully functional Samba-based network that is suit-able for the small office or home. If the network is located in the home, you may want to hide your server where it is less intrusive due to its physical presence or to the noise of its power supply fan or hard drive. A wireless net-work in some cases would be ideal. Chapter 13, "Linux Wireless Networking," discusses how to configure wireless NICs in Linux servers for this very reason.

Linux Wireless Networking

IN THIS CHAPTER

- ☞ Wireless Linux-Compatible NICs
- ☞ Common Wireless Networking Terms
- ☞ Networking with Linux Wireless Tools
- ☞ Networking with Linux-WLAN
- ☞ Troubleshooting Your Wireless LAN
- ☞ Wireless Networks in Businesses
- ☞ Conclusion

My very first Linux web server was an ancient desktop computer that I bought from a secondhand store that advertised it as being "very obsolete." It was cheap and it worked, but it was ugly and noisy—so noisy that it quickly became too loud to tolerate. Spending more money than I should have on the antique, I made it wireless so I could take it out of my bedroom where the DSL connection entered my apartment. Looking back, I really did it for the challenge, and also because we all get stupid some of the time. I thought wireless Linux would be easy, but at the time it wasn't. I had so many headaches with it that I thought one of my very first Web pages should be about my little nightmare warning people about how to do it right. This was how www.linux-homenetworking.com was born. This is the chapter about what started it all.

Wireless networks using the 802.11 standard have many advantages—not just the aesthetic one I mentioned. The hardware is commonly available, and wireless networks offer relatively easy and low cost deployment with security that's becoming increasingly better. Before you consider making a Linux server wireless capable, however, make sure you purchase a NIC that is Linux compatible. You also need to decide on the wireless Linux package you intend to use: Linux-WLAN or Wireless Tools. **Wireless Tools** is more convenient to use as it requires fewer configuration steps and the RPM package doesn't have to be reinstalled every time you upgrade your kernel as with **Linux-WLAN**. The packages support different NICs, so do your research before proceeding. Don't worry; I will explain all this later.

WIRELESS LINUX-COMPATIBLE NICS

Not all wireless NICs work with Linux. For this reason, do your homework. You can find hardware compatibility lists for Wireless Tools quite easily on popular search engines. For Linux-WLAN, check www.linux-wlan.org for the latest list of compatible hardware.

Wireless NIC manufacturers are notorious for changing the chip sets on their cards depending on the price of the components. They then supply different drivers with each new card to make them work. It is possible to buy cards with the same model number from the same vendor with very different circuitry. Frequently Linux drivers for the new cards are unavailable. Always check the compatibility lists before buying your wireless hardware.

The Linksys WMP11 wireless card is a good example of this confusion. The original version of the card used the Intersil Prisim chip set, which worked with Linux, but the newer version 2.7 (Broadcom chip set) and version 4 (InProComm chip set) do not. Even so, the original WMP won't work without upgrading the firmware.

COMMON WIRELESS NETWORKING TERMS

Learning the ins and outs of wireless Linux networks will be easier if we're all speaking the same language. Before proceeding, take time to become familiar with three key wireless terms: wireless access point, Service Set ID, and shared encryption key. Learn them now, because you'll see them throughout the chapter.

Wireless Access Points

A **wireless access point** (**WAP**) is a device that acts as the central hub of all wireless data communications. In the most common operating mode (Infrastructure mode), all wireless servers communicate with one another via the WAP, which is usually connected to a regular external or integrated router for communication to the Internet. WAPs are, therefore, analogous to switches in regular wired networks.

Servers can communicate with one another without a WAP if their NICs are configured in Ad Hoc mode, but this prevents them from communicating with any other communications path. For that, you need a WAP on your network.

Extended Service Set ID

The 802.11a/b wireless networks typically found in a home environment share the same frequency range with one another so it is possible for your computer to hear the traffic meant for somebody else's nearby network. The **Extended Service Set ID (ESSID)** helps prevent the garbling of messages. Each wireless network needs to be assigned an ESSID that doesn't match that of any neighboring networks within its range of operation. The desired ESSID is then set on both wireless NICs and WAPs, which in turn ignore all traffic using other identifiers.

Most wireless software packages enable you to view all the available ESSIDs within range and give you the option of selecting the corresponding wireless LAN (WLAN) to join. Unfortunately, this makes it easy to eavesdrop on a neighboring network, and therefore it is best to not only change your ESSID from the factory defaults, but also to encrypt your wireless data whenever possible.

The term ESSID is frequently interchangeably referred to as a Service Set ID (SSID) by many vendors. I'll stick with ESSID unless the term SSID is relevant to an application.

Encryption Keys

Encryption is a method of encoding data so that only people with the secret key to unlock the code can view the original data. As expected, if you encrypt your wireless network's data then you also need to use a **shared encryption key** on all the NICs and WAPs. Some software packages allow you to use a plain text key, but the more secure ones treat the key like a password and prompt you to enter your chosen key twice without your actually being able to ever see the unencrypted key again.

It is always best to encrypt your network data last to simplify troubleshooting. Make sure everything works normally first and then encrypt later.

NETWORKING WITH LINUX WIRELESS TOOLS

The Linux Wireless Tools package, installed by default, probably meets most of your 802.11a/b needs. Its main advantage is that, unlike Linux-WLAN, you don't have to reinstall it every time you upgrade your kernel.

Using *iwconfig* for Wireless Tools Configuration

After physically installing your Linux-compatible NIC, you need to configure your NIC's IP and wireless settings before Wireless Tools works.

You can configure your NIC's IP settings as if the NIC were a regular Ethernet device. After you use the `ifup` command the NIC becomes active, but it will not function correctly as its wireless settings haven't been configured yet.

The most commonly used command in Wireless Tools is iwconfig, which you can use to configure most of the wireless parameters, including the SSID and the wireless mode. For the wireless mode, Managed means that there is a wireless access point (WAP) on the network and Ad-hoc signifies that there is none.

For example, if your wireless NIC is named eth0 and your managed network's ESSID is homenet, then the commands would be:

```
iwconfig eth0 mode Managed
iwconfig eth0 essid homenet
```

Your NIC should now become fully functional. You will need to run these iwconfig commands each time you use the ifup command, however; forgetting to do so can be problematic. The next section shows how to make these iwconfig changes permanent.

Permanent Wireless Tools Configuration

Once your ad-hoc configuration has been completed, you need to make the changes permanent.

1. Configure your /etc/sysconfig/network-scripts/ifcfg-eth0 file normally as if it were a regular Ethernet NIC.

```
DHCP Version              Fixed IP Version
============              =================

DEVICE=eth0               DEVICE=eth0
USERCTL=yes               IPADDR=192.168.1.100
ONBOOT=yes                NETMASK=255.255.255.0
BOOTPROTO=dhcp            ONBOOT=yes
                          BOOTPROTO=static
```

2. Add the following statements to the end to specify that the NIC is wireless; provide the ESSID to use (in this case homenet), and finally choose Managed (a WAP on present of the network) or Ad-hoc (no WAP) for the wireless mode.

```
#
# Wireless configuration
#
TYPE=Wireless
MODE=Managed
ESSID=homenet
```

These commands need only be on the main interface file. They are not needed for IP aliases. Your wireless NIC should function as if it were a regular Ethernet NIC using the ifup and ifdown commands.

Wireless Tools Encryption

It is usually best to test your network in an unencrypted state before activating the additional security. This allows you to limit your troubleshooting activities to basic wireless settings, without the additional complications of encryption.

Encryption requires an encryption key that you can make up yourself or generate with the /sbin/nwepgen command that comes with the kernel-wlan-ng RPM (more on this coming up). The advantage of the nwepgen command is that you can provide an easily remembered string that it will consistently encode in to an ESSID key. You can use any one of the rows of characters to create a 40-bit key.

If you don't have nwepgen, then remember to use hexadecimal numbers, which are composed of numeric values between 0 and 9 and alphabetic characters between A and F:

```
[root@bigboy tmp]# /sbin/nwepgen ketchup
64:c1:a1:cc:db
2b:32:ed:37:16
b6:cc:9e:1b:37
d7:0e:51:3f:03
[root@bigboy tmp]#
```

When using iwconfig to add encryption, be sure that there are no colons or any other non-hexadecimal characters between the characters of the key. There should be ten characters in total:

```
iwconfig eth0 key 967136deac
```

The same rules (no colons or non-hexidecimals between the ten total characters) apply when using the /etc/sysconfig/network-scripts files to add encryption:

```
KEY=967136deac
```

NETWORKING WITH LINUX-WLAN

Linux-WLAN is one of the original wireless LAN products developed for Linux. It is generally more difficult to install than Wireless Tools and has fewer troubleshooting tools, but it does have wide ranging hardware support, making it a desirable alternative based on the NIC card you have available. You'll notice that Linux-WLAN uses the term SSID instead of ESSID in its configuration files.

Linux-WLAN Preparation

Here are some pointers you'll need to remember prior to using the Linux-WLAN product:

- ☞ **All devices on a wireless network must use the same Network Identifier or SSID to communicate with each other**: The default SSID for Linux-WLAN is `linux-wlan`, the default SSID for your windows NICs may be different. It's a good idea to decide on a common SSID and stick with it.

- ☞ **Once configured, Linux-WLAN doesn't identify the wireless NIC as an Ethernet `eth` device, but as a `wlan` device**: This is good to know in order to avoid confusion when troubleshooting.

- ☞ **Always be prepared to check your syslog** `/var/log/messages` **file for errors if things don't work**: It is a good source of information. Chapter 5, "Troubleshooting Linux with syslog," shows you how to set up syslog error logging to be more sensitive to errors.

- ☞ **You may get "device unknown" or "no such device" errors related to the `wlan` device in the** `/var/log/messages` **file if you use older unpatched versions of the Linux-WLAN software**: Always use the most recent versions to make the installation smoother.

- ☞ Before installing the Linux-WLAN software for PCMCIA cards such as the Linksys WPC11 you will need to install the RPM packages that support PCMCIA: This step isn't necessary for such true PCI cards as the Linksys WMP11.

    In Fedora Core, the package name is `pcmcia-cs` and in Red Hat 9 and earlier it is `kernel-pcmcia-cs`. When searching for the RPMs, remember that the filename usually starts with the software package name and a version number, as in `kernel-pcmcia-cs-3.1.31-13.i386.rpm`.

Identifying the Correct RPMs

You can find RPM versions of the driver files at `http://prism2.unixguru.raleigh.nc.us`. Remember to download the files for the correct kernel type, OS version, and kernel version. Downloading and installing RPMs isn't hard. If you need a refresher, Chapter 6, "Installing RPM Software," covers how to do this in detail.

Determine the Kernel Type

Use the `uname -p` command. The Bigboy server discussed in Chapter 1, "Why Host Your Own Site," is running an i686 version of Linux. The Linux version may not match the CPU you have installed, always use the `uname` version:

```
[root@bigboy tmp]# uname -p
i686
[root@bigboy tmp]#
```

Determine the OS Version

One of the easiest ways to determine the OS version is to view the /etc/ red-hat-release or the /etc/fedora-release file. In this case, server Bigboy is running Red Hat version 9.0, while Zero is running Fedora Core 1. You can also look at the /etc/issue file for other versions of Linux.

```
[root@bigboy tmp]# cat /etc/redhat-release
Red Hat Linux release 9 (Shrike)
[root@bigboy tmp]#

[root@zero root]# cat /etc/fedora-release
Fedora Core release 1 (Yarrow)
[root@zero root]#
```

Determine the Kernel Version

You can use the uname -r command to figure out the kernel version. In this case, Bigboy is running version 2.4.20-8:

```
[root@bigboy tmp]# uname -r
2.4.20-8
[root@bigboy tmp]#
```

Installing the RPMs

After you have all this Linux information, you need to download and install the base, module, and interface packages. When searching for the RPMs, remember that the filename usually starts with the software package name by a version number:

```
kernel-wlan-ng-0.2.1-pre14.i686.rpm
kernel-wlan-ng-modules-fc1.1.2115-0.2.1-pre14.i686.rpm
kernel-wlan-ng-pci-0.2.1-pre14.i686.rpm
kernel-wlan-ng-pcmcia-0.2.1-pre14.i686.rpm
```

Note

There are different RPMs for PCMCIA- and PCI-based NICs. The base and modules RPMs need to be installed in all cases.

Notice the sequence of installation in this sample output. Double-check your preparation steps and the RPM versions if the very last line of the installation gives a result code that is not success.

```
[root@bigboy tmp]# rpm -Uvh kernel-wlan-ng-0.2.1-pre14.i686.rpm
Preparing...                  ###################################
[100%]
    1:kernel-wlan-ng          ###################################
[100%]
[root@bigboy tmp]# rpm -Uvh  kernel-wlan-ng-modules-fc1.1.2115-0.2.1-
pre14.i686.rpm
Preparing...                  ###################################
[100%]
    1:kernel-wlan-ng-modules-###################################
[100%]
[root@bigboy tmp]#

[root@bigboy tmp]# rpm -Uvh kernel-wlan-ng-pcmcia-0.2.1-pre14.i686.rpm
Preparing...                  ###################################
[100%]
    1:kernel-wlan-ng-pci      ###################################
[100%]
Adding prism2_pci alias to /etc/modprobe.conf file...
***NOTE*** YOU MUST CHANGE THIS IF YOU HAVE A PLX CARD!!!
The default wlan0 network configuration is DHCP.  Adjust accordingly.

ACHTUNG!  ATTENTION!  WARNING!
    YOU MUST configure /etc/wlan/wlan.conf to define your SSID!
    YOU ALSO must configure /etc/wlan/wlancfg-SSID to match WAP
settings!
        (---> replace SSID in filename with the value of your SSID)

If you get an error after this point, there is either a problem with
your drivers or you don't have the hardware installed!  If the former,
get help!

Starting WLAN Devices:message=dot11req_mibset
  mibattribute=dot11PrivacyInvoked=false
  resultcode=success
message=dot11req_mibset
  mibattribute=dot11ExcludeUnencrypted=false
  resultcode=success
[root@bigboy tmp]#
```

Note

If you upgrade your Linux kernel, you'll have to reinstall Linux-WLAN all over again. This will also create new versions of your /etc/sysconfig/network-scripts/ifcfg-wlan0, /etc/wlan/wlan.conf, and /etc/pcmcia/wlan-ng.opts files. You may have to restore these from the automatically saved versions.

Linux-WLAN Post Installation Steps

After the RPMs are installed, you need to configure the new wlan0 wireless NIC to be compatible with your network.

Configure the New wlan0 *Interface*

Edit `/etc/sysconfig/network-scripts/ifcfg-wlan0` to include these new lines:

```
DHCP Version              Fixed IP Version
============              ==================

DEVICE=wlan0              DEVICE=wlan0
USERCTL=yes               IPADDR=192.168.1.100
ONBOOT=yes                NETMASK=255.255.255.0
BOOTPROTO=dhcp            ONBOOT=yes
                          BOOTPROTO=static
```

In the fixed IP version you also need to substitute your selected IP, net-mask, network, and broadcast address with those above. Plus, make sure you have the correct gateway statement in your `/etc/sysconfig/network` file, for example. `GATEWAY [eq] 192.168.1.1`.

Disable Your Existing Ethernet NIC

You may want to disable your existing `eth0` Ethernet interface after installing the drivers. Add an `ONBOOT=no` entry to the `/etc/sysconfig/network-scripts/ifcfg-eth0` file. This disables the interface on reboot or when `/etc/init.d/network` is restarted.

Select the Wireless Mode and SSID

All the configuration files are located in the `/etc/wlan` directory. The package allows your server to be connected to up to three wireless LANs. You specify the SSIDs (LAN IDs) for each wireless LAN in the `/etc/wlan/wlan.conf` file. In the example, I make the `wlan0` interface join the homenet WLAN, as well as instruct the WLAN driver to scan all wireless channels for SSIDs.

```
#
# Specify all the wlan interfaces on the server
#
WLAN_DEVICES="wlan0"

#
# Specify whether the server should scan the network channels
# for valid SSIDs
#
WLAN_SCAN=y

#
# Specify expected SSIDs and the wlan0 interface to which it should
# be tied
#
SSID_wlan0="homenet"
ENABLE_wlan0=y
```

Each WLAN specified in the /etc/wlan/wlan.conf file has its own configuration file. Copy the /etc/wlan/wlancfg-DEFAULT file to a file named /etc/wlan/wlancfg-SSID (replace SSID with the actual SSID for your WAP). This line configures for the homenet SSID:

```
[root@bigboy wlan]# cp wlancfg-DEFAULT wlancfg-homenet
```

Start Linux-WLAN

Start the wlan process and test for errors in the file /var/log/messages. All the result codes in the status messages should be success. You may receive the following error, however, which the WLAN RPM Web site claims is "harmless."

```
Error for wireless request "Set Encode" (8B2A) :
    SET failed on device wlan0 ; Function not implemented.
Error for wireless request "Set ESSID" (8B1A) :
    SET failed on device wlan0 ; Function not implemented.
```

With PCI cards, you can restart Linux-WLAN by restarting the WLAN daemon:

```
[root@bigboy tmp]# service wlan restart
[root@bigboy tmp]# ifup wlan0
```

With PCMCIA cards, you can start Linux-WLAN by restarting the Linux PCMCIA daemon:

```
[root@bigboy tmp]# service pcmcia restart
[root@bigboy tmp]# service network restart
```

Testing Linux-WLAN

Now check to see if the IP address of the wlan0 interface is okay. Refer to the upcoming troubleshooting section if you cannot ping the network's gateway.

```
[root@bigboy tmp]# ifconfig -a
[root@bigboy tmp]# ping <gateway-address>
```

Linux-WLAN Encryption for Security

One of the flaws of wireless networking is that all the wireless clients can detect the presence of all available network SSIDs and have the option of joining any of them. With encryption, the client must have a membership encryption password that can also be represented as a series of **Wireless Encryption Protocol** (**WEP**) keys. The `wlan.conf` file (Red Hat 8.0 RPMs), `wlan-SSID` file (Red Hat 9/Fedora Core 1 RPMs), or `/etc/pcmcia/wlan-ng.opts` file (PCMCIA-type NICs) is also used to activate this feature.

Tip

I *strongly* recommend that you first set up your network *without* encryption. Only migrate to an encrypted design after you are satisfied that the unencrypted design works correctly.

To invoke encryption, you have to set the `dot11PrivacyInvoked` parameter to `true`. You also must state which of the keys will be used as the default starting key via the `dot11WEPDefaultKeyID` parameter. You then have the option of either providing a key-generating string (simple password) or all four of the keys. In the example below, ketchup is the password used to automatically generate the keys.

```
#=======WEP========================================
# [Dis/En]able WEP. Settings only matter if PrivacyInvoked is true
lnxreq_hostWEPEncrypt=false # true|false
lnxreq_hostWEPDecrypt=false # true|false
dot11PrivacyInvoked=true
dot11WEPDefaultKeyID=1
dot11ExcludeUnencrypted=true # true|false, in AP this means WEP
# is required for all STAs

# If PRIV_GENSTR is not empty, use PRIV_GENTSTR to generate
# keys (just a convenience)
PRIV_GENERATOR=/sbin/nwepgen # nwepgen, Neesus compatible
PRIV_KEY128=false # keylength to generate
PRIV_GENSTR="ketchup"

# or set them explicitly. Set genstr or keys, not both.
dot11WEPDefaultKey0= # format: xx:xx:xx:xx:xx or

dot11WEPDefaultKey1= # xx:xx:xx:xx:xx:xx:xx:xx:xx:xx:xx:xx:xx
dot11WEPDefaultKey2= # e.g. 01:20:03:40:05 or
dot11WEPDefaultKey3= # 01:02:03:04:05:06:07:08:09:0a:0b:0c:0d
```

Not all devices on your network will use the same algorithm method to generate the encryption keys. You may find the same generator string will not create the same keys, rendering intra-network communication impossible. If this is the case, you can use the `/sbin/nwepgen` program to generate the keys after you provide an easy to remember key generator string. Once you have the four sets of keys, you'll have to add them individually and in sequence to

the wlan.conf, wlan-SSID or /etc/pcmcia/wlan-ng.opts file and set the PRIV_
GENSTR parameter to a null string of `″` (the quotes are important). Here is how
you can use nwepgen to create the keys with a generator string of ketchup.

```
[root@bigboy tmp]# /sbin/nwepgen ketchup
64:c1:a1:cc:db
2b:32:ed:37:16
b6:cc:9e:1b:37
d7:0e:51:3f:03
[root@bigboy tmp]#
```

In this case, your wlan.conf or wlan-SSID file would look like this:

```
PRIV_GENSTR=""

# or set them explicitly. Set genstr or keys, not both.
dot11WEPDefaultKey0= 64:c1:a1:cc:db
dot11WEPDefaultKey1= 2b:32:ed:37:16
dot11WEPDefaultKey2= b6:cc:9e:1b:37
dot11WEPDefaultKey3= d7:0e:51:3f:03
```

Remember that all devices on your network, including all wireless NICs
and WAPs, need to have the same keys and default key for this to work.

De-activating Encryption

In some cases, NICs without full Linux-WLAN compatibility freeze up after a
number of hours of working with encryption. The steps to reverse encryption
are:

1. Set the configuration file parameter dot11PrivacyInvoked to false.

2. Stop Linux-WLAN, and disable the wireless wlan0 interface.

```
[root@bigboy tmp]# service wlan stop
Shutting Down WLAN Devices:message=lnxreq_ifstate
  ifstate=disable
  resultcode=success
[root@bigboy tmp]# ifdown wlan0
```

3. The driver is still loaded in memory with the old encryption parameters,
even though it is not active. Linux frequently loads device driver software, such as those that govern the operation of NICs, as modules that
the **kernel**, or Linux master program, uses in its regular operation. Use
the lsmod command to display a list of loaded modules. You'll be most
interested in the modules associated with 802.11 wireless protocols,
which appear here as p80211 and prism2_pci:

```
[root@bigboy tmp]# lsmod
Module                    Size  Used by     Not tainted
...
...
```

```
prism2_pci                    66672   1   (autoclean)
p80211                        20328   1   [prism2_pci]
...
...
[root@bigboy tmp]#
```

Sometimes your NIC may use the `orinoco` chip set drivers instead of the `prism` drivers:

```
[root@bigboy tmp]# lsmod
Module                    Size   Used by
...
...
orinoco                   45517  1 orinoco_pci
hermes                    6721   2 orinoco_pci,orinoco
...
...
[root@bigboy tmp]#
```

4. Now that you have identified the driver modules in memory, unload them with the `rmmod` command:

```
[root@bigboy tmp]# rmmod prism2_pci
[root@bigboy tmp]# rmmod p80211
```

5. Restart Linux-WLAN, reactivate the `wlan0` interface, and you should be functional again:

```
[root@bigboy tmp]# service wlan start
Starting WLAN Devices:message=lnxreq_hostwep
  resultcode=no_value
  decrypt=false
  encrypt=false
[root@bigboy tmp]# ifup wlan0
```

If you fail to reload the driver modules, you'll get errors in your `/var/log/messages` file and your NIC card will operate in an encrypted mode only:

```
Jan 2 18:11:12 bigboy kernel: prism2sta_ifstate: hfa384x_drvr_start()
failed,result=-110
Jan 2 18:11:18 bigboy kernel: hfa384x_docmd_wait: hfa384x_cmd
timeout(1), reg=0x8021.
Jan 2 18:11:18 bigboy kernel: hfa384x_drvr_start: Initialize command
failed.
Jan 2 18:11:18 bigboy kernel: hfa384x_drvr_start: Failed, result=-110
```

TROUBLESHOOTING YOUR WIRELESS LAN

Linux wireless troubleshooting tools are quite extensive and provide a variety of useful information to help you get your network working. This section covers many important strategies that will complement the use of more conventional procedures such as scanning your `/var/log/messages` file.

Check the NIC Status

When using WLAN methodology, the iwconfig, iwlist, and iwspy commands can provide useful information about the status of your wireless network. Take a closer look.

The iwconfig *Command*
In addition to using the regular ifconfig command to check the status of your NIC, you can use the iwconfig command to view the state of your wireless network, just don't specify any parameters. Specifically, you can see such important information as the link quality, WAP MAC address, data rate, and encryption keys, which can be helpful in ensuring the parameters across your network are the same. For example:

```
[root@bigboy tmp]# iwconfig
eth0        IEEE 802.11-DS  ESSID:"homenet"  Nickname:"bigboy"
            Mode:Managed  Frequency:2.462GHz  Access Point:
00:09:5B:C9:19:22
            Bit Rate:11Mb/s   Tx-Power=15 dBm   Sensitivity:1/3
            Retry min limit:8   RTS thr:off   Fragment thr:off
            Encryption key:98D1-26D5-AC   Security mode:restricted
            Power Management:off
            Link Quality:36/92  Signal level:-92 dBm  Noise level:-148
dBm
            Rx invalid nwid:0  Rx invalid crypt:2  Rx invalid frag:0
            Tx excessive retries:10  Invalid misc:0   Missed beacon:0
[root@bigboy tmp]#
```

The iwlist *Command*
The iwlist command can provide further information related to not just the NIC, but the entire network, including the number of available frequency channels, the range of possible data rates, and the signal strength. This example uses the command to verify the encryption key being used by the NIC, which can be very helpful in troubleshooting security related difficulties on your network:

```
[root@bigboy tmp]# iwlist key
...
...
eth0        2 key sizes : 40, 104bits
            4 keys available :
                [1]: 9671-36DE-AC (40 bits)
                [2]: off
                [3]: off
                [4]: off
            Current Transmit Key: [1]
            Security mode:open
...
...
[root@bigboy tmp]#
```

The `iwlist` command can verify the speed of the NIC being used, 11Mb/s in this case. This can be helpful in determining possible reasons for network slowness, especially as poor signal quality can result in the NIC negotiating a low bit rate with its WAP.

```
[root@bigboy tmp]# iwlist rate
...
...
eth0      4 available bit-rates :
          1Mb/s
          2Mb/s
          5.5Mb/s
          11Mb/s
          Current Bit Rate:11Mb/s
...
...
[root@bigboy tmp]#
```

For further information on the `iwlist` command, consult the `man` pages.

The iwspy Command

The `iwspy` command provides statistics on the quality of the link between your NIC and another wireless device on the network. It doesn't run all the time; you have to activate `iwspy` on your interface first. When not activated, `iwspy` gives a "no statistics to collect" message:

```
[root@bigboy root]# iwspy eth0
eth0       No statistics to collect
[root@bigboy root]#
```

To activate the command, specify the target IP address and the wireless NIC interface through which it can be found:

```
[root@bigboy tmp]# iwspy eth0 192.168.1.1
```

If you use the `iwspy` command without the IP address, it provides WLAN statistics with a typical/reference value against which it can be compared. In the example that follows the signal is considered fairly strong, with a 64/92 quality value versus a typical 36/92 value, but it could be weak by the historical values on your network. It's good to check this from time to time for fluctuations.

```
[root@bigboy tmp]# iwspy eth0
eth0       Statistics collected:
    00:09:5B:C9:19:22 : Quality:0  Signal level:0  Noise level:0
    Link/Cell/AP      : Quality:64/92  Signal level:-51 dBm  Noise
level:-149 dBm (updated)
```

```
     Typical/Reference : Quality:36/92  Signal level:-62 dBm  Noise
level:-98 dBm
[root@bigboy tmp]#
```

To switch off `iwspy` monitoring, add the `off` argument:

```
[root@bigboy root]# iwspy eth0 off
```

Check for Interrupt Conflicts

Devices slotted into your PCI bus are generally assigned an interrupt value by the system, which the system uses to signal its need to communicate with the device. Multiple devices on the bus can have the same interrupt, but the system will access each one using a different memory address to avoid confusion. Sometimes this automatic allocation of **interrupt** (**IRQ**) values and memory locations is flawed and overlaps do occur, causing devices to fail.

Before configuring your WLAN software, you should ensure that the wireless NIC card doesn't have an interrupt that clashes with another device in your computer. Insert the card in an empty slot in your Linux box according to the instructions in its manual, reboot, and inspect your `/var/log/messages` file again:

```
[root@bigboy tmp]# tail -300 /var/log/messages
```

Look carefully for any signs that the card is interfering with existing card IRQs. If there is a conflict, there will usually be a warning or "IRQ also used by..." message. If that is the case, move the card to a different slot or otherwise eliminate the conflict by disabling the conflicting device if you don't really need it.

You should also inspect your `/proc/interrupts` file for multiple devices having the same interrupt:

```
[root@bigboy tmp]# cat /proc/interrupts
11:     4639     XT-PIC     wlan0, eth0       (potentially bad)

[root@bigboy tmp]# cat /proc/interrupts
11:     4639     XT-PIC     wlan0             (good)
```

Interrupt conflicts are usually more problematic with old style PC-AT buses; newer PCI-based systems generally handle conflicts better. The prior (potentially bad) `/proc/interrupts` example came from a functioning PCI-based Linux box. It worked because, although the interrupt was the same, the base memory addresses that Linux used to communicate with the cards were different. You can check both the interrupts and base memory of your NICs by using the `ifconfig -a` command:

```
[root@bigboy tmp]# ifconfig -a
eth0 Link encap:Ethernet HWaddr 00:08:C7:10:74:A8
BROADCAST MULTICAST MTU:1500 Metric:1
RX packets:0 errors:0 dropped:0 overruns:0 frame:0
TX packets:0 errors:0 dropped:0 overruns:0 carrier:0
collisions:0 txqueuelen:100
RX bytes:0 (0.0 b) TX bytes:0 (0.0 b)
Interrupt:11 Base address:0x1820

wlan0 Link encap:Ethernet HWaddr 00:06:25:09:6A:B5
inet addr:192.168.1.100 Bcast:192.168.1.255 Mask:255.255.255.0
UP BROADCAST RUNNING MULTICAST MTU:1500 Metric:1
RX packets:215233 errors:0 dropped:0 overruns:0 frame:0
TX packets:447594 errors:0 dropped:0 overruns:0 carrier:0
collisions:0 txqueuelen:100
RX bytes:39394014 (37.5 Mb) TX bytes:126738425 (120.8 Mb)
Interrupt:11 Memory:c887a000-c887b000
[root@bigboy tmp]#
```

Kernel Log Errors

When you find p80211 Kernel errors in `/var/log/messages`, they usually point to an incorrectly configured SSID or may also be caused by a NIC card with an outdated firmware version. For example:

```
Nov 13 22:24:54 bigboy kernel: p80211knetdev_hard_start_xmit: Tx
attempt prior to association, frame dropped.
```

Can't Ping Default Gateway

If you can't ping the default gateway, first check for kernel log errors.

If there are no errors in `/var/log/messages` and you can't ping your gateways or obtain an IP address, then check your `/etc/sysconfig/network-scripts/` configuration files for a correct IP configuration and your routing table to make sure your routes are OK. You can also check to see if your Linux box is out of range of the WAP using the `iwconfig` command.

Unknown Device Errors

Look for "unknown device" or "no such device" errors in your log files or on your screen during installation or configuration. These may be caused by:

☞ An NIC that hasn't been correctly inserted in the PCI slot.
☞ Incompatible hardware.

For example, you might see incompatible hardware errors in /var/log/ messages:

```
00:0c.0 Network controller: BROADCOM Corporation: Unknown device 4301
(rev01)
Subsystem: Unknown device 1737:4301
Flags: bus master, fast devsel, latency 64, IRQ 5
Memory at f4000000 (32-bit, non-prefetchable) [size=3D8K]
Capabilities: [40] Power Management version 2
```

Or, you might see errors on the screen:

```
Dec 1 01:28:14 bigboy insmod: /lib/modules/2.4.18-14/net/prism2_pci.o:
init_module: No such device
Dec 1 01:28:14 bigboy insmod: Hint: insmod errors can be caused by
incorrect module parameters, including invalid IO or IRQ parameters.
You may find more information in syslog or the output from dmesg
Dec 1 01:28:14 bigboy insmod: /lib/modules/2.4.18-14/net/prism2_pci.o:
insmod wlan0 failed
```

A Common Problem with Linux-WLAN and Fedora Core 1

In older versions of Fedora Core 1, the operating system will auto-detect Linux-WLAN-compatible NIC cards and enter a line similar to:

```
alias        eth2        orinoco_pci
```

in the /etc/modprobe.conf file. In other words, it detects them as an Ethernet eth device instead of a WLAN wlan device.

This seems to conflict with the WLAN RPMs, and you'll get errors like this when starting Linux-WLAN:

```
Starting WLAN Devices: /etc/init.d/wlan: line 119: Error: Device wlan0
does not seem to be present.: command not found
/etc/init.d/wlan: line 120: Make sure you've inserted the appropriate:
command not found
/etc/init.d/wlan: line 121: modules or that your modules.conf file
contains: command not found
/etc/init.d/wlan: line 122: the appropriate aliase(s).: command not
found
```

You can fix the problem with the proper steps. This example refers to a compatible Orinoco chipset card:

1. Remove the orinoco_pci line from the /etc/modprobe.conf file. Do *not* remove the entry for device wlan0.

2. Edit your `/etc/sysconfig/hwconf` file, search for `orinoco_pci`, and remove the `orinoco_pci` section that refers to your wireless card. (Each section starts and ends with a single - on a new line.)

3. Reboot.

4. The Linux boot process always runs `kudzu`, the program that detects new hardware. `Kudzu` detects the wireless card and asks whether you want to configure it. Choose `ignore`. This will reinsert the wireless card in the `/etc/sysconfig/hwconf file`, but not in the `/etc/modprobe.conf` file.

5. Your NIC should start to function as expected as device `wlan0` when you use the `ifconfig -a` command. Configure the IP address, and activate the NIC as shown earlier in this chapter.

The procedure removes all reference to the Orinoco driver in the Linux configuration files and then forces `kudzu` not to configure the NIC card according to the Linux defaults. The `eth` device will be recreated, but the `ignore` option provided to `kudzu` will prevent the Orinoco entry in the `/etc/modprobe.conf` from being reinserted, preventing conflict with the Linux-WLAN package's `wlan` device.

WIRELESS NETWORKS IN BUSINESSES

Sometimes implementing a wireless network inside a business place becomes necessary. Visiting managers may need a quick connection in a conference room; sales people sharing cubicles my need it as the number of work spaces get exhausted. Perhaps someone is going to set one up on your network anyway—you might as well control this from the beginning.

Apart from people who download infected software and e-mail attachments, mobile employees' notebook computers are usually viewed as a high risk source of unintentional malicious activity as there is even less control over what these employees do than those with fixed workstations. With this in mind, it is usually best to isolate this type of wireless network completely from your internal, trusted, and wired one. Some types of network architectures make the wireless router only have access to the Internet, and no where else, via its own dedicated DSL line. The wireless users then have to use some form of a VPN client to gain access to the office servers just as if they were doing so from home. To reduce the risk of the network being hijacked, be sure to encrypt the traffic and use a proxy server running such software as Squid (see Chapter 32, "Controlling Web Access with Squid") to limit Internet access to authorized users via some form of pop-up username and password authentication. With this sort of architecture, if the wireless network gets hijacked, your office systems should remain relatively safe.

Many WAPs have the option of not advertising their ESSIDs, which prevents users from browsing around to select the nearest available WLAN. Activation of this feature can be inconvenient to users as wireless clients will need to know the predefined ESSID to gain LAN access, but more importantly, reduces the risk of an outsider connecting to your wireless LAN by roaming the airwaves for an available WAP. Your WAP may also have the additional security feature of only allowing connections from a list of predefined MAC addresses of all the wireless NICs in your company or department. The more expensive ones have the ability to refer to a database server for this information.

There are many other types of wireless methodologies. Please investigate a variety of options before coming to a final conclusion.

CONCLUSION

With the knowledge gained in the chapters in Part 1 of the book you will be able to configure a Linux file and DHCP server on small networks with relative ease. Part 2 will explore the possibility of making your server also become the core of your self-managed dedicated Web site.

## PART II

The Linux Web Site Project

Linux Firewalls Using *iptables*

Network security is a primary consideration in any decision to host a Web site as the threats are becoming more widespread and persistent every day. One means of providing additional protection is to invest in a firewall. Though prices are always falling, in some cases you may be able to create a comparable unit using the Linux `iptables` package on an existing server for little or no additional expenditure.

This chapter shows how to convert a Linux server into:

- ☞ A firewall while simultaneously being your home Web site's mail, Web, and DNS server

☞ A router that will use **NAT** and **port forwarding** to both protect your home network and have another Web server on your home network while sharing the public IP address of your firewall

Creating an `iptables` firewall script requires many steps, but with the aid of the sample tutorials, you should be able to complete a configuration relatively quickly.

WHAT IS *IPTABLES*?

Originally, the most popular firewall/NAT package running on Linux was `ipchains`, but it had a number of shortcomings. To rectify this, the **Netfilter** organization decided to create a new product called `iptables`, giving it such improvements as:

☞ Better integration with the Linux kernel with the capability of loading `iptables`-specific kernel modules designed for improved speed and reliability.

☞ Stateful packet inspection. This means that the firewall keeps track of each connection passing through it and in certain cases will view the contents of data flows in an attempt to anticipate the next action of certain protocols. This is an important feature in the support of active FTP and DNS, as well as many other network services.

☞ Filtering packets based on a MAC address and the values of the flags in the TCP header. This is helpful in preventing attacks using malformed packets and in restricting access from locally attached servers to other networks in spite of their IP addresses.

☞ System logging that provides the option of adjusting the level of detail of the reporting.

☞ Better network address translation.

☞ Support for transparent integration with such Web proxy programs as Squid.

☞ A rate limiting feature that helps `iptables` block some types of denial of service (DoS) attacks.

Considered a faster and more secure alternative to `ipchains`, `iptables` has become the default firewall package installed under Red Hat and Fedora Linux.

DOWNLOAD AND INSTALL THE *IPTABLES* PACKAGE

Before you begin, you need to make sure that the `iptables` software RPM is installed. (See Chapter 6, "Installing RPM Software," if you need a refresher.) When searching for the RPMs, remember that the filename usually starts with the software package name by a version number, as in `iptables-1.2.9-1.0.i386.rpm`.

HOW TO START *IPTABLES*

You can start, stop, and restart `iptables` after booting by using the commands:

```
[root@bigboy tmp]# service iptables start
[root@bigboy tmp]# service iptables stop
[root@bigboy tmp]# service iptables restart
```

To get `iptables` configured to start at boot, use the `chkconfig` command:

```
[root@bigboy tmp]# chkconfig iptables on
```

DETERMINING THE STATUS OF *IPTABLES*

You can determine whether `iptables` is running or not via the `service iptables status` command. Fedora Core will give a simple status message. For example:

```
[root@bigboy tmp]# service iptables status
Firewall is stopped.
[root@bigboy tmp]#
```

PACKET PROCESSING IN *IPTABLES*

All packets inspected by `iptables` pass through a sequence of built-in **tables** (**queues**) for processing. Each of these queues is dedicated to a particular type of packet activity and is controlled by an associated packet transformation/filtering chain.

There are three tables in total. The first is the `mangle` table, which is responsible for the alteration of quality of service bits in the TCP header. This is hardly used in a home or SOHO environment.

The second table is the `filter` queue, which is responsible for packet filtering. It has three built-in chains in which you can place your firewall policy rules:

☞ **FORWARD chain:** Filters packets to servers protected by the firewall.

☞ **INPUT chain:** Filters packets destined for the firewall.

☞ **OUTPUT chain:** Filters packets originating from the firewall.

The third table is the `nat` queue, which is responsible for network address translation. It has two built-in chains:

☞ **PREROUTING chain:** NATs packets when the destination address of the packet needs to be changed.

☞ **POSTROUTING chain:** NATs packets when the source address of the packet needs to be changed.

Table 14.1 provides more details on each queue.

Table 14.1   Processing for Packets Routed by the Firewall

Queue Type	Queue Function	Packet Transformation Chain in Queue	Chain Function
`filter`	Packet filtering	FORWARD	Filters packets to servers accessible by another NIC on the firewall.
		INPUT	Filters packets destined to the firewall.
		OUTPUT	Filters packets originating from the firewall.
NAT	Network Address Translation	PREROUTING	Address translation occurs before routing. Facilitates the transformation of the destination IP address to be compatible with the firewall's routing table. Used with NAT of the destination IP address, also known as destination NAT or DNAT.
		POSTROUTING	Address translation occurs after routing. This implies that there was no need to modify the destination IP address of the packet as in prerouting. Used with NAT of the source IP address using either one to one or many to one NAT. This is known as source NAT or SNAT.

Queue Type	Queue Function	Packet Transformation Chain in Queue	Chain Function
		OUTPUT	Network address translation for packets generated by the firewall. (Rarely used in SOHO environments.)
mangle	TCP header modification	PREROUTING, POSTROUTING, OUTPUT, INPUT, FORWARD	Modification of the TCP packet quality of service bits before routing occurs. (Rarely used in SOHO environments.)

You need to specify the table and the chain for each firewall rule you create. There is an exception: Most rules are related to filtering, so `iptables` assumes that any chain that's defined without an associated table will be a part of the `filter` table. The `filter` table is therefore the default.

To help make this clearer, take a look at the way packets are handled by `iptables`. In Figure 14.1 a TCP packet from the Internet arrives at the firewall's interface on Network A to create a data connection.

The packet is first examined by your rules in the `mangle` table's PREROUTING chain, if any. It is then inspected by the rules in the `nat` table's PREROUTING chain to see whether the packet requires DNAT. It is then routed.

If the packet is destined for a protected network, then it is filtered by the rules in the FORWARD chain of the `filter` table and, if necessary, the packet undergoes SNAT before arriving at Network B. When the destination server decides to reply, the packet undergoes the same sequence of steps.

If the packet is destined for the firewall itself, then it is filtered by the rules in the INPUT chain of the `filter` table before being processed by the intended application on the firewall. At some point, the firewall needs to reply. This reply is inspected by your rules in the OUTPUT chain of the mangle table, if any. The rules in the OUTPUT chain of the `nat` table determine whether address translation is required and the rules in the OUTPUT chain of the `filter` table are then inspected before the packet is routed back to the Internet.

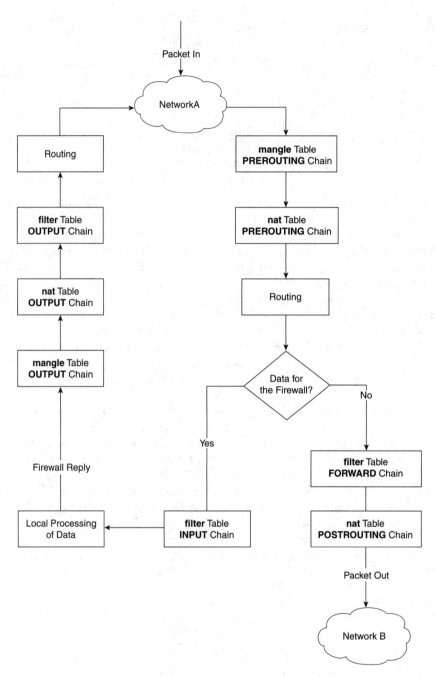

Figure 14.1   A diagram of the iptables packet flow.

It is now time to discuss the ways in which you add rules to these chains.

TARGETS AND JUMPS

Each firewall rule inspects each IP packet and then tries to identify it as the **target** of some sort of operation. Once a target is identified, the packet needs to **jump** over to it for further processing. Table 14.2 lists the built-in targets that `iptables` uses.

Table 14.2   Descriptions of the Most Commonly Used Targets

Target	Description	Most Common Options
ACCEPT	`iptables` stops further processing. The packet is handed over to the end application or the operating system for processing.	N/A
DROP	`iptables` stops further processing. The packet is blocked.	N/A
LOG	The packet information is sent to the syslog daemon for logging. `iptables` continues processing with the next rule in the table. As you can't log and drop at the same time, it is common to have two similar rules in sequence. The first logs the packet, the second drops it.	`--log-prefix "string"` Tells `iptables` to prefix all log messages with a user defined string. Frequently used to tell why the logged packet was dropped.
REJECT	Works like the DROP target, but also returns an error message to the host sending the packet that the packet was blocked.	`--reject-with` *qualifier* The qualifier tells what type of reject message is returned. Qualifiers include `icmp-port-unreachable` (default) `icmp-net-unreachable` `icmp-host-unreachable` `icmp-proto-unreachable` `icmp-net-prohibited` `icmp-host-prohibited` `tcp-reset` `echo-reply`
DNAT	Used to do **destination network address translation**, rewriting the destination IP address of the packet.	`--to-destination` *ipaddress* Tells `iptables` what the destination IP address should be.
SNAT	Used to do source network address translation, rewriting the source IP address of the packet.	`--to-source <address> [-<address>] [:<port>-<port>]` The source IP address is user defined. Specifies the source IP address and ports to be used by SNAT.

continues

Table 14.2   continued

Target	Description	Most Common Options
MASQUERADE	Used to do source network address translation. By default the source IP address is the same as that used by the firewall's interface.	`[--to-ports <port>[-<port>]]` Specifies the range of source ports to which the original source port can be mapped.

IMPORTANT *IPTABLES* COMMAND SWITCH OPERATIONS

Each line of an `iptables` script not only has a jump, but they also have a number of command line options that are used to append rules to chains that match your defined packet characteristics, such the source IP address and TCP port. There are also options that can be used to just clear a chain so you can start all over again. Tables 14.3 through 14.7 list the most common options.

Table 14.3   General `iptables` Match Criteria

`iptables` Command Switch	Description
`-t <table>`	If you don't specify a table, then the filter table is assumed. The possible built-in tables include: filter, nat, mangle.
`-j <target>`	Jump to the specified target chain when the packet matches the current rule.
`-A`	Append rule to end of a chain.
`-F`	Flush. Deletes all the rules in the selected table.
`-p <protocol-type>`	Match protocol. Types include `icmp`, `tcp`, `udp` and `all`.
`-s <ip-address>`	Match source IP address.
`-d <ip-address>`	Match destination IP address.
`-i <interface-name>`	Match input interface on which the packet enters.
`-o <interface-name>`	Match output interface on which the packet exits.

In this command switches example:

```
iptables -A INPUT -s 0/0 -i eth0 -d 192.168.1.1  -p TCP -j ACCEPT
```

`iptables` is being configured to allow the firewall to accept TCP packets coming in on interface `eth0` from any IP address destined for the firewall's IP address of 192.168.1.1. The `0/0` representation of an IP address means any.

Table 14.4   Common TCP and UDP Match Criteria

Switch	Description
`-p tcp --sport <port>`	TCP source port; can be a single value or a range in the format:start-port-number: end-port-number
`-p tcp --dport <port>`	TCP destination port; can be a single value or a range in the format: starting-port: ending-port
`-p tcp --syn`	Used to identify a new connection request; ! --syn means, not a new connection request
`-p udp --sport <port>`	UDP source port; Can be a single value or a range in the format: starting-port: ending-port
`-p udp --dport <port>`	UDP destination port; can be a single value or a range in the format:starting-port: ending-port

In this example:

```
iptables -A FORWARD -s 0/0 -i eth0 -d 192.168.1.58 -o eth1 -p TCP \
        --sport 1024:65535 --dport 80 -j ACCEPT
```

`iptables` is being configured to allow the firewall to accept TCP packets for routing when they enter on interface `eth0` from any IP address and are destined for an IP address of 192.168.1.58 that is reachable via interface `eth1`. The source port is in the range 1024 to 65535 and the destination port is port 80 (www/http).

Table 14.5   Common ICMP (Ping) Match Criteria

Matches used with `--icmp-type`	Description
`--icmp-type <type>`	The most commonly used types are `echo-reply` and `echo-request`

In this example:

```
iptables -A OUTPUT -p icmp --icmp-type echo-request -j ACCEPT
iptables -A INPUT  -p icmp --icmp-type echo-reply   -j ACCEPT
```

`iptables` is being configured to allow the firewall to send ICMP echo-requests (pings) and in turn, accept the expected ICMP echo-replies.

Consider another example:

```
iptables -A INPUT -p icmp --icmp-type echo-request \
        -m limit --limit 1/s -i eth0 -j ACCEPT
```

The `limit` feature in `iptables` specifies the maximum average number of matches to allow per second. You can specify time intervals in the format

/second, /minute, /hour, or /day, or you can use abbreviations so that 3/second is the same as 3/s.

In this example, ICMP echo requests are restricted to no more than one per second. When tuned correctly, this feature allows you to filter unusually high volumes of traffic that characterize denial of service (DOS) attacks and Internet worms.

```
iptables -A INPUT -p tcp --syn -m limit --limit 5/s -i eth0 -j ACCEPT
```

You can expand on the limit feature of iptables to reduce your vulnerability to certain types of denial of service attacks. Here a defense for SYN flood attacks was created by limiting the acceptance of TCP segments with the SYN bit set to no more than five per second.

Table 14.6   Common Extended Match Criteria

Switch	Description
-m --sport <port, port>	A variety of TCP/UDP source ports separated by commas. Unlike when -m isn't used, they do not have to be within a range.
-m --dport <port, port>	A variety of TCP/UDP destination ports separated by commas. Unlike when -m isn't used, they do not have to be within a range.
-m --ports <port, port>	A variety of TCP/UDP ports separated by commas. Source and destination ports are assumed to be the same and they do not have to be within a range.
-m --state <state>	The most frequently tested states are: **ESTABLISHED**: The packet is part of a connection that has seen packets in both directions. **NEW**: The packet is the start of a new connection. **RELATED**: The packet is starting a new secondary connection. This is a common feature of such protocols as an FTP data transfer, or an ICMP error. **INVALID**: The packet couldn't be identified. Could be due to insufficient system resources or ICMP errors that don't match an existing data flow.

This is an expansion on the previous example:

```
iptables -A FORWARD -s 0/0 -i eth0 -d 192.168.1.58 -o eth1 -p TCP \
        --sport 1024:65535 -m multiport --dport 80,443 -j ACCEPT

iptables -A FORWARD -d 0/0 -o eth0 -s 192.168.1.58 -i eth1 -p TCP \
        -m state --state ESTABLISHED -j ACCEPT
```

Here `iptables` is being configured to allow the firewall to accept TCP packets to be routed when they enter on interface `eth0` from any IP address destined for IP address of 192.168.1.58 that is reachable via interface `eth1`. The source port is in the range 1024 to 65535 and the destination ports are port 80 (www/http) and 443 (https). The return packets from 192.168.1.58 are allowed to be accepted too. Instead of stating the source and destination ports, you can simply allow packets related to established connections using the `-m state` and `--state ESTABLISHED` options.

USING USER-DEFINED CHAINS

As you may remember, you can configure `iptables` to have user-defined chains. This feature is frequently used to help streamline the processing of packets. For example, instead of using a single, built-in chain for all protocols, you can use the chain to determine the protocol type for the packet and then hand off the actual final processing to a user-defined, protocol-specific chain in the filter table. In other words, you can replace a long chain with a stubby main chain pointing to multiple stubby chains, thereby shortening the total length of all chains the packet has to pass through. For example:

```
iptables -A INPUT -i eth0   -d 206.229.110.2 -j fast-input-queue
iptables -A OUTPUT -o eth0 -s 206.229.110.2 -j fast-output-queue

iptables -A fast-input-queue  -p icmp -j icmp-queue-in
iptables -A fast-output-queue -p icmp -j icmp-queue-out

iptables -A icmp-queue-out -p icmp --icmp-type echo-request \
         -m state --state NEW -j ACCEPT

iptables -A icmp-queue-in -p icmp --icmp-type echo-reply -j ACCEPT
```

Here six queues help assist in improving processing speed. Table 14.8 summarizes the function of each.

Table 14.8 Custom Queues Example Listing

Chain	Description
INPUT	The regular built-in INPUT chain in `iptables`
OUTPUT	The regular built-in OUTPUT chain in `iptables`
`fast-input-queue`	Input chain dedicated to identifying specific protocols and shunting the packets to protocol specific chains
`fast-output-queue`	Output chain dedicated to identifying specific protocols and shunting the packets to protocol specific chains
`icmp-queue-out`	Output queue dedicated to ICMP
`icmp-queue-in`	Input queue dedicated to ICMP

SAVING YOUR *IPTABLES* SCRIPTS

The service iptables save command permanently saves the iptables configuration in the /etc/sysconfig/iptables file. When the system reboots, the iptables-
restore program reads the configuration and makes it the active configuration.

The format of the /etc/sysconfig/iptables file is slightly different from
that of the scripts shown in this chapter. The initialization of built-in chains is
automatic and the string "iptables" is omitted from the rule statements.

Here is a sample /etc/sysconfig/iptables configuration that allows
ICMP, IPSec (ESP and AH packets), already established connections, and
inbound SSH:

```
[root@bigboy tmp]# cat /etc/sysconfig/iptables
# Generated by iptables-save v1.2.9 on Mon Nov 8 11:00:07 2004
*filter
:INPUT ACCEPT [0:0]
:FORWARD ACCEPT [0:0]
:OUTPUT ACCEPT [144:12748]
:RH-Firewall-1-INPUT - [0:0]
-A INPUT -j RH-Firewall-1-INPUT
-A FORWARD -j RH-Firewall-1-INPUT
-A RH-Firewall-1-INPUT -i lo -j ACCEPT
-A RH-Firewall-1-INPUT -p icmp -m icmp --icmp-type 255 -j ACCEPT
-A RH-Firewall-1-INPUT -p esp -j ACCEPT
-A RH-Firewall-1-INPUT -p ah -j ACCEPT
-A RH-Firewall-1-INPUT -m state --state RELATED,ESTABLISHED -j ACCEPT
-A RH-Firewall-1-INPUT -p tcp -m state --state NEW -m tcp --dport 22 -
j ACCEPT
-A RH-Firewall-1-INPUT -j REJECT --reject-with icmp-host-prohibited
COMMIT
# Completed on Mon Nov 8 11:00:07 2004
[root@bigboy tmp]#
```

It is never a good idea to edit this script directly because it is always
overwritten by the save command and it doesn't save any comments at all,
which can also make it extremely difficult to follow. For these reasons, you're
better off writing and applying a customized script and then using the service
iptables save command to make the changes permanent.

FEDORA'S *IPTABLES* RULE GENERATOR

Fedora comes with a program called lokkit that you can use to generate a very
rudimentary firewall rule set. It prompts for the level of security and then
gives you the option of doing simple customizations. It is a good place
for beginners to start on a test system so that they can see a general rule
structure.

Like the service iptables save command, lokkit saves the firewall rules
in a new /etc/sysconfig/iptables file for use on the next reboot.

Once you have become familiar with the `iptables` syntax, it's best to write scripts that you can comment and then save them to `/etc/sysconfig/iptables`. It makes them much more manageable and readable.

RECOVERING FROM A LOST SCRIPT

Sometimes the script you created to generate `iptables` rules may get corrupted or lost, or you might inherit a new system from an administer and cannot find the original script used to protect it. In these situations, you can use the `iptables-save` and `iptables-restore` commands to assist you with the continued management of the server.

Unlike the `service iptables save` command, which actually saves a permanent copy of the firewall's active configuration in the `/etc/sysconfig/iptables` file, `iptables-save` displays the active configuration to the screen in `/etc/sysconfig/iptables` format. If you redirect the `iptables-save` screen output to a file with the > symbol, then you can edit the output and reload the updated rules when they meet your new criteria with the `iptables-restore` command.

This example exports the `iptables-save` output to a text file named `firewall-config`:

```
[root@bigboy tmp]# iptables-save > firewall-config
[root@bigboy tmp]# cat firewall-config
# Generated by iptables-save v1.2.9 on Mon Nov 8 11:00:07 2004
*filter
:INPUT ACCEPT [0:0]
:FORWARD ACCEPT [0:0]
:OUTPUT ACCEPT [144:12748]
:RH-Firewall-1-INPUT - [0:0]
-A INPUT -j RH-Firewall-1-INPUT
-A FORWARD -j RH-Firewall-1-INPUT
-A RH-Firewall-1-INPUT -i lo -j ACCEPT
-A RH-Firewall-1-INPUT -p icmp -m icmp --icmp-type 255 -j ACCEPT
-A RH-Firewall-1-INPUT -p esp -j ACCEPT
-A RH-Firewall-1-INPUT -p ah -j ACCEPT
-A RH-Firewall-1-INPUT -m state --state RELATED,ESTABLISHED -j ACCEPT
-A RH-Firewall-1-INPUT -p tcp -m state --state NEW -m tcp --dport 22 -
j ACCEPT
-A RH-Firewall-1-INPUT -j REJECT --reject-with icmp-host-prohibited
COMMIT
# Completed on Mon Nov 8 11:00:07 2004
[root@bigboy tmp]#
```

After editing the `firewall-config` file with the commands you need, you can reload it into the active firewall rule set with the `iptables-restore` command:

```
[root@bigboy tmp]# iptables-restore < firewall-config
```

Finally, you should permanently save the active configuration so that it will be loaded automatically when the system reboots:

```
[root@bigboy tmp]# service iptables save
```

If desired, you can eventually convert this `firewall-config` file into a regular `iptables` script so that it becomes more easily recognizable and manageable.

LOADING KERNEL MODULES NEEDED BY *IPTABLES*

The `iptables` application requires you to load certain kernel modules to activate some of its functions. Whenever any type of NAT is required, the `iptable_nat` module needs to be loaded. The `ip_conntrack_ftp` module needs to be added for FTP support and should always be loaded with the `ip_conntrack` module, which tracks TCP connection states. As most scripts probably will keep track of connection states, the `ip_conntrack` module will be needed in any case. The `ip_nat_ftp` module also needs to be loaded for FTP servers behind a NAT firewall.

Unfortunately, the `/etc/sysconfig/iptables` file doesn't support the loading of modules, so you'll have to add the statements to your `/etc/rc.local` file, which is run at the end of every reboot.

The script samples in this chapter include these statements only as a reminder to place them in the `/etc/rc.local` file:

```
# File: /etc/rc.local

# Module to track the state of connections
modprobe ip_conntrack

# Load the iptables active FTP module, requires ip_conntrack
modprobe ip_conntrack_ftp

# Load iptables NAT module when required
modprobe iptable_nat

# Module required for active an FTP server using NAT
modprobe ip_nat_ftp
```

SAMPLE *IPTABLES* SCRIPTS

This section provides some sample scripts you can use to get `iptables` working for you. Pay special attention to the logging example at the end.

The basic initialization script snippet should also be included in all your scripts to ensure the correct initialization of your chains should you decide to restart your script after startup. Other snippets will help you get basic functionality. It should be a good guide to get you started.

Note

Once you feel more confident, you can use Appendix II, "Codes, Scripts, and Configurations," to find detailed scripts. The appendix shows you how to allow your firewall to:

☞ Be used as a Linux Web, mail, and DNS server
☞ Be the NAT router for your home network
☞ Prevent various types of attacks using corrupted TCP, UDP, and ICMP packets
☞ Provide outbound passive FTP access from the firewall

There are also simpler code snippets in Appendix II for Inbound and Outbound FTP connections to and from your firewall.

Basic Operating System Defense

You can do several things before employing your firewall script to improve the resilience of your firewall to attack. For example, the Linux operating system has a number of built-in protection mechanisms that you should activate by modifying the system kernel parameters in the `/proc` filesystem via the `/etc/sysctl.conf` file. Using of `/etc/sysctl.conf` to modify kernel parameters is explained in more detail in Appendix I, "Miscellaneous Linux Topics."

Here is a sample configuration:

```
# File: /etc/sysctl.conf

#--------------------------------------------------------------------
# Disable routing triangulation. Respond to queries out
# the same interface, not another. Helps to maintain state
# Also protects against IP spoofing
#--------------------------------------------------------------------

net/ipv4/conf/all/rp_filter = 1


#--------------------------------------------------------------------
# Enable logging of packets with malformed IP addresses
#--------------------------------------------------------------------

net/ipv4/conf/all/log_martians = 1
```

```
#------------------------------------------------------------------
# Disable redirects
#------------------------------------------------------------------

net/ipv4/conf/all/send_redirects = 0


#------------------------------------------------------------------
# Disable source routed packets
#------------------------------------------------------------------

net/ipv4/conf/all/accept_source_route = 0


#------------------------------------------------------------------
# Disable acceptance of ICMP redirects
#------------------------------------------------------------------

net/ipv4/conf/all/accept_redirects = 0


#------------------------------------------------------------------
# Turn on protection from Denial of Service (DOS) attacks
#------------------------------------------------------------------

net/ipv4/tcp_syncookies = 1


#------------------------------------------------------------------
# Disable responding to ping broadcasts
#------------------------------------------------------------------

net/ipv4/icmp_echo_ignore_broadcasts = 1

#------------------------------------------------------------------
# Enable IP routing. Required if your firewall is protecting a
# network, NAT included
#------------------------------------------------------------------

net/ipv4/ip_forward = 1
```

This configuration will become active after the next reboot, but changes won't become active in the current boot session until you run the sysctl -p command:

```
[root@bigboy tmp]# sysctl -p
...
...
net.ipv4.conf.all.rp_filter = 1
net.ipv4.conf.all.log_martians = 1
net.ipv4.conf.all.send_redirects = 0
net.ipv4.conf.all.accept_source_route = 0
net.ipv4.conf.all.accept_redirects = 0
net.ipv4.tcp_syncookies = 1
net.ipv4.icmp_echo_ignore_broadcasts = 1
[root@bigboy tmp]#
```

Basic *iptables* Initialization

It is a good policy, in any `iptables` script you write, to initialize your chain and table settings with known values. The `filter` table's INPUT, FORWARD, and OUTPUT chains should drop packets by default for the best security. It is not good policy, however, to make your `nat` and `mangle` tables drop packets by default. These tables are queried before the `filter` table, and if all packets that don't match the `nat` and `mangle` table rules are dropped, then they will not reach the INPUT, FORWARD, and OUTPUT chains for processing.

Additional ALLOW rules should be added to the end of this script snippet.

```
#-------------------------------------------------------------------
# Load modules for FTP connection tracking and NAT - You may need
# them later
#
# Note: It is best to use the /etc/rc.local example in this
#        chapter. This value will not be retained in the
#        /etc/sysconfig/iptables file. Included only as a reminder.
#-------------------------------------------------------------------

modprobe ip_conntrack
modprobe ip_nat_ftp
modprobe ip_conntrack_ftp
modprobe iptable_nat

#-------------------------------------------------------------------
# Initialize all the chains by removing all the rules
# tied to them
#-------------------------------------------------------------------

iptables -flush
iptables -t nat -flush
iptables -t mangle -flush

#-------------------------------------------------------------------
# Now that the chains have been initialized, the user defined
# chains should be deleted. We'll recreate them in the next step
#-------------------------------------------------------------------

iptables --delete-chain
iptables -t nat --delete-chain
iptables -t mangle --delete-chain

#-------------------------------------------------------------------
# If a packet doesn't match one of the built in chains, then
# The policy should be to drop it
#-------------------------------------------------------------------

iptables --policy INPUT DROP
iptables --policy OUTPUT DROP
iptables --policy FORWARD DROP
iptables -t nat --policy POSTROUTING ACCEPT
iptables -t nat --policy PREROUTING ACCEPT

#-------------------------------------------------------------------
# The loopback interface should accept all traffic
```

```
# Necessary for X-Windows and other socket based services
#----------------------------------------------------------------

iptables -A INPUT  -i lo -j ACCEPT
iptables -A OUTPUT -o lo -j ACCEPT
```

Advanced *iptables* Initialization

You may also want to add some more advanced initialization steps to your script, including checks for Internet traffic from RFC1918 private addresses. The sample script snippet below outlines how to do this. More complex initializations would include checks for attacks using invalid TCP flags and directed broadcasts, which are beyond the scope of this book.

The script also uses multiple user-defined chains to make the script shorter and faster as the chains can be repeatedly accessed. This removes the need to repeat the same statements over and over again.

You can take even more precautions to further protect your network. The complete firewall script in Appendix II outlines most of them.

```
#=#=#=#=#=#=#=#=#=#=#=#=#=#=#=#=#=#=#=#=#=#=#=#=#=#=#=#=#=#=#=#=
#
# Define networks: NOTE!! You may want to put these "EXTERNAL"
# definitions at the top of your script.
#
#=#=#=#=#=#=#=#=#=#=#=#=#=#=#=#=#=#=#=#=#=#=#=#=#=#=#=#=#=#=#=#=

EXTERNAL_INT="eth0"              # External Internet interface
EXTERNAL_IP="97.158.253.25"     # Internet Interface IP address

#------------------------------------------
# Initialize our user-defined chains
#------------------------------------------

iptables -N valid-src
iptables -N valid-dst

#------------------------------------------
# Verify valid source and destination addresses for all packets
#------------------------------------------

iptables -A INPUT   -i $EXTERNAL_INT -j valid-src
iptables -A FORWARD -i $EXTERNAL_INT -j valid-src
iptables -A OUTPUT  -o $EXTERNAL_INT -j valid-dst
iptables -A FORWARD -o $EXTERNAL_INT -j valid-dst

#=#=#=#=#=#=#=#=#=#=#=#=#=#=#=#=#=#=#=#=#=#=#=#=#=#=#=#=#=#=#=#
#
# Source and Destination Address Sanity Checks
#
# Drop packets from networks covered in RFC 1918 (private nets)
# Drop packets from external interface IP
#
```

```
#=#=#=#=#=#=#=#=#=#=#=#=#=#=#=#=#=#=#=#=#=#=#=#=#=#=#=#=#=#=#=#
iptables -A valid-src -s $10.0.0.0/8      -j DROP
iptables -A valid-src -s $172.16.0.0/12   -j DROP
iptables -A valid-src -s $192.168.0.0/16  -j DROP
iptables -A valid-src -s $224.0.0.0/4     -j DROP
iptables -A valid-src -s $240.0.0.0/5     -j DROP
iptables -A valid-src -s $127.0.0.0/8     -j DROP
iptables -A valid-src -s 0.0.0.0/8        -j DROP
iptables -A valid-src -d 255.255.255.255  -j DROP
iptables -A valid-src -d 169.254.0.0/16   -j DROP
iptables -A valid-src -s $EXTERNAL_IP     -j DROP
iptables -A valid-dst -d $224.0.0.0/4     -j DROP
```

Allowing DNS Access to Your Firewall

You'll almost certainly want your firewall to make DNS queries to the Internet. This is not because it is required for the basic functionality of the firewall, but because of Fedora Linux's yum RPM updater, which will help to keep the server up to date with the latest security patches. The following statements will apply not only for firewalls acting as DNS clients but also for firewalls working in a caching or regular DNS server role.

```
#----------------------------------------------------------------
# Allow outbound DNS queries from the FW and the replies too
#
# - Interface eth0 is the internet interface
#
# Zone transfers use TCP and not UDP. Most home networks
# / websites using a single DNS server won't require TCP statements
#
#----------------------------------------------------------------

iptables -A OUTPUT -p udp -o eth0 --dport 53 --sport 1024:65535 \
         -j ACCEPT

iptables -A INPUT -p udp -i eth0 --sport 53 --dport 1024:65535 \
         -j ACCEPT
```

Allowing WWW and SSH Access to Your Firewall

This sample snippet is for a firewall that doubles as a Web server that is managed remotely by its system administrator via **secure shell (SSH)** sessions. Inbound packets destined for ports 80 and 22 are allowed, thereby making the first steps in establishing a connection. It isn't necessary to specify these ports for the return leg as outbound packets for all established connections are allowed. Connections initiated by users logged into the Web server will be denied as outbound NEW connection packets aren't allowed.

```
#------------------------------------------------------------------
# Allow previously established connections
# - Interface eth0 is the internet interface
#------------------------------------------------------------------

iptables -A OUTPUT -o eth0 -m state --state ESTABLISHED,RELATED \
   -j ACCEPT

#------------------------------------------------------------------
# Allow port 80 (www) and 22 (SSH) connections to the firewall
#------------------------------------------------------------------

iptables -A INPUT -p tcp -i eth0 --dport 22 --sport 1024:65535 \
   -m state --state NEW -j ACCEPT

iptables -A INPUT -p tcp -i eth0 --dport 80 --sport 1024:65535 \
   -m state --state NEW -j ACCEPT
```

Allowing Your Firewall to Access the Internet

This `iptables` script enables a user on the firewall to use a Web browser to surf the Internet. HTTP traffic uses TCP port 80, and HTTPS uses port 443.

Note

HTTPS (secure HTTP) is used for credit card transactions frequently, as well as by Red Hat Linux servers running up2date. FTP and HTTP are frequently used with yum.

```
#------------------------------------------------------------------
# Allow port 80 (www) and 443 (https) connections from the firewall
#------------------------------------------------------------------

iptables -A OUTPUT -j ACCEPT -m state \
   --state NEW,ESTABLISHED,RELATED -o eth0 -p tcp \
   -m multiport --dport 80,443 -m multiport --sport 1024:65535

#------------------------------------------------------------------
# Allow previously established connections
# - Interface eth0 is the internet interface
#------------------------------------------------------------------
iptables -A INPUT -j ACCEPT -m state --state ESTABLISHED,RELATED  \
-i eth0 -p tcp
```

If you want all TCP traffic originating from the firewall to be accepted, then remove the line:

```
-m multiport --dport 80,443 -m multiport --sport 1024:65535
```

Allow Your Home Network to Access the Firewall

In this example, eth1 is directly connected to a home network using IP addresses from the 192.168.1.0 network. All traffic between this network and the firewall is simplistically assumed to be trusted and allowed.

Further rules will be needed for the interface connected to the Internet to allow only specific ports, types of connections, and possibly even remote servers to have access to your firewall and home network.

```
#------------------------------------------------------------------
# Allow all bidirectional traffic from your firewall to the
# protected network
# - Interface eth1 is the private network interface
#------------------------------------------------------------------

iptables -A INPUT   -j ACCEPT -p all -s 192.168.1.0/24 -i eth1
iptables -A OUTPUT  -j ACCEPT -p all -d 192.168.1.0/24 -o eth1
```

Masquerading (Many to One NAT)

As explained in Chapter 2, "Introduction to Networking," **masquerading** is another name for what many call **many to one NAT**. In other words, traffic from all devices on one or more protected networks will appear as if it originated from a single IP address on the Internet side of the firewall.

Note

The masquerade IP address always defaults to the IP address of the firewall's main interface. The advantage of this is that you never have to specify the NAT IP address. This makes it much easier to configure iptables NAT with DHCP.

You can configure many to one NAT to an IP alias, using the POSTROUTING and not the MASQUERADE statement. An example of this can be seen in the static NAT section that follows.

Keep in mind that iptables requires the iptables_nat module to be loaded with the modprobe command for the masquerade feature to work. Masquerading also depends on the Linux operating system being configured to support routing between the Internet and private network interfaces of the firewall. This is done by enabling **IP forwarding** or routing by giving the file /proc/sys/net/ipv4/ip_forward the value 1 as opposed to the default disabled value of 0.

Once masquerading has been achieved using the POSTROUTING chain of the nat table, you will have to configure iptables to allow packets to flow between the two interfaces. To do this, use the FORWARD chain of the filter table. More specifically, packets related to NEW and ESTABLISHED connections will be allowed outbound to the Internet, but only packets related to

ESTABLISHED connections will be allowed inbound. This helps to protect the
home network from anyone trying to initiate connections from the Internet.

```
#------------------------------------------------------------------
# Load the NAT module
#
# Note: It is best to use the /etc/rc.local example in this
#        chapter. This value will not be retained in the
#        /etc/sysconfig/iptables file. Included only as a reminder.
#------------------------------------------------------------------

modprobe iptable_nat

#------------------------------------------------------------------
# Enable routing by modifying the ip_forward /proc filesystem file
#
# Note: It is best to use the /etc/sysctl.conf example in this
#        chapter. This value will not be retained in the
#        /etc/sysconfig/iptables file. Included only as a reminder.
#------------------------------------------------------------------

echo 1 > /proc/sys/net/ipv4/ip_forward

#------------------------------------------------------------------
# Allow masquerading
# - Interface eth0 is the internet interface
# - Interface eth1 is the private network interface
#------------------------------------------------------------------

iptables -A POSTROUTING -t nat -o eth0 -s 192.168.1.0/24 -d 0/0 \
         -j MASQUERADE

#------------------------------------------------------------------
# Prior to masquerading, the packets are routed via the filter
# table's FORWARD chain.
# Allowed outbound: New, established and related connections
# Allowed inbound : Established and related connections
#------------------------------------------------------------------

iptables -A FORWARD -t filter -o eth0 -m state \
         --state NEW,ESTABLISHED,RELATED -j ACCEPT

iptables -A FORWARD -t filter -i eth0 -m state \
         --state ESTABLISHED,RELATED -j ACCEPT
```

Note

If you configure your firewall to do masquerading, then it should be used as the
default gateway for all your servers on the network.

Port Forwarding Type NAT (DHCP DSL)

In many cases home users may get a single DHCP public IP address from
their ISPs. If a Linux firewall is also your interface to the Internet and you

want to host a Web site on one of the NAT protected home servers, then you will have to use port forwarding. Here the combination of the firewall's single IP address, the remote server's IP address, and the source/destination port of the traffic can be used to uniquely identify a traffic flow. All traffic that matches a particular combination of these factors may then be forwarded to a single server on the private network.

Port forwarding is handled by the PREROUTING chain of the nat table. As in masquerading, the iptables_nat module has to be loaded and routing has to be enabled for port forwarding to work. Routing too must be allowed in iptables with the FORWARD chain, this includes all NEW inbound connections from the Internet matching the port forwarding port plus all future packets related to the ESTABLISHED connection in both directions.

```
#-------------------------------------------------------------------
# Load the NAT module
#
# Note: It is best to use the /etc/rc.local example in this
#       chapter. This value will not be retained in the
#       /etc/sysconfig/iptables file. Included only as a reminder.
#-------------------------------------------------------------------

modprobe iptable_nat

#-------------------------------------------------------------------
# Get the IP address of the Internet interface eth0 (linux only)
#
# You'll have to use a different expression to get the IP address
# for other operating systems which have a different ifconfig output
# or enter the IP address manually in the PREROUTING statement
#
# This is best when your firewall gets its IP address using DHCP.
# The external IP address could just be hard coded ("typed in
# normally")
#-------------------------------------------------------------------

external_int="eth0"
external_ip="`ifconfig $external_int | grep 'inet addr' | \
                  awk '{print $2}' | sed -e 's/.*://'`"

#-------------------------------------------------------------------
# Enable routing by modifying the ip_forward /proc filesystem file
#
# Note: It is best to use the /etc/sysctl.conf example in this
#       chapter. This value will not be retained in the
#       /etc/sysconfig/iptables file. Included only as a reminder.
#-------------------------------------------------------------------

echo 1 > /proc/sys/net/ipv4/ip_forward

#-------------------------------------------------------------------
# Allow port forwarding for traffic destined to port 80 of the
# firewall's IP address to be forwarded to port 8080 on server
# 192.168.1.200
#
# - Interface eth0 is the internet interface
```

```
# - Interface eth1 is the private network interface
#-----------------------------------------------------------------

iptables -t nat -A PREROUTING -p tcp -i eth0 -d $external_ip \
     --dport 80 --sport 1024:65535 -j DNAT --to 192.168.1.200:8080

#-----------------------------------------------------------------
# After DNAT, the packets are routed via the filter table's
# FORWARD chain.
# Connections on port 80 to the target machine on the private
# network must be allowed.
#-----------------------------------------------------------------

iptables -A FORWARD -p tcp -i eth0 -o eth1 -d 192.168.1.200 \
     --dport 8080 --sport 1024:65535 -m state --state NEW -j ACCEPT

iptables -A FORWARD -t filter -o eth0 -m state \
       --state NEW,ESTABLISHED,RELATED -j ACCEPT

iptables -A FORWARD -t filter -i eth0 -m state \
       --state ESTABLISHED,RELATED -j ACCEPT
```

Static NAT

In this example, all traffic to a particular public IP address, not just to a particular port, is translated to a single server on the protected subnet. Because the firewall has more than one IP address, I can't recommend MASQUERADE; it will force masquerading as the IP address of the primary interface and not as any of the alias IP addresses the firewall may have. Instead, use SNAT to specify the alias IP address to be used for connections initiated by all other servers in the protected network.

Note

Although the nat table translates all traffic to the target servers (192.168.1.100 to 102), only connections on ports 80, 443, and 22 are allowed through by the FORWARD chain. Also notice how you have to specify a separate -m multiport option whenever you need to match multiple nonsequential ports for both source and destination.

In this example, the firewall:

☞ Uses one to one NAT to make the server 192.168.1.100 on your home network appear on the Internet as IP addresses 97.158.253.26.

☞ Creates a many to one NAT for the 192.168.1.0 home network in which all the servers appear on the Internet as IP address 97.158.253.29. This is different from masquerading.

You will have to create alias IP addresses for each of these Internet IPs for one to one NAT to work.

```
#----------------------------------------------------------------
# Load the NAT module
#
# Note: It is best to use the /etc/rc.local example in this
#       chapter. This value will not be retained in the
#       /etc/sysconfig/iptables file. Included only as a reminder.
#----------------------------------------------------------------

modprobe iptable_nat


#----------------------------------------------------------------
# Enable routing by modifying the ip_forward /proc filesystem file
#
# Note: It is best to use the /etc/sysctl.conf example in this
#       chapter. This value will not be retained in the
#       /etc/sysconfig/iptables file. Included only as a reminder.
#----------------------------------------------------------------

echo 1 > /proc/sys/net/ipv4/ip_forward

#----------------------------------------------------------------
# NAT ALL traffic:
##########
# REMEMBER to create aliases for all the internet IP addresses below
##########
#
# TO:              FROM:            MAP TO SERVER:
# 97.158.253.26    Anywhere         192.168.1.100 (1:1 NAT - Inbound)
# Anywhere         192.168.1.100    97.158.253.26 (1:1 NAT - Outbound)
# Anywhere         192.168.1.0/24   97.158.253.29 (FW IP)
#
# SNAT is used to NAT all other outbound connections initiated
# from the protected network to appear to come from
# IP address 97.158.253.29
#
# POSTROUTING:
#    NATs source IP addresses. Frequently used to NAT connections from
#    your home network to the Internet
#
# PREROUTING:
#    NATs destination IP addresses. Frequently used to NAT
#    connections from the Internet to your home network
#
# - Interface eth0 is the internet interface
# - Interface eth1 is the private network interface
#----------------------------------------------------------------

# PREROUTING statements for 1:1 NAT
# (Connections originating from the Internet)

iptables -t nat -A PREROUTING -d 97.158.253.26 -i eth0 \
         -j DNAT --to-destination 192.168.1.100

# POSTROUTING statements for 1:1 NAT
```

```
# (Connections originating from the home network servers)

iptables -t nat -A POSTROUTING -s 192.168.1.100 -o eth0 \
        -j SNAT --to-source 97.158.253.26

# POSTROUTING statements for Many:1 NAT
# (Connections originating from the entire home network)

iptables -t nat -A POSTROUTING -s 192.168.1.0/24 \
        -j SNAT -o eth0 --to-source 97.158.253.29

# Allow forwarding to each of the servers configured for 1:1 NAT
# (For connections originating from the Internet. Notice how you
# use the real IP addresses here)

iptables -A FORWARD -p tcp -i eth0 -o eth1 -d 192.168.1.100 \
       -m multiport --dport 80,443,22 \
       -m state --state NEW -j ACCEPT


# Allow forwarding for all New and Established SNAT connections
# originating on the home network AND already established
# DNAT connections

iptables -A FORWARD -t filter -o eth0 -m state \
        --state NEW,ESTABLISHED,RELATED -j ACCEPT

# Allow forwarding for all 1:1 NAT connections originating on
# the Internet that have already passed through the NEW forwarding
# statements above

iptables -A FORWARD -t filter -i eth0 -m state \
        --state ESTABLISHED,RELATED -j ACCEPT
```

TROUBLESHOOTING *IPTABLES*

A number of tools are at your disposal for troubleshooting iptables firewall
scripts. One of the best methods is to log all dropped packets to the
/var/log/messages file.

Checking the Firewall Logs

You track packets passing through the iptables list of rules using the LOG
target. You should be aware that the LOG target:

☞ Logs all traffic that matches the iptables rule in which it is located.

☞ Automatically writes an entry to the /var/log/messages file and then executes the next rule.

If you want to log only unwanted traffic, therefore, you have to add a
matching rule with a DROP target immediately after the LOG rule. If you

don't, you'll find yourself logging both desired and unwanted traffic with no way of discerning between the two, because by default `iptables` doesn't state why the packet was logged in its log message.

This example logs a summary of failed packets to the file /var/log/mes-sages. You can use the contents of this file to determine which TCP/UDP ports you need to open to provide access to specific traffic that is currently stopped.

```
#-------------------------------------------------------------
# Log and drop all other packets to file /var/log/messages
# Without this we could be crawling around in the dark
#-------------------------------------------------------------

iptables -A OUTPUT -j LOG
iptables -A INPUT -j LOG
iptables -A FORWARD -j LOG

iptables -A OUTPUT -j DROP
iptables -A INPUT -j DROP
iptables -A FORWARD -j DROP
```

Here are some examples of the output of this file:

☞ Firewall denies replies to DNS queries (UDP port 53) destined to server 192.168.1.102 on the home network

```
Feb 23 20:33:50 bigboy kernel: IN=wlan0 OUT=
MAC=00:06:25:09:69:80:00:a0:c5:e1:3e:88:08:00 SRC=192.42.93.30
DST=192.168.1.102 LEN=220 TOS=0x00 PREC=0x00 TTL=54 ID=30485
PROTO=UDP SPT=53 DPT=32820 LEN=200
```

☞ Firewall denies Windows NetBIOS traffic (UDP port 138)

```
Feb 23 20:43:08 bigboy kernel: IN=wlan0 OUT=
MAC=ff:ff:ff:ff:ff:ff:00:06:25:09:6a:b5:08:00
SRC=192.168.1.100 DST=192.168.1.255 LEN=241 TOS=0x00 PREC=0x00
TTL=64 ID=0 DF PROTO=UDP SPT=138 DPT=138 LEN=221
```

☞ Firewall denies Network Time Protocol (NTP UDP port 123)

```
Feb 23 20:58:48 bigboy kernel: IN= OUT=wlan0
SRC=192.168.1.102 DST=207.200.81.113 LEN=76 TOS=0x10 PREC=0x00
TTL=64 ID=0 DF PROTO=UDP SPT=123 DPT=123 LEN=56
```

The traffic in all these examples isn't destined for the firewall; therefore, you should check your INPUT, OUTPUT, FORWARD, and NAT related statements. If the firewall's IP address is involved, then you should focus on the INPUT and OUTPUT statements

If nothing shows up in the logs, then follow the steps in Chapter 4, "Simple Network Troubleshooting," to determine whether the data is reaching your firewall at all and, if it is not, the location on your network that could be causing the problem.

As a general rule, you won't be able to access the public NAT IP addresses from servers on your home network. Basic NAT testing requires you to ask a friend to try to connect to your home network from the Internet.

You can then use the logging output in /var/log/messages to make sure that the translations are occurring correctly and iptables isn't dropping the packets after translation occurs.

iptables Won't Start

The iptables startup script expects to find the /etc/sysconfig/iptables before it starts. If none exists, then symptoms include the firewall status always being stopped and the /etc/init.d/iptables script running without the typical [OK] or [FAILED] messages.

If you have just installed iptables and have never applied a policy, then you will face this problem. Unfortunately, running the service iptables save command before restarting won't help either. You have to create this file:

```
[root@bigboy tmp]# service iptables start
[root@bigboy tmp]#

[root@bigboy tmp]# touch /etc/sysconfig/iptables
[root@bigboy tmp]# chmod 600 /etc/sysconfig/iptables

[root@bigboy tmp]# service iptables start
Applying iptables firewall rules: [  OK  ]
[root@bigboy tmp]#
```

CONCLUSION

A firewall is a critical part of any establishment that connects to an unprotected network such as the Internet, but a firewall is never sufficient. Web site security involves not just protection from corrupted packets or maliciously overwhelming volumes of traffic, but also involves daily data backups to help recovery from device failures, regular application patching, enforced password policies, restricted and monitored physical access to your servers, reliable power and cooling, secured cabling, redundant hardware, and, probably most importantly, well trained and motivated employees. Security should be viewed as anything that contributes to the desired risk-free functioning of your site, and it is well worth the money to invest in and learn from a book that specializes in the topic.

Linux FTP Server Setup

IN THIS CHAPTER

☞ FTP Overview
☞ Problems with FTP and Firewalls
☞ How to Download and Install VSFTPD
☞ How to Get VSFTPD Started
☞ Testing the Status of VSFTPD
☞ The `vsftpd.conf` File
☞ FTP Security Issues
☞ Troubleshooting FTP
☞ Tutorial
☞ Conclusion

The **File Transfer Protocol** (**FTP**) is one of the most common means of copying files between servers over the Internet. Most Web-based download sites use the built-in FTP capabilities of Web browsers, and, therefore, most server-oriented operating systems usually include an FTP server application as part of the software suite. Linux is no exception.

This chapter will show you how to convert your Linux box into an FTP server using the default **Very Secure FTP Daemon** (**VSFTPD**) package included in Fedora.

FTP OVERVIEW

FTP relies on a pair of TCP ports to get the job done. It operates using two connection channels:

237

☞ **FTP control channel, TCP Port 21**: All commands you send, as well as the FTP server's responses to those commands, go over the control connection, but any data sent back (such as `ls` directory lists or actual file data in either direction) will go over the data connection.

☞ **FTP data channel,** TCP Port 20: This port is used for all subsequent data transfers between the client and server.

In addition to these channels, there are several varieties of FTP.

Types of FTP

From a networking perspective, the two main types of FTP are active and passive. In **active FTP**, the FTP server initiates a data transfer connection back to the client. For **passive FTP,** the connection is initiated from the FTP client. These are illustrated in Figure 15.1.

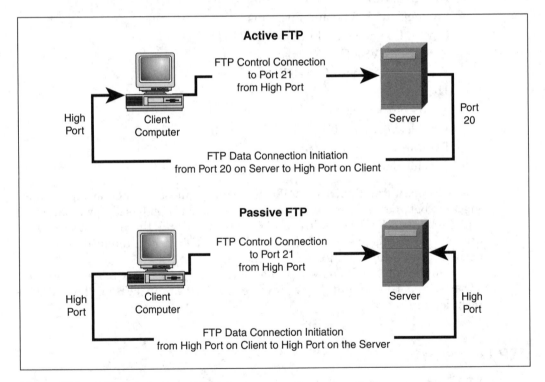

Figure 15.1   Active and passive FTP.

From a user management perspective, there are two additional types of FTP: **regular FTP**, in which files are transferred using the username and password of a regular user FTP server, and **anonymous FTP,** in which general access is provided to the FTP server using a well known universal login method.

Take a closer look at each type.

Active FTP

The sequence of events for active FTP is:

1. Your client connects to the FTP server by establishing an FTP control connection to port 21 of the server. Your commands such as `ls` and `get` are sent over this connection.
2. Whenever the client requests data over the control connection, the server initiates data transfer connections back to the client. The source port of these data transfer connections is always port 20 on the server, and the destination port is a high port (greater than 1024) on the client.
3. Thus the `ls` listing that you asked for comes back over the port 20 to high port connection, not the port 21 control connection.

FTP active mode, therefore, transfers data in a counter intuitive way to the TCP standard, as it selects port 20 as its source port (not a random high port that's greater than 1024) and connects back to the client on a random high port that has been pre-negotiated on the port 21 control connection.

Active FTP may fail in cases where the client is protected from the Internet via many to one NAT (masquerading), because the firewall will not know which of the many servers behind it should receive the return connection.

Passive FTP

Passive FTP works differently:

1. Your client connects to the FTP server by establishing an FTP control connection to port 21 of the server. Your commands such as `ls` and `get` are sent over that connection.
2. Whenever the client requests data over the control connection, the client initiates the data transfer connections to the server. The source port of these data transfer connections is always a high port on the client with a destination port of a high port on the server.

Passive FTP should be viewed as the server never making an active attempt to connect to the client for FTP data transfers. Because the client always initiates the required connections, passive FTP works better for clients protected by a firewall.

As Windows defaults to active FTP and Linux defaults to passive, you'll probably have to accommodate both forms when deciding upon a security policy for your FTP server.

Regular FTP

By default, the VSFTPD package allows regular Linux users to copy files to and from their home directories with an FTP client using their Linux usernames and passwords as their login credentials.

VSFTPD also has the option of allowing this type of access to only a group of Linux users, enabling you to restrict the addition of new files to your system to authorized personnel.

The disadvantage of regular FTP is that it isn't suitable for general download distribution of software as everyone either has to get a unique Linux user account or has to use a shared username and password. Anonymous FTP allows you to avoid this difficulty.

Anonymous FTP

Anonymous FTP is the choice of Web sites that need to exchange files with numerous unknown remote users. Common uses include downloading software updates and MP3s and uploading diagnostic information for a technical support engineers' attention. Unlike regular FTP where you login with a pre-configured Linux username and password, anonymous FTP requires only a username of anonymous and your e-mail address for the password. Once logged into a VSFTPD server, you automatically have access to only the default anonymous FTP directory (/var/ftp in the case of VSFTPD) and all its subdirectories.

As seen in Chapter 6, "Installing RPM Software," using anonymous FTP as a remote user is fairly straightforward. VSFTPD can be configured to support user-based and/or anonymous FTP in its configuration file, as you'll see later.

PROBLEMS WITH FTP AND FIREWALLS

FTP frequently fails when the data has to pass through a firewall, because firewalls are designed to limit data flows to predictable TCP ports and FTP uses a wide range of unpredictable TCP ports. You have a choice of methods to overcome this.

Note

Appendix II, "Codes, Scripts, and Configurations," contains examples of how to configure the **VSFTPD** Linux firewall to function with both active and passive FTP.

Client Protected by a Firewall Problem

Typically firewalls don't allow any incoming connections at all, which frequently blocks active FTP from functioning. With this type of FTP failure, the active FTP connection appears to work when the client initiates an outbound connection to the server on port 21. The connection then appears to hang, however, as soon as you use the ls, dir, or get commands. The reason is that the firewall is blocking the return connection from the server to the client (from port

20 on the server to a high port on the client). If a firewall allows all outbound connections to the Internet, then passive FTP clients behind a firewall will usually work correctly as the clients initiate all the FTP connections.

Solution

Table 15.1 shows the general rules you'll need to allow FTP clients through a firewall.

Table 15.1 Client Protected by Firewall: Required Rules for FTP

Method	Source Address	Source Port	Destination Address	Destination Port	Connection Type
Allow outgoing control connections to server					
Control channel	FTP client/ network	High[1]	FTP server[2]	21	New
	FTP server[2]	21	FTP client/ network	High	Established[3]
Allow the client to establish data channels to remote server					
Active FTP	FTP server[2]	20	FTP client/ network	High	New
	FTP client/ network	High	FTP server[2]	20	Established[3]
Passive FTP	FTP client/ network	High	FTP server[2]	High	New
	FTP server[2]	High	FTP client/ network	High	Established[3]

1 Greater than 1024.

2 In some cases, you may want to allow all Internet users to have access, not just a specific client, server, or network.

3 Many home-based firewall routers automatically allow traffic for already established connections. This rule may not be necessary in all cases.

Server Protected by a Firewall Problem

Typically, firewalls don't let any connections come in at all. When an incorrectly configured firewall protects an FTP server, the FTP connection from the client doesn't appear to work at all for both active and passive FTP.

Solution

Table 15.2 outlines the general rules needed to allow FTP servers through a firewall.

Table 15.2   Server Protected by Firewall: Required Rules for FTP

Method	Source Address	Source Port	Destination Address	Destination Port	Connection Type
Allow incoming control connections to server					
Control channel	FTP client/ network[1]	High[2]	FTP server	21	New
	FTP server	21	FTP client/ network[1]	High	Established[3]
Allow server to establish data channel to remote client					
Active FTP	FTP server	20	FTP client/ network[1]	High	New
	FTP client/ network[1]	High	FTP server	20	Established[3]
Passive FTP	FTP client/ network[1]	High	FTP server	High	New
	FTP server	High	FTP client/ network[1]	High	Established[3]

1   In some cases, you may want to allow all Internet users to have access, not just a specific client, server, or network.

2   Greater than 1024.

3   Many home-based firewall routers automatically allow traffic for already established connections. This rule may not be necessary in all cases.

How to Download and Install VSFTPD

Most Red Hat and Fedora Linux software products are available in the RPM format. Downloading and installing RPMs isn't hard. If you need a refresher, Chapter 6 covers how to do this in detail. It is best to use the latest version of VSFTPD.

When searching for the file, remember that the VSFTPD RPM's filename usually starts with the word "vsftpd" followed by a version number, as in vsftpd-1.2.1-5.i386.rpm.

How to Get VSFTPD Started

You can start, stop, or restart VSFTPD after booting using these commands:

```
[root@bigboy tmp]# service vsftpd start
[root@bigboy tmp]# service vsftpd stop
[root@bigboy tmp]# service vsftpd restart
```

To configure VSFTPD to start at boot, use the `chkconfig` command:

```
[root@bigboy tmp]# chkconfig vsftpd on
```

Note

In Red Hat Linux version 8.0 and earlier, VSFTPD operation is controlled by the `xinetd` process, which is covered in Chapter 16, "TELNET, TFTP, and XINETD." You can find a full description of how to configure these versions of Linux for VSFTPD in Appendix III, "Fedora Version Differences."

TESTING THE STATUS OF VSFTPD

You can always test whether the VSFTPD process is running by using the `netstat -a` command, which lists all the TCP and UDP ports on which the server is listening for traffic. This example shows the expected output:

```
[root@bigboy root]# netstat -a | grep ftp
tcp        0          0        *:ftp        *:*         LISTEN
[root@bigboy root]#
```

If VSFTPD wasn't running, there would be no output at all.

THE VSFTPD.CONF FILE

VSFTPD reads the contents of its `vsftpd.conf` configuration file only when it starts, so you'll have to restart VSFTPD each time you edit the file in order for the changes to take effect.

This file uses a number of default settings you need to know about:

☞ **VSFTPD runs as an anonymous FTP server:** Unless you want any remote user to log into to your default FTP directory using a username of `anonymous` and a password that's the same as their e-mail address, I suggest turning this off. You can set the configuration file's `anonymous_enable` directive to no to disable this feature. You'll also need to simultaneously enable local users to be able to log in by removing the comment symbol (#) before the `local_enable` instruction.

☞ **VSFTPD allows only anonymous FTP downloads to remote users, not uploads from them**: You can change this by modifying the `anon_upload_enable` directive shown later.

☞ **VSFTPD doesn't allow anonymous users to create directories on your FTP server**: You can change this by modifying the anon_mkdir_write_enable directive.

☞ **VSFTPD logs FTP access to the /var/log/vsftpd.log log file**: You can change this by modifying the xferlog_file directive.

☞ **VSFTPD expects files for anonymous FTP to be placed in the /var/ftp directory**: You can change this by modifying the anon_root directive. There is always the risk with anonymous FTP that users will discover a way to write files to your anonymous FTP directory. You run the risk of filling up your /var partition if you use the default setting. It is best to make the anonymous FTP directory reside in its own dedicated partition.

The configuration file is fairly straightforward as you can see in the snippet:

```
# Allow anonymous FTP?
anonymous_enable=YES



# Uncomment this to allow local users to log in.
local_enable=YES

# Uncomment this to enable any form of FTP write command.
# (Needed even if you want local users to be able to upload files)
write_enable=YES

# Uncomment to allow the anonymous FTP user to upload files. This only
# has an effect if global write enable is activated. Also, you will
# obviously need to create a directory writable by the FTP user.
#anon_upload_enable=YES

# Uncomment this if you want the anonymous FTP user to be able to
create
# new directories.
#anon_mkdir_write_enable=YES

# Activate logging of uploads/downloads.
xferlog_enable=YES

# You may override where the log file goes if you like.
# The default is shown# below.
#xferlog_file=/var/log/vsftpd.log

# The directory which vsftpd will try to change
# into after an anonymous login. (Default = /var/ftp)
#anon_root=/data/directory
```

To activate or deactivate a feature, remove or add the # at the beginning of the appropriate line.

Other *vsftpd.conf* Options

There are many other options you can add to this file:

☞ Limiting the maximum number of client connections (`max_clients`)
☞ Limiting the number of connections by source IP address (`max_per_ip`)
☞ Setting the maximum rate of data transfer per anonymous login (`anon_max_rate`)
☞ Setting the maximum rate of data transfer per non-anonymous login (`local_max_rate`)

Descriptions on this and more can be found in the `vsftpd.conf` man pages.

FTP SECURITY ISSUES

FTP has a number of security drawbacks, but you can overcome them in some cases. You can restrict an individual Linux user's access to non-anonymous FTP, and you can change the configuration to not display the FTP server's software version information, but unfortunately, though very convenient, FTP logins and data transfers are not encrypted.

The */etc/vsftpd.ftpusers* File

For added security, you may restrict FTP access to certain users by adding them to the list of users in the `/etc/vsftpd.ftpusers` file. The VSFTPD package creates this file with a number of entries for privileged users that normally shouldn't have FTP access. As FTP doesn't encrypt passwords, thereby increasing the risk of data or passwords being compromised, it is a good idea to let these entries remain and add new entries for additional security.

Anonymous Upload

If you want remote users to write data to your FTP server, then you should create a write-only directory within `/var/ftp/pub`. This will allow your users to upload but not access other files uploaded by other users. The commands you need are:

```
[root@bigboy tmp]# mkdir /var/ftp/pub/upload
[root@bigboy tmp]# chmod 722 /var/ftp/pub/upload
```

FTP Greeting Banner

Change the default greeting banner in the `vsftpd.conf` file to make it harder for malicious users to determine the type of system you have. The directive in this file is:

```
ftpd_banner= New Banner Here
```

Using SCP as Secure Alternative to FTP

One of the disadvantages of FTP is that it does not encrypt your username and password. This could make your user account vulnerable to an unauthorized attack from a person eavesdropping on the network connection. **Secure Copy (SCP)** and **Secure FTP (SFTP)** provide encryption and could be considered as an alternative to FTP for trusted users. `scp` does not support anonymous services, however, a feature that FTP does support.

TROUBLESHOOTING FTP

You should always test your FTP installation by attempting to use an FTP client to log into your FTP server to transfer sample files.

The most common sources of day-to-day failures are incorrect usernames and passwords.

Initial setup failures could be caused by firewalls along the path between the client and server blocking some or all types of FTP traffic. Typical symptoms of this are either connection timeouts or the ability to use the `ls` command to view the contents of a directory without the ability to either upload or download files. Follow the firewall rule guidelines to help overcome this problem. Connection problems could also be the result of typical network issues outlined in Chapter 4, "Simple Network Troubleshooting."

TUTORIAL

FTP has many uses, one of which is allowing numerous unknown users to download files. You have to be careful, because you run the risk of accidentally allowing unknown persons to upload files to your server. This sort of unintended activity can quickly fill up your hard drive with illegal software, images, and music for the world to download, which in turn can clog your server's Internet access and drive up your bandwidth charges.

FTP Users with Read-Only Access to a Shared Directory

In this example, anonymous FTP is not desired, but a group of trusted users need to have read-only access to a directory for downloading files. Here are the steps:

1. Disable anonymous FTP. Comment out the `anonymous_enable` line in the `vsftpd.conf` file:

```
# Allow anonymous FTP?
# anonymous_enable=YES
```

2. Enable individual logins by making sure you have the `local_enable` line uncommented in the `vsftpd.conf` file:

```
# Uncomment this to allow local users to log in.
local_enable=YES
```

3. Start VSFTP.

```
[root@bigboy tmp]# service vsftpd start
```

4. Create a user group and shared directory. In this case, use `/home/ftp-users` and a user group name of ftp-users for the remote users:

```
[root@bigboy tmp]# groupadd ftp-users
[root@bigboy tmp]# mkdir /home/ftp-docs
```

5. Make the directory accessible to the ftp-users group:

```
[root@bigboy tmp]# chmod 750 /home/ftp-docs
[root@bigboy tmp]# chown root:ftp-users /home/ftp-docs
```

6. Add users, and make their default directory `/home/ftp-docs`:

```
[root@bigboy tmp]# useradd -g ftp-users -d /home/ftp-docs user1
[root@bigboy tmp]# useradd -g ftp-users -d /home/ftp-docs user2
[root@bigboy tmp]# useradd -g ftp-users -d /home/ftp-docs user3
[root@bigboy tmp]# useradd -g ftp-users -d /home/ftp-docs user4
[root@bigboy tmp]# passwd user1
[root@bigboy tmp]# passwd user2
[root@bigboy tmp]# passwd user3
[root@bigboy tmp]# passwd user4
```

7. Copy files to be downloaded by your users into the `/home/ftp-docs` directory.

8. Change the permissions of the files in the `/home/ftp-docs` directory to read-only access by the group:

```
[root@bigboy tmp]# chown root:ftp-users /home/ftp-docs/*
[root@bigboy tmp]# chmod 740 /home/ftp-docs/*
```

Users should now be able to log in via FTP to the server using their new usernames and passwords. If you absolutely don't want any FTP users to be able to write to any directory, then you should set the `write_enable` line in your `vsftpd.conf` file to no:

```
write_enable = NO
```

Remember, you must restart VSFTPD for the configuration file changes to take effect.

Sample Login Session to Test Functionality

Here is a simple test procedure you can use to make sure everything is working correctly:

1. Check for the presence of a test file on the FTP client server.

```
[root@smallfry tmp]# ll
total 1
-rw-r--r-- 1 root root 0 Jan 4 09:08 testfile
[root@smallfry tmp]#
```

2. Connect to Bigboy via FTP:

```
[root@smallfry tmp]# ftp 192.168.1.100
Connected to 192.168.1.100 (192.168.1.100)
220 ready, dude (vsFTPd 1.1.0: beat me, break me)
Name (192.168.1.100:root): user1
331 Please specify the password.
Password:
230 Login successful. Have fun.
Remote system type is UNIX.
Using binary mode to transfer files.
ftp>
```

As expected, you can't do an upload transfer of testfile to bigboy:

```
ftp> put testfile
local: testfile remote: testfile
227 Entering Passive Mode (192,168,1,100,181,210)
553 Could not create file.
ftp>
```

But we can view and download a copy of the VSFTPD RPM on the FTP server bigboy:

```
ftp> ls
227 Entering Passive Mode (192,168,1,100,35,173)
150 Here comes the directory listing.
-rwxr----- 1 0 502 76288 Jan 04 17:06 vsftpd-1.1.0-1.i386.rpm
```

```
226 Directory send OK.
ftp> get vsftpd-1.1.0-1.i386.rpm vsftpd-1.1.0-1.i386.rpm.tmp
local: vsftpd-1.1.0-1.i386.rpm.tmp remote: vsftpd-1.1.0-
1.i386.rpm
227 Entering Passive Mode (192,168,1,100,44,156)
150 Opening BINARY mode data connection for vsftpd-1.1.0-
1.i386.rpm (76288 bytes).
226 File send OK.
76288 bytes received in 0.499 secs (1.5e+02 Kbytes/sec)
ftp> exit
221 Goodbye.
[root@smallfry tmp]#
```

As expected, an anonymous FTP fails:

```
[root@smallfry tmp]# ftp 192.168.1.100
Connected to 192.168.1.100 (192.168.1.100)
220 ready, dude (vsFTPd 1.1.0: beat me, break me)
Name (192.168.1.100:root): anonymous
331 Please specify the password.
Password:
530 Login incorrect.
Login failed.
ftp> quit
221 Goodbye.
[root@smallfry tmp]#
```

Now that testing is complete, you can make this a regular part of your FTP server's operation.

CONCLUSION

FTP is a very useful software application that can have enormous benefit to a Web site or to collaborative computing in which files need to be shared between business partners. Although insecure, it is universally accessible, because FTP clients are a part of all operating systems and Web browsers. If data encryption security is of great importance to you, then you should probably consider SCP as a possible alternative. You can find more information on it in Chapter 17, "Secure Remote Logins and File Copying."

TELNET, TFTP, and *xinetd*

In This Chapter

☞ Managing xinetd Programs
☞ TELNET
☞ Conclusion

Many network-enabled Linux applications don't rely on themselves to provide restricted access or bind to a particular TCP port; instead they often offload a lot of this work to a program suite made just for this purpose: xinetd.

Managing *xinetd* Programs

The xinetd RPM is installed by default in Fedora Linux and uses /etc/xinetd.conf as its main configuration file. Fortunately you usually don't have to edit this file, so day-to-day xinetd operation is frequently limited to only starting and stopping xinetd-managed applications.

Controlling *xinetd*

The scripts in the /etc/init.d directory control the starting and stopping of the xinetd daemon, and chkconfig controls its behavior at boot time.

You can start, stop, and restart xinetd after booting by using:

```
[root@bigboy tmp]# service xinetd start
[root@bigboy tmp]# service xinetd stop
[root@bigboy tmp]# service xinetd restart
```

251

To get `xinetd` configured to start at boot, you can use the `chkconfig` command.

```
[root@bigboy tmp]# chkconfig xinetd on
```

Controlling *xinetd*-Managed Applications

`Xinetd`-managed applications all store their configuration files in the `/etc/xinetd.d` directory. Each configuration file has a `disable` statement that you can set to yes or no. This governs whether `xinetd` is allowed to start them or not.

You don't have to edit these files to activate or deactivate the application. The `chkconfig` command does that for you automatically and also stops or starts the application accordingly too! Here is an example of the activation and deactivation of the Samba SWAT Web GUI management application:

```
[root@bigboy tmp]# chkconfig swat on
[root@bigboy tmp]# chkconfig swat off
```

TELNET

TELNET is a program that allows users to log into your server and get a command prompt just as if they were logged into the VGA console. The TELNET server RPM is installed and disabled by default on Fedora Linux.

One of the disadvantages of Telnet is that the data is sent as **clear text**. This means that it is possible for someone to use a network analyzer to peek into your data packets and see your username and password. A more secure method for remote logins would be via **Secure Shell (SSH),** which uses varying degrees of encryption.

In spite of this, the older TELNET application remains popular. Many network devices don't have SSH clients, making Telnet the only means of accessing other devices and servers from them. I'll show you how to limit your exposure to TELNET's insecurities later in this chapter.

Using The TELNET Client

The command to do remote logins via TELNET from the command line is simple. You enter the word "telnet" and then the IP address or server name to which you want to connect.

Here is an example of someone logging into a remote server named smallfry from server Bigboy. The user looks at the routing table and then logs out.

```
[root@bigboy tmp]# telnet 192.168.1.105
Trying 192.168.1.105...
Connected to 192.168.1.105.
Escape character is '^]'.

Linux 2.4.18-14 (smallfry.my-web-site.org) (10:35 on Sunday, 05
January 2003)

Login: peter
Password:
Last login: Fri Nov 22 23:29:44 on ttyS0
You have new mail.
[peter@smallfry peter]$
[peter@smallfry peter]$ netstat -nr
Kernel IP routing table
Destination       Gateway         Genmask            Flags  MSS Window irtt
Iface
255.255.255.255 0.0.0.0         255.255.255.255 UH       40  0       0
wlan0
192.168.1.0     0.0.0.0         255.255.255.0   U        40  0       0
wlan0
127.0.0.0       0.0.0.0         255.0.0.0       U        40  0       0
lo
0.0.0.0         192.168.1.1     0.0.0.0         UG       40  0       0
wlan0
[peter@smallfry peter]$ exit
logout

Connection closed by foreign host.
[root@bigboy tmp]#
```

Installing the TELNET Server Software

Older versions of Red Hat had the TELNET server installed by default. Fedora Linux doesn't do this, and you will have to install it yourself.

Most Red Hat and Fedora Linux software products are available in the RPM format. Downloading and installing RPMs isn't hard. If you need a refresher, Chapter 6, "Installing RPM Software," covers how to do this in detail.

When searching for the file, remember that the TELNET server RPM's filename usually starts with telnet-server followed by a version number, as in telnet-server-0.17-28.i386.rpm.

Setting Up a TELNET Server

To set up a TELNET server, use the `chkconfig` command to activate TELNET:

```
[root@bigboy tmp]# chkconfig telnet on
```

You can test whether the TELNET process is running with the `netstat` command, which is used to check the TCP/UDP ports on which your server is listening. If it isn't running, then there will be no response.

```
[root@bigboy tmp]# netstat -a | grep telnet
tcp         0         0          *:telnet          *:*
LISTEN
[root@bigboy tmp]#
```

You can also use the `chkconfig --list` command to verify that TELNET will be started on the next reboot:

```
[root@bigboy tmp]# chkconfig --list | grep telnet
        telnet: on
[root@bigboy tmp]#
```

Stopping a TELNET Server

Use the `chkconfig` command to deactivate TELNET, even after the next reboot:

```
[root@bigboy tmp]# chkconfig telnet off
```

Basic TELNET Security

There are a number of things you can do to improve the security of TELNET. For example, you should also try to ensure that TELNET sessions run over secure internal networks or across VPNs to reduce the risk of exposing sensitive data to unauthorized eyes. Check out some other options.

Let Telnet Listen on Another TCP Port

Letting TELNET run on an alternate TCP port doesn't encrypt the traffic, but it makes it less likely to be detected as TELNET traffic. Remember that this isn't a foolproof strategy; good port scanning programs can detect TELNET and other applications running on alternative ports. The steps are:

1. Edit your `/etc/services` file, and add an entry for a new service. Call it stelnet.

```
# Local services
stelnet             7777/tcp                              # "secure"
telnet
```

2. Copy the TELNET configuration file called `/etc/xinetd.d/telnet` and call it `/etc/xinetd.d/stelnet`:

```
[root@bigboy tmp]# cp /etc/xinetd.d/telnet /etc/xinetd.d/stel-
net
```

3. Edit the new `/etc/xinetd.d/stelnet` file. Make the new service stelnet, and add a `port` statement for TCP port 7777:

```
# default: on
# description: The telnet server serves telnet sessions
# unencrypted username/password pairs for authentication.
service stelnet
{
        flags           = REUSE
        socket_type     = stream
        wait            = no
        user            = root
        server          = /usr/sbin/in.telnetd
        log_on_failure  += USERID
        disable         = no
    port                = 7777
}
```

4. Use `chkconfig` to activate stelnet:

```
[root@bigboy tmp]# chkconfig stelnet on
```

5. Check to make sure your server is now listening on port 7777 with the `netstat` command:

```
[root@bigboy tmp]# netstat -an | grep 777
tcp   0  0 0.0.0.0:7777         0.0.0.0:*              LISTEN
[root@bigboy tmp]#
```

You should now be able to log into the new stelnet server on port 7777. This is done using the telnet command with the TCP port as the second argument.

```
[root@smallfry tmp]# telnet 192.168.1.100 7777
Trying 192.168.1.100...
Connected to 192.168.1.100.
Escape character is '^]'.
Fedora Core release 2 (Tettnang)
Kernel 2.6.8-1.521 on an i686
login:
```

Let TELNET Allow Connections from Trusted Addresses

You can restrict TELNET logins' access to individual remote servers by using the `only_from` keyword in the TELNET configuration file. Here's how:

1. Add a list of trusted servers to the `/etc/xinetd.d/telnet` file separated by spaces:

```
# default: on
# description: The telnet server serves telnet sessions
```

```
# unencrypted username/password pairs for authentication.
service telnet
{
        flags             = REUSE
        socket_type       = stream
        wait              = no
        user              = root
        server            = /usr/sbin/in.telnetd
        log_on_failure    += USERID
        disable           = no
        only_from         = 192.168.1.100 127.0.0.1
192.168.1.200
}
```

2. Restart TELNET:

```
[root@bigboy tmp]# chkconfig telnet off
[root@bigboy tmp]# chkconfig telnet on
```

3. Test the TELNET session. Servers that are not on the trusted list get the message "Connection closed by foreign host."

```
[root@smallfry tmp]# telnet 192.168.1.100
Trying 192.168.1.100...
Connected to 192.168.1.100.
Escape character is '^]'.
Connection closed by foreign host.
[root@smallfry tmp]#
```

TFTP

Many networking equipment manufacturers allow you to back up live configurations of their devices to centralized servers via the TFTP protocol. TFTP can be used with great versatility as a network management tool and not just for saving files. TFTP servers can be used to upload new configurations to replacement devices after serious hardware failures. They also can be used for uploading new versions of software to be run as network devices. Finally, they can be used to upload even partial configurations, such as files containing updated **access control lists (ACLs)** that restrict access to networks and even the regular application of new passwords.

TFTP may not be an application used regularly in a home, but it will become increasingly important in an expanding small office/home office (SOHO) environment, which is why the topic is covered here. The provided TFTP examples use equipment from Cisco Systems, a leading networking hardware manufacturer.

Installing the TFTP Server Software

Most Red Hat and Fedora Linux software products are available in the RPM
format. Downloading and installing RPMs isn't hard. If you need a refresher,
see Chapter 6.

When searching for the file, remember that the TFTP server RPM's filename usually starts with word `tftp-server` and is followed by a version number, as in: `tftp-server-0.33-3.i386.rpm`.

Configuring the TFTP Server

The procedure to set up a TFTP Server is straightforward.

By default, the TFTP application expects files to be located in the `/tftp-
boot` directory. Change this in the `/etc/xinetd.d/tftp` file via the `server_args`
option, or create your own directory just for this purpose and create a `/tftp-
boot` symbolic link to it.

It is usually best to place the TFTP files in a partition other than the root
partition. TFTP files of increasing size could eventually fill the partition,
affecting your ability to install new software or even the overall performance
of your system. This example creates a new `tftpboot` directory in the `/var` partition, and then creates a symbolic link that makes this directory appear to
also be the `/tftpboot` directory:

```
[root@bigboy tmp]# mv /tftpboot /var
[root@bigboy tmp]# ln -s /var/tftpboot /tftpboot
```

You must restart `xinetd` for the new configuration to take effect:

```
[root@bigboy tmp]# chkconfig tftp on
```

Each device must have a configuration file in the `/tftpboot` directory.
Here's an example of what to do for a SOHO firewall named pixfw and a configuration filename that matches Cisco's standard naming scheme of device-
name-config:

```
[root@bigboy tmp]# touch /tftpboot/pixfw-config
[root@bigboy tmp]# chmod 666 /tftpboot/pixfw-config
[root@bigboy tmp]# ll /tftpboot/
total 1631
-rw-rw-rw- 1 root root 3011 Oct 29 14:09 pixfw-config
[root@bigboy tmp]#
```

You can test whether the TFTP process is running with the `netstat` command, which is used to check the TCP/UDP ports on which your server is listening. If it isn't running then there will be no response.

```
[root@bigboy tmp]# netstat -a | grep tftp
udp        0        0 *:tftp                          *:*
[root@bigboy tmp]#
```

Saving Cisco Configurations to the TFTP Server

You'll now have to configure your Cisco router/firewall to use the TFTP server. The examples assume that the TFTP server's IP address is 192.168.1.100.

Cisco PIX Firewall

Follow these steps on a PIX firewall:

1. Log onto the device, get into Enable mode, and then enter the TFTP commands to initially configure TFTP:

```
pixfw> enable
Password: ********
pixfw# configure terminal
pixfw(config)# tftp-server inside 192.168.1.100 /pixfw-config
pixfw(config)# exit
```

2. Save the configuration to non-volatile memory:

```
pixfw# write memory
Building configuration...
Cryptochecksum: 3af43873 d35d6f06 51f8c999 180c2342
[OK]
pixfw#
```

3. Save the configuration to the TFTP server:

```
pixfw# write network
Building configuration...
TFTP write '/pixfw-config' at 192.168.1.100 on interface 1
[OK]
pixfw#
```

Your firewall configuration has now been successfully saved for later use in the event of unrecoverable human error or hardware failure.

Cisco Switch Running CATOS

To save the configuration of a Catalyst-series switch running CATOS, you need to log onto the device, get into Enable mode, and then enter the `write net` TFTP command:

```
ciscoswitch> (enable) wr net
This command shows non-default configurations only.
Use 'write network all' to show both default and non-default
configurations.
IP address or name of remote host? [192.168.1.100]
Name of configuration file? [ciscoswitch-config]
Upload configuration to ciscoswitch-config on 192.168.1.100 (y/n) [n]?
y
.........
Finished network upload. (30907 bytes)
ciscoswitch> (enable)
```

Cisco Router

To save the configuration of a router, log onto the device, get into Enable mode, switch to Configure mode, and then enter the TFTP commands:

```
ciscorouter> enable
ciscorouter# write net
Remote host [192.168.1.100]? 192.168.1.100
Name of configuration file to write [ciscorouter-config]? ciscorouter-
config
Write file ciscorouter-config on host 192.168.1.100? [confirm] y
ciscorouter# exit
```

Cisco CSS 11000 Arrowpoints

To save the configuration of a Cisco CSS-series load balancer, log onto the device and enter the TFTP commands as seen below:

```
ciscocss# copy running-config tftp 192.168.1.100 ciscocss-config
Working..(\) 100%
Connecting (/)
Completed successfully.

ciscocss# exit
```

Cisco Local Director

To save the configuration of a Cisco Local Director load balancer, log onto the device, get into Enable mode, switch to Configure mode, and then enter the TFTP commands:

```
ciscold> ena
Password:
ciscold# write net 192.168.1.100 ciscold-config
Building configuration...

writing configuration to //ciscold-config on 192.168.1.100:69 ...
[OK]
ciscold# exit
```

Uploading Cisco Configurations from the TFTP Server

From time to time you may have to upload configurations from your TFTP server to your network equipment. In this example, a small file containing a new encrypted password and access control list is uploaded from the TFTP server and inserted into a router configuration.

Sample Upload Configuration File

The configuration file is named `config.file`, and it looks like this:

```
!
! Set the console password
!
line con 0
 password 7 $1$qDwqJEjunK$tuff0HE/g31/b7G/IZ
!
! Delete and recreate access list #10
!
no access-list 10
access-list 10 permit 192.168.1.0  0.0.0.255
access-list 10 permit 192.168.10.0 0.0.0.255
```

Procedure to Upload Configuration File

Uploading the file can be done using either the `copy tftp: running-config` or the older `configure network` commands. In both cases, you are prompted for the IP address of the TFTP server and the name of the file with the configuration commands. The filename provided is always relative to the `/tftpboot` directory. So if the file was located in the `/tftpboot` directory, it would be referred to as `config.file`, but if it were in the `/tftpboot/configs` directory, it would be referred to as `/tftpboot/configs/config.file`.

Consider this sample `configure network` command:

```
ciscorouter>ena
Password:
ciscorouter#configure network
Host or network configuration file [host]?
This command has been replaced by the command:
        'copy <url> system:/running-config'
Address or name of remote host []? 192.168.1.100
Source filename []? config.file
Configure using tftp://192.168.1.100/config.file? [confirm]
Loading config.file from 192.168.1.100 (via FastEthernet0/0): !!!!!!
[OK - 26521/52224 bytes]

ciscorouter#
```

Here's a sample `copy tftp: running-config` command:

```
ciscorouter#copy tftp: running-config
Address or name of remote host []? 192.168.1.100
Source filename []? config.file
Destination filename [running-config]?
Accessing tftp://192.168.1.100/config.file...
Loading config.file from 192.168.1.100 (via FastEthernet0/0): !!!!!!
[OK - 26521/52224 bytes]

26521 bytes copied in 1.912 secs (26521 bytes/sec)
ciscorouter#
```

Always remember to permanently save your configurations to non-volatile RAM (NVRAM) afterwards with the `write memory` or `copy running-config startup-config`.

Using TFTP to Restore Your Router Configuration

In disastrous cases, where you have to replace a router completely, you can use TFTP to completely restore the configuration to the replacement device. If the replacement unit is identical, then you need to do very little editing of the saved configuration file, but expect to edit it if the interface names and software versions are different.

The procedure for restoring your configuration is simple:

1. Connect your router to the local network of the TFTP server.
2. Give your router the bare minimum configuration that allows it to ping your TFTP server (no access controls or routing protocols).
3. Use the `copy` command to copy the backup configuration from the TFTP server to your startup configuration in NVRAM.
4. Disconnect the router from the network.
5. Reload the router without saving the live running configuration to overwrite the startup configuration. On rebooting, the router will copy the startup configuration stored in NVRAM into a clean running configuration environment.
6. Log into the router via the console and verify the configuration is OK.
7. Reconnect the router to the networks on which it was originally connected.

The commands you need are:

```
ciscorouter> enable
Password: ********
ciscorouter# write erase
...
...
! Enter the commands to provide a bare minimum of connectivity to
! your TFTP server here. This includes IP addresses, a default route
! and the TFTP setup commands.
...
```

```
. . .
ciscorouter# copy tftp:file-name startup-config
ciscorouter# reload
```

Please be aware that the `write erase` command erases your NVRAM startup configuration; always use it with great care.

CONCLUSION

TELNET and TFTP are important applications in an overall systems administration strategy. They both have the shortcoming of not encrypting their data and therefore need to be used on secured networks for improved security. TFTP sessions don't even need a username and password, and the TFTP server process overwrites any existing file beneath its root directory in keeping with the instructions of the network engineer. Making mistakes with TFTP can be fairly easy to do, and you may want to consider automating the process by using a helper application, such as `expect`.

TELNET is a greater security risk as the connections are longer, and valuable usernames and passwords are exchanged, making eavesdropping easier and more lucrative for the hacker. I'd suggest that you use an encrypted TELNET replacement whenever possible. One such product, SSH, will be covered in Chapter 17, "Secure Remote Logins and File Copying."

Secure Remote Logins and File Copying

IN THIS CHAPTER

- ☞ A Quick Introduction to SSH Encryption
- ☞ Starting OpenSSH
- ☞ Testing the Status of SSH
- ☞ The `/etc/ssh/sshd_config` File
- ☞ Using SSH to Log Into a Remote Machine
- ☞ What to Expect with Your First Login
- ☞ Deactivating TELNET After Installing SSH
- ☞ Executing Remote Commands on Demand with SSH
- ☞ SCP: A Secure Alternative to FTP
- ☞ SFTP: Another Secure Alternative to FTP
- ☞ Using SSH and SCP Without a Password
- ☞ Conclusion

One of the most popular file transfer and remote login Linux applications is **OpenSSH**, which provides a number of ways to create encrypted remote terminal and file transfer connections between clients and servers. The OpenSSH **Secure Copy** (SCP) and **Secure FTP** (SFTP) programs are secure replacements for FTP, and **Secure Shell** (SSH) is often used as a stealthy alternative to TELNET. OpenSSH isn't limited to Linux; SSH and SCP clients are available for most operating systems including Windows.

A QUICK INTRODUCTION TO SSH ENCRYPTION

Data encryption is accomplished by using special mathematical equations to scramble the bits in a data stream to make it unreadable to anyone who does not have access to the corresponding decryption equation. The process is usually made even harder through the use of an encryption key that is used to modify the way the equations do the scrambling. You can recover the original data only if you have access to this key and the corresponding programs. Data encryption helps to prevent unauthorized users from having access to the data.

SSH uses the concept of randomly generated private and public keys to do its encryption. The keys are usually created only once, but you have the option of regenerating them should they become compromised.

A successful exchange of encrypted data requires the receiver to have a copy of the sender's public key beforehand. Here's how it's done with SSH.

When you log into an SSH server, you are prompted as to whether you want to accept the download of the server's public key before you can proceed. The SSH client's public key is uploaded to the server at the same time. This creates a situation in which the computers at each end of the SSH connection have each other's public keys and are able to decrypt the data sent from the other end of the encrypted link or "tunnel".

All the public keys that an SSH client's Linux user encounters are stored in a file named ~/.ssh/known_hosts along with the IP address that provided it. If a key and IP address no longer match, then SSH knows that something is wrong. For example, reinstalling the operating system or upgrading the SSH application might regenerate the keys. Of course, key changes can be caused by someone trying some sort of cyber attack as well. Always investigate changes to be safe. Your server's own public and private SSH keys are stored in the /etc/ssh/ directory.

Note

The .ssh directory is a hidden directory, as are all files and directories whose names begin with a period. The ls -a command lists all normal and hidden files in a directory. The ~/ notation is a universally accepted way of referring to your home directory and is recognized by all Linux commands.

Linux also uses other key files at the user level to provide the capability of password-less logins and file copying to remote servers using SSH and SCP. In this case, the SSH connection is established, and then the client automatically sends its public key which the server uses to match against a predefined list in the user's directory. If there is a match then the login is authorized. These files are also stored in your ~/.ssh directory and need to be specially generated. The id_dsa and id_dsa.pub files are your private and public keys respectively, and authorized_keys stores all the authorized public keys from remote hosts that may log into your account without the need for passwords (more on this later).

STARTING OPENSSH

OpenSSH is installed by default during Linux installations. Because SSH and SCP are part of the same application, they share the same configuration file and are governed by the same /etc/init.d/sshd startup script.

You can configure SSH to start at boot by using the chkconfig command.

```
[root@bigboy tmp]# chkconfig sshd on
```

You can also start, stop, and restart SSH after booting by running the sshd initialization script.

```
[root@bigboy tmp]# service sshd start
[root@bigboy tmp]# service sshd stop
[root@bigboy tmp]# service sshd restart
```

Remember to restart the SSH process every time you make a change to the configuration files for the changes to take effect on the running process.

TESTING THE STATUS OF SSH

You can test whether the SSH process is running with:

```
[root@bigboy tmp]# pgrep sshd
```

You should get a response of plain old process ID numbers.

THE /ETC/SSH/SSHD_CONFIG FILE

The SSH configuration file is called /etc/ssh/sshd_config. By default SSH listens on all your NICs and uses TCP port 22. Take a look at a snippet from configuration:

```
# The strategy used for options in the default sshd_config shipped
with
# OpenSSH is to specify options with their default value where
# possible, but leave them commented. Uncommented options change a
# default value.

#Port 22
#Protocol 2,1
#ListenAddress 0.0.0.0
#ListenAddress ::
```

SSH Versions 1 and 2

The original encryption scheme of SSH was adequate for its time but was eventually found to have a number of limitations. The answer to these was version 2. Always force your systems to operate exclusively with version 2 by setting the protocol statement in the /etc/ssh/sshd_config file to 2. Remember to restart SSH to make this take effect.

```
#
# File: /etc/ssh/sshd_config
#

Protocol 2
```

Change the TCP Port on Which SSH Listens

If you are afraid of people trying to hack in on a well known TCP port, then you can change port 22 to a location that won't interfere with other applications on your system, such as port 435. This is a rudimentary precaution only, because good network scanning programs can detect SSH running on alternative ports.

What you need to do is:

1. Use the netstat command to make sure your system isn't listening on port 435, using grep to filter out everything that doesn't have the string "435":

```
[root@bigboy root]# netstat -an | grep 435
[root@bigboy root]#
```

2. No response allows us to proceed. Change the Port line in /etc/ssh/sshd_config to mention 435 and remove the # at the beginning of the line. If port 435 is being used, pick another port and try again:

```
Port 435
```

3. Restart SSH:

```
[root@bigboy tmp]# service sshd restart
```

4. Check to ensure SSH is running on the new port:

```
[root@bigboy root]# netstat -an | grep 435
tcp    0    0    192.168.1.100:435    0.0.0.0:*    LISTEN
[root@bigboy root]#
```

Next, you'll discover how to actually log into systems using SSH.

USING SSH TO LOG INTO A REMOTE MACHINE

Using SSH is similar to TELNET. To log in from another Linux box use the `ssh` command with a `-l` to specify the username you wish to log in as. If you leave out the `-l`, your username will not change. Here are some examples for a server named Smallfry in your `/etc/hosts` file. You can also use the user-name@remote_server format as an alternative.

If you are user root and you want to log into Smallfry as yourself, use the command:

```
[root@bigboy tmp]# ssh smallfry
```

User root can also log into Smallfry as user peter via the default port 22:

```
[root@bigboy tmp]# ssh -l peter smallfry
```

or via port 435 using the `username@remote_server` alternative login format:

```
[root@bigboy tmp]# ssh -p 435 peter@smallfry
```

WHAT TO EXPECT WITH YOUR FIRST LOGIN

The first time you log in, you get a warning message saying that the remote host doesn't know about your machine and prompting you to store a copy of the remote host's SSH identification keys on your local machine. It will look something like this:

```
[root@bigboy tmp]# ssh smallfry
The authenticity of host 'smallfry (smallfry)' can't be established.
RSA key fingerprint is
5d:d2:f5:21:fa:07:64:0d:63:1b:3b:ee:a6:58:58:bb.
Are you sure you want to continue connecting (yes/no)? yes
Warning: Permanently added 'smallfry' (RSA) to the list of known
hosts. root@smallfry's password:
Last login: Thu Nov 14 10:18:45 2002 from 192.168.1.98
No mail.
[root@smallfry tmp]#
```

The key is stored in your `~/.ssh/known_hosts` file and you should never be prompted for this again.

SSH Failures Due to Linux Reinstallations

If Linux or SSH is reinstalled on the remote server, then the keys are regenerated and your SSH client will detect that this new key doesn't match the saved value in the known_hosts file. The SSH client will fail, erring on the side of caution to alert you to the possibility of a form of hacking attack:

```
[root@bigboy tmp]# ssh 192.168.1.102
@@@@@@@@@@@@@@@@@@@@@@@@@@@@@@@@@@@@@@@@@@@@@@@@@@@@@@@@@@@@@@
@    WARNING: REMOTE HOST IDENTIFICATION HAS CHANGED!      @
@@@@@@@@@@@@@@@@@@@@@@@@@@@@@@@@@@@@@@@@@@@@@@@@@@@@@@@@@@@@@@
IT IS POSSIBLE THAT SOMEONE IS DOING SOMETHING NASTY!
Someone could be eavesdropping on you right now (man-in-the-middle
attack)!
It is also possible that the RSA host key has just been changed.
The fingerprint for the RSA key sent by the remote host is
5d:d2:f5:21:fa:07:64:0d:63:1b:3b:ee:a6:58:58:bb.
Please contact your system administrator.
Add correct host key in /root/.ssh/known_hosts to get rid of this
message.
Offending key in /root/.ssh/known_hosts:2
RSA host key for 192.168.1.102 has changed and you have requested
strict checking.
Host key verification failed.
[root@bigboy tmp]#
```

If you are confident that the error is due to a reinstallation, then edit your ~/.ssh/known_hosts text file, removing the entry for the offending remote server. When you try connecting via SSH again, you'll be prompted to add the new key to your ~/.ssh/known_hosts file and the login session should proceed as normal after that.

DEACTIVATING TELNET AFTER INSTALLING SSH

You should always consider SSH over TELNET, because of the inherent data encryption features of SSH and the current widespread availability of SSH clients for both Linux and Windows.

By default, the TELNET server isn't installed with Fedora Linux. If you do decide to deactivate an active TELNET server on Fedora, then use the chkconfig command as detailed in Chapter 16, "TELNET, TFTP, and xinetd."

```
[root@bigboy tmp]# chkconfig telnet off
```

EXECUTING REMOTE COMMANDS ON DEMAND WITH SSH

A nice feature of SSH is that it is capable of logging in and executing single commands on a remote system. You just have to place the remote command, enclosed in quotes, at the end of the ssh command of the local server. In the example below, a user on server Smallfry who needs to know the version of the kernel running on server Bigboy (192.168.1.100) remotely runs the uname -a command. The command returns the version of 2.6.8-1.521 and the server's name, Bigboy:

```
[root@smallfry tmp]# ssh 192.168.1.100 "uname -a"
root@192.168.1.100's password:
Linux bigboy 2.6.8-1.521 #1 Mon Aug 16 09:01:18 EDT 2004 i686 i686
i386 GNU/Linux
[root@smallfry tmp]#
```

This feature can be very useful. You can combine it with password-free login, explained later in this chapter, to get the status of a remote server whenever you need it. More comprehensive monitoring may best be left to such purpose built programs as MRTG, which is covered in Chapter 22, "Monitoring Server Performance."

SCP: A SECURE ALTERNATIVE TO FTP

From a networking perspective, FTP isn't very secure, because usernames, passwords, and data are sent across the network unencrypted. More secure forms such as SFTP (Secure FTP) and SCP (Secure Copy) are available as a part of the OpenSSH package that is normally installed by default on Red Hat and Fedora Core. Remember, unlike FTP, SCP doesn't support anonymous downloads like FTP.

The Linux scp command for copying files has a format similar to that of the regular Linux cp command. The first argument is the source file and the second is the destination file. When copying to or from a remote server, SCP logs into the server to transfer the data and this therefore requires you to supply a remote server name, username, and password to successfully execute the command. The remote filename is therefore preceded by a prefix of the remote username and server name separated by an @ symbol. The remote filename or directory then follows separated by a colon. The format therefore looks like this:

```
username@servername:filename
username@servername:directoryname
```

For example, file `/etc/syslog.conf` on a server with IP address 192.168.1.100 that needs to be retrieved as user peter would have the format `peter@192.168.1.000:/etc/syslog.conf`, the entire `/etc` directory would be `peter@192.168.1.000:/etc/`.

Tip
You can download an easy-to-use Windows SCP client called WinSCP from `http://winscp.vse.cz/eng/`.

Copying Files to the Local Linux Box

If you understand how `scp` represents remote filenames, you can start copying files fairly easily. For example, to copy file `/tmp/software.rpm` on the remote machine to the local directory `/usr/rpm` use the commands:

```
[root@bigboy tmp]# scp root@smallfry:/tmp/software.rpm /usr/rpm
root@smallfry's password:
software.rpm                    100% 1011    27.6KB/s    00:00
[root@bigboy tmp]#
```

To copy the file `/tmp/software.rpm` on the remote machine to the local directory `/usr/rpm` using TCP port 435, use the commands:

```
[root@bigboy tmp]# scp -P 435 root@smallfry:/tmp/software.rpm /usr/rpm
root@smallfry's password:
software.rpm                    100% 1011    27.6KB/s    00:00
[root@bigboy tmp]#
```

Copying Files to the Remote Linux Box

Copying files to the local Linux server now becomes intuitive. For example, to copy file `/etc/hosts` on the local machine to directory `/tmp` on the remote server:

```
[root@bigboy tmp]# scp /etc/hosts root@192.168.1.103:/tmp
root@192.168.1.103's password:
hosts                           100% 1011    27.6KB/s    00:00
[root@bigboy tmp]#
```

To copy file `/etc/hosts` on the local machine to directory `/tmp` on the remote server via TCP port 435, use the commands:

```
[root@bigboy tmp]# scp -P 435 /etc/hosts root@192.168.1.103:/tmp
hosts                           100% 1011    27.6KB/s    00:00
[root@bigboy tmp]#
```

SFTP: ANOTHER SECURE ALTERNATIVE TO FTP

OpenSSH also has the SFTP program, which runs over an encrypted SSH session but whose commands mimic those of FTP. SFTP can be more convenient to use than SCP when you are uncertain of the locations of the files you want to copy, because it has the directory browsing abilities of FTP. Unlike FTP, SFTP doesn't support anonymous logins.

Here is a sample login sequence that logs in, gets help on the available commands, and downloads a file to the local server:

```
[root@bigboy tmp]# sftp 192.168.1.200
Connecting to 192.168.1.200...
root@192.168.1.200's password:
sftp> help
Available commands:
cd path                              Change remote directory to 'path'
lcd path                             Change local directory to 'path'
chgrp grp path                       Change group of file 'path' to 'grp'
chmod mode path                      Change permissions of file 'path' to
'mode'
...
...
sftp> ls
..

..

anaconda-ks.cfg
install.log
install.log.syslog
..

..
sftp> get install.log
install.log                          100%    17KB   39.4KB/s    00:00
sftp> exit
[root@bigboy tmp]#
```

USING SSH AND SCP WITHOUT A PASSWORD

From time to time you may want to write scripts that will allow you to copy files to a server, or login, without being prompted for passwords. This can make them simpler to write and also prevents you from having to embed the password in your code.

SCP has a feature that allows you to do this. You no longer have to worry about prying eyes seeing your passwords nor worry about your script breaking when someone changes the password. You can configure SSH to do this by generating and installing data transfer encryption keys that are tied to the IP addresses of the two servers. The servers then use these pre-installed keys to authenticate one another for each file transfer. As you may expect, this feature doesn't work well with computers with IP addresses that periodically change, such as those obtained via DHCP.

There are some security risks though. The feature is automatically applied to SSH as well. Someone could use your account to log into the target server by entering the username alone. It is therefore best to implement this using unprivileged accounts on both the source and target servers.

The example that follows enables this feature in one direction (from server Bigboy to server Smallfry) and only uses the unprivileged account called filecopy.

Configuration: Client Side

Here are the steps you need to do on the computer that acts as the SSH client:

1. Generate your SSH encryption key pair for the filecopy account. Press the Enter key each time you are prompted for a password to be associated with the keys. (Do *not* enter a password.)

```
[filecopy@bigboy filecopy]# ssh-keygen -t dsa
Generating public/private dsa key pair.
Enter file in which to save the key
(/filecopy/.ssh/id_dsa):
Enter passphrase (empty for no passphrase):
Enter same passphrase again:
Your identification has been saved in
/filecopy/.ssh/id_dsa.
Your public key has been saved in
/filecopy/.ssh/id_dsa.pub.
The key fingerprint is:
1e:73:59:96:25:93:3f:8b:50:39:81:9e:e3:4a:a8:aa
filecopy@bigboy
[filecopy@bigboy filecopy]#
```

2. These keyfiles are stored in the .ssh subdirectory of your home directory. View the contents of that directory. The file named id_dsa is your private key, and id_dsa.pub is the public key that you will be sharing with your target server. Versions other than Red Hat/Fedora may use different filenames, use the SSH man pages to verify this.

```
[filecopy@bigboy filecopy]# cd ~/.ssh
[filecopy@bigboy filecopy]# ls
id_dsa   id_dsa.pub   known_hosts
[filecopy@bigboy .ssh]#
```

3. Copy *only* the public key to the home directory of the account to which you will be sending the file.

```
[filecopy@bigboy .ssh]# scp id_dsa.pub \
filecopy@smallfry:public-key.tmp
```

Now, on to the server side of the operation.

Configuration: Server Side

Here are the steps you need to do on the computer that will act as the SSH server.

   1. Log into Smallfry as user filecopy. Create an `.ssh` subdirectory in your home directory and then go to it with `cd`.

```
[filecopy@smallfry filecopy]# ls
public-key.tmp
[filecopy@smallfry filecopy]# mkdir .ssh
[filecopy@smallfry filecopy]# chmod 700 .ssh
[filecopy@smallfry filecopy]# cd .ssh
```

   2. Append the `public-key.tmp` file to the end of the `authorized_keys` file using the `>>` append redirector with the `cat` command. The `authorized_keys` file contains a listing of all the public keys from machines that are allowed to connect to your Smallfry account without a password. Versions other than Red Hat/Fedora may use different filenames, use the SSH man pages to verify this.

```
[filecopy@smallfry .ssh]# cat ~/public-key.tmp >>
authorized_keys
[filecopy@smallfry .ssh]# rm ~/public-key.tmp
```

From now on you can use `ssh` and `scp` as user filecopy from server Bigboy to Smallfry without being prompted for a password.

CONCLUSION

Most Linux security books strongly recommend using SSH and SCP over TEL-NET and FTP because of their encryption capabilities. Despite this, there is still a place for FTP in the world thanks to its convenience in providing simple global access to files and TELNET, which is much easier to implement in price-sensitive network appliances than SSH. Consider all options when choosing your file transfer and remote login programs and select improved security whenever possible as the long-term benefits eventually outweigh the additional cost over time.

Configuring DNS

In This Chapter

- ☞ Introduction to DNS
- ☞ Downloading and Installing the BIND Packages
- ☞ Starting BIND
- ☞ The /etc/resolv.conf File
- ☞ Configuring a Caching Name Server
- ☞ Important File Locations
- ☞ Configuring a Regular Name Server
- ☞ Troubleshooting BIND
- ☞ Migrating Your Web Site In-House
- ☞ DHCP Considerations for DNS
- ☞ Simple DNS Security
- ☞ Conclusion

Domain Name System (DNS) converts the name of a Web site (www.linuxhome-networking.com) to an IP address (65.115.71.34). This step is important, because the IP address of a Web site's server, not the Web site's name, is used in routing traffic over the Internet. This chapter will explain how to configure your own DNS server to help guide Web surfers to your site.

INTRODUCTION TO DNS

Before you dig too deep in DNS, you need to understand a few foundation concepts on which the rest of the chapter will be built.

DNS Domains

Everyone in the world has a first name and a last, or family, name. The same thing is true in the DNS world: A family of Web sites can be loosely described as a **domain**. For example, the domain linuxhomenetworking.com has a number of children, such as www.linuxhomenetworking.com and mail.linuxhomenetworking.com for the Web and mail servers, respectively.

BIND

BIND is an acronym for the **Berkeley Internet Name Domain Project**, which is a group that maintains the DNS-related software suite that runs under Linux. The most well-known program in BIND is named, the daemon that responds to DNS queries from remote machines.

DNS Clients

A DNS client doesn't store DNS information; it must always refer to a DNS server to get it. The only DNS configuration file for a DNS client is the /etc/resolv.conf file, which defines the IP address of the DNS server it should use. You shouldn't need to configure any other files. You'll become well acquainted with the /etc/resolv.conf file soon.

Authoritative DNS Servers

Authoritative servers provide the definitive information for your DNS domain, such as the names of servers and Web sites in it. They are the last word in information related to your domain.

How DNS Servers Find Your Site Information

There are 13 **root authoritative DNS servers** (super duper authorities) that all DNS servers query first. These root servers know all the authoritative DNS servers for all the main domains—.com, .net, and the rest. This layer of servers keep track of all the DNS servers that Web site systems administrators have assigned for their sub domains.

For example, when you register your domain my-web-site.org, you are actually inserting a record on the .com DNS servers that point to the authoritative DNS servers you assigned for your domain. (More on how to register your site later.)

When to Use a DNS Caching Name Server

Most servers don't ask authoritative servers for DNS directly, they usually ask a **caching DNS server** to do it on their behalf. The caching DNS servers then store (or cache) the most frequently requested information to reduce the lookup overhead of subsequent queries.

If you want to advertise your Web site `www.my-web-site.org` to the rest of the world, then a regular DNS server is what you require. Setting up a caching DNS server is fairly straightforward and works whether or not your ISP provides you with a static or dynamic IP address.

After you set up your caching DNS server, you must configure each of your home network PCs to use it as their DNS server. If your home PCs get their IP addresses using DHCP, then you have to configure your DHCP server to make it aware of the IP address of your new DNS server, so that the DHCP server can advertise the DNS server to its PC clients. Off-the-shelf router/firewall appliances used in most home networks usually can act as both the caching DNS and DHCP server, rendering a separate DNS server is unnecessary.

You can find the configuration steps for a Linux DHCP server in Chapter 8, "Configuring the DHCP Server."

When to Use a Static DNS Server

If your ISP provides you with a fixed or static IP address, and you want to host your own Web site, then a regular authoritative DNS server would be the way to go. A caching DNS **name server** is used as a reference only, regular name servers are used as the authoritative source of information for your Web site's domain.

Note
Regular name servers are also caching name servers by default.

When To Use A Dynamic DNS Server

If your ISP provides your router/firewall with its IP address using DHCP, then you must consider **dynamic DNS** covered in Chapter 19, "Dynamic DNS." For now, I'm assuming that you are using static IP addresses.

How to Get Your Own Domain

Whether or not you use static or dynamic DNS, you need to register a domain.

Dynamic DNS providers frequently offer you a subdomain of their own site, such as `my-web-site.dnsprovider.com`, in which you register your domain on their site.

If you choose to create your very own domain, such as `my-web-site.org`, you have to register with a company specializing in static DNS registration and then point your registration record to the intended authoritative DNS for your domain. Popular domain registrars include VeriSign, Register Free, and Yahoo.

If you want to use a dynamic DNS provider for your own domain, then you have to point your registration record to the DNS servers of your dynamic DNS provider. (More details on domain registration are coming later in the chapter.)

Basic DNS Testing of DNS Resolution

As you know, DNS resolution maps a **fully qualified domain name** (FQDN), such as www.linuxhomenetworking.com, to an IP address. This is also known as a **forward lookup**. The reverse is also true: By performing a reverse lookup, DNS can determining the fully qualified domain name associated with an IP address.

Many different Web sites can map to a single IP address, but the reverse isn't true; an IP address can map to only one FQDN. This means that forward and reverse entries frequently don't match. The reverse DNS entries are usually the responsibility of the ISP hosting your site, so it is quite common for the reverse lookup to resolve to the ISP's domain. This isn't an important factor for most small sites, but some e-commerce applications require matching entries to operate correctly. You may have to ask your ISP to make a custom DNS change to correct this.

There are a number of commands you can use to do these lookups. Linux uses the host command, for example, but Windows uses nslookup.

The host Command

The host command accepts arguments that are either the fully qualified domain name or the IP address of the server when providing results. To perform a forward lookup, use the syntax:

```
[root@bigboy tmp]# host www.linuxhomenetworking.com
www.linuxhomenetworking.com has address 65.115.71.34
[root@bigboy tmp]#
```

To perform a reverse lookup:

```
[root@bigboy tmp]# host 65.115.71.34
34.71.115.65.in-addr.arpa domain name pointer 65-115-71-34.my-isp-
provider.net.
[root@bigboy tmp]#
```

As you can see, the forward and reverse entries don't match. The reverse entry matches the entry of the ISP.

The nslookup Command

The nslookup command provides the same results on Windows PCs. To perform forward lookup, use:

```
C:\> nslookup www.linuxhomenetworking.com
Server:   192-168-1-200.my-web-site.org
Address:  192.168.1.200

Non-authoritative answer:
Name:     www.linuxhomenetworking.com
Address:  65.115.71.34

C:\>
```

To perform a reverse lookup:

```
C:\> nslookup 65.115.71.34
Server:  192-168-1-200.my-web-site.org
Address:  192.168.1.200

Name:    65-115-71-34.my-isp-provider.net
Address:  65.115.71.34

C:\>
```

DOWNLOADING AND INSTALLING THE BIND PACKAGES

Most Red Hat and Fedora Linux software products are available in the RPM format. When searching for the file, remember that the BIND RPM's filename usually starts with the word "bind" followed by a version number, as in `bind-9.2.2.P3-9.i386.rpm`. (For more details on downloading RPMs, see Chapter 6, "Installing RPM Software.")

STARTING BIND

You can use the `chkconfig` command to get BIND configured to start at boot:

```
[root@bigboy tmp]# chkconfig named on
```

To start, stop, and restart BIND after booting, use:

```
[root@bigboy tmp]# service named start
[root@bigboy tmp]# service named stop
[root@bigboy tmp]# service named restart
```

Remember to restart the BIND process every time you make a change to the configuration file for the changes to take effect on the running process.

THE */ETC/RESOLV.CONF* FILE

DNS clients (servers not running BIND) use the `/etc/resolv.conf` file to determine both the location of their DNS server and the domains to which they belong. The file generally has two columns; the first contains a keyword, and the second contains the desired values separated by commas. See Table 18.1 for a list of keywords.

Table 18.1   Keywords in `/etc/resolv.conf`

Keyword	Value
nameserver	IP address of your DNS name server. There should be only one entry per `nameserver` keyword. If there is more than one name server, use multiple `nameserver` lines.
domain	The local domain name to be used by default. If the server is `bigboy.my-web-site.org`, then the entry would just be `my-web-site.org`.
search	If you refer to another server just by its name without the domain added on, DNS on your client appends the server name to each domain in this list and does a DNS lookup on each to get the remote servers' IP addresses. This is a handy time-saving feature, enabling you to refer to servers in the same domain by only their server name without having to specify the domain. The domains in this list must be separated by spaces.

Take a look at a sample configuration in which the client server's main domain is `my-web-site.org`, but it also is a member of domains `another-web-site.org` and `my-web-business.org`, which should be searched for shorthand references to other servers. Two name servers, 192.168.1.100 and 192.168.1.102, provide DNS name resolution:

```
search my-web-site.org another-web-site.org my-web-business.org
nameserver 192.168.1.100
nameserver 192.168.1.102
```

The first domain listed after the search directive *must* be the home domain of your network, in this case `my-web-site.org`. Placing a domain and search entry in the `/etc/resolv.conf` is redundant, therefore.

CONFIGURING A CACHING NAME SERVER

The Red Hat/Fedora default installation of BIND is configured to convert your Linux box into a caching name server. The only file you have to edit is `/etc/resolv.conf`; you'll have to comment out the reference to your previous DNS server (most likely your router) with a # or make it point to the server itself using the universal localhost IP address of 127.0.0.1.

So, your old entry of:

```
nameserver 192.168.1.1
```

would be replaced by a new entry of:

```
# nameserver 192.168.1.1
```

or

```
nameserver 127.0.0.1
```

The next step is to make all the other machines on your network point to the caching DNS server as their primary DNS server.

IMPORTANT FILE LOCATIONS

Red Hat/Fedora BIND normally runs as the **named** process owned by the unprivileged **named** user.

Sometimes BIND is also installed using Linux's chroot feature to not only run named as user named, but also to limit the files named can see. When installed, named is fooled into thinking that the directory /var/named/chroot is actually the root or / directory. Therefore, named files normally found in the /etc directory are found in /var/named/chroot/etc directory instead, and those you'd expect to find in /var/named are actually located in /var/named/chroot/var/named.

The advantage of the chroot feature is that if a hacker enters your system via a BIND exploit, the hacker's access to the rest of your system is isolated to the files under the chroot directory and nothing else. This type of security is also known as a **chroot jail**.

You can determine whether you have the chroot add-on RPM by using this command, which returns the name of the RPM:

```
[root@bigboy tmp]# rpm -q bind-chroot
bind-chroot-9.2.3-13
[root@bigboy tmp]#
```

There can be confusion with the locations: Regular BIND installs its files in the normal locations, and the chroot BIND add-on RPM installs its own versions in their chroot locations. Unfortunately, the chroot versions of some of the files are empty. Before starting Fedora BIND, copy the configuration files to their chroot locations:

```
[root@bigboy tmp]# cp -f /etc/named.conf /var/named/chroot/etc/
[root@bigboy tmp]# cp -f /etc/rndc.* /var/named/chroot/etc/
```

Before you go to the next step of configuring a regular name server, it is important to understand exactly where the files are located. Table 18.2 provides a map.

Table 18.2   Differences in Fedora and Red Hat DNS File Locations

File	Purpose	BIND `chroot` Location	Regular BIND Location
`named.conf`	Tells the names of the zone files to be used for each of your Web site domains	`/var/named/chroot/etc`	`/etc`
`rndc.key,` `rndc.conf`	Named authentication	`/var/named/chroot/etc`	`/etc`
zone files	Link all the IP addresses in your domain to their corresponding servers	`/var/named/chroot/var/named`	`/var/named`

Note

Fedora Core installs BIND `chroot` by default. Red Hat 9 and earlier versions don't.

CONFIGURING A REGULAR NAME SERVER

For the purposes of this tutorial, assume your ISP assigned you the subnet 97.158.253.24 with a subnet mask of 255.255.255.248 (/29).

Configuring *resolv.conf*

You'll have to make your DNS server refer to itself for all DNS queries by configuring the `/etc/resolv.conf` file to reference localhost only.

```
nameserver 127.0.0.1
```

Configuring *named.conf*

The `named.conf` file contains the main DNS configuration and tells BIND where to find the configuration files for each domain you own. This file usually has two zone areas:

☞ **Forward zone** file definitions list files to map domains to IP addresses
☞ **Reverse zone** file definitions list files to map IP addresses to domains

In this example, you'll set up the forward zone for www.my-web-site.org by placing entries at the bottom of the `named.conf` file. The zone file is named `my-site.zone`, and, although not explicitly stated, the file `my-site.zone` should be located in the default directory of `/var/named/chroot/var/named` in a `chroot` or in `/var/named` in a regular one. Use the code:

```
zone "my-web-site.org" {

        type master;
        notify no;
        allow-query { any; };
        file "my-site.zone";

};
```

In addition, you can insert additional entries in the `named.conf` file to reference other Web domains you host. Here is an example for `another-site.com` using a zone file named `another-site.zone`:

```
zone "another-site.com" {

        type master;
        notify no;
        allow-query { any; };
        file "another-site.zone";

};
```

Note

The `allow-query` directive defines the networks that are allowed to query your DNS server for information on any zone. For example, to limit queries to only your 192.168.1.0 network, you could modify the directive to:

```
allow-query { 192.168.1.0/24; };
```

Next, you have to format entries to handle the reverse lookups for your IP addresses. In most cases, your ISP handles the reverse zone entries for your public IP addresses, but you will have to create reverse zone entries for your SOHO/home environment using the 192.168.1.0/24 address space. This isn't important for the Windows clients on your network, but some Linux applications require valid forward and reverse entries to operate correctly.

The forward domain lookup process for `mysite.com` scans the FQDN from right to left to get increasingly more specific information about the authoritative servers to use. Reverse lookups operate similarly by scanning an IP address from left to right to get increasingly specific information about an address.

The similarity in both methods is that increasingly specific information is sought, but the noticeable difference is that for forward lookups the scan is from right to left, and for reverse lookups the scan is from left to right. This difference can be seen in the formatting of the zone statement for a reverse zone in `/etc/named.conf` file where the main `in-addr.arpa` domain, to which all IP addresses belong, is followed by the first three octets of the IP address in reverse order. This order is important to remember or else the configuration will fail. This reverse zone definition for `named.conf` uses a reverse zone file named `192-168-1.zone` for the 192.168.1.0/24 network:

```
zone "1.168.196.in-addr.arpa" {
    type master;
    notify no;
    file "192-168-1.zone";
};
```

Configuring the Zone Files

You need to keep a number of things in mind when configuring DNS zone files:

☞ In all zone files, you can place a comment at the end of any line by inserting a semi-colon character then typing in the text of your comment.

☞ By default, your zone files are located in the directory `/var/named` or
  `/var/named/chroot/var/named`.

☞ Each zone file contains a variety of records (SOA, NS, MX, A, and
  CNAME) that govern different areas of BIND.

Take a closer look at these entries in the zone file.

Time to Live Value

The very first entry in the zone file is usually the zone's **time to live (TTL)**
value. Caching DNS servers cache the responses to their queries from authoritative DNS servers. The authoritative servers not only provide the DNS
answer but also provide the information's time to live, which is the period for
which it's valid.

The purpose of a TTL is to reduce the number of DNS queries the authoritative DNS server has to answer. If the TTL is set to three days, then caching servers
use the original stored response for three days before making the query again:

```
$TTL 3D
```

BIND recognizes several suffixes for time-related values. A D signifies
days, a W signifies weeks, and an H signifies hours. In the absence of a suffix,
BIND assumes the value is in seconds.

DNS Resource Records

The rest of the records in a zone file are usually BIND resource records. They
define the nature of the DNS information in your zone files that's presented to
querying DNS clients. They all have the general format:

```
Name    Class    Type    Data
```

There are different types of records for **mail (MX)**, **forward lookups**
(A), **reverse lookups (PTR)**, **aliases (CNAME)** and overall zone definitions,

Start of Authority (SOA). The data portion is formatted according to the record type and may consist of several values separated by spaces. Similarly, the name is also subject to interpretation based on this factor.

The SOA Record

The first resource record is the SOA record, which contains general administrative and control information about the domain. It has the format:

```
Name Class Type Name-Server Email-Address Serial-No Refresh Retry
Expiry Minimum-TTL
```

The record can be long, and will sometimes wrap around on your screen. For the sake of formatting, you can insert new line characters between the fields as long as you insert parenthesis at the beginning and end of the insertion to alert BIND that part of the record will straddle multiple lines. You can also add comments to the end of each new line separated by a semicolon when you do this. Here is an example:

```
@        IN       SOA      ns1.my-web-site.org. hostmaster.my-web-site.org. (
                           2004100801            ; serial #
                           4H                    ; refresh
                           1H                    ; retry


             1W                        ; expiry
                1D  )                    ; minimum
```

Table 18.3 explains what each field in the record means.

Table 18.3 The SOA Record Format

Field	Description
Name	The root name of the zone. The @ sign is a shorthand reference to the current origin (zone) in the /etc/named.conf file for that particular database file.
Class	There are a number of different DNS classes. Home/SOHO will be limited to the IN or Internet class used when defining IP address mapping information for BIND. Other classes exist for non-Internet protocols and functions but are very rarely used.
Type	The type of DNS resource record. In the example, this is an SOA resource record. Other types of records exist, which I'll cover later.
Name-server	Fully qualified name of your primary name server. Must be followed by a period.
Email-address	The e-mail address of the name server administrator. The regular @ in the e-mail address must be replaced with a period instead. The e-mail address must also be followed by a period.
Serial-no	A serial number for the current configuration. You can use the format YYYYMMDD with single digit incremented number tagged to the end to provide an incremental value that provides some editing information.

continues

Table 18.3   continued

Field	Description
Refresh	Tells the slave DNS server how often it should check the master DNS server. Slaves aren't usually used in home/SOHO environments.
Retry	The slave's retry interval to connect the master in the event of a connection failure. Slaves aren't usually used in home/SOHO environments.
Expiry	Total amount of time a slave should retry to contact the master before expiring the data it contains. Future references will be directed towards the root servers. Slaves aren't usually used in home/SOHO environments.
Minimum-TTL	There are times when remote clients will make queries for subdomains that don't exist. Your DNS server will respond with a no domain or NXDOMAIN response that the remote client caches. This value defines the caching duration your DNS includes in this response.

So in the example, the primary name server is defined as `ns1.my-web-site.org` with a contact e-mail address of `hostmaster@my-web-site.org`. The serial number is 2004100801 with refresh, retry, expiry, and minimum values of 4 hours, 1 hour, 1 week, and 1 day, respectively.

NS, MX, A, PTR, and CNAME Records
Like the SOA record, the NS, MX, A, PTR, and CNAME records each occupy a single line with a very similar general format. Table 18.4 outlines the way they are laid out.

Table 18.4   NS, MX, A, PTR, and CNAME Record Formats

Record Type	Field Descriptions			
	Name Field	Class Field[2]	Type Field	Data Field
NS	Usually blank[1]	IN	NS	IP address or CNAME of the name server
MX	Domain to be used for mail; usually the same as the domain of the zone file itself.	IN	MX	Mail server DNS name
A	Name of a server in the domain	IN	A	IP address of server
CNAME	Server name alias	IN	CNAME	"A" record name for the server
PTR	Last octet of server's IP address	IN	PTR	Fully qualified server name

[1] If the search key to a DNS resource record is blank, it reuses the search key from the previous record. For the example, this is the SOA @ sign.

[2] For most home/SOHO scenarios, the Class field will always be IN or Internet. You should also be aware that IN is the default Class, and BIND assumes a record is of this type unless otherwise stated.

If you don't put a period at the end of a host name in a SOA, NS, A, or CNAME record, BIND will automatically tack on the zone file's domain name to the name of the host. So, BIND assumes an A record with www refers to www.my-web-site.org. This may be acceptable in most cases, but if you forget to put the period after the domain in the MX record for my-web-site.org, BIND attaches the my-web-site.org at the end, and you will find your mail server accepting mail only for the domain my-web-site.org.mysite.com.

Sample Forward Zone File

Now that you know the key elements of a zone file, it's time to examine a working example for the domain my-web-site.org:

```
;
; Zone file for my-web-site.org
;
; The full zone file
;
$TTL 3D
@        IN      SOA      ns1.my-web-site.org. hostmaster.my-web-
site.org. (
                         200211152        ; serial#
                         3600             ; refresh, seconds
                         3600             ; retry, seconds
                         3600             ; expire, seconds
                         3600 )           ; minimum, seconds
;
                 NS       www             ; Inet Address of nameserver

my-web-site.org.    MX       10 mail          ; Primary Mail Exchanger

;
localhost        A        127.0.0.1
bigboy           A        97.158.253.26
mail             CNAME    bigboy
ns1              CNAME    bigboy
www              CNAME    bigboy
```

Notice that in this example:

☞ Server ns1.my-web-site.org is the name server for my-web-site.org. In corporate environments there may be a separate name server for this purpose. Primary name servers are more commonly called ns1 and secondary name servers ns2.

☞ The minimum TTL value ($TTL) is three days, therefore remote DNS caching servers will store learned DNS information from your zone for three days before flushing it out of their caches.

☞ The MX record for my-web-site.org points to the server named mail.my-web-site.org

☞ ns1 and mail are actually CNAMEs or aliases for the Web server www. So here you have an example of the name server, mail server, and Web server being the same machine. If they were all different machines, then you'd have an A record entry for each:

```
www                    A           97.158.253.26
mail                   A           97.158u.253.134
ns                     A           97.158.253.125
```

It is a required practice to increment your serial number whenever you edit your zone file. When DNS is set up in a redundant configuration, the slave DNS servers periodically poll the master server for updated zone file information, and use the serial number to determine whether the data on the master has been updated. Failing to increment the serial number, even though the contents of the zone file have been modified, could cause your slaves to have outdated information.

Sample Reverse Zone File

Now you need to make sure that you can do a host query on all your home network's PCs and get their correct IP addresses. This is very important if you are running a mail server on your network, because sendmail typically relays mail only from hosts whose IP addresses resolve correctly in DNS. NFS, which is used in network-based file access, also requires valid reverse lookup capabilities.

This is an example of a zone file for the 192.168.1.x network. All the entries in the first column refer to the last octet of the IP address for the network, so the IP address 192.168.1.100 points to the name bigboy.my-web-site.org.

Notice how the main difference between forward and reverse zone files is that the reverse zone file only has PTR and NS records. Also the PTR records cannot have CNAME aliases.

```
;
; Filename: 192-168-1.zone
;
; Zone file for 192.168.1.x
;
$TTL 3D
@       IN      SOA     www.my-web-site.org.   hostmaster.my-web-
site.org. (
                        200303301              ; serial number
                        8H                     ; refresh, seconds
                        2H                     ; retry, seconds
                        4W                     ; expire, seconds
                        1D )                   ; minimum, seconds
;
                NS      www                    ; Nameserver Address
;
    100         PTR     bigboy.my-web-site.org.
```

```
103                    PTR          smallfry.my-web-site.org.
102                    PTR          ochorios.my-web-site.org.
105                    PTR          reggae.my-web-site.org.

32                     PTR          dhcp-192-168-1-32.my-web-site.org.
33                     PTR          dhcp-192-168-1-33.my-web-site.org.
34                     PTR          dhcp-192-168-1-34.my-web-site.org.
35                     PTR          dhcp-192-168-1-35.my-web-site.org.
36                     PTR          dhcp-192-168-1-36.my-web-site.org.
```

I included entries for addresses 192.168.1.32 to 192.168.1.36, which are the addresses the DHCP server issues. SMTP mail relay wouldn't work for PCs that get their IP addresses via DHCP if these lines weren't included.

You may also want to create a reverse zone file for the public NAT IP addresses for your home network. Unfortunately, ISPs won't usually delegate this ability for anyone with less than a Class C block of 256 IP addresses. Most home DSL sites wouldn't qualify.

What You Need to Know About NAT and DNS

The previous examples assume that the queries will be coming from the Internet with the zone files returning information related to the external 97.158.253.26 address of the Web server.

What do the PCs on your home network need to see? They need to see DNS references to the real IP address of the Web server, 192.168.1.100, because NAT won't work properly if a PC on your home network attempts to connect to the external 97.158.253.26 NAT IP address of your Web server.

Don't worry. BIND has a way around this called views. The views feature allows you to force BIND to use predefined zone files for queries from certain subnets. This means it's possible to use one set of zone files for queries from the Internet and another set for queries from your home network.

Here's a summary of how it's done:

1. Place your zone statements in the /etc/named.conf file in one of two views sections. The first section is called **internal** and lists the zone files to be used by your internal network. The second view called **external** lists the zone files to used for Internet users.

   For example, you could have a reference to a zone file called my-site.zone for lookups related to the 97.158.253.X network, which Internet users would see. This /etc/named.conf entry would be inserted in the external section. You could also have a file called my-site-home.zone for lookups by home users on the 192.168.1.0 network. This entry would be inserted in the internal section. Creating the my-site-home.zone file is fairly easy: Copy it from the my-site.zone file and replace all references to 97.158.253.X with references to 192.168.1.X.

2. You must also tell the DNS server which addresses you feel are internal and external. To do this, you must first define the internal and external networks with access control lists (ACLs) and then refer to these lists within their respective `view` section with the `match-clients` statement. Some built-in ACLs can save you time:

☞   `localhost`: Refers to the DNS server itself

☞   `localnets`: Refers to all the networks to which the DNS server is directly connected

☞   `any`: which is self explanatory

Note

You must place your `localhost`, `0.0.127.in-addr.arpa.` and period "." zone statements in the internal `views` section. Remember to increment your serial numbers!

Here is a sample configuration snippet for the `/etc/named.conf` file I use for my home network. All the statements below were inserted after the `options` and `controls` sections in the file.

```
// ACL statement

acl "trusted-subnet" { 192.168.17.0/24; };


view "internal" { // What the home network will see

    match-clients { localnets; localhost; "trusted-subnet"; };

        zone "." IN {
                type hint;
                file "named.ca";
        };

        zone "localhost" IN {
                type master;
                file "localhost.zone";
                allow-update { none; };
        };

        zone "0.0.127.in-addr.arpa" IN {
                type master;
                file "named.local";
                allow-update { none; };
        };

        // IPv6 Support
        zone
"0.0.0.0.0.0.0.0.0.0.0.0.0.0.0.0.0.0.0.0.0.0.0.0.0.0.0.0.0.0.0.0.ip6.arp
a" IN {
                type master;
                file "named.ip6.local";
                allow-update { none; };
```

```
                };

                // Prevents lookups for broadcast addresses ending in ".255"
                zone "255.in-addr.arpa" IN {
                        type master;
                        file "named.broadcast";
                        allow-update { none; };
                };

                // Prevents lookups for network addresses ending in ".0"
                zone "0.in-addr.arpa" IN {
                        type master;
                        file "named.zero";
                        allow-update { none; };
                };

                zone "1.168.192.in-addr.arpa" IN {
                        type master;
                        file "192-168-1.zone";
                        allow-update { none; };
                };

                zone "my-web-site.org" {
                        type master;
                        notify no;
                        file "my-site-home.zone";
                        allow-query { any; };
                };

                zone "another-site.com" {
                        type master;
                        notify no;
                        file "another-site-home.zone";
                        allow-query { any; };
                };

        };


    view "external" { // What the Internet will see

        match-clients { any; };
        recursion no;

                zone "my-web-site.org" {
                        type master;
                        notify no;
                        file "my-site.zone";
                        allow-query { any; };
                };


                zone "another-site.com" {
                        type master;
                        notify no;
                        file "another-site.zone";
                        allow-query { any; };
                };

        };
```

In this example, I included an ACL for network 192.168.17.0 /24 called `trusted-subnet` to help clarify the use of ACLs in more complex environments. Once the ACL was defined, I then inserted a reference to the `trusted-subnet` in the `match-clients` statement in the internal view. So in this case the local network (192.168.1.0 /24), the other trusted network (192.168.17.0), and `localhost` get DNS data from the zone files in the internal view. Remember, this is purely an example. The example home network doesn't need to have the ACL statement at all as the built in ACLs `localnets` and `localhost` are sufficient. The network won't need the `trusted-subnet` section in the `match-clients` line either.

Loading Your New Configuration Files

To load your new configuration files, first make sure your file permissions and ownership are okay in the `/var/named` directory:

```
[root@bigboy tmp]# cd /var/named
[root@bigboy named]# ll
total 6
-rw-r--r-- 1 named named 195  Jul 3 2001   localhost.zone
-rw-r--r-- 1 named named 2769 Jul 3 2001   named.ca
-rw-r--r-- 1 named named 433  Jul 3 2001   named.local
-rw-r--r-- 1 root  root  763  Oct 2 16:23 my-site.zone
[root@bigboy named]# chown named *
[root@bigboy named]# chgrp named *
[root@bigboy named]# ll
total 6
-rw-r--r-- 1 named named 195  Jul 3 2001   localhost.zone
-rw-r--r-- 1 named named 2769 Jul 3 2001   named.ca
-rw-r--r-- 1 named named 433  Jul 3 2001   named.local
-rw-r--r-- 1 named named 763  Oct 2 16:23 my-site.zone
[root@bigboy named]#
```

The configuration files above will not be loaded until you issue the proper command to restart the named process that controls DNS, but be sure to increment your configuration file serial number before doing this:

```
[root@bigboy tmp]# service named restart
```

Take a look at the end of your `/var/log/messages` file to make sure there are no errors.

Make Sure Your */etc/hosts* File is Correctly Updated

Chapter 3, "Linux Networking," explains how to correctly configure your `/etc/hosts` file. Some programs, such as `sendmail`, require a correctly configured `/etc/hosts` file even though DNS is correctly configured.

Configure Your Firewall

The sample network assumes that the BIND name server and Apache Web server software run on the same machine protected by a router/firewall. The actual IP address of the server is 192.168.1.100, which is a private IP address. You'll have to use NAT for Internet users to be able to gain access to the server via the chosen public IP address, namely 97.158.253.26. If your firewall is a Linux box, you may want to consider taking a look at Chapter 14, "Linux Firewalls Using `iptables`," which describes how to do the network address translation and allow DNS traffic through to your name server.

Fix Your Domain Registration

Remember to edit your domain registration for `my-web-site.org`, or whatever it is, so that at least one of the name servers is your new name server (97.158.253.26 in this case). Domain registrars, such as VeriSign and RegisterFree, usually provide a Web interface to help you manage your domain.

Once you've logged in with the registrar's username and password, you'll have to take two steps:

1. Create a new name server record entry for the IP address 97.158.253.26 to map to `ns.my-web-site.org` or `www.my-web-site.org` or whatever your name server is called. (This screen prompts you for both the server's IP address and name.)

2. Assign `ns.my-web-site.org` to handle your domain. This screen will prompt you for the server name only.

   Sometimes, the registrar requires at least two registered name servers per domain. If you only have one, then you could either create a second name server record entry with the same IP address, but different name, or you could give your Web server a second IP address using an IP `alias,` create a second NAT entry on your firewall and then create the second name server record entry with the new IP address, and different name.

It normally takes about three to four days for your updated DNS information to be propagated to all 13 of the world's root name servers. You'll therefore have to wait about this amount of time before starting to notice people hitting your new Web site.

You can use the chapter's troubleshooting section to test specific DNS servers for the information they have on your site. You'll most likely want to test your new DNS server, which should be up to date, plus a few well-known ones, which should have delayed values.

TROUBLESHOOTING BIND

One of the most common culprits of BIND problems is incorrectly located
chroot files. If you have the BIND chroot package installed, make sure the
configuration files are located in the chroot directory.

Here's a quick list of symptoms that indicate your files may not be
located correctly.

☞ The named daemon starts without loading any zone files. Here is a sample of the /var/log/messages file that shows that named doesn't load
them:.

```
Nov  9 17:35:41 bigboy named[1157]: starting BIND 9.2.3 -u
named -t /var/named/chroot
Nov  9 17:35:41 bigboy named[1157]: using 1 CPU
Nov  9 17:35:41 bigboy named[1157]: loading configuration
from '/etc/named.conf'
Nov  9 17:35:41 bigboy named[1157]: listening on IPv4 inter-
face lo, 127.0.0.1#53
Nov  9 17:35:41 bigboy named[1157]: listening on IPv4 inter-
face eth0, 10.41.32.71#53
Nov  9 17:35:41 bigboy named[1157]: command channel listening
on 127.0.0.1#953
Nov  9 17:35:41 bigboy named[1157]: command channel listening
on ::1#953
Nov  9 17:35:41 bigboy named[1157]: running
```

☞ Restarting named gives rndc "connect failed" messages:

```
[root@bigboy tmp]# service named restart
Stopping named: rndc: connect failed: connection refused
[  OK  ]
Starting named: [  OK  ]
[root@bigboy tmp]#
```

☞ The chroot files are empty:

```
[root@bigboy tmp]# cat /var/named/chroot/etc/named.conf
[root@bigboy tmp]# cat /var/named/chroot/etc/rndc.key
[root@bigboy tmp]#
```

To correctly relocate the files:

1. Copy the /etc/rndc.* and /etc/named.conf files to the
/var/named/chroot/etc/ directory:

```
[root@bigboy tmp]# cp -f /etc/rndc.* /var/named/chroot/etc/
[root@bigboy tmp]# cp /etc/named.conf /var/named/chroot/etc/
```

2. Restart named twice; it should shutdown correctly without error the
second time.

```
[root@bigboy tmp]# service named restart
Stopping named: rndc: connect failed: connection refused
```

```
[  OK  ]
Starting named: [  OK  ]
[root@bigboy tmp]# service named restart
Stopping named: [  OK  ]
Starting named: [  OK  ]
[root@bigboy tmp]#
```

3. Check your /var/log/messages file for the loading of the zone files:

```
Nov  9 17:36:34 bigboy named[1180]: zone 0.0.127.in-addr.arpa/IN:
loaded serial 1997022700
Nov  9 17:36:34 bigboy named[1180]: zone localhost/IN: loaded
serial 42
Nov  9 17:36:34 bigboy named[1180]: running
Nov  9 09:36:35 bigboy named: named startup succeeded
```

General Troubleshooting Steps

Once your files are in the right place, you can continue with the following troubleshooting steps:

1. Determine whether your DNS server is accessible on DNS UDP/TCP port 53. Lack of connectivity could be caused by a firewall with incorrect permit, NAT, or port forwarding rules to your DNS server. Failure could also be caused by the named process being stopped. It is best to test this from both inside your network and from the Internet.

Troubleshooting with TELNET is covered in Chapter 4, "Simple Network Troubleshooting."

2. Linux status messages are logged to the file /var/log/messages. Use it to make sure all your zone files are loaded when you start BIND/named. Check your /etc/named.conf file if they fail to do so. (Linux logging is covered in Chapter 5, "Troubleshooting with syslog."

```
Feb 21 09:13:13 bigboy named: named startup succeeded
Feb 21 09:13:13 bigboy named[12026]: loading configuration from
'/etc/named.conf'
Feb 21 09:13:13 bigboy named[12026]: no IPv6 interfaces found
Feb 21 09:13:13 bigboy named[12026]: listening on IPv4 interface
lo, 127.0.0.1#53
Feb 21 09:13:13 bigboy named[12026]: listening on IPv4 interface
wlan0, 192.168.1.100#53
Feb 21 09:13:13 bigboy named[12026]: listening on IPv4 interface
eth0, 172.16.1.100#53
Feb 21 09:13:14 bigboy named[12026]: command channel listening on
127.0.0.1#953
Feb 21 09:13:14 bigboy named[12026]: zone 0.0.127.in-addr.arpa/IN:
loaded serial 1997022700
Feb 21 09:13:14 bigboy named[12026]: zone 1.16.172.in-
addr.arpa/IN: loaded serial 51
Feb 21 09:13:14 bigboy named[12026]: zone 1.168.192.in-
addr.arpa/IN: loaded serial 51
```

```
Feb 21 09:13:14 bigboy named[12026]: zone my-web-site.org/IN:
loaded serial 2004021401
Feb 21 09:13:14 bigboy named[12026]: zone localhost/IN: loaded
serial 42
Feb 21 09:13:14 bigboy named[12026]: zone my-web-site.org/IN:
loaded serial 200301114
Feb 21 09:13:14 bigboy named[12026]: running
```

3. Use the `host` (`nslookup` in Windows) command for both forward and reverse lookups to make sure the zone files were configured correctly.

If this fails, try:

☞ Double check for your updated serial numbers in the modified files and also inspect the individual records within the files for mistakes.

☞ Ensure there isn't a firewall that could be blocking DNS traffic on TCP and/or UDP port 53 between your server and the DNS server.

☞ Use the `dig` command to determine whether the name server for your domain is configured correctly.

Here is an example of querying DNS server `ns1.my-web-site.org` for the IP address of `www.linuxhomenetworking.com`. (You can also replace the name server's name with its IP address.)

```
[root@bigboy tmp]# host www.linuxhomenetworking.com ns1.my-site.com
Using domain server:
Name: ns1.my-web-site.org
Address: 192.168.1.100#53
Aliases:

www.linuxhomenetworking.com has address 65.115.71.34
[root@bigboy tmp]#
```

Here is an example of querying your default DNS server for the IP address of `www.linuxhomenetworking.com`. As you can see, the name of the specific DNS server to query has been left off the end. Failure in this case could be due not only to an error on your BIND configuration or domain registration but also to an error in your DNS client's DNS server entry in your Linux /etc/resolv.conf file or the Windows TCP/IP properties for your NIC.

```
[root@bigboy tmp]# host www.linuxhomenetworking.com
www.linuxhomenetworking.com has address 65.115.71.34
[root@bigboy tmp]#
```

☞ You can also use the `dig` command to determine whether known DNS servers on the Internet have received a valid update for your zone. (Remember if you decide to change the DNS servers for your domain that it could take up to four days for it to propagate across the Internet.)

The format for the command is:

```
dig <domain-name> <name-server> soa
```

The name server is optional. If you specify a name server, then `dig` queries that name server instead of the Linux server's default name server. It is sometimes good to query both your name server, as well as a well-known name server such as `ns1.yahoo.com` to make sure your DNS records have propagated properly. The `dig` command only works with fully qualified domain names, because it doesn't refer to the `/etc/resolv.conf` file.

This command uses the local DNS server for the query. It returns the SOA record information and the addresses of the domain's DNS servers in the authority section.

```
[root@bigboy tmp]# dig linuxhomenetworking.com SOA
...
...
;; AUTHORITY SECTION:
linuxhomenetworking.com. 3600    IN      NS       ns1.my-isp-
provider.net.
linuxhomenetworking.com. 3600    IN      NS       ns2.my-isp-
provider.net.

;; ADDITIONAL SECTION:
ns1.my-isp-provider.net.         3600    IN      A        65.115.70.68
ns2.my-isp-provider.net.         3600    IN      A        65.115.70.69
...
...
[root@bigboy tmp]#
```

Here is a successful dig using DNS server `ns1.yahoo.com` for the query. As before, it returns the SOA record for the zone.

```
[root@bigboy tmp]# dig ns1.yahoo.com linuxhomenetworking.com SOA
...
...
;; AUTHORITY SECTION:
linuxhomenetworking.com. 3600    IN     NS       ns2.my-isp-provider.net.
linuxhomenetworking.com. 3600    IN     NS       ns1.my-isp-provider.net.

;; ADDITIONAL SECTION:
ns1.my-isp-provider.net.         3600    IN     A        65.115.70.68
ns2.my-isp-provider.net.         3600    IN     A        65.115.70.69
...
...[root@bigboy tmp]#
```

Sometimes your SOA dig will fail. This command uses the DNS server `ns1.yahoo.com` for the query. In this case the authority section doesn't know of the domain and points to the name server for the entire `.com` domain at VeriSign.

```
[root@bigboy tmp]# dig  ns1.yahoo.com linuxhomeqnetworking.com SOA
...
...

;; QUESTION SECTION:
;linuxhomeqnetworking.com.       IN      SOA

;; AUTHORITY SECTION:
com.                    0       IN      SOA     a.gtld-servers.net.
nstld.verisign-grs.com. 1077341254 1800 900 604800 900
...
...
[root@bigboy tmp]#
```

Possible causes of failure include:

☞ Typographical errors. In this case the misspelling "linuxhomeqnetwork-ing.com" was entered on the command line.

☞ Incorrect domain registration.

☞ Correct domain registration, but there is a lag in the propagation of the domain information across the Internet. Delays of up to four days are not uncommon.

☞ A firewall could be blocking DNS traffic on TCP and/or UDP port 53 between your server and the DNS server.

MIGRATING YOUR WEB SITE IN-HOUSE

It is important to have a detailed migration plan if you currently use an external company to host your Web site and wish to move the site to a server at home or in your office. At the very least your plan should include these steps:

1. There is no magic bullet that will allow you to tell all the caching DNS servers in the world to flush their caches of your zone file entries. Your best alternative is to request your existing service provider to set the TTL on my-web-site.org in the DNS zone file to a very low value, say one minute. As the TTL is usually set to a number of days, it will take at least three to five days for all remote DNS servers to recognize the change. Once the propagation is complete, it will take only one minute to see the results of the final DNS configuration switch to your new server. If anything goes wrong, you can then revert to the old configuration, knowing it will rapidly recover within minutes rather than days.

2. Set up your test server in-house. Edit the /etc/hosts file to make www.my-web-site.org refer to its own IP address, not that of the www.my-web-site.org site that is currently in production. This file is usually given a higher priority than DNS, therefore the test server will begin to think that www.my-web-site.org is really hosted on itself. You may also want to add an entry for mail.my-web-site.org if the new Web server is going to also be your new mail server.

3. Test your server-based applications from the server itself. This should include mail, Web, and so on.

4. Test the server from a remote client. You can test the server running as `www.my-web-site.org` even though DNS hasn't been updated. Just edit your `/etc/hosts` file on your Web browsing Linux PC to make `www.my-web-site.org` map to the IP address of the new server. In the case of Windows, the file would be `C:\WINDOWS\system32\drivers\etc`. You may also want to add an entry for `mail.my-web-site.org` if the new Web server is going to also be your new mail server. Your client will usually refer to these files first before checking DNS, hence you can use them to predefine some DNS lookups at the local client level only.

5. Once testing is completed, coordinate with your Web hosting provider to update your domain registration's DNS records for `www.my-web-site.org` to point to your new Web server. As the TTLs were set to one minute previously, you'll be able to see results of the migration within minutes.

6. Once complete, you can set the TTL back to the original value to help reduce the volume of DNS query traffic hitting your DNS server.

7. Fix your `/etc/hosts` files by deleting the test entries you had before.

8. You may also want to take over your own DNS. Edit your `my-web-site.org` DNS entries with VeriSign, RegisterFree or whoever you bought your domain from to point to your new DNS servers.

Remember, you don't have to host DNS or mail in-house, this could be left in the hands of your service provider. You can then migrate these services in-house as your confidence in hosting becomes greater.

Finally, if you have concerns that your service provider won't cooperate, then you could explain to the provider that you want to test its failover capabilities to a duplicate server that you host in-house. You can then decide whether the change will be permanent once you have failed over back and forth a few times.

DHCP CONSIDERATIONS FOR DNS

If you have a DHCP server on your network, you'll need to make it assign the IP address of the Linux box as the DNS server it tells the DHCP clients to use. If your Linux box is the DHCP server, then you may need to refer to Chapter 8, "Configuring the DHCP Server."

SIMPLE DNS SECURITY

DNS can reveal a lot about the nature of your domain. You should take some precautions to conceal some of the information for the sake of security.

Zone Transfer Protection

The `host` command does one DNS query at a time, but the `dig` command is much more powerful. When given the right parameters it can download the entire contents of your domain's zone file.

In this example, the AFXR zone transfer parameter is used to get the contents of the `my-web-site.org` zone file:

```
[root@smallfry tmp]# dig my-web-site.org AXFR

; <<>> DiG 9.2.3 <<>> my-web-site.org AXFR
;; global options:  printcmd
my-web-site.org.                3600     IN      SOA      www.my-web-
site.org. hostmaster.my-web-site.org. 2004110701 3600 3600 3600 3600
my-web-site.org.                3600     IN      NS       ns1.my-web-
site.org.
my-web-site.org.                3600     IN      MX       10 mail.my-web-
site.org.
192-168-1-96.my-web-site.org.  3600     IN      A        192.168.1.96
192-168-1-97.my-web-site.org.  3600     IN      A        192.168.1.97
192-168-1-98.my-web-site.org.  3600     IN      A        192.168.1.98
bigboy.my-web-site.org.        3600     IN      A        192.168.1.100
gateway.my-web-site.org.       3600     IN      A        192.168.1.1
localhost.my-web-site.org.     3600     IN      A        127.0.0.1
mail.my-web-site.org.          3600     IN      CNAME    www.my-web-
site.org.
ns1.my-web-site.org.           3600     IN      CNAME    www.my-web-
site.org.
ntp.my-web-site.org.           3600     IN      CNAME    www.my-web-
site.org.
smallfry.my-web-site.org.      3600     IN      A        192.168.1.102
www.my-web-site.org.           3600     IN      A        192.168.1.100
my-web-site.org.               3600     IN      SOA      www.my-web-
site.org. hostmaster.my-web-site.org. 2004110701 3600 3600 3600 3600
;; Query time: 16 msec
;; SERVER: 192.168.1.100#53(192.168.1.100)
;; WHEN: Sun Nov 14 20:21:07 2004
;; XFR size: 16 records
[root@smallfry tmp]#
```

This may not seem like an important security threat at first glance, but it is. Anyone can use this command to determine all your server's IP addresses and from the names determine what type of server it is and then launch an appropriate cyber attack.

In a simple home network, without master and slave servers, zone transfers should be disabled. You can do this by applying the `allow-transfer` directive to the global `options` section of your `named.conf` file.

```
options {
    allow-transfer {none;};
};
```

Once applied, your zone transfer test should fail.

```
[root@smallfry tmp]# dig my-web-site.org AXFR
...
...
; <<>> DiG 9.2.3 <<>> my-web-site.org AXFR
;; global options:  printcmd
; Transfer failed.
[root@smallfry tmp]#
```

Naming Convention Security

Your my-web-site.org domain will probably have a www and a mail subdomain, and they should remain obvious to all. You may want to adjust your DNS views so that to external users, your MySQL database server doesn't have the letters "DB" or "SQL" in the name, or that your firewall doesn't have the letters "FW" in its name either. This may be good for ease of reference within the company, but to the Internet these names provide rapid identification of the types of malicious exploits a hacker could use to break in. Web site security refers to anything that helps to guarantee the availability of the site; this is just one of many methods you can use.

CONCLUSION

DNS management is a critical part of the maintenance of any Web site. Fortunately, although they can be a little complicated, DNS modifications are usually infrequent, because the IP address of a server is normally fixed or static. This is not always the case. There are situations in which a server's IP address will change unpredictably and frequently, making DNS management extremely difficult. Dynamic DNS was created as a solution to this and is explained in Chapter 19, "Dynamic DNS."

Dynamic DNS

IN THIS CHAPTER

☞ Dynamic DNS Preparation

☞ Dynamic DNS and NAT Router/Firewalls

☞ DDNS Client Software: SOHO Router/Firewalls

☞ DDNS Client Software: Linux DDclient

☞ Testing Your Dynamic DNS

☞ Conclusion

In many home networking environments, the DSL or cable modem IP address is provided by DHCP and therefore changes from time to time. This can cause problems with the DNS zone files explained in Chapter 18, "Configuring DNS," which assume the IP address of a server won't change continuously. For this reason there are two broad types of DNS:

☞ **Static DNS:** This is used when your ISP provides you with unchanging fixed or static IP addresses. Your DNS server acts as the authoritative source of information for your my-web-site.org domain. You can consider static DNS as the "traditional" or "regular" form of DNS.

☞ **Dynamic DNS (DDNS):** Used when you get a changing dynamic IP addresses via DHCP from your ISP. You will have to use the services of a third-party DNS provider to provide DNS information for your my-web-site.org domain.

This chapter will explain the details of dynamic DNS configuration.

DYNAMIC DNS PREPARATION

Unlike DSL, most cable modem providers may not allow you to host sites at home by blocking inbound HTTP (TCP port 80) and SMTP mail (TCP port 25) while allowing most other TCP traffic through. Many DDNS providers are aware of this and provide a redirect service to bypass the problem. Under the system, Web queries first hit their servers on the regular TCP ports and then these servers automatically redirect the Web clients to use the IP address of your server on a different TCP port. Although this works well, it has disadvantages. The cost of the service can make hosting with a $10 /month virtual hosting service look very attractive, and many search engines do not index redirected pages.

Testing ISP Connectivity for Your Web Site

The very first thing you need to do is to determine whether your ISP allows inbound connections on your DSL or cable modem line. The easiest way to do this is to phone them and ask, but in some cases they'll say no when in fact the answer is yes. Here is how you can test it out for yourself.

Setup
You need to do some basic setup before testing can begin.

1. Configure and start Apache on your Linux Web server as described in Chapter 20, "The Apache Web Server."
2. Connect your Linux server directly to your cable or DSL modem, and configure the Ethernet NIC for DHCP as described in Chapter 3, "Linux Networking."
3. Make sure you can ping your default gateway.
4. Use the `ipconfig` command to determine the new IP address of your Web server. (This command is explained in Chapter 3 also.)
5. From the Linux Web server itself, try to TELNET to this IP address on port 80 as explained in Chapter 4, "Simple Network Troubleshooting."

If you can get through to the IP address on port 80, then you most likely have Apache configured correctly

Testing from the Internet
You may be able to see Web pages from the Web server itself. Ask a friend somewhere else on the Internet to try to TELNET to this IP address on port 80.

If port 80 works, then ask the friend to point a Web browser to the IP address and see whether a valid Web page appears. If your Linux server will eventually be placed behind a firewall, then adjust your network topology accordingly and test port 80 port forwarding to your Web server.

If the TELNET to port 80 fails, your ISP probably doesn't allow HTTP access to its networks. Configure your Web server to run on a different TCP port, preferably above 1024. The Apache `httpd.conf` file uses the `listen` directive to do this. Change it to your new value and restart `httpd`:

```
# httpd.conf listen directive, change "80" to some other value.
Listen 80
```

Test again with TELNET on this new port. If it works, try the Web browser test too. If the test port is 1234, then use a URL of `http://server-ip-address:1234`.

Note

If you are running `iptables`, remember to adjust the rules to match this new port or stop `iptables` temporarily while doing this testing.

If you can get a connection with correctly displayed pages on a nonstandard port, then you can additionally sign up for a redirect service with your DDNS provider as explained earlier.

Test Port Forwarding

If your Linux server will eventually be placed behind a firewall, then adjust your network topology accordingly. Let Apache run on port 80, and test port forwarding from the nonstandard port to port 80 on your Web server from the Internet.

One of the features of the `curl` troubleshooting utility is that it allows you to download a Web page's HTML code to your screen without interpreting it. You can determine the external IP address of your router or firewall by logging onto your Linux Web server and issuing the `curl` command to query the DynDNS.org IP information server. In this case, you are interested in only the line that tells you what the server thinks your IP address is; use the `grep` command to extract just that part. In this example, the IP address is 24.4.97.110:

```
[root@bigboy tmp]# curl -s http://checkip.dyndns.org/ | grep -i
address
<html><head><title>Current IP Check</title></head><body>Current IP
Address: 24.4.97.110</body></html>
[root@bigboy tmp]#
```

Registering DDNS

Once you decide to go ahead with DDNS, you need to choose between the broad categories of Dynamic DNS service:

☞ **Free Dynamic DNS:** Your Web site name will be a subdomain of the DDNS provider's domain. For example, if the DDNS provider's domain is `isp.net`, then your site will become `my-site.my-isp.net`. You can perform all the necessary steps on your DDNS service provider's Web site. Remember that this type of service may be undesirable for a company that wants to establish its own corporate identity. Another disadvantage is that you must rely on your DDNS provider staying in business or else you may lose your domain. When you own your own domain this worry largely goes away as you are fully in control of the DNS registration and renewal process.

☞ **Paid Customized DNS:** You can register the domain name of your choice and still host your Web site on a DHCP line.

If you choose to create your own domain and use a paid DDNS service, follow these steps:

1. Register your domains (such as `my-web-site.org`) with such companies as Verisign and RegisterFree.
2. Create an account with the DDNS provider, and register your Web sites (sometimes called hosts) as part of your domain (as in `www.my-web-site.org` and `mail.my-web-site.org`) with them. Your DDNS registration process will provide you with a username and password, which you'll need to use when configuring your DDNS client.
3. Update your domain information with your main DNS registrar (Verisign and RegisterFree) to tell them to direct queries to `*.my-web-site.org` to the DNS name servers of the DDNS provider.
4. Install a DDNS client on your Web servers that continuously runs, only updating the DDNS provider's DNS servers with the most current DHCP IP address of the site whenever it detects a change.

You should also be prepared for slower response times for your home-based site than if you were using a static IP and a regular DNS service.

Install a DDNS Client on Your Server

All DDNS service providers require that you use a DDNS client on your Web server that will periodically update the IP address information in your provider's DDNS record. The very popular one DDclient, for example, now comes in a RPM format.

DYNAMIC DNS AND NAT ROUTER/FIREWALLS

As discussed in Chapter 2, "Introduction to Networking," to conserve the limited number of IP addresses available for Internet purposes, most home router/firewalls use **network address translation** (**NAT**) to map a single, public, DHCP-obtained IP address to the many private IP addresses within your network.

NAT can fool the operation of some DDNS client software. In these cases, the software can report only the true IP address of the Linux box's NIC interface. If the Linux box is being protected behind a NAT router/firewall, then the NIC reports in its data stream to the DDNS provider a private IP address that no one can reach directly via the Internet. The reported value is therefore invalid.

Some DDNS providers use more intelligent clients, such as DDclient, that can be configured to let the DDNS provider record the public IP address from which the data stream is originating. Once this is done, you'll have to also configure your router/firewall to do **port forwarding** to make all HTTP traffic destined for the IP address of the router/firewall to be exclusively address translated using NAT and forwarded to a single server on your home network. If your firewall is Linux based, then the examples in Chapter 14, "Linux Firewalls Using `iptables`," will be helpful. Many Web-based small office/home office (SOHO) firewalls have easy interfaces to configure port forwarding; please refer to your manufacturer's manual on how to do this.

DDNS CLIENT SOFTWARE: SOHO ROUTER/FIREWALLS

Most new SOHO router/firewalls have built in dynamic DNS clients for one or more of the major DDNS service providers. There is usually a Dynamic DNS Web menu that prompts for the name of the service provider and your DDNS username and password. With this support, there is no need to install software on your Web server.

DDNS CLIENT SOFTWARE: LINUX DDCLIENT

One of the most commonly used clients is DDclient, which can overcome the NAT limitations of DDNS by actually logging into your SOHO firewall to determine the latest IP address information. Like most Red Hat and Fedora Linux software products, DDclient is available in the RPM format. (If you need a refresher on RPMs, consult Chapter 6, "Installing RPM Software.") You can usually download the software from your DDNS provider, or you can find it at `rpmfind.net`. The RPM name usually starts with `ddclient` followed by a version number, as in `ddclient-3.6.3-1.noarch.rpm`.

The /etc/ddclient.conf File

The ddclient.conf file is usually installed completely commented out, but provides many configuration examples for the most popular DDNS providers.

The most important general parameters to configure are:

☞ **Username:** Your DDNS account's login name
☞ **Password:** Your DDNS account's password
☞ **Use:** The method used to determine the IP address to advertise to the DDNS server

Some important DDNS provider parameters are:

☞ **Server:** The name of the DDNS provider's main DNS server
☞ **Protocol:** The methodology the DDNS client should use to communicate with the DDNS server
☞ **Your domain:** The domain to which your Web server will belong

You can use the `ddclient` command to determine the best `use` parameter to use in the `ddclient.conf` file. In this example, only the `use=web` option gives a valid Internet IP address and should be considered as a first option:

```
[root@bigboy tmp]# ddclient -daemon=0 -query
use=if, if=lo address is 127.0.0.1
use=if, if=wlan0 address is 192.168.1.100
use=web, web=dyndns address is 97.158.253.26
[root@bigboy tmp]#
```

Take a look at a sample configuration. This example specifies a username of my-account-login-name and a password of my-account-password using the dyndns DDNS service provider's settings to track the Web site named mysite-example.dnsalias.com.

```
# General Parameter Section
login=my-account-login-name
password=my-account-password

# DDNS Provider Parameters Section
server=members.dyndns.org,                        \
protocol=dyndns2                                   \
mysite-example.dnsalias.com
```

You can add *one* of the following `use` lines to the General Parameter Section near the top of the file to define the method that will be used to determine the correct IP address:

☞ **Query a well-known Internet server**: The Web method queries two well known servers run by DynDNS.org and DNSpark to determine the public Internet IP address of the Web server running the DDclient software. This method is the simplest as it requires no further information and handles NAT correctly.

```
use=web
```

☞ **Use the IP address of a specific server NIC**: You can also query the IP address of the DDclient Web server's NIC interface of your choice. This is probably most valuable for servers connected directly to the Internet, and not via NAT.

```
use=if, if=eth0
```

☞ **Login to your SOHO firewall for information**: The `ddclient.conf` file has a list of `use` statements for various vendor's firewalls. If your model isn't listed, you can create your own parameters as outlined in the DDclient read-me file. This option is good for NAT environments where the `use=web` option isn't considered a good alternative.

After editing your configuration file, you'll have to start ddclient as shown in the next section.

How to Get DDclient Started

You can configure DDclient to start at boot time using the `chkconfig` command:

```
[root@bigboy tmp]# chkconfig ddclient on
```

You can start, stop, and restart DDclient after boot time using the DDclient initialization script, as in:

```
[root@bigboy tmp]# service ddclient start
[root@bigboy tmp]# service ddclient stop
[root@bigboy tmp]# service ddclient restart
```

Remember to restart the DDclient process every time you make a change to the `ddclient.conf` file for the changes to take effect on the running process.

You can test whether the DDclient process is running with the `pgrep` command; you should get a response of plain old process ID numbers:

```
[root@bigboy tmp]# pgrep ddclient
```

Finding DDclient Help

The DDclient read-me and `ddclient.conf` files are good sources of information for doing custom configurations and troubleshooting. You can find the read-me file by using DDclient RPMs or the `locate` command.

Use the `rpm` command to get a list of installed DDclient files, one of which is the read-me file:

```
[root@bigboy tmp]# rpm -ql ddclient
...
/usr/doc/ddclient-3.6.3/README
...
[root@bigboy tmp]#
```

Alternately, you can use the `locate` command to find all the DDclient files:

```
[root@bigboy tmp]# locate ddclient | grep READ
/usr/doc/ddclient-3.6.3/README
/usr/doc/ddclient-3.6.3/README.cisco
[root@bigboy tmp]#
```

If the command doesn't work, try updating your locate database with the `locate -u` command followed by the `locate ddclient` command once more:

```
[root@bigboy tmp]# locate -u
```

TESTING YOUR DYNAMIC DNS

You can test your dynamic DNS by:

☞ Looking at the status page of your DNS provider and making sure the IP address that matches your www site is the same as your router/firewall's public IP address.

☞ Using the `host www.my-web-site.org` command from your Linux command prompt to determine whether you are getting a valid response. If you failed to add your host record, you will get an error message like:

```
[root@bigboy tmp]# host www.my-web-site.org

Server: 127.0.0.1
Address: 127.0.0.1#53

** server can't find www.my-web-site.org: NXDOMAIN
```

This error could be because your domain hasn't propagated fully throughout the Internet. You can test to make sure everything is okay by forcing NS lookup to query the name servers directly. The example below queries the miniDNS name server ns1.minidns.net:

```
[root@bigboy tmp]# host www.my-web-site.org ns1.minidns.net
www.my-web-site.org has address 97.158.253.26
[root@bigboy tmp]#
```

CONCLUSION

Always remember that dynamic DNS works, but it is frequently unreliable as residential class broadband data circuits are not monitored, maintained, or managed as closely as business class lines. It is a good starting place to help you become familiar with Web hosting, but as your Web site becomes busier and more financially important to you, you may need to consider a regular data center far away from spilt coffee and the washing machine that always trips the circuit breakers.

The Apache Web Server

IN THIS CHAPTER

- ☞ Downloading and Installing the Apache Package
- ☞ Starting Apache
- ☞ Configuring DNS for Apache
- ☞ DHCP and Apache
- ☞ General Configuration Steps
- ☞ Configuration: Multiple Sites and IP Addresses
- ☞ Using Data Compression on Web Pages
- ☞ Apache Running on a Server Behind a NAT Firewall
- ☞ Protecting Web Page Directories with Passwords
- ☞ The /etc/httpd/conf.d Directory
- ☞ Troubleshooting Apache
- ☞ Conclusion

Apache is probably the most popular Linux-based Web server application in use. Once you have DNS correctly set up and your server has access to the Internet, you'll need to configure Apache to accept surfers wanting to access your Web site.

This chapter explains how to configure Apache in a number of commonly encountered scenarios for small Web sites.

DOWNLOADING AND INSTALLING THE APACHE PACKAGE

Most Red Hat and Fedora Linux software products are available in the RPM format. When searching for the file, remember that the Apache RPM's filename usually starts with the word httpd followed by a version number, as in httpd-2.0.48-1.2.rpm. It is best to use the latest version of Apache. (For more on RPMs, see Chapter 6, "Installing RPM Software.")

STARTING APACHE

Use the chkconfig command to configure Apache to start at boot:

```
[root@bigboy tmp]# chkconfig httpd on
```

Use the httpd init script in the /etc/init.d directory to start, stop, and restart Apache after booting:

```
[root@bigboy tmp]# service httpd start
[root@bigboy tmp]# service httpd stop
[root@bigboy tmp]# service httpd restart
```

You can test whether the Apache process is running with:

```
[root@bigboy tmp]# pgrep httpd
```

You should get a response of plain old process ID numbers.

CONFIGURING DNS FOR APACHE

Remember that you will never receive the correct traffic unless you configure DNS for your domain to make your new Linux box Web server the target of the DNS domain's www entry. To do this, refer to Chapter 18, "Configuring DNS," or Chapter 19, "Dynamic DNS."

DHCP AND APACHE

As you remember, if your Internet connection uses DHCP to get its IP address, then you need to use dynamic DNS to get the correct Internet DNS entry for your Web server. If your Web server and firewall are different machines, then you probably also need to set up port forwarding for your Web traffic to reach the Web server correctly. (Chapter 19 explains port forwarding, as well.)

DHCP on your protected home network is different. In the book's sample topology, the Web server lives on the 192.168.1.0 home network protected by a firewall. The firewall uses NAT and port forwarding to pass Internet traffic on to the Web server. Remember that the IP address of your Web server can change if it gets its IP address using DHCP. This could cause your firewall port forwarding, not dynamic DNS, to break.

In this case, I recommend that your Web server on the 192.168.1.0 network uses a fixed, or static IP address that is outside of the range of the DHCP server to prevent you from having this problem.

GENERAL CONFIGURATION STEPS

The configuration file used by Apache is `/etc/httpd/conf/httpd.conf`. As for most Linux applications, you must restart Apache before changes to this configuration file take effect.

Where to Put Your Web Pages

All the statements that define the features of each Web site are grouped together inside their own `<VirtualHost>` section, or **container**, in the `httpd.conf` file. The most commonly used statements, or **directives,** inside a `<VirtualHost>` container are:

☞ `servername`: Defines the name of the Web site managed by the `<VirtualHost>` container. This is needed in named virtual hosting only, as I'll explain soon.

☞ `DocumentRoot`: Defines the directory in which the Web pages for the site can be found.

By default, Apache searches the `DocumentRoot` directory for an index, or home, page named `index.html`. So for example, if you have a `servername` of `www.my-web-site.org` with a `DocumentRoot` directory of `/home/www/site1/`, Apache displays the contents of the file `/home/www/site1/index.html` when you enter `http://www.my-web-site.org` in your browser.

Some editors, such as Microsoft FrontPage, create files with an .htm extension, not .html. This isn't usually a problem if all your HTML files have hyperlinks pointing to files ending in .htm as FrontPage does. The problem occurs with Apache not recognizing the topmost `index.htm` page. The easiest solution is to create a symbolic link (known as a shortcut to Windows users) called `index.html` pointing to the file `index.htm`. This then enables you to edit or copy the file `index.htm` with `index.html` being updated automatically. You'll almost never have to worry about `index.html` and Apache again!

This example creates a symbolic link to `index.html` in the `/home/www/site1` directory:

```
[root@bigboy tmp]# cd /home/www/site1
[root@bigboy site1]# ln -s index.htm index.html
[root@bigboy site1]# ll index.*
-rw-rw-r--    1 root     root        48590 Jun 18 23:43 index.htm
lrwxrwxrwx    1 root     root            9 Jun 21 18:05 index.html ->
index.htm
[root@bigboy site1]#
```

The `l` at the very beginning of the `index.html` entry signifies a link and the `->` indicates the link target.

The Default File Location

By default, Apache expects to find all its Web page files in the /var/www/html/ directory with a generic DocumentRoot statement at the beginning of httpd.conf. The examples in this chapter use the /home/www directory to illustrate how you can place them in other locations successfully.

File Permissions and Apache

Apache will display Web page files as long as they are world readable. You have to make sure all the files and subdirectories in your DocumentRoot have the correct permissions.

It is a good idea to have the files owned by a nonprivileged user so that Web developers can update the files using FTP or SCP without requiring the root password.

To do this:

1. Create a user with a home directory of /home/www.
2. Recursively change the file ownership permissions of the /home/www directory and all its subdirectories.
3. Change the permissions on the /home/www directory to 755, which allows all users, including the Apache's httpd daemon, to read the files inside.

The code you need is:

```
[root@bigboy tmp]# useradd -g users www
[root@bigboy tmp]# chown -R www:users /home/www
[root@bigboy tmp]# chmod 755 /home/www
```

Now test for the new ownership with the ll command:

```
[root@bigboy tmp]# ll /home/www/site1/index.*
-rw-rw-r--    1 www      users        48590 Jun 25 23:43 index.htm
lrwxrwxrwx    1 www      users            9 Jun 25 18:05 index.html ->
index.htm
[root@bigboy tmp]#
```

Tip
Be sure to FTP or SCP new files to your Web server as this new user. This will make all the transferred files automatically have the correct ownership.

If you browse your Web site after configuring Apache and get a "403 Forbidden" permissions-related error on your screen, then your files or directories under your DocumentRoot most likely have incorrect permissions. Appendix II, "Codes, Scripts, and Configurations," has a short script that you can use to recursively set the file permissions in a directory to match those expected by Apache. You may also have to use the Directory directive to make Apache serve the pages once the file permissions have been correctly set. If you have your files in the default /home/www directory, then this second step becomes unnecessary.

Security Contexts for Web Pages

Fedora Core 3 introduced the concept of security contexts as part of the Security Enhanced Linux (SELinux) definition. (See Appendix I, "Miscellaneous Linux Topics," for details.) A Web page may have the right permissions, but the Apache httpd daemon won't be able to read it unless you assign it the correct security context or daemon access permissions. Context-related configuration errors will give "403 Forbidden" browser messages, and in some cases, you will get the default Fedora Apache page where your expected Web page should be.

When a file is created, it inherits the security context of its parent directory. If you decide to place your Web pages in the default /var/www/ directory, then they will inherit the context of that directory and you should have very few problems.

The context of a file depends on the SELinux label it is given. The most important types of security label are listed in Table 20.1.

Table 20.1   SELinux Security Context File Labels

HTTP Code	Description
httpd_sys_content_t	The type used by regular static Web pages with .html and .htm extensions.
httpd_sys_script_ro_t	Required for CGI scripts to read files and directories.
httpd_sys_script_ra_t	Same as the httpd_sys_script_ro_t type, but also allows appending data to files by the CGI script.
httpd_sys_script_rw_t	Files with this type may be changed by a CGI script in any way, including deletion.
httpd_sys_script_exec_t	The type required for the execution of CGI scripts.

As expected, security contexts become important when Web pages need to be placed in directories that are not the Apache defaults. In this example, user root creates a directory /home/www/site1 in which the pages for a new Web site will be placed. Using the ls -Z command, you can see that the user_home_t security label has been assigned to the directory and the index.html page created in it. This label is not accessible by Apache.

```
[root@bigboy tmp]# mkdir /home/www/site1
[root@bigboy tmp]# ls -Z /home/www/
drwxr-xr-x   root     root      root:object_r:user_home_t    site1
[root@bigboy tmp]# touch /home/www/site1/index.html
[root@bigboy tmp]# ls -Z /home/www/site1/index.html
-rw-r--r--   root     root      root:object_r:user_home_t
/home/www/site1/index.html
[root@bigboy tmp]#
```

Accessing the `index.html` file via a Web browser gets a "Forbidden 403" error on your screen, even though the permissions are correct. Viewing the `/var/log/httpd/error_log` gives a "Permission Denied" message and the `/var/log/` messages file shows kernel audit errors.

```
[root@bigboy tmp]# tail /var/log/httpd/error_log
[Fri Dec 24 17:59:24 2004] [error] [client 216.10.119.250]
(13)Permission denied: access to / denied
[root@bigboy tmp]# tail /var/log/messages
Dec 24 17:59:24 bigboy kernel: audit(1103939964.444:0): avc:  denied
{ getattr } for  pid=2188 exe=/usr/sbin/httpd path=/home/www/site1
dev=hda5 ino=73659 scontext=system_u:system_r:httpd_t
tcontext=root:object_r:user_home_t tclass=dir
[root@bigboy tmp]#
```

SELinux security context labels can be modified using the `chcon` command. Recognizing the error, user root uses `chcon` with the `-R` (recursive) and `-h` (modify symbolic links) qualifiers to modify the label of the directory to `httpd_sys_content_t` with the `-t` qualifier.

```
[root@bigboy tmp]# chcon  -R -h -t httpd_sys_content_t /home/www/site1
[root@bigboy tmp]# ls -Z /home/www/site1/
-rw-r--r--  root      root      root:object_r:httpd_sys_content_t
index.html
[root@bigboy tmp]#
```

Browsing now works without errors. User root won't have to run the `chcon` command again for the directory, because new files created in the directory will inherit the SELinux security label of the parent directory. You can see this when the file `/home/www/site1/test.txt` is created:

```
[root@bigboy tmp]# touch /home/www/site1/test.txt
[root@bigboy tmp]# ls -Z /home/www/site1/
-rw-r--r--  root      root      root:object_r:httpd_sys_content_t
index.html
-rw-r--r--  root      root      root:object_r:httpd_sys_content_t
test.txt
[root@bigboy tmp]#
```

Security Contexts for CGI Scripts

You can use Apache to trigger the execution of programs called **Common Gateway Interface** (**CGI**) scripts. CGI scripts can be written in a variety of languages, including PERL and PHP, and can be used to do such things as generate new Web page output or update data files. A Web page's Submit button usually has a CGI script lurking somewhere beneath. By default, CGI scripts are placed in the `/var/www/cgi-bin/` directory as defined by the

ScriptAlias directive you'll find in the httpd.conf file, which I'll discuss in more detail later.

```
ScriptAlias /cgi-bin/ "/var/www/cgi-bin/"
```

In the default case, any URL with the string /cgi-bin/ will trigger Apache to search for an equivalent executable file in this directory. So, for example, the URL http://192.168.1.100/cgi-bin/test/test.cgi actually executes the script file /var/www/cgi-bin/test/test.cgi.

SELinux contexts have to be modified according to the values in Table 20.1 for a CGI script to be run in another directory or to access data files. In the example case, the PERL script test.cgi was created to display the word "Success" on the screen of your Web browser.

```
#!/usr/bin/perl

# CGI Script "test.cgi"

print qq(
<html>
<head>
<meta http-equiv="Content-Language" content="en-us">
<meta http-equiv="Content-Type" content="text/html">
<title>Linux Home Networking</title>
</head>
<body>
<p align="center"><font size="7">Success!</font></p>
</body>
</html>
);
```

The ScriptAlias directive was set to point to /home/www/cgi-bin/ instead of /var/www/cgi-bin/.

```
ScriptAlias /cgi-bin/ "/home/www/cgi-bin/"
```

User root creates the /home/www/cgi-bin/ directory, changes the directory's security context label to httpd_sys_script_exec_t, and then creates the script /home/www/cgi-bin/test/test.cgi with the correct executable file permissions.

```
[root@bigboy tmp]# mkdir -p /home/www/cgi-bin/test
[root@bigboy tmp]# chcon -h -t httpd_sys_script_exec_t /home/www/cgi-bin/
[root@bigboy tmp]# mkdir /home/www/cgi-bin/test
[root@bigboy tmp]# ls -Z /home/www/cgi-bin
drwxr-xr-x  root     root       root:object_r:httpd_sys_script_exec_t test
[root@bigboy tmp]# vi /home/www/cgi-bin/test/test.cgi
[root@bigboy tmp]# chmod o+x /home/www/cgi-bin/test/test.cgi
[root@bigboy tmp]#
```

Accessing the URL `http://192.168.1.100/cgi-bin/test/test.cgi` is successful. Problems occur when the same `test.cgi` file needs to be used by a second Web site housed on the same Web server. The file is copied to a directory `/web/cgi-bin/site2/` governed by the `ScriptAlias` in the second Web site's `<VirtualHost>` container (explained later), but the security context label isn't copied along with it.

```
ScriptAlias /cgi-bin/ "/web/cgi-bin/site2/"
```

The file inherits the context of its new parent.

```
[root@bigboy tmp]# cp /home/www/cgi-bin/test/test.cgi /web/cgi-
bin/site2/test.cgi
[root@bigboy tmp]# ls -Z /web/cgi-bin/site2/test.cgi
-rw-r--r-x  root       root       root:object_r:tmp_t
/web/cgi-bin/site2/test.cgi
[root@bigboy tmp]#
```

Permission denied and kernel audit errors occur once more; you can fix them only by changing the security context of the `test.cgi` file.

```
[root@bigboy tmp]# tail /var/log/httpd/error_log
[Fri Dec 24 18:36:08 2004] [error] [client 216.10.119.250]
(13)Permission denied: access to /cgi-bin/texcelon/test.cgi denied
[root@bigboy tmp]# tail /var/log/messages
Dec 24 18:36:08 bigboy kernel: audit(1103942168.549:0): avc:   denied
{ getattr } for  pid=2191 exe=/usr/sbin/httpd path=/web/cgi-
bin/site2/test.cgi dev=hda5 ino=77491
scontext=system_u:system_r:httpd_t tcontext=root:object_r:tmp_t
tclass=file
[root@bigboy tmp]#
```

Note

If you find security contexts too restrictive, you can turn them off system wide by editing your `/etc/selinux/config` file, modifying the SELINUX parameter to disabled. SELinux will be disabled after your next reboot.

Named Virtual Hosting

You can make your Web server host more than one site per IP address by using Apache's **named virtual hosting** feature. You use the `NameVirtualHost` directive in the `/etc/httpd/conf/httpd.conf` file to tell Apache which IP addresses will participate in this feature.

The <VirtualHost> containers in the file then tell Apache where it should look for the Web pages used on each Web site. You must specify the IP address for which each <VirtualHost> container applies.

Named Virtual Hosting Example

Consider an example in which the server is configured to provide content on 97.158.253.26. In the code that follows, notice that within each <VirtualHost> container you specify the primary Web site domain name for that IP address with the ServerName directive. The DocumentRoot directive defines the directory that contains the index page for that site.

You can also list secondary domain names that will serve the same content as the primary ServerName using the ServerAlias directive.

Apache searches for a perfect match of NameVirtualHost, <VirtualHost>, and ServerName when making a decision as to which content to send to the remote user's Web browser. If there is no match, then Apache uses the first <VirtualHost> in the list that matches the target IP address of the request.

This is why the first <VirtualHost> statement contains an asterisk: to indicate it should be used for all other Web queries.

```
NameVirtualHost 97.158.253.26

<VirtualHost *>
    Default Directives. (In other words, not site #1 or site #2)
</VirtualHost>

<VirtualHost 97.158.253.26>
    servername www.my-web-site.org
    Directives for site #1
</VirtualHost>

<VirtualHost 97.158.253.26>
    servername www.another-web-site.org
    Directives for site #2
</VirtualHost>
```

Be careful with using the asterisk in other containers. A <VirtualHost> with a specific IP address always gets higher priority than a <VirtualHost> statement with an * intended to cover the same IP address, even if the ServerName directive doesn't match. To get consistent results, try to limit the use of your <VirtualHost *> statements to the beginning of the list to cover any other IP addresses your server may have.

You can also have multiple NameVirtualHost directives, each with a single IP address, in cases where your Web server has more than one IP address.

IP-Based Virtual Hosting

The other virtual hosting option is to have one IP address per Web site, which is also known as **IP-based virtual hosting**. In this case, you will *not* have a

NameVirtualHost directive for the IP address, and you must only have a single `<VirtualHost>` container per IP address.

Also, because there is only one Web site per IP address, the ServerName directive isn't needed in each `<VirtualHost>` container, unlike in named virtual hosting.

IP Virtual Hosting Example: Single Wild Card

In this example, Apache listens on all interfaces, but gives the same content. Apache displays the content in the first `<VirtualHost *>` directive even if you add another right after it. Apache also seems to enforce the single `<VirtualHost>` container per IP address requirement by ignoring any ServerName directives you may use inside it.

```
<VirtualHost *>
    DocumentRoot /home/www/site1
</VirtualHost>
```

IP Virtual Hosting Example: Wild Card and IP Addresses

In this example, Apache listens on all interfaces, but gives different content for addresses 97.158.253.26 and 97.158.253.27. Web surfers get the site1 content if they try to access the Web server on any of its other IP addresses.

```
<VirtualHost *>
    DocumentRoot /home/www/site1
</VirtualHost>

<VirtualHost 97.158.253.26>
    DocumentRoot /home/www/site2
</VirtualHost>

<VirtualHost 97.158.253.27>
    DocumentRoot /home/www/site3
</VirtualHost>
```

Virtual Hosting and SSL

Because it makes configuration easier, system administrators commonly replace the IP address in the `<VirtualHost>` and NameVirtualHost directives with the * wildcard character to indicate all IP addresses.

If you installed Apache with support for secure HTTPS/SSL, which is used frequently in credit card and shopping cart Web pages, then wild cards won't work. The Apache SSL module demands at least one explicit `<VirtualHost>` directive for IP-based virtual hosting. When you use wild cards, Apache interprets it as an overlap of name-based and IP-based `<VirtualHost>`

directives and gives error messages because it can't make up its mind about which method to use:

```
Starting httpd: [Sat Oct 12 21:21:49 2002] [error] VirtualHost
_default_:443 -- mixing * ports and non-* ports with a NameVirtualHost
address is not supported, proceeding with undefined results
```

If you try to load any Web page on your Web server, you'll also see the error:

```
Bad request!

Your browser (or proxy) sent a request that this server could not
understand.
If you think this is a server error, please contact the webmaster
```

The best solution to this problem is to use wild cards more sparingly. Don't use virtual hosting statements with wild cards except for the very first <VirtualHost> directive that defines the Web pages to be displayed when matches to the other <VirtualHost> directives cannot be found. Here is an example:

```
NameVirtualHost *

<VirtualHost *>
    Directives for other sites
</VirtualHost>

<VirtualHost 97.158.253.28>
    Directives for site that also run on SSL
</VirtualHost>
```

CONFIGURATION: MULTIPLE SITES AND IP ADDRESSES

To help you better understand the edits needed to configure the /etc/httpd/conf/httpd.conf file, I'll walk you through an example scenario. The parameters are:

☞ The Web site's systems administrator previously created DNS entries for www.my-web-site.org, my-web-site.org, www.my-web-business.org, and default.my-web-site.org to map to the IP address 97.158.253.26 on this Web server. The domain www.another-web-site.org is also configured to point to alias IP address 97.158.253.27. The administrator wants to be able to get to test.my-web-site.org on all the IP addresses.

☞ Traffic to www.my-web-site.org, my-web-site.org, and www.my-web-business.org must get content from subdirectory site2. Hitting these URLs causes Apache to display the contents of index.html in this directory.

☞ Traffic to test.my-web-site.org must get content from subdirectory site3.

☞ Named virtual hosting will be required for 97.158.253.26 as in this case we have a single IP address serving different content for a variety of domains. A NameVirtualHost directive for 97.158.253.26 is therefore required.

☞ Traffic going to www.another-web-site.org will get content from directory site4.

☞ All other domains pointing to this server that don't have a matching ServerName directive will get Web pages from the directory defined in the very first <VirtualHost> container: directory site1. Site default.my-web-site.org falls in this category.

Table 20.2 summarizes these requirements.

Table 20.2   Web Hosting Scenario Summary

Domain	IP address	Directory	Type of Virtual Hosting
www.my-web-site.org my-web-site.org www.my-web-business.org	97.158.253.26	Site2	Name based
test.my-web-site.org	97.158.253.27	Site3	Name based (Wild card)
www.another-web-site.org	97.158.253.27	Site1	Name based
default.my-web-site.org All other domains	97.158.253.26	Site1	Name based

How do these requirements translate into code? Here is a sample snippet of a working httpd.conf file:

```
ServerName localhost
NameVirtualHost 97.158.253.26
NameVirtualHost 97.158.253.27

#
# Match a webpage directory with each website
#
<VirtualHost *>
    DocumentRoot /home/www/site1
</VirtualHost>

<VirtualHost 97.158.253.26>
    DocumentRoot /home/www/site2
    ServerName www.my-web-site.org
    ServerAlias my-web-site.org, www.my-web-business.org
</VirtualHost>
```

```
<VirtualHost 97.158.253.27>
    DocumentRoot /home/www/site3
    ServerName test.my-web-site.org
</VirtualHost>

<VirtualHost 97.158.253.27>
    DocumentRoot /home/www/site4
    ServerName www.another-web-site.org
</VirtualHost>


#
# Make sure the directories specified above
# have restricted access to read-only.
#
<Directory "/home/www/*">
    Order allow,deny
    Allow from all

    AllowOverride FileInfo AuthConfig Limit
    Options MultiViews -Indexes SymLinksIfOwnerMatch IncludesNoExec
    <Limit GET POST OPTIONS>
      Order allow,deny
      Allow from all
    </Limit>

    <LimitExcept GET POST OPTIONS>
      Order deny,allow
      Deny from all
    </LimitExcept>

</Directory>
```

These statements would normally be found at the very bottom of the file where the virtual hosting statements reside. The last section of this configuration snippet has some additional statements to ensure read-only access to your Web pages with the exception of Web-based forms using POSTs (pages with "submit" buttons). Remember to restart Apache every time you update the `httpd.conf` file for the changes to take effect on the running process.

Note

You will have to configure your DNS server to point to the correct IP address used for each of the Web sites you host. Chapter 18 shows you how to configure multiple domains, such as `my-web-site.org` and `another-web-site.org`, on your DNS server.

Testing Your Web Site Before DNS Is Fixed

You may not be able to wait for DNS to be configured correctly before starting your project. The easiest way to temporarily bypass this is to modify the hosts file on the Web developer's client PC or workstation (not the Apache server).

By default, PCs and Linux workstations query the hosts file first before checking DNS, so if a value for `www.my-web-site.org` is listed in the file, that's what
the client will use.

The Windows equivalent of the Linux `/etc/hosts` file is named `C:\`
`WINDOWS\system32\drivers\etc\hosts`. You need to open and edit it with a text
editor, such as Notepad. Here you could add an entry similar to:

```
97.158.253.26              www.my-web-site.org
```

Do not remove the localhost entry in this file.

Disabling Directory Listings

Be careful to include any `index.html` pages in each subdirectory under your
`DocumentRoot` directory, because if one isn't found, Apache will default to giving
a listing of all the files in that subdirectory. Say, for example, you create a subdirectory named `/home/www/site1/example` under `www.my-web-site.org`'s
`DocumentRoot` of `/home/www/site1/`. Now you'll be able to view the contents of the
file `my-example.html` in this subdirectory if you point your browser to:

```
http://www.my-web-site.org/example/my-example.html
```

If curious surfers decide to see what the index page is for `www.my-web-`
`site.org/example`, they would type the link:

```
http://www.my-web-site.org/example
```

Apache lists all the contents of the files in the `example` directory if it can't
find the `index.html` file. You can disable the directory listing by using a -
`Indexes` option in the `<Directory>` directive for the `DocumentRoot` like this:

```
<Directory "/home/www/*">
   . . .
   . . .
   . . .
   Options MultiViews -Indexes SymLinksIfOwnerMatch IncludesNoExec
```

Remember to restart Apache after the changes. Users attempting to
access the nonexistent index page will now get a "403 Access Denied" message.

Note

When setting up a `yum` server it's best to enable directory listings for the RPM subdirectories. This allows Web surfers to double-check the locations of files through
their browsers.

Handling Missing Pages

You can tell Apache to display a predefined HTML file whenever a surfer attempts to access a non-index page that doesn't exist. You can place this statement in the `httpd.conf` file, which will make Apache display the contents of `missing.htm` instead of a generic "404 File Not Found" message:

```
ErrorDocument 404 /missing.htm
```

Remember to put a file with this name in each `DocumentRoot` directory. You can see the `missing.htm` file I use by trying the nonexistent link:

```
http://www.linuxhomenetworking.com/bogus-file.htm
```

Notice that this gives the same output as:

```
http://www.linuxhomenetworking.com/missing.htm.
```

USING DATA COMPRESSION ON WEB PAGES

Apache also has the ability to dynamically compress static Web pages into `gzip` format and then send the result to the remote Web surfers' Web browser. Most current Web browsers support this format, transparently uncompressing the data and presenting it on the screen. This can significantly reduce bandwidth charges if you are paying for Internet access by the megabyte.

First you need to load Apache version 2's `deflate` module in your `httpd.conf` file and then use `Location` directives to specify which type of files to compress. After making these modifications and restarting Apache, you will be able to verify from your `/var/log/httpd/access_log` file that the sizes of the transmitted HTML pages have shrunk.

Compare the file sizes in this Apache log:

```
[root@ bigboy tmp]# grep dns-static /var/log/httpd/access_log
...
...
67.119.25.115 - - [15/Feb/2003:23:06:51 -0800] "GET /dns-static.htm
HTTP/1.1" 200 15190 "http://www.linuxhomenetworking.com/sendmail.htm"
"Mozilla/4.0 (compatible; MSIE 5.5; Windows NT 4.0; AT&T CSM6.0; YComp
5.0.2.6)"
...
...
[root@ bigboy tmp]#
```

and the corresponding directory listing:

```
[root@ bigboy tmp]# ll /web-dir/dns-static.htm
-rw-r--r--     1 user         group        78350 Feb 15 00:53
/home/www/ccie/dns-static.htm
[root@bigboy tmp]#
```

As you can see, 78,350 bytes shrunk to 15,190 bytes—that's almost 80% compression.

Compression Configuration Example

You can insert these statements just before your virtual hosting section of your httpd.conf file to activate the compression of static pages. Remember to restart Apache when you do.

Note

Fedora's version of httpd.conf loads the compression module mod_deflate by default. This means that the LoadModule line (the first line of the example snippet) is not required for Fedora. The location statements are required, however.

```
LoadModule deflate_module modules/mod_deflate.so

<Location />

    # Insert filter
    SetOutputFilter DEFLATE

    # Netscape 4.x has some problems...
    BrowserMatch ^Mozilla/4 gzip-only-text/html

    # Netscape 4.06-4.08 have some more problems
    BrowserMatch ^Mozilla/4\.0[678] no-gzip

    # MSIE masquerades as Netscape, but it is fine
    BrowserMatch \bMSIE !no-gzip !gzip-only-text/html

    # Don't compress images
    SetEnvIfNoCase Request_URI \
        \.(?:gif|jpe?g|png)$ no-gzip dont-vary


    # Make sure proxies don't deliver the wrong content
    Header append Vary User-Agent env=!dont-vary

</Location>
```

APACHE RUNNING ON A SERVER BEHIND A NAT FIREWALL

If your Web server is behind a NAT firewall and you are logged on a machine behind the firewall as well, then you may encounter problems when trying to access www.mysite.com of www.another-web-site.org. Because of NAT (network address translation), firewalls frequently don't allow access from their protected network to IP addresses that they masquerade on the outside.

For example, Linux Web server Bigboy has an internal IP address of 192.168.1.100, but the firewall presents it to the world with an external IP address of 97.158.253.26 via NAT/masquerading. If you are on the inside, 192.168.1.X network, you may find it impossible to hit URLs that resolve in DNS to 97.158.253.26.

There is a two-part solution to this problem:

Step 1: Configure Virtual Hosting on Multiple IPs

You can configure Apache to serve the correct content when accessing www.mysite.com or www.another-web-site.org from the outside, and also when accessing the specific IP address 192.168.1.100 from the inside. Fortunately Apache allows you to specify multiple IP addresses in the <VirtualHost> statements to help you overcome this problem.

Here is an example:

```
NameVirtualHost 192.168.1.100
NameVirtualHost 97.158.253.26

<VirtualHost 192.168.1.100 97.158.253.26>
    DocumentRoot /www/server1
    ServerName www.my-web-site.org
    ServerAlias bigboy, www.another-web-site.org
</VirtualHost>
```

Step 2: Configure DNS Views

You now need to fix the DNS problem that NAT creates. Users on the Internet need to access IP address 97.158.253.26 when visiting www.my-web-site.org and users on your home network need to access IP address 192.168.1.100 when visiting the same site.

You can configure your DNS server to use views which makes your DNS server give different results depending on the source IP address of the Web surfer's PC doing the query. Chapter 18 explains how to do this in detail.

> **Tip**
>
> If you have to rely on someone else to do the DNS change, then you can edit your
> PC's hosts file as a quick and dirty temporary solution to the problem. Remember
> that this will fix the problem on your PC alone.

PROTECTING WEB PAGE DIRECTORIES WITH PASSWORDS

You can password protect content in both the main and subdirectories of your
DocumentRoot fairly easily. I know people who allow normal access to their regular Web pages, but require passwords for directories or pages that show MRTG
or Webalizer data. This example shows how to password protect the /home/www
directory:

1. Use Apache's htpasswd password utility to create username/password
   combinations independent of your system login password for Web page
   access. You have to specify the location of the password file, and if it does-
   n't yet exist, you have to include a -c, or create, switch on the command
   line. I recommend placing the file in your /etc/httpd/conf directory, away
   from the DocumentRoot tree where Web users could possibly view it. Here
   is an example for a first user named peter and a second named paul:

   ```
   [root@bigboy tmp]# htpasswd -c /etc/httpd/conf/.htpasswd peter
   New password:
   Re-type new password:
   Adding password for user peter
   [root@bigboy tmp]#

   [root@bigboy tmp]# htpasswd /etc/httpd/conf/.htpasswd paul
   New password:
   Re-type new password:
   Adding password for user paul
   [root@bigboy tmp]#
   ```

2. Make the .htpasswd file readable by all users:

   ```
   [root@bigboy tmp]# chmod 644 /etc/httpd/conf/.htpasswd
   ```

3. Create a .htaccess file in the directory to which you want password control with these entries:

   ```
   AuthUserFile /etc/httpd/conf/.htpasswd
   AuthGroupFile /dev/null
   AuthName EnterPassword
   AuthType Basic
   require user peter
   ```

   Remember this password protects the directory and all its subdirectories.
   The AuthUserFile tells Apache to use the .htpasswd file. The require user
   statement tells Apache that only user peter in the .htpasswd file should

have access. If you want all `.htpasswd` users to have access, replace this line with `require valid-user`. `AuthType Basic` instructs Apache to accept basic unencrypted passwords from the remote users' Web browser.

4. Set the correct file protections on your new `.htaccess` file in the directory `/home/www`:

```
[root@bigboy tmp]# chmod 644 /home/www/.htaccess
```

5. Make sure your `/etc/httpd/conf/http.conf` file has an `AllowOverride` statement in a `<Directory>` directive for any directory in the tree above `/home/www`. In this example below, all directories below `/var/www/` require password authorization:

```
<Directory /home/www/*>
    AllowOverride AuthConfig
</Directory>
```

6. Make sure that you have a `<VirtualHost>` directive that defines access to `/home/www` or another directory higher up in the tree:

```
<VirtualHost *>
    ServerName 97.158.253.26
    DocumentRoot /home/www
</VirtualHost>
```

7. Restart Apache.

Now, when you try accessing the Web site, you'll be prompted for a password.

THE /ETC/HTTPD/CONF.D DIRECTORY

Files in the `/etc/httpd/conf.d` directory are read and automatically appended to the configuration in the `httpd.conf` file every time Apache is restarted. In complicated configurations, in which a Web server has to host many Web sites, you can create one configuration file per Web site each with its own set of `<VirtualHost>` and `<Directory>` containers. This can make Web site management much simpler. To do this correctly:

1. Back up your `httpd.conf` file, in case you make a mistake.
2. Create the files located in this directory that contain the Apache required `<VirtualHost>` and `<Directory>` containers and directives.
3. If each site has a dedicated IP address, then place the `NameVirtualHost` statements in the corresponding `/etc/httpd/conf.d` directory file. If it is shared, it'll need to remain in the main `httpd.conf` file.
4. Remove the corresponding directives from the `httpd.conf` file.
5. Restart Apache, and test.

The files located in the `/etc/httpd/conf.d` directory don't have to have any special names, and you don't have to refer to them in the `httpd.conf` file.

TROUBLESHOOTING APACHE

Troubleshooting a basic Apache configuration is fairly straightforward; you'll find errors in the /var/log/httpd/error_log file during normal operation or displayed on the screen when Apache starts up. Most of the errors you'll encounter will probably be related to incompatible syntax in the <VirtualHosts> statement caused by typing errors.

Testing Basic HTTP Connectivity

The very first step is to determine whether your Web server is accessible on TCP port 80 (HTTP).

Lack of connectivity could be caused by a firewall with incorrect permit, NAT, or port forwarding rules to your Web server. Other sources of failure include Apache not being started at all, the server being down, or network-related failures.

If you can connect on port 80 but no pages are being served, then the problem is usually due to a bad Web application, not the Web server software itself.

It is best to test this from both inside your network and from the Internet. Troubleshooting with TELNET is covered in Chapter 4, "Simple Network Troubleshooting."

Browser 403 Forbidden Messages

Browser 403 Forbidden messages are usually caused by file permissions and security context issues. Please refer to the "General Configuration Steps" section for further details.

A sure sign of problems related to security context are "avc: denied" messages in your /var/log/messages log file.

```
Nov 21 20:41:23 bigboy kernel: audit(1101098483.897:0): avc:   denied
{ getattr } for   pid=1377 exe=/usr/sbin/httpd
path=/home/www/index.html dev=hda5 ino=12
scontext=root:system_r:httpd_t tcontext=root:object_r:home_root_t
tclass=file
```

Only the Default Apache Page Appears

When only the default Apache page appears, there are two main causes. The first is the lack of an index.html file in your Web site's DocumentRoot directory. The second cause is usually related to an incorrect security context for the Web page's file. Please refer to the "General Configuration Steps" section for further details.

Incompatible */etc/httpd/conf/http.conf* Files When Upgrading

Your old configuration files will be incompatible when upgrading from Apache version 1.3 to Apache 2.X. The new version 2.X default configuration file is stored in `/etc/httpd/conf/httpd.conf.rpmnew`. For the simple virtual hosting example above, it would be easiest to:

1. Save the old `httpd.conf` file with another name, `httpd.conf-version-1.x` for example. Copy the `ServerName`, `NameVirtualHost`, and `VirtualHost` containers from the old file and place them in the new `httpd.conf.rpmnew` file.
2. Copy the `httpd.conf.rpmnew` file, and name it `httpd.conf`.
3. Restart Apache.

Server Name Errors

All `ServerName` directives must list a domain that is resolvable in DNS, or else you'll get an error similar to these when starting `httpd`:

```
Starting httpd: httpd: Could not determine the server's fully
qualified domain name, using 127.0.0.1 for ServerName

Starting httpd: [Wed Feb 04 21:18:16 2004] [error] (EAI 2)Name or
service not known: Failed to resolve server name for 192.16.1.100
(check DNS) -- or specify an explicit ServerName
```

You can avoid this by adding a default generic `ServerName` directive at the top of the `httpd.conf` file that references `localhost` instead of the default `new.host.name:80`:

```
#ServerName new.host.name:80
ServerName localhost
```

The Apache Status Log Files

The `/var/log/httpd/access_log` file is updated after every HTTP query and is a good source of general purpose information about your Web site. There is a fixed formatting style with each entry separated by spaces or quotation marks. Table 20.3 lists the layout.

Table 20.3   Apache Log File Format

Field Number	Description	Separator
1	IP address of the remote Web surfer	Spaces
2	Time stamp	Square Brackets []
3	HTTP query including the Web page served	Quotes ""
4	HTTP result code	Spaces
5	The amount of data in bytes sent to the remote Web browser	Spaces
6	The Web page that contained the link to the page served	Quotes ""
7	The version of the Web browser used to get the page	Quotes ""

Upon examining the entry, you can determine that someone at IP address 67.119.25.115 on February 15 looked at the Web page /dns-static.htm returning a successful 200 status code. The amount of data sent was 15190 bytes and the surfer got to the site by clicking on the link http://www.linuxhomenetworking.com/sendmail.htm using Microsoft Internet Explorer version 5.5.

```
67.119.25.115 - - [15/Feb/2003:23:06:51 -0800] "GET /dns-static.htm
HTTP/1.1" 200 15190 "http://www.linuxhomenetworking.com/sendmail.htm"
"Mozilla/4.0 (compatible; MSIE 5.5; Windows NT 4.0; AT&T CSM6.0; YComp
5.0.2.6)"
```

The HTTP status code can provide some insight into the types of operations surfers are trying to attempt and may help to isolate problems with your pages, not the operation of the Apache server. For example, 404 errors are generated when someone tries to access a Web page that doesn't exist anymore. This could be caused by incorrect URL links in other pages on your site. Table 20.4 has some of the more common examples.

Table 20.4   HTTP Status Codes

HTTP Code	Description
200	Successful request.
304	Successful request, but the Web page requested hasn't been modified since the current version in the remote Web browser's cache. This means the Web page will not be sent to the remote browser, it will just use its cached version instead. Frequently occurs when a surfer is browsing back and forth on a site.
401	Unauthorized access. Someone entered an incorrect username or password on a password-protected page.
403	Forbidden. File permissions prevent Apache from reading the file. Often occurs when the Web page file is owned by user root, even though it has universal read access.

HTTP Code	Description
404	Not found. Page requested doesn't exist.
500	Internal server error. Frequently generated by CGI scripts that fail from bad syntax. Check your error_log file for further details on the script's error message.

The Apache Error Log Files

The `/var/log/httpd/error_log` file is a good source for error information. Unlike the `/var/log/httpd/access_log` file, there is no standardized formatting.

Typical errors that you'll find here are HTTP queries for files that don't exist or forbidden requests for directory listings. The file will also include Apache startup errors, which can be very useful.

The `/var/log/httpd/error_log` file also is the location where CGI script errors are written. Many times CGI scripts fail with a blank screen on your browser; the `/var/log/httpd/error_log` file most likely lists the cause of the problem.

CONCLUSION

Web sites both personal and commercial can be very rewarding exercises as they share your interests with the world and allow you to meet new people with whom to develop friendships or transact business.

Unfortunately, even the best Web sites can be impersonal as they frequently only provide information that the designer expects the visitor to need. E-mail, although ancient in comparison to newer personalized interactive Internet technologies, such as IP telephony and instant messaging, has the advantage of being able to relay documents and other information without interrupting the addressee. This allows them to schedule a response when they are better prepared to answer, a valuable quality when replies need to be complex.

Chapter 21, "Configuring Linux Mail Servers," explains how to configure a Linux e-mail server to reduce spam and provide personalized addresses across multiple domains. No Web site should be without one.

Configuring Linux Mail Servers

IN THIS CHAPTER

☞ Configuring `sendmail`
☞ Fighting Spam
☞ Configuring Your POP Mail Server
☞ Conclusion

E-mail is an important part of any Web site you create. In a home environment, a free Web-based e-mail service may be sufficient, but if you are running a business, then a dedicated mail server will probably be required.

This chapter will show you how to use `sendmail` to create a mail server that will relay your mail to a remote user's mailbox or incoming mail to a local mailbox. You'll also learn how to retrieve and send mail via your mail server using a mail client such as Outlook Express or Evolution.

CONFIGURING *SENDMAIL*

One of the tasks in setting up DNS for your domain (`my-web-site.org`) is to use the MX record in the configuration zone file to state the hostname of the server that will handle the mail for the domain. The most popular Unix mail transport agent is `sendmail`, but others, such as `postfix` and `qmail`, are also gaining popularity with Linux. The steps used to convert a Linux box into a `sendmail` mail server will be explained here.

How *sendmail* Works

As stated before, `sendmail` can handle both incoming and outgoing mail for your domain. Take a closer look.

Incoming Mail

Usually each user in your home has a regular Linux account on your mail server. Mail sent to each of these users (username@my-web-site.org) eventually arrives at your mail server and sendmail then processes it and deposits it in the mailbox file of the user's Linux account.

Mail isn't actually sent directly to the user's PC. Users retrieve their mail from the mail server using client software, such as Microsoft's Outlook or Outlook Express, that supports either the POP or IMAP mail retrieval protocols.

Linux users logged into the mail server can read their mail directly using a text-based client, such as mail, or a GUI client, such as Evolution. Linux workstation users can use the same programs to access their mail remotely.

Outgoing Mail

The process is different when sending mail via the mail server. PC and Linux workstation users configure their e-mail software to make the mail server their outbound SMTP mail server.

If the mail is destined for a local user in the mysite.com domain, then sendmail places the message in that person's mailbox so that they can retrieve it using one of the methods above.

If the mail is being sent to another domain, sendmail first uses DNS to get the MX record for the other domain. It then attempts to relay the mail to the appropriate destination mail server using the **Simple Mail Transport Protocol (SMTP)**. One of the main advantages of mail relaying is that when a PC user A sends mail to user B on the Internet, the PC of user A can delegate the SMTP processing to the mail server.

Note

If mail relaying is not configured properly, then your mail server could be commandeered to relay spam. Simple sendmail security will be covered later.

---

sendmail Macros

When mail passes through a sendmail server the mail routing information in its header is analyzed, and sometimes modified, according to the desires of the systems administrator. Using a series of highly complicated regular expressions listed in the /etc/mail/sendmail.cf file, sendmail inspects this header and then acts accordingly.

In recognition of the complexity of the /etc/mail/sendmail.cf file, a much simpler file named /etc/sendmail.mc was created, and it contains more understandable instructions for systems administrators to use. These are then interpreted by a number of macro routines to create the sendmail.cf file. After editing sendmail.mc, you must always run the macros and restart sendmail for the changes to take effect.

Each `sendmail.mc` directive starts with a keyword, such as DOMAIN, FEATURE, or OSTYPE, followed by a subdirective and in some cases arguments. A typical example is:

```
FEATURE(`virtusertable',`hash -o /etc/mail/virtusertable.db')dnl
```

The keywords usually define a subdirectory of `/usr/share/sendmail-cf`, in which the macro may be found and the subdirective is usually the name of the macro file itself. So in the example, the macro name is `/usr/share/sendmail-cf/feature/virtusertable.m4`, and the instruction `\ hash -o /etc/mail/virtusertable.db` is being passed to it.

Notice that `sendmail` is sensitive to the quotation marks used in the m4 macro directives. They open with a grave mark and end with a single quote:

```
FEATURE(`masquerade_envelope')dnl
```

Some keywords, such as `define` for the definition of certain `sendmail` variables and MASQUERADE_DOMAIN, have no corresponding directories with matching macro files. The macros in the `/usr/share/sendmail-cf/m4` directory deal with these.

Once you finish editing the `sendmail.mc` file, you can then execute the `make` command while in the `/etc/mail` directory to regenerate the new `sendmail.cf` file.

```
[root@bigboy tmp]# cd /etc/mail
[root@bigboy mail]# make
```

If there have been no changes to the files in `/etc/mail` since the last time `make` was run, then you'll get an error like this:

```
[root@bigboy mail]# make
make: Nothing to be done for `all'.
[root@bigboy mail]#
```

The `make` command actually generates the `sendmail.cf` file using the m4 command. The m4 usage is simple, you just specify the name of the macro file as the argument, in this case `sendmail.mc`, and redirect the output, which would normally go to the screen, to the `sendmail.cf` file with the > redirector symbol.

```
# m4 /etc/mail/sendmail.mc > /etc/mail/sendmail.cf
```

I'll discuss many of the features of the `sendmail.mc` file later in the chapter.

Installing *sendmail*

Most Red Hat and Fedora Linux software products are available in the RPM format. You will need to make sure that the `sendmail`, `sendmail-cf`, and `m4` software RPMs are installed. (Chapter 6, "Installing RPM Software," will tell you how.) When searching for the RPMs, remember that the filename usually starts with the software package name by a version number, as in `sendmail-8.12.10-1.1.1.i386.rpm`.

Starting *sendmail*

You can use the `chkconfig` command to get `sendmail` configured to start at boot:

```
[root@bigboy tmp]# chkconfig sendmail on
```

To start, stop, and restart `sendmail` after booting, use:

```
[root@bigboy tmp]# service sendmail start
[root@bigboy tmp]# service sendmail stop
[root@bigboy tmp]# service sendmail restart
```

Remember to restart the `sendmail` process every time you make a change to the configuration files for the changes to take effect on the running process. You can also test whether the `sendmail` process is running with the `pgrep` command.

```
[root@bigboy tmp]# pgrep sendmail
```

You should get a response of plain old process ID numbers.

How to Restart *sendmail* After Editing Your Configuration Files

In this chapter, you'll see that `sendmail` uses a variety of configuration files that require different treatments for their commands to take effect. This little script encapsulates all the required post configuration steps:

```
#!/bin/bash
cd /etc/mail
make
newaliases
/etc/init.d/sendmail restart
```

It first runs the `make` command, which creates a new `sendmail.cf` file from the `sendmail.mc` file and compiles supporting configuration files in the `/etc/mail` directory according to the instructions in the file `/etc/mail/Makefile`.

It then generates new e-mail aliases with the `newaliases` command, (this will be covered later), and then restarts `sendmail`.

Use this command to make the script executable:

```
chmod 700 filename
```

You'll need to run the script each time you change any of the `sendmail` configuration files.

The line in the script that restarts `sendmail` is only needed if you have made changes to the `/etc/mail/sendmail.mc` file, but I included it so that you don't forget. This may not be a good idea in a production system.

Note

When `sendmail` starts, it reads the file `sendmail.cf` for its configuration. `sendmail.mc` is a more user friendly configuration file and really is much easier to fool around with without getting burned. The `sendmail.cf` file is located in different directories depending on the version of Red Hat you use. The `/etc/sendmail.cf` file is used for versions up to 7.3, and `/etc/mail/sendmail.cf` is used for versions 8.0 and higher and Fedora Core.

The */etc/mail/sendmail.mc* File

As discussed earlier, you can define most of `sendmail`'s configuration parameters in the `/etc/mail/sendmail.mc` file, which is then used by the `m4` macros to create the `/etc/mail/sendmail.cf` file. Configuration of the `sendmail.mc` file is much simpler than configuration of `sendmail.cf`, but it is still often viewed as an intimidating task with its series of structured **directive** statements that get the job done. Fortunately, in most cases you won't have to edit this file very often.

How to Put Comments in sendmail.mc

In most Linux configuration files a # symbol is used at the beginning of a line to convert it into a comment line or to deactivate any commands that may reside on that line.

The `sendmail.mc` file doesn't use this character for commenting, but instead uses the string "`dnl`". Here are some valid examples of comments used with the `sendmail.mc` configuration file:

These statements are disabled by `dnl` commenting:

```
dnl DAEMON_OPTIONS(`Port=smtp,Addr=127.0.0.1, Name=MTA')
dnl # DAEMON_OPTIONS(`Port=smtp,Addr=127.0.0.1, Name=MTA')
```

This statement is incorrectly disabled:

```
# DAEMON_OPTIONS(`Port=smtp,Addr=127.0.0.1, Name=MTA')
```

This statement is active:

```
DAEMON_OPTIONS(`Port=smtp,Addr=127.0.0.1, Name=MTA')
```

Configuring DNS for *sendmail*

Remember that you will never receive mail unless you have configured DNS for your domain to make your new Linux box mail server the target of the DNS domain's MX record. See either Chapter 18, "Configuring DNS," or Chapter 19, "Dynamic DNS," for details on how to do this.

Configure Your Mail Server's Name In DNS

You first need to make sure that your mail server's name resolves in DNS correctly. For example, if your mail server's name is Bigboy and you intend for it to mostly handle mail for the domain my-web-site.org, then bigboy.my-web-site.org must correctly resolve to the IP address of one of the mail server's interfaces. You can test this using the host command:

```
[root@smallfry tmp]# host bigboy.my-site.com
bigboy.my-web-site.org has address 192.168.1.100
[root@smallfry tmp]#
```

You will need to fix your DNS server's entries if the resolution isn't correct.

Configure the /etc/resolv.conf File

The sendmail program expects DNS to be configured correctly on the DNS server. The MX record for your domain must point to the IP address of the mail server.

The program also expects the files used by the mail server's DNS client to be configured correctly. The first one is the /etc/resolv.conf file in which there must be a domain directive that matches one of the domains the mail server is expected to handle mail for.

Finally, sendmail expects a nameserver directive that points to the IP address of the DNS server the mail server should use to get its DNS information.

For example, if the mail server is handling mail for my-web-site.org and the IP address of the DNS server is 192.168.1.100, there must be directives that look like this:

```
domain my-web-site.org
nameserver 192.168.1.100
```

An incorrectly configured `resolv.conf` file can lead to errors when running the `m4` command to process the information in your `sendmail.mc` file:

```
WARNING: local host name (smallfry) is not qualified; fix $j in config
file
```

The /etc/hosts File

The `/etc/hosts` file also is used by DNS clients and also needs to be correctly configured. Here is a brief example of the first line you should expect to see in it:

```
127.0.0.1 bigboy.my-web-site.org localhost.localdomain localhost
bigboy
```

The entry for 127.0.0.1 must always be followed by the fully qualified domain name (FQDN) of the server. In the case above, it would be `bigboy.my-web-site.org`. Then you *must* have an entry for `localhost` and `localhost.localdomain`. Linux does not function properly if the 127.0.0.1 entry in `/etc/hosts` doesn't also include `localhost` and `localhost.localdomain`. Finally, you can add any other aliases your host may have to the end of the line.

How to Configure Linux *sendmail* Clients

All Linux mail clients in your home or company need to know which server is the mail server. This is configured in the `sendmail.mc` file by setting the `SMART_HOST` statement to include the mail server. In the example below, the mail server has been set to `mail.my-web-site.org`, the mail server for the `my-web-site.org` domain.

```
define(`SMART_HOST',`mail.my-web-site.org')
```

If you don't have a mail server on your network, you can either create one or use the one offered by your ISP.

Once this is done, you need to process the `sendmail.mc` file and restart `sendmail`. To do this, run the restarting script from earlier in the chapter.

If the `sendmail` server is a Linux server, then the `/etc/hosts` file will also have to be correctly configured.

Converting From a Mail Client to a Mail Server

All Linux systems have a virtual **loopback** interface that lives only in memory with an IP address of 127.0.0.1. As mail must be sent to a target IP address even when there is no NIC in the box, `sendmail` therefore uses the loopback address to send mail between users on the same Linux server. To become a mail server, and not a mail client, `sendmail` needs to be configured to listen for messages on NIC interfaces, as well:

1. Determine which NICs `sendmail` is running on. You can see the interfaces on which `sendmail` is listening with the `netstat` command. Because `sendmail` listens on TCP port 25, you use `netstat` and `grep` for 25 to see a default configuration listening only on IP address 127.0.0.1 (loopback):

```
[root@bigboy tmp]# netstat -an | grep :25 | grep tcp
tcp 0 0 127.0.0.1:25 0.0.0.0:* LISTEN
[root@bigboy tmp]#
```

2. Edit `sendmail.mc` to make `sendmail` listen on all interfaces. If `sendmail` is listening on the loopback interface only, you should comment out the `daemon_options` line in the `/etc/mail/sendmail.mc` file with `dnl` statements. It is also good practice to take precautions against spam by not accepting mail from domains that don't exist by commenting out the `accept_unresolvable_domains` feature too. See the sixth and next to last lines in the example:

```
dnl
dnl This changes sendmail to only listen on the loopback
dnl device 127.0.0.1 and not on any other network
dnl devices. Comment this out if you want
dnl to accept email over the network.
dnl DAEMON_OPTIONS(`Port=smtp,Addr=127.0.0.1, Name=MTA')
dnl
...
...
...
dnl
dnl We strongly recommend to comment this one out if you want
dnl to protect yourself from spam. However, the laptop and
dnl users on computers that do
dnl not have 24x7 DNS do need this.
dnl FEATURE(`accept_unresolvable_domains')dnl
dnl FEATURE(`relay_based_on_MX')dnl
dnl
```

Note

You need to be careful with the `accept_unresolvable_names` feature. In the sample network, Bigboy the mail server does not accept e-mail relayed from any of the other PCs on your network if they are not in DNS. Chapter 18 shows how to create your own internal domain just for this purpose.

Note

If your server has multiple NICs and you want it to listen to only one of them, then you can uncomment the `localhost DAEMON_OPTIONS` entry and add another one for the IP address of the NIC on which you wish to accept SMTP traffic.

3. Comment out the SMART_HOST entry in sendmal.mc. The mail server doesn't need a SMART_HOST entry in its sendmail.mc file. Comment this out with a dnl at the beginning.

```
dnl define(`SMART_HOST',`mail.my-web-site.org')
```

4. Regenerate the sendmail.cf file, and restart sendmail. Again, you can do this with the restart script from the beginning of the chapter.

5. Make sure sendmail is listening on all interfaces (0.0.0.0).

```
[root@bigboy tmp]# netstat -an | grep :25 | grep tcp
tcp 0 0 0.0.0.0:25 0.0.0.0:* LISTEN
[root@bigboy tmp]#
```

You have now completed the first phase of converting your Linux server into a sendmail server by enabling it to listen to SMTP traffic on its interfaces. The following sections will show you how to define what type of mail it should handle and the various ways this mail can be processed.

A General Guide to Using the sendmail.mc File

The sendmail.mc file can seem jumbled. To make it less cluttered, I usually create two easily identifiable sections in it with all the custom commands I've ever added.

The first section is near the top where the FEATURE statements usually are, and the second section is at the very bottom.

Sometimes sendmail will archive this file when you do a version upgrade. Having easily identifiable modifications in the file will make post upgrade reconfiguration much easier. Here is a sample:

```
dnl ***** Customised section 1 start *****
dnl
dnl
FEATURE(delay_checks)dnl
FEATURE(masquerade_envelope)dnl
FEATURE(allmasquerade)dnl
FEATURE(masquerade_entire_domain)dnl
dnl
dnl
dnl ***** Customised section 1 end *****
```

The /etc/mail/relay-domains File

The /etc/mail/relay-domains file is used to determine domains from which it will relay mail. The contents of the relay-domains file should be limited to those domains that can be trusted not to originate spam. By default, this file does not exist in a standard Red Hat/Fedora install. In this case, all mail sent from another-web-site.org and not destined for this mail server will be forwarded:

```
another-web-site.org
```

One disadvantage of this file is that it controls mail based on the source domain only, and source domains can be spoofed by spam e-mail servers. The `/etc/mail/access` file has more capabilities, such as restricting relaying by IP address or network range and is more commonly used. If you delete `/etc/mail/relay-domains`, then relay access is fully determined by the `/etc/mail/access` file.

Be sure to run the restart `sendmail` script from the beginning of the chapter for these changes to take effect.

The */etc/mail/access* File

You can make sure that only trusted PCs on your network have the ability to relay mail via your mail server by using the `/etc/mail/access` file. That is to say, the mail server will relay mail only for those PCs on your network that have their e-mail clients configured to use the mail server as their outgoing SMTP mail server. (In Outlook Express, you set this using: Tools>Accounts>Properties>Servers.)

If you don't take the precaution of using this feature, you may find your server being used to relay mail for spam e-mail sites. Configuring the `/etc/mail/access` file will not stop spam coming to you, only spam flowing through you.

The `/etc/mail/access` file has two columns. The first lists IP addresses and domains from which the mail is coming or going. The second lists the type of action to be taken when mail from these sources or destinations is received. Keywords include RELAY, REJECT, OK (not ACCEPT), and DISCARD. There is no third column to state whether the IP address or domain is the source or destination of the mail, `sendmail` assumes it could be either and tries to match both. All other attempted relayed mail that doesn't match any of the entries in the `/etc/mail/access` file, `sendmail` will reject. Despite this, my experience has been that control on a per e-mail address basis is much more intuitive via the `/etc/mail/virtusertable` file.

The sample file that follows allows relaying for only the server itself (127.0.0.1, localhost), two client PCs on your home 192.168.1.X network, everyone on your 192.168.2.X network, and everyone passing e-mail through the mail server from servers belonging to `my-web-site.org`. Remember that a server will be considered a part of `my-web-site.org` only if its IP address can be found in a DNS reverse zone file:

```
localhost.localdomain          RELAY
localhost                      RELAY
127.0.0.1                      RELAY
192.168.1.16                   RELAY
192.168.1.17                   RELAY
192.168.2                      RELAY
my-web-site.org                RELAY
```

You'll then have to convert this text file into a `sendmail` readable database file named `/etc/mail/access.db`. Here are the commands you need:

```
[root@bigboy tmp]# cd /etc/mail
[root@bigboy mail]# make
```

The `sendmail` restart script configured at the beginning of the chapter does this for you too.

Remember that the relay security features of this file may not work if you don't have a correctly configured `/etc/hosts` file.

The */etc/mail/local-host-names* File

When `sendmail` receives mail, it needs a way of determining whether it is responsible for the mail it receives. It uses the `/etc/mail/local-host-names` file to do this. This file has a list of hostnames and domains for which `sendmail` accepts responsibility. For example, if this mail server was to accept mail for the domains `my-web-site.org` and `another-site` then the file would look like this:

```
my-web-site.org
another-web-site.org
```

In this case, remember to modify the MX record of the `another-web-site.org` `DNS zone file` to point to `my-web-site.org`. Here is an example. (Remember each is important.)

```
; Primary Mail Exchanger for another-web-site.org
another-web-site.org. MX 10 mail.my-web-site.org.
```

Which User Should Really Receive the Mail?

After checking the contents of the `virtusertable`, `sendmail` checks the `aliases` files to determine the ultimate recipient of mail.

The /etc/mail/virtusertable *file*

The `/etc/mail/virtusertable` file contains a set of simple instructions on what to do with received mail. The first column lists the target e-mail address, and the second column lists the local user's mail box, a remote e-mail address, or a mailing list entry in the `/etc/aliases` file to which the e-mail should be forwarded.

If there is no match in the `virtusertable` file, `sendmail` checks for the full e-mail address in the `/etc/aliases` file:

```
webmaster@another-web-site.org   webmasters
@another-web-site.org            marc
sales@my-web-site.org             sales@another-web-site.org
paul@my-web-site.org             paul
finance@my-web-site.org          paul
@my-web-site.org                 error:nouser User unknown
```

In this example, mail sent to:

☞ webmaster@another-web-site.org goes to local user (or mailing list) web-masters, all other mail to another-web-site.org goes to local user marc

☞ sales at my-web-site.org goes to the sales department at my-othersite.com

☞ paul and finance at my-web-site.org goes to local user (or mailing list) paul

All other users at my-web-site.org receive a bounce back message stating "User unknown."

After editing the /etc/mail/virtusertable file, you have to convert it into a sendmail-readable database file named /etc/mail/virtusertable.db with two commands:

```
[root@bigboy tmp]# cd /etc/mail
[root@bigboy mail]# make
```

If these lines look like you've seen them before, you have: They're in your all-purpose sendmail restart script.

The /etc/aliases File

You can think of the /etc/aliases file as a mailing list file. The first column has the mailing list name (sometimes called a **virtual mailbox**), and the second column has the members of the mailing list separated by commas.

To start, sendmail searches the first column of the file for a match. If there is no match, then sendmail assumes the recipient is a regular user on the local server and deposits the mail in their mailbox.

If it finds a match in the first column, sendmail notes the nickname entry in the second column. It then searches for the nickname again in the first column to see if the recipient isn't on yet another mailing list.

If sendmail doesn't find a duplicate, it assumes the recipient is a regular user on the local server and deposits the mail in their mailbox.

If the recipient is a mailing list, then sendmail goes through the process all over again to determine if any of the members is on yet another list, and when it is all finished, they all get a copy of the e-mail message.

In the example that follows, you can see that mail sent to users bin, dae-mon, lp, shutdown, apache, named, and so on by system processes will all be sent to user (or mailing list) root. In this case, root is actually an alias for a mailing list consisting of user marc and webmaster@my-web-site.org.

Note

The default /etc/aliases file installed with Red Hat/Fedora has the last line of this sample commented out with a #. You may want to delete the comment and change user marc to another user.

Also, after editing this file, you'll have to convert it into a sendmail readable database file named /etc/aliases.db. The newaliases command is used to do this.

```
[root@bigboy tmp]# newaliases

# Basic system aliases -- these MUST be present.
mailer-daemon:          postmaster
postmaster:             root

# General redirections for pseudo accounts.
bin:                    root
daemon:                 root
...
...
abuse:                  root

# trap decode to catch security attacks
decode:                 root

# Person who should get root's mail
root:                   marc,webmaster@my-web-site.org
```

Notice that there are no spaces between the mailing list entries for root: You will get errors if you add spaces.

In this simple mailing list example, mail sent to root actually goes to user account marc and webmaster@my-web-site.org. Because aliases can be very useful, here are a few more list examples for your /etc/aliases file.

☞ Mail to directors@my-web-site.org goes to users peter, paul, and mary:

```
# Directors of my SOHO company
directors:      peter,paul,mary
```

☞ Mail sent to family@my-web-site.org goes to users grandma, brother, and sister:

```
# My family
family:         grandma,brother,sister
```

☞ Mail sent to admin-list gets sent to all the users listed in the file /home/mailings/admin-list.

```
# My mailing list file
admin-list:     ":include:/home/mailings/admin-list"
```

The advantage of using mailing list files is that the `admin-list` file can be a file that trusted users can edit, user root is only needed to update the aliases file. Despite this, there are some problems with mail reflectors. One is that bounce messages from failed attempts to broadcast go to all users. Another is that all subscriptions and unsubscriptions have to be done manually by the mailing list administrator. If either of these are a problem for you, then consider using a mailing list manager, such as `majordomo`.

One important note about the /etc/aliases file: By default your system uses `sendmail` to mail system messages to local user root. When `sendmail` sends e-mail to a local user, the mail has no To: in the e-mail header. If you then use a mail client with a spam mail filtering rule to reject mail with no To: in the header, such as Outlook Express or Evolution, you may find yourself dumping legitimate mail.

To get around this, try making root have an alias for a user with a fully qualified domain name, this forces `sendmail` to insert the correct fields in the header; for example:

```
# Person who should get root's mail
root:                   webmaster@my-web-site.org
```

sendmail Masquerading Explained

If you want your mail to appear to come from `user@mysite.com` and not `user@bigboy.mysite.com`, then you have two choices:

☞ Configure your e-mail client, such as Outlook Express, to set your e-mail address to `user@mysite.com`. (I'll explain this in the "Configuring Your POP Mail Server" section.)

☞ Set up masquerading to modify the domain name of all traffic originating from and passing trough your mail server.

Configuring Masquerading

In the DNS configuration, you made Bigboy the mail server for the domain `my-web-site.org`. You now have to tell Bigboy in the `sendmail` configuration file `sendmail.mc` that all outgoing mail originating on Bigboy should appear to be coming from `my-web-site.org`; if not, based on the settings in the `/etc/hosts` file, mail will appear to come from `mail.my-web-site.org`. This isn't terrible, but you may not want your Web site to be remembered with the word "mail" in front of it. In other words, you may want your mail server to handle all e-mail by assigning a consistent return address to all outgoing mail, no matter which server originated the e-mail.

You can solve this by editing your `sendmail.mc` configuration file and adding some masquerading commands and directives:

```
FEATURE(always_add_domain)dnl
FEATURE(`masquerade_entire_domain')dnl
FEATURE(`masquerade_envelope')dnl
FEATURE(`allmasquerade')dnl
MASQUERADE_AS(`my-web-site.org')dnl
MASQUERADE_DOMAIN(`my-web-site.org.')dnl
MASQUERADE_DOMAIN(localhost)dnl
MASQUERADE_DOMAIN(localhost.localdomain)dnl
```

The result is that:

☞ The MASQUERADE_AS directive makes all mail originating on Bigboy appear
to come from a server within the domain my-web-site.org by rewriting
the e-mail header.

☞ The MASQUERADE_DOMAIN directive makes mail relayed via Bigboy from all
machines in the another-web-site.org and localdomain domains appear
to come from the MASQUERADE_AS domain of my-web-site.org. Using DNS,
sendmail checks the domain name associated with the IP address of the
mail relay client sending the mail to help it determine whether it should
do masquerading or not.

☞ FEATURE masquerade_entire_domain makes sendmail masquerade servers
named *my-web-site.org and *another-web-site.org as my-web-site.org.
In other words, mail from sales.my-web-site.org would be masqueraded
as my-web-site.org. If this wasn't selected, then only servers named my-
web-site.org and my-othersite.com would be masqueraded. Use this with
caution when you are sure you have the necessary authority.

☞ FEATURE allmasquerade makes sendmail rewrite both recipient addresses
and sender addresses relative to the local machine. If you cc: yourself on
an outgoing mail, the other recipient sees a cc: to an address he knows
instead of one on localhost.localdomain.

Note

Use FEATURE allmasquerade with caution if your mail server handles e-mail for
many different domains and the mailboxes for the users in these domains reside
on the mail server. The allmasquerade statement causes all mail destined for these
mailboxes to appear to be destined for users in the domain defined in the MASQUER-
ADE_AS statement. In other words, if MASQUERADE_AS is my-web-site.org and you use
allmasquerade, then mail for peter@another-web-site.org enters the correct mailbox
but sendmail rewrites the To:, making the e-mail appear to be sent to peter@my-
ste.com originally.

☞ FEATURE always_add_domain always masquerades e-mail addresses, even if
the mail is sent from a user on the mail server to another user on the
same mail server.

☞ FEATURE masquerade_envelope rewrites the e-mail envelope just as
MASQUERADE_AS rewrote the header.

Masquerading is an important part of any mail server configuration as it enables systems administrators to use multiple outbound mail servers, each providing only the global domain name for a company and not the fully qualified domain name of the server itself. All e-mail correspondence then has a uniform e-mail address format that complies with the company's brand marketing policies.

Note

E-mail clients, such as Outlook Express, consider the To: and From: statements as the **e-mail header**. When you choose Reply or Reply All in Outlook Express, the program automatically uses the To: and From: in the header. It is easy to fake the header, as spammers often do; it is detrimental to e-mail delivery, however, to fake the envelope.

The e-mail **envelope** contains the To: and From: used by mail servers for protocol negotiation. It is the envelope's From: that is used when e-mail rejection messages are sent between mail servers.

Testing Masquerading

The best way of testing masquerading from the Linux command line is to use the `mail -v username` command. I have noticed that `sendmail -v username` ignores masquerading altogether. You should also tail the `/var/log/maillog` file to verify that the masquerading is operating correctly and check the envelope and header of test e-mail received by test e-mail accounts.

Other Masquerading Notes

By default, user root will not be masqueraded. To remove this restriction use the

```
EXPOSED_USER(`root')dnl
```

command in `/etc/mail/sendmail.mc`. You can comment this out if you like with a "dnl" at the beginning of the line and running the `sendmail` start script.

Using *sendmail* to Change the Sender's E-mail Address

Sometimes masquerading isn't enough. At times you may need to change not only the domain of the sender but also the username portion of the sender's e-mail address. For example, perhaps you bought a program for your SOHO office that sends out notifications to your staff, but the program inserts its own address as sender's address, not that of the IT person.

Web-based CGI scripts tend to run as user apache and, therefore, send mail as user apache too. Often you won't want this, not only because apache's e-mail address may not be suitable, but also because some anti-spam programs check to ensure that the From:, or source e-mail address, actually exists as a real user. If your `virtusertable` file allows e-mail to only predefined users, then queries about the apache user will fail, and your valid e-mail may be classified as being spam.

With `sendmail`, you can change both the domain and username on a case-by-case basis using the `genericstable` feature:

1. Add these statements to your `/etc/mail/sendmail.mc` file to activate the feature:

```
FEATURE(`genericstable',`hash -o
/etc/mail/genericstable.db')dnl
GENERICS_DOMAIN_FILE(`/etc/mail/generics-domains')dnl
```

2. Create a `/etc/mail/generics-domains` file that is just a list of all the domains that should be inspected. Make sure the file includes your server's canonical domain name, which you can obtain using the command:

```
sendmail -bt -d0.1 </dev/null
```

Here is a sample `/etc/mail/generics-domains` file:

```
my-web-site.org
another-web-site.org
bigboy.my-web-site.org
```

3. Create your `/etc/mail/genericstable` file. First `sendmail` searches the `/etc/mail/generics-domains` file for a list of domains to reverse map. It then looks at the `/etc/mail/genericstable` file for an individual e-mail address from a matching domain. The format of the file is:

```
linux-username     username@new-domain.com
```

Here is an example:

```
alert          security-alert@my-web-site.org
peter          urgent-message@my-web-site.org
apache         mailer@my-web-site.org
```

4. Run the `sendmail` restart script from the beginning of the chapter and then test.

Your e-mails from linux-username should now appear to come from `username@new-domain.com`.

Troubleshooting *sendmail*

When `sendmail` doesn't appear to work correctly, you can test it in a number of ways. Here are a few tests and techniques you can use to fix some of the most common problems.

Test TCP Connectivity

The very first step is to determine whether your mail server is accessible on the `sendmail` SMTP TCP port 25. Lack of connectivity could be caused by a firewall with incorrect permit, NAT, or port forwarding rules to your mail server. Failure could also be caused by the `sendmail` process being stopped. It is best to test this from both inside your network and from the Internet.

Chapter 4, "Simple Network Troubleshooting," covers troubleshooting with TELNET.

Test TCP Connectivity

You can also mimic a full mail session using TELNET to make sure everything is working correctly. If you get a "500 Command not recognized" error message along the way, the cause is probably a typographical error. Follow these steps carefully:

1. TELNET to the mail server on port 25. You should get a response with a 220 status code.

```
[root@bigboy tmp]# telnet mail.my-web-site.org 25
Trying mail.my-web-site.org...
Connected to mail.my-web-site.org.
Escape character is '^]'.
220 mail.my-web-site.org ESMTP server ready
```

2. Use the `hello` command to tell the mail server the domain to which you belong. You should receive a message with a successful status 250 code at the beginning of the response.

```
hello another-web-site.org
250 mail.my-web-site.org Hello c-24-4-97-
110.client.comcast.net [24.4.97.110], pleased to meet you.
```

3. Inform the mail server from which the test message is coming with the MAIL FROM: statement:

```
MAIL FROM:sender@another-web-site.org
250 2.1.0 sender@another-web-site.org... Sender ok
```

4. Using the RCPT TO: statement, tell the mail server to whom the test message is going:

```
RCPT TO: user@my-web-site.org
250 2.1.5 user@my-web-site.org... Recipient ok
```

5. Prepare the mail server to receive data with the DATA statement:

```
DATA
354 Enter mail, end with "." on a line by itself
```

6. Type the string "subject:" then type a subject. Type in your text message, ending it with a single period on the last line. For example:

```
Subject: Test Message
Testing sendmail interactively
.


250 2.0.0 iA75r9si017840 Message accepted for delivery
```

7. Use the QUIT command to end the session.

```
QUIT
221 2.0.0 mail.my-web-site.org closing connection
Connection closed by foreign host.
[root@bigboy tmp]#
```

Now verify that the intended recipient received the message, and check the system logs for any mail application errors.

The /var/log/maillog *File*

Because sendmail writes all its status messages in the /var/log/maillog file, always monitor this file whenever you are doing changes. Open two TELNET, SSH, or console windows. Work in one of them and monitor the sendmail status output in the other using the command:

```
[root@bigboy tmp]# tail -f /var/log/maillog
```

Common Errors Due to Incomplete RPM Installation

Both the newaliases and m4 commands require the sendmail-cf and m4 RPM packages. These must be installed. If they are not, you'll get errors when running various sendmail related commands:

☞ Sample errors when running newaliases

```
[root@bigboy mail]# newaliases
Warning: .cf file is out of date: sendmail 8.12.5 supports
version 10, .cf file is version 0
No local mailer defined
QueueDirectory (Q) option must be set
[root@bigboy mail]#
```

☞ Sample errors when processing the sendmail.mc file

```
[root@bigboy mail]# m4 /etc/mail/sendmail.mc > /etc/mail/send-
mail.cf
/etc/mail/sendmail.mc:8: m4: Cannot open /usr/share/sendmail-
cf/m4/cf.m4: No such file or directory
[root@bigboy mail]#
```

☞ Sample errors when restarting sendmail

```
[root@bigboy mail]# service sendmail restart
Shutting down sendmail: [ OK ]
Shutting down sm-client: [FAILED]
Starting sendmail: 554 5.0.0 No local mailer defined
```

```
554 5.0.0 QueueDirectory (Q) option must be set
[FAILED]
Starting sm-client: [ OK ]
[root@bigboy mail]#
```

If these errors occur, make sure your m4, sendmail, and sendmail-cf RPM packages are installed correctly.

Incorrectly Configured /etc/hosts Files

By default, Fedora inserts the host name of the server between the 127.0.0.1 and the localhost entries in /etc/hosts:

```
127.0.0.1      bigboy     localhost.localdomain    localhost
```

Unfortunately in this configuration, sendmail will think that the server's FQDN is Bigboy, which it will identify as being invalid because there is no extension at the end, such as .com or .net. It will then default to sending e-mails in which the domain is localhost.localdomain.

The /etc/hosts file is also important for configuring mail relay. You can create problems if you fail to place the server name in the FDQN for 127.0.0.1 entry. Here sendmail thinks that the server's FDQN was my-site and that the domain was all of .com:

```
127.0.0.1      my-web-site.org  localhost.localdomain   localhost
(Wrong!!!)
```

The server would therefore be open to relay all mail from any .com domain and would ignore the security features of the access and relay-domains files I'll describe later.

As mentioned, a poorly configured /etc/hosts file can make mail sent from your server to the outside world appear as if it came from users at local-host.localdomain and not bigboy.my-web-site.org.

Use the sendmail program to send a sample e-mail to someone in verbose mode. Enter some text after issuing the command and end your message with a single period all by itself on the last line, for example:

```
[root@bigboy tmp]# sendmail -v example@another-web-site.org
test text
test text
.
example@another-web-site.org... Connecting to mail.another-web-
site.org. via esmtp...
220 ltmail.another-web-site.org LiteMail v3.02(BFLITEMAIL4A); Sat, 05
Oct 2002 06:48:44 -0400
>>> EHLO localhost.localdomain
250-mx.another-web-site.org Hello [67.120.221.106], pleased to meet
you
250 HELP
```

```
>>> MAIL From:<root@localhost.localdomain>
250 <root@localhost.localdomain>... Sender Ok
>>> RCPT To:<example@another-web-site.org>
250 <example@another-web-site.org>... Recipient Ok
>>> DATA
354 Enter mail, end with "." on a line by itself
>>> .
250 Message accepted for delivery
example@another-web-site.org... Sent (Message accepted for delivery)
Closing connection to mail.another-web-site.org.
>>> QUIT
[root@bigboy tmp]#
```

Localhost.localdomain is the domain that all computers use to refer to themselves; it is therefore an illegal Internet domain. Consider an example: Mail sent from computer PC1 to PC2 appears to come from a user at local-host.localdomain on PC1 and is rejected. The rejected e-mail is returned to localhost.localdomain. PC2 sees that the mail originated from localhost.localdomain and thinks that the rejected e-mail should be sent to a user on PC2 that may not exist. You end up with an error in /var/log/maillog:

```
Oct 16 10:20:04 bigboy sendmail[2500]: g9GHK3iQ002500: SYSERR(root):
savemail: cannot save rejected email anywhere
Oct 16 10:20:04 bigboy sendmail[2500]: g9GHK3iQ002500: Losing
./qfg9GHK3iQ002500: savemail panic
```

You may also get this error if you are using a spam prevention program, such as a script based on the PERL module Mail::Audit. An error in the script could cause this type of message, too.

Another set of telltale errors caused by the same problem can be generated when trying to send mail to a user (the example uses root) or creating a new alias database file. (I'll explain the newaliases command later.)

```
[root@bigboy tmp]# sendmail -v  root
WARNING: local host name (bigboy) is not qualified; fix $j in config
file
[root@bigboy tmp]# newaliases
WARNING: local host name (bigboy) is not qualified; fix $j in config
file
[root@bigboy tmp]#
```

An accompanying error in /var/log/maillog log file looks like this:

```
Oct 16 10:23:58 bigboy sendmail[2582]: My unqualified host name
(bigboy) unknown; sleeping for retry
```

FIGHTING SPAM

Unsolicited commercial e-mail (UCE or spam) can be annoying, time consuming to delete, and in some cases dangerous when they contain viruses and worms. Fortunately, you can use your mail server to combat spam.

Using Public Spam Blacklists with *sendmail*

There are many publicly available lists of known open mail relay servers and spam generating mail servers on the Internet. Some are maintained by volunteers, others are managed by public companies, but in all cases they rely heavily on complaints from spam victims. Some spam blacklists simply try to determine whether the e-mail is coming from a legitimate IP address.

The IP addresses of offenders usually remain on the list for six months to two years. In some cases, to provide additional pressure on the spammers, the blacklists include not only the offending IP address but also the entire subnet or network block to which it belongs. This prevents the spammers from easily switching their servers' IP addresses to the next available ones on their networks. Also, if the spammer uses a public data center, it is possible that their activities could also cause the IP addresses of legitimate e-mailers to be black listed too. It is hoped that these legitimate users will pressure the data center's management to evict the spamming customer.

You can configure `sendmail` to use its `dnsbl` feature to both query these lists and reject the mail if a match is found. Here are some sample entries you can add to your `/etc/sendmail.mc` file; they should all be on one line:

☞ **RFC-Ignorant**: A valid IP address checker.

```
FEATURE(`dnsbl', `ipwhois.rfc-ignorant.org',`"550 Mail from "
$&{client_addr} " refused. Rejected for bad WHOIS info on IP
of your SMTP server - see http://www.rfc-ignorant.org/"')
```

☞ **Easynet**: An open proxy list.

```
FEATURE(`dnsbl', `proxies.blackholes.easynet.nl', `"550 5.7.1
ACCESS DENIED to OPEN PROXY SERVER "$&{client_name}" by easynet.nl
DNSBL  (http://proxies.blackholes.easynet.nl/errors.html)"', `')dnl
```

☞ **The Open Relay Database**: An open mail relay list.

```
FEATURE(`dnsbl', `relays.ordb.org', `"550 Email rejected due
to sending server misconfiguration - see
http://www.ordb.org/faq/\#why_rejected"')dnl
```

☞ **Spamcop**: A spammer blacklist.

```
FEATURE(`dnsbl', `bl.spamcop.net', `"450 Mail from "
$`'&{client_addr} " refused - see http://spamcop.net/bl.shtml"')
```

☞ **Spamhaus**: A spammer blacklist.

```
FEATURE(`dnsbl',`sbl.spamhaus.org',`Rejected - see
http://spamhaus.org/')dnl
```

Be sure to visit the URLs listed to learn more about the individual services.

spamassassin

Once `sendmail` receives an e-mail message, it hands the message over to `procmail`, which is the application that actually places the e-mail in user mailboxes on the mail server. You can make `procmail` temporarily hand over control to another program, such as a spam filter. The most commonly used filter is `spamassassin`.

`spamassassin` doesn't delete spam, it merely adds the word "spam" to the beginning of the subject line of suspected spam e-mails. You can then configure the e-mail filter rules in Outlook Express or any other mail client to either delete the suspect message or store it in a special Spam folder.

Downloading and Installing spamassassin

Most Red Hat and Fedora Linux software products are available in the RPM format. When searching for the RPMs, remember that the filename usually starts with the software package name and is followed by a version number, as in `spamassassin-2.60-2.i386.rpm`. (For help downloading, see Chapter 6.)

Starting spamassassin

You can use the `chkconfig` command to get `spamassassin` configured to start at boot:

```
[root@bigboy tmp]# chkconfig --level 35 spamassassin on
```

To start, stop, and restart spamassassin after booting:

```
[root@bigboy tmp]# service spamassassin start
[root@bigboy tmp]# service spamassassin stop
[root@bigboy tmp]# service spamassassin restart
```

Configuring procmail *for* spamassassin

The `/etc/procmailrc` file is used by `procmail` to determine the `procmail` helper programs that should be used to filter mail. This file isn't created by default.

`spamassassin` has a template you can use called `/etc/mail/spamassassin/spamassassin-spamc.rc`. Copy the template to the `/etc` directory:

```
[root@bigboy tmp]# cp /etc/mail/spamassassin/spamassassin-spamc.rc
/etc/procmailrc
```

This file forces all mail arriving for your mail server's users through Spamassassin.

Configuring spamassassin

The `spamassassin` configuration file is named `/etc/mail/spamassassin/local.cf`. You can customize this fully commented sample configuration file to meet your needs:

```
###################################################################
# See 'perldoc Mail::SpamAssassin::Conf' for
# details of what can be adjusted.
###################################################################

#
# These values can be overridden by editing
# ~/.spamassassin/user_prefs.cf (see spamassassin(1) for details)
#

# How many hits before a message is considered spam. The lower the
# number the more sensitive it is.

required_hits           5.0


# Whether to change the subject of suspected spam (1=Yes, 0=No)
rewrite_subject         1


# Text to prepend to subject if rewrite_subject is used
subject_tag             *****SPAM*****


# Encapsulate spam in an attachment (1=Yes, 0=No)
report_safe             1


# Use terse version of the spam report (1=Yes, 0=No)
use_terse_report        0


# Enable the Bayes system (1=Yes, 0=No)
use_bayes               1


# Enable Bayes auto-learning (1=Yes, 0=No)
auto_learn              1


# Enable or disable network checks (1=Yes, 0=No)
skip_rbl_checks         0
use_razor2              1
use_dcc                 1
use_pyzor               1


# Mail using languages used in these country codes will not be marked
# as being possibly spam in a foreign language.
# - english

ok_languages            en
```

```
# Mail using locales used in these country codes will not be marked
# as being possibly spam in a foreign language.

ok_locales                en
```

Be sure to restart spamassassin for your changes to take effect.

Startup spamassassin

The final steps are to configure spamassassin to start on booting and then to start it.

```
[root@bigboy tmp]# chkconfig spamassassin on
[root@bigboy tmp]# service spamassassin start
Starting spamd: [  OK  ]
[root@bigboy tmp]#
```

A Simple PERL Script to Help Stop Spam

Blacklists won't stop everything, but you can limit the amount of unsolicited spam you receive by writing a small script to intercept your mail before it is written to your mailbox.

This is fairly simple to do, because sendmail always checks the .forward file in your home directory for the name of this script. The sendmail program then looks for the filename in the directory /etc/smrsh and executes it.

By default, PERL doesn't come with modules that are able to check e-mail headers and envelopes so you have to download them from CPAN (www.cpan.org). The most important modules are:

☞ MailTools
☞ IO-Stringy
☞ MIME-tools
☞ Mail-Audit

I have written a script called mail-filter.pl that effectively filters out spam e-mail for my home system. A few steps are required to make the script work:

1. Install PERL and the PERL modules you downloaded from CPAN.
2. Place an executable version of the script in your home directory and modify the script's $FILEPATH variable point to your home directory.
3. Update file mail-filter.accept, which specifies the subjects and e-mail addresses to accept, and file mail-filter.reject, which specifies those to reject.
4. Update your .forward file and place an entry in /etc/smrsh.

Mail-filter first rejects all e-mail based on the reject file and then accepts all mail found in the accept file. It then denies everything else.

For a simple script with instructions on how to install the PERL modules, see Appendix II, "Codes, Scripts, and Configurations."

CONFIGURING YOUR POP MAIL SERVER

Each user on your Linux box will get mail sent to their account's mail folder, but sendmail just handles mail sent to your my-web-site.org domain. If you want to retrieve the mail from your Linux box's user account using a mail client such as Evolution, Microsoft Outlook or Outlook Express, then you have a few more steps. You'll also have to make your Linux box a POP mail server.

Fedora Linux comes with its Cyrus IMAP/POP server RPM package, but I have found the IMAP-2002 RPMs found on rpmfind.net and featured in this section much more intuitive to use for the SOHO environment.

Installing Your POP Mail Server

You need to install the imap RPM that contains the POP server software. It isn't yet a part of the Fedora RPM set, and you will probably have to download it from rpmfind.net. Remember that the filename is probably similar to imap-2002d-3.i386.rpm.

Starting Your POP Mail Server

POP mail is started by xinetd. To configure POP mail to start at boot, therefore, you have to use the chkconfig command to make sure xinetd starts up on booting. As with all xinetd-controlled programs, the chkconfig command also immediately activates application.

```
[root@bigboy tmp]# chkconfig pop3 on
```

To stop POP mail after booting, once again use chkconfig:

```
[root@bigboy tmp]# chkconfig pop3 off
```

Remember to restart the POP mail process every time you make a change to the configuration files to ensure the changes take effect on the running process.

How to Configure Your Windows Mail Programs

All your POP e-mail accounts are really only regular Linux user accounts in which `sendmail` has deposited mail. You can now configure your e-mail client such as Outlook Express to use your new POP/SMTP mail server quite easily. To configure `POP Mail`, set your POP mail server to be the IP address of your Linux mail server. Use your Linux user username and password when prompted.

Next, set your SMTP mail server to be the IP address/domain name of your Linux mail server.

Configuring Secure POP Mail

If you need to access your e-mail from the mail server via the Internet or some other insecure location, you may want to configure POP to work over an encrypted data channel. For this, use `/etc/xinetd.d/pop3s` file instead of `/etc/xinetd.d/ipop3`. Encrypted POP runs on TCP port 995, so firewall rules may need to be altered as well.

Most POP clients support secure POP. For example, Windows configures it in the Advanced menu of the Outlook Express Account Configuration window.

How to Handle Overlapping E-mail Addresses

If you have user overlap, such as John Smith (`john@my-web-site.org`) and John Brown (`john@another-web-site.org`), both users will get sent to the Linux user account john by default. You have two options for a solution:

☞ Make the user part of the e-mail address different—`john1@my-web-site.org` and `john2@another-web-site.org`, for example—and create Linux accounts john1 and john2. If the users insist on overlapping names, then you may need to modify your `virtusertable` file.

☞ Create the user accounts john1 and john2 and point `virtusertable` entries for `john@my-web-site.org` to account john1 and point `john@another-web-site.org` entries to account john2. The POP configuration in Outlook Express for each user should retrieve their mail via POP using john1 and john2, respectively.

With this trick you'll be able to handle many users belonging to multiple domains without many address overlap problems.

Troubleshooting POP Mail

The very first troubleshooting step is to determine whether your POP server is accessible on the POP TCP port 110 or the secure POP port of 995. Lack of connectivity could be caused by a firewall with incorrect permit, NAT, or port forwarding rules to your server. Failure could also be caused by the xinetd process being stopped or the configuration files being disabled. Test this from both inside your network and from the Internet. (Troubleshooting TCP with TELNET is covered in Chapter 4.)

Linux status messages are logged to the file /var/log/messages. Use it to make sure all your files are loaded when you start xinetd. Check your configuration files if it fails to do so. This example starts xinetd and makes a successful secure POP query from a remote POP client. (Linux logging is covered in Chapter 5, "Troubleshooting with syslog.")

```
Aug 11 23:20:33 bigboy xinetd[18690]: START: pop3s pid=18693
from=172.16.1.103
Aug 11 23:20:33 bigboy ipop3d[18693]: pop3s SSL service init from
172.16.1.103
Aug 11 23:20:40 bigboy ipop3d[18693]: Login user=labmanager host=172-
16-1-103.my-web-site.org [172.16.1.103] nmsgs=0/0
Aug 11 23:20:40 bigboy ipop3d[18693]: Logout user=labmanager host=172-
16-1-103.my-web-site.org [172.16.1.103] nmsgs=0 ndele=0
Aug 11 23:20:40 bigboy xinetd[18690]: EXIT: pop3s pid=18693
duration=7(sec)
Aug 11 23:20:52 bigboy xinetd[18690]: START: pop3s pid=18694
from=172.16.1.103
Aug 11 23:20:52 bigboy ipop3d[18694]: pop3s SSL service init from
172.16.1.103
Aug 11 23:20:52 bigboy ipop3d[18694]: Login user=labmanager host=172-
16-1-103.my-web-site.org [172.16.1.103] nmsgs=0/0
Aug 11 23:20:52 bigboy ipop3d[18694]: Logout user=labmanager host=172-
16-1-103.my-web-site.org [172.16.1.103] nmsgs=0 ndele=0
Aug 11 23:20:52 bigboy xinetd[18690]: EXIT: pop3s pid=18694
duration=0(sec)
```

CONCLUSION

E-mail is an important part of any Web site, and you need to plan its configuration carefully to make it a seamless part of the Web experience of your visitors. Without it, your Web site won't seem complete.

A fully functioning Web site is just the beginning. It needs to be maintained to reduce the risk of failure and monitored to help detect potential problems. Chapter 22, "Monitoring Server Performance," discusses many Linux-based tools that you can use to track the health of your Linux server.

Monitoring Server Performance

IN THIS CHAPTER

You can monitor your system's Web performance quite easily with graphical Linux tools. You'll learn how to use several in this chapter, including MRTG, which is based on SNMP and monitors raw network traffic, and Webalizer, which tracks Web site hits.

SNMP

Most servers, routers and firewalls keep their operational statistics in **object identifiers** (**OID**s) that you can remotely retrieve via the **Simple Network Management Protocol** (**SNMP**). For ease of use, equipment vendors provide **Management Information Base** (**MIB**) files for their devices that define the functions of the OIDs they contain. That's a lot of new terms to digest in two sentences, so take a moment to look more closely.

OIDs and MIBs

OIDs are arranged in a **structure of management information** (**SMI**) tree defined by the SNMP standard. The tree starts from a **root node**, which then descends through **branches** and **leaves** that each add their own reference value to the path separated by a period. Figure 22.1 shows an OID structure in which the path to the `enterprises` OID branch passes through the `org`, `dod`, `internet`, and `private` branches first. The OID path for `enterprises` is, therefore, `1.3.6.1.4.1`.

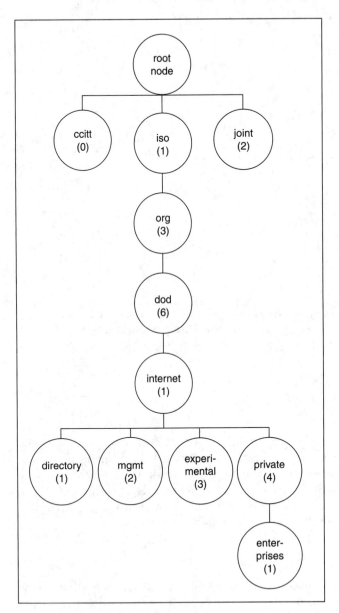

Figure 22.1   The SNMP OID structure.

Management Information Bases (MIBs) are text definitions of each of the OID branches. Table 22.1 shows how some commonly used OIDs map to their MIB definitions. For example, the SMI `org` MIB defines all the topmost OIDs found at the next layer, which is named `dod`; the `internet` MIB under `dod` defines the function of the topmost OIDs in the `directory`, `mgmt`, `experimental`, and `private` branches. This MIB information is very useful for SNMP management programs, enabling you to click on an OID and see its value, type, and description.

Table 22.1 OIDs and Their Equivalent MIBs

OID	MIB
1.3	org
1.3.6	dod
1.3.6.1	internet
1.3.6.1.1	directory
1.3.6.1.2	mgmt
1.3.6.1.3	experimental
1.3.6.1.4	private
1.3.6.1.4.1	enterprises

You can refer to an OID by substituting the values in a branch with one of these more readable MIB aliases. For example, you can reference the OID `1.3.6.1.4.1.9.9.109.1.1.1.1.5` as `enterprises.9.9.109.1.1.1.1.5.1` by substituting the branch name (`enterprises`) for its OID numbers (`1.3.6.1.4.1`).

Remember, only the OID value at the very tip of a branch, the —leaf— actually has a readable value. Think of OIDs like the directory structure on a hard disk. Each branch is equivalent to a subdirectory, and the very last value at the tip (the leaf) correlates to a file containing data.

The Linux `snmpget` command outputs the value of a single leaf, and the `snmpwalk` command provides the values of all leaves under a branch. I'll discuss these commands later; for now, all you need to know is that the command output frequently doesn't list the entire OID, just the MIB file in which it was found and the alias within the MIB. For example:

```
SNMPv2-MIB::sysUpTime.0
```

Here the OID value was found in the SNMPv2-MIB file and occupies position zero in the sysUpTime alias.

Equipment manufacturers are usually assigned their own dedicated OID branch under the `enterprises` MIB, and they must also provide information in universally accepted OIDs for ease of manageability. For example, NIC interface data throughput values must always be placed in a predefined location in the general tree, but a memory use value on a customized processor card may be defined in a MIB under the manufacturer's own OID branch.

SNMP Community Strings

As a security measure, you need to know the SNMP password, or **community string**, to query OIDs. There are a number of types of community strings, the most commonly used ones are the Read Only or "get" community string that only provides access for viewing statistics and system parameters. In many cases the Read Only community string or password is set to the word "public"; you should change it from this easy-to-guess value whenever possible. The Read/Write or "set" community string is for not only viewing statistics and system parameters but also for updating the parameters.

SNMP Versions

There are currently three versions of SNMP:

- ☞ **SNMP Version 1**: The first version of SNMP to be implemented, version 1 was designed to be a protocol to provide device statistics and error reporting without consuming a lot of system resources. Security was limited to community strings and access controls based on the IP address of the querying server. Data communication wasn't encrypted.
- ☞ **SNMP Version 2**: The second version of SNMP, often referred to as **v2c**, expanded the number of supported error codes, increased the size of counters used to track data, and had the ability to do bulk queries that more efficiently loaded response packets with data. SNMP v2c is backward compatible with version 1.
- ☞ **SNMP Version 3**: This version provides greater security and remote configuration capabilities than its predecessors. Access isn't limited to a single community string for read-only and read/write access, as usernames and passwords have been introduced. Views of OIDs in a MIB can also be limited on a per-user basis. Support for encrypted SNMP data transfer and transfer error detection is also provided.

Remember their differences, because you will need to specify the version number when doing SNMP queries.

Doing SNMP Queries

Configuring SNMP on a server isn't hard, but it does require a number of detailed steps.

Installing SNMP Utilities on a Linux Server

If you intend to use your Linux box to query your network devices, other servers or even itself using MRTG or any other tool, you need to have the SNMP utility tools package net-snmp-utils installed. When searching for the file, remember that the SNMP utility tools RPM's filename usually starts with net-snmp-utils, which is followed by a version number, as in net-snmp-utils-5.1.1-2.i386.rpm. (If you need an installation refresher, see Chapter 6, "Installing RPM Software.")

SNMP Utilities Command Syntax

The SNMP utility tools package installs a number of new commands on your system for doing SNMP queries, most notably snmpget for individual OIDs and snmpwalk for obtaining the contents of an entire MIB. Both commands require you to specify the community string with a -c operator. They also require you to specify the version of the SNMP query to be used with a -v 1, -v 2c, or -v 3 operator for versions 1, 2, and 3, respectively. The first argument is the name or IP address of the target device and all other arguments list the MIBs to be queried.

This example gets all the values in the interface MIB of the local server using SNMP version 1 and the community string of craz33guy.

```
[root@bigboy tmp]# snmpwalk -v 1 -c craz33guy localhost interface
...

...
IF-MIB::ifDescr.1 = STRING: lo
IF-MIB::ifDescr.2 = STRING: eth0
IF-MIB::ifDescr.3 = STRING: eth1
...

...
IF-MIB::ifPhysAddress.1 = STRING:
IF-MIB::ifPhysAddress.2 = STRING: 0:9:5b:2f:9e:d5
IF-MIB::ifPhysAddress.3 = STRING: 0:b0:d0:46:32:71
...

...
[root@bigboy tmp]#
```

Upon inspecting the output of the snmpwalk command, you can see that the second interface seems to have the name eth0 and the MAC address 0:9:5b:2f:9e:d5. You can now retrieve the individual MAC address using the snmpget command:

```
[root@bigboy tmp]# snmpget -v 1 -c const1payted localhost
ifPhysAddress.2
IF-MIB::ifPhysAddress.2 = STRING: 0:9:5b:2f:9e:d5
[root@bigboy tmp]#
```

You can confirm this information using the `ifconfig` command for interface `eth0`; the very first line shows a matching MAC address:

```
[root@bigboy tmp]# ifconfig -a eth0
eth0      Link encap:Ethernet  HWaddr 00:09:5B:2F:9E:D5
          inet addr:216.10.119.244  Bcast:216.10.119.255
Mask:255.255.255.240
...
...
[root@bigboy tmp]#
```

You'll now see how you can configure SNMP on your Linux server to
achieve these results.

Configuring SNMP on a Linux Server

By default Fedora, installs the `net-snmp` package as its SNMP server product.
This package uses a configuration file named `/etc/snmp/snmpd.conf` in which
the community strings and other parameters may be set. The version of the
configuration file that comes with `net-snmp` is quite complicated. I suggest
archiving it and using a much simpler version with only a single line containing the keyword `rocommunity` followed by the community string. Here is an
example:

1. Save the old configuration file:

   ```
   [root@bigboy tmp]# cd /etc/snmp/
   [root@bigboy snmp]# mv snmpd.conf snmpd.conf.old
   [root@bigboy snmp]# vi snmpd.conf
   ```

2. Enter this line in the new configuration file to set the Read Only community string to `craz33guy`:

   ```
   rocommunity craz33guy
   ```

3. Configure Linux to start SNMP services on each reboot with the
   `chkconfig` command:

   ```
   [root@bigboy root]# chkconfig snmpd on
   [root@bigboy root]#
   ```

4. Start SNMP to load the current configuration file:

   ```
   [root@bigboy root]# service snmpd start
   Starting snmpd: [ OK ]
   [root@bigboy root]#
   ```

5. Test whether SNMP can read the `system` and `interface` MIBs using the
   `snmpwalk` command:

   ```
   [root@bigboy snmp]# snmpwalk -v 1 -c craz33guy localhost system
   SNMPv2-MIB::sysDescr.0 = STRING: Linux bigboy 2.4.18-14 #1 Wed Sep
   4 11:57:57 EDT 2002 i586
   ```

```
SNMPv2-MIB::sysObjectID.0 = OID: NET-SNMP-MIB::netSnmpAgentOIDs.10
SNMPv2-MIB::sysUpTime.0 = Timeticks: (425) 0:00:04.25
SNMPv2-MIB::sysContact.0 = STRING: root@localhost
SNMPv2-MIB::sysName.0 = STRING: bigboy
...
...
...
[root@bigboy snmp]# snmpwalk -v 1 -c craz33guy localhost interface
IF-MIB::ifNumber.0 = INTEGER: 3
IF-MIB::ifIndex.1 = INTEGER: 1
IF-MIB::ifIndex.2 = INTEGER: 2
IF-MIB::ifIndex.3 = INTEGER: 3
IF-MIB::ifDescr.1 = STRING: lo
IF-MIB::ifDescr.2 = STRING: wlan0
IF-MIB::ifDescr.3 = STRING: eth0
...
...
...
[root@bigboy snmp]#
```

Now that you know SNMP is working correctly on your Linux server, you can configure SNMP statistics gathering software, such as MRTG, to create online graphs of your traffic flows.

SNMP on Other Devices

In the example, you were polling localhost. You can poll any SNMP-aware network device that has SNMP enabled. All you need is the IP address and SNMP Read Only string and you'll be able to get similar results. Here is an example of a query of a device with an IP address of 192.168.1.1.

```
[root@bigboy snmp]# snmpwalk -v 1 -c chir1qui 192.168.1.1 interface
```

Different SNMP Versions

There are currently three versions of SNMP; versions 1, 2 and 3. The Linux snmpwalk and snmpget commands have -v 1, -v 2c, and -v 3 switches for specifying the SNMP version to be used for queries. Always make sure you are using the correct one.

Basic SNMP Security

The most commonly supported versions of SNMP don't encrypt your community string password so you shouldn't do queries over insecure networks, such as the Internet. You should also make sure that you use all reasonable security measures to allow queries only from trusted IP addresses either via a firewall or the SNMP security features available in the snmp.conf file. You can also configure your server to use the TCP wrappers feature outlined in Appendix I,

"Miscellaneous Linux Topics," to limit access to specific servers without the need of a firewall.

In case you need it, the snmpd.conf file can support limiting MIB access to trusted hosts and networks.

The snmpd.conf file has two security sections; a section with very restrictive access sits at the top of the file and is immediately followed by a less restrictive section. The example that follows is a modification of the less restrictive section. You will have to comment out the more restrictive statements at the top of the file for it to work correctly.

```
##         sec.name    source          community
##         ========    ======          =========
com2sec    local       localhost       craz33guy
com2sec    network_1   172.16.1.0/24   craz33guy
com2sec    network_2   192.16.1.0/24   craz33guy


##         Access.group.name  sec.model    sec.name
##         =================  =========    ========
group      MyROGroup          v1           local
group      MyROGroup          v1           network_1
group      MyROGroup          v1           network_2


##    MIB.view.name    incl/excl   MIB.subtree   mask
##    =============    =========   ===========   ====
view  all-mibs         included    .1            80


##         MIB
##         group.name context sec.model sec.level prefix read      write
notif
##         ========== ======= ========= ========= ====== ====      =====
=====

access MyROGroup      ""       v1        noauth    0      all-mibs none
none
```

In the example:

☞ Only three networks (localhost, 172.16.1.0/24, and 192.168.1.0/24) are allowed to access the server with the craz33guy community string.

☞ Each network is matched to a group called MyROGroup using SNMP version 1, and all the MIBs on the server are defined by the view named all-mibs.

☞ An access statement ensures that only the defined networks have read only access to all the MIBs.

☞ Modification of the MIBs via SNMP is denied because the word "none" is in the write section of the `access` statement.

These precautions are probably unnecessary in a home environment where access is generally limited to devices on the home network by an NAT firewall.

Simple SNMP Troubleshooting

If your SNMP queries fail, then verify that:

☞ You restarted your `snmp.conf` file so the configuration settings become active. Remember, the `snmpd.conf` file is only read by the `snmpd` daemon when it starts up.

☞ You are using the correct community string.

☞ Firewalls aren't preventing SNMP queries from the SNMP client to the SNMP target.

☞ Your SNMP security policy allows the query from your network.

☞ Any TCP wrappers configuration on your SNMP target machine allows SNMP queries from your SNMP client. Generally speaking in a home environment protected by NAT your TCP wrappers files (`/etc/hosts.allow`) and (`/etc/hosts.deny`) should be blank.

☞ Network routing between the client and target devices is correct. A simple ping or `traceroute` test should be sufficient.

☞ The `snmpd` daemon is running on the SNMP client.

☞ You are querying using the correct SNMP version.

☞ Your `/var/log/messages` file does not contain errors that may have occurred while starting `snmpd`.

Troubleshooting to get functioning SNMP queries is important as many other supporting applications such as MRTG—which I'll discuss next—rely on them in order to work correctly.

MRTG

MRTG (Multi-Router Traffic Grapher) is a public domain package for producing graphs of various router statistics via a Web page. You can easily create graphs of traffic flow statistics through your home network's firewall/router or even your Linux box's NIC cards using MRTG. The product is available from the MRTG Web site (`www.mrtg.org`) and also on your distribution CDs. Figure 22.2 shows a sample MRTG graph.

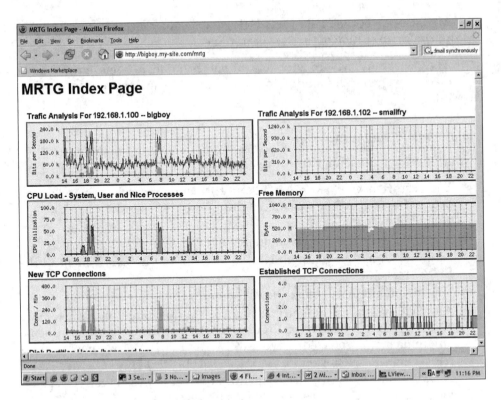

Figure 22.2   A typical MRTG Web page.

MRTG Download and Installation

You need to install MRTG before proceeding. Most Red Hat and Fedora Linux software products are available in the RPM format. When searching for the file, remember that the MRTG RPM's filename usually starts with mrtg and a version number, as in mrtg-2.10.5-3.i386.rpm.

   In addition to MRTG, you need to install the SNMP utility tools as explained earlier and you need to have a Web server package installed for MRTG to work. Red Hat Linux usually comes with the Apache Web server software preinstalled. The easiest way to tell if Apache is installed is to run the rpm -q httpd command. If you don't get a positive response, you can refer to Chapter 20, "The Apache Web Server," for installation details. By default Apache expects the HTML files for your Web site to be located in /var/www/html. MRTG places its HTML files in /var/www/mrtg.

Configuring MRTG

By default, MRTG maps the inbound and outbound data throughput rates on the device it is polling. Methods for specifying other OIDs, such as CPU and memory usage, are discussed in Chapter 23, "Advanced MRTG for Linux." For now, I'll stick with the default configuration.

When the MRTG RPM is installed, it creates a directory called /etc/mrtg in which all future configuration files are stored. To create a replacement default /etc/mrtg/mrtg.cfg configuration file for the server, follow these steps:

1. Use MRTG's cfgmaker command to create a configuration file named mrtg.cfg for the server (Bigboy) using a Read Only community string of craz33guy. Place all data files in the directory /var/www/mrtg:.

```
[root@bigboy tmp]# cfgmaker --output=/etc/mrtg/mrtg.cfg \
--global "workdir: /var/www/mrtg" -ifref=ip \
--global 'options[_]: growright,bits' \
craz33guy@localhost


--base: Get Device Info on craz33guy@localhost:
--base: Vendor Id:
--base: Populating confcache
--snpo: confcache craz33guy@localhost: Descr lo --> 1
--snpo: confcache craz33guy@localhost: Descr wlan0 --> 2
...
...
...
--base: Walking ifAdminStatus
--base: Walking ifOperStatus
--base: Writing /etc/mrtg/mrtg.cfg
[root@bigboy tmp]#
```

Tip

Using the -ifref=ip cfgmaker command option instructs MRTG to use the interface's IP address as the title for each graph. Unfortunately, this causes errors when Fedora Core 1 polls another Fedora Core 1 server; the errors prevent the graphs from being created correctly. You can avoid this problem by removing the option to get graph titles using the much less recognizable MAC address of the interfaces.

Tip
As explained in the SNMP section, there are different versions of SNMP. If your
query doesn't work, check to make sure you are using the required version and
then check other SNMP configuration parameters on the target device. You can
specify MRTG's SNMP query version with the `--snmp-options cfgmaker` option.
Here is an example of `cfgmaker` using an SNMP version 2 query of a router with an
IP address of 192.168.1.3. The `--snmp-options` option's five colons before the 2 are
important:

```
[root@bigboy tmp]# cfgmaker --
output=/etc/mrtg/192.168.1.3.cfg \
-ifref=ip --global "workdir: /var/www/mrtg" \
--snmp-options=::::::2 craz33guy@192.168.1.3
```

2. Edit `/etc/mrtg/mrtg.cfg`, and remove the sections related to interfaces
you don't need to monitor. A certain candidate would be the virtual loopback interface `Lo:` (with the IP address of 127.0.0.1), which doesn't pass
any network traffic at all.

3. Run MRTG using `/etc/mrtg/mrtg.cfg` as your argument three times.
You'll get an error the two times as MRTG tries to move old data files,
and naturally, the first time it is run, MRTG has no data files to move.

```
[root@bigboy tmp]# env LANG=C /usr/bin/mrtg /etc/mrtg/mrtg.cfg
Rateup WARNING: /usr/bin/rateup could not read the primary log
file for localhost_192.168.1.100
Rateup WARNING: /usr/bin/rateup The backup log file for local-
host_192.168.1.100 was invalid as well
Rateup WARNING: /usr/bin/rateup Can't remove local-
host_192.168.1.100.old updating log file
Rateup WARNING: /usr/bin/rateup Can't rename local-
host_192.168.1.100.log to localhost_192.168.1.100.old updating
log file
[root@bigboy tmp]# env LANG=C /usr/bin/mrtg /etc/mrtg/mrtg.cfg
Rateup WARNING: /usr/bin/rateup Can't remove local-
host_192.168.1.100.old updating log file
[root@bigboy tmp]# env LANG=C /usr/bin/mrtg /etc/mrtg/mrtg.cfg
[root@bigboy tmp]#
```

4. Use MRTG's `indexmaker` command to create a Web index page using your
new `mrtg.cfg` file as a guide. The MRTG Web GUI expects to find the
index file in the default MRTG Web directory of `/var/www/mrtg/`, so the
format of the command would be:

```
[root@bigboy tmp]# indexmaker --output=/var/www/mrtg/index.html \
/etc/mrtg/mrtg.cfg
```

5. MRTG is run every five minutes by default, and the file that governs this
is `/etc/cron.d/mrtg`. For MRTG to work correctly, edit this file, replacing
all occurrences of `/usr/bin/mrtg` with `env LANG[eq]C /usr/bin/mrtg`. The
explanation for changing the language character set for MRTG is given
in the "Troubleshooting MRTG" section.

This isn't all—you need to view the graphs too. This will be covered later, but first I'll show you how to poll multiple devices.

Getting MRTG to Poll Multiple Devices

The Fedora Core MRTG installation process creates a `cron` file named `/etc/cron.d/mrtg`. This file tells the `cron` daemon to run MRTG using the `/etc/mrtg/mrtg.cfg` file every five minutes to poll your network devices. You can configure MRTG to poll multiple devices, each with a separate configuration file. Here's how:

1. Create a new configuration file using the steps from the previous section; choose a filename that is not `mrtg.cfg`.

2. Add a new MRTG line in `/etc/cron.d/mrtg` for each new configuration file you create:

```
0-59/5 * * * * root env LANG=C /usr/bin/mrtg /etc/mrtg/mrtg.cfg
0-59/5 * * * * root env LANG=C /usr/bin/mrtg /etc/mrtg/device1.cfg
0-59/5 * * * * root env LANG=C /usr/bin/mrtg /etc/mrtg/device2.cfg
```

3. Run the `indexmaker` command, and include all of your `/etc/mrtg` configuration files, to regenerate your Web index page.

```
[root@bigboy tmp]# indexmaker --output=/var/www/mrtg/index.html \
/etc/mrtg/mrtg.cfg /etc/mrtg/device1.cfg /etc/mrtg/device2.cfg
```

4. Other versions of Linux keep their MRTG `cron` entries inside the `/etc/crontab` file. Edit this file using the same syntax as the Fedora `/etc/cron.d/mrtg` file, and then restart the `cron` daemon to re-read the configuration:

```
[root@bigboy tmp]# service crond restart
```

You could also create a script with the `/usr/bin/mrtg/etc/mrtg/device.cfg` entries in it and make `cron` run it every five minutes. This way you can just edit the script each time you add a device without having to restart `cron`.

Configuring Apache to Work with MRTG

MRTG is useful because it can provide a graphical representation of your server's performance statistics via a Web browser.

With Fedora Core, MRTG creates an add-on configuration file named `/etc/httpd/conf.d/mrtg.conf` that includes all the necessary Apache commands for MRTG to work.

Some configuration may need to be done, because by default MRTG accepts Web requests from the Linux console only. You can add your home network to the file by inserting the network on the `Allow from` line, or you can allow universal access by commenting out that line along with the `Deny from` line. This example adds access from the 192.168.1.0 network:

```
<Location /mrtg>
    Order deny,allow
    Deny from all
    Allow from localhost 192.168.1.0/24
</Location>
```

If you want to access MRTG from the Internet, then you'll have to comment out the Deny statement and allow from all IP addresses:

```
<Location /mrtg>
    Order deny,allow
    Allow from all
</Location>
```

Remember to restart Apache after you make these modifications for the changes to take effect.

Note

With newer versions of Fedora, Apache automatically reads the add-on files in the /etc/httpd/conf.d/ directory. With Fedora Core 1, you have to specifically configure the Apache configuration file /etc/httpd/conf/httpd.conf to find it. You can do this yourself by inserting this line at the very bottom of the main Apache configuration file before restarting Apache for the change to take effect:

```
include "/etc/httpd/conf.d/mrtg.conf"
```

Basic Security

If you are accessing MRTG graphs from the Internet, you may want to add password protection to the directory by using a .htaccess file as described in Chapter 20.

How to View the MRTG Graphs in Your Web Browser

You can now access your MRTG graphs by pointing your browser to the URL:

```
http://server-ip-address/mrtg/
```

Using MRTG to Monitor Other Subsystems

MRTG will generate HTML pages with daily, weekly, monthly, and yearly statistics for your interfaces. By default, MRTG provides only network interface statistics. Chapter 23 has detailed examples and explanations of how to monitor Linux disk, CPU, memory, and Web connection data. The MRTG Web site, www.mrtg.org, also has links to other sites that show you how to monitor many other subsystems on a variety of devices and operating systems.

Troubleshooting MRTG

There are many simple steps you can use to troubleshoot MRTG. Take a look at some of the most common ones.

Basic Steps

MRTG won't work if SNMP queries don't work. Make sure you follow the SNMP troubleshooting steps if you have any difficulties.

Setting the Correct Character Set

MRTG usually works only if your system uses an ASCII-based (Western European) character set. If it isn't set, then you'll get errors such as this every time you run MRTG from the command line or as part of a `cron` job:

```
root@bigboy tmp]# mrtg /etc/mrtg/mrtg.cfg
------------------------------------------------------------------
ERROR: Mrtg will most likely not work propperly when the environment
       variable LANG is set to UTF-8. Please run mrtg in an envir..
       where this is not the case:

       env LANG=C /usr/bin/mrtg ...
------------------------------------------------------------------
[root@bigboy tmp]#
```

Your system's character set is defined in `/etc/sysconfig/i18n`, and the current Fedora default of `en_US.UTF-8` won't work, but `en_US` will after a system reboot. This is not necessarily a good idea, especially if the native language Linux uses on your system is not ASCII based, other things may fail to work.

A better solution is to always run MRTG using this command instead of using just plain `/usr/bin/mrtg`:

```
env LANG=C /usr/bin/mrtg
```

This will modify the character set used by MRTG alone and shouldn't affect anything else.

Fedora Core 1 MRTG Errors with net-snmp

A bug appears in the MRTG implementation for some Fedora Core 1 MRTG versions when polling another Fedora Core 1 server.

When using a `-ifref=ip` statement with the `cfgmaker` command, every line in the configuration file that is generated becomes commented out. When it works, this statement is very convenient, because it makes MRTG provide graphs sorted by the IP addresses of the interfaces instead of the default, which is the much harder to recognize interface MAC address. Upgrading to the most current Core 1 version of MRTG will fix the problem:

```
### Interface 6 >> Descr: `' | Name: `' | Ip: `192.168.1.100'
###
### The following interface is commented out because:
### * has a speed of which makes no sense
### * got `Received SNMP response with error code
###        error status: noSuchName
###        index 1 (OID: 1.3.6.1.2.1.2.2.1.10.6)
###     SNMPv1_Session (remote host: "localhost" [127.0.0.1].161)
###                      community: "craz33guy"
###                     request ID: 824482716
###                    PDU bufsize: 8000 bytes
###                        timeout: 2s
###                        retries: 5
#
# Target[localhost_192.168.1.100]: /192.168.1.100:craz33guy@localhost:
# SetEnv[localhost_192.168.1.100]: MRTG_INT_IP="192.168.1.100"
MRTG_INT_DES
# MaxBytes[localhost_192.168.1.100]: 0
# Title[localhost_192.168.1.100]: Traffic Analysis for 192.168.1.100
# PageTop[localhost_192.168.1.100]: <H1>Traffic Analysis for
192.168.1.100
#   <TABLE>
#     <TR><TD>System:</TD>      <TD>bigboy in Unknown</TD></TR>
#     <TR><TD>Maintainer:</TD>  <TD>root@localhost</TD></TR>
#     <TR><TD>Description:</TD><TD>   </TD></TR>
#     <TR><TD>ifType:</TD>      <TD> ()</TD></TR>
#     <TR><TD>ifName:</TD>      <TD></TD></TR>
#     <TR><TD>Max Speed:</TD>   <TD>0.0 bits/s</TD></TR>
#   </TABLE>
```

As all the lines in the configuration file are commented out with a # character, indexmaker fails to create an index.html file and gives errors:

```
[root@bigboy tmp]# indexmaker --output=/var/www/mrtg/stats/index.html
/etc/mrtg/mrtg.cfg
Use of uninitialized value in hash element at /usr/bin/indexmaker line
307.
[root@bigboy tmp]#
```

WEBALIZER

Webalizer is a Web server log file analysis tool that comes installed by default on Red Hat/Fedora Linux. Each night, Webalizer reads your Apache log files and creates a set of Web pages that enable you to view Web surfer statistics for your site. The information provided includes a list of your Web site's most popular pages sorted by hits along with traffic graphs showing the times of day when your site is most popular.

How to View Your Webalizer Statistics

Fedora creates an add-on configuration file named /etc/httpd/conf.d/webal-izer.conf that includes all the necessary Apache commands for Webalizer to work. As in the case of the MRTG add-on file mentioned above, you have to edit it to allow access to the Webalizer pages from locations other than the Linux console. You also have to restart Apache to make the changes take effect.

By default, Webalizer places its index page in the directory /var/www/html/usage and allows you to view your data by visiting the URL http://server-ip-address/usage.

The Webalizer Configuration File

Webalizer stores its configuration in the file /etc/webalizer.conf. The default settings should be sufficient for your Web server, but you may want to adjust the directory in which Webalizer places your graph statistics. This can be adjusted with the OutputDir directive in the file. After adjustments, Webalizer functions with few annoyances; however, be aware that running in quiet mode could hide deeper problems that could occur in the future.

THE *TOP* COMMAND

You can monitor the amount of memory and CPU resources your system is using with the top command:

```
[root@bigboy tmp]# top
top - 20:00:54 up 61 days, 23:35, 2 users, load average: 0.00, 0.00
Tasks: 72 total, 1 running, 71 sleeping, 0 stopped, 0 zombie
Cpu(s): 4.3% us, 0.5% sy, 0.0% ni, 95.1% id, 0.1% wa, 0.0% hi,
Mem:  1027784k total, 868484k used,  159300k free, 276272k
Swap: 4192924k total,     80k used, 4192844k free, 356256k
PID USER PR NI VIRT RES  SHR S %CPU %MEM TIME+    COMMAND
  1 root 16  0 2268 516 1420 S  0.0  0.1 0:03.85 init
  2 root 34 19    0   0    0 S  0.0  0.0 0:00.32 ksoftirqd/0
  3 root 5 -10    0   0    0 S  0.0  0.0 0:00.00 events/0
  4 root 7 -10    0   0    0 S  0.0  0.0 0:00.02 khelper
[root@bigboy tmp]#
```

Here the CPU usage is running 95.1% idle and 15% of memory (159300k) is free. The amount of free memory may appear low, but in this case, the server doesn't seem to be swapping idle processes from memory to the swap disk partition as it isn't being used at all. Excessive swapping can cause your system to slow down dramatically, the simplest ways to avoid this is to add more RAM or reduce the number of processes or users that are active on your system.

If your system seems slow but the CPU and memory usage is low, then start looking at networking problems, such as poor duplex negotiation, bad cables, and network congestion due to excessive traffic.

THE *VMSTAT* COMMAND

You can also determine memory and swap usage with the vmstat command, which provides a summary of what top produces. In the example, memory is still 15% free (158,196MB used from a total of 130,780) and only 80MB of the swap partition is being used.

```
[root@bigboy tmp]# vmstat
procs ------memory----- --swap- ---io-- -system- --cpu--
 r  b   swpd   free   buff  cache   si   so   bi   bo   in    cs us
sy id wa
 0  0      80 158196 276272 357236    0    0    1    0    0    4  4
 1 95  0
[root@bigboy tmp]#
```

As your memory fills up, your system temporarily stores programs and data on your hard disk's swap partition. Excess swapping of programs and data between disk and memory can cause your system to slow down significantly and memory usage should be monitored to allow you to plan ways to either increase RAM or tune the way your system operates.

THE *FREE* UTILITY

The free utility can determine the amount of free RAM on your system. The output is easier to understand than vmstat's. Here's a sample:

```
[root@bigboy tmp]# vmstat
procs ------memory------ --swap- ---io-
 r  b   swpd   free   buff  cache   si   so   bi   bo
 0  0      80 158196 276272 357236    0    0    1    0
[root@bigboy tmp]#
```

You should generally try to make your system run with at least 20% free memory on average, which should allow it to handle moderate spikes in usage caused by running memory-intensive `cron` batch jobs or tape backups. If you cannot achieve this, consider running more efficient versions of programs, offloading some applications to servers with less load, and, of course, upgrading the capacity of your RAM.

CONCLUSION

Server monitoring is always a good practice, because it can help you predict when things are going to go wrong or long-term trends in your Web traffic.

MRTG can be expanded not only to monitor traffic on your server's NIC cards, but also to graph many of the statistics listed in `top`, `free`, and `vmstat`. Chapter 23 shows you how.

CHAPTER **23**

Advanced MRTG for Linux

IN THIS CHAPTER

- ☞ Locating and Viewing the Contents of Linux MIBs
- ☞ Testing Your MIB Value
- ☞ Differences in MIB and MRTG Terminology
- ☞ The CPU and the Memory Monitoring MIB
- ☞ The TCP/IP Monitoring MIB
- ☞ Manually Configuring Your MRTG File
- ☞ Implementing Advanced Server Monitoring
- ☞ Monitoring Non-Linux MIB Values
- ☞ Troubleshooting
- ☞ Conclusion

In many cases using MRTG in a basic configuration to monitor the volume of network traffic to your server isn't enough. You may also want to see graphs of CPU, disk, and memory usage. This chapter explains how to find the values you want to monitor in the SNMP MIB files and then how to use this information to configure MRTG.

All the chapter's examples assume that the SNMP Read Only string is `craz33guy` and that the `net-snmp-utils` RPM package is installed (see Chapter 22, "Monitoring Server Performance").

LOCATING AND VIEWING THE CONTENTS OF LINUX MIBS

Residing in memory, MIBs are data structures that are constantly updated via the SNMP daemon. The MIB configuration text files are located on your hard disk and loaded into memory each time SNMP restarts.

385

You can easily find your Fedora Linux MIBs by using the `locate` command and filtering the output to include only values with the word "snmp" in them. As you can see in this case, the MIBs are located in the `/usr/share/snmp/mibs` directory:

```
[root@bigboy tmp]# locate mib | grep snmp
/usr/share/doc/net-snmp-5.0.6/README.mib2c
/usr/share/snmp/mibs
/usr/share/snmp/mibs/DISMAN-SCHEDULE-MIB.txt
...
...
[root@bigboy tmp]#
```

As the MIB configurations are text files you can search for keywords in them using the `grep` command. This example searches for the MIBs that keep track of TCP connections and returns the RFC1213 and TCP MIBs as the result.

```
[root@silent mibs]# grep -i tcp /usr/share/snmp/mibs/*.txt \
   | grep connections
...
RFC1213-MIB.txt: "The limit on the total number of TCP connections
RFC1213-MIB.txt: "The number of times TCP connections have made a
...
TCP-MIB.txt:     "The number of times TCP connections have made a
...
...
[root@silent mibs]#
```

You can use the `vi` editor to look at the MIBs. Don't change them, because doing so could cause SNMP to fail. MIBs are very complicated, but fortunately the key sections are commented.

Each value tracked in a MIB is called an **object** and is often referred to by its **object ID** or **OID**. In this snippet of the RFC1213-MIB.txt file, you can see that querying the `tcpActiveOpens` object returns the number of active open TCP connections to the server. The SYNTAX field shows that this is a counter value.

MIBs usually track two types of values. **Counter** values are used for items that continuously increase as time passes, such as the amount of packets passing through a NIC or amount of time the CPU has been busy since boot time. **Integer** values change instant by instant and are useful for tracking such statistics as the amount of memory currently being used.

```
tcpActiveOpens OBJECT-TYPE
      SYNTAX   Counter
      ACCESS   read-only
      STATUS   mandatory
      DESCRIPTION
             "The number of times TCP connections have made a
             direct transition to the SYN-SENT state from the
```

```
                    CLOSED state."
       ::= { tcp 5 }
```

You'll explore the differences between SNMP and MRTG terminologies in more detail later. Understanding them will be important in understanding how to use MRTG to track MIB values.

TESTING YOUR MIB VALUE

Once you identify an interesting MIB value for your Linux system, you can use the snmpwalk command to poll it. Many times the text aliases in an MIB reference the OID branch only and not the data located in a leaf ending in an additional number, such as .0 or .1. The snmpget command doesn't work with branches, giving an error stating that the MIB variable couldn't be found.

In the example below, the ssCpuRawUser OID alias was found to be interesting, but the snmpget command fails to get a value. Follow up with the snmpwalk command shows that the value is located in ssCpuRawUser.0 instead. The snmpget is then successful in retrieving the counter32 type data with a current value of 396271.

```
[root@bigboy tmp]# snmpget -v1 -c craz33guy localhost ssCpuRawUser
Error in packet
Reason: (noSuchName) There is no such variable name in this MIB.
Failed object: UCD-SNMP-MIB::ssCpuRawUser
[root@bigboy tmp]#

[root@bigboy tmp]# snmpwalk -v1 -c craz33guy localhost ssCpuRawUser
UCD-SNMP-MIB::ssCpuRawUser.0 = Counter32: 396241
[root@bigboy tmp]# snmpget -v1 -c craz33guy localhost ssCpuRawUser.0
UCD-SNMP-MIB::ssCpuRawUser.0 = Counter32: 396271
[root@bigboy tmp]#
```

The MIB values that work successfully with snmpget are the ones you should use with MRTG.

DIFFERENCES IN MIB AND MRTG TERMINOLOGY

Always keep in mind that MRTG refers to MIB counter values as counter values. It refers to MIB integer and gauge values as gauge. By default, MRTG considers all values to be counters.

MRTG doesn't plot counter values as a constantly increasing graph; it plots only how much the value has changed since the last polling cycle. CPU usage is typically tracked by MIBs as a counter value; fortunately, you can edit your MRTG configuration file to make it graph this information in a percentage use format (more on this later).

The syntax type, the MIB object name, and the description of what it does are the most important things you need to know when configuring MRTG; I'll come back to these later.

THE CPU AND THE MEMORY MONITORING MIB

The UCD-SNMP-MIB MIB keeps track of a number of key performance MIB objects, including the commonly used ones in Table 23.1.

Table 23.1   Important Objects in the UCD-SNMP-MIB MIB

UCD-SNMP-MIB Object Variable	MIB Type	MRTG Type	Description
ssCpuRawUser	Counter	Counter	Total CPU usage by applications run by nonprivileged users since the system booted. Adding the user, system, and nice values can give a good approximation of total CPU usage.
ssCpuRawSystem	Counter	Counter	Total CPU usage by applications run by privileged system processes since the system booted.
ssCpuRawNice	Counter	Counter	Total CPU usage by applications running at a nondefault priority level.
ssCpuRawIdle	Counter	Counter	The percentage of the time the CPU is running idle. Subtracting this value from 100 can give a good approximation of total CPU usage.
memAvailReal	Integer	Gauge	Available physical memory space on the host.

THE TCP/IP MONITORING MIB

The TCP-MIB MIB keeps track of data connection information and contains the very useful tcpActiveOpens and tcpCurrEstab objects. Table 23.2 details the most important objects in TCP-MIB.

Table 23.2 Important Objects in the `TCP-MIB` MIB

`TCP-MIB` Object Variable	MIB Type	MRTG Type	Description
`tcpActiveOpens`	Counter	Counter	Measures the number of completed TCP connections.
`tcpCurrEstab`	Gauge	Gauge	Measures the number of TCP connections in the established state.
`tcpInErrs`	Counter	Counter	Total number of TCP segments with bad checksum errors.

MANUALLY CONFIGURING YOUR MRTG FILE

The MRTG `cfgmaker` program creates configuration files for network interfaces only, simultaneously tracking two OIDs: the NIC's input and output data statistics. The `mrtg` program then uses these configuration files to determine the type of data to record in its data directory. The `indexmaker` program also uses this information to create the overview, or **Summary View** Web page for the MIB OIDs you're monitoring.

This Summary View page shows daily statistics only. You have to click on the Summary View graphs to get the **Detailed View** page behind it with the daily, weekly, monthly, and annual graphs. Some of the parameters in the configuration file refer to the Detailed View, others refer to the Summary View.

If you want to monitor any other pairs of OIDs, you have to manually create the configuration files, because `cfgmaker` isn't aware of any OIDs other than those related to a NIC. The `mrtg` and `indexmaker` program can be fed individual OIDs from a customized configuration file and will function as expected if you edit the file correctly.

Parameter Formats

MRTG configuration parameters are always followed by a graph name surrounded by square brackets and a colon. The format looks like this:

```
Parameter[graph name]: value
```

For ease of editing, the parameters for a particular graph are usually grouped together. Each graph can track two OIDS listed in the `Target` parameter, which is usually placed at the very top of the `graph name` list. The two OID values are separated by an & symbol; the first one is the input OID, and the second one is the output OID.

Legend Parameters

On the Detailed View Web page, each graph has a legend that shows the max, average, and current values of the graph's OID statistics. You can use the legendI parameter for the description of the input graph (first graph OID) and the legendO for the output graph (second graph OID).

The space available under each graph's legend is tiny so MRTG also has legend1 and legend2 parameters that are placed at the very bottom of the page to provide more details. Parameter legend1 is the expansion of legendI, and legend2 is the expansion of legendO.

The Ylegend is the legend for the Y axis, the value you are trying to compare. In the case of a default MRTG configuration this would be the data flow through the interface in bits or bytes per second. Here is an example of the legends of a default MRTG configuration:

```
YLegend[graph1]: Bits per second
Legend1[graph1]: Incoming Traffic in Bits per Second
Legend2[graph1]: Outgoing Traffic in Bits per Second
LegendI[graph1]: In
LegendO[graph1]: Out
```

You can prevent MRTG from printing the legend at the bottom of the graph by leaving the value of the legend blank like this:

```
LegendI[graph1]:
```

Later you'll learn how to match the legends to the OIDs for a variety of situations.

Options Parameters

Options parameters provide MRTG with graph formatting information. The growright option makes sure the data at the right of the screen is for the most current graph values. This usually makes the graphs more intuitively easy to read. MRTG defaults to growing from the left.

The nopercent option prevents MRTG from printing percentage style statistics in the legends at the bottom of the graph. The gauge option alerts MRTG to the fact that the graphed values are of the gauge type. If the value you are monitoring is in bytes, then you can convert the output to bits using the bits option. Likewise, you can convert per second values to per minute graphs using the perminute option. Here are some examples for two different graphs:

```
options[graph1]: growright,nopercent,perminute

options[graph2]: gauge,bits
```

If you place this parameter at the top with a label of `[_]` it gets applied to all the graphs defined in the file:

```
options[_]: growright
```

Title Parameters

The title on the Summary Page is provided by the `Title` parameter, the `PageTop` parameter tells the title for the Detailed View page. The `PageTop` string must start with `<H1>` and end with `</H1>`.

```
Title[graph1]: Interface eth0
PageTop[graph1]: <H1>Detailed Statistics For Interface eth0</H1>
```

Scaling Parameters

The `MaxBytes` parameter is the maximum amount of data MRTG will plot on a graph. Anything more than this seems to disappear over the edge of the graph.

MRTG also tries to adjust its graphs so that the largest value plotted on the graph is always close to the top. This is so even if you set the `MaxBytes` parameter.

When you are plotting a value that has a known maximum and you always want to have this value at the top of the vertical legend, you may want to turn off MRTG's auto scaling. If you are plotting percentage CPU usage, and the server reaches a maximum of 60%, with scaling, MRTG will have a vertical plot of 0% to 60%, so that the vertical peak is near the top of the graph image.

When scaling is off, and `MaxBytes` is set to 100, then the peak will be only 60% of the way up as the graph plots from 0% to 100%. The example removes scaling from the yearly, monthly, weekly, and daily views on the Detailed View page and gives them a maximum value of 100:

```
Unscaled[graph1]: ymwd
MaxBytes[graph1]: 100
```

Defining The MIB Target Parameters

As stated before, MRTG always tries to compare two MIB OID values that are defined by the `Target` parameter. You have to specify the two MIB OID objects—the SNMP password and the IP address of the device you are querying in this parameter—and separate them with an & character:

```
Target[graph1]: mib-object-1.0&mib-object-2.0:<SNMP-password>@<IP-address>
```

The numeric value, in this case `.0`, at the end of the MIB is required. The next example uses the SNMP command to return the user mode CPU utilization of a Linux server. Notice how the `.0` is tagged onto the end of the output.

```
[root@silent mibs]# snmpwalk -v 1 -c craz33guy localhost ssCpuRawUser
UCD-SNMP-MIB::ssCpuRawUser.0 = Counter32: 926739
[root@silent mibs]#
```

The MRTG legends map to the MIBs listed in the target as shown in Table 23.3.

Table 23.3   Mapping MIBs to the Graph Legends

Legend	Maps to Target MIB
Legend1	1
Legend2	2
LegendI	1
LegendO	2

So in the example below, `legend1` and `legendI` describe `mib-object-1.0`, and `legend2` and `legendO` describe `mib-object-2.0`.

```
Target [graph1]: mib-object-1.0&mib-object-2.0:<SNMP-password>@<IP-
address>
```

Plotting Only One MIB Value

If you want to plot only one MIB value, you can just repeat the target MIB in the definition as in the next example, which plots only `mib-object-1`. The resulting MRTG graph actually superimposes the input and output graphs one on top of the other.

```
Target [graph1]: mib-object-1.0&mib-object-1.0:<SNMP-password>@<IP-
address>
```

Adding MIB Values Together for a Graph

You can use the plus sign between the pairs of MIB object values to add them together. The next example adds `mib-object-1.0` and `mib-object-3.0` for one graph and adds `mib-object-2.0` and `mib-object-4.0` for the other.

```
Target [graph1]: mib-object-1.0&mib-object-2.0:<SNMP-password>@<IP-
address> + mib-object-3.0&mib-object-4.0:<SNMP-password>@<IP-address>
```

You can use other mathematical operators, such as subtract (-), multiply (*), and divide (%). Left and right parentheses are also valid. There *must* be white spaces before and after all these operators for MRTG to work correctly. If not, you'll get oddly shaded graphs.

Sample Target: Total CPU Usage

Linux CPU usage is occupied by system processes, user mode processes, and a few processes running in nice mode. This example adds them all together in a single plot:

```
Target[graph1]:ssCpuRawUser.0&ssCpuRawUser.0:<SNMP-password>@<IP-
address> + ssCpuRawSystem.0&ssCpuRawSystem.0:<SNMP-password>@<IP-
address> + ssCpuRawNice.0&ssCpuRawNice.0:<SNMP-password>@<IP-address>
```

Be sure to place this command on a single line.

Sample Target: Memory Usage

Here is an example for plotting the amount of free memory versus the total RAM installed in the server. Notice that this is a gauge type variable:

```
Target[graph1]: memAvailReal.0&memTotalReal.0:<SNMP-password>@<IP-
address>
options[graph1]: nopercent,growright,gauge
```

Next, plot the percentage of available memory. Notice how the mandatory white spaces separate the mathematical operators from the next target element.

```
Target[graph1]: ( memAvailReal.0& memAvailReal.0:<SNMP-password>@<IP-
Address> ) * 100 / ( memTotalReal.0&memTotalReal.0:<SNMP-
password>@<IP-Address> )
options[graph1]: nopercent,growright,gauge
```

Sample Target: Newly Created Connections

HTTP traffic caused by Web browsing usually consists of many very short-lived connections. The `tcpPassiveOpens` MIB object tracks newly created connections and is suited for this type of data transfer. The `tcpActiveOpens` MIB object monitors new connections originating from the server. On smaller Web sites you may want to use the `perminute` option to make the graphs more meaningful:

```
Target[graph1]: tcpPassiveOpens.0& tcpPassiveOpens.0:<SNMP-
password>@<IP-address>
MaxBytes[graph1]: 1000000
Options[graph1]: perminute
```

Sample Target: Total TCP Established Connections

Other protocols, such as FTP and SSH, create longer established connections while people download large files or stay logged into the server. The tcpCurrEstab MIB object measures the total number of connections in the established state and is a gauge value:

```
Target[graph1]: tcpCurrEstab.0&tcpCurrEstab.0:<SNMP-password>@<IP-
address>
MaxBytes[graph1]: 1000000
Options[graph1]: gauge
```

Sample Target: Disk Partition Usage

In this example, you'll monitor the /var and /home disk partitions on the system:

1. First use the df -k command to get a list of the partitions in use:

```
[root@bigboy tmp]# df -k
Filesystem              1K-blocks       Used Available Use% Mounted
on
/dev/hda8                  505605     128199    351302  27% /
/dev/hda1                  101089      19178     76692  21% /boot
/dev/hda5                 1035660     122864    860188  13% /home
/dev/hda6                  505605       8229    471272   2% /tmp
/dev/hda3                 3921436     890092   2832140  24% /usr
/dev/hda2                 1510060     171832   1261520  73% /var
[root@bigboy tmp]#
```

2. Add two entries to your snmpd.conf file:

```
disk        /home
disk        /var
```

3. Restart the SNMP daemon to reload the values:

```
[root@bigboy tmp]# service snmpd restart
```

4. Use the snmpwalk command to query the the dskPercent MIB. Object dskPercent.1 refers to the first disk entry in snmpd.conf (/home), and dskPercent.2 refers to the second (/var).

```
[root@bigboy tmp]# snmpwalk -v 1 -c craz33guy localhost \
  dskPercent.1
UCD-SNMP-MIB::dskPercent.1 = INTEGER: 13
[root@bigboy tmp]# snmpwalk -v 1 -c craz33guy localhost \
  dskPercent.2
UCD-SNMP-MIB::dskPercent.2 = INTEGER: 73
[root@bigboy tmp]#
```

Your MRTG target for these gauge MIB objects should look like this:

```
Target[graph1]: dskPercent.1& dskPercent.1:<SNMP-password>@<IP-
address>
options[graph1]: growright,gauge
```

Defining Global Variables

You have to make sure MRTG knows where the MIBs you're using are located. The default location MRTG uses may not be valid. Specify their locations with the global LoadMIBs parameter. You must also define where the HTML files will be located; the example specifies the default Fedora MRTG HTML directory:

```
LoadMIBs: /usr/share/snmp/mibs/UCD-SNMP-MIB.txt,
/usr/share/snmp/mibs/TCP-MIB.txt
workdir: /var/www/mrtg/
```

IMPLEMENTING ADVANCED SERVER MONITORING

You now can combine all you have learned to create a configuration file that monitors all these variables, and then you can integrate it into the existing MRTG configuration.

A Complete Sample Configuration

Here is a sample configuration file that is used to query server localhost for CPU, memory, disk, and TCP connection information:

```
#
# File: /etc/mrtg/server-info.cfg
#
# Configuration file for non bandwidth server statistics
#


#
# Define global options
#

LoadMIBs: /usr/share/snmp/mibs/UCD-SNMP-
MIB.txt,/usr/share/snmp/mibs/TCP-MIB.txt

workdir: /var/www/mrtg/


#
# CPU Monitoring
# (Scaled so that the sum of all three values doesn't exceed 100)
#

Target[server.cpu]:ssCpuRawUser.0&ssCpuRawUser.0:craz33guy@localhost +
ssCpuRawSystem.0&ssCpuRawSystem.0:craz33guy@localhost +
ssCpuRawNice.0&ssCpuRawNice.0:craz33guy@localhost
Title[server.cpu]: Server CPU Load
PageTop[server.cpu]: <H1>CPU Load - System, User and Nice
Processes</H1>
```

```
MaxBytes[server.cpu]: 100
ShortLegend[server.cpu]: %
YLegend[server.cpu]: CPU Utilization
Legend1[server.cpu]: Current CPU percentage load
LegendI[server.cpu]: Used
LegendO[server.cpu]:
Options[server.cpu]: growright,nopercent
Unscaled[server.cpu]: ymwd


#
# Memory Monitoring (Total Versus Available Memory)
#

Target[server.memory]:
memAvailReal.0&memTotalReal.0:craz33guy@localhost
Title[server.memory]: Free Memory
PageTop[server.memory]: <H1>Free Memory</H1>
MaxBytes[server.memory]: 100000000000
ShortLegend[server.memory]: B
YLegend[server.memory]: Bytes
LegendI[server.memory]: Free
LegendO[server.memory]: Total
Legend1[server.memory]: Free memory, not including swap, in bytes
Legend2[server.memory]: Total memory
Options[server.memory]: gauge,growright,nopercent
kMG[server.memory]: k,M,G,T,P,X


#
# Memory Monitoring (Percentage usage)
#
Title[server.mempercent]: Percentage Free Memory
PageTop[server.mempercent]: <H1>Percentage Free Memory</H1>
Target[server.mempercent]: (
memAvailReal.0&memAvailReal.0:craz33guy@localhost ) * 100 / (
memTotalReal.0&memTotalReal.0:craz33guy@localhost )
options[server.mempercent]: growright,gauge,transparent,nopercent
Unscaled[server.mempercent]: ymwd
MaxBytes[server.mempercent]: 100
YLegend[server.mempercent]: Memory %
ShortLegend[server.mempercent]: Percent
LegendI[server.mempercent]: Free
LegendO[server.mempercent]: Free
Legend1[server.mempercent]: Percentage Free Memory
Legend2[server.mempercent]: Percentage Free Memory



#
# New TCP Connection Monitoring (per minute)
#

Target[server.newconns]:
tcpPassiveOpens.0&tcpActiveOpens.0:craz33guy@localhost
Title[server.newconns]: Newly Created TCP Connections
PageTop[server.newconns]: <H1>New TCP Connections</H1>
MaxBytes[server.newconns]: 10000000000
ShortLegend[server.newconns]: c/s
```

```
YLegend[server.newconns]: Conns / Min
LegendI[server.newconns]: In
LegendO[server.newconns]: Out
Legend1[server.newconns]: New inbound connections
Legend2[server.newconns]: New outbound connections
Options[server.newconns]: growright,nopercent,perminute


#
# Established TCP Connections
#

Target[server.estabcons]:
tcpCurrEstab.0&tcpCurrEstab.0:craz33guy@localhost
Title[server.estabcons]: Currently Established TCP Connections
PageTop[server.estabcons]: <H1>Established TCP Connections</H1>
MaxBytes[server.estabcons]: 10000000000
ShortLegend[server.estabcons]:
YLegend[server.estabcons]: Connections
LegendI[server.estabcons]: In
LegendO[server.estabcons]:
Legend1[server.estabcons]: Established connections
Legend2[server.estabcons]:
Options[server.estabcons]: growright,nopercent,gauge


#
# Disk Usage Monitoring
#

Target[server.disk]: dskPercent.1&dskPercent.2:craz33guy@localhost
Title[server.disk]: Disk Partition Usage
PageTop[server.disk]: <H1>Disk Partition Usage /home and /var</H1>
MaxBytes[server.disk]: 100
ShortLegend[server.disk]: %
YLegend[server.disk]: Utilization
LegendI[server.disk]: /home
LegendO[server.disk]: /var
Options[server.disk]: gauge,growright,nopercent
Unscaled[server.disk]: ymwd
```

Testing the Configuration

The next step is to test that MRTG can load the configuration file correctly.

Restart SNMP to make sure the disk monitoring commands in the `snmpd.conf` file are activated. Run the `/usr/bin/mrtg` command followed by the name of the configuration file three times. If all goes well, MRTG will complain only about the fact that certain database files don't exist. MRTG then creates the files. By the third run, all the files are created and MRTG should operate smoothly.

```
[root@bigboy tmp]# service snmpd restart
[root@bigboy tmp]# env LANG=C /usr/bin/mrtg /etc/mrtg/server-stats.cfg
```

Creating a New MRTG Index Page to Include this File

Use the `indexmaker` command and include your original MRTG configuration file from Chapter 22 (`/etc/mrtg/mrtg.cfg`) plus the new one you created (`/etc/mrtg/server-stats.cfg`).

```
[root@bigboy tmp]# indexmaker --output=/var/www/mrtg/index.html \
/etc/mrtg/mrtg.cfg /etc/mrtg/server-stats.cfg
```

Configuring CRON to Use the New MRTG File

The final step is to make sure that MRTG is configured to poll your server every five minutes using this new configuration file. To do so, add this line to your `/etc/cron.d/mrtg` file:

```
0-59/5 * * * * root env LANG=C /usr/bin/mrtg /etc/mrtg/server-
stats.cfg
```

Some versions of Linux require you to edit your `/etc/crontab` file instead. See Chapter 22 for more details. You will also have to restart cron with the service crond restart for it to read its new configuration file that tells it to additionally run MRTG every five minutes using the new MRTG configuration file.

```
[root@bigboy tmp]# service crond restart
```

MONITORING NON-LINUX MIB VALUES

All the MIBs mentioned so far are for Linux systems; other types of systems will need additional MIBs whose correct installation may be unclear in user guides or just not available. In such cases, you'll need to know the exact value of the OID.

Scenario

Imagine that your small company has purchased a second-hand Cisco switch to connect its Web site servers to the Internet. The basic MRTG configuration shown in Chapter 22 provides the data bandwidth statistics, but you want to measure the CPU load the traffic is having on the device, as well. Downloading MIBs from Cisco and using them with the `snmpget` command was not a success. You do not know what to do next.

Find the OIDs

When MIB values fail, it is best to try to find the exact OID value. Like most network equipment manufacturers, Cisco has an FTP site from which you can download both MIBs and OIDs. The SNMP files for Cisco's devices can be found at `ftp.cisco.com` in the `/pub/mibs` directory; OIDs are in the `oid` directory beneath that.

After looking at all the OID files, you decide that the file CISCO-PROCESS-MIB.oid will contain the necessary values and find these entries inside it:

```
"cpmCPUTotalPhysicalIndex"   "1.3.6.1.4.1.9.9.109.1.1.1.1.2"
"cpmCPUTotal5sec"            "1.3.6.1.4.1.9.9.109.1.1.1.1.3"
"cpmCPUTotal1min"            "1.3.6.1.4.1.9.9.109.1.1.1.1.4"
"cpmCPUTotal5min"            "1.3.6.1.4.1.9.9.109.1.1.1.1.5"
"cpmCPUTotal5secRev"         "1.3.6.1.4.1.9.9.109.1.1.1.1.6"
"cpmCPUTotal1minRev"         "1.3.6.1.4.1.9.9.109.1.1.1.1.7"
"cpmCPUTotal5minRev"         "1.3.6.1.4.1.9.9.109.1.1.1.1.8"
```

Testing The OIDs

As you can see, all the OIDs are a part of the same tree starting with `1.3.6.1.4.1.9.9.109.1.1.1.1`. The OIDs provided may be incomplete, so it is best to use the `snmpwalk` command to try to get all the values below this root first:

```
[root@bigboy tmp]# snmpwalk -v1 -c craz33guy cisco-switch
1.3.6.1.4.1..9.9.109.1.1.1.1
SNMPv2-SMI::enterprises.9.9.109.1.1.1.1.2.1 = INTEGER: 0
SNMPv2-SMI::enterprises.9.9.109.1.1.1.1.3.1 = Gauge32: 32
SNMPv2-SMI::enterprises.9.9.109.1.1.1.1.4.1 = Gauge32: 32
SNMPv2-SMI::enterprises.9.9.109.1.1.1.1.5.1 = Gauge32: 32
[root@bigboy tmp]#
```

Although listed in the OID file, `1.1.1.1.6`, `1.1.1.1.7`, and `1.1.1.1.8` are not supported. Notice also how SNMP has determined that the first part of the OID value (`1.3.6.1.4.1`) in the original OID file maps to the word "enterprise".

Next, you can use the `snmpget` command to set only one of the OID values returned by `snmpwalk`:

```
[root@bigboy tmp]# snmpwalk -v1 -c craz33guy cisco-switch
1.3.6.1.4.1.9.9.109.1.1.1.1
SNMPv2-SMI::enterprises.9.9.109.1.1.1.1.5.1 = Gauge32: 33
[root@bigboy tmp]#
```

Success! Now you can use this OID value, `enterprises.9.9.109.1.1.1.1.5.1`, for your MRTG queries.

TROUBLESHOOTING

The troubleshooting techniques for advanced MRTG are similar to those mentioned in Chapter 22, but because you have done some customizations you'll have to go the extra mile:

1. Verify the IP address and community string of the target device you intend to poll.
2. Make sure you can do an SNMP walk of the target device. If not, revise your access controls on the target device and any firewall rules that may impede SNMP traffic.
3. Ensure you can do an SNMP get of the specific OID value listed in your MRTG configuration file.
4. Check your MRTG parameters to make sure they are correct. Gauge values defined as counter and vice versa will cause your graphs to have continuous zero values. Graph results that are eight times what you expect may have the `bits` parameter set.

These quick steps should be sufficient in most cases and will reward you with a more manageable network.

CONCLUSION

Using the guidelines in this chapter you should be able to graph most SNMP MIB values available on any type of device. MRTG is an excellent, flexible monitoring tool and should be considered as a part of any systems administrator's server management plans.

The NTP Server

IN THIS CHAPTER

☞ Download and Install the NTP Package
☞ The /etc/ntp.conf File
☞ How to Get NTP Started
☞ Testing and Troubleshooting NTP
☞ Configuring Cisco Devices to Use an NTP Server
☞ Firewalls and NTP
☞ Configuring a Windows NTP Client
☞ Conclusion

The **Network Time Protocol** (**NTP**) is a protocol used to help synchronize your Linux system's clock with an accurate time source. There are a number of sites that allow the general public to synchronize with them. They are divided into two types:

☞ **Stratum 1**: NTP sites using an atomic clock for timing
☞ **Stratum 2**: NTP sites with slightly less accurate time sources

It is good practice to have at least one server on your network be the local time server for all your other devices. This makes the correlation of system events on different systems much easier. It also reduces Internet bandwidth usage due to NTP traffic and reduces the need to manage firewall rules for each NTP client on your network. Sometimes, not all your servers will have Internet access; in such cases, you'll need a central server that all can access. For a list of available Stratum 1 and 2 servers, consult www.ntp.org.

DOWNLOAD AND INSTALL THE NTP PACKAGE

Most Red Hat and Fedora Linux software products are available in the RPM format. Downloading and installing RPMs isn't hard. If you need a refresher, Chapter 6, "Installing RPM Software," has all the details.

When searching for the file, remember that the NTP RPM's filename usually starts with ntp followed by a version number, as in `ntp-4.1.2-5.i386.rpm`.

THE /ETC/NTP.CONF FILE

The `/etc/ntp.conf file` is the main configuration file for Linux NTP in which you place the IP addresses of the Stratum 1 and Stratum 2 servers you want to use. Here are the steps to create a configuration file using a pair of sample Internet-based NTP servers:

1. Specify the servers you're interested in:

```
server   otherntp.server.org     # A stratum 1 server at server.org
server   ntp.research.gov        # A stratum 2 server at research.gov
```

2. Restrict the type of access you allow these servers. In this example, the servers are not allowed to modify the run-time configuration or query your Linux NTP server

```
restrict otherntp.server.org    mask 255.255.255.255 nomodify
notrap noquery
restrict ntp.research.gov       mask 255.255.255.255 nomodify
notrap noquery
```

   The `mask 255.255.255.255` statement is really a subnet mask limiting access to the single IP address of the remote NTP servers.

3. If this server is also going to provide time for other computers, such as PCs, other Linux servers, and networking devices, then you'll have to define the networks from which this server will accept NTP synchronization requests. You do so with a modified restrict statement with the `noquery` replaced with a `notrust` keyword. This allows the network to query your NTP server, but it won't be trusted to be a source of NTP synchronization data. The syntax is:

```
restrict 192.168.1.0 mask 255.255.255.0 notrust nomodify notrap
```

   In this case the `mask` statement has been expanded to include all 255 possible IP addresses on the local network.

4. Make sure that `localhost` (the universal IP address used to refer to a Linux server itself) has full access without any restricting keywords:

```
restrict 127.0.0.1
```

5. Save the file and restart NTP for the settings to take effect.

You can now configure other Linux hosts on your network to synchronize with this new master NTP server in a similar fashion.

How to Get NTP Started

You have to restart the NTP process every time you make a change to the configuration file for the changes to take effect on the running process.

☞ To get NTP configured to start at boot, use the line:

```
[root@bigboy tmp]# chkconfig ntpd on
```

☞ To start, stop, and restart NTP after booting, follow these examples:

```
[root@bigboy tmp]# service ntpd start
[root@bigboy tmp]# service ntpd stop
[root@bigboy tmp]# service ntpd restart
```

Testing and Troubleshooting NTP

After configuring and starting NTP, you should test it to make sure it is working. Here are some guidelines you can follow to get NTP working correctly.

Verifying NTP is Running

To test whether the NTP process is running, use the command:

```
[root@bigboy tmp]# pgrep ntpd
```

You should get a response of plain old process ID numbers.

Doing an Initial Synchronization

If the time on the local server is very different from that of its primary time server, your NTP daemon will eventually terminate itself leaving an error message in the /var/log/messages file. Run the ntpdate -u command to force your server to become instantly synchronized with its NTP servers before starting the NTP daemon for the first time. The ntpdate command doesn't run continuously in the background, you still have to run the ntpd daemon to get continuous NTP updates.

Take a look at some sample output of the ntpdate command in which a server whose initial time was set to midnight, was correctly set to 8:03 a.m.

☞ The date was originally set to midnight which was verified by using the date command:

```
[root@smallfry tmp]# date
Thu Aug 12 00:00:00 PDT 2004
[root@smallfry tmp]#
```

☞ The ntpdate command is run three times to synchronize smallfry's clock to server 192.168.1.100, but it must be run while the ntpd process is stopped. So you'll have to stop ntpd, run ntpdate and then start ntpd again:

```
[root@smallfry tmp]# service ntpd stop
[root@smallfry tmp]# ntpdate -u 192.168.1.100
Looking for host 192.168.1.100 and service ntp
host found : bigboy.my-web-site.org
12 Aug 08:03:38 ntpdate[2472]: step time server 192.168.1.100 off-
set 28993.084943 sec
[root@smallfry tmp]# ntpdate -u 192.168.1.100
Looking for host 192.168.1.100 and service ntp
host found : bigboy.my-web-site.org
12 Aug 08:03:40 ntpdate[2472]: step time server 192.168.1.100 off-
set 2.467652 sec
[root@smallfry tmp]# ntpdate -u 192.168.1.100
Looking for host 192.168.1.100 and service ntp
host found : bigboy.my-web-site.org
12 Aug 08:03:42 ntpdate[2472]: step time server 192.168.1.100 off-
set 0.084943 sec
[root@smallfry tmp]# service ntpd start
[root@smallfry tmp]#
```

☞ The date is now corrected:

```
[root@smallfry tmp]# date
Thu Aug 12 08:03:45 PDT 2004
[root@smallfry tmp]#
```

Determining If NTP Is Synchronized Properly

Use the ntpq command to see the servers with which you are synchronized. It provided you with a list of configured time servers and the delay, offset, and jitter that your server is experiencing with them. For correct synchronization, the delay and offset values should be non-zero and the jitter value should be under 100.

```
[root@bigboy tmp]# ntpq -p
```

Here is some sample output of the command:

```
      remote          refid         st t when poll reach  delay    offset
jitter
==================================================================================
========
-jj.cs.umb.edu    gandalf.sigmaso  3 u   95 1024  377  31.681  -18.549
1.572
milo.mcs.anl.go   ntp0.mcs.anl.go  2 u  818 1024  125  41.993  -15.264
1.392
-mailer1.psc.edu ntp1.usno.navy.   2 u  972 1024  377  38.206   19.589
28.028
-dr-zaius.cs.wis ben.cs.wisc.edu   2 u  502 1024  357  55.098    3.979
0.333
+taylor.cs.wisc. ben.cs.wisc.edu   2 u  454 1024  347  54.127    3.379
0.047
-ntp0.cis.strath harris.cc.strat   3 u  507 1024  377 115.274   -5.025
1.642
*clock.via.net   .GPS.             1 u  426 1024  377 107.424   -3.018
2.534
ntp1.conectiv.c  0.0.0.0          16 u    - 1024    0  0.000     0.000
4000.00
```

Your Linux NTP Clients Cannot Synchronize Properly

A telltale sign that you haven't got proper synchronization is when all the remote servers have jitters of 4000 with delay and reach values of 0.

```
      remote          refid         st t when poll reach  delay    offset
jitter
==================================================================================
======
LOCAL(0)          LOCAL(0)         10 1    -   64    7  0.000     0.000
0.008
ntp-cup.externa 0.0.0.0           16 u    -   64    0  0.000     0.000
4000.00
snvl-smtp1.trim 0.0.0.0           16 u    -   64    0  0.000     0.000
4000.00
nist1.aol-ca.tr 0.0.0.0           16 u    -   64    0  0.000     0.000
4000.00
```

This could be caused by:

☞ Older versions of the NTP package that don't work correctly if you use the DNS name for the NTP servers. In these cases, you use the actual IP addresses instead.

☞ A firewall blocking access to your Stratum 1 and 2 NTP servers. This could be located on one of the networks between the NTP server and its time source, or firewall software, such as iptables, could be running on the server itself.

☞ The notrust nomodify notrap keywords are present in the restrict statement for the NTP client. In some versions of the Fedora Core 2's implementation of NTP, clients will not be able to synchronize with a Fedora Core 2 time server unless the notrust nomodify notrap keywords are removed from the NTP client's restrict statement.

In this example, the `restrict` statement has only the client network defined without any keywords and the configuration line that works with other NTP versions has been commented out:

```
# -- CLIENT NETWORK -------
#restrict 172.16.1.0 mask 255.255.255.0 notrust nomodify notrap
restrict 172.16.1.0 mask 255.255.255.0
```

Fedora Core 2 File Permissions

All the Fedora/Red Hat NTP daemons write temporary files to the `/etc/ntp` directory. Unfortunately, in Fedora Core 2, the permissions on this directory don't allow the writing of temporary files. Instead, you have to set the group and owner of the directory to be `ntp`:

```
[root@bigboy tmp]# chown ntp:ntp /etc/ntp
```

If you don't, you'll get errors in the `/var/log/messages` file:

```
Aug 12 00:29:45 smallfry ntpd[2097]: can't open /etc/ntp/drift.TEMP:
Permission denied
```

CONFIGURING CISCO DEVICES TO USE AN NTP SERVER

You can use NTP to synchronize time on a variety of devices including networking equipment. I have included the necessary NTP commands for a variety of Cisco Systems products, because it is one of the most popular manufacturers of networking equipment and would feature in the overall architectures of many small office/home office (SOHO) environments and corporate departments.

Cisco IOS

To make your router synchronize with NTP servers with IP addresses 192.168.1.100 and 192.168.1.201, use the commands:

```
ciscorouter> enable
password: ********
ciscorouter# config t
ciscorouter(config)# ntp update-calendar
ciscorouter(config)# ntp server 192.168.1.100
ciscorouter(config)# ntp server 192.168.1.201
ciscorouter(config)# exit
ciscorouter# wr mem
```

The `ntp server` command forms a server association with another system, and `ntp update-calendar` configures the system to update its hardware clock from the software clock at periodic intervals.

CAT OS

To make your router synchronize with NTP servers with IP addresses 192.168.1.100 and 192.168.1.201, use the commands:

```
ciscoswitch> enable
password: *********
ciscoswitch# set ntp client enable
ciscoswitch# ntp server 192.168.1.100
ciscoswitch# ntp server 192.168.1.201
ciscoswitch# exit
```

The `ntp server` command forms a server association with another system, and `set ntp client enable` activates the NTP client.

FIREWALLS AND NTP

NTP servers communicate with one another using UDP with a destination port of 123. Unlike most UDP protocols, the source port isn't a high port (above 1023), but 123 also. You'll have to allow UDP traffic on source/destination port 123 between your server and the Stratum 1/2 server with which you are synchronizing.

A sample Linux `iptables` firewall script snippet is in Appendix II, "Codes, Scripts, and Configurations."

CONFIGURING A WINDOWS NTP CLIENT

You can add your new NTP server to your Windows client:

1. Click on the time at the bottom right of your screen.
2. Click on the Internet Time tab of the dialog box
3. Click the check box labeled Automatically Synchronize with an Internet Time Server, and enter the name or IP address in the box underneath it.
4. Click on the Update Now button

You will get a message saying "Your time has been successfully synchronized" when the operation is complete.

Conclusion

It is important that all the systems under your control have the same accurate time. It can help to give a very clear indication of a chain of events that involve multiple devices, and it can also help in the synchronization of time-sensitive transactions.

Having an NTP server on your local network can make this easier to do. Sometimes it isn't desirable for all your NTP clients to have access to the Internet to synchronize with Stratum 1 and 2 servers; even when they all have access there is the risk of them losing synchronization if the central connection to the Internet is lost. The maintenance of firewall rules for multiple NTP connections to the Internet can also be daunting, especially if the management of the firewall is handled by another group.

A local NTP server can ensure that the clients all have the same time relative to the server even when Internet connectivity is temporarily lost, thereby reducing the problems of them being out of synchronization with each other. The firewall rules can also be greatly simplified. A local NTP server is frequently a good thing to have for these reasons.

Advanced Topics

Network-Based Linux Installation

Fedora Linux allows you to do operating system installations via a network connection using a Kickstart server. It is frequently much faster than using CDs, and the process can be automated. The procedure is fairly simple:

1. Connect the new server (installation client) to the same network as the server with the preloaded installation files (installation server).
2. Boot the installation client from a specially created boot CD.
3. Enter your preferred installation method (FTP, HTTP, NFS) and the needed network parameters to do this.
4. The installation procedure will then continue with the more familiar Fedora Linux installation screens. Enter your selections, and complete the installation.

This chapter will briefly explain three methods of installing operating systems over a network connection, using a single installation server (Bigboy) with an IP address of 192.168.1.100 as an example.

SETTING UP THE INSTALLATION SERVER

Kickstart can be configured on an FTP, NFS, or Apache server. Each method is explained below, but my experience is that the Apache server has a number of advantages over the other two.

Using a Web server for Kickstart is generally easier because:

☞ Sometimes a Kickstart server has to be located on a remote network, often passing through a firewall. Strict firewall rules for HTTP are generally easier to configure than those for FTP or NFS.

☞ The http:// nomenclature used by Kickstart for accessing files is more familiar to users than that used for NFS and FTP. This may be important for you when configuring files for automated Kickstart installation.

Basic Preparation

The first example sets up a Kickstart server for use in Fedora Core 2 installations. You will place all the necessary files in the /data/network-install directory.

Create the Installation Directories

Create the directories /data/network-install/Fedora/base, /data/network-install/Fedora/RPMS, and /data/network-install/ISO in which you will copy the necessary files.

```
[root@bigboy tmp]# mkdir -p /data/network-install/Fedora/base
[root@bigboy tmp]# mkdir -p /data/network-install/Fedora/RPMS
[root@bigboy tmp]# mkdir -p /data/network-install/ISO
```

You now need to place the network installation driver files into the base directory.

Copying the Files

The HTTP, NFS, and FTP Kickstart methods all require the base set of Fedora files to be installed on the Kickstart server:

1. Mount your first Fedora CD-ROM:
   ```
   [root@bigboy tmp]# mount /dev/cdrom /mnt/cdrom
   ```

2. Copy the files from the CD-ROM base directory to the hard disk:
   ```
   [root@bigboy tmp]# cd /mnt/cdrom/Fedora/base
   [root@bigboy base]# cp -r * /data/network-install/Fedora/base
   ```

3. Unmount your CD-ROM, and use the eject command to retrieve it from the drive bay:

```
[root@bigboy base]# cd /tmp
[root@bigboy tmp]# umount /dev/cdrom
[root@bigboy tmp]# eject cdrom
```

You also have the option to FTP all the files from the base directory of the desired version of Fedora from the Fedora Web site to the /data/network-install/Fedora/base directory.

HTTP and FTP Preparation

Copy all the contents of the /Fedora directory of each of the installation CDs to the /data/network-install/ directory. You need about 2GB of space. When copying is complete, your /data/network-install/Fedora/ directory should look like this:

```
[root@bigboy tmp]# ls /data/network-install/Fedora/
base   RPMS   TRANS.TBL
[root@bigboy tmp]#
```

NFS Preparation

Create ISO images of the installation CDs, and place them in the /data/network-install/ISO directory. This requires about 2GB of space as well. You can download the ISO images from the Fedora Web site or use the Fedora CDs. If you create the ISO files from CDs, make sure they have the same file names as the ones you can download from the Fedora Web site.

For the first CD, the code you need is:

```
[root@bigboy tmp]# cd /data/network-install/ISO
[root@bigboy ISO]# dd if=/dev/cdrom of=FC2-i386-disc1.iso bs=32k
...
...
[root@bigboy ISO]# eject cdrom
```

For the second CD, use:

```
[root@bigboy ISO]# dd if=/dev/cdrom of=FC2-i386-disc2.iso bs=32k
[root@bigboy ISO]# eject cdrom
```

For the third, use:

```
[root@bigboy ISO]# dd if=/dev/cdrom of=FC2-i386-disc3.iso bs=32k
[root@bigboy ISO]# eject cdrom
```

Finally, use this code to install the fourth CD:

```
[root@bigboy ISO]# dd if=/dev/cdrom of=FC2-i386-disc4.iso bs=32k
[root@bigboy ISO]# eject cdrom
```

> **Note**
>
> Here is a sample procedure to make ISO files with the older `mkisofs` command. You may have to install the `mkisofs` RPM on newer Fedora versions. The command requires a mounted CD-ROM drive, so don't forget the `mount` command.

```
[root@bigboy ISO]# mount /mnt/cdrom
[root@bigboy ISO]# mkisofs -J -r -T -o filename.iso
/mnt/cdrom
[root@bigboy ISO]# eject cdrom
```

Set Up Your Web Server

You will now have to set up Apache to give the file listings of your /data/net-work-install/Fedora and /data/network-install/ISO directories by pointing your browser to the URL http://192.168.1.100/network-install/Fedora/RPMS/ or http://192.168.1.100/network-install/Fedora/ISO/, respectively. Here is a sample httpd.conf configuration:

```
NameVirtualHost 192.168.1.100

#
# For HTTP Installations
#
<VirtualHost 192.168.1.100>
    DocumentRoot /data/
</VirtualHost>

<Directory /data/network-install>
   Options +Indexes
   AllowOverride AuthConfig
   order allow,deny
   allow from all
</Directory>
```

Remember to restart Apache to make these settings take effect.

Set Up Your FTP Server

You also have to set up your VSFTPD server to make incoming anonymous FTP connections log into the /data/network-install directory by default. Here is a sample snippet of the vsftpd.conf file:

```
#
# Anonymous FTP Root Directory
#
anon_root=/data/network-install/
#
```

Remember to restart VSFTPD to make these settings take effect.

Create a Special FTP User

You can create a special user for non-anonymous FTP installations with the user's home directory as /. You must also make sure that the user has read access to the /data/network-install directory. For example:

```
[root@bigboy tmp]# useradd -g users ftpinstall
[root@bigboy tmp]# passwd ftpinstall
Changing password for user ftpinstall.
New password:
Retype new password:
passwd: all authentication tokens updated successfully.
[root@bigboy tmp]#
[root@bigbot tmp]# usermod -d / ftpinstall
[root@bigbot tmp]#
```

Set Up Your NFS Server

The steps for setting up an NFS server are more complicated:

1. Create a /etc/exports file with the following entry in it. You must use tabs, not spaces between the entries:

   ```
   /data/network-install          *(ro,sync)
   ```

2. Make sure that the portmap, nfs, nfslock, and netfs daemons are all running to create an NFS server. The startup scripts for these are found in the /etc/init.d directory. Chapter 29, "Remote Disk Access with NFS," explains this in more detail.

3. Run the exportfs command to add this directory to the NFS database of network available directories:

   ```
   [root@bigboy tmp]# exportfs -ra
   ```

Keep in mind that the installation client must have a matching pair of forward and reverse DNS entries on your DNS server. In other words, a DNS lookup on the IP address of the installation client must return a server name that maps back to the original IP address when a DNS lookup is done on that same server name. For example:

```
[root@bigboy tmp]# host 192.168.1.96
96.1.168.192.in-addr.arpa domain name pointer 192-168-1-96.my-
web-site.org.
[root@bigboy tmp]#

[root@bigboy tmp]# host 192-168-1-96.my-site.com
192-168-1-96.my-web-site.org has address 192.168.1.96
[root@bigboy tmp]#
```

This may mean that you must create entries for all your DHCP IP addresses if you choose to use a DHCP method of assigning IP addresses during installation.

Configure Your DHCP Server

During the installation procedure, the installation client prompts you for the IP address it should use for the installation process. I recommend selecting the option that makes the installation client get its address via DHCP. This automates the installation more, thereby making it faster. It also reduces the possibility of human error.

Setting up the Installation Server as a DHCP server is fairly straight forward; for details see Chapter 8, "Configuring the DHCP Server."

CREATING A BOOT CD

You will need the first CD in your set of Fedora CDs prior to actually starting the installation. You can either copy an existing disk or burn a copy of the `FC2-i386-disc1.iso` file onto a CD.

THE NETWORK INSTALLATION

From here on, the installation procedure mimics the regular Linux installation, except for the first couple steps:

1. Connect your client Linux box to the DHCP network.
2. Boot your system using the first Fedora installation CD. This is the only CD you'll need for future network installations.
3. Enter the command `linux askmethod` at the `boot:` prompt
4. Press the Enter key.
5. Go through the usual steps until prompted for the installation method.
6. From the list of choices

   ```
   Local CDROM
   Hard Drive
   NFS Image
   FTP
   HTTP
   ```

   select the network option of your choice (NFS, FTP, or HTTP).
7. Select the Ethernet device with which the installation client is connected to the installation server network. This would most likely be interface `eth0`.
8. Select DHCP in the Configure TCP/IP screen, making the Installation client use DHCP during the installation.

If you selected the NFS method, you now come to the NFS Setup menu. Enter the IP address of the installation server for NFS Server Name, in this case 192.168.1.100. For Red Hat Directory specify `/data/network-install/ISO`. The remaining menus will be the usual Fedora GUI installation screens.

If you selected the HTTP method, you are shown the HTTP Setup menu. Enter the IP address of the installation server when prompted for a Web site name, in this case 192.168.1.100. Do not add an `http://` to the beginning. The Red Hat directory is `/network-install`. The remaining menus will be text-based versions of the usual Fedora installation screens.

If you selected the FTP method, you are given the FTP Setup menu. Enter the IP address of the installation server as the FTP site name (192.168.1.100 again). If you do *not* select the Non-Anonymous FTP box, the Red Hat directory is simply `/`, and the remaining menus will be text-based versions of the usual Fedora installation screens. If you *do* select the Non-Anonymous FTP box, then the Red Hat directory is `/data/network-install`. Enter the username and password of your special FTP user account. The remaining menus will be text-based versions of the usual Fedora installation screens.

TROUBLESHOOTING THE NETWORK INSTALLATION

You can do some basic troubleshooting by accessing the various installation status screens available:

- ☞ To view the installation logs, press Ctrl+Alt+F3 at any time.
- ☞ To see kernel messages, press Ctrl+Alt+F4.
- ☞ To access a limited BASH shell kernel, press Ctrl+Alt+F2.
- ☞ To return to the main installation screen at any time, press Ctrl+Alt+F1 from text-based installations or Ctrl+Alt+F7 from the GUI.

DIFFERENCES BETWEEN FEDORA AND RED HAT INSTALLATION

The RPM file locations have to be different when using the HTTP and FTP methods. Fedora expects the files to be placed in a directory named Fedora under `/data/network-install`, but Red Hat expects the files to be placed in a directory named RedHat under `/data/network-install`. This is the only difference between both operating systems when configuring network installations.

AUTOMATING INSTALLATION WITH KICKSTART

Both Fedora and Red Hat Linux save all the parameters you used during installation in the `/root/anaconda-ks.cfg` Kickstart configuration file. You can use this file to create an automated installation of a duplicate system, which can be useful if you have a large number of servers to install.

This section shows you how to automate network installations using the Kickstart application and NFS. You can use HTTP and FTP, but I omitted them to keep the discussion brief.

How to Create New Kickstart Configuration Files

You can create a customized Kickstart configuration file by using the `ksconfig` command from a GUI console. It brings up a menu from which you can select all your installation options. When finished, you save the configuration with the filename of your choice.

You may want to then edit the configuration file, adding # signs to comment out certain parameters that may change from system to system, including the system's name and IP address. During the Kickstart process you will be prompted for these unspecified values.

Note

Do not change the order of the entries in the Kickstart configuration file.

Note

The IP address you assign must be on the same subnet as that of the DHCP server for Kickstart to work. If the server is going to reside on a different network after the installation, then you'll have to run a separate script to change the IP addressing information after the installation is complete.

Adding post Installation Commands

You may want to run some commands on the newly created Linux installation after Kickstart is complete. Some processes that Fedora activates by default may not be suitable for your server and may need to be disabled. You can disable them by placing a `%post` section at the end of the Kickstart file with all the `post` installation commands you wish to run. For example:

```
%post
chkconfig isdn off
chkconfig pcmcia off
chkconfig portmap off
chkconfig apmd off
chkconfig nfslock off
chkconfig nfs off
```

A Note about Using anaconda-ks.cfg

It is possible to use the `/root/anaconda-ks.cfg` file as a template for future installations. Fedora comments out the partitioning information in this file, so you have to uncomment it and then make your partitioning modifications or be prepared to be prompted for your portioning information.

How to Run a Kickstart Installation

It is best to place your Kickstart files in a subdirectory under the /data/net-work-install directory. The upcoming examples assume the subdirectory is called /data/network-install/kickstart. Remember that you may want to remove the # comments from the partition section of the file. If not, you will be prompted for this information.

When using a NFS server, verify that the first two lines of the file look like this:

```
install
nfs --server=192.16.1.100 --dir=/data/network-install/ISO
```

If they don't you may be prompted for NFS ISO file location information.

When using a Web server, verify that the first two lines of the file look like this:

```
install
url --url http://192.168.1.100/network-install/
```

If they don't, you may be prompted for RPM base file location information.

Booting With Your Kickstart Files

There are two ways to specify the name of the Kickstart file to use. The first is to enter it manually from the boot: prompt when you insert the boot CD. The second is to have your DHCP server automatically tell the Kickstart client the name of the Kickstart file when the server assigns the IP address.

Manually Specifying the Kickstart Filename

After you boot from your boot CD-ROM, you need to issue a command at the boot: prompt to continue with the installation. The ks.cfg file is the Kickstart configuration file you want to use, but the command syntax changes depending on whether you choose NFS or HTTP. For the NFS method, use:

```
boot: linux ks=nfs:192.168.1.100:/kickstart/ks.cfg
```

For the HTTP method, use:

```
boot: linux ks=http://192.168.1.100/network-install/kickstart/ks.cfg
```

Configuring the Filename Automatically

Whenever you have to create lots of cloned Linux servers, you may want to configure your DHCP server to specify the single Kickstart configuration file you wish to use. Here is how it's done:

1. Place your Kickstart file in the `/data/network-install/kickstart` directory.

2. Edit your `dhcpd.conf` file, and add the following lines to the section for the interface that will be serving DHCP IP addresses. The next-server value is the IP address of the Kickstart server.

   ```
   filename "/data/network-install/kickstart/ks.cfg";
   next-server 192.168.1.100;
   ```

3. Insert the boot CD into the Kickstart client Linux box, and connect it to the DHCP network. At the `boot:` prompt type:

   ```
   boot: linux ks
   ```

Kickstart first searches for a configuration file named `ks.cfg` on the boot CD. It then automatically attempts to get a DHCP IP address and see if the DHCP server will specify a configuration file.

Kickstart next uses NFS to get both the configuration file and the installation ISOs. The rest should be automatic.

CONCLUSION

The Kickstart method of Fedora Linux installation can greatly reduce the length of time it takes to install the operating system. Time is saved not only because a network connection can be faster than using CDs, but also because it can be left unattended to install a predetermined Linux configuration. A Kickstart server connected to an isolated wireless network dedicated to the purpose may be a good idea for data centers with hundreds of Linux servers.

A recent standard called PXE enables you to run Kickstart without a CD-ROM if you configure the NIC to do a network boot from a specially configured DHCP server. The topic is beyond the scope of this book, but you may want to research this option some more, if you have more complex projects.

Linux Software RAID

In This Chapter

☞ RAID Types
☞ Before You Start
☞ Configuring Software RAID
☞ Conclusion

The main goals of using **redundant arrays of inexpensive disks (RAID)** are to improve disk data performance and provide data redundancy.

RAID can be handled either by the operating system software or it may be implemented via a purpose built RAID disk controller card without having to configure the operating system at all. This chapter will explain how to configure the software RAID schemes supported by Red Hat/Fedora Linux.

For the sake of simplicity, the chapter focuses on using RAID for partitions that include neither the /boot or the root (/) filesystems.

RAID Types

Whether hardware- or software-based, RAID can be configured using a variety of standards. Take a look at the most popular.

Linear Mode RAID

In the **Linear RAID**, the RAID controller views the RAID set as a chain of disks. Data is written to the next device in the chain only after the previous one is filled.

The aim of Linear RAID is to accommodate large filesystems spread over multiple devices with no data redundancy. A drive failure will corrupt your data.

Linear mode RAID is not supported by Fedora Linux.

RAID 0

With **RAID 0**, the RAID controller tries to evenly distribute data across all disks in the RAID set.

Envision a disk as if it were a plate, and think of the data as a cake. You have four cakes—chocolate, vanilla, cherry and strawberry—and four plates. The initialization process of RAID 0 divides the cakes and distributes the slices across all the plates. The RAID 0 drivers make the operating system feel that the cakes are intact and placed on one large plate. For example, four 9GB hard disks configured in a RAID 0 set are seen by the operating system to be one 36GB disk.

Like Linear RAID, RAID 0 aims to accommodate large filesystems spread over multiple devices with no data redundancy. The advantage of RAID 0 is data access speed. A file that is spread over four disks can be read four times as fast. You should also be aware that RAID 0 is often called **striping**.

RAID 0 can accommodate disks of unequal sizes. When RAID runs out of **striping space** on the smallest device, it then continues the striping using the available space on the remaining drives. When this occurs, the data access speed is lower for this portion of data, because the total number of RAID drives available is reduced. For this reason, RAID 0 is best used with drives of equal size.

RAID 0 is supported by Fedora Linux. Figure 26.1 illustrates the data allocation process in RAID 0.

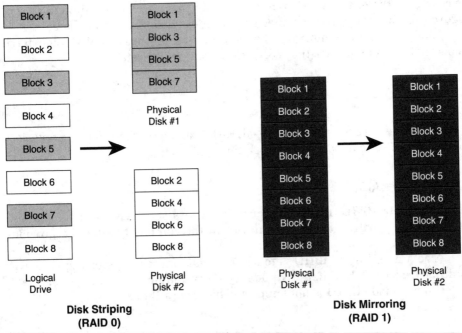

Figure 26.1   RAID 0 and RAID 1 operation.

RAID 1

With **RAID 1**, data is cloned on a duplicate disk. This RAID method is therefore frequently called **disk mirroring**. Think of telling two people the same story so that if one forgets some of the details you can ask the other one to remind you.

When one of the disks in the RAID set fails, the other one continues to function. When the failed disk is replaced, the data is automatically cloned to the new disk from the surviving disk. RAID 1 also offers the possibility of using a **hot standby** spare disk that will be automatically cloned in the event of a disk failure on any of the primary RAID devices.

RAID 1 offers data redundancy, without the speed advantages of RAID 0. A disadvantage of software-based RAID 1 is that the server has to send data twice to be written to each of the mirror disks. This can saturate data busses and CPU use. With a hardware-based solution, the server CPU sends the data to the RAID disk controller once, and the disk controller then duplicates the data to the mirror disks. This makes RAID-capable disk controllers the preferred solution when implementing RAID 1.

A limitation of RAID 1 is that the total RAID size in gigabytes is equal to that of the smallest disk in the RAID set. Unlike RAID 0, the extra space on the larger device isn't used.

RAID 1 is supported by Fedora Linux. Figure 26.1 illustrates the data allocation process in RAID 1.

RAID 4

RAID 4 operates like RAID 0 but inserts a special error-correcting or **parity** chunk on an additional disk dedicated to this purpose.

RAID 4 requires at least three disks in the RAID set and can survive the loss of a single drive only. When this occurs, the data in it can be recreated on the fly with the aid of the information on the RAID set's parity disk. When the failed disk is replaced, it is repopulated with the lost data with the help of the parity disk's information.

RAID 4 combines the high speed provided of RAID 0 with the redundancy of RAID 1. Its major disadvantage is that the data is striped, but the parity information is not. In other words, any data written to any section of the data portion of the RAID set must be followed by an update of the parity disk. The parity disk can therefore act as a bottleneck. For this reason, RAID 4 isn't used very frequently.

RAID 4 is not supported by Fedora Linux.

RAID 5

RAID 5 improves on RAID 4 by striping the parity data between all the disks in the RAID set. This avoids the parity disk bottleneck, while maintaining many of the speed features of RAID 0 and the redundancy of RAID 1. Like RAID 4, RAID 5 can survive the loss of a single disk only.

RAID 5 is supported by Fedora Linux. Figure 26.2 illustrates the data allocation process in RAID 5.

Linux RAID 5 requires a minimum of three disks or partitions.

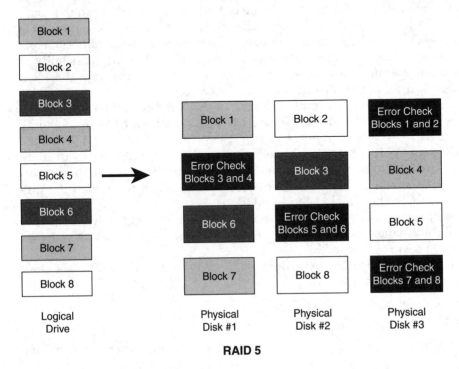

RAID 5

Figure 26.2   RAID 5 operation.

BEFORE YOU START

Specially built hardware-based RAID disk controllers are available for both IDE and SCSI drives. They usually have their own BIOS, so you can configure them right after your system's power on self test (POST). Hardware-based RAID is transparent to your operating system; the hardware does all the work.

If hardware RAID isn't available, then you should be aware of these basic guidelines to follow when setting up software RAID.

IDE Drives

To save costs, many small business systems will probably use IDE disks, but they do have some limitations:

☞ The total length of an IDE cable can be only a few feet long, which generally limits IDE drives to small home systems.

☞ IDE drives do not hot swap. You cannot replace them while your system is running.

☞ Only two devices can be attached per controller.

☞ The performance of the IDE bus can be degraded by the presence of a second device on the cable.

☞ The failure of one drive on an IDE bus often causes the malfunctioning of the second device. This can be fatal if you have two IDE drives of the same RAID set attached to the same cable.

For these reasons, I recommend you use only one IDE drive per controller when using RAID, especially in a corporate environment. In a home or SOHO setting, IDE-based software RAID may be adequate.

Serial ATA Drives

Serial ATA type drives are rapidly replacing IDE, or ultra ATA, drives as the preferred entry-level disk storage option because of a number of advantages:

☞ The drive data cable can be as long as one meter in length versus IDE's 18 inches.

☞ Serial ATA has better error checking than IDE.

☞ There is only one drive per cable, which makes hot swapping or the ability to replace components while the system is still running, possible without the fear of affecting other devices on the data cable.

☞ There are no jumpers to set on Serial ATA drives to make it a master or slave, which makes them easier to configure.

☞ IDE drives have a 133Mbytes/s data rate whereas the Serial ATA specification starts at 150 Mbytes/sec with a goal of reaching 600 Mbytes/s over the expected ten year life of the specification.

If you can't afford more expensive and faster SCSI drives, Serial ATA would be the preferred device for software and hardware RAID.

SCSI Drives

SCSI hard disks have a number of features that make them more attractive for RAID use than either IDE or Serial ATA drives:

☞ SCSI controllers are more tolerant of disk failures. The failure of a single drive is less likely to disrupt the remaining drives on the bus.

☞ SCSI cables can be up to 25 meters long, making them suitable for data center applications.

☞ Much more than two devices may be connected to a SCSI cable bus. It can accommodate 7 (single-ended SCSI) or 15 (all other SCSI types) devices.

☞ Some models of SCSI devices support hot swapping, which allows you to replace them while the system is running.

☞ SCSI currently supports data rates of up to 640 Mbytes/s making them highly desirable for installations where rapid data access is imperative.

SCSI drives tend to be more expensive than IDE drives, however, which may make them less attractive for home use.

Should I Use Software RAID Partitions or Entire Disks?

It is generally not a good idea to share RAID-configured partitions with non-RAID partitions. The reason for this is obvious: A disk failure could still incapacitate a system.

If you decide to use RAID, all the partitions on each RAID disk should be part of a RAID set. Many people simplify this problem by filling each disk of a RAID set with only one partition.

Back up Your System First

Software RAID creates the equivalent of a single RAID virtual disk drive made up of all the underlying regular partitions used to create it. You have to format this new RAID device before your Linux system can store files on it. Formatting, however, causes all the old data on the underlying RAID partitions to be lost. It is best to back up the data on these and any other partitions on the disk drive on which you want implement RAID. A mistake could unintentionally corrupt valid data.

Configure RAID in Single-User Mode

As you will be modifying the disk structure of your system, you should also consider configuring RAID while your system is running in single-user mode from the VGA console. This makes sure that most applications and networking are shutdown and that no other users can access the system, reducing the risk of data corruption during the exercise.

```
[root@bigboy tmp]# init 1
```

Once finished, issue the `exit` command, and your system will boot in the default runlevel provided in the `/etc/inittab` file.

CONFIGURING SOFTWARE RAID

Configuring RAID using Fedora Linux requires a number of steps that need to be followed carefully. In the tutorial example, you'll be configuring RAID 5 using a system with three pre-partitioned hard disks. The partitions to be used are:

☞ /dev/hde1

☞ /dev/hdf2

☞ /dev/hdg1

Be sure to adapt the various stages outlined below to your particular environment.

RAID Partitioning

You first need to identify two or more partitions, each on a separate disk. If you are doing RAID 0 or RAID 5, the partitions should be of approximately the same size, as in this scenario. RAID limits the extent of data access on each partition to an area no larger than that of the smallest partition in the RAID set.

Determining Available Partitions

First use the `fdisk -1` command to view all the mounted and unmounted filesystems available on your system. You may then also want to use the `df -k` command, which shows only mounted filesystems but has the big advantage of giving you the mount points too.

These two commands should help you to easily identify the partitions you want to use. Here is some sample output of these commands:

```
[root@bigboy tmp]# fdisk -1

Disk /dev/hda: 12.0 GB, 12072517632 bytes
255 heads, 63 sectors/track, 1467 cylinders
Units = cylinders of 16065 * 512 = 8225280 bytes

     Device Boot    Start       End    Blocks   Id  System
/dev/hda1     *         1        13    104391   83  Linux
/dev/hda2              14       144   1052257+  83  Linux
/dev/hda3             145       209    522112+  82  Linux swap
/dev/hda4             210      1467  10104885    5  Extended
/dev/hda5             210       655   3582463+  83  Linux
...
...
/dev/hda15          1455      1467    104391   83  Linux
[root@bigboy tmp]#
```

```
[root@bigboy tmp]# df -k
Filesystem                1K-blocks         Used Available Use%
Mounted on
/dev/hda2                  1035692         163916    819164  17% /
/dev/hda1                   101086           8357     87510   9% /boot
/dev/hda15                  101086           4127     91740   5% /data1
...
...
...
/dev/hda7                  5336664         464228   4601344  10% /var
[root@bigboy tmp]#
```

Unmount the Partitions

You don't want anyone else accessing these partitions while you are creating the RAID set, so you need to make sure they are unmounted:

```
[root@bigboy tmp]# umount /dev/hde1
[root@bigboy tmp]# umount /dev/hdf2
[root@bigboy tmp]# umount /dev/hdg1
```

Prepare the Partitions with fdisk

You have to change each partition in the RAID set to be of type FD (Linux raid autodetect), and you can do this with fdisk. Here is an example using /dev/hde1:

```
[root@bigboy tmp]# fdisk /dev/hde

The number of cylinders for this disk is set to 8355.
There is nothing wrong with that, but this is larger than 1024,
and could in certain setups cause problems with:
1) software that runs at boot time (e.g., old versions of LILO)
2) booting and partitioning software from other OSs
    (e.g., DOS FDISK, OS/2 FDISK)

Command (m for help):
```

Use fdisk Help

Now use the fdisk m command to get some help:

```
Command (m for help): m

   ...
   ...
   p   print the partition table
   q   quit without saving changes
   s   create a new empty Sun disklabel
   t   change a partition's system id
   ...
   ...

Command (m for help):
```

Set the ID Type to FD

Partition /dev/hde1 is the first partition on disk /dev/hde. Modify its type using the t command, and specify the partition number and type code. You also should use the L command to get a full listing of ID types in case you forget:

```
Command (m for help): t
Partition number (1-5): 1
Hex code (type L to list codes): L

 . . .
 . . .
 . . .
16  Hidden FAT16    61 SpeedStor    a9 NetBSD      f2 DOS secondary
17  Hidden HPFS/NTF 63 GNU HURD or Sys ab Darwin boot fd Linux raid auto
18  AST SmartSleep  64 Novell Netware b7 BSDI fs    fe LANstep
1b  Hidden Win95 FA 65 Novell Netware b8 BSDI swap  ff BBT
Hex code (type L to list codes): fd
Changed system type of partition 1 to fd (Linux raid autodetect)

Command (m for help):
```

Make Sure the Change Occurred

Use the p command to get the new proposed partition table:

```
Command (m for help): p

Disk /dev/hde: 4311 MB, 4311982080 bytes
16 heads, 63 sectors/track, 8355 cylinders
Units = cylinders of 1008 * 512 = 516096 bytes

   Device Boot    Start      End      Blocks   Id  System
/dev/hde1             1      4088    2060320+  fd  Linux raid
                                               autodetect
/dev/hde2          4089      5713     819000   83  Linux
/dev/hde4          6608      8355     880992    5  Extended
/dev/hde5          6608      7500     450040+  83  Linux
/dev/hde6          7501      8355     430888+  83  Linux

Command (m for help):
```

Save the Changes

Use the w command to permanently save the changes to disk /dev/hde:

```
Command (m for help): w
The partition table has been altered!

Calling ioctl() to re-read partition table.
```

```
WARNING: Re-reading the partition table failed with error 16: Device
or resource busy.
The kernel still uses the old table.
The new table will be used at the next reboot.
Syncing disks.
[root@bigboy tmp]#
```

The error above will occur if any of the other partitions on the disk is mounted.

Repeat for the Other Partitions

For the sake of brevity, I won't show the process for the other partitions. It's enough to know that the steps for changing the IDs for /dev/hdf2 and /dev/hdg1 are very similar.

Edit the RAID Configuration File

The Linux RAID configuration file is /etc/raidtab. You can find templates for this file in the /usr/share/doc/raidtools* directory. For an explanation of the various parameters, issue the man raidtab command.

To ensure success, remember these general guidelines:

☞ When configuring RAID 5, you *must* use a parity-algorithm setting.

☞ The raid-disk parameters for each partition in the /etc/raidtab file are numbered starting at 0. For example, if you have four partitions for RAID, they would be numbered 0, 1, 2, and 3.

☞ For RAID levels 1, 4, and 5, the /etc/raidtab persistent-superblock must be set to 1 for the RAID autodetect feature (partition type FD) to work. For all other RAID versions, persistent-superblock must be set to 0.

Consider an example. Here, RAID 5 is configured to use each of the desired partitions on the three disks, and the set of three is called /dev/md0. The data is distributed across the drives in 32KB chunks:

```
#
# sample raiddev configuration file
# 'old' RAID0 array created with mdtools.
#
raiddev /dev/md0
    raid-level              5
    nr-raid-disks           3
    persistent-superblock   1
    chunk-size              32
    parity-algorithm        left-symmetric
    device                  /dev/hde1
    raid-disk               0
    device                  /dev/hdf2
    raid-disk               1
    device                  /dev/hdg1
    raid-disk               2
```

Create the RAID Set

The mkraid command creates the RAID set by reading the /etc/raidtab file. The example creates the logical RAID device /dev/md0:

```
[root@bigboy tmp]# mkraid /dev/md0
analyzing super-block
disk 0: /dev/hde1, 104391kB, raid superblock at 104320kB
disk 1: /dev/hdf2, 104391kB, raid superblock at 104320kB
disk 2: /dev/hdg1, 104391kB, raid superblock at 104320kB
[root@bigboy tmp]#
```

Confirm RAID Is Correctly Initialized

The /proc/mdstat file provides the current status of all RAID devices. Confirm that the initialization is finished by inspecting the file and making sure that there are no initialization-related messages:

```
[root@bigboy tmp]# cat /proc/mdstat
Personalities : [raid5]
read_ahead 1024 sectors
md0 : active raid5 hdg1[2] hde1[1] hdf2[0]
      4120448 blocks level 5, 32k chunk, algorithm 3 [3/3] [UUU]

unused devices: <none>
[root@bigboy tmp]#
```

Format the New RAID Set

Your new RAID device now has to be formatted. The next example uses the -j qualifier to ensure that a journaling filesystem is created. Here a block size of 4KB (4096 bytes) is used with each chunk, which is comprised of 8 blocks. It is very important that the chunk-size parameter in the /etc/raidtab file match the value of the block size multiplied by the stride value in the command below. If the values don't match, you will get parity errors.

```
[root@bigboy tmp]# mke2fs -j -b 4096 -R stride=8 /dev/md0
mke2fs 1.32 (09-Nov-2002)
Filesystem label=
OS type: Linux
Block size=4096 (log=2)
Fragment size=4096 (log=2)
516096 inodes, 1030160 blocks
51508 blocks (5.00%) reserved for the super user
First data block=0
32 block groups
32768 blocks per group, 32768 fragments per group
16128 inodes per group
```

```
Superblock backups stored on blocks:
        32768, 98304, 163840, 229376, 294912, 819200, 884736

Writing inode tables: done
Creating journal (8192 blocks): done
Writing superblocks and filesystem accounting information: done

This filesystem will be automatically checked every 26 mounts or
180 days, whichever comes first.  Use tune2fs -c or -i to override.
[root@bigboy tmp]#
```

Load the RAID Driver for the New RAID Set

Next, make the Linux operating system fully aware of the RAID set by loading the driver for the new RAID set using the raidstart command:

```
[root@bigboy tmp]# raidstart /dev/md0
[root@bigboy tmp]#
```

Create a Mount Point for the RAID Set

After the driver loads, create a mount point for /dev/md0, such as this one called /mnt/raid:

```
[root@bigboy mnt]# mkdir /mnt/raid
```

Edit the */etc/fstab* File

The /etc/fstab file lists all the partitions that need to mount when the system boots. Add an Entry for the RAID set, the /dev/md0 device:

```
/dev/md0        /mnt/raid       ext3    defaults    1 2
```

Do not use labels in the /etc/fstab file for RAID devices; just use the real device name, such as /dev/md0. On startup, the /etc/rc.d/rc.sysinit script checks the /etc/fstab file for device entries that match RAID set names in the /etc/raidtab file. The script will not automatically start the RAID set driver for the RAID set if it doesn't find a match. Device mounting then occurs later on in the boot process. Mounting a RAID device that doesn't have a loaded driver can corrupt your data and produce this error:

```
Starting up RAID devices: md0 (skipped)
Checking filesystems
```

```
/raiddata: Superblock has a bad ext3 journal(inode8)
CLEARED.
***journal has been deleted - file system is now ext 2 only***

/raiddata: The filesystem size (according to the superblock) is
2688072 blocks.
The physical size of the device is 8960245 blocks.
Either the superblock or the partition table is likely to be corrupt!
/boot: clean, 41/26104 files, 12755/104391 blocks

/raiddata: UNEXPECTED INCONSISTENCY; Run fsck manually (ie without -a
or -p options).
```

If you are not familiar with the /etc/fstab file, use the man fstab command to get a comprehensive explanation of each data column it contains.

The /dev/hde1, /dev/hdf2, and /dev/hdg1 partitions were replaced by the combined /dev/md0 partition. You therefore don't want the old partitions to be mounted again. Make sure that all references to them in this file are commented with a # at the beginning of the line or deleted entirely:

```
#/dev/hde1       /data1        ext3      defaults       1 2
#/dev/hdf2       /data2        ext3      defaults       1 2
#/dev/hdg1       /data3        ext3      defaults       1 2
```

Start the New RAID Set's Driver

You now can start the new RAID set's driver with the raidstart command. This command is run automatically at boot time, so you'll only have to do this once.

```
[root@bigboy tmp]# raidstart /dev/md0
```

Mount the New RAID Set

Use the mount command to mount the RAID set. You have your choice of methods:

☞ The mount command's -a flag causes Linux to mount all the devices in the /etc/fstab file that have automounting enabled (default) and that are also not already mounted.

```
[root@bigboy tmp]# mount -a
```

☞ You can also mount the device manually.

```
[root@bigboy tmp]# mount /dev/md0 /mnt/raid
```

Check the Status of the New RAID

The /proc/mdstat file provides the current status of all the devices. When the RAID driver is stopped, the file has very little information, as seen here:

```
[root@bigboy tmp]# raidstop /dev/md0
[root@bigboy tmp]# cat /proc/mdstat
Personalities : [raid5]
read_ahead 1024 sectors
unused devices: <none>
[root@bigboy tmp]#
```

More information, including the partitions of the RAID set, is provided after you load the driver using the raidstart command.

```
[root@bigboy tmp]# raidstart /dev/md0
[root@bigboy tmp]# cat /proc/mdstat
Personalities : [raid5]
read_ahead 1024 sectors
md0 : active raid5 hdg1[2] hde1[1] hdf2[0]
        4120448 blocks level 5, 32k chunk, algorithm 3 [3/3] [UUU]

unused devices: <none>
[root@bigboy tmp]#
```

CONCLUSION

Linux software RAID provides redundancy across partitions and hard disks, but it tends to be slower and less reliable than RAID provided by a hardware-based RAID disk controller.

Hardware RAID configuration is usually done via the system BIOS when the server boots up, and once configured, it is absolutely transparent to Linux. Unlike software RAID, hardware RAID requires entire disks to be dedicated to the purpose and when combined with the fact that it usually requires faster SCSI hard disks and an additional controller card, it tends to be expensive.

Remember to take these factors into consideration when determining the right solution for your needs and research the topic thoroughly before proceeding. Weighing cost versus reliability is always a difficult choice in systems administration.

Expanding Disk Capacity

The lack of available disk storage frequently plagues Linux systems administrators. The most common reasons for this are expanding databases, increasing numbers of users, and the larger number of tasks your Linux server is expected to perform until a replacement is found.

This chapter explores how to add a disk to a Linux system in two ways. The first is by moving directories from a full partition to an empty one made available by the new disk and then linking the directory structures of the two disks together. The second is by merging the partitions together to create a combined partition using the Linux Logical Volume Manager (LVM).

ADDING DISKS TO LINUX

At some stage you'll be faced with the task of installing an additional hard drive into your Linux server. Perhaps an existing device failed, or maybe you ran out of available space. To provide more space, this section will cover adding a hard disk with only one partition and will then explain how to migrate data from the full disk to the new one.

Scenario

Things are getting crowded on bigboy: Even after you removed all unwanted data, the /var partition would still be over 95% full. You need to add a new hard drive to the system. You can verify this situation with the `df -k` command's output, which also shows that the other partitions are too full to accept any more data:

```
[root@bigboy tmp]# df -k
Filesystem              1K-blocks      Used Available Use% Mounted on
/dev/hda3                  505636    118224    361307  25% /
/dev/hda1                  101089     14281     81589  15% /boot
none                        63028         0     63028   0% /dev/shm
/dev/hda5                  248895      6613    229432   3% /tmp
/dev/hda7                 3304768   2720332    416560  87% /usr
/dev/hda2                 3304768   3300536      4232  99% /var
[root@bigboy tmp]#
```

A new hard disk was added according to the manufacturer's instructions, but you now need to know how to proceed.

Determining the Disk Types

Linux stores the names of all known disk partitions in the `/proc/partitions` file. The entire hard disk is represented by an entry with a minor number of 0, and all the partitions on the drive are sequentially numbered after that. In the example, the system has two hard disks; disk `/dev/hda` has been partitioned, but the new disk (`/dev/hdb`) needs to be prepared to accept data.

```
[root@bigboy tmp]# cat /proc/partitions
major minor  #blocks   name

   3      0   7334145 hda
   3      1    104391 hda1
   3      2   1052257 hda2
   3      3   2040255 hda3
   3      4         1 hda4
   3      5   3582463 hda5
   3      6    554211 hda6
  22      0  78150744 hdb
[root@bigboy tmp]#
```

Note

Linux hard disk device names follow a specific standard. SCSI disks all start with sd and IDE disks with hd. After this comes a letter that identifies the unit number of the disk, so for example, the first disk would be a, the second would be b, the third would be c, and so on. Finally, a two-digit number defines the partition number. Using this convention the fifth partition on the fourth IDE drive would be `/dev/hdd5`.

Preparing Partitions on New Disks

Linux partition preparation is very similar to that in a Windows environment, because both operating systems share the fdisk partitioning utility. The steps are:

1. The first Linux step in adding a new disk is to partition it in preparation of adding a filesystem to it. Type the fdisk command followed by the name of the disk. You want to run fdisk on the /dev/hdb disk, so the command is

```
[root@bigboy tmp]# fdisk /dev/hdb

The number of cylinders for this disk is set to 9729.
There is nothing wrong with that, but this is larger than 1024,
and could in certain setups cause problems with:
1) software that runs at boot time (e.g., old versions of LILO)
2) booting and partitioning software from other OSs
   (e.g., DOS FDISK, OS/2 FDISK)

Command (m for help):
```

2. Just to make sure you're on the correct device, issue the p command to print all the known partitions on the disk. In this case, there are none, which is good:

```
Command (m for help): p

Disk /dev/hdb: 80.0 GB, 80026361856 bytes
255 heads, 63 sectors/track, 9729 cylinders
Units = cylinders of 16065 * 512 = 8225280 bytes

   Device Boot        Start          End      Blocks   Id  System

Command (m for help):
```

3. The fdisk m command prints a small help manual of valid commands. You will see that n is the command to add a new partition. Add a new primary partition, number 1, and use the defaults to make the partition occupy the entire disk:

```
Command (m for help): n
Command action
   e   extended
   p   primary partition (1-4)
p
Partition number (1-4): 1
First cylinder (1-9729, default 1):<RETURN>
Using default value 1
Last cylinder or +size or +sizeM or +sizeK (1-9729, default 9729):
```

4. Run the print (p) command to confirm that you successfully created the partition.

```
Command (m for help): p

Disk /dev/hdb: 80.0 GB, 80026361856 bytes
```

```
255 heads, 63 sectors/track, 9729 cylinders
Units = cylinders of 16065 * 512 = 8225280 bytes

    Device Boot       Start       End       Blocks   Id  System
/dev/hdb1                  1      9726     78148161   83  Linux

Command (m for help):
```

Tip

If you make a mistake, you can use the d command to delete the partition and start over. The t command enables you to change partition type from the default of 83 for regular Linux partitions to something else, such as 82 for swap space. In most cases, this won't be necessary, the default value is sufficient.

Note

When you created the new partition, you may have noticed that fdisk queried you as to whether it was going to be a primary or secondary partition. Linux allows only four primary partitions; if you need more, you can convert one of the primary ones into an extended one. Here is an example of a partition table that includes an extended partition followed by two regular partitions within it:

```
Command (m for help): p

Disk /dev/hda: 7510 MB, 7510164480 bytes
255 heads, 63 sectors/track, 913 cylinders
Units = cylinders of 16065 * 512 = 8225280 bytes

    Device Boot  Start   End    Blocks   Id  System
/dev/hda1    *       1    13    104391   83  Linux
/dev/hda2           14   144   1052257+  83  Linux
/dev/hda3          145   398   2040255   82  Linux swap
/dev/hda4          399   913   4136737+   5  Extended
/dev/hda5          399   844   3582463+  83  Linux
/dev/hda6          845   913    554211   83  Linux

Command (m for help):
```

Adding more partitions is just a question of repeating the previous steps the required number of times, while remembering that at some stage, you may need to add an extended partition.

---

5. Changes won't be made to the disk's partition table until you use the w command to write, or save, the changes. Do that now, and, when finished, exit with the q command.

```
Command (m for help): w
Command (m for help): q
```

After this is complete, you'll need to verify your work and start migrating your data to the new disk. These steps will be covered next.

Verifying Your New Partition

You can take a look at the /proc/partitions file or use the fdisk -l command to see the changes to the disk partition structure of your system:

```
[root@bigboy tmp]# cat /proc/partitions
major minor  #blocks   name
 . . .
 . . .
 . . .
   22    0   78150744 hdb
   22    1   78150744 hdb1
[root@bigboy tmp]#


[root@bigboy tmp]# fdisk -1
 . . .
 . . .
 . . .
Disk /dev/hdb: 80.0 GB, 80026361856 bytes
255 heads, 63 sectors/track, 9729 cylinders
Units = cylinders of 16065 * 512 = 8225280 bytes

   Device Boot      Start         End      Blocks   Id  System
/dev/hdb1               1        9729    76051710   83  Linux
[root@bigboy tmp]#
```

Putting a Directory Structure on Your New Partition

You now need to format the partition, giving it a new directory structure by using the mkfs command. The Fedora installation procedure defaults to an ext3 type, which is what you should use here:

```
[root@bigboy tmp]# mkfs -t ext3 /dev/hdb1
```

Next, you must create a special **mount point directory**, to which the new partition will be attached. Create directory /mnt/hdb1 for this purpose:

```
[root@bigboy tmp]# mkdir /mnt/hdb1
```

When Linux boots, it searches the /etc/fstab file for a list of all partitions and their mounting characteristics, and then it mounts the partitions automatically. You'll have to add an entry for your new partition that looks like this:

```
#
# File: /etc/fstab
#
/dev/hdb1  /mnt/hdb1  ext3   default 1 2
```

The first entry is the name of the partition followed by the mount point directory and the filesystem type. The fourth entry defines the mounting options, which need be only default for most scenarios. The fifth entry governs whether the dump filesystem backup command can be used for the filesystem. A value of 0 means no, and 1 means yes. The final entry defines the order in which a filesystem check is done at boot time. The check is done twice. The root (or master) filesystem has a value of 1 and is checked on the first pass, all other filesystems should have a value of 2. If you are not familiar with the /etc/fstab file use the man fstab command to get a full explanation of its various options.

You don't have to wait for a reboot to mount your partition. You can use the mount command with the -a option to read the /etc/fstab file for new entries:

```
[root@bigboy tmp]# mount -a
```

You are now able to access your new partition as device /mnt/hdb1.

Migrating Data to Your New Partition

As you remember from investigating with the df -k command, the /var partition is almost full.

```
[root@bigboy tmp]# df -k
Filesystem             1K-blocks      Used Available Use% Mounted on
/dev/hda3                 505636    118224    361307  25% /
/dev/hda1                 101089     14281     81589  15% /boot
none                       63028         0     63028   0% /dev/shm
/dev/hda5                 248895      6613    229432   3% /tmp
/dev/hda7                3304768   2720332    416560  87% /usr
/dev/hda2                3304768   3300536      4232  99% /var
[root@bigboy tmp]#
```

The du -sk * command shows the disk usage of all subdirectories in a directory. You can recursively use the command by using the cd command to step down through all the subdirectories until you discover the one with the

greatest file usage. In this case, you only had to go to the /var directory to see
that the /var/transactions directory was the culprit.

```
[root@bigboy tmp]# cd /var
[root@bigboy var]# du -sk *
2036     cache
4        db
8        empty
...
...
133784   transactions
...
...
[root@bigboy var]#
```

As a solution, the /var partition will be expanded to the new /dev/hdb1
partition mounted on the /mnt/hdb1 directory mount point. To migrate the
data, use these steps:

1. Back up the data on the partition you are about to work on.

2. Use the who command to see who's logged in. If other users are present,
   send a message with the wall command informing them that the system
   is about to shutdown.

```
[root@bigboy tmp]# who
root      pts/0        Nov  6 14:46 (192-168-1-242.my-web-site.org)
bob       pts/0        Nov  6 12:01 (192-168-1-248.my-web-site.org)
bunny     pts/0        Nov  6 16:25 (192-168-1-250.my-web-site.org)
[root@bigboy tmp]# wall The system is shutting down now!

Broadcast message from root (pts/0) (Sun Nov  7 15:04:27 2004):

The system is shutting down now!
[root@bigboy tmp]#
```

3. Log into the VGA console, and enter single-user mode:

```
[root@bigboy tmp]# init 1
```

4. Rename the /var/transactions directory /var/transactions-save to make
   sure you have an easy to restore backup of the data, not just the tapes:

```
sh-2.05b# mv /var/transactions /var/transactions-save
```

5. Create a new, empty /var/transactions directory; this will later act as a
   mount point:

```
sh-2.05b# mkdir /var/transactions
```

6. Copy the contents of the /var/transactions-save directory to the root
   directory of /dev/hdb1, which is actually /mnt/hdb1:

```
sh-2.05b# cp -r /var/transactions-save /mnt/hdb1
```

7. Unmount the new /dev/hdb1 partition:

```
sh-2.05b# umount /mnt/hdb1
```

8. Edit the /etc/fstab file, removing our previous entry for /dev/hdb1 replacing it with one using the new mount point.

```
#
# File: /etc/fstab
#

#/dev/hdb1   /mnt/hdb1   ext3   default 1 2

/dev/hdb1   /var/transactions   ext3   default 1 2
```

9. Remount /dev/hdb1 on the new mount point using the mount -a command, which reads /etc/fstab and automatically mounts any entries that are not mounted already:

```
sh-2.05b# mount -a
```

10. Test to make sure that the contents of the new /var/transactions directory is identical to /var/transactions-save.

11. Return to multi-user mode by typing exit. The system will return to its default runlevel.

```
sh-2.05b# exit
```

12. Make sure your applications are working correctly and delete both the /var/transactions-save directory and the /mnt/hdb1 mount point directory at some later date.

This exercise showed you how to migrate the entire contents of a subdirectory to a new disk. Linux also allows you to merge partitions together in order to create a larger combined one. The reasons and steps for doing so will be explained next.

EXPANDING PARTITIONS WITH LVM

The **Logical Volume Manager** (**LVM**) enables you to resize your partitions without having to modify the partition tables on your hard disk. This is most useful when you find yourself running out of space on a filesystem and want to expand into a new disk partition versus migrating all or a part of the filesystem to a new disk.

LVM Terms

Before you run through the LVM tutorial, you need to become familiar with some LVM concepts:

☞ **Physical Volume**: A physical volume (**PV**) is another name for a regular physical disk partition that is used or will be used by LVM.

☞ **Volume Group**: Any number of physical volumes (PVs) on different disk drives can be lumped together into a volume group (**VG**). Under LVM, volume groups are analogous to a virtual disk drive.

☞ **Logical Volumes**: Volume groups must then be subdivided into logical volumes. Each logical volume can be individually formatted as if it were a regular Linux partition. A logical volume is, therefore, like a virtual partition on your virtual disk drive.

This may seem complicated, but it allows you to create new virtual partitions with sizes you can change from groups of real disk partitions whose sizes you probably cannot change. Another advantage of LVM is that this can all be done without disturbing other partitions on your hard disks.

☞ **Physical Extent**: Real disk partitions are divided into chunks of data called physical extents (**PEs**) when you add them to a logical volume. PEs are important as you usually have to specify the size of your volume group not in gigabytes, but as a number of physical extents.

Make sure you understand these terms fully as they will be used repeatedly in many of the following sections. Let's go!

Configuring LVM Devices

It is probably best to learn about the features of LVM through a scenario. Suppose a small company needs to expand disk capacity, but there isn't the budget to purchase an adequately sized hard drive. The /home filesystem, which resides on /dev/hde5, has become too full. You just added a new hard drive /dev/hdf with 50% of the capacity of /dev/hde5 into which you want to expand /home. The device /dev/hdf has a single partition named /dev/hdf1 into which /dev/hde5 will be merged. Take a look at the required steps.

Back up Your Data

Use the tar command or some other method to backup your data in /home. The LVM process will destroy the data on all physical volumes.

Unmount Your /home Filesystem

As /home stores most users' data, you'll need to do some preparatory work before unmounting the filesystem:

1. Use the who command to see who's logged in. If other users are present, send a message with the wall command informing them that the system is about to shutdown.

```
[root@bigboy tmp]# who
root      pts/0        Nov  6 14:46 (192-168-1-242.my-web-site.org)
bob       pts/0        Nov  6 12:01 (192-168-1-248.my-web-site.org)
bunny     pts/0        Nov  6 16:25 (192-168-1-250.my-web-site.org)
[root@bigboy tmp]# wall The system is shutting down now!
```

```
Broadcast message from root (pts/0) (Sun Nov  7 15:04:27 2004):

The system is shutting down now!
[root@bigboy tmp]#
```

2. Log into the VGA console, and enter single-user mode:

```
[root@bigboy tmp]# init 1
```

3. Unmount the filesystem:

```
sh-2.05b# umount /home
```

Now we're ready to start modifying the partitions, which is covered next.

Determine the Partition Types

You have to change each LVM partition used to be of type 8e (Linux LVM). You can test this with the fdisk -l command. Here is an example using /dev/hde that shows your target partitions are of the incorrect type:

```
sh-2.05b# fdisk -l /dev/hde

Disk /dev/hde: 4311 MB, 4311982080 bytes
16 heads, 63 sectors/track, 8355 cylinders
Units = cylinders of 1008 * 512 = 516096 bytes

   Device Boot     Start        End      Blocks   Id  System
/dev/hde1              1       4088    2060320+   fd  Linux raid
                                                      autodetect
/dev/hde2           4089       5713     819000    83  Linux
/dev/hde3           5714       6607     450576    83  Linux
/dev/hde4           6608       8355     880992     5  Extended
/dev/hde5           6608       7500     450040+   83  Linux
sh-2.05b#
```

Start fdisk

You can change the partition type using fdisk with the disk name as its argument. Use it to modify both partitions /dev/hde5 and /dev/hdf1. The fdisk examples that follow are for /dev/hde5; repeat them for /dev/hdf1.

```
sh-2.05b# fdisk /dev/hde

The number of cylinders for this disk is set to 8355.
There is nothing wrong with that, but this is larger than 1024,
and could in certain setups cause problems with:
1) software that runs at boot time (e.g., old versions of LILO)
2) booting and partitioning software from other OSs
     (e.g., DOS FDISK, OS/2 FDISK)

Command (m for help):
```

Set the ID Type to 8e

You now need to set the partition types to the LVM value of 8e. Partitions /dev/hde5 and /dev/hdf1 are the fifth and sixth partitions on disk /dev/hde. Modify their type using the t command, and then specify the partition number and type code. You can also use the L command to get a full listing of ID types in case you forget.

```
Command (m for help): t
Partition number (1-6): 5
Hex code (type L to list codes): 8e
Changed system type of partition 5 to 8e (Linux LVM)

Command (m for help): t
Partition number (1-6): 6
Hex code (type L to list codes): 8e
Changed system type of partition 6 to 8e (Linux LVM)

Command (m for help):
```

Make Sure the Change Occurred

Use the p command to get the new proposed partition table:

```
Command (m for help): p

Disk /dev/hde: 4311 MB, 4311982080 bytes
16 heads, 63 sectors/track, 8355 cylinders
Units = cylinders of 1008 * 512 = 516096 bytes

   Device Boot    Start      End    Blocks   Id  System
/dev/hde1             1     4088   2060320+  fd  Linux raid
                                                 autodetect
/dev/hde2          4089     5713    819000   83  Linux
/dev/hde3          5714     6607    450576   83  Linux
/dev/hde4          6608     8355    880992    5  Extended
/dev/hde5          6608     7500    450040+  8e  Linux LVM

Command (m for help):
```

Save the Partition Changes

Use the w command to permanently save the changes to disk /dev/hde:

```
Command (m for help): w
The partition table has been altered!

Calling ioctl() to re-read partition table.

WARNING: Re-reading the partition table failed with error 16: Device
or resource busy.
The kernel still uses the old table.
```

```
The new table will be used at the next reboot.
Syncing disks.
[root@bigboy updates]#
```

The error above will occur if any of the other partitions on the disk is mounted. This shouldn't be grave as you are already in single user mode in which most of the system's processes that would be accessing the partition have been shutdown.

Define Each Physical Volume

After modifying the partition tables of /dev/hde and /dev/hdf, initialize the target partitions with the pvcreate command. This wipes out all the data on them in preparation for the next step. If you haven't backed up your data yet, do it now!

```
sh-2.05b# pvcreate /dev/hde5
pvcreate -- physical volume "/dev/hde5" successfully created

sh-2.05b# pvcreate /dev/hdf1
pvcreate -- physical volume "/dev/hdf1" successfully created

sh-2.05b#
```

Run VGscan

The next step is to make Linux scan for any new LVM disk partitions and automatically create the LVM configuration files in the /etc directory. To do this, use the vgscan command:

```
sh-2.05b# vgscan
vgscan -- reading all physical volumes (this may take a while...)
sh-2.05b#
```

Create a Volume Group for the PVs

Use the vgcreate command to combine the two physical volumes into a single unit called a volume group. The LVM software effectively tricks the operating system into thinking the volume group is a new hard disk. In the example, the volume group is called **lvm-hde**.

```
sh-2.05b# vgcreate lvm-hde /dev/hdf1 /dev/hde5
Volume group "lvm-hde" successfully created
sh-2.05b#
```

Therefore, the vgcreate syntax uses the name of the volume group as the first argument followed by the partitions that it will be comprised of as all subsequent arguments.

Create a Logical Volume from the Volume Group

Now you're ready to partition the volume group into logical volumes with the lvcreate command. Like hard disks, which are divided into blocks of data, logical volumes are divided into units called physical extents (PEs).

You'll have to know the number of available PEs before creating the logical volume. This is done with the vgdisplay command using the new lvm-hde volume group as the argument:

```
sh-2.05b# vgdisplay lvm-hde
--- Volume group ---
VG Name                 lvm-hde
VG Access               read/write
VG Status               available/resizable
VG #                    0
MAX LV                  256
Cur LV                  0
Open LV                 0
MAX LV Size             255.99 GB
Max PV                  256
Cur PV                  2
Act PV                  2
VG Size                 848 MB
PE Size                 4 MB
Total PE                212
Alloc PE / Size         0 / 0
Free  PE / Size         212 / 848 MB
VG UUID                 W7bgLB-1AFW-wtKi-wZET-jDJF-8VYD-snUaSZ

sh-2.05b#
```

As you can see, 212 PEs are available as free. You can now use all 212 of them to create a logical volume named lvm0 from volume group lvm-hde.

```
sh-2.05b# lvcreate -l 212 lvm-hde -n lvm0
Logical volume "lvm0" created
sh-2.05b#
```

Format the Logical Volume

After the logical volume is created, you can format it as if it were a regular partition. In this case, use the -t switch to specify to the mkfs formatting program that you want a type ext3 partition:

```
sh-2.05b# mkfs -t ext3 /dev/lvm-hde/lvm0
mke2fs 1.32 (09-Nov-2002)
```

```
Filesystem label=
OS type: Linux
Block size=4096 (log=2)
Fragment size=4096 (log=2)
108640 inodes, 217088 blocks
10854 blocks (5.00%) reserved for the super user
First data block=0
7 block groups
32768 blocks per group, 32768 fragments per group
15520 inodes per group
Superblock backups stored on blocks:
        32768, 98304, 163840

Writing inode tables: done
Creating journal (4096 blocks): done
Writing superblocks and filesystem accounting information: done

This filesystem will be automatically checked every 38 mounts or
180 days, whichever comes first.  Use tune2fs -c or -i to override.
sh-2.05b#
```

Create a Mount Point

When you formatted the /dev/hde5 partition, you lost the /home directory. Now you have to recreate /home on which you'll later mount your new logical volume:

```
sh-2.05b# mkdir /home
```

Update the /etc/fstab File

The /etc/fstab file lists all the partitions that need to be automatically mounted when the system boots. This snippet configures the newly labeled partition to be mounted on the /home mount point:

```
/dev/lvm-hde/lvm0   /home       ext3    defaults        1 2
```

The /dev/hde5 and /dev/hdf1 partitions are replaced by the combined /lvm0 logical volume. You, therefore, don't want the old partitions to be mounted again. Make sure that any reference to them in this file has either been commented with a # character at the beginning of each line or deleted entirely.

```
#/dev/hde5       /data1      ext3    defaults        1 2
#/dev/hdf1       /data2      ext3    defaults        1 2
```

Mount the Volume

The `mount -a` command reads the `/etc/fstab` file and mounts all the devices that haven't been mounted already. After mounting, test the volume by listing its directory contents. It should just contain the `lost+found` directory.

```
sh-2.05b# mount -a
sh-2.05b# ls /home
lost+found
sh-2.05b#
```

Restore Your Data

You can now restore your backed up data to `/home`.

Get Out of Single User Mode

Return to your original run state by using either the `init 3` or `init 5` commands. The `exit` command will make you return to your default runlevel.

CONCLUSION

The demise of the hard disk has been predicted for many years. Faster, denser memory chips were supposed to eliminate their need, but hard disk technology has evolved, dramatically increasing their speed and capacity too. They will be around for a long time to come.

It seems as if when drives get bigger, so does the data they are intended to store. Expanding the existing disk capacity of your server may become an everyday occurrence and the tools described in this chapter should make the task easier.

Managing Disk Usage with Quotas

IN THIS CHAPTER

- ☞ Setting Up Quotas
- ☞ Other Quota Topics
- ☞ Conclusion

Eventually, you may need to restrict the amount of disk space used on each partition by each user or group of users as your disk drives become filled with data. The **disk quota** feature of Red Hat/Fedora Linux enables you to do this, and the setup is fairly simple.

SETTING UP QUOTAS

For example, your family Linux server is running out of space in the /home filesystem because of an abundance of MP3 downloads.

Enter Single-User Mode

As you'll need to remount the /home filesystem, you make sure that no other users or processes are using it by first entering single-user mode from the console. If you are certain that you're the only user on the system, you might be able to skip this step.

Entering single-user mode automatically logs off all users and stops cron jobs, so wait until after hours to do this in a business environment. The procedure is quick:

1. Use the who command to see which users are logged in. If there are any, besides yourself, send a message stating that the system is about to shutdown with the wall command:

```
[root@bigboy tmp]# who
root        pts/0           Nov  6 14:46  (192-168-1-242.my-web-site.org)
bob         pts/0           Nov  6 12:01  (192-168-1-248.my-web-site.org)
bunny       pts/0           Nov  6 16:25  (192-168-1-250.my-web-site.org)
[root@bigboy tmp]# wall The system is shutting down now!

Broadcast message from root (pts/0) (Sun Nov  7 15:04:27 2004):

The system is shutting down now!
[root@bigboy tmp]#
```

2. Log into the VGA console, and enter single user mode:

```
[root@bigboy tmp]# init 1
```

Simple, eh?

Edit Your */etc/fstab* File

The /etc/fstab file lists all the partitions that need to be auto-mounted when the system boots. You have to alert Linux that quotas are enabled on the filesystem by editing the /etc/fstab file and modifying the options for the /home directory. You'll need to add the usrquota option. In case you forget the name, the usrquota option is mentioned in the fstab man pages.

The old fstab looked like:

```
LABEL=/home          /home        ext3    defaults            1 2
```

but your new fstab should be:

```
LABEL=/home          /home        ext3    defaults,usrquota   1 2
```

Remount the Filesystem

Editing the /etc/fstab file isn't enough; Linux needs to reread the file to get its instructions for /home. You can do this using the mount command with the -o remount qualifier.

```
sh-2.05b# mount -o remount /home
```

Get Out of Single-User Mode

Return to your original run state by using either the init 3 or init 5 commands. Continue to the next step once the system is back to its normal state. You can also use the exit command to return to your default runlevel.

Create the Partition Quota Configuration Files

The uppermost directory of the filesystem needs to have an `aquota.user` file (defines quotas by user), an `aquota.group` file (defines quotas by group), or both. The man page for `quota` lists them at the bottom.

In this case, just enable per-user quotas for the `/home` filesystem:

```
[root@bigboy tmp]# touch /home/aquota.user
[root@bigboy tmp]# chmod 600 /home/aquota.user
[root@bigboy tmp]#
```

Initialize the Quota Table

Editing the `/etc/fstab` file and remounting the file system only alerted Linux to the fact that the filesystem has quota capabilities. You have to generate a quota table, separate from the `aquota` files, that lists all the current allocations for each user on the file system. This table will be automatically and transparently updated each time a file is modified. Linux compares the values in this table with the quota limitations that the systems administrator has placed in the `aquota` files and uses this information to determine whether the user has rights to increased disk usage.

You initialize the table with the `quotacheck` command. Be prepared: You'll get an error the first time you enter the command, because Linux will realize that the `aquota` file wasn't created using one of the quota commands:

```
[root@bigboy tmp]# quotacheck -vagum
quotacheck: WARNING -  Quotafile /home/aquota.user was probably
truncated. Can't save quota settings...
quotacheck: Scanning /dev/hda3 [/home] done
quotacheck: Checked 185 directories and 926 files
[root@bigboy tmp]#
```

Edit the User's Quota Information

Now you need to edit the user's quota information. The `edquota` command enables you to selectively edit a portion of the `aquota.user` file on a per-user basis:

```
[root@bigboy tmp]# edquota -u mp3user
```

The command invokes the `vi` editor.

```
Disk quotas for user mp3user (uid 503):
  Filesystem  blocks      soft      hard    inodes     soft     hard
    /dev/hda3      24         0         0         7        0        0
```

From here, you can edit a number of fields:

☞ **Blocks:** The amount of space, in 1K blocks, that the user is currently using.

☞ **Inodes:** The number of files the user is currently using.

☞ **Soft limit:** The maximum blocks/inodes a quota user may have on a partition. The role of a soft limit changes if you use grace periods. With grace periods, the user is warned only that their soft limit has been exceeded. When the grace period expires, the user is barred from using additional disk space or files. When set to zero, limits are disabled.

☞ **Hard limit:** The maximum blocks/inodes a quota user may have on a partition when a grace period is set. Users may exceed a soft limit, but they can never exceed their hard limit.

Here user mp3user is limited to a maximum of 5MB of data storage on /dev/hda3 (**/home**):

```
Disk quotas for user mp3user (uid 503):
    Filesystem  blocks      soft      hard    inodes     soft     hard
    /dev/hda3       24      5000         0         7        0        0
```

Testing

Linux checks the total amount of disk space a user uses each time a file is accessed and compares it against the values in the quota file. If the values are exceeded, depending on the configuration, then Linux prevents the creation of new files or the expansion of existing files to use more disk space.

OTHER QUOTA TOPICS

Creating disk quotas frequently isn't enough. You also have to manage the process by reviewing the quota needs of each user and adjusting them according to the policies of your company. You'll need to make Linux scan its hard disks periodically to check for exceeded quotas. This section describes the most common quota management activities.

Editing Grace Periods

The edquota -t command sets the grace period for each filesystem. Like the edquota -u command, it invokes the vi editor.

The grace period is a time limit before the soft limit is enforced for a quota-enabled file system. You can use time units of seconds, minutes, hours, days, weeks, and months. This is what you'll see with the command edquota -t:

```
[root@bigboy tmp]# edquota -t

Grace period before enforcing soft limits for users:
Time units may be: days, hours, minutes, or seconds
  Filesystem              Block grace period      Inode grace period
  /dev/hda3                     7days                   7days
```

Note

There should be no spaces between the number and the unit of time measure. Therefore, 7days is correct, but 7 days is wrong.

Editing Group Quotas

Editing quotas on a per-group basis can be done similarly with the edquota -g command.

Getting Quota Reports

The repquota command lists quota usage limits of all users on the system:

```
[root@bigboy tmp]# repquota /home
*** Report for user quotas on device /dev/hda3
Block grace time: 7days; Inode grace time: 7days
                        Block limits            File limits
User            used    soft    hard  grace   used  soft  hard  grace
----------------------------------------------------------------------
root      --   52696       0       0          1015     0     0
...
...
...
mp3user   --      24       0       0             7     0     0

[root@bigboy tmp]#
```

CONCLUSION

Disk quotas are good to put in place for specific users whose disk usage activities need to be curtailed. It helps to not only limit the use of physical disk resources that could potentially be put to better use, but also reduces the likelihood of having fragmented disk structures that slow disk access due to the presence of too many files. User education must play a major role in your strategy too; users must be made aware of the challenges you face as a result of excessive disk usage. Of course, there comes a time when you are faced with no option but to expand the number of disks in your system. Chapter 27, "Expanding Disk Capacity," covers a variety of approaches to increasing your storage capacity.

Remote Disk Access With NFS

IN THIS CHAPTER

- ☞ NFS Operation Overview
- ☞ Installing nfs
- ☞ Scenario
- ☞ Configuring NFS on the Server
- ☞ Configuring NFS on the Client
- ☞ Activating Modifications to the /etc/exports File
- ☞ The NFS automounter
- ☞ Troubleshooting NFS
- ☞ Other NFS Considerations
- ☞ Conclusion

Samba is usually the solution of choice when you want to share disk space between Linux and Windows machines. The **Network File System protocol** (**NFS**) is used when disks need to be shared between Linux servers. Basic configuration is fairly simple, and this chapter will explain all the essential steps.

NFS OPERATION OVERVIEW

Linux data storage disks contain files stored in **filesystems** with a standardized directory structure. New disks are added by attaching, or **mounting**, the directories of their filesystems to a directory of an already existing filesystem. This in effect makes the new hard disk transparently appear to be a subdirectory of the filesystem to which it is attached.

NFS was developed to allow a computer system to access directories on remote computers by mounting them on a local filesystem as if they were a local disk. The systems administrator on the NFS server has to define the directories that need to be activated, or **exported,** for access by the NFS clients, and administrators on the clients need to define both the NFS server and the subset of its exported directories to use.

General NFS Rules

You should follow some general rules when configuring NFS:

☞ Only export directories beneath the / directory.

☞ Do not export a subdirectory of a directory that has already been exported—the exception being when the subdirectory is on a different physical device. Likewise, do not export the parent of a subdirectory unless it is on a separate device.

☞ Only export local filesystems.

Keep in mind that when you mount any filesystem on a directory, the original contents of the directory are ignored, or obscured, in favor of the files in the mounted filesystem. When the filesystem is unmounted, then the original files in the directory reappear unchanged.

Key NFS Concepts

Data access over a network always introduces a variety of challenges, especially if the operation is intended to be transparent to the user, as in the case of NFS. Here are some key NFS background concepts that will help in your overall understanding.

VFS

The **virtual filesystem** (**VFS**) interface is the mechanism used by NFS to transparently and automatically redirect all access to NFS-mounted files to the remote server. This is done in such a way that files on the remote NFS server appear to the user to be no different than those on a local disk.

VFS also translates these requests to match the actual filesystem format on the NFS server's disks. This allows the NFS server to be not only a completely different operating system, but also use different naming schemes for files with different file attribute types.

Stateless Operation

Programs that read and write to files on a local filesystem rely on the operating system to track their access location within the file with a **pointer**. As NFS is a network-based file system, and networks can be unreliable, it was decided that the NFS client daemon would act as a failsafe intermediary between regular programs running on the NFS client and the NFS server.

Normally, when a server fails, file accesses timeout and the file pointers are reset to zero. With NFS, the NFS server doesn't maintain the file pointer information, the NFS client does. This means that if an NFS server suddenly fails, the NFS client can precisely restart the file access once more after patiently waiting until the server returns online.

Caching
NFS clients typically request more data than they need and cache the results in memory locally so that further sequential access of the data can be done locally versus over the network. This is also known as a **read ahead cache**. Data that's to be written to the NFS server is cached with the data being written to the server when the cache becomes full. Caching therefore helps to reduce the amount of network traffic while simultaneously improving the speed of some types of data access.

The NFS server caches information too, such as the directory information for the most recently accessed files and a read ahead cache for recently read files.

NFS and Symbolic Links
You have to be careful with the use of symbolic links on exported NFS directories. If an absolute link points to a directory on the NFS server that hasn't been exported, then the NFS client won't be able to access it.

Unlike absolute links, relative symbolic links are interpreted relative to the client's filesystem. Consider an example where the /data1 directory on the server is mounted on the /data1 directory. If there is a link to the ../data2 directory on the NFS server and a directory corresponding to ../data2 doesn't exist on the NFS client, then an error will occur.

Also, mounting a filesystem on a symbolic link actually mounts the filesystem on the target of the symbolic link. You'll have to be careful not to obscure the contents of this original directory in the process. Plan carefully before doing this.

NFS Background Mounting
NFS clients use the **remote procedure call** (**RPC**) suite of network application helper programs to mount remote filesystems. If the mount cannot occur during the default RPC timeout period, then the client retries the mount process until the NFS number of retries has been exceeded. The default is 10,000 minutes, which is approximately a week. The difficulty here is that if the NFS server is unavailable, the mount command will hang for a week until it returns online. It is possible to use a bg option to spawn the retries off as a subprocess so that the main mount command can continue to process other requests.

Hard and Soft Mounts
The process of continuous retrying, whether in the background or foreground, is called a **hard mount**. NFS attempts to guarantee the consistency of your data with these constant retries. With **soft mounts**, repeated RPC failures

cause the NFS operation to fail not hang and data consistency is therefore not guaranteed. The advantage is that the operation completes quickly, whether it fails or not. The disadvantage is that the use of the soft option implies that you are using an unreliable NFS server; if this is the case it is best not to place critical data that needs to be updated regularly or executable programs in such a location.

NFS Versions

Three versions of NFS are available currently: versions 2, 3, and 4. Version 1 was a prototype. This chapter focuses on version 2, which:

☞ Supports files up to 4GB long

☞ Requires an NFS server to successfully write data to its disks before the write request is considered successful

☞ Has a limit of 8KB per read or write request

The main differences with version 3 are that it:

☞ Supports extremely large file sizes of up to 264 - 1 bytes

☞ Supports the NFS server data updates as being successful when the data is written to the server's cache

☞ Negotiates the data limit per read or write request between the client and server to a mutually decided optimal value

Version 4 maintains many of version 3's features, but with the additions that:

☞ File locking and mounting are integrated in the NFS daemon and operate on a single, well known TCP port, making network security easier

☞ File locking is mandatory, whereas before it was optional

☞ Support for the bundling of requests from each client provides more efficient processing by the NFS server

It is important to match the versions of NFS running on clients and servers to help ensure the necessary compatibility to get NFS to work predictably.

Important NFS Daemons

NFS isn't a single program, but a suite of interrelated programs that work together to get the job done:

☞ `portmap`: The primary daemon upon which all the others rely, `portmap` manages connections for applications that use the RPC specification. By default, `portmap` listens to TCP port 111 on which an initial connection is made. This is then used to negotiate a range of TCP ports, usually above port 1024, to be used for subsequent data transfers. You need to run `portmap` on both the NFS server and client.

☞ **nfs**: Starts the RPC processes needed to serve shared NFS file systems. The `nfs` daemon needs to be run on the NFS server only.

☞ **nfslock**: Used to allow NFS clients to lock files on the server via RPC processes. The `nfslock` daemon needs to be run on both the NFS server and client.

☞ **netfs**: Allows RPC processes run on NFS clients to mount NFS filesystems on the server. The `nfslock` daemon needs to be run on the NFS client only.

Now take a look at how to configure these daemons to create functional NFS client/server peering.

INSTALLING *NFS*

Red Hat Linux installs `nfs` by default, and also by default `nfs` is activated when the system boots. You can determine whether you have `nfs` installed using the RPM command in conjunction with the `grep` command to search for all installed `nfs` packages:

```
[root@bigboy tmp]# rpm -qa | grep nfs
redhat-config-nfs-1.1.3-1
nfs-utils-1.0.1-3.9
[root@bigboy tmp]#
```

A blank list means that you'll have to install the required packages.

You also need to have the RPC `portmap` package installed, and the `rpm` command can tell you whether it's on your system already. When you use `rpm` in conjunction with `grep`, you can determine all the `portmap` applications installed:

```
[root@bigboy tmp]# rpm -q portmap
portmap-4.0-57
[root@bigboy tmp]#
```

A blank list means that you'll have to install the required packages.

If `nfs` and `portmap` are not installed, they can be added fairly easily once you find the `nfs-utils` and `portmap` RPMs. (If you need a refresher, see Chapter 6, "Installing RPM Software.") Remember that RPM filenames usually start with the software's name and a version number, as in `nfs-utils-1.1.3-1.i386.rpm`.

SCENARIO

A small office has an old Linux server that is running out of disk space. The office cannot tolerate any down time, even after hours, because the server is accessed by overseas programmers and clients at night and local ones by day.

Budgets are tight and the company needs a quick solution until it can get a purchase order approved for a hardware upgrade. Another Linux server on the network has additional disk capacity in its /data partition and the office would like to expand into it as an interim expansion NFS server.

CONFIGURING NFS ON THE SERVER

Both the NFS server and NFS client have to have parts of the NFS package installed and running. The server needs portmap, nfs, and nfslock operational, as well as a correctly configured /etc/exports file. Here's how to do it.

The /etc/exports File

The /etc/exports file is the main NFS configuration file, and it consists of two columns. The first column lists the directories you want to make available to the network. The second column has two parts. The first part lists the networks or DNS domains that can get access to the directory, and the second part lists NFS options in brackets.

For the scenario you need:

☞ Read-only access to the /data/files directory to all networks

☞ Read/write access to the /home directory from all servers on the 192.168.1.0 /24 network, which is all addresses from 192.168.1.0 to 192.168.1.255

☞ Read/write access to the /data/test directory from servers in the my-web-site.org DNS domain

☞ Read/write access to the /data/database directory from a single server, 192.168.1.203

In all cases, use the sync option to ensure that file data cached in memory is automatically written to the disk after the completion of any disk data copying operation.

```
#/etc/exports
/data/files           *(ro,sync)
/home                 192.168.1.0/24(rw,sync)
/data/test            *.my-web-site.org(rw,sync)
/data/database        192.168.1.203/32(rw,sync)
```

After configuring your /etc/exports file, you need to activate the settings, but first make sure that NFS is running correctly.

Starting NFS on the Server

Configuring an NFS server is straightforward:

1. Use the `chkconfig` command to configure the required `nfs` and RPC `portmap` daemons to start at boot. You also should activate NFS file locking to reduce the risk of corrupted data.

```
[root@bigboy tmp]# chkconfig --level 35 nfs on
[root@bigboy tmp]# chkconfig --level 35 nfslock on
[root@bigboy tmp]# chkconfig --level 35 portmap on
```

2. Use the `init` scripts in the `/etc/init.d` directory to start the `nfs` and RPC `portmap` daemons. The examples use the `start` option, but when needed, you can also stop and restart the processes with the `stop` and `restart` options:

```
[root@bigboy tmp]# service portmap start
[root@bigboy tmp]# service nfs start
[root@bigboy tmp]# service nfslock start
```

3. Test whether NFS is running correctly with the `rpcinfo` command. You should get a listing of running RPC programs that must include `mountd`, `portmapper`, `nfs`, and `nlockmgr`:

```
[root@bigboy tmp]# rpcinfo -p localhost
   program vers proto   port
    100000    2   tcp    111  portmapper
    100000    2   udp    111  portmapper
    100003    2   udp   2049  nfs
    100003    3   udp   2049  nfs
    100021    1   udp   1024  nlockmgr
    100021    3   udp   1024  nlockmgr
    100021    4   udp   1024  nlockmgr
    100005    1   udp   1042  mountd
    100005    1   tcp   2342  mountd
    100005    2   udp   1042  mountd
    100005    2   tcp   2342  mountd
    100005    3   udp   1042  mountd
    100005    3   tcp   2342  mountd
[root@bigboy tmp]#
```

CONFIGURING NFS ON THE CLIENT

NFS configuration on the client requires you to start the NFS application; create a directory on which to mount the NFS server's directories that you exported via the `/etc/exports` file, and finally to mount the NFS server's directory on your local directory, or **mount point**. Here's how to do it all.

Starting NFS on the Client

Three more steps easily configure NFS on the client:

1. Use the `chkconfig` command to configure the required `nfs` and RPC `portmap` daemons to start at boot. Activate `nfslock` to lock the files and reduce the risk of corrupted data:

```
[root@smallfry tmp]# chkconfig --level 35 netfs on
[root@smallfry tmp]# chkconfig --level 35 nfslock on
[root@smallfry tmp]# chkconfig --level 35 portmap on
```

2. Use the `init` scripts in the `/etc/init.d` directory to start the `nfs` and RPC `portmap` daemons. As on the server, the examples use the `start` option, but you can also stop and restart the processes with the `stop` and `restart` options:

```
[root@smallfry tmp]# service portmap start
[root@smallfry tmp]# service netfs start
[root@smallfry tmp]# service nfslock start
```

3. Test whether NFS is running correctly with the `rpcinfo` command. The listing of running RPC programs you get must include `status`, `portmapper`, and `nlockmgr`:

```
[root@smallfry root]# rpcinfo -p
   program vers proto   port
    100000    2   tcp    111  portmapper
    100000    2   udp    111  portmapper
    100024    1   udp  32768  status
    100024    1   tcp  32768  status
    100021    1   udp  32769  nlockmgr
    100021    3   udp  32769  nlockmgr
    100021    4   udp  32769  nlockmgr
    100021    1   tcp  32769  nlockmgr
    100021    3   tcp  32769  nlockmgr
    100021    4   tcp  32769  nlockmgr
    391002    2   tcp  32770  sgi_fam
[root@smallfry root]#
```

NFS and DNS

The NFS client must have a matching pair of forward and reverse DNS entries on the DNS server used by the NFS server. In other words, a DNS lookup on the NFS server for the IP address of the NFS client must return a server name that will map back to the original IP address when a DNS lookup is done on that same server name.

```
[root@bigboy tmp]# host 192.168.1.102
201.1.168.192.in-addr.arpa domain name pointer 192-168-1-102.my-web-
site.org.
```

```
[root@bigboy tmp]# host 192-168-1-102.my-web-site.org
192-168-1-102.my-web-site.org has address 192.168.1.102
[root@bigboy tmp]#
```

This is a security precaution added into the nfs package that lessens the likelihood of unauthorized servers from gaining access to files on the NFS server. Failure to correctly register your server IPs in DNS can result in "fake hostname" errors:

```
Nov  7 19:14:40 bigboy rpc.mountd: Fake hostname smallfry.my-web-
site.org for 192.168.1.1 - forward lookup doesn't exist
```

Making NFS Mounting Permanent

In most cases, users want their NFS directories to be permanently mounted. This requires an entry in the /etc/fstab file in addition to the creation of the mount point directory.

The /etc/fstab File

The /etc/fstab file lists all the partitions that need to be auto-mounted when the system boots. Therefore, you need to edit the /etc/fstab file if you need the NFS directory to be made permanently available to users on the NFS. For the example, mount the /data/files directory on server Bigboy (IP address 192.16801.100) as an NFS-type filesystem using the local /mnt/nfs mount point directory:

```
#/etc/fstab
#Directory                   Mount Point    Type    Options        Dump
FSCK
192.168.1.100:/data/files    /mnt/nfs       nfs     soft,nfsvers=2  0
0
```

This example used the soft and nfsvers options; Table 29.1 outlines these and other useful NFS mounting options you may want to use. See the NFS man pages for more details.

Table 29.1 Possible NFS Mount Options

Option	Description
bg	Retry mounting in the background if mounting initially fails.
fg	Mount in the foreground.
soft	Use soft mounting.
hard	Use hard mounting.

continues

Table 29.1   continued

Option	Description
rsize=n	The amount of data NFS will attempt to access per read operation. The default is dependent on the kernel. For NFS version 2, set it to 8192 to assure maximum throughput.
wsize=n	The amount of data NFS will attempt to access per write operation. The default is dependent on the kernel. For NFS version 2, set it to 8192 to assure maximum throughput.
nfsvers=n	The version of NFS the mount command should attempt to use,
tcp	Attempt to mount the filesystem using TCP packets; the default is UDP.
intr	If the filesystem is hard mounted and the mount times out, allow for the process to be aborted using the usual methods such as CTRL-C and the kill command.

The steps to mount the directory are fairly simple, as you'll see.

Permanently Mounting the NFS Directory

You'll now create a mount point directory, /mnt/nfs, on which to mount the remote NFS directory and then use the mount -a command to activate the mount. Notice how before mounting there were no files visible in the /mnt/nfs directory, this changes after the mounting is completed:

```
[root@smallfry tmp]# mkdir /mnt/nfs
[root@smallfry tmp]# ls /mnt/nfs
[root@smallfry tmp]# mount -a
[root@smallfry tmp]# ls /mnt/nfs
ISO  ISO-RedHat  kickstart  RedHat
[root@smallfry tmp]#
```

Each time your system boots, it reads the /etc/fstab file and executes the mount -a command, thereby making this a permanent NFS mount.

Note

There are multiple versions of NFS, the most popular of which is version 2, which most NFS clients use. Newer NFS servers may also be able to handle NFS version 4. To be safe, it is best to force the NFS server to export directories as version 2 using the nfsvers=2 option in the /etc/fstab file as shown in the example. Failure to do so may result in an error message:

```
[root@probe-001 tmp]# mount -a
mount to NFS server '192.168.1.100' failed: server is
down.
[root@probe-001 tmp]#
```

Manually Mounting NFS File Systems

If you don't want a permanent NFS mount, then you can use the mount command without the /etc/fstab entry to gain access only when necessary. This is a manual process; for an automated process, see the section "The NFS automounter."

In this case, you're mounting the /data/files directory as an NFS-type filesystem on the /mnt/nfs mount point. The NFS server is Bigboy whose IP address is 192.168.1.100.

Notice how before mounting there were no files visible in the /mnt/nfs directory, this changes after the mounting is complete:

```
[root@smallfry tmp]# mkdir /mnt/nfs
[root@smallfry tmp]# ls /mnt/nfs
[root@smallfry tmp]# mount -t nfs 192.168.1.100:/data/files /mnt/nfs
[root@smallfry tmp]# ls /mnt/nfs
ISO   ISO-RedHat   kickstart   RedHat
[root@smallfry tmp]#
```

Congratulations! You've made your first steps towards being an NFS administrator.

ACTIVATING MODIFICATIONS TO THE /ETC/EXPORTS FILE

You can force your system to re-read the /etc/exports file by restarting NFS. In a nonproduction environment, this may cause disruptions when an exported directory suddenly disappears without prior notification to users. Here are some methods you can use to update and activate the file with the least amount of inconvenience to others.

New Exports File

When no directories have yet been exported to NFS, use the exportfs -a command:

```
[root@bigboy tmp]# exportfs -a
```

Adding a Shared Directory To An Existing Exports File

When adding a shared directory, you can use the exportfs -r command to export only the new entries:

```
[root@bigboy tmp]# exportfs -r
```

Deleting, Moving, or Modifying a Share

Removing an exported directory from the `/etc/exports` file requires work on both the NFS client and server. The steps are:

1. Unexport the mount point directory on the NFS client using the `umount` command. In this case, you're unmounting the `/mnt/nfs` mount point:

```
[root@smallfry tmp]# umount /mnt/nfs
```

Note

You may also need to edit the `/etc/fstab` file of any entries related to the mount point if you want to make the change permanent even after rebooting.

---

2. Comment out the corresponding entry in the NFS server's `/etc/exports` file and reload the modified file:

```
[root@bigboy tmp]# exportfs -ua
[root@bigboy tmp]# exportfs -a
```

You have now completed a seamless removal of the exported directory with much less chance of having critical errors.

THE NFS *AUTOMOUNTER*

The permanent mounting of filesystems has its disadvantages. For example, the `/etc/fstab` file is unique per Linux server and has to be individually edited on each. NFS client management, therefore, becomes more difficult. Also, the mount is permanent, tying up system resources even when the NFS server isn't being accessed.

NFS uses an `automounter` feature that overcomes these shortcomings by allowing you to bypass the `/etc/fstab` file for NFS mounts, instead using an NFS-specific **map file** that can be distributed to multiple clients. In addition, you can use the file to specify the expected duration of the NFS mount, after which time it is unmounted automatically. However, `automounter` continues to report to the operating system kernel that the mount is still active. When the kernel makes an NFS file request, `automounter` intercepts it and mounts the remote directory on the mount point defined in the map file. The mount point directory is dynamically created by the `automounter` when needed, after the time-out period the remote directory is unmounted and the mount point is deleted.

automounter Map Files

The master map file of `automounter` has a simple format that defines the name of the mount point directory in the first column and the subsidiary map file that controls its mounting in the second. You can add mounting options to a third column.

In the example, the /home directory needs to be automounted on an NFS server and the configuration information is defined in the /etc/auto.home file. Finally, the mount will only last for five minutes (300 seconds), and this value will act as a default for all the entries in the /etc/auto.home file.

Irregular entries that don't match /home are placed in the /etc/auto.direct file.

```
#
# File: /etc/auto.master
#
/home    /etc/auto.home --timeout=300
/-       /etc/auto.direct
```

Direct Maps
Direct maps are used to define NFS filesystems that are mounted on different servers or that don't all start with the same prefix.

Indirect Maps
Indirect maps define directories that can be mounted under the same mount point. A good example would be all the users' directories under /home.

Note

Based on preliminary testing, an early release of Fedora Core 3 doesn't appear to work correctly with automounter. You have to have one indirect map defined to avoid startup errors, and after doing so, the maps don't appear to be activated. No errors occur in the logs either.

The Structure of Direct and Indirect Map Files

The format of these map files is similar to that of the /etc/auto.master file, except that columns two and three have been switched.

Column one lists all the directory **keys** that will activate the automounter feature. It is also the name of the mount point under the directory listed in the /etc/auto.master file. The second column provides all the NFS options to be used, and the third column lists the NFS servers and the filesystems that map to the keys.

When the NFS client accesses a file, it refers to the keys in the /etc/auto.master file to see whether any fall within the realm of the automounter's responsibility. If one does, then automounter checks the subsidiary map file for a subdirectory mount point key. If it finds one, then automounter mounts the files for the system.

Indirect Map File Example

In the previous example, the `/etc/auto.master` file redirected all references to the `/home` directory to the `/etc/auto.home` file. This second file has entries for peter, bob, and bunny; these directories are actually mount points for directories on servers Bigboy, Ochorios, and Waitabit.

```
#
# File: /etc/auto.home
#
peter    bigboy:/home/peter
bob      ochorios:/home/bob
bunny    waitabit:/home/bunny
```

Direct Map File Example

The second entry in the `/etc/auto.master` file was specifically created to handle all references to one of a kind directory prefixes. In the example the `/data/sales` and `/sql/database` are the mount points for directories on servers Bigboy and Waitabit.

```
#
# File: /etc/auto.direct
#
/data/sales          -rw           bigboy:/disk1/data/sales
/sql/database        -ro,soft      waitabit:/var/mysql/database
```

Note

The `automounter` treats direct mounts as if they were files in a directory, not as individual directories. This means all direct mount points in the same directory are mounted simultaneously even if only one of them is being accessed. This can cause excessive mounting activity that can slow response times. There are tricks you can use to avoid this, perhaps the simplest is just to place direct mount points in different directories.

Note

Direct map entries in the `/etc/auto.master` file must all begin with `/-`, and you can use absolute path names with direct map files only, if you don't then you'll get an error like this in your `/var/log/messages` file:

```
Nov  7 19:24:12 smallfry automount[31801]: bad map format:
found indirect, expected direct exiting
```

Wildcards in Map Files

You can use two types of wildcards in a map file. The asterisk (*), which means all, and the ampersand (&), which instructs automounter to substitute the value of the key for the & character.

Using the Ampersand Wildcard

In the example below, the key is peter, so the ampersand wildcard is interpreted to mean peter too. This means you'll be mounting the bigboy:/home/peter directory.

```
#
# File: /etc/auto.home
#
peter    bigboy:/home/&
```

Using the Asterisk Wildcard

In the example below, the key is *, meaning that automounter will attempt to mount any attempt to enter the /home directory. But what's the value of the ampersand? It is actually assigned the value of the key that triggered the access to the /etc/auto.home file. If the access was for /home/peter, then the ampersand is interpreted to mean peter, and bigboy:/home/peter is mounted. If access was for /home/bob, then bigboy:/home/bob would be mounted.

```
#
# File: /etc/auto.home
#
*    bigboy:/home/&
```

Starting *automounter*

Fedora Linux installs the automounter RPM, called autofs, by default. Here are some quick steps to get automounter started:

1. Use the chkconfig command to configure the automounter daemons to start at boot. Activate NFS file locking to reduce the risk of corrupted data.

   ```
   [root@bigboy tmp]# chkconfig autofs on
   ```

2. Use the init scripts in the /etc/init.d directory to start the automounter daemons. The example uses the start option, but you can also stop and restart the process with the stop and restart options.

   ```
   [root@bigboy tmp]# service autofs start
   ```

3. Use the `pgrep` command to determine whether `automounter` is running. If it is, the command will return the process ID of the `automount` daemon.

```
[root@bigboy tmp]# pgrep automount
32261
[root@bigboy tmp]#
```

As you can see, managing the startup of `automounter` is very similar to that of other Linux applications and should be easy to remember.

automounter Examples

Now that you understand NFS `automounter`, you may benefit from an example. Chapter 30, "Centralized Logins Using NIS," contains a full scenario in which a school computer laboratory uses `automounter` to centrally house all the home directories of its students. Additional centralization is also achieved by using NIS for login authentication, access, and accounting control.

TROUBLESHOOTING NFS

A basic NFS configuration usually works without problems when the client and server are on the same network. The most common problems are caused by forgetting to start NFS, to edit the `/etc/fstab` file, or to export the `/etc/exports` file. Another common cause of failure is the `iptables` firewall daemon running on either the server or client without the administrator realizing it.

When the client and server are on different networks, these checks still apply, but you'll also have to make sure basic connectivity has been taken care of as outlined in Chapter 4, "Simple Network Troubleshooting." Sometimes a firewall being present on the path between the client and server can cause difficulties.

As always, no troubleshooting plan would be complete without frequent reference to the `/var/log/messages` file when searching for additional clues. Table 29.2 shows some common NFS errors you'll encounter.

Table 29.2   Some Common NFS Error Messages

Option	Description
Too many levels of remote in path	Attempting to mount a filesystem that has already been mounted.
Permission denied	User is denied access. This could be the client's root user who has unprivileged status on the server due to the `root_squash` option. Could also be because the user on the client doesn't exist on the server.
No such host	Typographical error in the name of the server.
No such file or directory	Typographical error in the name of the file or directory; they don't exist.

Table 29.2   Some Common NFS Error Messages

Option	Description
NFS server is not responding	The server could be overloaded or down.
Stale file handle	A file that was previously accessed by the client was deleted on the server before the client closed it.
Fake hostname	Forward and reverse DNS entries don't exist for the NFS client.

The *showmount* Command

When run on the server, the showmount -a command lists all the currently exported directories. It also shows a list of NFS clients accessing the server, in this case one client has an IP address of 192.168.1.102:

```
[root@bigboy tmp]# showmount -a
All mount points on bigboy:
*:/home
192.168.1.102:*
[root@bigboy tmp]#
```

The *df* Command

The df command lists the disk usage of a mounted filesystem. Run it on the NFS client to verify that NFS mounting has occurred. In many cases, the root_squash mount option will prevent the root user from doing this, so it's best to try it as an unprivileged user.

```
[nfsuser@smallfry nfsuser]$ df -F nfs
Filesystem              1K-blocks        Used Available Use% Mounted on
192.168.1.100:/home/nfsuser
                        1032056      346552    633068  36% /home/nfsuser
[nfsuser@smallfry nfsuser]$
```

The *nfsstat* Command

The nfsstat command provides useful error statistics. The -s option provides NFS server stats, while the -c option provides them for clients. Threshold guidelines are provided in Table 29.3.

```
[root@bigboy tmp]# nfsstat -s
Server rpc stats:
calls       badcalls    badauth     badclnt     xdrcall
1547        0           0           0           0
Server nfs v2:
null        getattr     setattr     root        lookup      readlink
```

```
244       100% 0       0% 0        0% 0        0% 0        0% 0        0%
read          wrcache      write       create      remove      rename
0         0% 0        0% 0        0% 0        0% 0        0% 0        0%
link          symlink      mkdir       rmdir       readdir     fsstat
0         0% 0        0% 0        0% 0        0% 0        0% 0        0%

Server nfs v3:
null          getattr      setattr     lookup       access      readlink
251       19% 332    25% 0        0% 265    20% 320    24% 0        0%
read          write        create      mkdir        symlink     mknod
39        2% 14     1% 1        0% 1        0% 0        0% 0        0%
remove        rmdir        rename      link         readdir     readdirplus
0         0% 0        0% 0        0% 0        0% 0        0% 31       2%
fsstat        fsinfo       pathconf    commit
1         0% 34     2% 0        0% 14     1%

[root@bigboy tmp]#
```

Table 29.3   Error Thresholds for the `nfsstat` Command

Value	Threshold	Description
Readlink	> 10%	Excessive numbers of symbolic links slowing performance. Try to replace them with a directory and mount the filesystem directly on this new mount point.
Getattr	> 50%	File attributes, like file data, is cached in NFS. This value tracks the percentage of file attribute reads that are not from cache refresh requests. Usually caused by the NFS `noac` mount option, which prevents file attribute caching.
badcalls	> 0	Bad RPC requests. Could be due to poorly configured authentication, the root user attempting to access data governed by the `root_squash` directive, or having a user in too many groups.
retrans	> 5%	Percentage of requests for service that the client had to retransmit to the servers. Could be due to slow NFS servers or poor network conditions.
Writes	> 10%	Writes are slow due to poor caching values. Check the `noac` and `wsize` mount options.
Read	> 10%	Reads are slow due to poor caching values. Check the `noac` and `rsize` mount options.

OTHER NFS CONSIDERATIONS

NFS can be temperamental. An incorrect configuration can cause it to be unresponsive. Its security is relatively weak, and you have to be aware of the file permissions on both the NFS client and server to get it to work correctly. Often these issues can be resolved with some basic guidelines outlined in this section.

Security

NFS and `portmap` have had a number of known security deficiencies in the past. As a result, I don't recommended using NFS over insecure networks. NFS doesn't encrypt data and it is possible for root users on NFS clients to have root access to the server's filesystems. You can exercise security-related caution with NFS by following a few guidelines:

☞ Restrict its use to secure networks.

☞ Export only the most needed data.

☞ Consider using read-only exports whenever data updates aren't necessary.

☞ Use the `root_squash` option in `/etc/exports` file (default) to reduce the risk of the possibility of a root user on the NFS client having root file permission access on the NFS server. This is normally an undesirable condition, especially if the NFS client and NFS server are being managed by different sets of administrators.

These points should be the foundation of your NFS security policy; the list, however, isn't comprehensive due to the concise scope of this book. I'd suggest that you refer to a dedicated NFS reference for more detailed advice.

NFS Hanging

As stated before, if the NFS server fails, the NFS client waits indefinitely for it to return. This also forces programs relying on the same client server relationship to wait indefinitely too.

For this reason, use the `soft` option in the NFS client's `/etc/fstab` file. This causes NFS to report an I/O error to the calling program after a long timeout.

You can reduce the risk of NFS hanging by taking a number of precautions:

☞ Run NFS on a reliable network.

☞ Avoid having NFS servers that NFS mount each other's filesystems or directories.

☞ Always use the sync option whenever possible.

☞ Do not have mission-critical computers rely on an NFS server to operate, unless the server's reliability can be guaranteed.

☞ Do not include NFS-mounted directories as part of your search path, because a hung NFS connection to a directory in your search path could cause your shell to pause at that point in the search path until the NFS session is regained.

Following these simple but important guidelines will help to make NFS operate more predictably, allowing you more time to focus on other important administrative tasks.

File Locking

NFS allows multiple clients to mount the same directory, but NFS has a history of not handling file locking well, although more recent versions are said to have rectified the problem. Test your network-based applications thoroughly before considering using NFS.

Nesting Exports

NFS doesn't allow you to export directories that are subdirectories of directories that have already been exported unless they are on different partitions.

Limiting *root* Access

NFS doesn't allow a root user on a NFS client to have root privileges on the NFS server. This can be disabled with the `no_root_squash` export option in the `/etc/exports` file. This is normally an undesirable condition, especially if the NFS client and NFS server are being managed by different sets of administrators.

Restricting Access to the NFS Server

NFS doesn't provide restrictions on a per-user basis. If a user named nfsuser exists on the NFS client, then they will have access to all the files of a user named nfsuser on the NFS server. It is best, therefore, to use the `/etc/exports` file to limit access to certain trusted servers or networks.

You may also want to use a firewall to protect access to the NFS server. A main communication control channel is usually created between the client and server on TCP port 111, but the data is frequently transferred on a randomly chosen TCP port negotiated between them. There are ways to limit the TCP ports used, but that is beyond the scope of this book.

You may also want to eliminate any wireless networks between your NFS server and client, and it is not wise to mount an NFS share across the Internet as access could be either slow, intermittent or insecure.

File Permissions

The NFS file permissions on the NFS server are inherited by the client. It can become complicated especially if the users and user groups on the NFS client that are expected to access data on the NFS server don't exist on the NFS server.

For simplicity, make the key users and groups on both systems match and make sure the permissions on the NFS client mount point and the exported directories of the NFS server are in keeping with your operational objectives.

CONCLUSION

As you have seen NFS can be a very powerful tool in providing clients with access to large amounts of data, such as a database stored on a centralized server. Many of the new network-attached storage products currently available on the market rely on NFS—a testament to its popularity, increasing stability, and improving security.

Centralized Logins Using NIS

IN THIS CHAPTER

Network Information Services (**NIS**) enables you to create user accounts that can be shared across all systems on your network. The user account is created only on the NIS server. NIS clients download the necessary username and password data from the NIS server to verify each user login.

An advantage of NIS is that users need to change their passwords on the NIS server only, instead of every system on the network. This makes NIS popular in computer training labs, distributed software development projects or any other situation where groups of people have to share many different computers.

The disadvantages are that NIS doesn't encrypt the username and password information sent to the clients with each login and that all users have access to the encrypted passwords stored on the NIS server. A detailed analysis of NIS security is beyond the scope of this book, but I suggest that you restrict its use to highly secure networks or to networks where access to non-NIS networks is highly restricted.

SCENARIO

To understand the benefits of NFS, consider an example. A school wants to set up a small computer lab for its students:

☞ The main Linux server, Bigboy, has a large amount of disk space and will be used as both the NIS server and NFS-based file server for the Linux PCs in the lab.

☞ Users logging into the PCs will be assigned home directories on Bigboy and not on the PCs themselves.

☞ Each user's home directory will be automatically mounted with each user login on the PCs using NFS.

☞ The lab instructor will practice with a Linux PC named Smallfry before implementing NIS on all the remaining PCs.

☞ The suite of NIS RPMs have been installed on the server and client: `ypserve` and `yp-tools` are on the server, and `ypbind` and `yp-tools` are on the client.

Downloading and installing RPMs isn't hard, as discussed in Chapter 6, "Installing RPM Software." When searching for the RPMs, remember that the filename usually starts with the software package name followed by a version number, as in `yp-tools-2.8-3.i386.rpm`.

The lab instructor did some research and created an implementation plan:

1. Configure Bigboy as an NFS server to make its `/home` directory available to the Linux workstations.
2. Configure Smallfry as an NFS client that can access Bigboy's `/home` directory.
3. Configure Bigboy as an NIS server.
4. Create a user account (nisuser) on Bigboy that doesn't exist on Smallfry. Convert the account to a NIS user account.
5. Configure Smallfry as an NIS client.
6. Test a remote login from Bigboy to Smallfry using the username and password of the account nisuser.

You have the scenario and the plan, it's time to get to work.

CONFIGURING THE NFS SERVER

Here are the steps to configure the school's NFS server:

1. Edit the `/etc/exports` file to allow NFS mounts of the `/home` directory with read/write access:

```
/home                          *(rw,sync)
```

2. Let NFS read the `/etc/exports` file for the new entry, and make `/home` available to the network with the `exportfs` command:

```
[root@bigboy tmp]# exportfs -a
[root@bigboy tmp]#
```

3. Make sure the required `nfs`, `nfslock`, and `portmap` daemons are both running and configured to start after the next reboot.

```
[root@bigboy tmp]# chkconfig nfslock on
[root@bigboy tmp]# chkconfig nfs on
[root@bigboy tmp]# chkconfig portmap on
[root@bigboy tmp]# service portmap start
Starting portmapper: [  OK  ]
[root@bigboy tmp]# service nfslock start
Starting NFS statd: [  OK  ]
[root@bigboy tmp]# service nfs start
Starting NFS services:   [  OK  ]
Starting NFS quotas: [  OK  ]
Starting NFS daemon: [  OK  ]
Starting NFS mountd: [  OK  ]
[root@bigboy tmp]#
```

After configuring the NIS server, we have to configure its clients. This will be covered next.

CONFIGURING THE NFS CLIENT

You also need to configure the NFS clients to mount their `/home` directories on the NFS server.

These steps archive the `/home` directory. In a production environment in which the `/home` directory would be actively used, you'd have to force the users to log off, back up the data, restore it to the NFS server, and then follow the steps below. As this is a lab environment, these prerequisites aren't necessary.

1. Make sure the required `netfs`, `nfslock`, and `portmap` daemons are running and configured to start after the next reboot:

```
[root@smallfry tmp]# chkconfig nfslock on
[root@smallfry tmp]# chkconfig netfs on
[root@smallfry tmp]# chkconfig portmap on
[root@smallfry tmp]# service portmap start
Starting portmapper: [  OK  ]
[root@smallfry tmp]# service netfs start
Mounting other filesystems:  [  OK  ]
[root@smallfry tmp]# service nfslock start
Starting NFS statd: [  OK  ]
[root@smallfry tmp]#
```

2. Keep a copy of the old /home directory, and create a new directory /home on which you'll mount the NFS server's directory.

```
[root@smallfry tmp]# mv /home /home.save
[root@smallfry tmp]# mkdir /home
[root@smallfry tmp]# ll /
...
...
drwxr-xr-x    1 root    root        11 Nov 16 20:22 home
drwxr-xr-x    2 root    root      4096 Jan 24  2003 home.save
...
...
[root@smallfry tmp]#
```

3. Make sure you can mount Bigboy's /home directory on the new /home directory you just created. Unmount it once everything looks correct:

```
[root@smallfry tmp]# mount 192.168.1.100:/home /home/
[root@smallfry tmp]# ls /home
ftpinstall   nisuser   quotauser   smallfry   www
[root@smallfry tmp]# umount /home
[root@smallfry tmp]#
```

4. Start configuring autofs automounting. Edit your /etc/auto.master file to refer to file /etc/auto.home for mounting information whenever the /home directory is accessed. After five minutes, autofs unmounts the directory:

```
#/etc/auto.master
/home          /etc/auto.home --timeout 600
```

5. Edit file /etc/auto.home to do the NFS mount whenever the /home direc-tory is accessed. If the line is too long to view on your screen, you can add a \ character at the end to continue on the next line:

```
#/etc/auto.home
*      -fstype=nfs,soft,intr,rsize=8192,wsize=8192,nosuid,tcp \
       192.168.1.100:/home:&
```

6. Start autofs and make sure it starts after the next reboot with the chkconfig command:

```
[root@smallfry tmp]# chkconfig autofs on
[root@smallfry tmp]# service autofs restart
Stopping automount:[  OK  ]
Starting automount:[  OK  ]
[root@smallfry tmp]#
```

After doing this, you won't be able to see the contents of the /home direc-tory on Bigboy as user root. This is because by default NFS activates the root squash feature, which disables this user from having privileged access to directories on remote NFS servers. You'll be able to test this later after NIS is configured.

> **Note**
>
> This `automounter` feature doesn't appear to function correctly in my preliminary testing of Fedora Core 3. See Chapter 29, "Remote Disk Access With NFS," for details.

All newly added Linux users will now be assigned a home directory under the new remote `/home` directory. This scheme will make the users feel their home directories are local, when in reality they are automatically mounted and accessed over your network.

CONFIGURING THE NIS SERVER

NFS only covers file sharing over the network. You now have to configure NIS login authentication for the lab students before the job is done. The configuration of the NIS server is not difficult, but requires many steps that you may overlook. Don't worry, we'll review each one in detail.

> **Note**
>
> In the early days, NIS was called Yellow Pages. The developers had to change the name after a copyright infringement lawsuit, yet many of the key programs associated with NIS have kept their original names beginning with yp.

Edit Your */etc/sysconfig/network* File

You need to add the NIS domain you wish to use in the `/etc/sysconfig/network` file. For the school, call the domain NIS-SCHOOL-NETWORK:

```
#/etc/sysconfig/network
NISDOMAIN="NIS-SCHOOL-NETWORK"
```

Edit Your */etc/yp.conf* File

NIS servers also have to be NIS clients themselves, so you'll have to edit the NIS client configuration file `/etc/yp.conf` to list the domain's NIS server as being the server itself or `localhost`:

```
# /etc/yp.conf - ypbind configuration file
ypserver 127.0.0.1
```

Start the Key NIS Server-Related Daemons

Start the necessary NIS daemons in the /etc/init.d directory and use the chkconfig command to ensure they start after the next reboot.

```
[root@bigboy tmp]# service portmap start
Starting portmapper: [  OK  ]
[root@bigboy tmp]# service yppasswdd start
Starting YP passwd service: [  OK  ]
[root@bigboy tmp]# service ypserv start
Setting NIS domain name NIS-SCHOOL-NETWORK:   [  OK  ]
Starting YP server services: [  OK  ]
[root@bigboy tmp]#

[root@bigboy tmp]# chkconfig portmap on
[root@bigboy tmp]# chkconfig yppasswdd on
[root@bigboy tmp]# chkconfig ypserv on
[root@bigboy tmp]#
```

Table 30.1 lists a summary of the daemon's functions.

Table 30.1   Required NIS Server Daemons

Daemon Name	Purpose
portmap	The foundation RPC daemon upon which NIS runs
yppasswdd	Lets users change their passwords on the NIS server from NIS clients
ypserv	Main NIS server daemon
ypbind	Main NIS client daemon
ypxfrd	Used to speed up the transfer of very large NIS maps

Make sure they are all running before continuing to the next step. You can use the rpcinfo command to do this:

```
[root@bigboy tmp]# rpcinfo -p localhost
   program vers proto   port
    100000    2   tcp    111  portmapper
    100000    2   udp    111  portmapper
    100009    1   udp    681  yppasswdd
    100004    2   udp    698  ypserv
    100004    1   udp    698  ypserv
    100004    2   tcp    701  ypserv
    100004    1   tcp    701  ypserv
[root@bigboy tmp]#
```

The ypbind and ypxfrd daemons won't start properly until after you initialize the NIS domain. You'll start these daemons after initialization is completed.

Initialize Your NIS Domain

Now that you have decided on the name of the NIS domain, you'll have to use the `ypinit` command to create the associated authentication files for the domain. You will be prompted for the name of the NIS server, which in this case is Bigboy.

With this procedure, all nonprivileged accounts are automatically accessible via NIS:

```
[root@bigboy tmp]# /usr/lib/yp/ypinit -m

At this point, we have to construct a list of the hosts which will run
NIS servers.  bigboy is in the list of NIS server hosts.  Please
continue to add the names for the other hosts, one per line.  When you
are done with the list, type a <control D>.
        next host to add:  bigboy
        next host to add:
The current list of NIS servers looks like this:

bigboy

Is this correct?  [y/n: y]   y
We need a few minutes to build the databases...
Building /var/yp/NIS-SCHOOL-NETWORK/ypservers...
Running /var/yp/Makefile...
gmake[1]: Entering directory `/var/yp/NIS-SCHOOL-NETWORK'
Updating passwd.byname...
Updating passwd.byuid...
Updating group.byname...
Updating group.bygid...
Updating hosts.byname...
Updating hosts.byaddr...
Updating rpc.byname...
Updating rpc.bynumber...
Updating services.byname...
Updating services.byservicename...
Updating netid.byname...
Updating protocols.bynumber...
Updating protocols.byname...
Updating mail.aliases...
gmake[1]: Leaving directory `/var/yp/NIS-SCHOOL-NETWORK'

bigboy has been set up as a NIS master server.

Now you can run ypinit -s bigboy on all slave server.
[root@bigboy tmp]#
```

Note
Make sure `portmap` is running before trying this step or you'll get errors, such as:

```
failed to send `clear' to local ypserv: RPC: Port mapper
failureUpdating group.bygid...
```

You will have to delete the /var/yp/NIS-SCHOOL-NETWORK directory and restart portmap, yppasswd, and ypserv before you'll be able to do this again successfully.

Start the *ypbind* and *ypxfrd* Daemons

You can now start the ypbind and the ypxfrd daemons because the NIS domain files have been created:

```
[root@bigboy tmp]# service ypbind start
Binding to the NIS domain: [  OK  ]
Listening for an NIS domain server.
[root@bigboy tmp]# service ypxfrd start
Starting YP map server: [  OK  ]
[root@bigboy tmp]# chkconfig ypbind on
[root@bigboy tmp]# chkconfig ypxfrd on
```

Make Sure the Daemons Are Running

All the NIS daemons use RPC port mapping and, therefore, are listed using the rpcinfo command when they are running correctly.

```
[root@bigboy tmp]# rpcinfo -p localhost
   program vers proto   port
    100000    2   tcp    111  portmapper
    100000    2   udp    111  portmapper
    100003    2   udp   2049  nfs
    100003    3   udp   2049  nfs
    100021    1   udp   1024  nlockmgr
    100021    3   udp   1024  nlockmgr
    100021    4   udp   1024  nlockmgr
    100004    2   udp    784  ypserv
    100004    1   udp    784  ypserv
    100004    2   tcp    787  ypserv
    100004    1   tcp    787  ypserv
    100009    1   udp    798  yppasswdd
 600100069    1   udp    850  fypxfrd
 600100069    1   tcp    852  fypxfrd
    100007    2   udp    924  ypbind
    100007    1   udp    924  ypbind
    100007    2   tcp    927  ypbind
    100007    1   tcp    927  ypbind
[root@bigboy tmp]#
```

ADDING NEW NIS USERS

New NIS users can be created by logging into the NIS server and creating the new user account. In this case, you'll create a user account called nisuser and give it a new password.

Once this is complete, you then have to update the NIS domain's authentication files by executing the make command in the /var/yp directory.

This procedure makes all NIS-enabled, nonprivileged accounts become automatically accessible via NIS, not just newly created ones. It also exports all the user's characteristics stored in the /etc/passwd and /etc/group files, such as the login shell, the user's group, and home directory:

```
[root@bigboy tmp]# useradd -g users nisuser
[root@bigboy tmp]# passwd nisuser
Changing password for user nisuser.
New password:
Retype new password:
passwd: all authentication tokens updated successfully.
[root@bigboy tmp]# cd /var/yp
[root@bigboy yp]# make
gmake[1]: Entering directory `/var/yp/NIS-SCHOOL-NETWORK'
Updating passwd.byname...
Updating passwd.byuid...
Updating netid.byname...
gmake[1]: Leaving directory `/var/yp/NIS-SCHOOL-NETWORK'
[root@bigboy yp]#
```

You can check to see if the user's authentication information has been updated by using the ypmatch command, which should return the user's encrypted password string:

```
[root@bigboy yp]# ypmatch nisuser passwd
nisuser:$1$d6E2i79Q$wp3Eo0Qw9nFD/::504:100::/home/nisuser:/bin/bash
[root@bigboy yp]
```

You can also use the getent command, which has similar syntax. Unlike ypmatch, getent doesn't provide an encrypted password when run on an NIS server, it just provides the user's entry in the /etc/passwd file. On a NIS client, the results are identical with both showing the encrypted password.

```
[root@bigboy yp]# getent passwd nisuser
nisuser:x:504:100::/home/nisuser:/bin/bash
[root@bigboy yp]#
```

Configuring the NIS Client

Now that the NIS server is configured, it's time to configure the NIS clients. There are a number of related configuration files that you need to edit to get it to work. Take a look at the procedure.

Run *authconfig*

The `authconfig` program automatically configures your NIS files after prompting you for the IP address and domain of the NIS server:

```
[root@smallfry tmp]# authconfig
```

Once finished, it should create an `/etc/yp.conf` file that defines, amongst other things, the IP address of the NIS server for a particular domain. It also edits the `/etc/sysconfig/network` file to define the NIS domain to which the NIS client belongs.

```
# /etc/yp.conf - ypbind configuration file
domain NIS-SCHOOL-NETWORK server 192.168.1.100

#/etc/sysconfig/network
NISDOMAIN=NIS-SCHOOL-NETWORK
```

In addition, the `authconfig` program updates the `/etc/nsswitch.conf` file that lists the order in which certain data sources should be searched for name lookups, such as those in DNS, LDAP, and NIS. Here you can see where NIS entries were added for the important login files:

```
#/etc/nsswitch.conf
passwd:     files nis
shadow:     files nis
group:      files nis
```

Note

You can also locate a sample NIS `nsswitch.conf` file in the `/usr/share/doc/yp-tools*` directory.

Start the NIS Client-Related Daemons

Start the `ypbind` NIS client, `yppasswd,` and `portmap` daemons in the `/etc/init.d` directory and use the `chkconfig` command to ensure they start after the next reboot. Remember to use the `rpcinfo` command to ensure they are running correctly.

```
[root@smallfry tmp]# service portmap start
Starting portmapper: [  OK  ]
[root@smallfry tmp]# service ypbind start
Binding to the NIS domain:
Listening for an NIS domain server.
[root@smallfry tmp]# service yppasswdd start
Starting YP passwd service: [  OK  ]
[root@smallfry tmp]#
```

```
[root@smallfry tmp]# chkconfig ypbind on
[root@smallfry tmp]# chkconfig portmap on
[root@smallfry tmp]# chkconfig yppasswdd on
```

Remember to use the `rpcinfo -p localhost` command to make sure they all started correctly.

Verify Name Resolution

As the configuration examples refer to the NIS client and server by their host-names, you'll have to make sure the names resolve correctly to IP addresses. This can be configured either in DNS, when the hosts reside in the same domain, or more simply by editing the /etc/hosts file on both Linux boxes:

```
#
# File: /etc/hosts (smallfry)
#
192.168.1.100    bigboy
```

```
#
# File: /etc/hosts (bigboy)
#
192.168.1.102    smallfry
```

Test NIS Access to the NIS Server

You can run the `ypcat`, `ypmatch`, and `getent` commands to make sure communication to the server is correct.

```
[root@smallfry tmp]# ypcat passwd
nisuser:$1$Cs2GMe6r$1hohkyG7ALrDLjH1:505:100::/home/nisuser:/bin/bash
quotauser:!!:503:100::/home/quotauser:/bin/bash
ftpinstall:$1$8WjAVtes$SnRh9S1w07sYkFNJwpRKa.:502:100::/:/bin/bash
www:$1$DDCi/OPI$hwiTQ.LOXqYJUk09Bw.pJ/:504:100::/home/www:/bin/bash
smallfry:$1$qHni9dnR$iKDs7gfyt..BS9Lry3DAq.:501:100::/:/bin/bash
[root@smallfry tmp]#
```

```
[root@smallfry tmp]# ypmatch nisuser passwd
nisuser:$1$d6E2i79Q$wp3Eo0Qw9nFD/:504:100::/home/nisuser:/bin/bash
[root@smallfry tmp]#
```

```
[root@smallfry tmp]# getent passwd nisuser
nisuser:$1$d6E2i79Q$wp3Eo0Qw9nFD/:504:100::/home/nisuser:/bin/bash
[root@smallfry tmp]#
```

Possible sources of error include:

☞ Incorrect `authconfig` setup resulting in errors in the `/etc/yp.conf`, `/etc/sysconfig/network` and `/etc/nsswitch.conf` files

☞ Failure to run the `ypinit` command on the NIS server

☞ NIS not being started on the NIS server or client

☞ Poor routing between the server and client, or the existence of a firewall that's blocking traffic

Try to eliminate these areas as sources of error and refer to the syslog `/var/log/`messages file on the client and server for entries that may provide additional clues.

Test Logins via the NIS Server

Once your basic NIS functionality testing is complete, try to test a remote login. Failures in this area could be due to firewalls blocking TELNET or SSH access and the TELNET and SSH server process not being started on the clients.

Logging in via TELNET

Try logging into the NIS client via TELNET if it is enabled:

```
[root@bigboy tmp]# telnet 192.168.1.102
Trying 192.168.1.102...
Connected to 192.168.1.102.
Escape character is '^]'.
Red Hat Linux release 9 (Shrike)
Kernel 2.4.20-6 on an i686
login: nisuser
Password:
Last login: Sun Nov 16 22:03:51 from 192-168-1-100. my-web-site.org
[nisuser@smallfry nisuser]$
```

Logging in via SSH

Try logging into the NIS client via SSH:

```
[root@bigboy tmp]# ssh -l nisuser 192.168.1.102
nisuser@192.168.1.102's password:
[nisuser@smallfry nisuser]$
```

In some versions of Linux, the NIS client's SSH daemon doesn't re-read the `/etc/nsswitch.conf` file you just modified until SSH is restarted. SSH logins, therefore, won't query the NIS server until this is done. Restart SSH on the NIS client:

```
[root@smallfry root]# service sshd restart
Stopping sshd:[  OK  ]
Starting sshd:[  OK  ]
[root@smallfry root]#
```

NIS SLAVE SERVERS

NIS relies a lot on broadcast traffic to operate, which prevents you from having an NIS server on a different network from the clients. You can avoid this problem on your local subnet by using slave servers that are configured to automatically synchronize their NIS data with that of the single master server.

You can also consider placing multiple NIS servers on a single subnet for the sake of redundancy. To do this, configure the NIS clients to have multiple NIS servers for the domain in the `/etc/yp.conf` file.

Configuring NIS Slave Servers

In this scenario, you need to add an NIS slave server named Nisslave (IP address 192.168.1.254) to the NIS-SCHOOL-NETWORK NIS domain. You also must configure the NIS master server, Bigboy, to push its database map information to the slave whenever there is an update. Here are the steps you need:

1. As you're referring to our servers by their hostnames, you'll have to make sure the names resolve correctly to IP addresses. This can be done either in DNS, when the hosts reside in the same domain, or more simply by editing the `/etc/hosts` files on both servers as seen in Table 30.2.

Table 30.2   NIS Master and Slave `/etc/hosts` Files

Master (Bigboy)	Slave (nisslave)
#	#
# File: /etc/hosts (Bigboy)	# File: /etc/hosts (Nisslave)
#	#
192.168.1.254 nisslave	192.168.1.100 bigboy

2. Configure the NIS slave as a NIS client of itself in the `/etc/yp.conf` file, and configure the NIS domain in the `/etc/sysconfig/network` file as seen in Table 30.3.

Table 30.3 NIS Master and Slave `/etc/yp.conf` Files

`/etc/yp.conf`	`/etc/sysconfig/network`
`#`	`#`
`# File: /etc/yp.conf (Bigboy)`	`# File: /etc/sysconfig/network`
`#`	`#`
`ypserver 127.0.0.1`	`NISDOMAIN="NIS-SCHOOL-NETWORK"`

3. On the slave server, run `ypbind` so the slave can query the master server:

```
[root@nisslave tmp]# service portmap start
Starting portmapper: [  OK  ]
[root@nisslave tmp]# service ypbind start
Binding to the NIS domain:
Listening for an NIS domain server.
[root@nisslave tmp]#

[root@nisslave tmp]# chkconfig portmap on
[root@nisslave tmp]# chkconfig ypbind on
```

4. Optimize database map transfers by the NIS map transfer daemon, which should be started on both the master and slave:

```
[root@nisslave tmp]# service ypxfrd start
Starting YP map server: [  OK  ]
[root@nisslave tmp]#
[root@nisslave tmp]# chkconfig ypxfrd on

[root@bigboy tmp]# service ypxfrd start
Starting YP map server: [  OK  ]
[root@bigboy tmp]#
[root@bigboy tmp]# chkconfig ypxfrd on
```

5. Do a simple database query of the master from the slave using the `ypwhich` command with the `-m` (master) switch. You should get a listing of all the tables.

```
[root@nisslave tmp]# ypwhich -m
mail.aliases bigboy
group.bygid bigboy
passwd.byuid bigboy
rpc.bynumber bigboy
...
...
[root@nisslave tmp]#
```

6. Do an initial database download to the slave from the master with the `ypinit` command using the `-s` switch for a slave-type operation and specifying server Bigboy as the master from which the data is to be obtained. You should see "Trying `ypxfrd` - success" messages. If the messages say "Trying `ypxfrd` - not running," then start `ypxfrd` on both servers.

```
[root@nisslave tmp]# /usr/lib/yp/ypinit -s bigboy
We will need a few minutes to copy the data from bigboy.
```

```
Transferring services.byservicename...
Trying ypxfrd ... success

Transferring group.byname...
Trying ypxfrd ... success
...
...


nisslave's NIS data base has been set up.
If there were warnings, please figure out what went wrong, and fix
it.

At this point, make sure that /etc/passwd and /etc/group have
been edited so that when the NIS is activated, the data bases you
have just created will be used, instead of the /etc ASCII files.
[root@nisslave tmp]#
```

If your database is corrupt or your /etc/hosts files are incorrect, you'll
get map enumeration errors as shown. Use the make command again to
rebuild your database on the master when necessary.

```
[root@nisslave tmp]# /usr/lib/yp/ypinit -s bigboy
Can't enumerate maps from bigboy. Please check that it is running.
[root@nisslave tmp]#
```

7. Now that the data has been successfully downloaded, make the slave
server serve NIS clients with ypserv.

```
[root@nisslave tmp]# service ypserv start
Starting YP server services:
[root@nisslave tmp]#
[root@nisslave tmp]# chkconfig ypxfrd on
```

8. Log on to the master server. Add the slave server to the master server's
database map by editing the /var/yp/ypservers file on the master:

```
[root@bigboy yp]# cd /tmp
[root@bigboy tmp]# cd /var/yp/
[root@bigboy yp]# vi ypservers
```

9. Add nisslave to the file.

```
#
# File: /var/yp/ypservers
#
bigboy
nisslave
```

10. The make file in the /var/yp directory defines how the NIS server will
build the database map and how the master will relate to the NIS slave.
Make a copy of the master's make file for safekeeping:

```
[root@bigboy yp]# cp Makefile Makefile.old
```

11. Edit the make file to allow the master to push maps to the slave:

```
#
# File: /var/vp/Makefile
#

#
# Allow the master to do database pushes to the slave
#
NOPUSH=false
```

12. Use the make command to rebuild the database. The make command automatically pushes database updates to the servers listed in the
/var/yp/servers file.

```
[root@bigboy yp]# make
gmake[1]: Entering directory `/var/yp/NIS-SCHOOL-NETWORK'
Updating ypservers...
YPPUSH: gethostbyname(): Success
YPPUSH: using not FQDN name
gmake[1]: Leaving directory `/var/yp/NIS-SCHOOL-NETWORK'
gmake[1]: Entering directory `/var/yp/NIS-SCHOOL-NETWORK'
Updating netid.byname...
YPPUSH: gethostbyname(): Success
YPPUSH: using not FQDN name
gmake[1]: Leaving directory `/var/yp/NIS-SCHOOL-NETWORK'
[root@bigboy yp]#
```

13. On the slave server, create a cron file in the /etc/crond.d directory, in this
case named nis_sync, that will run periodic database downloads from the
master server. This helps to ensure that the slave servers have current
databases even if they miss updates from the master in the event the
school goes offline for maintenance. Restart the cron daemon so that the
configuration in this file becomes active.

```
[root@nisslave yp]# vi /etc/cron.d/nis_sync

#
# File: /etc/cron.d/nis_sync
#
20 *     * * *    /usr/lib/yp/ypxfr_1perhour
40 6     * * *    /usr/lib/yp/ypxfr_1perday
55 6,18 * * *    /usr/lib/yp/ypxfr_2perday


[root@nisslave yp]# service crond restart
```

That's a lot of work but it's still not over. There is one final configuration
step that needs to be done on the NIS clients before you're finished.

Configuring NIS Clients with Slaves

Edit the /etc/yp.conf file on all the clients to include Nisslave, and restart ypbind.

```
#
# File: /etc/yp.conf (Smallfry)
#
domain NIS-SCHOOL-NETWORK server 192.168.1.100
domain NIS-SCHOOL-NETWORK server 192.168.1.254

[root@smallfry tmp]# service ypbind restart
Shutting down NIS services: [  OK  ]
Binding to the NIS domain: [  OK  ]
Listening for an NIS domain server..
[root@smallfry tmp]#
```

CHANGING YOUR NIS PASSWORDS

You should also test to make sure your users can change their NIS passwords from the NIS clients with the yppasswd command. The process is different whether there is only a single NIS master or a master-slave server relationship.

When There Is Only an NIS Master

When there is only a single NIS server, password changes can be made only on the NIS server using the yppasswd command.

Users Changing Their Own Passwords

Users can change their passwords by logging into the NIS server and issuing the yppasswd command:

```
[nisuser@bigboy nisuser]$ yppasswd
Changing NIS account information for nisuser on bigboy.my-web-
site.org.
Please enter old password:
Changing NIS password for nisuser on bigboy.my-web-site.org.
Please enter new password:
Please retype new password:

The NIS password has been changed on bigboy.my-web-site.org.

[nisuser@bigboy nisuser]$
```

User root Changing Passwords

The root user can change other users' passwords issuing the yppasswd command with the -p switch that specifies the username that needs the change.

```
[root@bigboy tmp]# yppasswd -p nisuser
Changing NIS account information for nisuser on bigboy.my-web-
site.org.
Please enter root password:
Changing NIS password for nisuser on bigboy.my-web-site.org.
Please enter new password:
Please retype new password:

The NIS password has been changed on bigboy.my-web-site.org.

[root@bigboy tmp]#
```

When There Is a NIS Master and Slave Pair

With an NIS master and slave pair configuration, passwords can be changed on the NIS clients or the NIS slave, but not on the NIS master.

Possible Password Errors

There are a number of unexpected errors you may find when changing passwords—errors that have nothing to do with bad typing.

Segmentation Faults

Running the yppasswd command on the wrong client or server depending on your NIS master and slave configuration can cause **segmentation fault** errors. (Make sure you follow the chapter's guidelines for password changes!) Here are some sample password change failures on an NIS client with only one NIS master server:

```
[nisuser@smallfry nisuser]$ yppasswd
Segmentation fault
[nisuser@smallfry nisuser]$

[root@smallfry root]# yppasswd -p nisuser
Segmentation fault
[root@smallfry root]#
```

Daemon Errors

The yppasswdd daemon must be running on both the client and server for password changes to work correctly. When they aren't running, you'll get errors:

```
[root@smallfry etc]# yppasswd -p nisuser
yppasswd: yppasswdd not running on NIS master host ("bigboy").
[root@smallfry etc]#
```

You'll also get a similar error if you attempt to change an NIS password on an NIS master server in a master and slave configuration.

CONSIDERATIONS FOR A NON-NFS ENVIRONMENT

In many cases NFS, isn't used to create a centralized home directory for users and, therefore, you'll have to create it on each NIS client and not on the server.

This example creates the home directory for the NIS client, Smallfry. After doing this, you have to copy a BASH login profile file into it and modify the ownership of the directory and all the files to user nisuser.

Logins should proceed normally once this has been done and all the other steps have been followed.

```
[root@smallfry tmp]# mkdir /home/nisuser
[root@smallfry tmp]# chmod 700 /home/nisuser/
[root@smallfry tmp]# ll /home
total 2
drwx------    2 nisuser users         1024 Aug  4 08:05 nisuser
[root@smallfry tmp]#
[root@smallfry tmp]# cp /etc/skel/.* /home/nisuser/
cp: omitting directory `/etc/skel/.'
cp: omitting directory `/etc/skel/..'
cp: omitting directory `/etc/skel/.kde'
[root@smallfry tmp]# chown -R nisuser:users /home/nisuser
[root@smallfry tmp]#
```

NIS TROUBLESHOOTING

Troubleshooting is always required as any part of your daily routine, NIS is no exception. Here are some simple steps to follow to get it working again.

1. The rpcinfo command provides a list of TCP ports that your NIS client or server is using. Make sure you can TELNET to these ports from the client to the server and vice versa. If this fails, make sure all the correct NIS daemons are running and that there are no firewalls blocking traffic on the network or on the servers themselves. These ports change from time to time, so memorizing them won't help much.

The example tests from the client to the server:

```
[root@bigboy tmp]# rpcinfo -p
   program vers proto   port
    100000    2   tcp    111  portmapper
    100000    2   udp    111  portmapper
    100024    1   udp  32768  status
    100024    1   tcp  32768  status
    391002    2   tcp  32769  sgi_fam
    100009    1   udp   1018  yppasswdd
```

```
            100004      2    udp     611    ypserv
            100004      1    udp     611    ypserv
            100004      2    tcp     614    ypserv
            100004      1    tcp     614    ypserv
            100007      2    udp     855    ypbind
            100007      1    udp     855    ypbind
            100007      2    tcp     858    ypbind
            100007      1    tcp     858    ypbind
         600100069      1    udp     874    fypxfrd
         600100069      1    tcp     876    fypxfrd
      [root@bigboy tmp]#
```

```
[root@smallfry tmp]# telnet 192.168.1.100 858
Trying 10.41.32.71...
Connected to 10.41.32.71.
Escape character is '^]'.
^]
telnet> quit
Connection closed.
[root@smallfry tmp]#
```

2. Always use the ypmatch, getent, and ypwhich commands to check your NIS connectivity. If there is any failure, check your steps over again and you should be able to find the source of your problem.

3. Do not fail to create a user's home directory, set its permissions, and copy the /etc/skel files correctly. If you forget, which is a common error, your users may have incorrect login prompts and no ability to create files in their home directories.

It can never be overemphasized that one of the best places to start troubleshooting is in your error log files in the /var/log directory. You'll save a lot of time and effort if you always refer to them whenever the problem doesn't appear to be obvious.

CONCLUSION

NIS is a very useful tool for centralized login management, but it has two shortcomings: NIS clients are typically limited to Unix or Linux operating systems, and the password information passes over the network unencrypted.

Newer authentication schemes overcome these issues. For example, LDAP, which is discussed in Chapter 31, "Centralized Logins Using LDAP and Radius," provides both encryption and the ability to be used on varied types of equipment. Unfortunately older operating systems don't support it, making NIS the preferred option in some cases.

As always, explore your options when deciding on a centralized login scheme. A wrong decision could haunt you for a long time.

Centralized Logins Using LDAP and RADIUS

Many centralized database programs have been developed to allow users to log in on multiple computers using a single password. NIS was one of the first, but it doesn't encrypt the password transaction. It also uses the `portmapper` daemon, which uses an unpredictable range of TCP ports that are difficult for firewalls to track. **LDAP (Lightweight Directory Access Protocol)** provides an alternative based on the **X.500** standard.

The X.500 standard defines how globally referenced directories of people should be structured. X.500 directories are organized under a common **root** directory in a **tree** hierarchy with different levels for each category of information, such as country, state, city, organization, organizational unit, and person. Designed to provide a simpler yet robust implementation of X.500, LDAP was originally used as the backbone of Microsoft's Active Directory Service and Novell's Novell Directory Services (NDS) products. LDAP can also interact with other login programs, such as Remote Authentication Dial-in User Service (RADIUS), which the network equipment of many ISPs use to manage dialup Internet access.

It was later recognized that LDAP had features that could make it a desirable replacement for NIS in some scenarios. For example, it uses a single TCP port (389) for regular communication and another port (636) for encrypted transactions. LDAP also can interact with many login authentication, authorization, and accounting programs external to Linux and UNIX.

This chapter will first show you how to install and use LDAP on Fedora Linux systems, then go on to explain how LDAP interacts with RADIUS.

THE LDAP DIRECTORY STRUCTURE

Like X.500, LDAP directory entries are arranged in a tree structure. Under the root, there are branches that represent countries, organizations, organizational units, and people.

In complicated LDAP deployments, in which you have to exchange information with the LDAP databases of other companies, you may want to get a formal organization number from the **Internet Assigned Numbers Authority (IANA)** to reduce any data conflicts. In the chapter's example this won't be necessary. Because there will be no data sharing, I'll just make up one.

SCENARIO

These concepts are easier to explain when working from an example, so imagine the IT department in a small organization called example.com has many Linux servers it needs to administer.

☞ The company wants a simple, secure, centralized login scheme for all of the servers.

☞ It has decided to use the LDAP domain example.com for its LDAP database, in which one **domain component (DC)** will be example, and the other will be com.

☞ The database will have only one organizational unit simply called People, which is the LDAP default.

☞ Each person will have such attributes as a username (User ID or UID), password, Linux home directory, and login shell.

☞ The Fedora Linux server named Bigboy with the IP address 192.168.1.100 will act as the LDAP server containing the database.

☞ The Fedora Linux server named Smallfry will be used to test the system as the LDAP client and has the IP address 192.168.1.102.

☞ Server Bigboy has a special user account named ldapuser that will be used to test the LDAP logins.

Here is how all that is accomplished.

DOWNLOADING AND INSTALLING THE LDAP PACKAGES

Most Red Hat and Fedora Linux software products are available in the RPM format. When searching for the file, remember that the FreeRADIUS RPM's filename usually starts with `openldap` followed by a version number, as in `openldap-servers-2.1.22-8.i386.rpm`. (For more detail on downloading and installing, see Chapter 6, "Installing RPM Software.")

Required LDAP Server RPMs

Make sure these required LDAP Server RPMs are installed on your LDAP server:

☞ `openldap`

☞ `openldap-clients`

☞ `openldap-devel`

☞ `nss_ldap`

☞ `openldap-servers`

Required LDAP Client RPMs

On your LDAP client, make sure you have these required RPMs:

☞ `openldap`

☞ `openldap-clients`

☞ `openldap-devel`

☞ `nss_ldap`

CONFIGURING THE LDAP SERVER

The first stage of the project is to correctly configure the LDAP server. To do so, you must create an LDAP database into which you import the `/etc/passwd` file. Take a closer look at the steps.

Create a Database Directory

Fedora LDAP defaults to putting all databases in the `/var/lib/ldap` directory. For the example, create a dedicated `example.com` directory owned by the user `ldap`. (The `ldap` user is always created during the RPM installation process.)

```
[root@bigboy tmp]# mkdir /var/lib/ldap/example.com
[root@bigboy tmp]# chown ldap:ldap /var/lib/ldap/example.com
```

Create an LDAP Root Password

Only the LDAP root user can create, import data, and export data into an LDAP database. This user needs an encrypted password. You can create it with the `slappasswd` command and use the result in the LDAP configuration file.

```
[root@bigboy tmp]# slappasswd
New password:
Re-enter new password:
{SSHA}v4qLq/qy01w9my60LLX9BvfNUrRhOjQZ
[root@bigboy tmp]#
```

Edit the *slapd.conf* File

The main LDAP server configuration file is the `/etc/openldap/slapd.conf` file. Update it with:

☞ A database of the default type `ldbm` using the domain suffix `example.com` made up of domain components (DCs) `example` and `com`.

☞ The root user with a common name (CN), or nickname, of Manager who, as expected, is part of the `example` and `com` DCs.

☞ The encrypted version of the LDAP root password as well as the location of the LDAP database.

The configuration file syntax to do this is:

```
database     ldbm
suffix       "dc=example,dc=com"
rootdn       "cn=Manager,dc=example,dc=com"
rootpw       {SSHA}v4qLq/qy01w9my60LLX9BvfNUrRhOjQZ
directory    /var/lib/ldap/example.com
```

Start the *ldap* Daemon

The `service` command uses the options `start`, `stop`, and `restart` to control the LDAP server's operation. Use the `start` option to load the contents of the `slapd.conf` file:

```
[root@bigboy tmp]# service ldap start
   Starting slapd: [  OK  ]
[root@bigboy tmp]#
```

Convert the */etc/passwd* File to LDIF Format

The data on the server's /etc/passwd file now needs to be converted to LDAP **Data Interchange Files** (**LDIF**) format before it can be imported into the LDAP database. You don't need to import all of the usernames, just the ones you need.

Create the ldapuser *Test Account*

To create the ldapuser account you'll use for testing, type the commands:

```
[root@bigboy tmp]# useradd -g users ldapuser
[root@bigboy tmp]# passwd ldapuser
Changing password for user ldapuser.
New password:
Retype new password:
passwd: all authentication tokens updated successfully.
[root@bigboy tmp]#
```

Extract the Desired Records from /etc/passwd

You need to extract the ldapuser information from the /etc/passwd file using the grep command and save it by appending the information to the /etc/openldap/passwd.ldapusers file with the > character:

```
[root@bigboy tmp]# grep ldapuser /etc/passwd > \
    /etc/openldap/passwd.ldapusers
[root@bigboy tmp]#
```

If this is your first time creating the LDAP database, you will also want to extract the information for the Linux root account from the /etc/passwd file to a brand new file called /etc/openldap/passwd.root:

```
[root@bigboy tmp]# grep root /etc/passwd > \
    /etc/openldap/passwd.root
[root@bigboy tmp]#
```

Find the Conversion Script

The /etc/passwd conversion program is called migrate_passw.pl; you can find it using the locate command. The locate utility updates its database every night and may not be able to find newly installed files. You can use the locate command to do the update ahead of schedule.

```
[root@bigboy tmp]# locate -u
[root@bigboy tmp]# locate migrate
...
/usr/share/openldap/migration/migrate_passwd.pl
...
[root@bigboy tmp]#
```

Convert the .ldapuser *File*

You now need to convert the extracted `/etc/passwd` data into an LDIF that will then be imported into the database. Give the file used by regular users the name `/etc/openldap/ldapuser.ldif` and the one for the root user the name `/etc/openldap/root.ldif`:

```
[root@bigboy tmp]# /usr/share/openldap/migration/migrate_passwd.pl \
/etc/openldap/passwd.ldapusers /etc/openldap/ldapusers.ldif
[root@bigboy tmp]#

[root@bigboy tmp]# /usr/share/openldap/migration/migrate_passwd.pl \
/etc/openldap/passwd.root /etc/openldap/root.ldif
[root@bigboy tmp]#
```

Modify the LDIF Files

With your two new LDIF files, the next step is to import this data into the LDAP database. To prepare for this, you must do some editing and create a new LDIF file that defines the organizational unit.

Edit the User LDIF File

The Fedora `migrate_passwd.pl` script creates users that are all part of the organizational unit called `People`, but everyone belongs to the `padl.com` domain. You now have to edit *both* LDIF files and convert the string "padl" to "example" in each record. A text editor is fine for the job. For example, at the `vi` editor's : prompt, use the command

```
%s/padl/example/g
```

to perform a **global substitution** of example for padl.

In the `slapd.conf` file, you gave the root user a common name (CN) of `Manager`. You now have to add this information to the root LDIF file by inserting this line under the `UID` line in the file:

```
cn: Manager
```

Create an LDIF File for the **example.com** *Domain*

The LDIF files you created from `/etc/passwd` referred to users only. The attributes of the `example.com` domain haven't yet been defined, and you also haven't defined the organizational unit called `People`. This can be done using a third LDIF file called `/etc/openldap/example.com.ldif`, which should look like this:

```
dn: dc=example,dc=com
dc: example
description: Root LDAP entry for example.com
objectClass: dcObject
objectClass: organizationalUnit
ou: rootobject

dn: ou=People, dc=example,dc=com
ou: People
description: All people in organisation
objectClass: organizationalUnit
```

Import the LDIF Files into the Database

Use the LDAP `add` command to import all three LDIF files into the database starting with the `example.com.ldif` file, followed by `root.ldif`, and lastly by `ldapusers.ldif`.

Enter the LDAP root password you created when you are prompted:

```
[root@bigboy tmp]# ldapadd -x -D "cn=Manager,dc=example,dc=com" \
     -W -f /etc/openldap/example.com.ldif
[root@bigboy tmp]# ldapadd -x -D "cn=Manager,dc=example,dc=com" \
     -W -f /etc/openldap/root.ldif
[root@bigboy tmp]# ldapadd -x -D "cn=Manager,dc=example,dc=com" \
     -W -f /etc/openldap/ldapusers.ldif
[root@bigboy tmp]#
```

Test the LDAP Database

You can view all the LDAP database entries all at once with the `ldapsearch` command; this is a good test to make sure you have all the correct functionality:

```
[root@bigboy tmp]# ldapsearch -x -b 'dc=example,dc=com' \
    '(objectclass=*)'
[root@bigboy tmp]#
```

CONFIGURING THE LDAP CLIENT

Now that the LDAP server is configured properly, you can turn your attention to configuring and testing the clients.

Edit the *ldap.conf* Configuration File

LDAP clients are configured using the `/etc/openldap/ldap.conf` file. You need to make sure that the file refers to the LDAP server's IP address for the domain `example.com`. The file should look like this:

```
HOST 192.168.1.100
BASE dc=example,dc=com
```

Edit the */etc/nsswitch* File

The `/etc/nsswitch.conf` file defines the order in which the Linux operating system searches login databases for login information.

You want to configure it to first search its `/etc/passwd` file. If it doesn't find the user password information there, it goes to the LDAP server. The easiest way set this up is to use the `/usr/bin/authconfig` command:

1. Run `/usr/bin/authconfig`.
2. Select LDAP.
3. Give the LDAP server's IP address, which is 192.168.1.100 in this case.
4. Give the base DN as `dc [eq] example, dc [eq] com`.
5. Do not select TLS.
6. Use MD5 and shadow passwords.

The screen should look like this:

```
[*] Use Shadow Passwords
[*] Use MD5 Passwords
[*] Use LDAP                    [ ] Use TLS
                    Server: 192.168.1.100
                    Base DN: dc=example,dc=com
```

When finished, look at the `/etc/nsswitch.conf` file and make sure it has references to LDAP.

Create Home Directories on the LDAP Client

You previously created a user named `ldapuser` in the group users on server Bigboy. You now need to make sure that this user has a home directory on the LDAP client Smallfry. The example in this section creates the directory and makes `ldapuser` the owner. As you can see, server Smallfry correctly gets its user information about ldapuser from Bigboy; the `chown` command doesn't complain about `ldapuser` not existing in Smallfry's `/etc/passwd` file.

Check If ldapuser Is Missing from the /etc/passwd File

You can look for `ldapuser` by searching the `/etc/passwd` file with the `grep` command. There should be no response.

```
[root@smallfry tmp]# grep ldapuser /etc/passwd
[root@smallfry tmp]#
```

Create the Home Directory for ldapuser on the LDAP Client

In this phase, you create the home directory, copy a BASH login profile file into it, and modify the ownership of the directory and all the files to user ldapuser.

Tip

If the `chown` command fails, it is probably because of an incorrect LDAP configuration in which the LDAP client cannot read the user information from the LDAP server.

In some cases, you may want to use NFS mounts to provide home directories for your users, which will significantly reduce the need to do this step. The benefits and disadvantages of NFS are covered in Chapter 29, "Remote Disk Access with NFS," and Chapter 30, "Centralized Logins Using NIS," covers using NFS for home directories.

```
[root@smallfry tmp]# mkdir /home/ldapuser
[root@smallfry tmp]# chmod 700 /home/ldapuser/
[root@smallfry tmp]# chown ldapuser:users /home/ldapuser/
[root@smallfry tmp]# ll /home
total 2
drwx------    2 ldapuser users          1024 Aug  4 08:05 ldapuser
[root@smallfry tmp]#
[root@smallfry tmp]# cp /etc/skel/.* /home/ldapuser/
cp: omitting directory `/etc/skel/.'
cp: omitting directory `/etc/skel/..'
cp: omitting directory `/etc/skel/.kde'
[root@smallfry tmp]# chown ldapuser:users /home/ldapuser/.*
[root@smallfry tmp]#
```

Testing

You next need to do basic testing. For details, see what is covered in the "Troubleshooting LDAP Logins" section.

CONFIGURING ENCRYPTED LDAP COMMUNICATION

The secure tunnel (stunnel) utility can be used to intercept regular LDAP communications and encrypt them over an SSL tunnel using the TCP port of your choice. Fortunately, stunnel is installed by default on Fedora Linux, making it even easier to use.

Tip

Add the SSL encryption, only after basic LDAP has been proven to work without encryption. This makes troubleshooting much easier.

Here's how to encrypt LDAP with Fedora Linux.

Configuring the *stunnel* LDAP Client

First, you configure the LDAP client to use stunnel:

1. Edit the ldap.conf file. You have to trick the LDAP client into thinking that the LDAP server is actually running locally as a daemon, so you need to set the HOST entry to localhost. You then configure the stunnel utility to intercept this traffic and relay it to the real LDAP server:

   ```
   HOST localhost
   BASE dc=example,dc=com
   ```

2. Create an stunnel user with the useradd command:

   ```
   [root@smallfry tmp]# useradd stunnel
   ```

3. Edit the stunnel.conf configuration file in the /etc/stunnel directory, configuring it as shown:

   ```
   #
   # File: /etc/stunnel (LDAP Client)
   #

   # Configure stunnel to run as user "stunnel" placing temporary
   # files in the /usr/var/run/stunnel/ directory
   chroot = /home/stunnel
   pid = /stunnel.pid
   setuid = stunnel
   setgid = stunnel

   # Configure logging
   debug = 7
   output = /var/log/messages

   # Use it for client mode
   client = yes

   # Service-level configuration
   [ldap]
   accept  = 389
   connect = 192.168.1.100:636
   ```

At the very end of the file, notice that traffic on the LDAP TCP port 389 is specifically redirected to the LDAP server on TCP port 636 over the secure tunnel.

4. Start `stunnel` with the `stunnel` command:

```
[root@smallfry tmp]# stunnel
```

5. Check the log files, especially the last 100 lines of the error log file `/var/log/messages`, to make sure there are no errors. If there are errors, double check your `stunnel` configuration file for mistakes.

```
[root@smallfry tmp]# tail -100 /var/log/messages
```

6. Make sure `stunnel` runs on the next reboot. The script `/etc/rc.local` is run at the end of every boot sequence. Use the `locate` command to find out where the `stunnel` program is and then place your `stunnel` command in `/etc/rc.local` as shown:

```
# Run stunnel for LDAP (Fedora file location)
/usr/sbin/stunnel
```

Configuring the *stunnel* LDAP Server

After you configure the client, you're ready to set up `stunnel` on the LDAP server:

1. Create an stunnel user using the `useradd` command:

```
[root@bigboy tmp]# useradd stunnel
```

2. Edit the `stunnel.conf` configuration file located in the `/etc/stunnel` directory. Configure it as shown:

```
#
# File: /etc/stunnel (LDAP Server)
#

# Configure stunnel to run as user "stunnel" placing temporary
# files in the /usr/var/run/stunnel/ directory
chroot = /home/stunnel/
pid = /stunnel.pid
setuid = stunnel
setgid = stunnel

# Some debugging stuff
debug = 7
output = /var/log/messages

# Use it for client mode
client  = no
cert = /usr/share/ssl/certs/stunnel.pem
key =   /usr/share/ssl/certs/stunnel.pem
```

```
# Service-level configuration
[ldap]
accept   =   636
connect =   389
```

There are a few differences between the client and server `stunnel.conf` files. The very bottom of the file shows that *all* traffic received on the secure LDAP port of 636 is redirected to the application listening on LDAP port 389. The file is configured for `server` mode and a special SSH certificate has been defined for the encryption process. You'll create the certificates next.

3. Go to the `/usr/share/ssl/certs` directory and create the certificate using the `make` command. Use all the defaults when prompted, but make sure you use the server's IP address when prompted for your server's Common Name or hostname.

```
[root@bigboy tmp]# cd /usr/share/ssl/certs
[root@bigboy certs]# make stunnel.pem
...
Common Name (eg, your name or your server's hostname) []:
192.168.1.100
...
[root@bigboy certs]#
```

Note

The certificate created only has a 365 day lifetime. Remember to repeat this process next year.

---

4. Modify certificate file permissions. The certificate needs to be read by root and the stunnel user. Use the `chmod` and `chgrp` commands to do this:

```
[root@bigboy certs]# chmod 640 stunnel.pem
[root@bigboy certs]# chgrp stunnel stunnel.pem

[root@bigboy certs]# ll /usr/share/ssl/certs
-rw-r-----  1 root stunnel   1991 Jul 31 21:50 stunnel.pem
[root@bigboy certs]#
```

5. Start `stunnel` with the `stunnel` command:

```
[root@bigboy tmp]# stunnel
```

6. Check the last 100 lines of the error log file `/var/log/messages` to make sure there are no errors. If you find errors, double check your `stunnel` configuration file for mistakes.

```
[root@bigboy tmp]# tail -100 /var/log/messages
```

The key things to look for are the loading of the certificate, the binding of LDAP to the 636 secure LDAP port, and the creation of the temporary `stunnel.pid` file:

```
2004.08.02 08:50:18 LOG7[12102:3210052320]: Certificate:
/usr/share/ssl/certs/stunnel.pem
2004.08.02 08:50:18 LOG7[12102:3210052320]: Key file:
/usr/share/ssl/certs/stunnel.pem
2004.08.02 08:50:18 LOG7[12102:3210052320]: ldap bound to
0.0.0.0:636
2004.08.02 08:50:18 LOG7[12103:3210052320]: Created pid file
/stunnel.pid
```

7. Make sure `stunnel` runs on the next reboot. The script `/etc/rc.local` is run at the end of every boot sequence. Use the `locate` command to find out where the `stunnel` program is and then place your `stunnel` command in `/etc/rc.local`:

```
#
# File : /etc/rc.local
#
# Run stunnel for LDAP (Fedora file location)
/usr/sbin/stunnel
```

The final step of the preparation is to create home directories for each user to use just like in the unencrypted LDAP example before this. After this is complete, you'll need to do some basic testing, which is covered in the troubleshooting section.

TROUBLESHOOTING LDAP LOGINS

You can never be certain about the functioning of any application unless you test it. LDAP is fairly complicated to install and should be as thoroughly tested as possible before you deploy it. Here are some steps you can take to help you sleep better at night.

Test Using *ldapsearch*

Always run the `ldapsearch` command on both the LDAP client and server to test your LDAP configuration:

```
[root@smallfry tmp]# ldapsearch -x -b 'dc=example,dc=com' \
    '(objectclass=*)'
```

When LDAP is configured correctly, the command sends a full database listing to your screen.

Use SSH or the Linux Console

Try to log in as user ldapuser to the LDAP client Linux system as an alterna-tive test. If it fails, try restarting SSH on the LDAP client so that the /etc/nsswitch.conf file can be reread with the new LDAP information. This step is not required in all versions of Linux.

Use the *tcpdump* Command

If the LDAP configuration files appear correct and LDAP still doesn't work, then you should try using the tcpdump command, outlined in Chapter 4, "Simple Network Troubleshooting," to see whether your systems can correctly communicate with one another. A failure to communicate could be due to poor routing, misconfigured firewalls along the way, or possibly LDAP being turned off on the server.

Test Secure LDAP

On the LDAP server, use the tcpdump command to listen for traffic on the secure LDAP port 636 or ldaps. Run the ldapsearch command on the LDAP client and if everything is configured correctly, you should see packet flows such as this one:

```
[root@bigboy tmp]# tcpdump -n tcp port ldaps
tcpdump: listening on eth0
09:20:02.281257 192.168.1.102.1345 > 192.168.1.100.ldaps: S
1665037104:1665037104(0) win 5840 <mss 1460,sackOK,timestamp 74401362
0,nop,wscale 0> (DF)
09:20:02.281356 192.168.1.100.ldaps > 192.168.1.102.1345: S
1911175072:1911175072(0) ack 1665037105 win 5792 <mss
1460,sackOK,timestamp 20737195 74401362,nop,wscale 0> (DF)
...
...
[root@bigboy tmp]#
```

Test Regular LDAP

On the LDAP server, use the tcpdump command to listen for traffic on the regu-lar LDAP port 389 or ldap. Run the ldapsearch command on the LDAP client:

```
[root@bigboy tmp]# tcpdump -n tcp port ldap
```

If everything is configured correctly, you should see LDAP packet flows similar to those in the last section.

Test Basic Connectivity

The very first step is to use TELNET to determine whether your LDAP server is accessible on TCP port 389 (LDAP) or 636 (LDAPS).

Lack of connectivity could be caused by a firewall in the path between the LDAP server and client or there could be firewall software running on the servers themselves.

Other sources of failure include LDAP not being started at all, the server could be down, or there could be a network related failure.

Troubleshooting with Telnet is covered in Chapter 4.

LDAP Works But Is Not Using LDAPS

An LDAPS configuration will default to using regular LDAP if there is an error with the SSL keys. This is usually caused by incorrect permissions and ownerships on the key file.

stunnel Doesn't Appear to Work

Changes to the `stunnel.conf` file take effect only after `stunnel` has been restarted. Unfortunately, there is no `stunnel` script in the `/etc/init.d` directory to do this. You have to use the `pkill` command to stop it and the `stunnel` command to start it again:

```
[root@bigboy tmp]# pkill stunnel ; stunnel
[root@bigboy tmp]#
```

LDAP *bind* Errors

The LDAP `bind` utility is used for each login and can give failure errors that are usually not very descriptive. Two of the main ones that usually occur when running the `ldapadd` command are:

☞ **Can't contact LDAP server (81)**: This is usually caused by not configuring the correct IP address in the LDAP client's `ldap.conf` file.
☞ **Invalid credentials (49)**: This is usually caused by incorrect `dc[eq]` statements in the configuration files or in commands used.

Possible *stunnel* Errors in Fedora Core 2

You may get a cryptonet error when starting `stunnel`:

```
Unable to open "/dev/cryptonet"
```

This is caused by an incompatibility with the hwcrypto RPM used for hardware-, not software-based encryption. You need to uninstall hwcrypto to get stunnel to work correctly:

```
[root@bigboy tmp]# rpm -e hwcrypto
```

COMMON LDAP ADMINISTRATIVE TASKS

Here are some explanations of how to do many common LDAP tasks. They are all based on our sample organization with DNs of example and com.

Note

You need to always make sure that there are no entries for regular users in the /etc/passwd files of the LDAP clients. These should only reside on the LDAP server.

Starting and Stopping LDAP

You can use the chkconfig command to get ldap configured to start at boot:

```
[root@bigboy tmp]# chkconfig ldap on
```

To start, stop, or restart ldap after booting, use:

```
[root@bigboy tmp]# service ldap start
[root@bigboy tmp]# service ldap stop
[root@bigboy tmp]# service ldap restart
```

Remember to restart the ldap process every time you make a change to the LDAP database file for the changes to take effect on the running process.

LDAP Users Changing Their Own Passwords

LDAP users can modify their LDAP passwords using the regular passwd command:

```
[ldapuser@smallfry ldapuser]$ passwd
Changing password for user ldapuser.
Enter login(LDAP) password:
New password:
Retype new password:
LDAP password information changed for ldapuser
passwd: all authentication tokens updated successfully.
[ldapuser@smallfry ldapuser]$
```

Modifying LDAP Users by User *root*

One easy way for the system administrator to manage LDAP users is to modify the regular Linux users' characteristics on the LDAP server in the regular way and then run a script to automatically modify the LDAP database.

The Modify LDAP User Script

You can use the very simple sample script /usr/local/bin/modifyldapuser to extract a particular user's information from /etc/passwd and import it into your LDAP database.

The script works by using the grep command to extract the /etc/passwd user record to a temporary file. It then runs the migrate_passwd script on this data and outputs the result to a temporary LDIF file. Next, the script replaces the default padl DC with the example DC and exports this to the final LDIF file. Finally, the ldapmodify command does the update, and then the temporary files are deleted.

```
#!/bin/bash

grep $1 /etc/passwd > /tmp/modifyldapuser.tmp

/usr/share/openldap/migration/migrate_passwd.pl \
    /tmp/modifyldapuser.tmp /tmp/modifyldapuser.ldif.tmp

cat /tmp/modifyldapuser.ldif.tmp | sed s/padl/example/ \
    > /tmp/modifyldapuser.ldif

ldapmodify -x -D "cn=Manager,dc=example,dc=com" -W -f \
    /tmp/modifyldapuser.ldif

rm -f /tmp/modifyldapuser.*
```

Remember to make the script executable and usable only by user root with the chmod command:

```
[root@bigboy tmp]# chmod 700 /usr/local/bin/modifyldapuser
[root@bigboy tmp]#
```

To use the script, modify the Linux user. In this case, modify the password for user ldapuser by running the modifyldapuser script using ldapuser as the argument. You will be prompted for the LDAP root password:

```
[root@bigboy tmp]# passwd ldapuser
Changing password for user ldapuser.
New password:
Retype new password:
passwd: all authentication tokens updated successfully.
[root@bigboy tmp]# modifyldapuser ldapuser
```

```
Enter LDAP Password:
modifying entry "uid=ldapuser,ou=People,dc=example,dc=com"

[root@bigboy tmp]#
```

Adding New LDAP Users

You can use the short script in this section to add LDAP users to your database. I'll also provide an example of how to use it.

Create an LDAP Add User Script

You can create a /usr/local/bin/addldapuser script based on the modifyldapuser script you created earlier. For example:

```
#!/bin/bash

grep $1 /etc/passwd > /tmp/changeldappasswd.tmp

/usr/share/openldap/migration/migrate_passwd.pl \
    /tmp/changeldappasswd.tmp /tmp/changeldappasswd.ldif.tmp

cat /tmp/changeldappasswd.ldif.tmp | sed s/padl/example/ \
    > /tmp/changeldappasswd.ldif

ldapadd -x -D "cn=Manager,dc=example,dc=com" -W -f \
    /tmp/changeldappasswd.ldif

rm -f /tmp/changeldappasswd.*
```

Add the User to the Database

Adding the user to the database takes three steps:

1. Create the Linux user on the LDAP server.
2. Run the addldapuser script with the username as the only argument. This example imports a previously created Linux user named ldapuser. The script prompts you for your LDAP root password:

```
[root@bigboy tmp]# addldapuser ldapuser
Enter LDAP Password:
adding new entry "uid=ldapuser,ou=People,dc=example,dc=com"

[root@bigboy tmp]#
```

3. Create home directories for the user on all the LDAP client Linux boxes.

Remember that this script adds existing Linux users to the LDAP database. The creation of Linux users still requires the use of the adduser command.

Deleting LDAP Users

Sometimes you want to get rid of users instead of add them. You can create a `/usr/local/bin/deleteldapuser` script to delete LDAP users from your database. For example:

```
#!/bin/bash

ldapdelete -x -W -D "cn=Manager,dc=example,dc=com" \
    "uid=$1,ou=People,dc=example,dc=com"
```

To delete the user from the database, run the `deleteldapuser` script with the username as the only argument. This example below deletes a previously created Linux user named ldapuser. The script prompts you for your LDAP root password:

```
[root@bigboy tmp]# deleteldapuser ldapuser
Enter LDAP Password:
[root@bigboy tmp]#
```

LDAP Web Management Tools

Once you understand the principles behind LDAP management, you may want to use a graphical tool to help with further administration. If the tool misbehaves, at least you'll now know how to try to fix it behind the scenes from the command line.

The **LDAP Account Manager** (**LAM**), which is available at `http://lam.sourceforge.net/`, is a well known, easy-to-use product. After you feel comfortable enough with the background tasks and concepts outlined in this chapter, you should give it a try.

CONFIGURING RADIUS FOR LDAP

Many network equipment manufacturers use an authorization scheme called **RADIUS** to filter the types of activities a user can do. The Linux **FreeRADIUS** server can be configured to talk to a Linux LDAP server to handle login authentication services. In other words, the user logs into the equipment, which then sends a username/password combination to the RADIUS server, the RADIUS server queries the LDAP server to see if the user is a valid one, and then replies to the network equipment with the desired login privileges if the LDAP query is successful.

You'll have to refer to your manufacturer's manuals on how to configure RADIUS, but fortunately researching how the FreeRADIUS server interacts with the Linux LDAP server is much simpler. Here are the steps.

Download and Install the FreeRADIUS Packages

Most Red Hat and Fedora Linux software products are available in the RPM format. When searching for the file, remember that the FreeRADIUS RPM's filename usually starts with `freeradius` followed by a version number, as in `freeradius-0.9.1-1.i386.rpm`.

Starting and Stopping FreeRADIUS

You can use the `chkconfig` command to get the FreeRADIUS daemon, `radiusd`, configured to start at boot:

```
[root@bigboy tmp]# chkconfig radiusd on
```

To start, stop, and restart `radiusd` after booting, use:

```
[root@bigboy tmp]# service radiusd start
[root@bigboy tmp]# service radiusd stop
[root@bigboy tmp]# service radiusd restart
```

Remember to restart the `radiusd` process every time you make a change to the configuration files for the changes to take effect on the running process.

Configuring the /etc/raddb/radiusd.conf File

The `/etc/raddb/radiusd.conf` file stores the main RADIUS configuration parameters. You'll have to update some of the settings to allow LDAP queries from RADIUS:

1. Activate the use of the LDAP module in the `authorize` section of the file by uncommenting the word `ldap`.

```
authorize {
    ...
    ...
    #
    #   The ldap module will set Auth-Type to LDAP if it has not
    #   already been set
    Ldap
    ...
    ...
}
```

2. Activate the use of the LDAP module in the `authenticate` section by uncommenting the `Auth-Type` block for LDAP:

```
Auth-Type LDAP {
    ldap
}
```

3. Define the LDAP domain, LDAP server, and password methods to be used in the `ldap` block. In the example, the LDAP and RADIUS server is the same machine, so you set the LDAP server IP address to `localhost`:

```
ldap {

    # Define the LDAP server and the base domain name

    server = "localhost"
    basedn = "dc=example,dc=com"

    # Define which attribute from an LDAP "ldapsearch" query
    # is the password. Create a filter to extract the password
    # from the "ldapsearch" output

    password_attribute = "userPassword"
    filter = "(uid=%{Stripped-User-Name:-%{User-Name}})"

    # The following are RADIUS defaults
    start_tls = no
    dictionary_mapping = ${raddbdir}/ldap.attrmap
    ldap_connections_number = 5
    timeout = 4
    timelimit = 3
    net_timeout = 1
}
```

These configuration steps only cover how to configure RADIUS to interact with LDAP. You'll have to define the login attributes and privileges each user will receive and the IP addresses of the various RADIUS clients. We'll cover these topics next.

Configuring the */etc/raddb/users* File

The `/etc/raddb/users` file defines the types of attributes a user receives upon login. In the case of a router, this may include allowing some user groups to login to a device in a privileged mode, while allowing other only basic access.

One of the first entries in this file is to check the local server's `/etc/passwd` file. The very next entry should be one referring to your LDAP server with a fall through statement that will allow additional authorizations to be granted to the LDAP user further down the file based on other sets of criteria.

```
#
# First setup all accounts to be checked against the UNIX /etc/passwd.
#
DEFAULT Auth-Type = System
    Fall-Through = 1

#
```

```
# Defaults for LDAP
#
DEFAULT Auth-Type := LDAP
   Fall-Through = 1
```

Configuring the */etc/raddb/clients.conf* File

You can define a shared secret password key to be used by the RADIUS server and its clients in the `/etc/raddb/clients.conf` file.

Passwords can be allocated for ranges of IP addresses in each network block using the secret keyword. The next example defines the password `test-ing123` for all queries from `localhost`, but `s3astar` for the 192.168.1.0/24 network and `shrtp3nc11` for the 172.16.1.0/24 network. All RADIUS clients have to peer with the RADIUS server from these networks using the correct password before logins are correctly accepted.

```
client 127.0.0.1 {
    secret = testing123
    shortname = localhost
}

client 192.168.1.0/24 {
    secret = s3astar
    shortname = home-network
}

client 172.16.1.0/24 {
    secret = shrtp3nc11
    shortname = office-network
}
```

Troubleshooting and Testing RADIUS

You can now test the various elements of the RADIUS setup.

Server Setup

To test the server, run `radiusd` in debug mode to see verbose messages about the status of the RADIUS queries. These messages are much more informative than those provided in the `/var/log/messages` and `/var/log/radius/radius.log` files.

```
[root@bigboy tmp]# /usr/sbin/radiusd -X -A
```

After testing is complete, you must start the `radiusd` daemon in the normal manner using the command `service radiusd start`.

Linux Client Setup

For Linux clients, you can perform RADIUS queries with the `radtest` command. The arguments are the LDAP username, the LDAP user's password, the LDAP server IP address, an NAS port value (any value between 1 and 100 will work here), and the RADIUS client-server shared secret password key. Successful queries will show an Access-Accept message.

A successful test from the RADIUS server looks like this:

```
[root@bigboy tmp]# radtest ldapuser "ldapuser-password" \
  localhost 2 testing123
...
rad_recv: Access-Accept packet from host 127.0.0.1:1812, id=99,
length=20
...
[root@bigboy tmp]#
```

A successful test from a Linux RADIUS client looks like this:

```
[root@smallfry bin]# radtest ldapuser "ldapuser-password"
192.168.1.100 2 s3astar
...
rad_recv: Access-Accept packet from host 192.168.1.100:1812, id=51,
length=20
...
[root@smallfry bin]#
```

In this case, `freeradius` was installed solely for the purposes of testing the shared secret password key from another network. This is a good troubleshooting tip to verify remote client access before deploying network equipment.

Cisco Client Setup

Here is a sample snippet of how to set up a Cisco device to use a RADIUS server. You can find full coverage of Cisco authentication, authorization, and accounting (AAA) setup using RADIUS on Cisco's corporate Web site at www.cisco.com.

```
aaa new-model
aaa authentication login default radius enable
aaa authentication ppp default radius
aaa authorization network radius

radius-server host 192.168.1.100
radius-server timeout 10
radius-server key shrtp3nc11
```

The important thing to note in relation to the example setup is that the `radius-server` statements define the RADIUS server's IP address and the shared secret password key.

Errors with Fedora Core 2

The interaction between LDAP and RADIUS on Fedora Core 2 seems to be plagued with a segmentation fault error that you can see on the RADIUS server when running in debug mode. The error looks like this:

```
ldap_get_conn: Got Id: 0
rlm_ldap: attempting LDAP reconnection
rlm_ldap: (re)connect to localhost:389, authentication 0
rlm_ldap: bind as / to localhost:389
Segmentation fault
```

The only solution I have found is to install the Fedora Core 1 versions of the RADIUS and LDAP RPMs and to edit the `/etc/yum.conf` file to prevent them from being automatically updated to newer versions.

CONCLUSION

LDAP is rapidly becoming a de facto standard for remote authentication and authorization of users, not only in the realm of Linux, but also in that of Windows where it is a key component of Active Directory. Usage of LDAP is also becoming increasingly widespread in wireless networking systems. For example in hot spots, ISPs will sacrifice data security for the sake of convenience by not using encryption, but will use LDAP to restrict access to the Internet to people who have purchased pre-paid access codes with a predefined lifetime.

Chapter 32, "Controlling Web Access with Squid," covers the use of the Linux Squid application to cache Web content, restrict Web access by the time of day and via password prompts. Although it is beyond the scope of this book, you should know that you can use LDAP to complement the functionality of Squid in larger implementations.

Controlling Web Access with Squid

Two important goals of many small businesses are to:

☞ Reduce Internet bandwidth charges
☞ Limit access to the Web to authorized users only

The Squid Web caching proxy server can achieve both these goals fairly easily.

Users configure their Web browsers to use the Squid proxy server instead of going to the Web directly. The Squid server then checks its Web cache for the Web information requested by the user. It returns any matching information that it finds in its cache. If it does not find any, it goes to the Web to find it on behalf of the user. Once it locates the information, Squid populates its cache with that information and also forwards it to the user's Web browser.

As you can see, this reduces the amount of data accessed from the Web. Another advantage is that you can configure your firewall to accept HTTP Web traffic from the Squid server only and no one else. Squid can then be configured to request usernames and passwords for each user that uses its services. This provides simple access control to the Internet.

DOWNLOAD AND INSTALL THE SQUID PACKAGE

Most Red Hat Linux software products, including Squid, are available in the RPM format. (If you need a refresher, Chapter 6, "Installing RPM Software," provides the details.) It is best to use the latest version of Squid.

STARTING SQUID

Use the chkconfig configure Squid to start at boot:

```
[root@bigboy tmp]# chkconfig squid on
```

Use the service command to start, stop, and restart Squid after booting:

```
[root@bigboy tmp]# service squid start
[root@bigboy tmp]# service squid stop
[root@bigboy tmp]# service squid restart
```

You can test whether the Squid process is running with the pgrep command:

```
[root@bigboy tmp]# pgrep squid
```

You should get a response of plain old process ID numbers.

THE /ETC/SQUID/SQUID.CONF FILE

The main Squid configuration file is squid.conf, and, like most Linux applications, Squid needs to be restarted for changes to the configuration file to take effect.

The Visible Host Name

Squid will fail to start if you don't give your server a hostname. You can set this with the visible_hostname parameter. Here, the hostname is set to the real name of the server Bigboy.

```
visible_hostname bigboy
```

Access Control Lists

You can limit users' ability to browse the Internet with **access control lists** (**ACLs**). Each ACL line defines a particular type of activity, such as an access time or source network; they are then linked to an http_access statement that tells Squid whether or not to deny or allow traffic that matches the ACL.

Squid matches each Web access request it receives by checking the http_access list from top to bottom. If it finds a match, it enforces the allow or deny statement and stops reading further. You have to be careful not to place a deny statement in the list that blocks a similar allow statement below it. The final http_access statement denies everything, so it is best to place new http_access statements above it.

Note

The very last http_access statement in the squid.conf file denies all access. You therefore have to add your specific permit statements above this line. In the chapter's examples, I've suggested that you place your statements at the top of the http_access list for the sake of manageability, but you can put them anywhere in the section above that last line.

Squid has a minimum required set of ACL statements in the ACCESS_CONTROL section of the squid.conf file. It is best to put new customized entries right after this list to make the file easier to read.

Restricting Web Access by Time

You can create access control lists with time parameters. For example, you can allow only business hour access from the home network:

```
#
# Add this to the bottom of the ACL section of squid.conf
#
acl home_network src 192.168.1.0/24
acl business_hours time M T W H F 9:00-17:00

#
# Add this at the top of the http_access section of squid.conf
#
http_access allow home_network business_hours
```

Or, you can allow morning access only:

```
#
# Add this to the bottom of the ACL section of squid.conf
#
acl mornings time 08:00-12:00

#
```

```
# Add this at the top of the http_access section of squid.conf
#
http_access allow mornings
```

Restricting Web Access by IP Address

You can create an access control list that restricts Web access to users on certain networks. In this case, it's an ACL that defines a home network of 192.168.1.0:

```
#
# Add this to the bottom of the ACL section of squid.conf
#
acl home_network src 192.168.1.0/255.255.255.0
```

You also have to add a corresponding `http_access` statement that allows traffic that matches the ACL:

```
#
# Add this at the top of the http_access section of squid.conf
#
http_access allow home_network
```

Password Authentication Using NCSA

You can configure Squid to prompt users for a username and password. Squid comes with a program called `ncsa_auth` that reads any NCSA-compliant encrypted password file. You can use the `htpasswd` program that comes installed with Apache to create your passwords. Here is how it's done:

1. Create the password file. The name of the password file should be `/etc/squid/squid_passwd`, and you need to make sure that it's universally readable.

    ```
    [root@bigboy tmp]# touch /etc/squid/squid_passwd
    [root@bigboy tmp]# chmod o+r /etc/squid/squid_passwd
    ```

2. Use the `htpasswd` program to add users to the password file. You can add users at anytime without having to restart Squid. In this case, you add a username called www:

    ```
    [root@bigboy tmp]# htpasswd /etc/squid/squid_passwd www
    New password:
    Re-type new password:
    Adding password for user www
    [root@bigboy tmp]#
    ```

3. Locate your ncsa_auth file using the rpm command:

```
[root@bigboy tmp]# rpm -ql squid | grep ncsa
/usr/lib/squid/ncsa_auth
[root@bigboy tmp]#
```

4. Edit squid.conf; specifically, you need to define the authentication program in squid.conf, which is[md]in this case—ncsa_auth. Next, create an ACL named ncsa_users with the REQUIRED keyword that forces Squid to use the NCSA auth_param method you defined previously. Finally, create an http_access entry that allows traffic that matches the ncsa_users ACL entry. Here's a simple user authentication example; the order of the statements is important:

```
#
# Add this to the auth_param section of squid.conf
#
auth_param basic program /usr/lib/squid/ncsa_auth
/etc/squid/squid_passwd


#
# Add this to the bottom of the ACL section of squid.conf
#
acl ncsa_users proxy_auth REQUIRED


#
# Add this at the top of the http_access section of
squid.conf
#
http_access allow ncsa_users
```

5. This requires password authentication and allows access only during business hours. Once again, the order of the statements is important.

```
#
# Add this to the auth_param section of squid.conf
#
auth_param basic program /usr/lib/squid/ncsa_auth
/etc/squid/squid_passwd


#
# Add this to the bottom of the ACL section of squid.conf
#
acl ncsa_users proxy_auth REQUIRED
acl business_hours time M T W H F 9:00-17:00


#
# Add this at the top of the http_access section of
squid.conf
#
http_access allow ncsa_users business_hours
```

Remember to restart Squid for the changes to take effect.

FORCING USERS TO USE YOUR SQUID SERVER

If you are using access controls on Squid, you may also want to configure your firewall to allow only HTTP Internet access to only the Squid server. This forces your users to browse the Web through the Squid proxy.

Making Your Squid Server Transparent to Users

It is possible to limit HTTP Internet access to only the Squid server without having to modify the browser settings on your client PCs. This called a **transparent proxy configuration**. It is usually achieved by configuring a firewall between the client PCs and the Internet to redirect all HTTP (TCP port 80) traffic to the Squid server on TCP port 3128, which is the Squid server's default TCP port.

The examples below are based on the discussion of Linux `iptables` in Chapter 14, "Linux Firewalls Using `iptables`." Additional commands may be necessary for you particular network topology.

In both cases below, the firewall is connected to the Internet on interface `eth0` and to the home network on interface `eth1`. The firewall is also the default gateway for the home network and handles network address translation on all the network's traffic to the Internet.

Only the Squid server has access to the Internet on port 80 (HTTP), because all HTTP traffic, except that coming from the Squid server, is redirected.

If the Squid server and firewall are the same server, all HTTP traffic from the home network is redirected to the firewall itself on the Squid port of 3128 and then only the firewall itself is allowed to access the Internet on port 80.

```
iptables -t nat -A PREROUTING -i eth1 -p tcp —dport 80 \
        -j REDIRECT —to-port 3128
iptables -A INPUT -j ACCEPT -m state \
        —state NEW,ESTABLISHED,RELATED -i eth1 -p tcp \
        —dport 3128
iptables -A OUTPUT -j ACCEPT -m state \
        —state NEW,ESTABLISHED,RELATED -o eth0 -p tcp \
        —dport 80
iptables -A INPUT -j ACCEPT -m state \
        —state ESTABLISHED,RELATED -i eth0 -p tcp \
        —sport 80
iptables -A OUTPUT -j ACCEPT -m state \
        —state ESTABLISHED,RELATED -o eth1 -p tcp \
        —sport 80
```

If the Squid server and firewall are different servers, the statements are different. You need to set up `iptables` so that all connections to the Web not originating from the Squid server are actually converted into three connections; one from the Web browser client to the firewall and another from the firewall to the Squid server. This triggers the Squid server to make its own connection to the Web to service the request. The Squid server then gets the data and replies to the firewall, which then relays this information to the Web browser client. The `iptables` program does all this using these NAT statements:

```
iptables -t nat -A PREROUTING -i eth1 -s ! 192.168.1.100 \
        -p tcp —dport 80 -j DNAT —to 192.168.1.100:3128
iptables -t nat -A POSTROUTING -o eth1 -s 192.168.1.0/24 \
        -d 192.168.1.100 -j SNAT —to 192.168.1.1
iptables -A FORWARD -s 192.168.1.0/24 -d 192.168.1.100 \
        -i eth1 -o eth1 -m state \
        —state NEW,ESTABLISHED,RELATED \
        -p tcp —dport 3128 -j ACCEPT
iptables -A FORWARD -d 192.168.1.0/24 -s 192.168.1.100 \
        -i eth1 -o eth1 -m state —state ESTABLISHED,RELATED \
        -p tcp —sport 3128 -j ACCEPT
```

In the first statement, all HTTP traffic from the home network except from the Squid server at IP address 192.168.1.100 is redirected to the Squid server on port 3128 using destination NAT. The second statement makes this redirected traffic also undergo source NAT to make it appear as if it is coming from the firewall itself. The FORWARD statements are used to ensure the traffic is allowed to flow to the Squid server after the NAT process is complete. The unusual feature is that the NAT all takes place on one interface, that of the home network (eth1).

Additionally, you will have to make sure your firewall has rules to allow your Squid server to access the Internet on HTTP TCP port 80 as covered in Chapter 14, "Linux Firewalls Using `iptables`."

You will also need to make a few transparent proxy modifications to your `squid.conf` file:

```
httpd_accel_host virtual
httpd_accel_port 80
httpd_accel_with_proxy on
httpd_accel_uses_host_header on
```

Manually Configuring Web Browsers to Use Your Squid Server

If you don't have a firewall that supports redirection, then you need to configure your firewall to only accept HTTP Internet access from the Squid server, as well as configure your PC browser's proxy server settings manually to use the Squid server. The method you use depends on your browser.

For example, to make these changes using Internet Explorer:

1. Click on the Tools item in the browser's menu bar.
2. Click on Internet Options.
3. Click on Connections.

4. Click on LAN Settings.

5. Configure with the address and TCP port (3128 default) used by your Squid server.

Here's how to make the same changes using Mozilla or Firefox:

1. Click on the Edit item in the browser's menu bar.

2. Click on Preferences.

3. Click on Advanced.

4. Click on Proxies.

5. Configure with the address and TCP port (3128 default) used by your Squid server under Manual Proxy Configuration.

SQUID DISK USAGE

Squid uses the `/var/spool/squid` directory to store its cache files. High usage Squid servers need a large amount of disk space in the `/var` partition to get optimum performance.

Every Web page and image accessed via the Squid server is logged in the `/var/log/squid/access.log` file. This can get quite large on high usage servers. Fortunately, the `logrotate` program automatically purges this file.

TROUBLESHOOTING SQUID

Squid logs both informational and error messages to files in the `/var/log/squid/` directory. It is best to review these files first whenever you have difficulties.

Another source of errors could be unintended statements in the `squid.conf` file that cause no errors; mistakes in the configuration of hours of access and permitted networks that were forgotten to be added are just two possibilities.

By default, Squid operates on port 3128, so if you are having connectivity problems, you'll need to follow the troubleshooting steps in Chapter 4, "Simple Network Troubleshooting," to help rectify them.

Note

Some of Squid's capabilities go beyond the scope of this book, but you should be aware of them. For example, for performance reasons, you can configure child Squid servers on which certain types of content are exclusively cached. Also, you can restrict the amount of disk space and bandwidth Squid uses.

CONCLUSION

Tools such as Squid are popular with many company managers. By caching images and files on a server shared by all, Internet bandwidth charges can be reduced.

Squid's password authentication feature is well liked because it allows only authorized users to access the Internet as a means of reducing usage fees and distractions in the office. Unfortunately, an Internet access password is usually not viewed as a major security concern by most users who are often willing to share it with their colleagues. Although it is beyond the scope of this book, you should consider automatically tying the Squid password to the user's regular login password. This will make them think twice about giving their passwords away. Internet access is one thing, letting your friends have full access to your e-mail and computer files is quite another.

Modifying the Linux Kernel to Improve Performance

IN THIS CHAPTER

- ☞ Download and Install the Kernel Sources Package
- ☞ Kernel Modules
- ☞ Creating a Custom Kernel
- ☞ Updating GRUB
- ☞ Updating the Kernel Using RPMs
- ☞ Conclusion

Like a government that rules a nation and all its provinces, the Linux kernel is the central program that not only governs how programs interact with one another, but also provides the guidelines on how they should use the computer's core infrastructure, such as memory, disks, and other input/output (I/O) devices for the user's benefit.

Linux drivers, the programs that manage each I/O device, are the staff that keeps all the government departments running. Continuing with the analogy, the more departments you make the kernel manage, the slower Linux becomes. Large kernels also reduce the amount of memory left over for user applications. These may then be forced to juggle their memory needs between RAM and the much slower swap partitions of disk drives, causing the whole system to become sluggish.

The Fedora installation CDs have a variety of kernel RPMs, and the installation process autodetects the one best suited to your needs. For this reason, the Fedora Linux kernel installed on your system is probably sufficient. The installation process chooses one of several prebuilt kernel types depending on the type of CPU and configuration you intend to use (Table 33.1).

Table 33.1   Kernels Found on Fedora Installation CDs

Processor Type	Configuration
I586	Single processor
I586	Multiprocessor (SMP)
I686	Single processor
I686	Multiprocessor (SMP)

The Pros and Cons of Kernel Upgrades

Despite this best fit installation, you may want to rebuild the kernel at times. For example, there is no installation RPM for multiprocessor systems with large amounts of memory. You may also want to experiment in making a high-speed Linux router without support for SCSI, USB, Bluetooth, and sound but *with* support for a few NIC drivers, an IDE hard drive, and a basic VGA console. This would require a kernel rebuild.

Rebuilding the kernel in a small business environment is usually unnecessary. If your system starts to slow down and you can't afford to replace hardware or are unable to add more RAM, however, you may want to tune the kernel by making it support only necessary functions or updating built-in parameters to make it perform better. Sometimes new features within the new kernel are highly desirable; for example, the version 2.6 kernel has much more efficient data handling capabilities than the older version 2.4, providing new life for old hardware.

Kernel tuning on a production server shouldn't be taken lightly, because the wrong parameters could cause your system to fail to boot, software to malfunction, or hardware peripherals to become unavailable. Always practice on a test system and keep a backup copy of your old kernel. Whenever possible, hire a consultant with kernel experience to help, and use this chapter and other references as a guide to prepare you for what to expect.

This chapter provides only an overview of the steps to take. It won't make you an expert, but it will expose you to the general process and provide greater confidence when you need to research the task with a specialized guide.

DOWNLOAD AND INSTALL THE KERNEL SOURCES PACKAGE

The Fedora Linux installation process installs a precompiled standardized version of your kernel for your system to use. If you need to compile a new customized version of your kernel, you must install the kernel source code files located in the `kernel-source` RPM package. (See Chapter 6, "Installing RPM Software," for details on downloading and installing.)

1. Start with a Linux system that has a standard kernel. If you have only used RPMs or the yum utility for kernel updates, you should be all set.

2. Determine which version of the kernel you are using with the uname command. The example is running version 2.6.5-1.358.

```
[root@bigboy tmp]# uname -r
2.6.5-1.358
[root@bigboy tmp]#
```

3. Install the matching kernel-source package using the rpm command from your CDs or using the yum utility. You may also have to install a C programming language compiler, such as gcc32, to convert the source text files into an executable kernel.

If you can't wait for the updated RPM to be created or your system doesn't support RPMs, then you can also consider downloading the latest Linux kernel code from the kernel.org Web site.

KERNEL MODULES

Over the years the Linux kernel has evolved. In the past, device drivers were included as part of this core program, for example, but now they are loaded on demand as modules.

Reasons for Kernel Modules

This new architecture has a number of advantages:

☞ Updates to a driver, such as a USB controller module, don't require a complete recompilation of the kernel; just the module itself needs recompiling. This reduces the likelihood of errors and ensures that the good, working base kernel remains unchanged.

☞ An error in a device driver is less likely to cause a fault that prevents your system from booting. A faulty device driver can be prevented from loading at boot time by commenting out its entry in the /etc/modprobe.conf file, or by using the rmmod command after boot time. In the past, the kernel would have to be recompiled.

☞ Updates to a driver don't require a reboot either, just the unloading of the old and reloading of the new module.

☞ You can add new devices to your system without requiring a new kernel, only the new module driver is needed. This adds a great deal of flexibility without a lot of systems administrator overhead.

There are some drivers that will always need to be compiled into the kernel to make sure your system boots correctly. For example, routines for basic system functions used in reading and writing files are an indispensable integrated part of any kernel.

Loadable kernel modules now include device drivers to manage various types of filesystems, network cards, and terminal devices to name a few. As they work so closely with the kernel, the modules need to be compiled specifically for the kernel they are intended to support. The kernel always looks for modules for its version number in the /lib/modules/<kernel version> directory and permanently loads them into RAM memory for faster access. Some critical modules are loaded automatically, others need to be specified in the /etc/modprobe.conf file.

The kernel recompilation process provides you with the option of compiling only the loadable modules. I won't specifically cover this, but simultaneous recompilation of all modules will be covered as part of the overall recompilation of your kernel.

How Kernel Modules Load When Booting

One question that must come to mind is "How does the kernel boot if the disk controller modules reside on a filesystem that isn't mounted yet?"

As stated in Chapter 7, "The Linux Boot Process," the GRUB boot loader resides on its own dedicated partition and uses the /boot/grub/grub.conf file to determine the valid kernels and their locations. The grub.conf file not only defines the available kernels, but also the location of the root partition and an associated ramdisk image that is automatically loaded into memory and that contains just enough modules to get the root filesystem mounted.

Note

In Fedora Linux, the /boot/grub/grub.conf file can also be referenced via the symbolic link file named /etc/grub.conf.

Modules and the grub.conf File

In this example of the /boot/grub/grub.conf file, the kernel in the /boot directory is named vmlinuz-2.6.8-1.521, its RAM disk image file is named initrd-2.6.8-1.521.img, and the root partition is (hd0,0).

```
#
# File: /boot/grub/grub.conf
#
default=0
timeout=10
splashimage=(hd0,0)/grub/splash.xpm.gz
title Fedora Core (2.6.8-1.521)
        root (hd0,0)
```

```
kernel /vmlinuz-2.6.8-1.521 ro root=LABEL=/
initrd /initrd-2.6.8-1.521.img
```

The .img file is created as part of the kernel compilation process, but can also be created on demand with the mkinitrd command.

The (hd0,0) disk definition may seem strange, but there is a file that maps the GRUB device nomenclature to that expected by Linux in the /boot/grub/device.map file.

```
#
# File: /boot/grub/device.map
#
(fd0)       /dev/fd0
(hd0)       /dev/hda
```

During the next phase of the boot process, the loaded kernel executes the init program located on the RAM disk, which mounts the root filesystem and loads the remaining modules defined in the /etc/modprobe.conf file before continuing with the rest of the startup process.

Loading Kernel Modules on Demand

It is possible to load add-on modules located under the /lib/modules/<kernel version> directory with the modprobe command. For example, the iptables firewall application installs kernel modules that it uses to execute NAT and pass FTP traffic. In this example, these modules are loaded with the modprobe command with the aid of the /etc/rc.local script.

```
#
# File: /etc/rc.local
#
# Load iptables FTP module when required
modprobe ip_conntrack_ftp

# Load iptables NAT module when required
modprobe iptable_nat
```

Kernel module drivers that are referenced by the operating system by their device aliases are placed in the /etc/modprobe.conf file and are loaded automatically at boot time. In the example, you can see that devices eth1 and eth0 use the natsemi and orinoco_pci drivers respectively.

```
#
# /etc/modprobe.conf
#
alias eth1 natsemi
alias eth0 orinoco_pci
```

Linux has a number of commands to help you with modules. The lsmod command lists all the ones loaded. In the example, you can see that iptables, NFS, and the Orinoco drivers are all kernel modules. You can use the modprobe command to load and unload modules or use the insmod and rmmod commands. See the man pages for details.

```
[root@bigboy tmp]# lsmod
Module                   Size    Used by
...
...
iptable_filter           2048    0
ip_tables               13440    1 iptable_filter
...
...
exportfs                 4224    1 nfsd
nfs                     142912    0
lockd                    47944    3 nfsd,nfs
autofs4                  10624    1
sunrpc                  101064    20 nfsd,nfs,lockd
...
...
natsemi                  18016    0
orinoco_pci               4876    0
orinoco                  31500    1 orinoco_pci
hermes                    6528    2 orinoco_pci,orinoco
...
...
[root@bigboy tmp]#
```

Finally, when in doubt about a device driver, try using the lspci command to take a look at the devices that use your PCI expansion bus. Here you can see that the natsemi module listed in the lsmod command has a high probability of belonging to the 01:08.0 Ethernet controller: device made by National Semiconductor.

```
[root@bigboy tmp]# lspci
...
...
01:07.0 Network controller: Intersil Corporation Prism 2.5 Wavelan
chipset (rev 01)
01:08.0 Ethernet controller: National Semiconductor Corporation
DP83815 (MacPhyter) Ethernet Controller
01:0c.0 Ethernet controller: 3Com Corporation 3c905C-TX/TX-M [Tornado]
(rev 78)
[root@bigboy tmp]#
```

CREATING A CUSTOM KERNEL

The installation of the kernel sources creates a file called README in the `/usr/src/linux-2.6.5-1.358` directory that briefly outlines the steps needed to create a new kernel. Take a look at a more detailed explanation of the required steps.

Make Sure Your Source Files Are in Order

Cleaning up the various source files is the first step. This isn't so important for a first time rebuild, but it is vital for subsequent attempts. You use the `make mrproper` command to do this; it must be executed in the Linux kernel version's subdirectory located under `/usr/src`. In this case, the subdirectory's name is `/usr/src/linux-2.6.5-1.358`:

```
[root@bigboy tmp]# cd /usr/src/linux-2.6.5-1.358/
[root@bigboy linux-2.6.5-1.358]# make mrproper
...
...
...
[root@bigboy linux-2.6.5-1.358]#
```

The .config File

You next need to run scripts to create a kernel configuration file called `/usr/src/linux-2.6.5-1.358/.config`. This file lists all the kernel options you wish to use.

Backup Your Configuration

The `.config` file won't exist if you've never created a custom kernel on your system before, but fortunately, Red Hat stores a number of default `.config` files in the `/usr/src/linux-2.6.5-1.358/configs` directory. You can automatically copy the `.config` file that matches your installed kernel by running the `make oldconfig` command in the `/usr/src/linux-2.6.5-1.358` directory:

```
[root@bigboy tmp]# cd /usr/src/linux-2.6.5-1.358
[root@bigboy linux-2.6.5-1.358]# ls .config
ls: .config: No such file or directory
[root@bigboy linux-2.6.5-1.358]# make oldconfig
...
...
...
[root@bigboy linux-2.6.5-1.358]#
```

If you've created a custom kernel before, the .config file that the previous custom kernel build used will already exist. Copy it to a safe location before proceeding.

Customizing the *.config* File

Table 33.2 lists three commands that you can run in the /usr/src/linux-2.6.5-1.358 directory to update the .config file.

Table 33.2 Scripts for Modifying the .config File

Command	Description
make config	Text-based utility that prompts you line by line. This method can become laborious.
make menuconfig	Text-menu-based utility.
make gconfig	X-Windows-based utility.

Each command prompts you in different ways for each kernel option, each of which generally provides you with the three choices shown in Table 33.3. A brief description of each kernel configuration option is given in Table 33.4.

Table 33.3 Kernel Option Choices

Kernel Option Choice	Description
M	The kernel loads the drivers for this option on an as-needed basis. Only the code required to load the driver on demand is included in the kernel.
Y	Includes all the code for the drivers needed for this option into the kernel itself. This generally makes the kernel larger and slower but makes it more self-sufficient. The Y option is frequently used in cases in which a stripped down kernel is one of the only programs Linux runs, such as purpose built home firewall appliances you can buy in a store. There is a limit to the overall size of a kernel. It fails to compile if you select parameters that make it too big.
N	Don't make the kernel support this option at all.

Table 33.4 Kernel Configuration Options

Option	Description
Code maturity level options	Determines whether Linux prompts you for certain types of development code or drivers.
Loadable module support	Support for loadable modules versus a monolithic kernel. Most of the remaining kernel options use loadable modules by default. It is best to leave this alone in most cases.
Processor type and features	SMP, Large memory, BIOS, and CPU type settings.

Option	Description
General setup	Support for power management, networking, and systems buses, such as PCI, PCMCIA, EISA, ISA.
Memory technology devices	Linux subsystem for memory devices, especially Flash devices.
Parallel port support	Self-explanatory.
Plug and Play configuration	Support of the automatic new hardware detection method called plug and play.
Block devices	Support for a number of parallel-port-based and ATAPI type devices. Support for your loopback interface and RAM disks can be found here too.
Multidevice support (RAID, LVM)	Support for RAID, 0, 1, and 5, as well as LVM.
Cryptography support (CryptoAPI)	Support for various types of encryption.
Networking options	TCP/IP, DECnet, Appletalk, IPX, ATM/LANE.
Telephony support	Support for voice to data I/O cards.
ATA/IDE/MFM/RLL support	Support for a variety of disk controller chipsets
SCSI support	Support for a variety of disk controller chipsets. Also sets limits on the maximum number of supported SCSI disks and CDROMs.
Fusion MPT support	High speed SCSI chipset support.
I2O device support	Support for specialized Intelligent I/O cards
Network device support	Support for Ethernet, Fibre Channel, FDDI, SLIP, PPP, ARCnet, Token Ring, ATM, PCMCIA networking, and specialized WAN cards.
Amateur Radio support	Support for packet radio.
IrDA subsystem support	Infrared wireless network support.
ISDN subsystem	Support for ISDN.
Old CD-ROM drivers (not SCSI, not IDE)	Support for non-SCSI, non-IDE, non-ATAPI CD-ROMs.
Input core support	Keyboard, mouse, and joystick support, in addition to the default VGA resolution.
Character devices	Support for virtual terminals and various serial cards for modems, joysticks, and basic parallel port printing.
Multimedia devices	Streaming video and radio I/O card support.
Crypto Hardware support	Web-based SSL hardware accelerator card support.
Console drivers	Support for various console video cards.
Filesystems	Support for all the various filesystems and strangely, the native languages supported by Linux.
Sound	Support for a variety of sound cards.
USB support	Support for a variety of USB devices.
Additional device driver support	Miscellaneous driver support.
Bluetooth support	Support for a variety of Bluetooth devices.
Kernel hacking device drivers	Support for detailed error messages for persons writing device drivers.

Configure Dependencies

As I mentioned before, the .config file you just created lists the options you'll need in your kernel. In version 2.4 of the kernel and older, the make dep command was needed at this step to prepare the needed source files for compiling. This step has been eliminated as of version 2.6 of the kernel.

Edit the Makefile to Give the Kernel a Unique Name

Edit the file Makefile, and change the line EXTRAVERSION [eq] to create a unique suffix at the end of the default name of the kernel.

For example, if your current kernel version is 2.6.5-1.358, and your EXTRAVERSION is set to -6-new, your new additional kernel will have the name vmlinuz-2.6.5-6-new.

Remember to change this for each new version of the kernel you create.

Compile a New Kernel

You can now use the make bzImage command to create a compressed version of your new kernel and its companion .img RAM disk file. This could take several hours on a 386 or 486 system. It will take about 20 minutes on a 400MHz Celeron.

```
[root@bigboy linux-2.6.5-1.358]# make bzImage
...
...
...
[root@bigboy linux-2.6.5-1.358]#
```

Build the Kernel's Modules

You can now use the make modules command to create all the modules the kernel needs. This command compiles the modules, but locates them within the Linux kernel source directory tree under the directory /usr/src/. The next step relocates them to where they should finally reside under the /lib/modules/<kernel version> directory.

```
[root@bigboy linux-2.6.5-1.358]# make modules
...
...
...
[root@bigboy linux-2.6.5-1.358]#
```

Install the Kernel Modules

The `make modules_install` command copies the newly created modules to the conventional module locations. This step allows you to test the module compilation process before placing them in directories that will make them immediately available to the kernel. The splitting of these two steps can make troubleshooting much easier.

```
[root@bigboy linux-2.6.5-1.358]# make modules_install
...
...
...
[root@bigboy linux-2.6.5-1.358]#
```

Copy the New Kernel to the */boot* Partition

The kernel and the `.img` you just created need to be copied to the `/boot` partition where all your systems active kernel files normally reside. This is done with the `make install` command.

This partition has a default size of 100MB, which is enough to hold a number of kernels. You may have to delete some older kernels to create enough space.

```
[root@bigboy linux-2.6.5-1.358]# make install
...
...
...
[root@bigboy linux-2.6.5-1.358]#
```

Here you can see that the new kernel `vmlinuz-2.6.5-1.358-new` is installed in the `/boot` directory.

```
[root@bigboy linux-2.6.5-1.358]# ls -l /boot/vmlinuz*
lrwxrwxrwx 1 root root       22 Nov 28 01:20 /boot/vmlinuz -> vmlinuz-
2.6.5-1.358-new
-rw-r--r-- 1 root root  1122363 Feb 27  2003 /boot/vmlinuz-2.6.5-1.358
-rw-r--r-- 1 root root  1122291 Nov 28 01:20 /boot/vmlinuz-2.6.5-
1.358-new
[root@bigboy linux-2.6.5-1.358]#
```

UPDATING *GRUB*

You should now update your /etc/grub.conf file to include an option to boot the new kernel. The make install command does this for you automatically.

In this example, default is set to 1, which means the system boots the second kernel entry, which happens to be that of the original kernel 2.6.5-1.358. You can set this value to 0, which makes it boot your newly compiled kernel (the first entry).

```
default=1
timeout=10
splashimage=(hd0,0)/grub/splash.xpm.gz
title Red Hat Linux (2.6.5-1.358-new)
        root (hd0,0)
        kernel /vmlinuz-2.6.5-1.358-new ro root=LABEL=/
        initrd /initrd-2.6.5-1.358-new.img
title Red Hat Linux (2.6.5-1.358)
        root (hd0,0)
        kernel /vmlinuz-2.6.5-1.358 ro root=LABEL=/
        initrd /initrd-2.6.5-1.358.img
```

Kernel Crash Recovery

Sometimes the new default kernel will fail to boot or work correctly with the new kernel. A simple way of recovering from this is to reboot your system, selecting the old version of the kernel from the Fedora splash screen. Once the system has booted with this stable version, edit the grub.conf file and set the default parameter to point to the older version instead. If this fails, you may want to boot from a CD with the original kernel. You can then try to either reinstall a good kernel RPM or rebuild the failed one over again after fixing the configuration problem that caused the trouble in the first place.

How to Create a Boot CD

The Fedora Core 2 kernel is too big to fit on a floppy disk, so you'll have to create a boot CD instead. Here are the steps.

1. Each installed kernel has a dedicated subdirectory for its modules in the /lib/modules directory. Get a listing of this directory. Here there are two installed kernels: versions 2.6.5-1.358 custom and 2.6.8-1.521:

```
[root@bigboy tmp]# ls /lib/modules/
2.6.5-1.358custom   2.6.8-1.521
[root@bigboy tmp]#
```

2. Select the desired kernel, and use the `mkbootdisk` command to create a CD ISO image named `/tmp/boot.iso` of one of the kernels, in this case 2.6.8-1.521:

```
[root@bigboy tmp]# mkbootdisk --iso --device /tmp/boot.iso \
                   2.6.8-1.521
```

3. Burn a CD using the image. This creates a boot CD with the specified kernel, named `vmlinuz`, and a scaled-down version of the `grub.conf` configuration file named `isolinux.cfg`, both located in the `isolinux` subdirectory of the CD. This example mounts the newly created CD-ROM and takes a look at the `isolinux.cfg` file to confirm that everything is okay.

```
[root@bigboy tmp]# mount /mnt/cdrom
[root@bigboy tmp]# ls /mnt/cdrom/isolinux/
boot.cat   boot.msg   initrd.img   isolinux.bin   isolinux.cfg
TRANS.TBL   vmlinuz
[root@bigboy tmp]# cat /mnt/cdrom/isolinux/isolinux.cfg
default linux
prompt 1
display boot.msg
timeout 100
label linux
        kernel vmlinuz
        append initrd=initrd.img ro   root=/dev/hda2
[root@bigboy tmp]#
```

When you reboot your system with the CD, the boot process automatically attempts to access your files in the `/root` partition and boot normally. The only difference is that the kernel used is on the CD.

UPDATING THE KERNEL USING RPMS

It is also possible to install a new standardized kernel from an RPM file. As you can see, it is much simpler than creating a customized one.

To create an additional kernel using RPMs, use the command:

```
[root@bigboy tmp]# rpm -ivh kernel-file.rpm
```

To replace an existing kernel using RPMs, you need only one line:

```
[root@bigboy tmp]# rpm -Uvh kernel-file.rpm
```

CONCLUSION

Building a customized Linux kernel is probably something that most systems administrators won't do themselves. The risk of having a kernel that may fail in some unpredictable way is higher when you modify it, and, therefore, many system administrators hire experts to do the work for them. After reading this chapter, at least you will have an idea of what is going on when the expert arrives—which can help considerably when things don't go according to plan.

Basic MySQL Configuration

IN THIS CHAPTER

Most home/SOHO administrators don't do any database programming, but they sometimes need to install applications that require a MySQL database. This chapter explains the basic steps of configuring MySQL for use with a MySQL-based application in which the application runs on the same server as the database.

PREPARING MySQL FOR APPLICATIONS

In most cases the developers of database applications expect the systems administrator to be able to independently prepare a database for their applications to use. The steps to do this include:

1. Install and start MySQL.
2. Create a MySQL root user.
3. Create a regular MySQL user that the application will use to access the database.
4. Create your application's database.
5. Create your database's data tables.
6. Perform some basic tests of your database structure.

The rest of the chapter is based on a scenario in which a Linux-based application named `sales-test` needs to be installed. After reading the `sales-test` manuals, you realize that you have to create a MySQL database, data tables, and a database user before you can start the application. Fortunately `sales-test` comes with a script to create the tables, but you have to do the rest yourself. Finally, as part of the planning for the installation, you decided to name the database `salesdata` and let the application use the MySQL user mysqluser to access it.

I'll cover all these common tasks in detail in the remaining sections.

INSTALLING MySQL

In most cases you'll probably want to install the MySQL server and MySQL client RPMs. The client RPM gives you the ability to test the server connection and can be used by any MySQL application to communicate with the server, even if the server software is running on the same Linux box.

You need to make sure that the `mysql-server` and `mysql` software RPMs are installed. When searching for the RPMs, remember that the filename usually starts with the software package name followed by a version number, as in `mysql-server-3.23.58-4.i386.rpm`.

There are a number of supporting RPMs that may be needed, so the `yum` utility may be the best RPM installation method to use. (For more on downloading and installing RPMs, see Chapter 6, "Installing RPM Software.")

STARTING MySQL

You have to start the MySQL process before you can create your databases. To configure MySQL to start at boot time, use the `chkconfig` command:

```
[root@bigboy tmp]# chkconfig mysqld on
```

You can start, stop, and restart MySQL after boot time using the service commands:

```
[root@bigboy tmp]# service mysqld start
[root@bigboy tmp]# service mysqld stop
[root@bigboy tmp]# service mysqld restart
```

Remember to restart the `mysqld` process every time you make a change to the configuration file for the changes to take effect on the running process.
You can test whether the `mysqld` process is running with:

```
[root@bigboy tmp]# pgrep mysqld
```

You should get a response of plain old process ID numbers.

THE /ETC/MY.CNF FILE

The `/etc/my.cnf` file is the main MySQL configuration file. It sets the default MySQL database location and other parameters. The typical home/SOHO user won't need to edit this file at all.

THE LOCATION OF MySQL DATABASES

According to the `/etc/my.cnf` file, MySQL databases are usually located in a subdirectory of the `/var/lib/mysql/` directory. If you create a database named test, the database files will be located in the directory `/var/lib/mysql/test`.

CREATING A MySQL ROOT ACCOUNT

MySQL stores all its username and password data in a special database named `mysql`. You can add users to this database and specify the databases to which they will have access with the `grant` command. The MySQL root or superuser account, which is used to create and delete databases, is the exception. You need to use the mysqladmin command to set your root password. Only two steps are necessary for a brand new MySQL installation:

1. Make sure MySQL is started.
2. Use the mysqladmin command to set the MySQL root password. The syntax is:

```
[root@tmp bigboy]# mysqladmin -u root password new-password
```

If you want to change your password later, you will probably have to do a **root password recovery**.

ACCESSING THE MySQL COMMAND LINE

MySQL has its own **command line interpreter** (CLI). You need to know how to access it to do very basic administration.

You can access the MySQL CLI using the mysql command followed by the -u option for the username and -p, which tells MySQL to prompt for a password. Here user root gains access:

```
[root@bigboy tmp]# mysql -u root -p
Enter password:
Welcome to the MySQL monitor.  Commands end with ; or \g.
Your MySQL connection id is 14 to server version: 3.23.58

Type 'help;' or '\h' for help. Type '\c' to clear the buffer.

mysql>
```

Note

Almost all MySQL CLI commands need to end with a semi-colon. Even the exit command used to get back to the Linux prompt needs one too!

CREATING AND DELETING MySQL DATABASES

Many Linux applications that use MySQL databases require you to create the database beforehand using the name of your choice. The procedure is relatively simple: Enter the MySQL CLI, and use the create database command:

```
mysql> create database salesdata;
Query OK, 1 row affected (0.00 sec)

mysql>
```

If you make a mistake during the installation process and need to delete the database, use the `drop database` command. The example deletes the newly created database named `salesdata`:

```
mysql> drop database salesdata;
Query OK, 0 rows affected (0.00 sec)

mysql>
```

Note

Sometimes a dropped database may still appear listed when you use the `show databases` command. This may happen even if your root user has been granted full privileges to the database, and it is usually caused by the presence of residual database files in your database directory. In such a case, you may have to physically delete the database subdirectory in `/var/lib/mysql` from the Linux command line. Make sure you stop MySQL before you do this.

```
[root@bigboy tmp]# service mysqld stop
```

GRANTING PRIVILEGES TO USERS

On many occasions you will not only have to create a database, but also have to create a MySQL username and password with privileges to access the database. It is not a good idea to use the root account to do this because of its universal privileges.

MySQL stores all its username and password data in a special database named `mysql`. You can add users to this database and specify the databases to which they will have access with the `grant` command, which has the syntax:

```
sql> grant all privileges on database.* to username@"servername"
identified by 'password';
```

So you can create a user named mysqluser with a password of pinksl1p to have full access to the database named `salesdata` on the local server (`localhost`) with the `grant` command. If the database application's client resides on another server, then you'll want to replace the `localhost` address with the actual IP address of that client.

```
sql> grant all privileges on salesdata.* to mysqluser@"localhost"
identified by 'pinksl1p';
```

The next step is to write the privilege changes to the `mysql.sql` database using the `flush privileges` command:

```
sql> flush privileges;
```

RUNNING MySQL SCRIPTS TO CREATE DATA TABLES

Another common feature of prepackaged applications written in MySQL is that they may require you to not only create the database, but also to create the tables of data inside them as part of the setup procedure. Fortunately, many of these applications come with scripts you can use to create the data tables automatically.

Usually you have to run the script by logging into MySQL as the MySQL root user and automatically importing all the script file's commands with a `<` on the command line.

The example runs a script named `create_mysql.script` whose commands are applied to the newly created database named `salesdata`. MySQL prompts for the MySQL root password before completing the transaction. (You have to create the database *first*, before you can run this command successfully.)

```
[root@bigboy tmp]# mysql -u root -p salesdata < create_mysql.script
Enter password:
[root@bigboy tmp]#
```

VIEWING YOUR NEW MySQL DATABASES

A number of commands can provide information about your newly created database. Here are some examples:

☞ **Log in as the database user**: It is best to do all your database testing as the MySQL user you want the application to eventually use. This will make your testing mimic the actions of the application and results in better testing in a more production-like environment than using the "root" account.

```
[root@bigboy tmp]# mysql -u mysqluser -p salesdata
```

☞ List all your MySQL databases: The `show databases` command gives you a list of all your available MySQL databases. In the example, you can see that the `salesdata` database has been successfully created:

```
mysql> show databases;
+-----------+
```

```
| Database  |
+-----------+
| salesdata |
+-----------+
1 row in set (0.00 sec)

mysql>
```

Listing the Data Tables in Your MySQL Database

The show tables command gives you a list of all the tables in your MySQL database, but you have to use the use command first to tell MySQL to which database it should apply the show tables command.

The example uses the salesdata database; notice that it has a table named test.

```
mysql> use salesdata;
Reading table information for completion of table and column names
You can turn off this feature to get a quicker startup with -A

Database changed
mysql> show tables;
+--------------------+
| Tables_in_salesdata |
+--------------------+
| test               |
+--------------------+
1 row in set (0.00 sec)

mysql>
```

Viewing Your MySQL Database's Table Structure

The describe command gives you a list of all the data fields used in your database table. In the example, you can see that the table named test in the salesdata database keeps track of four fields: name, description, num, and date_modified.

```
mysql> describe test;
+---------------+-------------+------+-----+------------+-------------
----+
| Field         | Type        | Null | Key | Default    | Extra
|
+---------------+-------------+------+-----+------------+-------------
----+
| num           | int(11)     |      | PRI | NULL       |
auto_increment |
| date_modified | date        |      | MUL | 0000-00-00 |
|
```

```
| name          | varchar(50)   |       | MUL |             |
|
| description   | varchar(75)   | YES   |     | NULL        |
|
+---------------+---------------+-------+-----+-------------+-------------
----+
6 rows in set (0.00 sec)

mysql>
```

Viewing the Contents of a Table

You can view all the data contained in the table named test by using the select command. In this example, you want to see all the data contained in the very first row in the table.

```
mysql> select * from test limit 1;
```

With a brand new database this will give a blank listing, but once the application starts and you enter data, you may want to run this command again as a rudimentary database sanity check.

CONFIGURING YOUR APPLICATION

After creating and testing the database, you need to inform your application of the database name, the IP address of the database client server, and the username and password of the application's special MySQL user that will be accessing the data.

Frequently this registration process is done by the editing of a special application-specific configuration file either via a Web GUI or from the command line. Read your application's installation guide for details.

RECOVERING AND CHANGING YOUR MySQL ROOT PASSWORD

Sometimes you may have to recover the MySQL root password because it was either forgotten or misplaced. The steps you need are:

1. Stop MySQL:

```
[root@bigboy tmp]# service mysqld stop
Stopping MySQL:  [  OK  ]
[root@bigboy tmp]#
```

2. Start MySQL in Safe mode with the `safe_mysqld` command and tell it not to read the `grant` tables with all the MySQL database passwords:

```
[root@bigboy tmp]# safe_mysqld --skip-grant-tables &
[1] 4815
[root@bigboy tmp]# Starting mysqld daemon with databases from
/var/lib/mysql
[root@bigboy tmp]#
```

3. Use the `mysqladmin` command to reset the root password. In this case, you are setting it to ack33nsaltf1sh:

```
[root@bigboy tmp]# mysqladmin -u root flush-privileges \
   password "ack33nsaltf1sh"
[root@bigboy tmp]#
```

4. Restart MySQL normally:

```
[root@bigboy tmp]# service mysqld restart
Stopping MySQL:   040517 09:39:38  mysqld ended
[  OK  ]
Starting MySQL:  [  OK  ]
[1]+  Done                        safe_mysqld --skip-grant-tables
[root@bigboy tmp]#
```

The MySQL root user will now be able to manage MySQL using this new password.

MySQL Database Backup

The syntax for backing up a MySQL database is:

```
mysqldump --add-drop-table -u [username] -p[password] [database] >
[backup_file]
```

In the previous section, you gave user mysqluser full access to the `salesdata` database when mysqluser used the password pinksl1p. You can now back up this database to a single file called `/tmp/salesdata-backup.sql` with the command

```
[root@bigboy tmp]# mysqldump --add-drop-table -u mysqluser \
  -ppinksl1p salesdata > /tmp/salesdata-backup.sql
```

Make sure there are no spaces between the `-p` switch and the password or you may get syntax errors.

Tip
Always back up the database named `mysql` too, because it contains all the database user access information.

MySQL Database Restoration

The syntax for restoring a MySQL database is:

```
mysql -u [username] -p[password] [database] < [backup_file]
```

So, using the previous example, you can restore the contents of the database with:

```
[root@bigboy tmp]# mysql -u mysqluser -ppinks11p salesdata \
  < /tmp/salesdata-backup.sql
```

Note

You may have to restore the database named `mysql` also, because it contains all the database user access information.

Very Basic MySQL Network Security

By default MySQL listens on all your interfaces for database queries from remote MySQL clients. You can see this using `netstat -an`. Your server will be seen to be listening on IP address 0.0.0.0 (all) on TCP port 3306.

```
[root@bigboy tmp]# netstat -an
Active Internet connections (servers and established)
Proto Recv-Q Send-Q Local Address           Foreign Address
State
...
...
tcp        0      0 0.0.0.0:3306             0.0.0.0:*
LISTEN
...
...
[root@bigboy tmp]#
```

The problem with this is that it exposes your database to MySQL queries from the Internet. If your SQL database is going to be accessed only by applications running on the server itself, then you can force it to listen only to the equivalent of its loopback interface. Here's how:

1. Edit the `/etc/my.cnf` file and use the `bind-address` directive in the `[mysqld]` section to define the specific IP address on which MySQL listens for connections:

```
[mysqld]
bind-address=127.0.0.1
```

2. Restart MySQL. The `netstat -an` command will show MySQL listening on only the loopback address on TCP port 3306, and your application should continue to work as expected.

BASIC MYSQL TROUBLESHOOTING

You can confirm whether your MySQL installation has succeeded by performing these few simple steps.

Connectivity Testing

In the example scenario, network connectivity between the database and the application will not be an issue because they are running on the same server.

In cases where they are not, you have to use the troubleshooting techniques in Chapter 4, "Simple Network Troubleshooting," to test both basic connectivity and access on the MySQL TCP port of 3306.

Test Database Access

The steps outlined earlier are a good test of database access. If the application fails, then retrace your steps to create the database and register the database information into the application. MySQL errors are logged automatically in the `/var/log/mysqld.log` file; investigate this file at the first sign of trouble. Sometimes, MySQL will fail to start because the `host` table in `mysql` database wasn't created during the installation; this can be rectified by running the `mysql_install_db` command.

A Common Fedora Core 1 MySQL Startup Error

You may notice that you can start MySQL correctly only once under Fedora Core 1. All subsequent attempts result in the message "Timeout error occurred trying to start MySQL Daemon."

```
[root@bigboy tmp]# /etc/init.d/mysqld start
Timeout error occurred trying to start MySQL Daemon.
Starting MySQL:   [FAILED]
[root@bigboy tmp]#
```

This is caused by the MySQL startup script incorrectly attempting to do a TCP port ping to contact the server. The solution is:

1. Edit the script `/etc/rc.d/init.d/mysqld`.
2. Search for the two `mysqladmin` lines with the word "ping" in them, and insert the string `"-u $RANDOM"` before the word "ping:"

```
if [ -n "`/usr/bin/mysqladmin -u $RANDOM ping 2> /dev/null`" ]; then
if !([ -n "`/usr/bin/mysqladmin -u $RANDOM ping 2> /dev/null`" ]); then
```

3. Restart MySQL.

After doing this, MySQL should function correctly—even after a reboot.

CONCLUSION

MySQL has become one of the most popular Linux databases on the market and it continues to improve each day. If you have a large project that requires the installation of a database, then I suggest seeking the services of a database administrator (DBA) to help install and fine-tune the operation of MySQL. I also suggest, no matter the size of the project, that you practice an application installation on a test Linux system to be safe. It doesn't necessarily have to be the same application. You can find free MySQL-based applications using a Web search engine, and you can use these to become familiar with the steps outlined in this chapter before beginning your larger project.

Configuring Linux VPNs

IN THIS CHAPTER

- ☞ VPN Guidelines
- ☞ Scenario
- ☞ Download and Install the Openswan Package
- ☞ Getting Openswan Started
- ☞ Get the Status of the Openswan Installation
- ☞ VPN Configuration Steps Using RSA Keys
- ☞ Possible Changes to IP Tables NAT/Masquerade Rules
- ☞ How to Ensure Openswan Starts When Rebooting
- ☞ Using Pre-Shared Keys (PSK)
- ☞ Troubleshooting Openswan
- ☞ Conclusion

As your SOHO grows, you'll eventually need to establish some form of secure data link with a supplier, vendor, branch office, business partner, or customer that will enable you to access their servers behind their Internet firewall.

One method of doing this is to create a **Virtual Private Network** (**VPN**) to provide an encrypted data stream between your firewall and theirs. A VPN is really convenient, because you can refer to the remote servers, not by their public network address translated IP addresses, but by their real, private IP addresses. This avoids problems inherent in connecting to servers behind a many to one NAT configuration.

This chapter will outline the configuration of a permanent site-to-site VPN link or **tunnel** using Openswan, one of the most popular VPN packages for Linux.

If you are new to VPNs, please refer to Appendix I, "Miscellaneous Linux Topics," for some important background information that will provide a deeper understanding of the steps outlined in this chapter.

VPN GUIDELINES

Here are some recommended guidelines that I suggest you consider before attempting a simple SOHO Linux VPN:

☞ The IPSec protocol on which VPNs are based will not tolerate its data packets being network address translated. If your firewall does NAT, then you'll have to disable it specifically for the packets that will traverse the VPN.

☞ Life will be much easier if you make your Linux VPN box also function as a firewall. Configure and test the firewall first and then configure the VPN. Chapter 14, "Linux Firewalls Using iptables," should help a lot.

☞ The networks at both ends of the VPN tunnel must use different IP address ranges. Many company networks operate using 192.168.0.x or 192.168.1.x addresses, you may have to reassign IP addresses to your network if overlaps occur.

☞ Permanent site-to-site VPNs require firewalls at both ends that use static, DHCP IP addresses.

SCENARIO

Figure 35.1 illustrates the topology of a VPN between two SOHO environments. Here's the scenario:

☞ The two sites need a VPN so that they can communicate with each other without the fear of eavesdropping.

☞ The network administrators at both sites are aware that permanent site-to-site VPNs require fixed Internet IP addresses and have upgraded from their basic DHCP services originally provided by their ISPs. The sites' IP addressing schemes do not overlap.

☞ Neither site wants to invest in a CA certificate service or infrastructure. The RSA key encryption methodology will be used for key exchange. (At the end of the chapter, I'll discuss an alternative Cisco-compatible method called alternately **shared secret, pre-shared,** or **symmetric key**.)

☞ Site 1 uses a private network of 172.168.1.0 /24 and has a Linux VPN/firewall device default gateway with an external Internet IP address of 97.158.253.25.

☞ Site 2 uses a private network of 10.0.0.0 /24 and has a Linux VPN/firewall device default gateway with an external Internet IP address of 6.25.232.1.

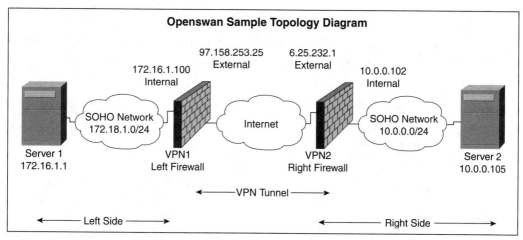

Figure 35.1   Openswan topolology diagram.

DOWNLOAD AND INSTALL THE OPENSWAN PACKAGE

You can download the Openswan RPM at www.openswan.org. The site has good instructions on how to install the product on Fedora and other versions of Linux. Be aware that to download the RPM version of Openswan you must have the ipsec-tools RPM package installed on your system. (Remember, RPM filenames usually start with the software's name and version number, as in openswan-2.1.4-1.fc2.i386.rpm. If you need more details, see Chapter 6, "Installing RPM Software.")

HOW TO GET OPENSWAN STARTED

You can configure Openswan to start at boot time using the chkconfig command:

```
[root@bigboy tmp]# chkconfig ipsec on
```

You can start, stop, and restart Openswan after booting using the ipsec initialization script as shown:

```
[root@bigboy tmp]# service ipsec start
[root@bigboy tmp]# service ipsec stop
[root@bigboy tmp]# service ipsec restart
```

Remember to restart the ipsec process every time you make a change to the ipsec.conf file for the changes to take effect on the running process.

GET THE STATUS OF THE OPENSWAN INSTALLATION

Immediately after installing Openswan, run the `ipsec verify` command. It should give an [OK] status for most of its checks:

```
[root@vpn2 tmp]# ipsec verify
Checking your system to see if IPsec got installed and started
correctly
Version check and ipsec on-path                              [OK]
Linux Openswan U2.2.0/K2.6.8-1.521 (native)
Checking for IPsec support in kernel                         [OK]
Checking for RSA private key (/etc/ipsec.secrets)           [OK]
Checking that pluto is running                               [OK]
Two or more interfaces found, checking IP forwarding        [OK]
Checking NAT and MASQUERADEing                              [N/A]
Checking for 'ip' command                                    [OK]
Checking for 'iptables' command                              [OK]
Checking for 'setkey' command for native IPsec stack support [OK]
[root@vpn2 tmp]#
```

How to Fix Common Status Errors

The status check may provide some errors. The most common ones are related to IP forwarding and opportunistic encryption.

IP Forwarding

Each Linux VPN device needs to have routing or IP forwarding enabled. To enable it, simply add an `ip_forward` entry to the `/etc/sysctl.conf` file:

```
#
# File: /etc/sysctl.conf
#
#--------------------------------------------------------------
# Enable routing (IP forwarding)
#--------------------------------------------------------------

net/ipv4/ip_forward = 1
```

Now use the `sysctl -p` command to activate the settings:

```
[root@bigboy tmp]# sysctl -p
...
...
net.ipv4.ip_forward = 1
[root@bigboy tmp]#
```

You can find more details on the `/etc/sysctl.conf` in Appendix I, "Miscellaneous Linux Topics."

Opportunistic Encryption DNS Checks

The opportunistic encryption DNS checks feature of Openswan allows gateways to encrypt their traffic, even if the two gateway administrators have had no prior contact and neither system has any preset information about the other. The rationale behind this is to make all connections to servers behind the VPN device automatically be encrypted using IPSec in the same way that HTTP traffic can be seamlessly encrypted to become HTTPS traffic.

This feature should be disabled by default in your configuration file; simply ignore the errors related to it.

VPN CONFIGURATION STEPS USING RSA KEYS

One of the more secure ways of setting up a VPN tunnel is to encrypt the data using certificate-based (**RSA**) keys. There are other VPN parameters too, but Openswan is very forgiving when it establishes a tunnel. It automatically goes through all the various combinations of IKE and IPSec settings with the remote VPN box until it finds a match. You don't have to configure most of these settings explicitly as you often have to do in the case of routers and firewall/VPN appliances.

The /etc/ipsec.conf File

Preparation work requires you to draw a basic network diagram such as Figure 35.1. The VPN box on the left is called the left-hand side and the one on the right is called the right-hand side. Left and right parameters must be configured in the /etc/ipsec.conf configuration file. Table 35.1 explains each parameter.

Table 35.1   Parameters of the /etc/ipsec.conf File

Parameter	Description
Left	Internet IP address of the left-hand side VPN device.
Leftsubnet	The network protected by the left-hand side VPN device.
Leftid	Fully qualified domain name in DNS of the left-hand side VPN device, which is preceded by an "@" sign. If DNS is set up for the IP addresses, remove this entry, because names that don't resolve correctly cause the VPN initialization to fail.
Leftrsasigkey	The entire left RSA sig public key for the left-hand side VPN device. This can be obtained by using the ipsec showhostkey --left command.
Leftnexthop	The next hop router from the left-hand side VPN device when trying to reach the right-hand side VPN device. You may use an auto-generated variable %defaultroute, which will be valid in most cases, or the actual IP address of the next hop router in cases where the next hop is not the default router.

continues

Table 35.1   continued

Parameter	Description
Right	Internet IP address of the right-hand side VPN device.
Rightsubnet	The network protected by the right-hand side VPN device.
Rightid	Fully qualified domain name in DNS of the right-hand side VPN device, which is preceded by an @ sign. If DNS isn't set up for the IP addresses, remove this entry, because names that don't resolve correctly cause the VPN initialization to fail.
Rightrsasigkey	The entire right RSA sig public key for the right-hand side VPN device. This can be obtained by using the `ipsec showhostkey --right` command.
Rightnexthop	The next hop router from the right-hand side VPN device when trying to reach the right-hand side VPN device. You may use an auto-generated variable `%defaultroute`, which will be valid in most cases, or the actual IP address of the next hop router in cases where the next hop is not the default router.

First you must gather all this information, then you have to enter it in the `/etc/ipsec.conf` configuration file.

Obtaining RSA Keys

To configure the `/etc/ipsec.conf` file, you need to get the left RSA public key for the left VPN device and the right key for the right VPN device. You need to generate these and insert them in the `/etc/ipsec.conf` file of the VPN peer device.

The best approach is to generate files containing these keys and then use the vi editor's read command (r) to read them into your `/etc/ipsec.conf` file. Cutting and pasting screen output over an SSH session may automatically insert carriage return and line feed characters at the end of each line where the text would normally wrap around on the screen. This can corrupt the keys.

Creating Your Own Keys

The Openswan installation automatically generates the keys. If you want to change them, you can issue the command:

```
[root@vpn2 tmp]# ipsec rsasigkey --verbose 2048 > keys.tmp
[root@vpn2 tmp]#
```

You can then edit the `/etc/ipsec.secrets` file and replace the contents between RSA: { and the final } with the contents of the keys.tmp file generated from the ipsec command above.

Get the Left Public Key

On the left VPN server, issue this command to export the left public key to a file named /tmp/left.pub:

```
[root@vpn1 tmp]# ipsec showhostkey --left > /tmp/left.pub
[root@vpn1 tmp]#
```

Get the Right Public Key

On the right VPN server, export the right public key to a file named /tmp/right.pub:

```
[root@vpn2 tmp]# ipsec showhostkey --right > /tmp/right.pub
[root@vpn2 tmp]#
```

Edit the */etc/ipsec.conf* Configuration File

Each VPN in the /etc/ipsec.conf file has its own subsection. The example creates a subsection called net-to-net, which then receives all the needed parameters:

```
#
# File: /etc/ipsec.conf
#
conn net-to-net
  left=97.158.253.25
  leftsubnet=172.16.1.0/24
  leftid=@vpn1.my-site.com
  #
  leftrsasigkey=0sAQNrV9AYdaW94FXvIxu5p54+MRaW0wy0+HHQrdGofklZYQ
  4TCBlL+Ym00Ahfc8mqXlerZY12Os41G8SIV+zzIO04WZ4wmOvEr8DZaldTbfCu
  vUvMhrTtCpZdm53yF5rCaUbg+Vmx71fgyVmGu8/kuhzB7nWtOYqDFO8OHDGePO
  yOVPQi73KfRoDbdb3ND0EtfnRhRPblKJ239OlIq1
  #
  leftnexthop=%defaultroute
  right=6.25.232.1
  rightsubnet=10.0.0.0/24
  rightid=@vpn2.another-site.com
  #
  rightrsasigkey=0sAQNNdxFPWCga+E/AnDgIM+uIDq4UXcZzpomwMFUpyQ9+r
  hUHT9w8nr3rjUR/qTZOKR2Vqd4XoBd1HkPDBQ8oNjtA3Oz+UQOU3KTMHN5ydFw
  e6MpTJV/hL6LvhB0OXQad/NhjMIx8vOnhM8g8SPRnj7pL3abgu7Sg7eFREV1MJ
  SVBhp0DJ0EbVMVV+Xvwlm9++9zbY3mlc+cSXMPAJZ
  #
  rightnexthop=97.158.253.25
  auto=start
```

Some Important Notes About the /etc/ipsec.conf File

Be sure to maintain the indentation before each parameter. The correct arrangement is:

```
conn net-to-net
    left=x.x.x.x
    leftsubnet=y.y.y.y/24
```

Do not use:

```
conn net-to-net
left=x.x.x.x
leftsubnet=y.y.y.y/24
```

The net-to-net subsections must be the *same* in the /etc/ipsec.conf for both the left- and right-hand side VPN devices. You can configure VPNs to other remote destinations in this file as long as they don't share a subsection name with other VPNs. So in this example, there should be only one net-to-net subsection which uniquely defines the VPN between our two sample sites.

Also, make sure no blank lines separate the net-to-net section's parameters. Lines commented with a # character are acceptable.

Restarting IPSec to reload the configuration file doesn't necessarily restart the tunnels. If you set the auto= parameter to add, you can start the tunnel only manually with the ipsec command. If the parameter is commented out, then the tunnel will never start. A value of start causes the tunnel to start automatically.

Restart Openswan

On *both* VPN devices, you need to start Openswan for the new /etc/ipsec.conf settings to take effect.

```
[root@vpn2 tmp]# service ipsec restart
ipsec_setup: Stopping Openswan IPsec...
ipsec_setup: Starting Openswan IPsec U2.2.0/K2.6.8-1.521...
[root@vpn2 tmp]#
```

Initialize the New Tunnel

To initialize the new tunnel, you can use the ipsec command to start the tunnel net-to-net. Be sure to issue the command simultaneously on the VPN boxes at both ends of the tunnel:

```
[root@vpn2 tmp]# ipsec auto --up net-to-net
104 "net-to-net" #1: STATE_MAIN_I1: initiate
106 "net-to-net" #1: STATE_MAIN_I2: sent MI2, expecting MR2
108 "net-to-net" #1: STATE_MAIN_I3: sent MI3, expecting MR3
004 "net-to-net" #1: STATE_MAIN_I4: ISAKMP SA established
112 "net-to-net" #2: STATE_QUICK_I1: initiate
004 "net-to-net" #2: STATE_QUICK_I2: sent QI2, IPsec SA established
{ESP=>0xe0bdd0e9 <0x13ac7645}
[root@vpn2 tmp]#
```

The "IPsec SA established" message signifies success.

Testing the New Tunnel

The troubleshooting section at the end of the chapter shows you how to test that everything is working correctly.

POSSIBLE CHANGES TO IP TABLES NAT/MASQUERADE RULES

If you are running `iptables` with masquerading/NAT for the VPN devices, then you must exclude packets traversing the tunnel from the NAT operation. This example assumes that interface `eth0` is the Internet facing interface on your Linux VPN/firewall.

Change the left-hand side VPN device's iptables statement from:

```
iptables -t nat -A POSTROUTING -o eth0 -s 172.168.1.0/24 -j MASQUERADE
```

to:

```
iptables -t nat -A POSTROUTING -o eth0 -s 172.168.1.0/24 -d \!
10.0.0.0/24 -j MASQUERADE
```

For the right-hand side VPN device, change the statement:

```
iptables -t nat -A POSTROUTING -o eth0 -s 10.0.0.0/24 -j MASQUERADE
```

to:

```
iptables -t nat -A POSTROUTING -o eth0 -s 10.0.0.0/24 -d \!
176.16.1.0/24 -j MASQUERADE
```

HOW TO ENSURE OPENSWAN STARTS WHEN REBOOTING

If your VPN subsection in the `/etc/ipsec.conf` file contains the line `auto=add`, then IPSec only authorizes but doesn't establish the connection at startup. You'll have to use the `ipsec auto --up <vpn-name>` command to start it manually.

You must change this to `auto=start` for Openswan to start the VPN automatically when IPSec restarts or when the system reboots.

USING PRE-SHARED KEYS (PSK)

You don't always have to use RSA type keys. Sometimes the VPN device at the other end of the tunnel won't support them, but will accept a simpler **pre-shared** key. Here is how to do it:

1. Create the PSK using one of two methods. You can create a random pre-shared key using the `ipsec` command:

   ```
   [root@vpn2 tmp]# ipsec ranbits --continuous 128
   0x33893a081b34d32a362a46c404ca32d8
   [root@vpn2 tmp]#
   ```

   Or, you can create them out of your head. Make them long (over 20 bytes), as in:

   ```
   Nonebutourselvescanfreeourminds
   ```

2. Update `/etc/ipsec.secrets` by adding text in this format at the beginning of the file:

   ```
   vpn1-ip-address vpn2-ip-address : PSK "key in quotations"
   ```

   For the example the line is:

   ```
   97.158.253.25 6.25.232.6 : PSK "nonebutourselvescanfreeourminds"
   ```

3. Update `/etc/ipsec.conf`. The PSK configuration is very similar to the RSA configuration with exception that the `leftid`, `rightid`, `leftrsasigkey`, and `rightrsasigkey` fields are omitted from the relevant `conn` subsection. Also add the `authtype=secret` command to the configuration:

   ```
   conn net-to-net
       authby=secret
       left=97.158.253.25
       leftsubnet=172.16.1.0/24
       leftnexthop=%defaultroute
       right=6.25.232.1
       rightsubnet=10.0.0.0/24
       rightnexthop=97.158.253.25
       auto=start
   ```

Remember to have the same configuration on the Linux VPN boxes on either side of the tunnel and to restart Openswan to activate the new settings.

TROUBLESHOOTING OPENSWAN

Troubleshooting is always important when setting up VPNs, because many things can go wrong. Here are some quick checks you can do to make sure all is working correctly.

Determine the Tunnel Status

The `ipsec auto --status` command provides a status on Opesnswan running on your VPN device. The output is divided into three sections:

☞ **IKE Section:** Defines the various encrypted key exchange algorithms and their parameters. At least one set of values must match between the left- and right-hand side VPN devices. This is also frequently referred to as the **Phase 1 parameters**, because the key exchange process is the first thing to occur in establishing a VPN.

☞ **ESP Section:** Defines the various data encryption algorithms and their parameters. At least one set of values must match between the left- and right-hand side VPN devices. This is also frequently referred to as the **Phase 2 parameters**, because the data encryption process is the second and final thing to occur in establishing a VPN.

☞ **VPN Section:** This is usually prefaced by the name of the VPN tunnel, in this case `net-to-net`. If there are no entries, then the VPN hasn't been established at all. If there are entries, but no `STATE_QUICK_R2` (`IPsec SA established`) lines then the IPSec parameters are configured, but the tunnel hasn't been established. This can be normal, tunnels become active once the Phase 1 and Phase 2 security associations are created, and this usually only occurs after traffic is flowing. The associations then get torn down after a timeout period. It is always best to pass traffic over the tunnel to activate them. An ICMP ping check is a good way to test this:

```
[root@vpn2 tmp]# ipsec auto --status
...
...
000 algorithm ESP encrypt: id=2, name=ESP_DES, ivlen=8, key-
sizemin=64, keysizemax=64
000 algorithm ESP encrypt: id=3, name=ESP_3DES, ivlen=8, key-
sizemin=192, keysizemax=192
000 algorithm ESP encrypt: id=7, name=ESP_BLOWFISH, ivlen=8, key-
sizemin=40, keysizemax=448
```

```
. . .
. . .
000 algorithm IKE encrypt: id=7, name=OAKLEY_AES_CBC, block-
size=16, keydeflen=128
000 algorithm IKE encrypt: id=5, name=OAKLEY_3DES_CBC, block-
size=8, keydeflen=192
000 algorithm IKE hash: id=2, name=OAKLEY_SHA, hashsize=20
. . .
. . .
000 "net-to-net":    IKE algorithms wanted: 5_000-1-5, 5_000-
1-2, 5_000-2-5, 5_000-2-2, flags=-strict
000 "net-to-net":    IKE algorithms found:  5_192-1_128-5,
5_192-1_128-2, 5_192-2_160-5, 5_192-2_160-2,
000 "net-to-net":    IKE algorithm newest: 3DES_CBC_192-MD5-
MODP1536
000 "net-to-net":    ESP algorithms wanted: 3_000-1, 3_000-2,
flags=-strict
000 "net-to-net":    ESP algorithms loaded: 3_000-1, 3_000-2,
flags=-strict
000 "net-to-net":    ESP algorithm newest: 3DES_0-HMAC_MD5;
pfsgroup=<Phase1>
. . .
. . .
000 #4: "net-to-net" STATE_QUICK_R2 (IPsec SA established);
EVENT_SA_REPLACE in 3635s; newest IPSEC; eroute owner
000 #4: "net-to-net" esp.aca08f86@192.168.1.100
esp.7b90ea53@192.168.1.1 tun.0@192.168.1.100 tun.0@192.168.1.1
000 #12: "net-to-net" STATE_MAIN_R3 (sent MR3, ISAKMP SA
established); EVENT_SA_REPLACE in 1153s; newest ISAKMP
[root@vpn2 tmp]#
```

It is important to know the status of your VPN as it can provide valuable troubleshooting clues when there are problems. This can be especially important when establishing a VPN between your Linux firewall and a non-Linux device. The IKE and ESP timers and encryption, hash, and key exchange algorithms must match at both ends to have success. This command allows you to see the value combinations Openswan is using and helps you configure the VPN device on the other end to have compatible settings.

Testing VPN Connectivity

You can test the VPN connectivity by sending a simple ping from one private network to the other. In this case, the ping goes to the Windows server 10.0.0.105, which is protected by vpn2, from server 172.16.1.1, which is protected by vpn1.

If the tunnel is up but ICMP pings don't work, then you need to check that the servers at both ends of the tunnel have routes pointing to the VPN firewalls. Also, check for additional network access controls between the servers and the VPN firewall. There may be additional firewalls in the way or the servers themselves may be running firewall software.

```
C:\>ping 10.0.0.105

Pinging 10.0.0.105 with 32 bytes of data:

Reply from 10.0.0.105: bytes=32 time=20ms TTL=253
Reply from 10.0.0.105: bytes=32 time<10ms TTL=253
Reply from 10.0.0.105: bytes=32 time=10ms TTL=253
Reply from 10.0.0.105: bytes=32 time<10ms TTL=253

Ping statistics for 10.0.0.105:
    Packets: Sent = 4, Received = 4, Lost = 0 (0% loss),
Approximate round trip times in milli-seconds:
    Minimum = 0ms, Maximum =  20ms, Average =  7ms

C:\>
```

Check the Routes

You'll need to check the routes after the VPN tunnel is up as well. As you can see, there is an additional route to the 172.16.1.0 network on firewall vpn2. Incorrect routing on the firewalls can cause problems, check your leftnexthop and rightnexthop values in your /etc/ipsec.conf file:

```
[root@vpn2 tmp]# netstat -nr
Kernel IP routing table
Destination Gateway       Genmask         Flags  MSS Window irtt Iface
10.0.0.0    0.0.0.0       255.255.255.0   U      40  0         0 eth1
6.25.232.0  0.0.0.0       255.255.255.248 U      40  0         0 eth0
172.16.1.0  97.158.253.25 255.255.255.0   UG     40  0         0 eth0
127.0.0.0   0.0.0.0       255.0.0.0       U      40  0         0 lo
0.0.0.0     6.25.232.6    0.0.0.0         UG     40  0         0 wlan0
[root@vpn2 tmp]#
```

Using *tcpdump*

If the tunnel doesn't appear to become established, use the tcpdump command as explained in Chapter 4, "Simple Network Troubleshooting," to determine whether the traffic is being seen at both ends of the tunnel. You need to know whether the IPSec packets are even reaching your VPN firewall. Check routing and your Openswan configuration if not.

Protected Interface TCPDUMP Output from vpn2

Here the TCPdump is done on server2 where you see unencrypted ICMP ping
traffic successfully passing back and forth between the two servers:

```
[root@server2 tmp]# tcpdump -n -i eth1 icmp
03:05:53.971308 IP 172.16.1.1 > 10.0.0.105: icmp 64: echo
request seq 89
03:05:53.995297 IP 10.0.0.105 > 172.16.1.1: icmp 64: echo reply seq 89
03:05:54.972759 IP 172.16.1.1 > 10.0.0.105: icmp 64: echo request seq
90
03:05:54.972789 IP 10.0.0.105 > 172.16.1.1: icmp 64: echo reply seq 90
03:05:55.972985 IP 172.16.1.1 > 10.0.0.105: icmp 64: echo request seq
91
03:05:55.972999 IP 10.0.0.105 > 172.16.1.1: icmp 64: echo reply seq 91
^C
[root@server2 tmp]#
```

Unprotected Interface TCPDUMP Output from vpn2

Here the encrypted ESP traffic is encapsulating the pings passing back and
forth between the two VPN boxes. The true source and destination IP
addresses (10.0.0.105 and 172.16.1.1) are hidden.

```
[root@vpn2 tmp]# tcpdump -n -i eth1  host 97.158.253.25
02:08:23.637149 IP 6.25.232.1 > 97.158.253.25:
ESP(spi=0xf4909a7e,seq=0x73)
02:08:24.635302 IP 97.158.253.25 > 6.25.232.1:
ESP(spi=0x808e9a87,seq=0x74)
02:08:24.637988 IP 6.25.232.1 > 97.158.253.25:
ESP(spi=0xf4909a7e,seq=0x74)
02:08:25.638015 IP 97.158.253.25 > 6.25.232.1:
ESP(spi=0x808e9a87,seq=0x75)
^C
[root@vpn2 tmp]#
```

Check *syslog* Error Messages

As always, check your /var/log/messages file for any messages that may provide clues as to the source of your problems.

Invalid Key Messages

If your left and right public keys were incorrectly applied to your
/etc/ipsec.conf file or your regenerated keys were not updated in your
/etc/ipsec.secrets file, then you will get messages stating that the keys are
invalid and that information is being ignored:

```
003 "net-to-net" #1: ignoring informational payload, type
INVALID_KEY_INFORMATION
003 "net-to-net" #1: received and ignored informational message
003 "net-to-net" #1: discarding duplicate packet; already
STATE_MAIN_I3
031 "net-to-net" #1: max number of retransmissions (2) reached
STATE_MAIN_I3.  Possible authentication failure: no acceptable
response to our first encrypted message
```

CONCLUSION

VPNs are increasingly becoming an everyday part of life on the Internet. Many people use them to gain access to many of the systems in their offices, such as e-mail and intranets. This trend is certain to become more popular as many companies are finding it cheaper for their employees to work from home, relieving them of the need to lease additional office space.

Site-to-site VPNs will also continue to be deployed as companies, both small and large, find it increasingly necessary to share access to their business systems. One notable area is in the realm of IP telephony, where VPNs enable all remote offices to use a single IP switchboard at the center of a VPN hub and spoke network. Intra-office communication is therefore encrypted and the use of a single switchboard saves costs.

Knowledge of VPNs is now indispensable for systems administrators.

Miscellaneous Linux Topics

From upgrades to headless operation to emulation—some topics, no matter how important, refuse to fit neatly into any one chapter. This appendix serves as a reference center for some of these need-to-know items.

FEDORA CORE 3

Released as this book was going to press, Fedora Core 3 has three main enhancements:

☞ Upgrades of the GCC C programming compiler, the GNOME and KDE desktops, the Evolution e-mail client, and the CUPS printer management software suite

☞ Support for Indic languages in both character sets and font rendering

☞ Mandatory application of the Security-Enhanced Linux (SE-Linux) feature

The first two items don't affect anything covered in the book, but SE Linux does. Applications that are registered with SE Linux have all their executable programs and data files listed in a database. The Linux operating system then authorizes access according to the rules defined in the registration database only. The intention is that a hacked SE Linux registered application would be able to affect only its own files and no one else's, even if file permissions in other areas would have normally allowed them access.

SE Linux shouldn't affect your server's operation if you locate your application data files in their default locations, and if it does, there will be ample warning messages in the `/var/log/messages` file. If you find SE Linux generally too complicated, you can deactivate it by editing your `/etc/selinux/config` file and setting the `SELINUX` variable to be `disabled` before rebooting your system. Remember that once this is done, newly created files won't be added to the SE Linux registration database so reactivating SE Linux correctly would be very difficult.

In Fedora Core 3, SE Linux support is provided for dhcpd, httpd, named, ntpd, portmap, snmpd, squid, and syslogd.

LINUX SECURITY WITH TCP WRAPPERS

The TCP Wrappers package is installed by default on Fedora Linux and provides host-based security separate from that provided by a firewall running on the server itself or elsewhere.

The application relies on two main files:

☞ /etc/hosts.allow: Defines the hosts and networks allowed to connect to the server. The TCP Wrappers enabled application searches this file for a matching entry, and if it finds one, then the connection is allowed.

☞ /etc/hosts.deny: Defines the hosts and networks prohibited from connecting to the server. If a match is found in this file, the connection is denied. No match means the connection proceeds normally.

The /etc/hosts.allow file is always read first and both files are always read from top to bottom, therefore the ordering of the entries is important.

The TCP Wrappers File Format

The format of the file is:

```
<TCP-daemon-name>      <client-list>  : <option>
```

This example allows all traffic from the 192.168.1.0/24 and the 192.168.2.0/255.255.255.0 networks and SSH from only two hosts, 172.16.1.1 and 216.10.119.244. All HTTP Web traffic is allowed. All other TCP traffic to the host is denied. Notice how the subnet masks can use the slash nomenclature or the dotted decimal 255.255.255.0 format.

```
#
# File: hosts.allow
#
ALL:    192.168.1.0/24 192.168.2.0/255.255.255.0
sshd:   172.16.1.1 216.10.119.244
httpd:  ALL

#
# File: hosts.deny
#
ALL:    ALL
```

Determining the TCP Daemon's Name

The easiest way of determining the name of a daemon is to use the ps command and then use grep to filter for the name of the service. Here, the example quickly determines the daemon name (/usr/sbin/sshd) for the SSH server process. Because TCP Wrappers only requires the program name and not the path, sshd therefore becomes the entry to place in the TCP-daemon-name column of the configuration file.

```
[root@bigboy tmp]# ps -ef | grep -i ssh
root       10053     1   0 Nov06 ?        00:00:00 /usr/sbin/sshd
root       14145 10053   0 Nov13 ?        00:00:02 sshd: root@pts/1
root       18100 14148   0 21:56 pts/1    00:00:00 grep ssh
[root@bigboy tmp]#
```

For a full explanation of all the options available, refer to section 5 of the man pages for hosts_access:

```
[root@bigboy tmp]# man 5 hosts_access
```

TCP Wrappers is simple to implement, but you have to set them on every host. Management is usually easier on a firewall that protects the entire network.

ADJUSTING KERNEL PARAMETERS

Unlike many Linux applications that need to be restarted before their configuration parameters are read, many of the Linux kernel's parameters can be instantaneously activated and deactivated.

The Linux kernel stores many of its dynamic parameters in the /proc filesystem, which resides on a virtual RAM disk in memory for maximum performance.

Parameters are generally categorized by function within subdirectories of the /proc; information on IDE hard drives is located in the /proc/ide directory, for example, and general system parameters are located in the /proc/sys directory.

System parameters are held within files with names that mimic their function. For example, a Linux system can become a rudimentary router if the IP forwarding networking parameter is set to 1, not 0. Networking parameters for IPv4 addressing schemes are located in the /proc/sys/net/ipv4/. The file that covers IP forwarding is named ip_forward and contains a single byte: 1 when it's active or 0 when it's not.

You can update these files by redirecting the output of the `echo` command to overwrite the file contents using the `>` redirection character. This line activates IP forwarding by overwriting the contents of the `ip_forward` file with the value 1:

```
[root@bigboy tmp] echo 1 > /proc/sys/net/ipv4/ip_forward
```

There are some disadvantages to doing this. It is not a permanent solution, and the system will revert back to its defaults after the next reboot. You can overcome this by adding the `echo` commands to the `/etc/rc.local` script that runs at the end of each reboot. This too has its disadvantages; it is the very last script to be run so if your parameters need to be set earlier, as most kernel parameters should be, it isn't a suitable solution.

Linux has a more elegant solution called the `/etc/sysctl.conf` file. It is a list of all the `/proc` filesystem files the systems administrator wants to customize and the values they should contain. The file has two columns, the first is the filename relative to the `/proc/sys` directory, and the second is the value the file should contain separated by an equals sign. You can also replace the slashes in the filename with periods. Continuing with the example, you can set the `/proc/sys/net/ipv4/ip_forward` file with a value of 1 using either of these configurations:

```
#
# Sample /etc/sysctl.conf file
#
# Activate IP forwarding
#
net.ipv4.ip_forward = 1

#
# Activate IP forwarding too!
#
net/ipv4/ip_forward = 1
```

Editing the `/etc/sysctl.conf` file isn't enough, because the update isn't instantaneous. You have to force Linux to reread the file and reset the kernel parameters using the `sysctl -p` command. In the example, the `/proc/sys/net/ipv4/ip_forward` file had a value of 0 until the `sysctl` command ran, after which time, IP forwarding was activated:

```
[root@bigboy tmp]# cat /proc/sys/net/ipv4/ip_forward
0
[root@bigboy tmp]# sysctl -p
net.ipv4.ip_forward = 1
net.ipv4.conf.default.rp_filter = 1
kernel.sysrq = 0
kernel.core_uses_pid = 1
```

```
[root@bigboy tmp]# cat /proc/sys/net/ipv4/ip_forward
1
[root@bigboy tmp]#
```

The use of the /etc/sysctl.conf is important in day-to-day administration.

RUNNING LINUX WITHOUT A MONITOR

You can reduce the cost of ownership of your Linux system by not using a VGA monitor. This creates what is also known as a **headless** system. Operating costs may not be important at home, but will be in a corporate environment with large numbers of Linux servers racked in data centers. In such cases, access to the Linux box can be more cheaply provided via the COM port.

I've included this section, largely because I have occasionally hosted the Web site www.linuxhomenetworking.com at friends' homes and felt badly about borrowing their monitors. Having access via the COM ports has also helped me in both the home and business situations. The most common occurrence is when the system is hung, locking out network access, and I need to get to it by using:

- ☞ A notebook PC with a console cable connected to the COM port
- ☞ A modem connected to the COM port
- ☞ TELNET to log into a terminal server that has one of its ports connected to the Linux box's COM port

Preparing to Go Headless

One of the advantages of this method is that you don't need a keyboard either. Unfortunately, your BIOS may halt the system during the Power On Self Test (POST) if it doesn't detect a keyboard. Make sure you disable this feature in the BIOS setup of your PC before proceeding. You can usually find the POST feature on the very first screen under the Halt On option.

You also need to make sure that you have activated your COM ports in your BIOS settings.

For connectivity that doesn't involve modems (PC to PC) connect a *null* modem cable to the COM port you want to test, connect the other end to the client PC running Hyperterm or whatever terminal emulation software you are using. One popular Linux equivalent to Hyperterm is minicom.

If you're using a modem for connectivity, then you'll need a *full* modem cable and you'll have to test via a dial up connection.

Configuration Steps

In Red Hat/Fedora Linux, the COM1 and COM2 ports are controlled by a program called `agetty`, but `agetty` usually isn't activated when you boot up unless its configuration file `/etc/inittab` is modified. In other versions of Linux, `agetty` may be called just plain `getty`. Table I.1 lists the physical ports to their equivalent Linux device names.

Table I.1   How Physical COM Ports Map to Linux TTYS Devices

Port	Linux `agetty` Device Name
COM1	ttyS0
COM2	ttyS1

To configure your COM ports for terminal access, add these lines to `/etc/inittab`:

```
# Run COM1 and COM2 gettys in standard runlevels
S0:235:respawn:/sbin/agetty -L 19200 ttyS0 vt102
S1:235:respawn:/sbin/agetty -L 19200 ttyS1 vt102
```

What do these lines mean? At boot time, when the system enters runlevels 2, 3, or 5, `agetty` must attach itself to devices `ttyS0` and `ttyS1` and emulate a VT102 terminal running at 19200 baud. The `-L` means ignore modem control signals, this option should be omitted if you are connecting the port to a modem. The respawn lines mean that `agetty` will restart automatically if, for whatever reason, it dies.

The next step is to restart the `init` process to re-read `/etc/inittab`:

```
[root@bigboy tmp]# init q
```

Now you need to configure the terminal client (Hyperterm) to match the speed settings in `/etc/inittab`. Connect the console/modem cable between the client and your Linux box. Press Enter a couple times, and celebrate when you see something like this:

```
Red Hat Linux release 8.0 (Psyche)
Kernel 2.4.18-14 on an i586

bigboy login:
```

By default, user root will not be able to log in from a terminal. To do this, you'll have to edit the `/etc/securetty` file, which contains the device names of TTY lines on which root is allowed to login. Just add `ttyS0` and `ttyS1` to the list if you need this access.

MAKE YOUR LINUX BOX EMULATE A VT100 DUMB TERMINAL

Dumb terminals are devices that allow you to log into your system via the COM port. You can make your Linux box emulate a dumb terminal quite easily. Why would you want to? For example, you run Linux on a notebook and you need to use it to access a hung headless Linux server via the COM port, Or, perhaps you need to gain access to a modem connected to the COM port. This section will focus on the notebook scenario, not using Linux to dial a modem.

Configuration Steps

The most commonly used Linux terminal emulation program is `minicom`. It is simple to use mainly because it uses a text-based GUI. You first need to go through all the relevant steps listed in the "Preparing to go Headless" section to ensure you have the right type of cable and correct BIOS settings.

Be warned, `minicom` will clash with your `agetty` configuration explained previously: A headless system cannot be used to access another headless system using the headless COM port. You, therefore, have to disable the `agetty` configuration for the port on which you wish to run `minicom`:

1. Disable `agetty` on COM1 by commenting out the `ttyS0 agetty` statements in the `/etc/inittab` file. COM1 now handles outbound `minicom` connections to other systems, and other systems using `minicom` can use COM2 to access this system. The next phase is to restart the `init` process to reload the new `/etc/inittab` settings.

2. Edit /etc/inittab:

```
# Run COM1 and COM2 gettys in standard runlevels
#S0:235:respawn:/sbin/agetty -L 19200 ttyS0 vt102
S1:235:respawn:/sbin/agetty -L 19200 ttyS1 vt102
```

3. Restart `init`:

```
[root@bigboy tmp]# init q
```

4. Run `minicom` in setup mode using the `minicom -s` command, which brings you to the setup menu:

```
[root@bigboy tmp]# minicom -s

------[configuration]-------
| Filenames and paths        |
| File transfer protocols    |
| Serial port setup          |
| Modem and dialing          |
| Screen and keyboard        |
| Save setup as dfl          |
| Save setup as..            |
| Exit                       |
| Exit from Minicom          |
----------------------------
```

5. Select the Serial Port Setup menu item. Make the speed match that of the remote headless system and make sure the correct serial COM device is chosen. Device `/dev/ttyS0` is COM1 and `/dev/ttyS1` is COM2. Also make sure that flow control is off.

```
---------------------------------------------
|  A -     Serial Device       : /dev/ttyS0 |
|  B - Lockfile Location        : /var/lock  |
|  C -    Callin Program        :            |
|  D -   Callout Program        :            |
|  E -     Bps/Par/Bits         : 19200 8N1  |
|  F - Hardware Flow Control : No            |
|  G - Software Flow Control : No            |
|                                            |
|      Change which setting?                 |
---------------------------------------------
```

6. Select the Modem and Dialing option and make sure the Init String and Reset String settings are blank.

7. Select the Save Setup as dfl to make this your saved default setting, and then choose Exit from Minicom.

8. Make sure the other system is correctly configured for headless operation. Connect the cables between the systems.

9. Re-enter `minicom`, this time without the `-s`:

```
[root@bigboy tmp]# minicom
```

10. Press Enter, and you should get a login prompt:

```
Welcome to minicom 2.00.0

OPTIONS: History Buffer, F-key Macros, Search History Buffer,
I18n
Compiled on Jun 23 2002, 16:41:20.

Press CTRL-A Z for help on special keys

bigboy login:
```

11. To exit `minicom`, type Ctrl-A, then Z, then X.

12. Users other than root will get a "permission denied" message if they use `minicom`, because the COM ports are not normally accessible to regular users. To get around this, user root can either give everyone read/write access using the `chmod` command or add selected trusted users to your `sudo` configuration.

Remember that `minicom` resets the privileges to the COM port each time you change the configuration with `minicom -s` so you may find yourself having to run `chmod` from time to time.

```
[root@bigboy tmp]# chmod o+rw /dev/ttyS0
```

VPN TERMS AND METHODS

A **virtual private network (VPN)** provides security for transmission of sensitive information over unprotected networks such as the Internet. VPN relationships are established between trusted sites on the Internet making the public network appear to be virtually the same as a private network to the VPN members. VPNs, however, have their own language. Once you know the terms, you'll be ready to get to work.

☞ Authentication: The process of ensuring that the VPN data received is both unchanged and from the expected source.

☞ Encryption: The use of special mathematical equations to scramble the bits in a data stream, rendering the data stream unreadable to anyone who does not have access to the corresponding decryption equation. The process is usually made even harder through the use of an encryption key, which modifies the way the equations do the scrambling. Only persons with access to this key and the corresponding programs are able to recover the original data. Data encryption helps to prevent unauthorized persons from having access to the data.

☞ IPSec: The name given to a number of data communications protocols designed to authenticate and encrypt VPN data to protect it from unauthorized viewing or modification as it is transmitted across a network.

☞ Authentication **header** (AH): One of two IPSec security protocols. Provides authentication and antireplay services, without encryption, by adding its own security header to the original IP packet.

☞ **Encapsulating security protocol** (**ESP**): The other IPSec security protocol. Provides authentication, encryption, and antireplay services. It encrypts the data within the packet and then adds its own security header to the original IP packet. Because ESP headers don't authenticate the outer IP header as AH headers do, AH and an ESP are often used in combination with each other. This is called **transport adjacency**.

☞ **Transport mode VPN**: A style of VPN in which the original source and destination address of the data sent over the VPN is unchanged. Figures I.1 and I.2 provide examples of transport mode VPN IP packets. (For more information on the IP protocol, please refer to Chapter 2, "Introduction to Networking," which introduces networking concepts.)

Original IP Header	Inserted AH Header	Original TCP Header	DATA

Figure I.1   Transport mode AH packet format.

Original IP Header	Inserted AH Header	Inserted ESP Header	Original TCP Header	DATA

Figure I.2   Transport mode AH/ESP packet format.

☞ Tunnel mode VPN: A style of VPN in which the original source and destination address of the data sent over the VPN is changed by encapsulating the original IP packet within another IP packet. The original packet is frequently encrypted, header and all, in an effort to provide an additional layer of security by not revealing the true identities of the servers communicating with each other. Figures I.3 and I.4 show examples of tunnel mode VPN IP packets.

New IP Header	Inserted AH Header	Original IP Header	Original TCP Header	DATA

Figure I.3   Tunnel mode AH packet format.

New IP Header	Inserted AH Header	Inserted ESP Header	Original IP Header	Original TCP Header	DATA

Figure I.4   Tunnel mode AH/ESP packet format.

Authentication and Encryption Methods

IPSec data integrity is usually provided by one of two **hashed message authentication code** (**HMAC**) methods:

☞ Message Digest 5 (MD5)
☞ Secure Hash Algorithm (SHA-1).

IPSec usually uses one of two methods to encrypt data:

☞ Data Encryption Standard (DES) using a 56-bit encryption key
☞ Triple DES using a 168-bit encryption key.

Internet Key Exchange (IKE)

IKE provides authentication of the IPSec peers, negotiates IPSec security associations, and establishes IPSec keys. There are two main methods of establishing a trusted relationship between two devices that want to create a VPN between themselves.

Public Encrypted Keys

The first method is **public key cryptography using RSA encryption pioneered by RSA Data Security, Inc.** Each VPN device has its own public and private keys. Anything encrypted with one of the keys can only be decrypted with the other. This allows you to create a signature when the message is encrypted with a sender's private key. The receiver verifies the signature by decrypting the message with the sender's public key.

A successful exchange requires the receiver to have a copy of the sender's public key and to know with a high degree of certainty that it really does belong to the sender, and not to someone pretending to be the sender. This certainty is assured using certificates and **Certification Authorities**.

A digital certificate contains information that identifies a user or device, such as a name, serial number, company, department, or IP address. It also contains a copy of the entity's public key. Certificates are managed and issued by Certification Authorities (CAs). A CA can either be a trusted public third party, such as VeriSign, or an in-house private server that you establish within your organization.

Prior to installing a certificate-based VPN, each VPN device must be pre-configured with the certificate generated for them by the CA. The VPN devices are also be preconfigured with the CA's certificate.

During the key exchange, the VPN peers authenticate by sending each other the certificate issued to them by the CA, but encrypted using their private key.

Each peer then uses the pre-installed CA certificate they have to authenticate with the CA and securely receive the other peer's certificate from the CA using public key cryptography.

Each peer then extracts the public key from the certificate they receive from the CA and uses it to decrypt the certificate they just received from the other peer.

Once the certificates received from the CA and the other peer match, authentication is complete.

Shared Private Keys

The second method of establishing a trusted relationship is to have the devices at each end of the VPN use a **shared key** or password. The disadvantage is that each pair of VPN connections needs set of keys, making it difficult for large scale implementations. Unlike the RSA method, there is no CA to provide an impartial audit trail of VPN connection initiations.

IKE's role in Creating Security Associations

Once authentication is complete, the VPN peers use IKE to negotiate the **security associations (SAs)** to be used at each end point. IKE, in turn, uses special ISAKMP IP packets using IP protocol 50 to establish a security association. SAs are comprised of transforms and shared keys. Transforms describe how the data will be transformed by the VPN and between which pre-defined networks at each end of the tunnel to provide the desired security, for example:

- ☞ Packet encryption methods
- ☞ Packet authentication methods
- ☞ Transport versus tunnel mode

☞ AH and or ESP usage

☞ SA lifetime before it is renegotiated. (SAs are permanent for when manually established.)

Shared keys are the actual keywords used by the encryption and authentication processes to protect the data.

VPN Security and Firewalls

All security devices in the path of a VPN connection have to allow IP protocol 50 between the two VPN devices to ensure that IKE works properly.

VPNs also use a separate channel through which the encrypted data passes as UDP packets through port 500. Unusually, the source and destination port is 500.

For the VPN to function correctly, these protocols must also be allowed to pass through unimpeded. In certificate based VPNs, you may have to open up these ports and protocols to the CA as well.

Note

VPN tunnels frequently don't operate correctly if they have to pass through a firewall that uses NAT. They will tend to work if the NAT firewall is the termination point of the VPN.

VPN User Authentication Methods for Temporary Connections

The discussion so far has been slanted towards a permanent connection between purpose built VPN devices. Frequently, however, the device at the other end of the connection is a PC. Table I.2 shows some authentication methods used in such cases.

Table I.2   Types of Dial Up VPN Authentication

Method	Description
IKE-XAUTH secured RADIUS	Usernames and passwords entered into the VPN remote login software are relayed by the VPN device at the remote end to a trusted RADIUS server. If the username/password combination is valid for remote login, then the RADIUS server authorizes the VPN device to continue with the IKE interchange.
ACE/SecurID	Software uses a username and password in conjunction with a small keyring token with a digital display, also known as a fob, whose authentication serial number changes every few minutes for a login to occur. To log in, the user not only has to enter the username and password, but also the PIN tied to the fob plus the fob's dynamic serial number which is synchronized with the authentication server at the other end of the VPN.

Method	Description
Windows Domain	Remote home user authentication relies on the same username/password combination of the Windows Domain Controller that the user would normally use to log in when they are at work.
Local user database	Valid usernames and passwords are configured into the VPN device at the other end of the VPN.

TCP/IP PACKET FORMAT

The TCP/IP packet contains an IP header followed by a TCP or UDP header followed by the TCP/UDP data as seen in Figure I.5.

IP Header	TCP/UDP Header	DATA

Figure I.5   The TCP/IP packet format.

Tables I.3 through I.5 show the general format of the various TCP/IP header fields you may encounter.

Table I.3   Contents of the IP Header

Field	Description
IP Version	The version of IP being used. Version 4 is the current version used by most devices on the Internet. Version 6 is a newer format that allows for a more vast range of addresses.
IHL	Internet header length. Total length of the IP header.
Total Length	Total length of the IP packet.
DF Bit	Indicator to tell whether the data in the packet may be fragmented into smaller packets due to limitations of the communications line.
MF Bit	Indicator to tell whether this data in this packet is the last one of a stream of fragments.
Fragment Offset	If the packet is part of a fragmented datagram, then this specifies where in the complete datagram the data in the packet should be inserted.
TTL	Time to live. This value is decremented by each router through which the packet passes. When the value reaches zero, the packet is discarded by the router. The server sending the data usually sets the TTL to a value high enough to reach its destination without being discarded. The TTL decrement feature is used by routers as an additional precaution to prevent the packet from mistakenly being routed around the Internet in an infinite loop caused by a routing error.
Protocol	Defines the type of protocol header to expect at the end of this header. For example `6 = TCP. 17 = UDP`

continues

Table I.3   continued

Field	Description
Header checksum	Used to ensure that the header contents are error free.
Source Address	Indicates the IP address of the server sending the data.
Destination Address	Indicates the IP address of the server intended to receive the data.

Table I.4   Contents of the TCP Header

Field	Description
Source and Destination Port	Identifies points at which upper-layer source and destination processes receive TCP services.
Sequence Number	Usually specifies the number assigned to the first byte of data in the current message. In the connection-establishment phase, this field also can be used to identify an initial sequence number to be used in an upcoming transmission.
Acknowledgment Number	Contains the sequence number of the next byte of data the sender of the packet expects to receive.
Data Offset	Length of the TCP header.
Flags	Carries a variety of control information, including the SYN and ACK bits used for connection establishment, and the FIN bit used for connection termination.
Window	Specifies the size of the sender's receive window (that is, the buffer space available for incoming data).
Checksum	Used to ensure that the header contents are error free.
Data	Contains upper-layer information.

Table I.5   Contents of the UDP Header

Field	Description
Source and Destination Port	Identifies points at which upper-layer source and destination processes receive TCP services.
Length	Specifies the length of the UDP header and data.
Checksum	Used to ensure that the header contents are error free.

ICMP CODES

You'll also encounter ICMP codes in your troubleshooting exercises, especially when viewing your `iptables` log files. Table I.6 lists the most commonly used codes.

Table I.6 ICMP Codes

Type	Name	Description
3		**Destination Unreachable Codes**
	Net Unreachable	The sending device knows about the network but believes it is not available at this time. Perhaps the network is too far away through the known route.
	Host Unreachable	The sending devices knows about host but doesn't get ARP reply, indicating the host is not available at this time.
	Protocol Unreachable	The protocol defined in IP header cannot be forwarded.
	Port Unreachable	The sending device does not support the port number you are trying to reach.
	Fragmentation Needed and Don't Fragment Was Set	The router needs to fragment the packet to forward it across a link that supports a smaller maximum transmission unit (MTU) size. However, application set the Don't Fragment bit.
	Source Route Failed	ICMP sender can't use the strict or loose source routing path specified in the original packet.
	Destination Network Unknown	ICMP sender does not have a route entry for the destination network, indicating this network may never have been available.
	Destination Host Unknown	ICMP sender does not have a host entry, indicating the host may never have been available on connected network.
	Source Host Isolated	ICMP sender (router) has been configured to not forward packets from source (the old electronic pink slip).
	Communication with Destination Network Is Administratively Prohibited	ICMP sender (router) has been configured to block access to the desired destination network.
	Communication with Destination Host Is Administratively Prohibited	ICMP sender (router) has been configured to block access to the desired destination host.
	Destination Network Unreachable for Type of Service	The sender is using a Type of Service (TOS) that is not available through this router for that specific network.
	Destination Host Unreachable for Type of Service	The sender is using a Type of Service (TOS) that is not available through this router for that specific host.
	Communication Administratively Prohibited	ICMP sender is not available for communications at this time.
	Host Precedence Violation	Precedence value defined in sender's original IP header is not allowed (for example, using Flash Override precedence).

continues

Table I.6   ICMP Codes

Type	Name	Description
5		**Redirect Codes**
	Redirect Datagram for the Network (or subnet)	ICMP sender (router) is not the best way to get to the desired network. Reply contains IP address of best router to destination. Dynamically adds a network entry in original sender's routing tables.
	Redirect Datagram for the Host	ICMP sender (router) is not the best way to get to the desired host. Reply contains IP address of best router to destination. Dynamically adds a host entry in original sender's route tables.
	Redirect Datagram for the Type of Service and Network	ICMP sender (router) does not offer a path to the destination network using the TOS requested. Dynamically adds a network entry in original sender's route tables.
	Redirect Datagram for the Type of Service and Host	ICMP sender (router) does not offer a path to the destination host using the TOS requested. Dynamically adds a host entry in original sender's route tables.
6		**Alternate Host Address Codes**
	Alternate Address for Host	Reply that indicates another host address should be used for the desired service. Should redirect application to another host.
11		**Time Exceeded Codes**
	Time to Live Exceeded in Transit	ICMP sender (router) indicates that originator's packet arrived with a Time to Live (TTL) of 1. Routers cannot decrement the TTL value to 0 and forward the packet.
	Fragment Reassembly Time Exceeded	ICMP sender (destination host) did not receive all fragment parts before the expiration (in seconds of holding time) of the TTL value of the first fragment received.
12		**Parameter Problem Codes**
	Pointer indicates the error	Error is defined in greater detail within the ICMP packet.
	Missing a Required Option	ICMP sender expected some additional information in the Option field of the original packet.
	Bad Length	Original packet structure had an invalid length.

Codes, Scripts, and Configurations

This appendix contains samples of all the scripts used in the previous chapters.

APACHE FILE PERMISSIONS SCRIPT

The first argument of the script is the target directory and must have a trailing /. The script prints an on-screen list of all the files it has modified.

```
[root@bigboy tmp]# ./fix-www-perms.sh /home/www/webpages/
/home/www/webpages/
/home/www/webpages/file1.htm
/home/www/webpages/file2.htm
...
    ...
    ...
[root@bigboy tmp]
```

Here's how it's done:

```
#!/bin/sh
#
# fix-www-perms.sh - Recursively fixes file permissions in a www
                     directory # so that Apache may serve the pages
correctly
#
# (c) SiliconValleyCCIE.com
#

for i in `find $1`
do
  if [ -d $i ] ; then
    chmod 755 $i
    echo $i
  else
    chmod 644 $i
    echo $i
  fi
done
```

591

SENDMAIL Spam Filter Script

One of the good things about having a Linux box at home is that you can create your own customized spam filter. Here's a summary of a script called `mail-filter.pl`, which I've used at home for some time:

☞ It uses two configuration files: `mail-filter.accept` lists all the mail to accept and `mail-filter.reject` lists all the mail to reject. Each file has two columns.

☞ The first column has either the word "subject:" or "address:" and the second column has either a subject string (inclusive of spaces) or a single address entry. Sometimes SPAM is sent to multiple addresses in the same domain, there is also a "repeataddress" keyword that can be used in the first column followed by the offending multiple entry domain name. If there are more than two repetitions of the domain, then the e-mail is rejected.

☞ The script matches addresses in both the To and From field of the received e-mail.

☞ The script reads the reject file and rejects any matching e-mails, it then reads the accept file and accepts any matching e-mails, then it denies everything else.

☞ The script rejects e-mails in which your e-mail address doesn't appear in the To, From, or CC field. BCC e-mails are therefore denied. If you receive e-mails as part of mailing lists, put the name of the mailing list in your accept file.

☞ The script is very tolerant of e-mail addresses. You do not have to have an @ sign in the configuration files' entries. The script matches on a partial address too.

☞ `Mail-filter.pl` logs all accepted and denied e-mails in a file called `mail-filter.log`. Look at this file from time to time as you may find yourself rejecting too much traffic, which will require you to modify the configuration files.

The script runs using the PERL scripting language, which is installed by default on Red Hat. If you don't have PERL, go to `www.cpan.org` to download and install a variety of PERL modules. Click on the CPAN home page's Modules link. Click the `All Modules` listing, and download and install the MailTools, IO-Stringy, MIME-tools, and Mail-Audit modules in that order. The CPAN modules page also has a link on how to install the modules.

Here's how to install the script:

1. Place `mail-filter.pl` in your `$HOME` directory (default login directory). In this case the username is mailiuser.

2. Use the `chmod` command to make it executable:

```
[root@bigboy mailuser]# chmod 700 mail-filter.pl
```

3. Go to the `/etc/smrsh` directory and create a symbolic link to the `mail-filter.pl` file there:

```
[root@bigboy mailuser]# cd /etc/smrsh
[root@bigboy smrsh]# ln -s /home/mailuser/mail-filter.pl
```

4. Create a .forward file in your home directory:

```
#!/bin/bash
| ~/mail-filter.pl
```

You should then be ready to go!

The *mail-filter.accept* File

```
address: my-address@mysite.com
address: cnn
subject: Alumni Association
```

The *mail-filter.reject* File

```
address: spammer@spammer.com
repeataddress: my-isp-provider.net
subject: porn
```

The *mail-filter* Script

```
#!/usr/bin/perl
#
#
# Mail-filter - PERL Script
#
#
# Reference pages
#
# http://search.cpan.org/author/SIMON/Mail-Audit-2.1/Audit.pm
# http://simon-cozens.org/writings/mail-audit.html
#
# PERL modules needed from
http://www.cpan.org/modules/01modules.index.html
#
# Need to install the following modules:
#
#       MailTools, IO-Stringy, MIME-tools & Mail-Audit in this order
#
#
# Need to have:
```

```
#
#        a logical link to this file in /etc/smrsh
#        .forward file with the following line in it
#
#            #!/bin/bash
#            | ~/mail-filter
#


use Mail::Audit;
use MIME::Lite;


#
# Spam filter variables
#

$FILEPATH            = "/home/mailuser/";
$ITEM                = Mail::Audit->new;
$FROM                = $ITEM->from();
$TO                  = $ITEM->to();
$CC                  = $ITEM->cc();
$SUBJECT             = $ITEM->subject();
$BODY                = $ITEM->body();
$DATE                = "";
$INBOX_LOG           = $FILEPATH . "mail-filter.log";
$ACCEPT_FILE         = $FILEPATH . "mail-filter.accept";
$REJECT_FILE         = $FILEPATH . "mail-filter.reject";


################### Don't edit below here ##################


chomp($DATE = `date '+ %m/%d/%Y %H:%M:%S'`);
$DATE =~ s/^\s*(.*?)\s*$/$1/;
chomp($FROM, $TO, $CC, $SUBJECT);
study $FROM;
study $SUBJECT;
study $TO;
study $CC;


&Mail_Filter;
exit;



sub Mail_Filter {


my %badsubjects          = ();
my %badaddresses         = ();
my %badrepeataddresses   = ();
my %goodsubjects         = ();
my %goodaddresses        = ();


#
```

```
                # Read in the configuration files
                #

                open (REJECT_FILE, "$REJECT_FILE");

                    while(<REJECT_FILE>){

                       my $record = $_;
                       my ($value, $type) = &Strip_Record($record);

                       #
                       # Get the bad subjects
                       #
                       if ($type =~ /^subject$/i){
                          $badsubjects{$value} = "$type";
                       }

                       #
                       # Get the bad address
                       #

                       if ($type =~ /^address$/i){
                          $badaddresses{$value} = "$type";
                       }

                       #
                       # Get the bad repeat address
                       #

                       if ($type =~ /^repeataddress$/i){
                          $badrepeataddresses{$value} = "$type";
                       }

                    }
                close (REJECT_FILE);


                open (ACCEPT_FILE, "$ACCEPT_FILE");

                    while(<ACCEPT_FILE>){

                       my $record = $_;
                       my ($value, $type) = &Strip_Record($record);

                       #
                       # Get the good subjects / address
                       #

                       if ($type =~ /subject/i){
                          $goodsubjects{$value} = "$type";
                       }

                       if ($type =~ /address/i){
                          $goodaddresses{$value} = "$type";
                       }

                    }
                close (ACCEPT_FILE);
```

```perl
#
# Reject by subject
#

foreach my $criteria (keys %badsubjects) {
    next unless $SUBJECT =~ /$criteria/i;
    &Reject_Mail("yes");
}


#
# Reject email to/from these addresses
#

foreach my $criteria (keys %badaddresses) {
    next unless ($TO =~ /$criteria/i) or ($CC =~ /$criteria/i) or
($FROM =~ /$criteria/i);
    &Reject_Mail("yes");
}


#
# Sometimes SPAM is sent to multiple addresses in the same domain. Reject email if
# the number of addresses in the to: or cc: >= 3
#

foreach my $criteria (keys %badrepeataddresses) {

    my $to_cc = $TO." ".$CC;
    my @repeat_test_string = split(/$criteria/,$to_cc);
    my $i = -1;
    foreach my $tmp_var (@repeat_test_string){
        $i++;
    }
    if($i >= 3){

        #
        # Reject
        #

        &Reject_Mail("yes");
    }
}


#
# Accept some subject lines
#

for my $criteria (keys %goodsubjects) {
    next unless $SUBJECT =~ /$criteria/i;
    &Reject_Mail("no");
}


#
# Accept emails to/from these addresses
```

```
        #

        for my $criteria (keys %goodaddresses) {
            next unless ($TO =~ /$criteria/i) or ($CC =~ /$criteria/i) or
($FROM =~ /$criteria/i);
            &Reject_Mail("no");
        }


        #
        # Reject everything else
        #

        &Reject_Mail("yes");
}



sub Strip_Record{

    my $record = shift(@_);

    #
    # Split out the fields in the record and strip out
leading/trailing white space
    #

    chomp $record;
    my @fields = split(/\:/,$record);
    $fields[0] =~ s/^\s*(.*?)\s*$/$1/;
    $fields[1] =~ s/^\s*(.*?)\s*$/$1/;

    #
    # Return the subjects
    #
    if ($fields[0] =~ /^subject$/i){
        return ($fields[1], "subject");
    }

    #
    # Return the addresses
    #
    elsif ($fields[0] =~ /^address$/i){
        if ($fields[1] =~ /\@/){
            my ($person, $domain) = split(/\@/, $fields[1]);
            return ($person ."\@" . $domain, "address");
        }
        else{
            return ($fields[1], "address");
        }
    }

    #
    # Return the repeat addresses
    #
    elsif ($fields[0] =~ /^repeataddress$/i){
        if ($fields[1] =~ /\@/){
            my ($person, $domain) = split(/\@/, $fields[1]);
            return ($person ."\@" . $domain, "repeataddress");
        }
```

```
            else{
                return ($fields[1], "repeataddress");
            }
        }


    }


    sub Reject_Mail {

        my $ok = shift(@_);

        open (LOG, ">> $INBOX_LOG");

        #
        # Log message receipt to file
        #

        if ($ok =~ /yes/i){

            print LOG "REJECT $DATE To: $TO From: $FROM Subject:
$SUBJECT\n";
            $ITEM->reject;
        }
        else{

            print LOG "ACCEPT $DATE To: $TO From: $FROM Subject:
$SUBJECT\n";
            $ITEM->accept;
        }

        close(LOG);
        exit;
    }
```

IPTABLES SCRIPTS

Here are a number of iptables script samples for such tasks as allowing FTP
and NTP traffic through your firewall, plus a detailed script suitable for a
home/small office.

FTP Client Script

```
# - Interface eth0 is the internet interface
# - Interface eth1 is the private network interface

modprobe ip_conntrack_ftp

#-------------------------------------------------------------------
# FTP connections from your Linux server
# Outbound FTP requests on control connection (port 21)
#-------------------------------------------------------------------
```

```
iptables -A OUTPUT-o eth0 -p tcp —sport 1024:65535 —dport 21 \
  -m state —state NEW -j ACCEPT
iptables -A INPUT -i eth0 -p tcp —sport 21 —dport 1024:65535 \
  -m state —state ESTABLISHED,RELATED -j ACCEPT

#================================================================
#================================================================
# Select one of the following two
#================================================================
#================================================================


#----------------------------------------------------------------
# FTP connections from your Linux server
# Active FTP data connection established back from remote server
#----------------------------------------------------------------

iptables -A INPUT -i eth0 -p tcp —sport 20 —dport 1024:65535 \
  -m state —state NEW -j ACCEPT
iptables -A OUTPUT -o eth0 -p tcp —dport 20 —sport 1024:65535 \
  -m state —state ESTABLISHED,RELATED -j ACCEPT

#----------------------------------------------------------------
# FTP connections from your Linux server
# Passive FTP data connection established from your Linux server
#----------------------------------------------------------------

iptables -A OUTPUT -o eth0 -p tcp —dport 1024:65535 \
        —sport 1024:65535 -m state —state  NEW -j ACCEPT
iptables -A INPUT -i eth0 -p tcp —sport 1024:65535 \
        —dport 1024:65535 -m state —state ESTABLISHED,RELATED \
        -j ACCEPT
```

FTP Server Script

```
# - Interface eth0 is the internet interface
# - Interface eth1 is the private network interface

modprobe ip_conntrack_ftp

#----------------------------------------------------------------
# FTP connections to your Linux server
# Inbound FTP requests on control connection (port 21)
#----------------------------------------------------------------

iptables -A INPUT -i eth0 -p tcp —dport 21 —sport 1024:65535 \
  -m state —state NEW -j ACCEPT
iptables -A OUTPUT-o eth0 -p tcp —dport 1024:65535 —sport 21 \
  -m state —state ESTABLISHED,RELATED -j ACCEPT

#================================================================
#================================================================
# Select one of the following two
#================================================================
#================================================================

#----------------------------------------------------------------
```

```
# FTP connections to your Linux server
# Active FTP data connection established back to client from
# your server
#----------------------------------------------------------------

iptables -A OUTPUT -o eth0 -p tcp —sport 20 —dport 1024:65535 \
   -m state —state NEW -j ACCEPT
iptables -A INPUT -i eth0 -p tcp —dport 20 —sport 1024:65535 \
   -m state —state ESTABLISHED,RELATED -j ACCEPT


#----------------------------------------------------------------
# FTP connections to your Linux server
# Passive FTP data connection established to your Linux server
# from remote client
#----------------------------------------------------------------

iptables -A INPUT -i eth0 -p tcp —sport 1024:65535 \
      —dport 1024:65535 -m state —state  NEW -j ACCEPT
iptables -A OUTPUT -o eth0 -p tcp —dport 1024:65535 \
      —sport 1024:65535 -m state —state ESTABLISHED,RELATED \
      -j ACCEPT
```

NTP Server Script

```
# - Interface eth0 is the internet interface
# - Interface eth1 is the private network interface

iptables -A OUTPUT -o eth0 -p udp -m multiport --ports 123 \
      -j ACCEPT

iptables -A INPUT -i eth0 -p udp -m multiport --ports 123 \
      -j ACCEPT
```

Home/Small Office Protection Script

```
#!/bin/bash


#----------------------------------------------------------------
# Set up variables for the firewall
#
# WEBSERVER_1 uses port forwarding for HTTP, DNS and SMTP mail
#----------------------------------------------------------------

EXTERNAL_INT="eth0"                    # External Internet interface
INTERNAL_INT="eth1"                    # Home Network Interface
HOME_NETWORK="192.168.1.0/24"          # Home network address range

WEBSERVER_1_INT="192.168.1.101"        # (Port fwding) Server Real IP
WEBSERVER_2_INT="192.168.1.100"        # (1 to 1 NAT) Server real IP
WEBSERVER_2_EXT="216.10.119.248"       # (1 to 1 NAT) Server NAT IP
```

```
TIME_SERVER1="192.6.38.127"          # Remote time server #1
TIME_SERVER2="216.27.190.202"        # Remote time server #2
TIME_SERVER3="204.123.2.5"           # Remote time server #1

# Uncomment this for 1:1 NAT PLUS (Remove Masquerade section)
# $MANY_TO_1_NAT="216.10.119.249"   # (Many to 1 NAT)

#################################################################
#################################################################
############## Load important iptables modules ##############
#################################################################
#################################################################

#------------------------------------------------------------------
# Load the NAT module
#------------------------------------------------------------------

modprobe iptable_nat

#------------------------------------------------------------------
# Load modules for FTP connection tracking and NAT - You may need
# them later
#------------------------------------------------------------------

modprobe ip_conntrack_ftp

#################################################################
#################################################################
######## Define our chains and important variables ##########
#################################################################
#################################################################

#------------------------------------------------------------------
# Get the IP address of the firewall's external interface
#------------------------------------------------------------------

EXTERNAL_IP="`ifconfig $EXTERNAL_INT | grep 'inet addr' | \
                awk '{print $2}' | sed -e 's/.*://'`"

INTERNAL_IP="`ifconfig $INTERNAL_INT | grep 'inet addr' | \
                awk '{print $2}' | sed -e 's/.*://'`"


#################################################################
#################################################################
############ Fix Linux settings for better security ##########
#################################################################
#################################################################

#------------------------------------------------------------------
# Disable routing triangulation. Respond to queries out
# the same interface, not another. Helps to maintain state
# Also protects against IP spoofing
#------------------------------------------------------------------

echo 1 > /proc/sys/net/ipv4/conf/all/rp_filter

#------------------------------------------------------------------
```

```
# Enable logging of packets with malformed IP addresses
#------------------------------------------------------------------

echo 1 > /proc/sys/net/ipv4/conf/all/log_martians


#------------------------------------------------------------------
# Disable redirects
#------------------------------------------------------------------

echo 0 > /proc/sys/net/ipv4/conf/all/send_redirects


#------------------------------------------------------------------
# Disable source routed packets
#------------------------------------------------------------------

echo 0 > /proc/sys/net/ipv4/conf/all/accept_source_route


#------------------------------------------------------------------
# Disable acceptance of ICMP redirects
#------------------------------------------------------------------

echo 0 > /proc/sys/net/ipv4/conf/all/accept_redirects


#------------------------------------------------------------------
# Turn on protection from Denial of Service (DOS) attacks
#------------------------------------------------------------------

echo 1 > /proc/sys/net/ipv4/tcp_syncookies


#------------------------------------------------------------------
# Disable responding to ping broadcasts
#------------------------------------------------------------------

echo 1 > /proc/sys/net/ipv4/icmp_echo_ignore_broadcasts


#------------------------------------------------------------------
# Enable routing (IP forwarding)
#------------------------------------------------------------------

echo 1 > /proc/sys/net/ipv4/ip_forward

################################################################
################################################################
############ Initialize all the chains we'll use #############
################################################################
################################################################


#------------------------------------------------------------------
# Initialize all the chains by removing all the rules
# tied to them
#------------------------------------------------------------------

iptables —flush
iptables -t nat —flush
```

```
iptables -t mangle —flush

#------------------------------------------------------------------
# Now that the chains have been initialized, the user defined
# chains should be deleted. We'll recreate them in the next step
#------------------------------------------------------------------

iptables —delete-chain
iptables -t nat —delete-chain
iptables -t mangle —delete-chain

#------------------------------------------------------------------
# If a packet doesn't match one of the built in chains, then
# The policy should be to drop it
#------------------------------------------------------------------

iptables —policy INPUT DROP
iptables —policy OUTPUT DROP
iptables —policy FORWARD DROP
iptables -t nat    —policy POSTROUTING ACCEPT
iptables -t nat    —policy PREROUTING  ACCEPT

#------------------------------------------------------------------
# The loopback interface should accept all traffic
# Necessary for X-Windows and other socket based services
#------------------------------------------------------------------

iptables -A INPUT  -i lo -j ACCEPT
iptables -A OUTPUT -o lo -j ACCEPT

################################################################
################################################################
################## Check for bad addresses ##################
################################################################
################################################################

#------------------------------------------------------------------
# Initialize our user-defined chains
#------------------------------------------------------------------

iptables -N valid-src
iptables -N valid-dst

#------------------------------------------------------------------
# Verify valid source and destination addresses for all packets
#------------------------------------------------------------------

iptables -A INPUT   -i $EXTERNAL_INT -j valid-src
iptables -A FORWARD -i $EXTERNAL_INT -j valid-src
iptables -A OUTPUT  -o $EXTERNAL_INT -j valid-dst
iptables -A FORWARD -o $EXTERNAL_INT -j valid-dst

#=#=#=#=#=#=#=#=#=#=#=#=#=#=#=#=#=#=#=#=#=#=#=#=#=#=#=#=#=#=#=#
#
# Source and Destination Address Sanity Checks
#
# Drop packets from networks covered in RFC 1918 (private nets)
# Drop packets from external interface IP
#
#=#=#=#=#=#=#=#=#=#=#=#=#=#=#=#=#=#=#=#=#=#=#=#=#=#=#=#=#=#=#=#
```

```
iptables -A valid-src -s $10.0.0.0/8      -j DROP
iptables -A valid-src -s $172.16.0.0/12   -j DROP
iptables -A valid-src -s $192.168.0.0/16  -j DROP
iptables -A valid-src -s $224.0.0.0/4     -j DROP
iptables -A valid-src -s $240.0.0.0/5     -j DROP
iptables -A valid-src -s $127.0.0.0/8     -j DROP
iptables -A valid-src -s 0.0.0.0/8        -j DROP
iptables -A valid-src -d 255.255.255.255  -j DROP
iptables -A valid-src -s 169.254.0.0/16   -j DROP
iptables -A valid-src -s $EXTERNAL_IP     -j DROP
iptables -A valid-dst -d $224.0.0.0/4     -j DROP


#=#=#=#=#=#=#=#=#=#=#=#=#=#=#=#=#=#=#=#=#=#=#=#=#=#=#=#=#=#
#
# Log and drop chain
#
#=#=#=#=#=#=#=#=#=#=#=#=#=#=#=#=#=#=#=#=#=#=#=#=#=#=#=#=#=#

iptables -A LOG-and-drop -j LOG —log-ip-options \
        —log-tcp-options —log-level debug
iptables -A LOG-and-drop -j DROP


##################################################################
##################################################################
################## Firewall Rules Section ####################
##################################################################
##################################################################

#------------------------------------------------------------------
# Allow outbound DNS queries from the FW and the replies too
#
# - Interface $EXTERNAL_INT is the internet interface
#
# Zone transfers use TCP and not UDP. Most home networks
# / websites using a single DNS server won't require TCP statements
#
#------------------------------------------------------------------

iptables -A OUTPUT -p udp -o $EXTERNAL_INT —dport 53 \
        —sport 1024:65535 -j ACCEPT

iptables -A INPUT -p udp -i $EXTERNAL_INT —sport 53 \
        —dport 1024:65535 \
        -j ACCEPT


#------------------------------------------------------------------
# Allow port 22 (SSH) connections to the firewall
#------------------------------------------------------------------

iptables -A INPUT -p tcp -i $EXTERNAL_INT —dport 22 \
  —sport 1024:65535 -m state —state NEW -j ACCEPT


#------------------------------------------------------------------
# Allow port 80 (www) and 443 (https) connections from the firewall
#------------------------------------------------------------------
```

```
iptables -A OUTPUT -j ACCEPT -m state --state NEW,ESTABLISHED,RELATED \
   -o $EXTERNAL_INT -p tcp --dport 80 --sport 1024:65535

iptables -A OUTPUT -j ACCEPT -m state --state NEW,ESTABLISHED,RELATED \
   -o $EXTERNAL_INT -p tcp --dport 443 --sport 1024:65535


#----------------------------------------------------------------
# Allow outbound ICMP echo requests & inbound echo replies
#----------------------------------------------------------------

iptables -A OUTPUT -j ACCEPT -o $EXTERNAL_INT -p icmp \
        --icmp-type echo-request
iptables -A INPUT  -j ACCEPT -i $EXTERNAL_INT -p icmp \
        --icmp-type echo-reply


#----------------------------------------------------------------
# Allow all bidirectional traffic from your firewall to the
# protected network
# - Interface $INTERNAL_INT is the private network interface
#----------------------------------------------------------------

iptables -A INPUT   -j ACCEPT -p all -s $HOME_NETWORK \
        -i $INTERNAL_INT
iptables -A OUTPUT  -j ACCEPT -p all -d $HOME_NETWORK \
        -o $INTERNAL_INT


################################################################
################################################################
################### 1 to 1 NAT Section #######################
################################################################
################################################################

#----------------------------------------------------------------
# NAT ALL traffic:
#
# TO:              FROM:          MAP TO SERVER:
# $WEBSERVER_1_EXT Anywhere       $WEBSERVER_1_INT
#
# SNAT is used to NAT all other outbound connections initiated
# from the protected network to appear to come from
# IP address $WEBSERVER_1_EXT
#
# POSTROUTING:
#   NATs source IP addresses. Frequently used to NAT connections from
#   your home network to the Internet
#
# PREROUTING:
#   NATs destination IP addresses. Frequently used to NAT
#   connections from the Internet to your home network
#
#----------------------------------------------------------------

# PREROUTING statements for 1:1 NAT
# (Connections originating from the Internet)

iptables -t nat -A PREROUTING -d $WEBSERVER_2_EXT \
        -i $EXTERNAL_INT \
```

```
                   -j DNAT —to-destination $WEBSERVER_2_INT

# POSTROUTING statements for 1:1 NAT
# (Connections originating from the home network servers)

iptables -t nat -A POSTROUTING -s $WEBSERVER_2_INT \
         -o $EXTERNAL_INT \
         -j SNAT —to-source $WEBSERVER_2_EXT


# Allow forwarding to each of the servers configured for 1:1 NAT
# (For connections originating from the Internet. Notice how you
# use the real IP addresses here)

# HTTP
iptables -A FORWARD -p tcp -i $EXTERNAL_INT -o $INTERNAL_INT \
    -d $WEBSERVER_2_INT —dport 80 —sport 1024:65535 \
    -m state —state NEW -j ACCEPT

# SSH
iptables -A FORWARD -p tcp -i $EXTERNAL_INT -o $INTERNAL_INT \
    -d $WEBSERVER_2_INT —dport 22 —sport 1024:65535 \
    -m state —state NEW -j ACCEPT

# DNS (TCP)
iptables -A FORWARD -p tcp -i $EXTERNAL_INT -o $INTERNAL_INT \
    -d $WEBSERVER_2_INT —dport 53 \
    -m state —state NEW -j ACCEPT

# DNS (UDP)
iptables -A FORWARD -p udp -i $EXTERNAL_INT -o $INTERNAL_INT
    -d $WEBSERVER_2_INT —dport 53 \
    -m state —state NEW -j ACCEPT

# NTP
iptables -A FORWARD -p udp \
         -d $TIME_SERVER1 —dport 123 —sport 123 \
         -s $WEBSERVER_2_EXT -j ACCEPT

iptables -A FORWARD -p udp \
         -d $TIME_SERVER2 —dport 123 —sport 123 \
         -s $WEBSERVER_2_EXT -j ACCEPT

iptables -A FORWARD -p udp \
         -d $TIME_SERVER3 —dport 123 —sport 123 \
         -s $WEBSERVER_2_EXT -j ACCEPT

#################################################################
#################################################################
################## Port Forwarding Section ##################
#################################################################
#################################################################

#-----------------------------------------------------------------
# Allow port forwarding for traffic on HTTP, HTTPS, SMTP and DNS
# to WEBSERVER_1 on the same ports
#-----------------------------------------------------------------

## Allow Port Forwarding
```

```
    # HTTP (Port Forwarding)
    iptables -t nat -A PREROUTING -p tcp -i $EXTERNAL_INT \
        -d $EXTERNAL_IP —dport 80 —sport 1024:65535 -j DNAT \
        —to $WEBSERVER_1_INT:80

    # SMTP Sendmail (Port Forwarding)
    iptables -t nat -A PREROUTING -p tcp -i $EXTERNAL_INT \
        -d $EXTERNAL_IP —dport 25 —sport 1024:65535 -j DNAT \
        —to $WEBSERVER_1_INT:25

    # SSH (Port Forwarding)
    iptables -t nat -A PREROUTING -p tcp -i $EXTERNAL_INT \
        -d $EXTERNAL_IP —dport 22 —sport 1024:65535 -j DNAT \
        —to $WEBSERVER_1_INT:22

    # DNS (TCP) (Port Forwarding)
    iptables -t nat -A PREROUTING -p tcp -i $EXTERNAL_INT \
        -d $EXTERNAL_IP \
        —dport 53 —sport 1024:65535 -j DNAT \
        —to $WEBSERVER_1_INT:53

    # DNS (UDP) (Port Forwarding)
    iptables -t nat -A PREROUTING -p udp -i $EXTERNAL_INT \
        -d $EXTERNAL_IP —dport 53 —sport 1024:65535 -j DNAT \
        —to $WEBSERVER_1_INT:53


    ## Allow routing after port forwarding


    # HTTP (Routing after port forwarding NAT)
    iptables -A FORWARD -p tcp -i $EXTERNAL_INT \
        -d $WEBSERVER_1_INT —dport 80 —sport 1024:65535 \
        -m state —state NEW -j ACCEPT

    # SMTP Sendmail (Routing after port forwarding NAT)
    iptables -A FORWARD -p tcp -i $EXTERNAL_INT \
        -d $WEBSERVER_1_INT —dport 25 —sport 1024:65535 \
        -m state —state NEW -j ACCEPT

    # SSH (Routing after port forwarding NAT)
    iptables -A FORWARD -p tcp -i $EXTERNAL_INT \
        -d $WEBSERVER_1_INT —dport 22 —sport 1024:65535 \
        -m state —state NEW -j ACCEPT

    # DNS (TCP) (Routing after port forwarding NAT)
    iptables -A FORWARD -p tcp -i $EXTERNAL_INT \
        -d $WEBSERVER_1_INT —dport 53 -m state —state NEW \
        -j ACCEPT

    # DNS (UDP) (Routing after port forwarding NAT)
    iptables -A FORWARD -p udp -i $EXTERNAL_INT \
        -d $WEBSERVER_1_INT \
        —dport 53 -j ACCEPT


    ################################################################
    ################################################################
    ############# (Many to one NAT) Not Masquerading ##############
    ################################################################
    ################################################################
```

```
# POSTROUTING statements for Many:1 NAT
# (Connections originating from the entire home network)

#iptables -t nat -A POSTROUTING -s $HOME_NETWORK \
#          -j SNAT -o INTERNAL_INT —to-source $MANY_TO_1_NAT


################################################################
################################################################
################ (Many to one NAT) Masquerading ##############
################################################################
################################################################

#-----------------------------------------------------------------
# Allow masquerading
# Enable routing by modifying the ip_forward /proc filesystem file
# - Interface $EXTERNAL_INT is the internet interface
# - Interface $INTERNAL_INT is the private network interface
#-----------------------------------------------------------------

iptables -A POSTROUTING -t nat -o $EXTERNAL_INT -s $HOME_NETWORK \
         -d 0/0 -j MASQUERADE


################################################################
################################################################
########### Allow  already established connections ##########
################################################################
################################################################

#-----------------------------------------------------------------
# Prior to masquerading, the packets are routed via the filter
# table's FORWARD chain.
# Allowed outbound: New, established and related connections
# Allowed inbound : Established and related connections
#-----------------------------------------------------------------

iptables -A FORWARD -t filter -o $EXTERNAL_INT -m state \
         —state NEW,ESTABLISHED,RELATED -j ACCEPT

iptables -A FORWARD -t filter -i $EXTERNAL_INT -m state \
         —state ESTABLISHED,RELATED     -j ACCEPT

#-----------------------------------------------------------------
# Allow previously established connections
# - Interface $EXTERNAL_INT is the internet interface
#-----------------------------------------------------------------

iptables -A INPUT -j ACCEPT -m state \
    —state ESTABLISHED,RELATED -i $EXTERNAL_INT -p tcp


################################################################
################################################################
############### Log and drop all other packets ##############
################################################################
################################################################

#-----------------------------------------------------------------
```

```
# Log and drop all other packets to file /var/log/messages
# Without this we could be crawling around in the dark
#-------------------------------------------------------------

iptables -A OUTPUT -j LOG-and-drop
iptables -A INPUT -j LOG-and-drop
iptables -A FORWARD -j LOG-and-drop
```

SAMPLE DNS ZONE FILES: USING BIND VIEWS

Here are some sample zone files for a home/small office network that requires the use of BIND views as explained in Chapter 18, "Configuring DNS."

The /etc/named.conf File

This first sample, named.conf, is for a network in which BIND views are being used.

An ACL named trusted-subnet was created to define the internal network 192.168.1.0. Two other built-in ACLs are used: localhost, which defines the DNS server itself, and localnets, which defines all the networks to which the server is directly connected. Together, the three are used to define the view named internal, which will return the data contained in the localhost.zone, 192.168.1.zone and my-site-internal.zone files for all queries from these networks. The view external is used for queries from all other networks and returns the contents of the my-site.zone file.

Reference to the 192.168.1.0/24 network in the ACL is actually redundant, because the network is directly connected to the server's NIC and therefore is also part of the localnets ACL too.

```
options {
        directory "/var/named";
        /*
         * If there is a firewall between you and nameservers you want
         * to talk to, you might need to uncomment the query-source
         * directive below.  Previous versions of BIND always asked
         * questions using port 53, but BIND 8.1 uses an unprivileged
         * port by default.
         */
        // query-source address * port 53;

        /*
        allow-query { 192.168.0.0/16; localhost; };
        allow-transfer { 192.168.0.0/16; localhost; };
        allow-recursion { 192.168.0.0/16; localhost; };
        */

};

//
// a caching only nameserver config
```

```
//
controls {
        inet 127.0.0.1 allow { localhost; } keys { rndckey; };
};


acl "trusted-subnet" { 192.168.1/24 };


view "internal" { // What the home network will see

    match-clients { localnets; localhost; "trusted-subnet"; };

        zone "." IN {
                type hint;
                file "named.ca";
        };

        zone "localhost" IN {
                type master;
                file "localhost.zone";
                allow-update { none; };
        };

        zone "0.0.127.in-addr.arpa" IN {
                type master;
                file "named.local";
                allow-update { none; };
        };

        zone "1.168.192.in-addr.arpa" IN {
                type master;
                file "192.168.1.zone";
            allow-update { none; };
        };
        zone "my-web-site.org" {
                type master;
                notify no;
                file "my-site-internal.zone";
                allow-query { any; };
        };

};


view "external" { // What the Internet will see

    match-clients { any; };
    recursion no;

        zone "my-web-site.org" {
                type master;
                notify no;
                file "my-site.zone";
                allow-query { any; };
        };


};
```

Zone File for *my-web-site.org* (External View)

Here is an example for the `external` zone file for `my-web-site.org`. The firewall rules NAT IP address 97.158.253.26 to server Bigboy's 192.168.1.100 IP address, so all references to Bigboy need to use the public IP address. As server Bigboy is the mail and Web server, the zone file also has an `A record` / `CNAME` combination so that so that you can access Bigboy by one of these two aliases depending on the role you wish it to play. For mail, you could access it as `mail.my-web-site.org` and for Web applications you could access it as `www.my-web-site.org`.

```
;
; Zone file for my-web-site.org - Filename my-site.zone
;
; The full zone file
;
$TTL 3D
@         IN      SOA      www.my-web-site.org. hostmaster.my-web-
site.org. (
                          200211152        ; serial, todays date + todays
serial #
                          3600             ; refresh, seconds
                          3600             ; retry, seconds
                          3600             ; expire, seconds
                          3600 )           ; minimum, seconds
;
                  NS       www             ; Inet Address of name server

my-web-site.org.    MX      10 mail          ; Primary Mail Exchanger

;
;
localhost     A       127.0.0.1
www           A       97.158.253.26
mail          CNAME   www
```

Zone File for *my-web-site.org* (Internal View)

Here is an example for the `internal` zone file for `my-web-site.org`. When the name server is accessed from the internal 192.168.0.0 network, `bigboy.my-web-site.org` maps to 192.168.1.100. There is also an entry for one of the home PCs named Smallfry, which you can now additionally access as `smallfry.my-web-site.org`. As server Bigboy is also a mail and Web server, CNAMES are added so that you can access 192.168.1.100 by one of two aliases depending on the role you wish it to play. For mail, you could access it as `mail.my-site-internal.com` and for Web applications you could access it as `www.my-web-site.org`.

```
;
; Zone file for my-web-site.org - Filename my-site-internal.zone
;
```

```
; The full zone file
;
$TTL 3D
@        IN      SOA     www.my-web-site.org. hostmaster.my-web-
site.org. (
                         200211151          ; serial, todays date + todays
serial #
                         3600               ; refresh, seconds
                         3600               ; retry, seconds
                         3600               ; expire, seconds
                         3600 )             ; minimum, seconds
;
                 NS      www                ; Inet Address of name server

my-web-site.org.  MX     10 mail.my-web-site.org. ; Primary Mail
Exchanger

;
;
localhost        A       127.0.0.1

bigboy           A       192.168.1.100
smallfry         A       192.168.1.102
firewall         A       192.168.1.1


www              CNAME   bigboy
mail             CNAME   bigboy
```

Reverse Zone File for a Home Network Using NAT

You can also create a reverse zone file for the home network on the
192.168.1.X network using the same principles you used for a public network.
Now you'll get correct responses for both forward and reverse lookups using
the host or nslookup commands.

```
;
; Reverse Zone file for 192.168.0.0 - Filename 192.168.1.zone
;
$TTL    86400
@                           1D IN SOA       @ root (
                                            51   ; serial (d. adams)
                                            3H   ; refresh
                                            15M  ; retry
                                            1W   ; expiry
                                            1D ) ; minimum

                            1D IN NS        @

100      PTR     bigboy.my-web-site.org.
102      PTR     smallfry.my-web-site.org.
1        PTR     firewall.my-web-site.org.
```

SENDMAIL SAMPLES

Chapter 21, "Configuring Linux Mail Servers," outlined the formats of numerous files. The features mentioned there are used in this complete set of files customized for a domain named `my-web-site.org`.

Sample */etc/mail/access* File

In this sample section of an `/etc/mail/access` file relaying is allowed for the local server and the 192.168.x.x network only.

```
# Check the /usr/share/doc/sendmail/README.cf file for a description
# of the format of this file. (search for access_db in that file)
# The /usr/share/doc/sendmail/README.cf is part of the sendmail-doc
# package.
#
# by default we allow relaying from localhost...
localhost.localdomain      RELAY
localhost                  RELAY
127.0.0.1                  RELAY

#
# Relay messages from the local subnet
192.168                    RELAY
```

Sample */etc/mail/local-host-names* File

In this sample section of a `local-host-names` file all the domains for which the mail server has mail responsibility are listed.

```
# local-host-names - include all aliases for your machine here.
#
my-web-site.org
www.my-web-site.org
mail.my-web-site.org
ns.my-web-site.org
#
my-other-site.com
www.my-other-site.com
mail.my-other-site.com
ns.my-other-site.com
```

Sample */etc/mail/sendmail.mc* File

Here is a sample section of a `sendmail.mc` file.

```
dnl # The following causes sendmail to only listen on the IPv4
loopback address
```

```
dnl # 127.0.0.1 and not on any other network devices. Remove the
loopback
dnl # address restriction to accept email from the internet or
intranet.
dnl #
dnl DAEMON_OPTIONS(`Port=smtp,Addr=127.0.0.1, Name=MTA')dnl
...
...
dnl ***** Customised section 1 start *****
dnl
dnl Kill The SPAM Using Blackholes
dnl
FEATURE(`dnsbl', `proxies.blackholes.easynet.nl', `"550 5.7.1 ACCESS
DENIED to OPEN PROXY SERVER "$&{client_name}" by easynet.nl DNSBL
(http://proxies.blackholes.easynet.nl/errors.html)"', `')dnl
FEATURE(`dnsbl', `relays.ordb.org', `"550 Email rejected due to
sending server misconfiguration - see
http://www.ordb.org/faq/\#why_rejected"')dnl
FEATURE(`dnsbl', `sbl.spamhaus.org', `"550 Mail from "
$`'&{client_addr} " refused - see http://www.spamhaus.org/sbl/"')
FEATURE(`dnsbl', `bl.spamcop.net', `"450 Mail from " $`'&{client_addr}
" refused - see http://spamcop.net/bl.shtml"')
FEATURE(`dnsbl', `ipwhois.rfc-ignorant.org',`"550 Mail from "
$&{client_addr} " refused. Rejected for bad WHOIS info on IP of your
SMTP server - see http://www.rfc-ignorant.org/"')
dnl
dnl Masquerading stuff
dnl
FEATURE(always_add_domain)dnl
FEATURE(`masquerade_entire_domain')dnl
FEATURE(`masquerade_envelope')dnl
dnl FEATURE(`allmasquerade')dnl Even masquerades messages destined for
local mailboxes but for other domains
FEATURE(delay_checks)dnl
dnl
dnl
dnl FEATURE(genericstable, `hash -o /etc/mail/genericstable')dnl
dnl GENERICS_DOMAIN_FILE(`/etc/mail/genericstable')dnl
dnl
dnl
define(`confPRIVACY_FLAGS', `goaway')dnl - Limits command usage
define(`confSMTP_LOGIN_MSG', `$j server ready at $b')dnl - Changes
login message
define(`confMAX_HEADERS_LENGTH',16384)dnl
dnl
MASQUERADE_DOMAIN(localhost)dnl
MASQUERADE_DOMAIN(localhost.localdomain)dnl
MASQUERADE_DOMAIN(`my-web-site.org.')dnl                      (for everyone
else)
MASQUERADE_AS(my-web-site.org)dnl                            (for local
machine)
dnl
dnl
dnl ***** Customised section 1 end *****
dnl
```

Sample */etc/mail/virtusertable* File

In this `virtusertable` file the server will accept e-mail to only three users in the various domains, rejecting everything else.

```
t689ndtw@my-web-site.org       paul
paul@my-other-site.com     paul
paul@my-web-site.org       paul
@my-other-site.com     error:nouser User unknown
@my-web-site.org           error:nouser User unknown
```

Fedora Version Differences

The book primarily covers the latest versions of Fedora Linux, but many systems administrators still use older versions. This appendix lists a number of features in configuration files and quirks in the operation of some of the older versions of Fedora/Red Hat Linux.

FTP DIFFERENCES

There are some well known differences in the configuration of the VSFTP package for version 8.0 and earlier of Red Hat/Fedora Linux.

For one, the starting and stopping of VSFTP is controlled by `xinetd` via the `/etc/xinetd.d/vsftpd` file. VSFTP is deactivated by default, so you'll have to edit this file to start the program. Make sure the contents look like the example. The `disable` feature must be set to no to accept connections.

```
service ftp
{
    disable = no
    socket_type = stream
    wait = no
    user = root
    server = /usr/sbin/vsftpd
    nice = 10
}
```

Linux will automatically edit this file to enable VSFTPD and restart `xinetd` with the `chkconfig` command.

```
[root@bigboy tmp]# chkconfig vsftpd on
[root@bigboy tmp]#
```

Naturally, to disable VSFTP once again, you'll use the `chkconfig vsftpd off` command.

617

DHCP Differences

There can be problems when upgrading from Red Hat 7.3 to 8.0 while maintaining the same dhcpd.conf file. You might run into a DHCP server error. This startup error is caused by not having this line at the very top of your /etc/dhcpd.conf file:

```
ddns-update-style interim
```

The error might look like:

```
Starting dhcpd: Internet Software Consortium DHCP Server V3.0pl1
Copyright 1995-2001 Internet Software Consortium.
All rights reserved.
For info, please visit http://www.isc.org/products/DHCP

** You must add a ddns-update-style statement to /etc/dhcpd.conf.
To get the same behaviour as in 3.0b2pl11 and previous
versions, add a line that says "ddns-update-style ad-hoc;"
Please read the dhcpd.conf manual page for more information. **

. . .
. . .
. . .


exiting.
[FAILED]
```

DNS Differences

You'll notice some differences running BIND on older versions of Red Hat/Fedora Linux. For example, Red Hat 9 doesn't shutdown BIND cleanly and gives a "named: already running" error when you try to restart it:

```
[root@bigboy tmp]# /etc/init.d/named restart
Stopping named:
named: already running[root@bigboy tmp]#
```

The pkill command enables you to kill processes by referring to them by name instead of their process ID number. In this case, you can forcefully stop the named daemon and restart it by issuing the command pkill named followed by /etc/init.d/named start.

```
[root@bigboy tmp]# pkill named
pkill: 29988 - No such process
pkill: 29992 - No such process
[root@bigboy tmp]# /etc/init.d/named start
[root@bigboy tmp]#
```

ROUTING DIFFERENCES

Some of the older versions of the Fedora stream of Linux had different methods of updating their routes. For example, in Red Hat versions 8 and 9, the file named `/etc/sysconfig/static-routes` was used to add permanent static routes that would be present after a reboot. The format is similar to that of the `route` command except that the interface comes first and the switches have no dashes in front of them. Here is a sample entry for a route to 10.0.0.0 via the 192.168.1.254 gateway:

```
wlan0 net 10.0.0.0 netmask 255.0.0.0 gw 192.168.1.254
```

The `/etc/sysconfig/static-routes` file is set to be deprecated in future releases, and you should consider the alternative solutions for newer operating systems.

IPTABLES DIFFERENCES

In Red Hat/Fedora 9 and earlier, `iptables` gave a different status message when the firewall was stopped. Instead of saying stopped, it presented a rule set that allowed all traffic through.

```
[root@bigboy tmp]# service iptables status
Table: filter
Chain INPUT (policy ACCEPT)
target     prot opt source              destination

Chain FORWARD (policy ACCEPT)
target     prot opt source              destination

Chain OUTPUT (policy ACCEPT)
target     prot opt source              destination

[root@bigboy tmp]#
```

SOFTWARE INSTALLATION DIFFERENCES

With some older Red Hat Linux versions, source RPM files are first exported into the directory `/usr/src/redhat/SPECS` with the `rpm` command. You then have to run the `rpm` command again to compile the source files into a regular RPM file, which will be placed in either the `/usr/src/packages/RPMS/i386/` or the `/usr/src/redhat/RPMS/i386/` directories. You then have to install the new RPM file from this directory.

```
[root@bigboy tmp]# rpm -Uvh filename.src.rpm
[root@bigboy tmp]# cd /usr/src/redhat/SPECS
[root@bigboy SPECS]# rpm -ba filename
[root@bigboy SPECS]# cd /usr/src/redhat/RPM/i386
[root@bigboy i386]# rpm -Uvh filename.rpm
```

WIRELESS NETWORKING DIFFERENCES

Under version 8.0 of Red Hat I have seen the `kernel-wlan-ng-pcmcia` RPM installation give errors stating that the `kernel-pcmcia-cs` RPM hadn't been previously installed even when it had been. Installing the RPM with `--force` and `--nodeps` switches does the trick by forcing the installation while not checking for dependencies. Always remember that under normal circumstances this wouldn't be a good idea, error messages are there for a reason.

```
[root@bigboy tmp]# rpm -Uvh kernel-wlan-ng-pcmcia-0.1.15-6.i686.rpm
error: Failed dependencies:
        kernel-pcmcia-cs is needed by kernel-wlan-ng-pcmcia-0.1.15-6
[root@bigboy tmp]# rpm -Uvh --force --nodeps kernel-wlan-ng-pcmcia-
0.1.15-6.i686.rpm
Preparing...                 ################################# [100%]
   1:kernel-wlan-ng-pcmcia   ################################# [100%]

Adding prism2_cs alias to /etc/modules.conf file...
Shutting down PCMCIA services: cardmgr modules.
Starting PCMCIA services: modules cardmgr.
The default wlan0 network configuration is DHCP.  Adjust accordingly.

ACHTUNG!  ATTENTION!  WARNING!
YOU MUST configure /etc/pcmcia/wlan-ng.opts to match WAP settings!!!

[root@bigboy tmp]#
```

Linux-WLAN File Locations Using Red Hat 8.0 RPMs

The main Linux-WLAN configuration file for version 8.0 is the /etc/wlan.conf file (PCI type NIC) or your /etc/pcmcia/wlan-ng.opts (PCMCIA type NICs) configuration file. Locate the lines containing ssid=linux_wlan, and set the SSID to whatever value you've decided to use on your wireless LAN. This example uses homenet.

Also modify the IS_ADHOC option to make your NIC either support Ad-hoc mode for peer-to-peer networks or Infrastructure mode if you are using a WAP. Here is a sample snippet:

```
#=======SELECT STATION MODE===================
IS_ADHOC=n               # y|n, y - adhoc, n - infrastructure
```

```
#=======INFRASTRUCTURE STATION START===================
# SSID is all we have for now
AuthType="opensystem" # opensystem | sharedkey (requires WEP)
# Use DesiredSSID="" to associate with any AP in range
DesiredSSID="homenet"
```

MRTG DIFFERENCES

You will need to take the several differences into account when configuring MRTG for various versions of Fedora and Red Hat.

File Locations

In Red Hat 9 and older, MRTG files are located in the /var/www/html/mrtg/. In Fedora Core, the files are located in the /var/www/mrtg/ directory. In both cases, the MRTG graphs can be accessed using a default Apache installation via the URL http://server-ip-address/mrtg.

indexmaker MRTG_LIB Errors with Red Hat 9 and 8.0

Red Hat versions 8 and 9 give an error when running indexmaker:

```
[root@bigboy mrtg]# indexmaker --output=index.html \
                    /etc/mrtg/mrtg.cfg
Can't locate package $VERSION for @MRTG_lib::ISA at
/usr/bin/indexmaker line 49
main::BEGIN() called at /usr/bin/../lib/mrtg2/MRTG_lib.pm line 49
eval {...} called at /usr/bin/../lib/mrtg2/MRTG_lib.pm line 49
[root@bigboy mrtg]#
```

This is caused by an incompatibility between MRTG and PERL 5.8, which MRTG uses to generate files. The MRTG site claims this was fixed in version 2.9.22, but this version of MRTG seems to fail under Red Hat.

The fix is simple: Edit the file /usr/lib/mrtg2/MRTG_lib.pm, replacing the line:

```
@ISA = qw(Exporter $VERSION);
```

with:

```
@ISA = qw(Exporter);
```

You'll then have to run indexmaker again.

Precedence Bitwise Error with Red Hat 9

`indexmaker` may also give an error related to a bitwise operation. It doesn't seem to affect the operation of MRTG or the HTML index page output. For example:

```
Possible precedence problem on bitwise | operator at
/usr/bin/../lib/mrtg2/BER.pm line 601
```

WEBALIZER DIFFERENCES

Older versions of Webalizer, especially those found with Red Hat 8.0 and earlier, have a tendency to create this message in your logs:

```
Error: Unable to open DNS cache file /var/lib/webalizer/dns_cache.db
```

According to the documentation on Webalizer's Web site, this is not a critical error. You can make the software run in quiet mode by editing the configuration file and changing the `Quiet` parameter to yes:

```
Quiet          yes
```

syslog Configuration and Cisco Devices

syslog reserves facilities local0 through local7 for log messages received from remote servers and network devices. Routers, switches, firewalls, and load balancers each logging with a different facility can each have their own log files for easy troubleshooting. This appendix will show you how to have a different log file for each class of device. All the network device configuration examples that follow log to the remote Linux logging server 192.168.1.100. Remember, if you have a large data center, you may also want to switch off all logging to /var/log/messages for the home/SOHO environment.

CISCO ROUTERS

By default Cisco routers send syslog messages to their logging server with a default facility of local7. Don't set the facility in this case, but do tell the router to timestamp the messages and make the messages have the source IP address of the loopback interface:

```
service timestamps log datetime localtime
no logging console
no logging monitor
logging 192.168.1.100
```

CATALYST CAT SWITCHES RUNNING CATOS

By default Cisco switches also send syslog messages to their logging server with a default facility of local7. Don't change this facility either, therefore making routers and switches log to the same file.

```
set logging server enable
set logging server 192.168.1.100
set logging level all 5
set logging server severity 6
```

CISCO LOCAL DIRECTOR

Local Directors use the `syslog output` command to set the logging facility and severity. The value provided must be in the format **FF.SS** (facility.severity) using the numbering scheme in Table IV.1.

Table IV.1   Numbering Scheme for Local Directors

Facility	FF Value		Severity	SS Value
local0	16		System unusable	0
local1	17		Immediate action required	1
local2	18		Critical condition	2
local3	19		Error conditions	3
local4	20		Warning conditions	4
local5	21		Normal but significant conditions	5
local6	22		Informational messages	6
local7	23		Debugging messages	7

This example uses facility local4 and the logging debugging messages from Table IV.1:

```
syslog output 20.7
no syslog console
syslog host 192.168.1.100
```

CISCO PIX FIREWALLS

PIX firewalls use the numbering scheme in Table IV.2 to determine their logging facilities.

Table IV.2   `syslog` Facility and Severity Numbering Scheme for PIX Firewalls

Facility	Logging Facility Command Value
local0	16
local1	17
local2	18

Facility	Logging Facility Command Value
local3	19
local4	20
local5	21
local6	22
local7	23

This configuration example assumes that the logging server is connected on the side of the "inside" protected interface. It sends log messages to facility local3 with a severity level of 5 (Notification) set by the logging trap command.

```
logging on
logging standby
logging timestamp
logging trap notifications
logging facility 19
logging host inside 192.168.1.100
```

Cisco CSS11000 (Arrowpoints)

The configuration for the Cisco CSS11000 load balancer series is more straightforward. You specify the facility with an intuitive number using the logging host command and set the severity with the logging subsystem command. This example shows the CSS11000 logging facility local6 and severity level 6 (Informational):

```
logging host 192.168.1.100 facility 6
set logging subsystem all info-6
logging commands enable
```

The Sample Cisco *syslog.conf* File

```
#
# All LOCAL3 messages (debug and above) go to the firewall file
ciscofw
#
local3.debug /var/log/cisco/ciscofw

#
```

```
# All LOCAL4 messages  (debug and above) go to the Local Director file
ciscold
#
local4.debug /var/log/cisco/ciscold

#
# All LOCAL6 messages  (debug and above) go to the CSS file ciscocss
#
local6.debug /var/log/cisco/ciscocss

#
# All LOCAL7 messages  (debug and above) go to the ciscoacl
# This includes ACL logs which are logged at severity debug
#
local7.debug /var/log/cisco/ciscoacl

#
# LOCAL7 messages  (notice and above) go to the ciscoinfo
# This excludes ACL logs which are logged at severity debug
#
local7.notice /var/log/cisco/ciscoinfo
```